About Aspen Law & Business

Aspen Law & Business is a leading publisher of authoritative treatises, practice manuals, services, and journals for attorneys, corporate and bank directors, accountants, auditors, environmental compliance professionals, financial and tax advisors, and other business professionals. Our mission is to provide practical solution-based how-to information keyed to the latest original pronouncements, as well as the latest legislative, judicial, and regulatory developments.

We offer publications in the areas of accounting and auditing; antitrust; banking and finance; bankruptcy; business and commercial law; construction law; corporate law; criminal law; environmental compliance; government and administrative law; health law; insurance law; intellectual property; international law; legal practice and litigation; matrimonial and family law; pensions, benefits, and labor; real estate law; securities; and taxation.

Other Aspen Law and Business products treating accounting and auditing issues include:

> Accounting Irregularities and Financial Fraud
> Audit Committees: A Guide for Directors, Management, and
>   Consultants
> Construction Accounting Deskbook
> CPA's Guide to Developing Effective Business Plans
> CPA's Guide to Effective Engagement Letters
> CPA's Guide to e-Business
> Federal Government Contractor's Manual
> How to Manage Your Accounting Practice
> Medical Practice Management Handbook
> Miller Audit Procedures
> Miller Compilations and Reviews
> Miller European Accounting Guide
> Miller GAAP Financial Statement Disclosures Manual
> Miller GAAP Guide
> Miller GAAP Practice Manual
> Miller GAAS Guide
> Miller GAAS Practice Manual
> Miller Governmental GAAP Guide
> Miller Local Government Audits
> Miller Not-for-Profit Organization Audits
> Miller Not-for-Profit Reporting
> Miller Single Audits
> Professional's Guide to Value Pricing

ASPEN LAW & BUSINESS
A Division of Aspen Publishers, Inc.
A Wolters Kluwer Company
www.aspenpublishers.com

SUBSCRIPTION NOTICE

This Aspen Law & Business product is updated on a periodic basis with supplements to reflect important changes in the subject matter. If you purchased this product directly from Aspen Law & Business, we have already recorded your subscription for the update service.

If, however, you purchased this product from a bookstore and wish to receive future updates and revised or related volumes billed separately with a 30-day examination review, please contact our Customer Service Department at 1-800-234-1660, or send your name, company name (if applicable), address, and the title of the product to:

ASPEN LAW & BUSINESS
A Division of Aspen Publishers, Inc.
7201 McKinney Circle
Frederick, MD 21704

2002

MILLER

INTERNATIONAL ACCOUNTING STANDARDS

GUIDE

David Alexander
Simon Archer

ASPEN LAW & BUSINESS
A Division of Aspen Publishers, Inc.
New York   Gaithersburg

(Formerly published by Harcourt Professional Publishing)

This publication is designed to provide accurate and authoritative information
in regard to the subject matter covered. It is sold with the understanding that
the publisher is not engaged in rendering legal, accounting, or other professional services. If legal advice or other professional assistance is required, the
services of a competent professional person should be sought.
— From a *Declaration of Principles* jointly adopted by
a Committee of the American Bar Association and a
Committee of Publishers and Associations

Contents

Foreword

A lot has changed since the printing of the first edition of the *Miller International Accounting Standards Guide*, just a year ago. The Trustees under Chairman Paul Volcker have had an impressive funding run to secure the financial support for the next several years. The reorganization of the IASC has been completed and the new 14-member board, renamed the International Accounting Standards Board (IASB), has held several meetings to address the most urgent issues and draft a plan to lay out a blueprint for convergence in financial reporting. The 49-member—geographically spread—Standards Advisory Council (SAC) met for the first time in July 2001. The new IASB standards will be called International Financial Reporting Standards (IFRS) and the body that provides timely guidance on financial reporting issues is now the International Financial Reporting Issues Committee (IFRIC). A preface has been approved which will create a different look and layout of the standards.

Probably one of the most important events will be the mandatory application of the standards in Europe. The experience gained from this effort will have a significant effect on the rest of the financial reporting world.

Finally, continue to look at our redesigned Web site, iasb.org.uk.

August 2001   Kurt P. Ramin
                                              Commercial Director, IASB

Preface

The new 2002 *Miller International Accounting Standards Guide (Miller IAS Guide)*, part of **The Complete Miller GAAP Library for Business**, explains and analyzes International Accounting Standards (IASs) promulgated by the International Accounting Standards Committee (IASC).

International accounting standards are playing an increasing role in the context of the globalization of capital markets. In particular, they provide a basis for the consolidated financial statements of multinational corporations based in countries where national GAAP are not considered to provide a basis that satisfies internationally accepted qualitative criteria for financial reporting. Some multinational corporations use U.S. GAAP for a similar reason. At the present time, IASs are not accepted as a substitute for U.S. GAAP as a basis for financial statements of foreign registrants with the U.S. Securities and Exchange Commission (SEC); but they are accepted by the London Stock Exchange and elsewhere in Europe. Consequently, they are used by an increasing number of multinational corporations based in Continental Europe and Asia as a basis for their consolidated financial statements. Such countries include Austria, France, Germany, Italy, and Switzerland. An understanding of IASs is therefore necessary for an understanding of the consolidated financial statements of such corporations.

Chapter 1, "The International Accounting Standards Committee—Past, Present, Future," explains in more detail the role and usage of IASs. It also examines their current status in terms of international acceptance as a basis for financial reporting in the context of cross-border securities listings (including that of foreign registrants in the United States). Their central role in the next phase of accounting harmonization within the European Union is explained. The recent major restructuring of the IASC, in the light of its intended role as a global accounting standard-setter for listed corporations, is described.

How to Use the 2002 *Miller IAS Guide*

Following an introductory section that covers the International Accounting Standards Committee, its Framework for the preparation and presentation of financial statements, and the key IAS 1, "Presentation of Financial Statements," the 2002 *Miller IAS Guide* organizes IASC accounting pronouncements into three parts (Overview, General Standards, and Industry-Specific Standards), then, alphabetically by topic. So that the authoritative information is immediately accessible, each chapter deals comprehensively with one, or in a few cases two, IASs and the related pronouncements of the IASC's Standing Interpretations Committee (SIC). Each chapter also indicates the main differences between IAS and U.S. GAAP on the matters dealt with in the chapter. However, the *Miller IAS Guide* is not written with the assumption that the reader is familiar with U.S. GAAP.

This edition is current through IAS 41, "Agriculture."

A few topics covered by IAS GAAP are not covered by U.S. GAAP, and vice versa. In a number of cases, the topic coverage in FASB pronouncements is narrower and more focused than it is in IASC pronouncements. (This is the main reason why the number of U.S. GAAP pronouncements is substantially greater than the number of IAS GAAP pronouncements.) Another reason is that current IASs include only two specialized accounting standards, IAS 30, "Disclosures in the Financial Statements of Banks and Similar Financial Institutions," and IAS 41, "Agriculture."

Chapters in the *Miller IAS Guide* also contain illustrations and examples to demonstrate and clarify specific accounting principles. They also contain **Practice Pointers**, which clarify issues of application, as well as **Observations**, which discuss issues of interpretation and bring apparent inconsistencies to your attention.

Material in the *Miller IAS Guide* can be located several ways: In addition to the Guide's **Table of Contents,** the **Cross-Reference** shows the chapter in which a particular pronouncement is discussed. The **Index** provides quick, accurate reference to needed information. In addition, an **Appendix** describes individual countries' usage and application of IASs.

For more information about international accounting and auditing standards, visit the Miller International Accounting Library at www.millerseries.com.

Acknowledgments

The authors and publisher wish to thank both Susan Harding, formerly Research Manager of the International Accounting Standards Committee, for reviewing the technical content of the *Miller IAS Guide*, and Kurt Ramin, Commercial Director of the IASC, for making this important addition to professional accounting literature possible. They would also like to thank Robert Sack, CPA, for his review of U.S. GAAP. Finally, they also would like to thank Anita Rosepka, Managing Editor, and Bernard Johnston, Senior Manuscript Editor, of Aspen Law & Business for their indispensable contributions in bringing this second edition of the *Miller IAS Guide* to press.

About the Authors

David Alexander is Professor of Accounting and Finance at the Birmingham Business School, The University of Birmingham, England. He has a degree in Economics and Accounting from the University of Bristol, England, and is a Fellow of the Institute of Chartered Accountants in England and Wales. Professor Alexander is a co-editor of the *Miller European Accounting Guide*.

Simon Archer, a former partner of Price Waterhouse, Paris, has had many years' experience working in Continental Europe. He is currently Professor of Financial Management at the University of Surrey, Guildford, United Kingdom. Professor Archer was educated at Oxford University, United Kingdom, and is a Fellow of the Institute of Chartered Accountants in England and Wales. Professor Archer is a co-editor of the *Miller European Accounting Guide*.

PART I

OVERVIEW

CHAPTER 1
THE INTERNATIONAL ACCOUNTING STANDARDS COMMITTEE— PAST, PRESENT, AND FUTURE

CONTENTS

INTRODUCTION

The International Accounting Standards Committee (IASC) was comprehensively restructured in 2001 and re-named the International Accounting Standards Board (hereinafter IASB). It describes itself on its Web site as

> an independent, private sector body, formed in 1973 with the objective of harmonising the accounting principles which are used by businesses and other organisations for financial reporting around the world.

IASB's formal objectives, as stated in its revised Constitution approved by members on May 24, 2000, are:

    (a) to develop, in the public interest, a single set of high quality, understandable and enforceable global accounting standards that require high quality, transparent and comparable information in financial statements and other financial reporting to help participants in the world's capital markets and other users make economic decisions;

    (b) to promote the use and rigorous application of those standards; and

    (c) to bring about convergence of national accounting standards and International Accounting Standards to high quality solutions.

As stated in the Home Page of IASB's Web site,

> The objective of the [IASB] is to achieve convergence in the accounting principles that are used by businesses and other organisations for financial reporting around the world. This, in turn, improves the ability of investors, creditors, governments, and others to make informed resource allocation and policy decisions.

Thus, the original objective of "harmonising accounting principles" has evolved into the objectives of "develop[ing]...a single set of *high quality...global accounting standards...*to help participants in the *world's capital markets* and others make *informed decisions,*" "promot[ing] the...*rigorous application* of those standards" and "bring[ing] about *convergence...[toward] high quality solutions.*"

This evolution of its objectives is associated with its collaboration with the International Organization of Securities Commissions since 1995, which led in 2000 to a comprehensive restructuring of IASC to take effect in 2001. This introductory chapter aims to provide an overview of IASC's history, its recent re-structuring as IASB, and the challenges facing it.

HISTORY OF IASC

IASC was created in 1973. Its creation was related to that of the International Federation of Accountants (IFAC). IFAC is the world-wide umbrella organization of accountancy bodies. It is independent of government or pseudo-government control. Its stated purpose is to develop and enhance a coordinated worldwide accountancy profession with harmonized standards. All members of the IFAC are automatically members of the IASC.

IASC's recent description of itself as an "independent private sector body" is accurate and revealing. It is, in essence, a private club, with no formal authority. This is in contrast to national regulatory or standard-setting bodies, which operate within a national jurisdiction and some form of legal and governmental framework that delineates, defines, and provides a level of authority. The IASC, however, has operated throughout its existence in the knowledge that in the last resort, it and its standards have no formal authority. It therefore has all along had to rely on persuasion and the quality of its analysis and argument. This can be seen to have had two major effects. First, the quality of logic and discussion in its publications has generally been high, and its conclusions—if sometimes debatable—have been feasible and clearly articulated. Second, however, the conclusions and recommendations of many of the earlier published IAS documents often had to accommodate two or more alternative acceptable treatments, simply because both or all were already being practiced in countries that were members of IASC and were too significant to be ignored.

The disadvantages of this state of affairs are obvious and were well recognized by the IASC itself. Toward the end of the 1980s, the IASC decided it would attempt a more proactive approach, and early in 1989 it published an Exposure Draft (E32) on the comparability of financial statements. This proposed the elimination of certain treatments permitted by particular IASs and the expression of a clear preference for one particular treatment, even where two alternatives were still to be regarded as acceptable.

This "comparability project" led to a whole raft of revised standards operative from the mid-1990s, which did indeed considerably narrow the degree of optionality compared with the earlier versions of the standards issued in the 1970s and 1980s. The comparability project, therefore, can be said to have made the set of IASs more meaningful and significant. Of course, it did nothing to increase the formal authority of the IASC.

In 1995, as the next stage in its development, IASC entered into an agreement with the International Organization of Securities Commissions (IOSCO) to complete a "core set" of IASs by 1999. With regard to the agreement, IOSCO's Technical Committee stated that completion of "comprehensive core standards acceptable to the Technical Committee" would allow it to "recommend endorsement" of those standards for "cross-border capital raising in all global markets." The potential significance of this agreement is great. If it all goes through successfully, it will mean that one set of financial statements, properly prepared in accordance with IAS GAAP, would automatically be acceptable for listing purposes without amendment and without any reconciliation to national (i.e., local) GAAP on each and all of the world's important stock exchanges. This would save huge resources at the international and multinational level, both for preparers and for users and analysts. The role of national standard-setters, except arguably for small and medium-sized enterprises, would simply disappear, if enforcement were left to other bodies.

From the IASC viewpoint, successful implementation of this process would provide the *de facto* authority that it needs and craves. Any enterprise failing to accept the authority of IASC would know that its shares would be likely to be de-listed.

This, of course, raises the issue of effective enforcement, for which IASB is dependent on securities regulators and other bodies with the power to impose de-listing and other sanctions, and on a mechanism for bringing breaches of IASs to the attention of such bodies.

In December 1998, the then IASC completed its "core standards" program with the approval of IAS 39, "Financial Instruments: Recognition and Measurement" (see Chapter 18). Following the publication of the report of IASC's Strategic Working Party, "Recommendations on Shaping IASC for the Future," in November 1999, the Board of IASC approved proposals in December 1999 to make significant changes to IASC's structure, in order to prepare it for an enhanced role as a global accounting standard-setter.

Following these preparations, the year 2000 was a momentous one for IASC. In May 2000 the proposed structural changes were approved by IASC's membership. (The results of these changes are outlined in "The New Structure," below.) Also in May 2000, IOSCO formally accepted the IASC's "core standards" as a basis for cross-border securities listing purposes worldwide (although for certain countries, notably the United States, reconciliations of items such as earnings and stockholders' equity to national GAAP are still required). In June 2000, the European Commission issued a Communication proposing that all listed companies in the European Union would be required to prepare their consolidated financial statements using IASs, a proposal that has since been adopted.

It is apparent, however, that acceptance of IASs by the SEC, for the financial reporting of foreign registrants for U.S. listings, is a crucial element in the new IASB's acceptance as the global accounting standard-setter. This is discussed further under "The Future," below.

CAUSES OF DIFFERENCES

Before we speculate about possible outcomes, it is helpful to think about the context in which this game is being played out. Moving back only twenty years, to the end of the 1970s, financial reporting practices, traditions, and philosophies differed enormously among key countries in the so-called developed world (to say nothing of the situation in developing and third-world countries). Ignorance of these differences was, and indeed in many respects still is, both widespread and deep-seated. The roots of these differences can, to a significant extent, be explained by considering four general factors, as follows.

1. *The relative importance of law.* The point at issue here is the extent to which the "law of the land" determines the details of accounting and financial reporting. Tradition in the Anglo-Saxon countries is that the law specifies general principle only, while in countries heavily influenced by Roman law tradition, the law tends to include more detail. Most of mainland Europe exemplifies the latter approach.

2. *Prescription or flexibility.* If regulation is not specified in full detail in legislation, then there are still two alternatives available. First, regulation might be created in detail by professional accounting bodies. Second, the broad regulation, whether created by legislation or by professional accounting bodies, may

be explicitly designed on the assumption that the individual expert, in each unique situation, can and should choose the appropriate course of action, within the broad parameters laid down. This was very much the approach in the Anglo-Saxon world before the creation of national standards bodies some thirty years ago.

3. *The providers of finance.* The national accounting systems developed before the 1970s predate the arguments of recent years that accounting statements must satisfy the needs of a wide variety of users. Generally, the suppliers of finance to business were the only users seriously considered until late in the last century (sometimes quite late). Different countries have very different financial institution structures and finance-raising traditions. It follows that accounting practice will have been adapted to suit the local dominant sources of finance. In some countries, tradition tends to focus on the shareholders and, therefore, on profit and on the reporting of expenses and revenues. Some other countries have more active banking sectors and fewer shareholder investors. Accounting in those countries will tend to focus on creditors, and therefore on the balance sheet and on the convention of prudence. Also, bankers tend to have access to "inside information" in those circumstances and are less reliant on annual reports.

A more obvious, but less often quoted, example of the influence of finance provision on financial reporting can be seen by considering the systems of eastern Europe as they begin to emerge from a half-century during which all finance was provided by the state.

4. *The influence of taxation.* The general point here is that the scope and extent of the influence of taxation law on financial statements vary considerably. Perceptions of this are often simplistic. In reality, no country can justly claim that tax considerations do not influence published results, and no country can be accused of simply taking tax-based results and publishing them just as they are. Within these nonexistent extremes, however, lies a variety of tradition and practice. It is common in many countries, for instance, for some tax allowances to be claimable only if the identical figure from the tax computation is also used in the published financial statements.

The most powerful of these causal factors creating and explaining historical differences is almost certainly the sources of finance. It is arguably this same factor that is now driving the move toward internationalism in financial reporting and its regulation. The market for the *supply* of finance for larger enterprises is now a single global market. If our analysis is correct, this means that the *demand* for finance is inevitably forced to operate in a single global market scenario. The demand for globally understood financial reports is therefore logically unstoppable.

As we have already hinted, the above arguments, while in our view fully justified at the "listed enterprise" level, do not necessarily imply any need to alter national financial reporting as it applies to small businesses. They certainly do not logically apply to the economies of many third-world countries. The implications for possible "two-tier" systems within countries and between economic regions raise significant issues, which both IASC and national regulatory systems have hardly begun to tackle, though discussion of such problems is outside the scope of this book. Unlike U.S. GAAP, at least as promulgated, which are intended to apply only to enterprises whose shares are tradeable, IAS GAAP seek applicability, in general, to all enterprises, in all types of economy. This intention is now beginning to be questioned within IASC. In its Statement in the IASC Annual Review 2000, the outgoing Board of IASC commented as follows (pars. 29–30):

> During the last few years, the [outgoing] Board has detected various indications that strong demand exists for more work on the application of accounting standards to reporting by small enterprises. The demand has been noted first in developing countries and countries in transition to market economies....The Board...wishes IASC to continue to meet the needs of constituents in developing countries and the needs of small businesses in general. It recognises that a case may exist for having different accounting standards for small businesses and large businesses...[but] inclines to the view that a case can be made rarely, if at all, for differences in standards for recognition and measurement...; a stronger case may exist with regard to disclosure standards and it may be possible to do more to help small businesses....

Given the position and role of IASC, and the widely differing practices and attitudes of its constituents, is it really valid to talk of Generally Accepted Accounting Principles in the IASC context? Is IAS GAAP the same species of animal as, say, U.S. GAAP, distinguished only by minor genetic individualities? Or is it of a different species or even genus?

One difference is clear, at least at the time of writing and at the time of the issuance of the International Accounting Standards described and discussed in this volume. IAS GAAP (we continue to use the term, if only for convenience) is, inevitably, designed to be "generally accepted" in a variety of different legal and cultural contexts. U.S. GAAP, U.K. GAAP, German regulation, and other national systems have no need for this consideration. This may sound like a weakness of IAS GAAP. From a national standpoint, perhaps it is, but national standpoints are no longer entirely valid. The very reason for the existence of the IASC is that financial reports must be comprehensible across countries, across jurisdictions, and across cultures. Country X may justifiably be able to say that its own national GAAP, as applied in its own national context, is "better" than IAS GAAP as applied in the *same* national context. But that is no longer the point. In a global market, the relevance of the national context is hugely reduced.

THE NEW STRUCTURE

Like the Financial Accounting Standards Board (FASB) in 1972, and the U.K. Accounting Standards Board in 1990, which replaced the APB and the ASC, respectively, the new IASB differs from its predecessor by having a two-tier structure, based on an organ of governance not involved in standard-setting (the Trustees), and a standard-setting Board. According to Clause 6 of the IASC Constitution:

> The governance of IASC shall rest with the Trustees and the Board and such other governing organs as may be appointed by the Trustees or the Board in accordance with the provisions of this Constitution. The Trustees shall use their best endeavors to ensure that the requirements of this Constitution are observed; however, they are empowered to make minor variations [in the Constitution] in the interest of feasibility of operation if such variations are agreed by 75% of all the Trustees.

The new structure is the one proposed in the Strategic Working Party's November 1999 report, "Recommendations on Shaping IASC for the Future." There are 19 Trustees, of whom six are to be from North America, six from Europe, four from the Asia/Pacific region, and three from any area, subject to establishing "overall geographical balance." The new Board differs significantly from its predecessor (the Committee) by having 12 full-time members as well as two part-time members. Moreover, its members are to be chosen for their technical expertise and background experience, and (in contrast to the Trustees) not on the basis of geographical representation. However, seven of the full-time members are expected to have "formal liaison responsibilities with national standard setters in order to promote convergence...but shall not be voting members of the national standard setters" (Constitution, clause 27). The seven countries with whose national standard-setters such liaison arrangements have been set up in the first Board are (in alphabetical order) Australia and New Zealand (together), Canada, France, Germany, Japan, the United Kingdom, and the United States.

A minimum of five members of the Board must have a background as practicing auditors, at least three must have a background as preparers of financial statements, at least three a background as users of financial statements, and at least one must have an academic background. Each member has one vote and most decisions are to be made by a simple majority of members attending in person or by a telecommunications link, with a quorum being such attendance by "at least 60% of the members" and the Chairman having a casting vote. The publication of an Exposure Draft, final IAS, or final Interpretation of the Standing Interpretations Committee requires approval by at least eight members of the Board. This change to majority voting is significant, as the old IASC required a 75% majority.

TRUSTEES

- 19 individuals with diverse geographic and functional backgrounds

- Trustees will:

— Appoint the Members of the Board, the Standing Interpretations Committee, and the Standards Advisory Council

— Monitor IASB's effectiveness

— Raise its funds

— Approve IASB's budget

— Have responsibility for constitutional change

STANDARDS ADVISORY COUNCIL	BOARD 14 members, 12 full-time, 2 part-time	STANDING INTERPRETATIONS COMMITTEE

The first Chairman of the IASC Trustees is Paul A. Volcker, former Chairman of the U.S. Federal Reserve Board. The first Chairman of the new Board is Sir David Tweedie, who moves from being Chairman of the U.K. Accounting Standards Board and was formerly U.K. technical partner for KPMG, after an academic career in Scotland.

As well as the Trustees and the Board, the new structure includes a Standing Interpretations Committee (SIC—similar to its predecessor in the previous structure) and a Standards Advisory Council; the members of both these bodies are appointed by the Trustees. The name of the SIC is due to be changed, and for Standards issued by IASB the term "International Financial Reporting Standard" (IFRS) will be used.

The Standards Advisory Council, with 49 members, provides a forum for participation by organizations and individuals with an interest in international financial reporting and having diverse geographic and functional backgrounds, with the objective of giving advice to the Board on agenda decisions and priorities, informing the Board of the view of members of the Council on major standard-setting projects, and giving other advice to the Board or the Trustees. The Council is chaired by the Chairman of the Board.

In addition to the seven "liaison" members mentioned above, the other seven members of the new Board are citizens of South Africa, Switzerland, the United Kingdom, and the United States, albeit with substantial international experience. Thus, the only "emerging economy" country that has one of its citizens on the Board is South Africa. One purpose of the Standards Advisory Council may be to give a greater voice to such countries. The orientation of the IASB toward global capital markets has left accountants in such countries (both practitioners and academics) feeling that their needs are not receiving sufficient attention and, in some cases, these feelings amount to bitterly expressed resentment. In "Causes of Differences" above, we quoted some words of the outgoing Board of IASC in which they expressed some concern for the needs of small enterprises and constituents in developing countries. It remains to be seen what attention the new IASB will devote to these needs, and what the role of national standard setters may be in this regard. For reasons discussed below, we do not believe that these needs will be high on the list of IASB's priorities in the near future.

THE FUTURE

In the report of the Strategic Working Party, "Recommendations on Shaping IASC for the Future," it was stated that:

> The primary attributes [considered desirable to establish the legitimacy of a standard setting organisation] identified were the representativeness of the decision making body, the independence of its members, and technical expertise....The proposed structure...provides a balanced approach to legitimacy based upon representativeness among members of the Trustees, the Standing Interpretations Committee (SIC), and the Standards Advisory Council, and technical competence and independence among Board Members.

The restructured IASB is undoubtedly much better equipped than its predecessor in these respects, as well as being far better resourced. Yet the key to IASB's future as a global accounting standard-setter will be the acceptance of its standards for cross-border listings by securities markets worldwide, by all members of IOSCO, *including the SEC for foreign registrants in the United States,* without the need for reconciliations to national GAAP. One of the watchwords of the new IASB is *convergence.* This is a two-way process: national sets of accounting standards are to converge toward one another, with IASs (or in the future, IFRSs) as the points of convergence, but IFRSs are also expected to converge toward certain national standards in some cases where the latter are recognized as conceptually or technically superior to existing IASs. On certain particularly important and difficult matters, such as financial instruments, IASB may look, as it has done in the past, to joint working parties composed of experts from countries such as Australia/New Zealand, Canada, the United Kingdom, and the United States, who with the former IASC formed the so-called G4+1.

Perhaps the major question for the future of the IASB is the extent to which the SEC will require IFRSs to "converge" *toward* U.S. solutions as set out by the FASB, as the price for IFRSs being accepted by the SEC for financial reporting by foreign registrants in the United States. In this respect, the role of the Board Member responsible for liaison with the FASB (of which he is a former member, with the role of observer on the former IASC Board) is likely to be particularly important. As the world's largest capital market, the United States undoubtedly provides a strong hand to the SEC and FASB in any bargaining over "convergence." The new IASB may be expected to resist anything that looks like U.S. arm-twisting, and to insist (as its Constitution requires) that convergence issues are dealt with in terms of conceptual and technical merits. But judgments about such merits tend to have an important subjective component. Watch this space!

IASB Web site: http://www.iasb.org.uk.

CHAPTER 2
FRAMEWORK FOR THE PREPARATION AND PRESENTATION OF FINANCIAL STATEMENTS

CONTENTS

OVERVIEW

The IASC's Framework belongs to the family of conceptual frameworks for financial reporting that have been developed by accounting standard-setters in a number of countries where accounting standard-setting is carried out by a private sector body. On one level, such conceptual frameworks may be considered attempts to assemble a body of accounting theory (or interrelated concepts) as a guide to standard-setting, so that standards are (as far as possible) formulated on a consistent basis and not in an *ad hoc* manner. On another but complementary level, they may be thought of as devices to confer legitimacy and authority on a private sector standard-setter that lacks the legal authority of a public body. The IASC, as a private sector standard-setter, shares these reasons for developing a conceptual framework.

Conceptual frameworks developed by accounting standard-setters are essentially based on identification of "good practice" from which principles are derived inductively. The criteria for identifying "good practice" are related to the assumed objectives of financial reporting. At the same time, attention is paid to conceptual coherence, and the development process typically involves "conceptual tidying up." Conceptual frameworks may be written in a prescriptive style or a descriptive style, or a mixture of the two. In any event, they are essentially *normative*, since they seek to provide a set of principles as a guide to setting and interpreting accounting standards. Such guidance, however, does not necessarily preclude a standard being issued that, for compelling pragmatic reasons, departs from a principle set out in the applicable conceptual framework.

The IASC's Framework is written in a descriptive style (in fact, it is IASC policy to use the word "should" only in standards) and seeks to avoid being excessively prescriptive. A principal reason for this is that it needs to have broad international applicability. In the final paragraph of the Framework, the IASC states:

> This Framework is applicable to a range of accounting models and provides guidance on preparing and presenting the financial statements constructed under the chosen model. At the present time [1989], it is not the intention of the Board of IASC to prescribe a particular model other than in exceptional circumstances, such as…a hyperinflationary economy.

In common with other conceptual frameworks, notably the FASB's set of Statements of Financial Accounting Concepts, the IASC's Framework covers the following topics:

1. *Objective of financial statements.* The IASC takes the position that, because investors are providers of risk capital to an enterprise, financial statements that meet investors' needs will also meet most of the needs of other users that financial statements can satisfy. On that basis, the objective of financial statements is to provide information about the financial position, performance, and changes in financial position of an enterprise that is useful to a wide range of users in making economic decisions, including assessment of the stewardship or accountability of management. The IASC states as "underlying assumptions" that, in order to meet their objectives, financial statements are prepared on the accrual basis of accounting and (normally) on the "going concern" basis.

2. *Qualitative characteristics of financial statement information.* The IASC cites four main qualitative characteristics: understandability, relevance, reliability, and comparability. Materiality is mentioned as an aspect of relevance. "Faithful representation," "substance over form," "neutrality" (freedom from bias), "prudence" (subject to neutrality), and "completeness" (within the bounds of materiality and cost) are mentioned as aspects of reliability. The Framework does not deal directly with the concepts of "true and fair view" (TFV) or "fair presentation" (FP), but states that "the application of the principal qualitative characteristics and of appropriate accounting standards normally results in financial statements that convey what is generally understood as [a TFV or FP] of such information." However, IAS 1, "Presentation of Financial Statements," as revised in 1997, states fair presentation as a requirement (see below).

3. *Elements of financial statements.* The Framework relates the elements to the measurement of financial position and performance. As elements of financial position, it provides definitions of assets, liabilities, and equity; and as elements of performance, it defines income (including revenue and gains) and expenses (including losses). The definitions given in the section on elements, and especially those of assets and liabilities, are the core of the Framework as a prescriptive basis for standard-setting.

4. *Principles for recognition of the elements.* The Framework states that recognition is the process of recording in the financial statements (subject to materiality) an item that meets the definition of an element and satisfies the two criteria for recognition,

namely, (a) it is *probable* that any future economic benefit associated with the item will flow to or from the enterprise and (b) the item has a cost or value that can be measured with reliability. Assessments of the degree of probability of the flow of future economic benefits "are made when the financial statements are prepared."

5. *Bases for measurement of the elements.* Unlike the section in which the elements of financial statements are defined, the treatment of measurement in the IASC's Framework avoids being prescriptive. It cites a number of different measurement bases and notes that the basis most commonly adopted is historical cost, usually combined with other bases.

The Framework also covers another topic, which is not necessarily dealt with specifically in other conceptual frameworks:

6. *Concepts of capital and capital maintenance.* The treatment of capital maintenance in the Framework also avoids being prescriptive. It distinguishes between (a) *financial* capital maintenance, in two forms, nominal (i.e., monetary units) or real (units of constant purchasing power) and (b) *physical* capital maintenance or operating capability. It states that the physical capital maintenance concept requires the use of a particular measurement basis, namely current cost, whereas neither form of the financial capital maintenance concept requires any particular measurement basis. It also states the implications of each concept of capital maintenance for profit measurement.

The IASC's Framework is a succinct document of 36 pages. It is thus much briefer than the FASB's set of six "Statements of Accounting Concepts," each of which is longer than the Framework. It is also shorter than the U.K. ASB's "Statement of Principles," which runs to some 130 pages. Succinctness is possible because of the limits that the IASC placed on its prescriptive aims. The IASC also benefited from the trailblazing work of the FASB, thanks to which most of the issues dealt with in the Framework had already been publicized.

BACKGROUND

The origins of the Framework go back to 1982, when the IASC initiated a limited study on the objectives of financial statements. The IASC stated at that time, however, that it did not intend to prepare an "international conceptual framework." The FASB had already issued in 1978 its SFAC 1, "Objectives of Financial Reporting by Business Enterprises," and in 1980 its SFACs 2 and 3 on "Qualitative Characteristics" and "Elements." In 1982–1984, the FASB's conceptual framework project was encountering some difficulties in dealing with issues of recognition and measurement.

In 1984, the IASC decided to revise IAS 1, "Disclosure of Accounting Policies," published in 1974, and it was also decided to merge the objectives project with this revision. In 1984 and 1985, new projects were started covering liabilities, equity and assets, and expenses. The decision to merge these into a Framework project occurred in November 1986, and the proposed revision of IAS 1 was deferred. The Framework was intended to be separate from the IASs and to avoid binding the IASC to particular accounting treatments in IASs. It was approved and issued in April 1989 and has not been revised since that time.

The status of the Framework vis-à-vis IAS GAAP may be compared with that of the FASB's SFACs vis-à-vis U.S. GAAP, as follows. As noted above, the IASC did not intend the Framework to be binding on it in its capacity as a standard-setter, just as the SFACs are not binding on the FASB in its standard-setting capacity. However, the Framework has been quite influential in the recent development of IASs and in major revisions. For example, its definitions (and especially those of assets and liabilities) were highly influential in the preparation of IAS 22, "Business Combinations"; IAS 37, "Provisions, Contingent Liabilities and Contingent Assets"; IAS 38, "Intangible Assets"; and IAS 39, "Financial Instruments: Recognition and Measurement."

The Framework is not an IAS and does not override any specific IAS; in case of conflict between it and an IAS, the requirements of the latter prevail. *One may, however, consider the Framework as embodying IAS GAAP in respect of issues that are not dealt with in any IAS.* This is apparent from the way in which the purpose and status of the Framework are described (see points 4 and 5 in the next section). For example, in the case of topics that have not yet been the subject of an IAS, the purpose of the Framework is to assist preparers in dealing with such topics. Moreover, the IASC will be guided by the Framework in the development of future IASs and in reviewing existing ones, so that the number of cases of conflict between the Framework and IASs are likely to diminish over time. The Framework itself will be subject to revision in the light of experience.

The relationship between the Framework and IAS 1, "Presentation of Financial Statements," is worthy of comment in the context of the comparison of IAS GAAP with U.S. GAAP. As noted above, originally the start of work on what became the Framework was linked to the revision of IAS 1. This revision was then deferred and not completed until 1997. The revised IAS 1 is a major standard that supersedes the former IASs 1, 5, and 13 (see Chapter 3). Although the Framework does not have the status of a standard, it and IAS 1 (revised) may to some extent be considered as complementary. The Framework itself does not conflict with U.S. GAAP in any important respect, but IAS 1 (revised) does. Its paragraphs 16–18 contain a provision to the effect that a specific requirement of an IAS may *need* to be departed from "in extremely rare circumstances...when the treatment required by the standard is clearly inappropriate and thus a fair presentation cannot be achieved either by applying the standard or through additional disclosure alone." This is the so-called "override," which is quite alien to U.S. GAAP. The override is *mandatory* if the circumstances require it.

While the override represents a major difference between IAS GAAP and U.S. GAAP in principle, the restrictions placed on its use by IAS 1 suggest that there should not be many cases of it in practice.

Purpose and Status

As indicated above, the Framework does not have the status of an IAS, does not override any specific IAS, and in case of conflict between the Framework and an IAS, the latter prevails (pars. 2–3). The purpose of the Framework is stated as follows (par. 1):

1. to assist the Board of IASC in the development of future IASs and in its review of existing IASs;

2. to assist the Board of IASC in promoting harmonization of regulations, accounting standards and procedures relating to the presentation of financial statements by providing a basis for reducing the number of alternative accounting treatments permitted by IASs;

3. to assist national standard-setting bodies in developing national standards;

4. to assist preparers of financial statements in applying IASs and in dealing with topics that have yet to form the subject of an IAS;

5. to assist auditors in forming an opinion as to whether financial statements conform with IASs;

6. to assist users of financial statements in interpreting the information contained in financial statements prepared in conformity with IASs;

7. to provide those who are interested in the work of the IASC with information about its approach to the formulation of accounting standards.

Scope

The scope of the Framework was indicated in the Overview given above. Paragraph 5 of the Framework mentions the following as constituting its scope:

1. Objectives of financial statements.
2. Qualitative characteristics that determine the usefulness of financial statement information.
3. Definition, recognition, and measurement of financial statement elements.
4. Concepts of capital and capital maintenance.

The Framework is concerned with "general purpose financial statements," including consolidated financial statements. These are described as being prepared and presented at least annually and being directed toward the common information needs of a wide range of users. They do not include special purpose reports such as prospectuses and tax computations (par. 6).

The term *financial statements* is understood as comprising a balance sheet, an income statement, a statement of changes in financial position (see the Observation below), and those notes and other statements and explanatory material that are an integral part of the financial statements. Supplementary schedules and information derived from, and expected to be read with, financial statements may also be included. Examples are segment reporting and information about the effects of changing prices. However, financial statements do not include such items as directors' reports, chairman's statements, management reports, and similar material that may be included in a financial or annual report (par. 7).

The Framework applies to the financial statements of all commercial, industrial, and business reporting enterprises, whether in the private or the public sectors (par. 8).

> **OBSERVATION:** The wording of paragraph 7 reads oddly in parts. The reference to the statement of changes in financial position states that this "may be presented in a variety of ways, for example as a statement of cash flows or a statement of funds flows." However, IAS 7 (revised in 1992) clearly requires a statement of cash flows (see Chapter 7). Likewise, it is stated that financial statements "*may*...include supplementary...information [such as]...financial information about industrial and geographical segments." Yet IAS 14, originally issued in 1981, *requires* such information (see Chapter 20). Hence, these apparent discrepancies are only partly the result of the Framework not having been revised. It seems that paragraph 7 does not set out fully to reflect the implications of IASs as to what should be considered as making up "financial statements."

USERS AND THEIR INFORMATION NEEDS, THE OBJECTIVE OF FINANCIAL STATEMENTS, AND UNDERLYING ASSUMPTIONS

Users and Their Information Needs

The Framework (par. 9) cites seven categories of "users" of financial statements, with comments on their needs. The seven categories are investors, employees, lenders, suppliers and other trade creditors, customers, governments and their agencies, and the public. The Framework argues that there are needs for financial statement information that are common to all users, and that, because investors are providers of risk capital to the enterprise, financial statements that meet their needs will also meet "most of the needs of other users that financial statements can satisfy" (par. 10).

> **OBSERVATION:** This argument to the effect that, as investors provide risk capital, basing financial statements on their needs will satisfy (as far as is practicable) most of the needs of other users, is not obviously correct and begs some questions that are not addressed in the Framework. The FASB employed similar but not identical wording in SFAC 1, referring to "investors and creditors" rather than just "investors." The FASB stated in support of its position that the information needs (or, at least, the decision models) of investors and creditors are reasonably well known, and better known than those of such other groups as customers and employees.

Objective of Financial Statements

The Framework states that the objective of financial statements is to provide information about the *financial position, performance,* and *changes in financial position* of an enterprise that is useful to a wide range of users in making economic decisions. It is acknowledged that financial statements do not provide all the information that users may need to make economic decisions, since they are largely oriented toward the *financial* effects of *past* events (pars. 12–13). Paragraph 14 mentions the use of financial statements for assessing the stewardship or accountability of management but sees such assessments as included within economic decisions.

Paragraphs 15–18 provide conventional explanations of the ways in which information about financial position, performance, and changes in financial position is useful. Information about financial position is primarily provided in a balance sheet, information about performance is primarily provided in an income statement, while information about changes in financial position is provided "by means of a separate statement" (par. 19). (As noted above, the Framework does not take a position as to what type of statement of changes in financial position is required.) Paragraph 20 draws attention to the interrelationships and complementarity of the three categories of financial statement, while paragraph 21 mentions notes and supplementary schedules as being part of the financial statements.

Underlying Assumptions

Paragraphs 22 and 23 discuss the underlying assumptions of the "accrual basis" and "going concern." Paragraph 22 presents conventional arguments as to why financial statements prepared on the accrual basis (rather than on a cash basis) "provide the type of information about past transactions and other events that is most useful to users in making economic decisions." If the going concern assumption cannot be applied because "the enterprise has...an intention or need...to liquidate or curtail materially the scale of its operations, the financial statements may have to be prepared on a different basis and, if so, the basis used is disclosed" (par. 23).

QUALITATIVE CHARACTERISTICS OF FINANCIAL STATEMENTS

The Framework (pars. 24–39) cites four main qualitative characteristics: understandability, relevance, reliability, and comparability. Materiality is mentioned as an aspect of relevance. "Faithful representation," "substance over form," "neutrality" (freedom from bias), "prudence" (subject to neutrality), and "completeness" (within the bounds of materiality and cost) are mentioned as aspects of reliability.

The subject of *understandability* is a difficult one, because of the notorious complexity of the financial statements of large multinational groups and of the accounting rules underlying them. The Framework states that "users are assumed to have a reasonable knowledge of business and economic activities, and accounting, and a willingness to study the information with reasonable diligence." Information about complex matters that is relevant should not be excluded just because it may be too difficult for some users to understand (par. 25). In this sense, relevance is more important than understandability.

On the subject of *relevance and materiality*, the Framework points out that in some cases the nature of an item of information is sufficient to determine its relevance, irrespective of materiality in the quantitative sense. An example (not given in the Framework) is a pending lawsuit from which the possible financial penalties are not of material size but which might lead to significant reputational damage and its commercial consequences. For this reason, such a pending lawsuit should be mentioned in a note, since it is relevant to users' economic decisions about the enterprise.

More generally, the Framework states that "information is material if its omission or misstatement could influence the economic decisions of users taken on the basis of the financial statements...the size of the item or error [being] judged in the particular circumstances of its omission or misstatement" (par. 30). Thus, the key characteristic is relevance, and materiality should be interpreted as a guide to relevance, since it is relevant to users' economic decisions about the enterprise.

The Framework presents *faithful representation* as a necessary condition of reliability, and *"substance over form"* as a necessary condition of faithful representation. There is a risk that financial information may be "less than a faithful representation of that which it seeks to portray...not due to bias, but rather to inherent difficulties either in identifying the transaction and other events to be measured or in devising and applying [appropriate] measurement and presentation techniques." This type of difficulty is given as a reason why internally generated goodwill is not recognized (par. 34).

Neutrality is also presented as a necessary condition of reliability. The well-known tension between neutrality (or freedom from bias) and *prudence* is considered in paragraphs 36 and 37. Financial statements are not neutral if, by the selection and presentation of information, they influence the making of a decision or judgment in order to achieve a predetermined outcome. Prudence is "the inclusion of a degree of caution in the exercise of judgments needed in making the estimates required under conditions of uncertainty, such that assets or income are not overstated and liabilities or expenses are not understated." But the exercise of prudence, as defined in the Framework, does not permit (for example) the creation of hidden reserves or excessive provisions, the deliberate understatement of assets or income, or the deliberate overstatement of liabilities or expenses, because this would fail to meet the requirement for neutrality and hence that for reliability.

> **OBSERVATION:** In fact, it is not obvious that neutrality or freedom from bias *as such* is a necessary condition of reliability, provided the bias is *known* to the user. Neutrality, as defined in the Framework, means the absence of the kind of bias that, by the selection or presentation of information, influences decisions or judgments in order to achieve a predetermined outcome (as in "creative accounting"). Hence, biases the effects of which can be reasonably assumed to be known to the user because they are part of IAS GAAP, such as the "prudently" asymmetric treatment of certain unrealized gains (unrecognized) and unrealized losses (recognized), do not imply lack of neutrality in the sense of the Framework.

It should be noted, however, that in its recent standards the IASC has shifted the balance between neutrality and prudence in favor of the former. It has done this by promoting both measurement on the basis of "fair values" and the recognition in income of the resultant unrealized gains and losses from remeasurement. An example is IAS 39, "Financial Instruments: Recognition and Measurement" (see Chapter 16). The result has been a substantial reduction in the extent of the asymmetric treatment of unrealized gains and losses in IAS GAAP.

Completeness (within the bounds of materiality and cost) is a necessary condition of reliability, since "an omission can cause information to be false or misleading and thus unreliable" (par. 38).

> **OBSERVATION:** The Framework does not make it clear how a trade-off between completeness and cost would be made, in the case of an omission that would cause the information to be unreliable. Some guidance on this matter is given in the disclosure requirements of individual IASs, which are fairly detailed.

Comparability of financial statements, both over time and cross-sectionally, is important to users. Comparability over time is needed in order to identify trends in an enterprise's financial position and performance. Cross-sectional comparability is necessary so that the financial statements of different enterprises may be used to evaluate their relative financial positions, performances, and changes in financial position (pars. 39–42).

Comparability requires consistency in the measurement and disclosure of the financial effects of similar transactions and other events. One important implication is that users need to be informed of the enterprise's accounting policies, of any changes in these, and of the effects of such changes. However, comparability over time should not be given precedence over the introduction of improvements in financial reporting (pars. 40–41). On the other hand, comparability over time makes the provision of corresponding prior-period information important (par. 42).

There are trade-offs to be made between timeliness and reliability, benefits and costs, and between different qualitative characteristics. There is, moreover, a need for professional judgment in making such trade-offs, given that "the overriding consideration is how best to meet…the objective of financial statements,…[that is,] to satisfy the economic decision-making needs of users" (pars. 43–45).

> **OBSERVATION:** In commenting on the trade-off between benefits and costs, the Framework (par. 44) states that "the costs do not necessarily fall on those users who enjoy the benefits. Benefits may also be enjoyed by users other than those for whom

the information is prepared." The latter sentence refers to the so-called "free rider" problem, but the formulation in the Framework seems to assume that the costs would be expected to be borne by those users for whom the information is prepared. In fact, costs are more usually considered to be borne by *preparers* of financial statements, whom the Framework seems to have left out of the equation. "Preparers," in this sense, are the enterprise's management and the common shareholders whom they represent, and it is the shareholders who effectively bear the costs.

There might seem to be a tacit assumption in the Framework that the users for whom the information is prepared can be identified with the preparers; in other words, those for whom the information is prepared (investors) are those on whose behalf management acts in preparing financial statements, and who end up bearing the cost. This identification would restrict the intended beneficiaries of the information to equity investors (common shareholders), to the exclusion of other investors.

However, the Framework gives as an example "the provision of further information to lenders [which] may reduce the borrowing costs of an enterprise." Yet, in that case, the lenders would not bear the cost of preparing such further information; it would be borne by the common shareholders (who would also benefit from the reduction in borrowing costs). One is forced to conclude that the comments on this issue in the Framework are somewhat confused.

The Framework does not deal directly with the concepts of "true and fair view" (TFV) or "fair presentation" (FP), but states that "the application of the principal qualitative characteristics and of appropriate accounting standards normally results in financial statements that convey what is generally understood as [a TFV or FP] of such information" (par. 46). As noted above, however, IAS 1, "Presentation of Financial Statements," as revised in 1997, states fair presentation as a requirement.

THE ELEMENTS OF FINANCIAL STATEMENTS

The section of the Framework concerning the elements of financial statements (pars. 47–80) consists essentially of definitions of the elements of financial statements as identified by the Framework.

> **OBSERVATION:** As noted in the Overview, the definitions given in this section, and especially those of assets and liabilities, are the core of the Framework as a prescriptive basis for standard-setting. The section on Recognition of Elements (pars. 82–98, see below) acts to reinforce this core. In particular:

1. The Framework defines income and expenses in terms of increases and decreases in economic benefits that are equated with changes in assets and liabilities;

2. The latter are defined in terms of "resources controlled" and "present obligations" to exclude some of the types of items that have been recognized as assets or liabilities (accruals and deferrals) in the name of "matching" expenses and revenues;

3. The effect of these tighter definitions, together with those of the recognition criteria set out in the section on recognition, can be seen particularly in the implications of the definition of a liability for the recognition of provisions (see Chapters 6 and 28 on IAS 22 and IAS 37), and in the implications of the definition of an asset for the recognition of intangible items (see Chapters 6 and 21 on IASs 22 and 38).

There is an overlap between definitions and recognition criteria, since satisfying the definition of an element is the principal criterion for recognition. The Framework, however, seeks to distinguish definition issues from recognition issues as far as possible.

The Framework relates the elements of financial statements to the measurement of financial position and performance. As elements of financial position (in the balance sheet), it provides definitions of assets, liabilities, and equity; and as elements of performance (in the income statement) , it defines income, including revenue and gains, and expenses, including losses. As for the statement of changes in financial position, this "usually reflects income statement elements and changes in balance sheet elements," and so the Framework does not identify any elements associated uniquely with this statement (par. 47).

Financial Position

The elements considered to be "directly related to the measurement of financial position" are assets, liabilities, and equity, which are defined as follows (par. 49):

1. An asset is a resource (a) controlled by the enterprise, (b) as a result of past events, and (c) from which future economic benefits are expected to flow to the enterprise. Recognition as an asset thus requires that the three components of the definition, (a), (b) and (c), be satisfied.

2. A liability is (a) a present obligation of the enterprise, (b) arising out of past events, (c) the settlement of which is expected to result in an outflow from the enterprise of resources

embodying economic benefits. Recognition as a liability thus requires that the three components of the definition, (a), (b) and (c), be satisfied.

3. Equity is defined as the residual interest in the assets of the enterprise after deducting all its liabilities.

> **OBSERVATION:** Financial position comprises a number of attributes, including liquidity, solvency, leverage, asset structure, reserves available to cover dividends, and so forth. While each of these attributes may be measured, it is not clear what is meant by "measurement" of financial position as such, which is the terminology used in paragraph 49. A term such as "evaluation of financial position" would be more usual.

Merely satisfying the above definitions does not entail recognition, since the recognition criteria in pars. 82–98 must also be satisfied, and also the principle of "substance over form" must be respected. For example, this principle requires fixed assets held under finance leases to be recognized by the lessee as fixed assets (with corresponding leasing liabilities), while the lessor recognizes a financial asset (pars. 50–51).

Balance sheets drawn up in accordance with "current" IASs may include items the treatment of which does not satisfy the *above* definitions, but the definitions will underlie "future" reviews of existing standards and the formulation of new ones (par. 52). As noted above, the IASC has acted accordingly, and it would now be unusual to find an item whose treatment according to a current IAS would conflict with the definitions.

Assets

The "future economic benefit embodied in an asset" is defined as "the potential to contribute, directly or indirectly, to the flow of cash and cash equivalents to the enterprise," including "a capability to reduce cash outflows." In case that definition should leave the status of cash itself as an asset unclear, it is stated that cash satisfies this definition, because it "renders a service to the enterprise because of its command over other resources." Assets embody future economic benefits that may flow to the enterprise by having one or more of the following capabilities: (a) being exchanged for other assets; (b) being used to settle a liability; or (c) being distributed to the enterprise's owners (three capabilities that cash conspicuously possesses); as well as that of being used singly or in combination with other assets in the production of goods and services to be sold by the enterprise (pars. 53–55).

Neither having physical form, nor being the object of a right of ownership, is an essential attribute of an asset. Intangible items such as patents and copyrights may satisfy the definition of an asset, as may a fixed asset held under a finance lease (by virtue of which it is a resource controlled though not owned by, and from which future benefits are expected to flow to, the enterprise). Moreover, knowledge obtained from development activity may meet the definition of an asset (capitalized development costs) even though neither physical form nor legal ownership is involved, provided there is *de facto* control such that, by keeping the knowledge secret, the enterprise controls the benefits that are expected to flow from it (pars. 56–57).

Assets may result from various types of past transactions and other past events. Normally, these are purchase transactions and the events associated with production; but they may include donation (for example, by way of a government grant) or discovery (as in the case of mineral deposits). Expected future transactions or events do not give rise to assets; for example, a binding contract by an enterprise to purchase inventory does not cause the inventory in question to meet the definition of an asset of that enterprise until the purchase transaction that fulfils the contract has occurred. While expenditure is a common way to acquire or generate an asset, expenditure undertaken with a view to generating future economic benefits may fail to result in an asset, for example, if the intended economic benefits cannot be expected or are not controlled by the enterprise (pars. 58–59).

Liabilities

An essential characteristic of (or necessary condition for) a liability is that the enterprise should have a "present obligation." An obligation is "a duty or responsibility to act or perform in a certain way." The duty or responsibility may arise from the law, for example, the law of contract; or it may arise from normal business practice, which leads to legitimate expectations that the enterprise will act or perform in a certain way (that is, a constructive obligation). An example of the latter is a constructive obligation to extend the benefits of a warranty for some period beyond the contractual warranty period, because this is an established practice (par. 60).

A present obligation (in the relevant sense) is not the same as a future commitment. An enterprise may have a commitment to purchase an asset in the future at an agreed price; however, this does not entail a net outflow of resources. The commitment does not give rise to a liability, which arises only when the purchase has actually taken place and title in the asset has passed to the enterprise, leaving the latter with an obligation to pay for it. (In the case of a cash transaction, no liability would arise.) (Paragraph 61.)

There are a number of ways in which a liability may be settled or discharged, which include replacement by another obligation, conversion into equity, and the creditor waiving or forfeiting his rights.

There are also various types of "past transactions or past events" from which liabilities may result (pars. 62–63). If a provision involves a present obligation and satisfies the rest of the definition of a liability given in the Framework, it is a liability even if the amount has to be estimated (par. 64).

> **OBSERVATION:** Paragraph 64 does not emphasize the equally important point that a provision that fails to satisfy the criterion of being an *obligation* arising from a past transaction or past event is not a liability. This point, however, was crucial in arriving at the requirements for recognition of provisions in IAS 22, "Business Combinations," and IAS 37, "Provisions, Contingent Liabilities, and Contingent Assets" (see Chapters 6 and 28).

Equity

Paragraphs 65–68 are concerned with equity. The fact that equity is defined as a residual interest (assets minus liabilities) does not mean that it cannot be meaningfully divided into subclassifications that are shown separately in the balance sheet. Examples are the differences among the following: (a) paid-in capital (capital stock and paid-in surplus); (b) retained earnings; (c) reserves representing appropriations of retained earnings; and (d) reserves representing the amounts required to be retained in order to maintain "real" capital, that is, either real financial capital or (real) physical capital (par. 65).

There are various legal, tax, and valuation considerations that affect equity, such as requirements for legal reserves, and whether or not the enterprise is incorporated. It is emphasized that transfers to legal, statutory, and tax reserves are appropriations of retained earnings and not expenses. (Likewise, releases from such reserves are credits to retained earnings and not income, but this is not spelled out.) The rather obvious point is made that the amount at which equity is shown in the balance sheet is not intended to be a measure of the market value of the enterprise, either as a going concern or in a piecemeal disposal. It is stated that the definition and treatment of equity in the Framework are appropriate for unincorporated enterprises, even if the legal considerations are different.

Performance

Paragraphs 69–81 contain the section of the Framework in which definitions of the financial statement elements relating to performance are given. "Profit is frequently used as a measure of performance or as the basis for other measures, such as return on investment and earnings per share" (par. 69). However, this section of the Framework does not discuss the relationship between the elements of performance and the profit measure, except to say that "the recognition and measurement of income and expenses, and hence profit, depends in part on the concepts of capital and capital maintenance used by the enterprise in preparing its financial statements." The determination of profit and related issues are discussed in a later section of the Framework (pars. 102–110).

The elements of income and expenses are defined as follows:

1. Income is increases in economic benefits during the accounting period in the form of inflows or enhancements of assets or decreases of liabilities that result in increases in equity, other than those relating to contributions from equity participants.

2. Expenses are decreases in economic benefits during the accounting period in the form of outflows or depletions of assets or incurrences of liabilities that result in decreases in equity, other than those relating to distributions to equity participants (par. 70).

These definitions identify the essential features of income and expenses but do not attempt to specify their recognition criteria (par. 71).

> **OBSERVATION:** The definitions given above make it clear that the Framework's approach treats the definitions of assets and liabilities as *logically prior to* those of income and expenses. This is sometimes characterized as a "balance sheet approach" to the relationship between financial statements. This term is potentially misleading, however. The Framework's approach should certainly not be understood as implying the subordination of the income statement to the balance sheet from an *informational* perspective.

Income and expenses may be presented in different ways in the income statement in order to provide relevant information. An example given is the distinction between items of income or expense that arise in the course of the ordinary business activities of the particular enterprise and those that do not (a distinction required by IAS 1, "Presentation of Financial Statements"; see Chapter 3). Combining items of income and expense in different ways also permits different measures of enterprise performance to be provided. Examples are the alternative income statement formats with different analyses of expenses, by nature and by function (pars. 72–73). (These different formats are discussed in IAS 1, pars. 80–82; see Chapter 3).

Income

The Framework's definition of income encompasses both revenue and gains. Revenue is described as arising in the course of the ordinary activities of an enterprise and includes sales, fees, interest, royalties, and rent. Gains may or may not arise in the course of ordinary activities. Gains may arise on the disposal of non-current assets and also include unrealized gains such as those arising on the revaluation of marketable securities and from increases in the carrying amount of long-term assets. Gains, when recognized in the income statement, are usually displayed separately because their economic significance tends to differ from that of revenue, and they are often reported net of related expenses (pars. 74–77).

The counterpart entry corresponding to a credit for income may be to various asset accounts (not only cash or receivables), or to a liability account such as when a loan is discharged by the provision of goods or services (par. 77).

Expenses

The Framework's definition of expenses encompasses losses as well as expenses that arise in the course of the ordinary activities of the enterprise. Examples given of expenses that arise in the course of ordinary activities are cost of sales, wages, and depreciation. They usually take the form (that is, are the accounting counterpart) of an outflow or depletion of assets such as cash and cash equivalents, inventory, property, or plant and equipment (par. 78).

Losses represent items that may or may not arise in the course of ordinary activities. They include those that result from such disasters as fire or flood, as well as those arising on the disposal of non-current assets, and also encompass unrealized losses, such as those arising from the effects of adverse currency exchange rate movements on financial assets or liabilities. Losses, when recognized in the income statement, are usually displayed separately because their economic significance tends to differ from that of other expenses, and they are often reported net of related income (pars. 79–80).

> **OBSERVATION:** Paragraphs 76 and 80 contain the phrases "when gains are recognized in the income statement" and "when losses are recognized in the income statement." IASs require or allow certain unrealized gains to be included directly in equity (for example, certain revaluation surpluses on non-current assets and foreign exchange gains), or to have their recognition deferred until realization occurs. IASs also require or allow certain losses, such as revaluation losses and foreign exchange losses, to be included directly in equity. Thus, the issue of recognition in the income statement needs to be considered in the context of individual IASs.

It is stated in paragraph 77 that "various kinds of assets may be received or enhanced by income." Likewise, expenses are described in paragraph 78 as "usually tak[ing] the form of an outflow or depletion of assets...." We believe that such points are made more clearly by using the accounting relationships, in virtue of which the income statement effect is the reflection or counterpart of (rather than merely consisting of) the related balance sheet movement. The importance of the accounting relationships in the context of recognition is mentioned in paragraph 84 (see below).

Capital Maintenance Adjustments

The effects on equity of revaluations or restatements of assets and liabilities meet the Framework's definitions of income and expenses, but their inclusion in the income statement depends on which concept of capital maintenance is being applied (par. 81). This matter is discussed further below.

RECOGNITION OF THE ELEMENTS OF FINANCIAL STATEMENTS

Recognition issues are dealt with in paragraphs 82–98. Recognition is described as "the process of incorporating in the balance sheet or [the] income statement an item that meets the definition of an element and satisfies the criteria for recognition set out in paragraph 83." (The statement of changes in financial position is not mentioned because its elements consist of those that are also elements of financial position or performance.) Failure to recognize *in the main financial statements* items that satisfy the relevant definition and recognition criteria is not rectified by disclosure of the accounting policies used or by use of notes or other explanatory material.

The recognition criteria set out in paragraph 83 are that an item which meets the definition of an element should be recognized if:

1. It is probable that any future economic benefit associated with the item will flow to or from the enterprise; and

2. The item has a cost or value that can be measured with reliability.

Recognition is subject to materiality. Accounting interrelationships are also significant, since recognition in the financial statements of an item that meets the definition and recognition criteria for a particular element, for example an asset, entails the recognition of another (counterpart) element, such as income or a liability (par. 84). (This refers, strictly speaking, to the initial recognition of an item. However, a similar point could be made about the implications of remeasurement or valuation adjustments.)

The Probability of Future Economic Benefit

The concept of *probability* is used in the recognition criteria "to refer to the degree of uncertainty [as to whether] the future economic benefits associated with the item will flow to or from the enterprise...in keeping with the uncertainty that characterizes the environment in which an enterprise operates." Assessments of such uncertainty are made on the basis of the evidence available when the financial statements are prepared. In regard to receivables, for example, for a large population of accounts, some statistical evidence will usually be available regarding collectibility (par. 85).

> **OBSERVATION:** The Framework does not offer any guidance, beyond that mentioned above, on the interpretation of "probable." IAS 37, "Provisions, Contingent Assets and Contingent Liabilities," contains an interpretation of "probable" as "more likely than not," that is, a probability in excess of 50%, but states that this interpretation is not intended to be applied in other contexts. Others have suggested an interpretation of "probable" in the present context as a probability of at least 75%. However, in the case of the receivables example mentioned above, the allowance to be made for probably uncollectible accounts would normally be based on past statistics, perhaps adjusted to take account of the current economic environment.

Reliability of Measurement

Reliability, the second recognition criterion, was discussed in the section "Qualitative Characteristics of Financial Statements" above. If an item does not possess a cost or value that can be measured with reliability (so that the information has that qualitative characteristic), then it is not appropriate to recognize it. However, in many cases, cost or (more particularly) value must be estimated; indeed, the use of reasonable estimates is an essential part of the financial reporting process and need not undermine reliability. In cases where an item satisfies the definition of an element but not the recognition criteria, it will not be recognized in the financial statements themselves, but its relevance is likely to require its disclosure in the notes to the financial statements or in other supplementary disclosures. This applies when the item meets the probability criterion of recognition but not the reliability criterion, but may also apply to an item that meets the definition of an element when neither recognition criterion is met. The key issue here is whether the item is considered to be relevant to the evaluation of financial position, performance, or changes in financial position. An item that does not satisfy the recognition criteria for an asset or a liability at one time may do so later, if more information relevant to estimating its probability, cost, or value becomes available (pars. 86–88).

> **OBSERVATION:** The concept of a "reasonable estimate" is clearly crucial in the application of the reliability criterion, but the Framework gives no guidance on how it is to be interpreted. While this will not generally be a problematic issue in relation to the ascertainment of cost, estimating value can be problematic. This issue is dealt with in individual IASs, such as the requirement for an active market on which to base estimates in IAS 39, "Financial Instruments: Recognition and Measurement" (see Chapter 16).
>
> On the issue of the retrospective recognition as an asset of an item of expenditure that has previously been recognized as an expense, IAS 38, "Intangible Assets" (see Chapter 21) does not permit the retrospective capitalization of development costs once they have been written off to expense.

Recognition of Assets

An asset is recognized in the balance sheet when it is probable that future economic benefits will flow to the enterprise (as a result of its control of the asset) and the asset's cost or value can be measured reliably. When expenditure has been incurred but it is not considered probable that economic benefits will flow to the enterprise beyond the current accounting period, this expenditure will be recognized as an expense, not as an asset. The intention of management in undertaking the expenditure is irrelevant (pars. 89–90).

Recognition of Liabilities

A liability is recognized in the balance sheet when it is probable that an outflow of resources embodying economic benefits will result from the settlement of a present obligation and the amount of that settlement can be measured reliably. Obligations under executory contracts, that is, non-cancelable contracts that are equally proportionately unperformed (such as the amount that will be a liability when inventory ordered and awaiting delivery is received), are not generally recognized as liabilities in the balance sheet, nor are the related assets recognized in the balance sheet. In some cases, however, recognition may be required (par. 91).

> **OBSERVATION:** The treatment of executory contracts is to some extent an open issue in IAS GAAP. Inventory ordered under a non-cancelable contract is not "a resource controlled by" the

enterprise that placed the order until title to the inventory has passed to it, and thus does not satisfy the Framework's definition of an asset of that enterprise. In such a case, it would be illogical to insist that the price to be paid for the inventory be recognized as a liability of that enterprise, since there would be no counterpart item to be recognized (recognition of an expense would make no sense).

There may, however, be other types of executory contract (for example, involving financial instruments) in respect of which recognition of an asset (or expense) and a related liability (or income) may be the most appropriate treatment.

Recognition of Income

Recognition of income occurs simultaneously with the recognition of increases in assets or decreases in liabilities (or a combination of the two). The normal recognition procedures used in practice are applications of the Framework's recognition criteria. An example is the requirement that revenue should be earned (that is, it should be associated with a simultaneous increase in assets or decrease in liabilities). These procedures are concerned with restricting the recognition of income to items that, in effect, meet the Framework's recognition criteria of *probability* (a sufficient degree of certainty that an economic benefit has flowed or will flow to the enterprise) and *reliability* of measurement (pars. 92–93).

Recognition of Expenses

Recognition of expenses occurs simultaneously with the recognition of an increase in liabilities or a decrease in assets (or a combination of the two). Expenses are commonly recognized in the income statement on the basis of an association (matching) between the incurrence of costs and the earning of specific items of revenue, that result directly and jointly from the same transactions or other events. An example is the matching of the cost of goods sold with the associated sales revenue. However, the Framework does not permit the application of the matching procedure to result in the recognition of items in the balance sheet that do not meet the definition of assets or liabilities (pars. 94–95).

> **OBSERVATION:** While the last sentence above is true of the Framework, individual IASs may require the recognition of balance sheet items that arguably do not meet the Framework's definitions. Examples include the deferral and amortization of government grants following the matching principle, required by

IAS 20 (see Chapter 18); and the similar treatment of gains on certain sale and leaseback transactions, required by IAS 17 (see Chapter 25).

Depreciation and amortization are procedures for dealing with a situation in which a decrease in the future economic benefits embodied in an asset takes place over several accounting periods. It may not be feasible or cost-effective to relate such decreases directly to revenue. In such cases, the expense is recognized in the income statement on the basis of procedures that systematically and rationally allocate it over those accounting periods in which the economic benefits embodied in the asset may be considered to be consumed or to expire (par. 96).

An expense is recognized immediately in the income statement in the case of an expenditure that produces no future economic benefits that qualify for recognition as an asset in the balance sheet. An expense is also recognized in the income statement when a liability is incurred without an asset being recognized. An example is the recognition of a liability under a product warranty and of the associated warranty expense (pars. 97–98).

> **OBSERVATION:** The paragraphs on the recognition of income and expenses use a terminology that we have avoided above. Income is described as being recognized in the income statement "when an increase in the future economic benefits related to an asset or a decrease of a liability has arisen that can be measured reliably." The description of the conditions for recognition of expenses is similar, with "decrease" being substituted for "increase" and vice versa. While logically correct in the Framework's terms, this terminology, with its reference to "future economic benefits," is rather cumbersome and is not essential to clarifying the criteria for recognition of income and expenses.

MEASUREMENT OF THE ELEMENTS OF THE FINANCIAL STATEMENTS

Paragraphs 99–101 deal with measurement issues, insofar as these are covered in the Framework. The treatment here is descriptive and avoids being prescriptive. Measurement is described as "the process of determining the monetary amounts at which the elements of the financial statements are to be recognized and carried in the balance sheet and income statement." It involves the selection of a particular basis of measurement.

Four different measurement bases are specifically mentioned and described (without any claim to exhaustiveness): historical cost, current cost (of replacement or settlement), realizable or (for liabilities) settlement value, and present value. Historical cost is mentioned as the measurement basis most commonly adopted by enterprises in preparing their financial statements, usually in combination with other measurement bases. An example of the latter is the carrying of inventories at the lower of historical cost and net realizable value. Marketable securities may be carried at market value, and pension liabilities are carried at their present value. Current cost may be used as a means of taking account of the effects of changing prices of nonmonetary assets.

CONCEPTS OF CAPITAL AND CAPITAL MAINTENANCE

Concepts of Capital

The Framework identifies two main concepts of capital: the financial concept and the physical concept. The financial concept of capital may take two forms: invested money (nominal financial) capital or invested purchasing power (real financial) capital. In either case, capital is identified with the equity of the enterprise (in either nominal or real financial terms) and with its net assets measured in those terms. The physical concept of capital is based on the notion of the productive capacity or operating capability of the enterprise, as embodied in its net assets. Most enterprises adopt a financial concept of capital, normally (in the absence of severe inflation) nominal financial capital (par. 102).

> **OBSERVATION:** The Framework does not distinguish clearly between nominal and real financial capital; however, the two are quite distinct and will be treated accordingly below. Physical capital is also a form of "real" capital concept.

Capital Maintenance and the Determination of Profit

Choice of a concept of capital is related to the concept of capital maintenance that is most meaningful, given the implications of the choice for profit measurement and the needs of the users of the financial statements in that regard, as follows:

1. *Maintenance of nominal financial capital.* Under this concept a profit is earned only if the money amount of the net assets at

the end of the period exceeds the money amount of the net assets at the beginning of the period, after excluding any distributions to, and contributions from, equity owners during the period.

2. *Maintenance of real financial capital.* Under this concept a profit is earned only if the money amount of the net assets at the end of the period exceeds the money amount of the net assets at the beginning of the period, restated in units of the same purchasing power, after excluding distributions to, and contributions from, owners. Normally, the units of purchasing power employed are those of the currency at the end of the period, into which the net assets at the beginning of the period are restated.

3. *Maintenance of real physical capital.* Under this concept a profit is earned only if the operating capability embodied in the net assets at the end of the period exceeds the operating capability embodied in the net assets at the beginning of the period, after excluding distributions to, and contributions from, owners. Operating capability embodied in assets may, in principle, be measured by employing the current cost basis of measurement.

(Pars. 103–106.)

The main difference among the three concepts of capital maintenance is the treatment of the effects of changes in the carrying amounts of the enterprise's assets and liabilities. Under nominal financial capital maintenance, increases in the money-carrying amounts of assets held over the period (to the extent that they are recognized as gains) are part of profit.

Under real financial capital maintenance, such increases are part of profit only if they are "real" increases, that is, increases that remain after money-carrying amounts have been restated in units of the same purchasing power. The total amount of the restatement is known as a "capital maintenance adjustment" and is transferred to a capital maintenance reserve, which is part of equity (but not of retained profits). Real financial capital maintenance may be used in conjunction with historical cost as a measurement basis but would more normally be used in conjunction with the current cost basis.

Under real physical capital maintenance, changes in the money prices (current costs) of assets and liabilities held over the period are considered not to affect the amount of operating capability embodied in those items, and therefore the total amount of those changes is treated as a capital maintenance adjustment and excluded from profit.

Illustration

Let us assume that a company begins with capital stock of $100 and cash of $100. At the beginning of the year, one item of inventory is bought for $100. The item of inventory is sold at the end of the year for $150, its replacement cost at that time is $120, and general inflation throughout the year is 10%. Profit measured using each of the capital maintenance concepts mentioned earlier would be as shown below.

	Nominal financial capital maintenance	Real financial capital maintenance	Real physical capital maintenance
Sales	$150	$150	$150
Less cost of sales	(100)	(100)	(120)
Operating profit	50	50	30
Less inflation adjustment	—	(10)	—
Total gain	$ 50	$ 40	$ 30
Capital maintenance adjustment	$ 0	$ 10	$ 20

Column 1 shows the gain after ensuring the maintenance of the stockholders' opening capital measured as a sum of money. Column 2 shows the gain after ensuring the maintenance of the stockholders' opening capital measured as a block of purchasing power. Both of these are concerned, under different definitions, with the maintenance of financial capital—in terms either of its money amount or of its general purchasing power. Column 3 shows the gain after ensuring the maintenance of the company's initial operating capacity and is therefore of a completely different nature.

Different combinations of measurement bases and capital maintenance concepts provide different accounting models, between which management should choose, taking into account relevance and reliability. The IASC does not "presently" intend to prescribe a particular model, other than in exceptional circumstances such as when reporting in the currency of a hyperinflationary economy (pars. 107–110).

> **OBSERVATION:** IAS 29, "Financial Reporting in Hyperinflationary Economies" (see Chapter 8) requires a choice between two different models: real financial capital, together with historical costs restated in units of the same purchasing power by use of a general price index; and real physical capital with adjustments for the purchasing power gain or loss on the net monetary position, together with current costs.

CHAPTER 3
PRESENTATION OF FINANCIAL STATEMENTS

CONTENTS

OVERVIEW

"Presentation of Financial Statements," the title of the recently revised IAS 1, represents an attempt to cover several important aspects. The objective of the standard is to prescribe the basis for presentation of general purpose financial statements in order to ensure comparability both with the enterprise's own financial statements of previous periods and with the financial statements of other enterprises. To achieve this objective, the standard sets out overall considerations for the presentation of financial statements, guidelines for their structure, and minimum requirements for the content of financial statements.

In principle, therefore, IAS 1 applies to all aspects of all businesses. Many aspects of financial reporting are covered additionally by other more specific International Accounting Standards, as detailed elsewhere in this volume. However, some other aspects are not further developed, and IAS 1, therefore, makes up the IAS GAAP in those respects. For example, disclosure of fixed assets is discussed in IAS 16, "Property, Plant, and Equipment" (see Chapter 27), but disclosure of current assets has no additional standard, except for component parts such as Inventories, covered by IAS 2, "Inventories" (see Chapter 23).

Broadly speaking, IAS 1 consists of two parts. Part 1 discusses a number of "overall considerations," consisting of general principles, conventions, and requirements. Much of Part 1 is a restatement of aspects of the Framework, discussed in Chapter 2. It should be remembered that the Framework does not have the status of a standard, whereas IAS 1 obviously does. Part 2 discusses in some detail the required contents of general purpose financial statements. It is worth noting that most national accounting standards operate, and are designed to operate, within the context of national legislation, especially for corporations. There is, of course, no single international company or corporation statute. To some extent, IAS 1 provides a minimal filling in of this lacuna.

BACKGROUND

To understand how and why IAS 1 as currently constituted came about, it is helpful to look at the chronology involved. The very first standard issued by IASC was the original IAS 1, "Disclosure of Accounting Policies," effective for accounting periods beginning on or after January 1, 1975. IAS 5, "Information to be Disclosed in Financial Statements," related to periods beginning on or after January 1, 1977 and IAS 13, "Presentation of Current Assets and Current Liabilities," related to periods beginning on or after January 1, 1981. All three of these were fairly short standards, with limited objectives accurately indicated by their titles.

Later, as its approach became generally more sophisticated, the IASC developed its "Framework for the Preparation and Presentation of Financial Statements." As discussed in detail in Chapter 2, this sets out the concepts that underlie the preparation and presentation of financial statements designed for external users. This document appeared in its agreed-upon form in 1989. It was intended to inform the preparation of standards and so improve consistency over time, but it is of a lower status than the standards, which override the Framework if any conflict occurs.

IAS 1, as revised in 1997, is the next step in this long process of development. It replaces the original IAS 1 and both IAS 5 and IAS

13, but it does a great deal more than merely update the three original standards. In particular, it deals not only with the disclosure of accounting policies, as did the original IAS 1, but also with the whole issue of policies and conventions, incorporating significant parts of the 1989 Framework (thereby increasing the status of those aspects so incorporated to full standard requirement).

The revised IAS 1, issued in 1997 and formally operative for financial statements covering accounting periods beginning on or after July 1, 1998, is an important and pervasive standard. It attempts to provide something approaching a philosophy of financial reporting, together with an overview of the complete required contents of published financial reports. Its gestation was at times fraught with disagreement, and further developments cannot be ruled out.

SCOPE

The scope and applicability of IAS 1 revised (hereafter IAS 1) are very wide. IAS 1 should be applied in the presentation of all general purpose financial statements prepared and presented in accordance with International Accounting Standards.

General purpose financial statements are those intended to meet the needs of users who are not in a position to demand reports tailored to meet their specific information needs. They include statements presented separately or those within another public document, such as an annual report or prospectus.

IAS 1 does not apply to condensed interim financial information, but it must be applied in full to all general purpose statements, as described above, that claim to be in accordance with International Accounting Standards. This includes banks and insurance companies, and IAS 1 notes that IAS 30, "Disclosures in the Financial Statements of Banks and Similar Financial Institutions," contains additional requirements that are "consistent with the requirements of" IAS 1. Not-for-profit organizations can also apply the standard (and IAS GAAP generally) by amending item descriptions in the financial statements as appropriate.

FINANCIAL STATEMENTS

IAS 1 repeats the objective of general purpose financial statements from the Framework, as being to provide information about the financial position, performance, and cash flows of an enterprise that is useful to a wide range of users in making economic decisions. Financial statements also show the results of management's stewardship of the resources entrusted to it. Financial statements provide information about an enterprise's (par. 5):

1. Assets,
2. Liabilities,
3. Equity,
4. Income and expenses, including gains and losses, and
5. Cash flows.

A complete set of financial statements, therefore, includes the following components (par. 7):

1. Balance sheet,
2. Income statement,
3. A statement showing either
   (a) all changes in equity, or
   (b) changes in equity other than those arising from capital transactions with owners and distribution to owners,
4. Cash flow statements, and
5. Accounting policies and explanatory notes.

Item 3 above may be a new concept in some jurisdictions. To deal with users' demands for more comprehensive information on "performance," measured more broadly than the "profit" shown in the income statement, the standard establishes a new requirement for a primary financial statement showing those gains and losses not presented in the income statement. This is discussed and illustrated in more detail later in this chapter.

IAS 1 encourages, but does not require, the additional presentation, "outside the financial statements," of a management report about the financial performance and financial position of the enterprise, and about its environment, risks, and uncertainties. Brief suggestions as to coverage are made in paragraph 8, but none of the suggestions are mandatory. Further additional statements and reports, for example, on environmental matters, are also encouraged.

FAIR PRESENTATION AND COMPLIANCE WITH INTERNATIONAL ACCOUNTING STANDARDS

The first substantive part of IAS 1 concerns the vexed question of the override. The issue at stake is whether or not the detailed regulations, that is, the standards in this case, are always and automatically both necessary and sufficient conditions for the preparation of adequate financial statements, or whether some more fundamental overriding criterion, such as the provision of a true and fair view, a requirement to present fairly, or a requirement not to mislead users, is, when a clash occurs, the determining requirement (hence "overriding" the standards). IAS 1 recognizes that compliance with the International Standards may be insufficient or inadequate "in extremely rare circumstances."

Enterprises that comply with IASs should say so. This requires that they comply with *all* applicable aspects of all applicable standards and with all applicable interpretations of the Standing Interpretations Committee. However, the overall requirement is that financial statements should present fairly the financial position, financial performance, and cash flows of an enterprise. The appropriate application of International Accounting Standards, with additional disclosure when necessary, results, in "virtually all circumstances," in financial statements that achieve a fair presentation.

In the extremely rare circumstances in which management concludes that compliance with a requirement in a standard would be misleading, and therefore that departure from a requirement is necessary to achieve a fair presentation, an enterprise should disclose (par. 13):

1. That management has concluded that the financial statements fairly present the enterprise's financial position, financial performance, and cash flows.

2. That it has complied in all material respects with applicable International Accounting Standards except that it has departed from a standard in order to achieve a fair presentation.

3. The standard from which the enterprise has departed, the nature of the departure, including the treatment that the standard would require, the reason why that treatment would be misleading in the circumstances and the treatment adopted.

4. The financial impact of the departure on the enterprise's net profit and loss, assets, equity and cash flows for each period presented.

> **OBSERVATION:** The question of terminology and national positions here is both important and potentially confusing. The U.S. requirement to present fairly in accordance with (U.S.) GAAP means, to follow GAAP, as the *Miller GAAP Guide*, which finds it unnecessary even to mention "fair presentation," makes clear. The U.K. requirement to give a true and fair view equally clearly means to follow standards where suitable but to depart from them if a true and fair view requires it. The U.K. position in essence found its way into the European Union Fourth Directive and, hence, subject to varying degrees of bastardization, into other European countries. IAS 1 follows the U.S. *wording* but the U.K./EU philosophy. The following table makes this clear.

Jurisdiction	Terminology	Overriding
U.K.	True and Fair View	Yes
European Union	True and Fair View	Yes
USA	Fair Presentation	No
IASC	Fair Presentation	Yes

This is not to imply that the override is likely to be used in similar ways or in similar volumes in the various jurisdictions where it exists. We predict that its usage under IASC will indeed be rare. But an important issue of principle is at stake. Can the qualitative characteristics required of financial reporting be ensured by *compliance* with a set of (static) rules, or is some *professional judgment* involved that may, in principle, entail departure from one or more rules?

Although no attempt to define "fair presentation" is provided (rightly in our view), the presumption "in virtually all circumstances" is that a fair presentation is achieved by compliance in all material respects with applicable International Accounting Standards. A fair presentation requires (par. 15):

1. Selecting and applying accounting policies as described below.
2. Presenting information, including accounting policies, in a manner that provides relevant, reliable, comparable, and understandable information.
3. Providing additional disclosures when the requirements in International Accounting Standards are insufficient to enable users to understand the impact of particular transactions or events on the enterprise's financial position and financial performance.

In extremely rare circumstances, application of a specific requirement in an International Accounting Standard might result in misleading financial statements. In such circumstances departure from the standard is *required*. IASC is at pains to minimize the likelihood of this happening. The override can be applied only when following the standard plus providing additional information would not give a fair presentation (i.e., presumably, would mislead). The existence of national regulations that conflict with IASC Standards is not an adequate reason for departing from an International Standard.

IAS 1 requires, in addition, if the override is employed, that full details of the departure be given in the financial statements, sufficient to enable users to make an informed judgment on whether the departure is necessary and to calculate the adjustments that would be required to comply with the standard. IASC will monitor instances of noncompliance that are brought to its attention (by enterprises, their auditors, and regulators, for example) and will consider the need for clarification through interpretations or amendments to standards, as appropriate, to ensure that departures remain necessary only in extremely rare circumstances.

> **OBSERVATION:** This last point strikes us as eminently sensible. It is at one and the same time a threat against opportunistic attempts to misuse the override facility and a recognition that business is dynamic and that the needs of dynamic reporting may move ahead of the laborious perceptions of standard-setters. Well-grounded departures from existing standards should lead to improved standards in the future.

ACCOUNTING POLICIES

Accounting policies are the specific principles, bases, conventions, rules, and practices adopted by an enterprise in preparing and presenting financial statements. Management should select and apply an enterprise's accounting policies so that the financial statements comply with all the requirements of each applicable International Accounting Standard and interpretation of the Standing Interpretations Committee. Where there are no specific requirements, management should develop policies to ensure that the financial statements provide information that is (par. 20):

1. Relevant to the decision-making needs of users.
2. Reliable in that they:
   (a) represent faithfully the results and financial position of the enterprise;
   (b) reflect the economic substance of events and transactions and not merely the legal form;
   (c) are neutral, that is, free from bias;
   (d) are prudent;
   (e) are complete in all material respects.

All the terms in 1 and 2 above are taken from the Framework, and their implications are discussed in Chapter 2.

In general, choosing appropriate accounting policies is a subjective process. The chosen policies should seek to provide "the most useful information to users" of the financial statements. In the absence of specific requirements in an IAS, the choice of policy should be informed by analogy with similar requirements in IASs or Interpretations, from the definitions, criteria, and logic of the Framework, and finally from national or industry pronouncements or practices if, but only if, they do not conflict with the contents or the spirit of the IASC Framework and body of standards.

IAS 1 proceeds to incorporate and discuss some, but not all, of the assumptions and qualitative characteristics of financial statements included in the Framework (see Chapter 2). The two "underlying assumptions" are going concern and the accrual basis of accounting. The going concern assumption means that it is assumed that the enterprise will continue in operation for the foreseeable future. Financial statements should be prepared on a going concern basis unless management either intends to liquidate the enterprise or to cease trading or has no realistic alternative but to do so. When management is aware, in making its assessment, of material uncertainties related to events or conditions that may cast significant doubt on the enterprise's ability to continue as a going concern, those uncertainties should be disclosed. When the financial statements are not prepared on a going concern basis, that fact should be disclosed, together with the basis on which the financial statements are prepared and the reason why the enterprise is not considered to be a going concern. When the financial statements are prepared on the going concern basis, it is not necessary to say so. Judgment and, in uncertain cases, detailed investigation may be required.

The accrual basis of accounting (except for cash flow statements) is also an automatic assumption that need not be explicitly stated. Under the accrual basis of accounting, transactions and events are recognized when they occur (and not as cash or its equivalent is received or paid), and they are recorded in the accounting records and reported in the financial statements of the periods to which they relate.

IAS 1, unlike the Framework, explicitly links together the alternative descriptions of accruals and matching for this concept. IAS 1 notes that the application of the matching concept in IAS GAAP does not allow the recognition of items in the balance sheet that do not meet the IAS definition of assets or liabilities.

The Framework states, however, that financial statements may include items not falling within these definitions if specific standards require their recognition. Some other standards do so require, for example, with regard to the deferral of government grants (IAS 20, see Chapter 18) and the deferral of income and expenses relating to operating leases (IAS 17, Chapter 25). Although there seems to be conflict between the Framework and IAS 1 on this point, standards, explicitly, override the Framework.

IAS 1 also incorporates the principle of consistency from paragraph 39 of the Framework, but, oddly, only regarding presentation. A change in presentation and classification of items in financial statements between one period and another is permitted only when it results in a more appropriate presentation (which is expected to continue) or is required by a specific International Standard or Interpretation. The Framework principle continues to relate, of course, to recognition and measurement.

The IASC has issued an Interpretation, SIC-18, "Consistency, Alternative Methods," which became effective for annual financial periods beginning on or after July 1, 2000. The issue is how the choice of accounting policy should be exercised in the context of those IASC Standards that allow an explicit choice of accounting policy but are silent on the manner of exercising that choice. The fundamental question is whether, once a choice of policy is made, that policy must be followed consistently for all items accounted for under the specific requirements that provide the choice.

SIC-18 requires that, if more than one accounting policy is available under an International Accounting Standard or Interpretation, an enterprise should choose and apply consistently one of those policies, unless the Standard or Interpretation specifically requires or permits categorization of items, the most appropriate accounting policy should be selected and applied consistently to each category.

The issue of materiality and aggregation raises some important considerations. Each material item should be presented separately in the financial statements. Immaterial amounts should be aggregated with amounts of a similar nature or function and need not be presented separately. In this context, information is material if its non-disclosure could influence the economic decisions of users taken on the basis of the financial statements. Materiality depends on the size and nature of the item judged in the particular circumstances of its omission. In deciding whether an item or an aggregate of items is material, the nature and the size of the item are evaluated together. Depending on the circumstances, either the nature or the size of the item could be the determining factor. For example, evidence of breaking the law causing a fine could be significant in principle, even if the amount is small. Similar items should be aggregated together however large they or the resulting total are in relation to the enterprise as a whole.

It is important that both assets and liabilities and income and expenses, when material, be reported separately. Offsetting in either the income statement or the balance sheet, except when offsetting reflects the substance of the transaction or event, would detract from the ability of users to understand the transactions undertaken and to assess the future cash flows of the enterprise. Assets and liabilities should not be offset except when offsetting is required or permitted by another International Accounting Standard. Items of income and expense should be offset when, and only when (par. 34):

1. An International Accounting Standard requires or permits it; or

2. Gains, losses, and related expenses arising from the same or similar transactions and events are not material. Such amounts should be aggregated in accordance with the principles discussed immediately above.

☞ **PRACTICE POINTER:** It is often not fully appreciated that the prevention of offsetting between assets and liabilities, and between income and expenses, is not at all the same thing as the prevention of netting out between debits and credits in a bookkeeping sense. Receipts and payments in relation to the purchase of one asset, for example, involve the netting out of debits and credits and are not examples of offsetting as discussed in IAS 1. We discuss this example in more detail in Chapter 18 relating to government grants.

It should also be noted that there are several examples where other International Accounting Standards do "require or permit" offsetting. One such example is IAS 11 (see Chapter 10), where contract costs plus recognized profits less losses are offset against progress billings to give a net figure of amount due from customers.

It is explicitly stated that the specific disclosure requirements of International Accounting Standards need not be met if the resulting information is not material. It thus follows that full compliance with IAS GAAP requires the following of complete IAS GAAP except for immaterial disclosure requirements, not the following of complete IAS GAAP period.

The "presentation" section of IAS 1 concludes with requirements about comparative figures. Unless an International Accounting Standard permits or requires otherwise, comparative information should be disclosed in respect of the previous period for all numerical information in the financial statements. Comparative narrative and descriptive information should be included when it is relevant to an understanding of the current period's financial statements.

Comparative information should be restated if necessary if the presentation or classification of items in the current financial statements is altered, unless it is impractical to do so, in which case the reason for not reclassifying should be disclosed together with "the nature of the changes that would have been made if amounts were reclassified." Five- or ten-year summaries should logically be changed as well, although IAS 1 does not consider this point.

It should be noted that IAS 8, "Net Profit or Loss for the Period, Fundamental Errors, and Changes in Accounting Policies," applies if changes constitute a change in accounting policy as discussed in that standard (see Chapter 26).

STRUCTURE AND CONTENT

The whole of the remainder of IAS 1 is concerned with the structure and content of financial statements. The standard requires certain disclosures on the face of the financial statements, requires other line items to be disclosed either on the face of the financial statements or in the notes, and sets out *recommended* formats as an appendix to the standard that an enterprise *may* follow as appropriate in its own circumstances.

IAS 1 requires that "financial statements" (to which IAS GAAP applies) be clearly distinguished from other information, of whatever kind and source, which is included in the same published document. Figures, components, and separate pages must be fully and clearly described. Financial statements should be presented at least annually, normally for a 12-month period. Explanations and clear narratives must be given for any exceptions (such as a change in reporting date after an acquisition by another enterprise). An enterprise "should be in a position" to issue audited financial statements within 6 months of its balance sheet date.

BALANCE SHEETS

It is usual, but not a requirement, to present current and non-current assets, and current and non-current liabilities, as separate classifications (i.e., separated into four) on the face of the balance sheet. When an enterprise chooses not to make this classification, assets and liabilities should be presented broadly in order of their liquidity. Whichever method of presentation is adopted, an enterprise should disclose, for each asset and liability item that combines amounts expected to be recovered or settled both before and after 12 months from the balance sheet date, the amount that is expected to be recovered or settled after more than 12 months.

If a business does not have a clearly defined operating cycle or has an operating cycle typically longer than 12 months, a balance sheet classified as above may not be appropriate. IAS 32, "Financial Instruments: Disclosure and Presentation" (see Chapter 16) requires disclosure of the maturity dates of financial assets and financial liabilities.

Where, as is usually the case, the current/non-current classification is followed, then IAS GAAP specifies the distinctions as described below. IAS 1 deals with assets first, by defining a current asset.

An asset should be classified as a current asset when it (par. 57):

1. Is expected to be realized in, or is held for sale or consumption in, the normal course of the enterprise's operating cycle; or

2. Is held primarily for trading purposes or for the short-term and expected to be realized within 12 months of the balance sheet date; or

3. Is cash or a cash equivalent that is not restricted in its use.

All other assets should be classified as non-current assets.

This definition of a current asset requires careful consideration. Only one of the three conditions needs to be met for classification as a current asset to be required. Thus, an asset that meets condition 1 in a business that has a 2-year operating cycle is a current asset. Conversely, under situation 2, an asset expected to be realized within 12 months of the balance sheet date is a current asset only if it is also held primarily for trading purposes or for the short-term.

> ☛ **PRACTICE POINTER:** The question arises of how to apply this definition to a non-current asset such as a machine, when it is near the end of its useful life and is scheduled for disposal within 12 months. Situation 2 above definitely does not apply, as the machine is not "held primarily for trading purposes or for the short-term." However, does situation 1 above apply and require reclassification as a current asset? It could be argued that (in most cases) it is "expected to be realized in the normal course of the enterprise's operating cycle."
>
> In our view, this would be a misreading of the wording and logic of IAS 1. It is clear that purpose rather than degree of market liquidity is the guiding factor in the current/non-current distribution.
>
> The definition also implies that the currently due portion of a long-term nontrading receivable is *not* to be reclassified as current.

The classification of liabilities, when undertaken by the reporting enterprise, must follow a comparable distinction. A liability should be classified as a current liability when it (par. 60):

1. Is expected to be settled in the normal course of the enterprise's operating cycle, or

2. Is due to be settled within 12 months of the balance sheet date.

All other liabilities should be classified as non-current liabilities.

Again, only one of these criteria needs to apply, so a long operating cycle could lead to the classification as current liabilities of items due to be settled in more than 12 months. In the case of liabilities the "current" (i.e., due within 12 months) portion of long-term interest-bearing liabilities *is* to be classified as "current" in most cases. However, an enterprise should continue to classify long-term interest-bearing liabilities as non-current, even when they are due to be settled within 12 months of the balance sheet date, if *all* of the following are satisfied:

1. The original term was for a period of more than 12 months.

2. The enterprise intends to refinance the obligation on a long-term basis.

3. The intention is supported by an agreement to refinance, or to reschedule payments, which is completed before the financial statements are approved.

The amount of any liability that has been so excluded from current liabilities, together with information in support of this presentation, should be disclosed in the notes to the balance sheet.

It is common for loan agreements to contain clauses such that, in the event of defined undertakings by the borrower not being satisfied (e.g., maintenance of an agreed maximum leverage ratio), the liability becomes payable on demand. If this happens, then the liability would, in general, immediately become "current" under IAS GAAP. The liability would continue to be classified as non-current, however, if (a) the lender has agreed, before the approval of the financial statements, not to demand payment, and (b) further breaches within 12 months of the balance sheet date are "not probable."

> **OBSERVATION:** It is worth repeating that IAS 1 provides a general definitional and disclosure framework. Many of the items in financial statements are the subject of specific and more detailed International Standards, as discussed throughout this book. Some of IAS 1's coverage is somewhat pragmatic. For example, the detailed discussion of the current/non-current distinction given above is included in IAS 1, arising from the simultaneous withdrawal of IAS 13, "Presentation of Current Assets and Current Liabilities." However, implications of non-current status are not mentioned in IAS 1, because these are covered by other standards, such as IAS 4, "Depreciation Accounting," and IAS 16, "Property, Plant, and Equipment" (see Chapter 27).

INFORMATION TO BE PRESENTED ON THE BALANCE SHEET

The remainder of IAS 1 consists, in essence, of a checklist and discussion of minimum disclosure requirements in a set of financial statements. We first consider the balance sheet. As a minimum, the face of the balance sheet (i.e., not the notes to the balance sheet) should include separate line items that present the following amounts (par. 66):

1. Property, plant, and equipment,
2. Intangible assets,
3. Financial assets (excluding amounts shown under 4, 6, and 7),
4. Investments accounted for using the equity method,
5. Inventories,
6. Trade and other receivables,
7. Cash and cash equivalents,
8. Trade and other payables,

9. Tax liabilities and assets as required by IAS 12, "Income Taxes,"

10. Provisions,

11. Non-current interest-bearing liabilities,

12. Minority interest,

13. Issued capital and reserves.

Logically, following from our earlier discussion of materiality, these separate line items are required only if "material."

The above represents a minimum. Additional line items, headings, and subtotals should also be presented on the face of the balance sheet when an International Accounting Standard requires it or when such presentation is necessary to present fairly the enterprise's financial position.

The first reason for additional line items is clearly objective, that is, nonjudgmental, except for the issue of materiality. The second "present fairly" reason, however, is inherently subjective. The judgment on whether additional line items are separately presented is based on an assessment of:

1. The nature and liquidity of assets and their materiality, leading, in most cases, to the separate presentation of goodwill and assets arising from development expenditure, monetary and non-monetary assets, and current and non-current assets.

2. Their function within the enterprise, leading, for example, to the separate presentation of operating and financial assets, inventories, receivables, and cash and cash equivalent assets.

3. The amounts, nature, and timing of liabilities, leading, for example, to the separate presentation of interest bearing and non-interest bearing liabilities and provisions, classified as current or non-current as appropriate.

It should be noted that IAS 1 does not prescribe any particular balance sheet format. The so-called horizontal and vertical formats are equally acceptable. As already discussed, enterprises are required *either* to present their balance sheet items classified into current and non-current, *or* to present them "broadly in order of their liquidity." This, at least theoretically, leaves a great deal of latitude. It says nothing, for example, about "which way up" the liquidity "order" should go. The descriptions used and the ordering of items may be amended according to the nature of the enterprise and its transactions, to provide information that is necessary for an overall understanding of the enterprise's financial position. For example, a bank amends the above descriptions in order to apply the more specific requirements in paragraphs 18 or 25 of IAS 30, "Disclosures in the Financial Statements of Banks and Similar Financial Institutions" (see Chapter 33). Other amendments not prescribed by promulgated IAS GAAP may be necessary in other industrial or commercial situations.

IAS 1 states that the use of different measurement bases for different classes of assets suggests that their nature or function differs and, therefore, that they should be presented as separate line items. It gives as an example the carrying of certain classes of property, plant, and equipment at cost, and other classes at revalued amounts, under IAS 16, "Property, Plant, and Equipment" (see Chapter 27).

> **OBSERVATION:** It seems to us that the above proposition, or at least the example given, is not logical. The recording of different subsets of property, plant, and machinery under different valuation bases does not necessarily suggest any difference in nature or function. Further disclosure *in the notes* may well be desirable, as discussed below, but that is a separate matter. A more logical example might be the different treatments allowed for investment properties (see Chapter 24), where the function of the property may affect the accounting treatment.

A third category of required disclosure relating to the balance sheet can be presented either on the face of the balance sheet or in the notes. Further subclassifications of the line items should be presented, classified in a manner appropriate to the enterprise's operations. Each item should be subclassified, when appropriate, by its nature, and amounts payable to and receivable from the parent enterprise, fellow subsidiaries, and associates and other related parties should be disclosed separately.

The detail provided in subclassifications, either on the face of the balance sheet or in the notes, depends on the requirements of International Accounting Standards and the size, nature, and function of the amounts involved. In some cases, other International Standards provide requirements (subject always to the materiality consideration). Tangible assets, for example, are classified by class as required by IAS 16, "Property, Plant, and Equipment" (see Chapter 27), and inventories are subclassified in accordance with IAS 2, "Inventories" (see Chapter 23). Other applications will be more subjective. For example, the standard states that receivables are analyzed between amounts receivable from trade customers, other members of the group, receivables from related parties, prepayments, and other amounts and that provisions are analyzed showing separately provisions for employee benefit costs and any other items classified in a manner appropriate to the enterprise's operations.

Extensive detailed disclosure regarding owner's equity is required, either on the face of the balance sheet or in the notes, as follows (par. 74):

1. For each class of share capital:
   (a) The number of shares authorized,
   (b) The number of shares issued and fully paid and issued but not fully paid,
   (c) Par value per share or that the shares have no par value,
   (d) A reconciliation of the number of shares outstanding at the beginning and at the end of the year,
   (e) The rights, preferences, and restrictions attaching to that class, including restrictions on the distribution of dividends and the repayment of capital,
   (f) Shares in the enterprise held by the enterprise itself or by subsidiaries or associates of the enterprise,
   (g) Shares reserved for issuance under options and sales contracts, including the terms and amounts.
2. A description of the nature and purpose of each reserve within owners' equity.
3. When dividends have been proposed but not formally approved for payment, the amount included (or not included) in liabilities.
4. The amount of any cumulative preference dividends not recognized.

Enterprises without share capital are required to present equivalent information showing details and movements of each category of equity interest.

> ☞ **PRACTICE POINTER:** In relation to point 3 above, the revised IAS 10, "Events after the Balance Sheet Date," operative from accounting periods beginning on or after January 1, 2000, states that dividends proposed but not yet formally approved for payment are not "obligations," and therefore requires that they should not be included as liabilities. (See Chapter 15.)

Item 1(f) above relates to so-called Treasury Shares. This issue has been further addressed in SIC-16, "Share Capital—Reacquired Own Equity Investments (Treasury Shares)," effective for financial periods beginning on or after July 1, 1999. This is presented largely as relating to IAS 32, "Financial Instruments: Disclosure and Presentation" (see Chapter 16) rather than to IAS 1. SIC-16 requires that treasury shares be included in the balance sheet as a deduction from equity and not as an asset. A variety of ways of including the acquisition cost of such shares, whether in the balance sheet or in the notes, are acceptable, "including for example" showing the total cost as a one-line adjustment of total equity, deducting the par value from share capital and adjusting premiums or discounts against other categories of equity, or by adjusting each category of equity (presumably pro rata). Explanation and transparency are obviously required if material. Note that no gain or loss should be recognized in the income statement relating to the sale, issuance, or cancellation of treasury shares.

INFORMATION TO BE PRESENTED IN THE INCOME STATEMENT

As with the balance sheet, IAS 1 requires certain disclosures on the face of the income statement, and other disclosures either on the face of the income statement or in the notes, at the discretion of the enterprise. As a minimum, the face of the income statement should include line items that present the following amounts (par. 75):

1. Revenue,
2. The results of operating activities,
3. Finance costs,
4. Share of profits and losses of associates and joint ventures accounted for using the equity method,
5. Tax expense,
6. Profit or loss from ordinary activities,
7. Extraordinary items,
8. Minority interest, and
9. Net profit or loss for the period.

Additional line items, headings, and subtotals should be presented on the face of the income statement when required by an International Accounting Standard or when such presentation is necessary to present fairly the enterprise's financial performance. IAS 33, "Earnings per Share," requires the disclosure of earnings per share data on the face of the income statement (see Chapter 12).

IAS 1 explicitly accepts that considerations of materiality and the nature of an enterprise's operations may require addition to, deletions from, or amendments of descriptions within the above list. The ordering of items may be changed from that given above "when this is necessary to explain the elements of performance" (which seems likely to occur only rarely).

The requirement for further disclosure is drawn widely and in general terms. An enterprise should present, either on the face of the income statement, which is "encouraged" but not obligatory, or in the notes to the income statement, an analysis of expenses using a classification based on either the nature of expenses or their function within the enterprise.

☞ **PRACTICE POINTER:** The implications of these two approaches to the classification of expenses are best shown by pro forma examples.

Nature of Expense Classification

Revenue		X
Other operating income		X
Changes in inventories of finished goods and work in progress (+ or –)	X	
Raw materials and consumables used	X	
Staff costs	X	
Depreciation and amortization expense	X	
Other operating expenses	X	
Total operating expenses	(X)	
Profit from operating activities		X

Function of Expense (or Cost of Sales) Classification

Revenue	X
Cost of sales	(X)
Gross profit	X
Other operating income	X
Distribution costs	(X)
Administrative expenses	(X)
Other operating expenses	(X)
Profit from operating activities	X

Both methods have advantages. The nature of expense method requires less analysis (and judgment) to prepare, but is arguably less informative and has the logical disadvantage that it might seem to imply that changes in inventory are an expense (or a revenue!), which they are not. Because each method of presentation has merit for different types of enterprises, the standard requires a choice between classifications based on that which most fairly presents the elements of an enterprise's performance. Because information on the nature of expenses is useful in predicting future cash flows, however, additional disclosure on the nature of expenses, including depreciation and amortization expenses and staff costs, is required when the cost of sales classification is used.

Dividends per share, declared or proposed for the period covered by the financial statements, must also be disclosed either on the face of the income statement or in the notes.

CHANGES IN EQUITY

IAS 1 requires the inclusion in financial statements of what in many jurisdictions will be an unfamiliar concept, a separate and distinct primary statement to record changes in equity. There are two acceptable ways of doing this. The first method is to prepare a separate statement of recognized gains and losses. This should show (par. 86):

1. The net profit or loss for the period.
2. Each item of income and expense, gain or loss which, as required by other standards is recognized directly in equity, and the total of these items.
3. The cumulative effect of changes in accounting policy and the correction of fundamental errors dealt with under the Benchmark treatments in IAS 8.

The following format is suggested.

**XYZ Group—Statement of Recognized Gains and Losses
for the Year Ended December 31, 20X2**
(in thousands of currency units)

	20X2	20X1
Surplus/(deficit) on revaluation of properties	(X)	X
Surplus/(deficit) on revaluation of investments	X	(X)
Exchange differences on translation of the financial statements of foreign entities	(X)	(X)
Net gains not recognized in the income statement	X	X
Net profit for the period	X	X
Total recognized gains and losses	X	X
Effect of changes in accounting policy		(X)

If this method is followed, then the enterprise should also present the following information in the notes:

4. Capital transactions with owners and distributions to owners.

5. The balance of accumulated profit or loss at the beginning of the period and at the balance sheet date and the movements for the period.

6. A reconciliation between the carrying amount of each class of equity capital, share premium, and each reserve at the beginning and the end of the period, separately disclosing each movement.

The effect of all this is to disclose movements of "gains and losses" in the new primary statement, and capital movements within equity in the notes. The alternative method of meeting these requirements of IAS 1 is to present *all* the information, that is, all of items 1 through 6 above, in a single statement of changes in equity, thus putting *all* equity movements together in the additional primary statement. This might have a format similar to that shown on the following page.

> **OBSERVATION:** The essential difference between either of these statements and the income statement is, of course, that the income statement is restricted to the inclusion of items recognized as revenues or expenses, whereas gains and losses are included in these separate primary statements whether or not they are recognized as part of income. Both of the suggested formats include the net result from the income statement as a separate line item.
>
> The whole issue of the appropriate format for presentation of these aspects of financial performance is in something of a state of flux. Much debate is under way within and between the world's major standard-setting bodies. There are two major questions. One concerns the question of what is known as recycling. Suppose an unrealized gain is recorded, outside the income statement, in year 1. In year 2 this gain becomes realized and now meets the criteria for inclusion in the income statement. How, *if at all*, should this be recorded in year 2? At the time of writing, to give two examples under IAS GAAP, IAS 16, "Property, Plant, and Equipment," requires in paragraph 41 that a transfer from revaluation surplus to retained earnings, on realization, "is not made through the income statement" (see Chapter 27). However, IAS 21, "The Effects of Changes in Foreign Exchange Rates," requires in paragraph 37 that, when a foreign entity is disposed of, related cumulative deferred exchange differences "should be recognized as income or as expenses" in the period in which the gain or loss is recognized. The issue requires clarification as a matter of general principle.
>
> The other major question, not entirely unrelated to the first one, concerns the very idea of the separation of the two statements (i.e., of income and of gains/losses in equity). Because the second is an extension of the first, or the first is merely a detailed breakdown of one element (net profit) of the second, why require separation at all? The idea of a single statement sounds

XYZ Group—Statement of Changes in Equity for the Year Ended December 31, 20X2

	Share Capital	Share Premium	Revaluation Reserve	Translation Reserve	Accumulated Profit	Total
Balance at December 31, 20X0	X	X	X	(X)	X	X
Changes in accounting policy					(X)	(X)
Restated balance	X	X	X	(X)	X	X
Surplus on revaluation of properties			X			X
Deficit on revaluation of investments			(X)			(X)
Currency translation differences				(X)		(X)
Net gains and losses not recognized in the income statement	—	—	X	(X)	—	X
Net profit for the period					X	X
Dividends					(X)	(X)
Issue of share capital	X	X				X
Balance at December 31, 20X1	X	X	X	(X)	X	X
Deficit on revaluation of properties			(X)			(X)
Surplus on revaluation of investments			X			X
Currency translation differences				(X)		(X)
Net gains and losses not recognized in the income statement	—	—	(X)	(X)	—	(X)
Net profit for the period					X	X
Dividends					(X)	(X)
Issue of share capital	X	X				X
Balance at December 31, 20X2	X	X	X	(X)	X	X

quite simple in one sense, but it carries the fundamental implication, objectionable to some, that the sanctity of the realization
convention regarding the income statement would be down-
graded or defiled. Nevertheless, there are signs of possible moves
in this direction. This debate will be ongoing. The precise outcome is unclear, but we expect to see further developments, and
changes to IAS 1 in the not too distant future.

CASH FLOW STATEMENTS

IAS 1 says nothing about cash flow statements, merely referring to
IAS 7, "Cash Flow Statements." The reader is in turn referred to our
full discussion in Chapter 7.

NOTES TO THE FINANCIAL STATEMENTS

In one sense, the notes to the financial statements are "where every-
thing else goes." IAS 1 summarizes the functions of the notes as
being to (par. 91):

1. Present information about the basis of preparation of the financial statements and the specific accounting policies selected
   and applied for significant transactions and events.
2. Disclose the information required by International Accounting
   Standards that is not presented elsewhere in the financial statements.
3. Provide additional information that is not presented on the face
   of the financial statements but that is necessary for a fair presentation.

Notes to the financial statements should be presented in a systematic manner. Each item on the face of the balance sheet, income
statement, and cash flow statement should be cross-referenced to
any related information in the notes.

The standard suggests that notes "are normally" presented in the
following order:

1. Statement of compliance with International Accounting Standards.
2. The measurement basis (or bases) used in preparing the financial statements.
3. Each specific accounting policy that is necessary for a proper
   understanding of the financial statements.

4. Supporting information for items presented on the face of each financial statement in the order in which each line item and each financial statements is presented.

5. Other disclosures, including:

   (a) contingencies, commitments, and other financial disclosures; and

   (b) non-financial disclosures.

Measurement basis refers to the valuation method, for example, historical cost, fair value. The standard gives a long list of areas of accounting policy that an enterprise "might consider presenting."

Many of the areas specifically require mention under the terms of the relevant IAS, but all significant policies (not the same as policies for all significant amounts) should be clearly disclosed.

Finally, additional disclosures are required, if not disclosed elsewhere in information published with the financial statements of:

1. The domicile and legal form of the enterprise, its country of incorporation, and the address of the registered office (or principal place of business, if different from the registered office).

2. A description of the nature of the enterprise's operations and its principal activities.

3. The name of the parent enterprise and the ultimate parent enterprise of the group.

4. Either the number of employees at the end of the period or the average for the period.

ILLUSTRATIONS

IAS 1 includes an appendix of illustrative financial statement structure, not part of the formal standard, which should be studied unless real examples of financial statements are available.

Part II

General Standards

CHAPTER 4
ACCOUNTING FOR INVESTMENTS

CONTENTS

OVERVIEW

This chapter is specifically concerned with IAS 25, "Accounting for Investments," which was withdrawn by IAS 41, "Investment Property," paragraph 2 (see Chapter 24), effective for annual financial statements covering periods beginning on or after January 1, 2001. IAS 25 had already been largely superseded by IAS 39, "Financial Instruments: Recognition and Measurement," with effect from the same date. This chapter on IAS 25 is retained in the 2002 *Miller IAS Guide* as it is applicable to financial statements for earlier periods.

BACKGROUND AND SCOPE

IAS 25, paragraph 4, defines an investment as "an asset held by an enterprise for the accretion of wealth through distribution (such as interest, dividends, royalties, and rentals) for capital appreciation or for other benefits to the investing enterprise such as those obtained through trading relationships."

However, IAS 25 was never applicable to investments in subsidiaries, associates, and joint ventures, for which the applicable IASs are IASs 27, 28, and 31 (see Chapters 6, 9, and 14). Investments in intangible assets are covered by IAS 38 (see Chapter 21). The bases for recognition of interest, royalties, dividends, and rentals earned on investments and the treatment of finance leases are dealt with in IASs 17 and 18 (see Chapters 25 and 30). Investments in financial assets are covered by IASs 32 and 39 (see Chapter 16).

Thus, prior to its withdrawal by IAS 41, the scope of IAS 25 included certain non-financial assets, such as investment properties, when an enterprise elects to account for them as long-term investments rather than as property, plant, and equipment. This chapter considers IAS 25 with its scope as amended by IAS 39, but before its withdrawal by IAS 41.

The main differences between IAS 25 and U.S. GAAP are as follows:

Under IAS 25 investment properties could be designated as long-term investments and: (a) exempted from depreciation, whereas no such exemption is permitted by U.S. GAAP; (b) revalued to a fair value in excess of cost, which is not permitted under U.S. GAAP.

Terminology

1. The *cost* of an investment includes acquisition charges such as brokerage fees, duties, and bank fees. If an investment is acquired or partly acquired for non-cash consideration, the cost of acquisition relating to that consideration is its fair value. If that cannot be readily determined, it may be appropriate to consider the fair value of the investment acquired (IAS 25, pars. 15–16).

2. *Fair value* is the amount for which an asset could be exchanged between a knowledgeable, willing buyer and a knowledgeable, willing seller in an arm's-length transaction. (This is consistent with the definition in IAS 39, par. 8.)

3. *Market value* is the amount obtainable from the sale of an investment in an active market.

Classification of Investments

IAS 25 distinguishes between:

current investments, that are by their nature readily realizable and are not intended to be held for more than one year; and

long-term investments, that is, any that are not current investments.

Current investments should be classified and accounted for as current assets, and long-term investments as long-term (non-current) assets, whether or not the enterprise's balance sheet presentation distinguishes between current and non-current assets (IAS 25, pars. 8–14).

> **OBSERVATION:** The balance sheet presentation shown as an illustration in the Appendix to IAS 1 distinguishes between non-current and current assets. IAS GAAP do not require such a presentation, however (IAS 1, par. 68).

Investments classified as current assets should be carried in the balance sheet at either:

- Market value, or
- The lower of cost and market value.

If current investments are carried at the lower of cost and market value, the carrying amount should be determined either on an aggregate portfolio basis, in total or by category of investment, or on an individual investment basis. IAS 25 expresses a preference for the aggregate portfolio basis, but does not identify it as a "benchmark" treatment (IAS 25, pars. 19–22).

Investments classified as long-term (non-current) assets should be carried in the balance sheet at either:

- Cost, or
- Revalued amounts.

If revalued amounts are used, a policy for the frequency of revaluations should be adopted and an entire category of long-term investments should be revalued at the same time.

The carrying value of all long-term investments should be reduced to recognize a decline other than temporary in the value of the investments, such reduction being determined and made for each investment individually. Thus, long-term investments carried at cost may need to be written down to reflect impairment of value (IAS 25, pars. 23–27).

> **OBSERVATION:** IAS 25, paragraph 23, mentions "marketable equity securities" and states that they should be carried at "the lower of cost and market value determined on a portfolio basis." However, this type of investment is a financial instrument, and these, as noted above, were withdrawn from the scope of IAS 25 by IAS 39.

INVESTMENT PROPERTIES

When investment properties are accounted for as long-term investments, they are revalued periodically at fair value on a systematic basis. The resultant fair values may be recognized in the carrying amount, in which case any changes in carrying amount are accounted for as described below. If they are not recognized in the carrying amount (i.e., the investment properties are carried at cost), fair values should nevertheless be disclosed (IAS 25, par. 30). If the cost basis is used but fair value is less than cost, this normally indicates that a write-down for impairment is required.

CHANGES IN THE CARRYING AMOUNT OF INVESTMENTS

For current investments carried at market value, one of the two following policies for accounting for changes in carrying amount should be consistently applied (IAS 25, par. 31):

1. Recognition of the change as income or expense, or
2. Treatment in accordance with the requirement for changes in the carrying amount of long-term investments in IAS 25, paragraph 32, as described below.

The treatment of charges in carrying value of long-term investments differs according to whether the change is an increase or a decrease. An increase is credited to a revaluation surplus that is a reserve within owners' equity, unless it is related to a previous decrease for the same investment that was recognized as an expense, in which case the increase is credited to income to the extent that it reverses the previously recorded decrease. A decrease is charged to a revaluation surplus to the extent that it is a reversal of a previously recorded increase for the same investment credited to that revaluation surplus; otherwise, it is recognized as an expense.

DISPOSALS OF INVESTMENTS

On disposal of an investment, the difference between the net disposal proceeds and the carrying amount should be recognized as income or expense. In the case of current investments carried on a portfolio basis, any reduction from cost to market value is considered to be made for the portfolio in aggregate; individual investments are considered to be still carried at cost. Hence, any profit or loss on sale should be calculated on the basis of cost. If the investment was previously revalued, or was carried at market value and an increase in carrying amount had been transferred to revaluation surplus, any revaluation surplus related to the investment being disposed of should be treated according to a consistent accounting policy, which may be either of the following:

1. To credit the related revaluation surplus to income (on the grounds that it is now "realized").
2. To transfer it to retained earnings (on the grounds, for example, that it has already been recognized in a "Statement of Total Gains and Losses").

When part of an enterprise's holding of a particular investment is disposed of, a carrying amount must be allocated to the part sold. IAS 25, paragraph 35, states that "[t]his carrying amount is usually determined from the average carrying amount of the total holding of the investment," but other methods of allocation, such as first in, first out, do not appear to be excluded.

Transfers (Reclassifications) of Investments

Investments may be reclassified between the current and long-term categories. For long-term investments reclassified as current, the rules in IAS 25 are as follows (par. 36):

1. if the valuation basis used for current investments is lower of cost and market, the transfer should be made at cost or carrying value, whichever is lower. Any remaining revaluation surplus from a previous upward revaluation should be reversed;
2. if current investments are carried at market value, the transfer should be made at the investments' carrying amount. If changes in market value of current investments are included in income, for consistency any remaining revaluation surplus from a previous upwards revaluation of the transferred investments should be transferred to income.

For current investments reclassified as long-term, the valuation basis used for them as current assets should be maintained (par. 37).

SWITCHES OF INVESTMENTS IN A PORTFOLIO

When one of the investments held in a portfolio is sold, IAS 25 permits two alternative methods regarding the recognition of the results of this transaction:

1. Any excess or deficiency of the net sales proceeds over the carrying amount should be recognized immediately in income as a profit or loss. This is normally the preferred method (the term *benchmark* is not used).

2. The disposal is treated as an adjustment of the constituents of the portfolio, with no increase or decrease in value; therefore, no profit or loss is recognized. This method is appropriate if, and only if, the market value basis is used for the carrying amount and changes in market value are included in income, in which case any adjustment to market value will already have been reflected in income (IAS 25, pars. 39–40).

INCOME STATEMENT TREATMENT

Investment income that should be included in the income statement comprises (IAS 25, par. 41):

1. Interest, dividends, and rentals from both long-term and current investments. IAS 25 also mentions royalties, but these would presumably relate to intangible assets such as patents and copyrights, which are outside the scope of IAS 25.

2. The following in relation to current investments:

   (a) Profits and losses on disposal.

   (b) Unrealized gains and losses on current investments carried at market value, if the enterprise has adopted the policy of recognizing these in income (see above under "Changes in the Carrying Amount of Investments").

   (c) Reductions to market value, and reversals of such reductions, required to state current investments at the lower of cost and market value.

3. The following in relation to long-term investments:

   (a) Reductions in carrying amount to reflect a nontemporary decline in value, and reversals of such reductions.

   (b) Profits and losses on disposal, calculated as described under "Disposals of Investments" above.

DISCLOSURE

The following should be disclosed:

1. The accounting policies for:

   (a) The determination of carrying amount of investments,

(b) The treatment of changes in market value of current investments carried at market value, and

(c) The treatment of a revaluation surplus on the sale of a revalued investment.

2. The significant amounts included in income for:

   (a) Interest, royalties, dividends, and rentals on long-term and current investments,

   (b) Profits and losses on disposal of current investments, and

   (c) Changes in value of such investments.

3. The market value of marketable investments if they are not carried at market value.

4. The fair value of investment properties if they are accounted for as long-term investments and not carried at fair value.

5. Significant restrictions on the realizability of investments or the remittance of income and proceeds of disposal.

6. For long-term investments stated at revalued amounts:

   (a) The policy for the frequency of revaluations,

   (b) The date of the latest revaluation, and

   (c) The basis of revaluation and whether an external valuer was involved.

7. The movements for the period in the revaluation surplus and the nature of such movements.

8. For enterprises whose main business is the holding of investments, an analysis of the portfolio of investments.

The following disclosures *may* be provided to assist a reader's understanding of the financial statements:

1. An analysis of long-term investments by category.

2. The directors' assessment of the fair value of investments that are not marketable.

3. Where investments are not marketable, the method of assessing value used for comparison with cost, where applicable.

4. The amount of any previous revaluation surplus that related to the investments disposed of during the year and that has been previously distributed or converted into share capital.

5. Details of any single investment that represents a significant proportion of the reporting enterprise's assets.

CHAPTER 5
BORROWING COSTS

CONTENTS

OVERVIEW

The accounting treatment of borrowing costs raises two types of issues: (a) the issue of definition, that is, what should be included in borrowing costs; and (b) the issue of recognition, that is, whether borrowing costs should be recognized as part of the expenses of the period or as part of the cost of an asset (capitalization). The former issue is obviously of much less importance if no borrowing costs are to be capitalized.

IAS GAAP take a broad view of what constitutes borrowing costs and include such items as amortization of ancillary costs incurred in connection with borrowings and preferred stock dividends if the preferred stock is classified as a liability in the balance sheet. By contrast, the imputed cost of financial instruments classed as equity capital is strictly excluded. On the issue of whether borrowing costs may be recognized as part of the cost of an asset, the "benchmark" (preferred) treatment under IAS GAAP is recognition as part of expense for the period. However, recognition as part of the cost of a "qualifying" asset (that is, an asset that necessarily takes a substantial period of time to get ready for its intended use or sale) is permitted as an alternative treatment.

BACKGROUND

IAS GAAP on the treatment of borrowing costs were originally set out in the 1984 version of IAS 23, "Capitalization of Borrowing Costs." This permitted a free choice between expensing these costs and capitalizing them when certain conditions were met. In its comparability project in the early 1990s, the IASC first proposed in E32 that the "benchmark" treatment should be for borrowing costs to be expensed, with capitalization as an alternative treatment when certain conditions were met. The responses to E32 were divided on this issue; however, the IASC then issued E39, according to which capitalization would be required if certain conditions were met, and expensing would be required otherwise. This position is similar to that in U.S. GAAP (FAS-34). Again, responses to E39 were also mixed. In particular, there is the argument that capitalization may lead to loss of comparability of asset measurements between enterprises with different capital structures (for an illustration, see the first Observation in the *Miller GAAP Guide,* Chapter 24). In any event, the IASC reverted to its position in E32 when the revised IAS 23, "Capitalization of Borrowing Costs," was issued in 1994.

IAS GAAP on borrowing costs are set out in:

- IAS 23, "Capitalization of Borrowing Costs"

- SIC-2, "Consistency—Capitalization of Borrowing Costs"

The main differences from U.S. GAAP are the following:

1. U.S. GAAP (FAS-34) *require* borrowing costs to be capitalized when the relevant conditions are met, namely, when the borrowing costs are part of the expenditures normally incurred in readying an asset for use and are thus part of the asset's acquisition cost. In IAS GAAP, this is *permitted* as the "alternative" treatment, but the "benchmark" treatment is to expense all borrowing costs.

2. U.S. GAAP (FAS-58) treat as qualifying assets equity investments in, and loans and advances to, investees accounted for under the equity method, if the latter are themselves acquiring qualifying assets as part of activities necessary to start their planned principal operations. IAS GAAP exclude from qualifying assets all investments except investment properties and the qualifying assets of an investee accounted for using proportionate consolidation.

3. FAS-34 considers borrowing costs to consist of interest costs actually incurred. IAS GAAP include in borrowing costs the effects of changes in exchange rates on the effective cost of borrowings in foreign currencies. These effects would not be

recognized in U.S. GAAP as borrowing costs for the purpose of capitalization.

SCOPE

IAS 23 applies to all borrowing costs of enterprises reporting under IAS GAAP, including the cost of preferred shares that are classified as a liability. It does not apply to the actual or imputed cost of equity or of preferred shares not classified as a liability (IAS 23, pars. 1–3).

DEFINITIONS

Borrowing costs are interest and other costs incurred by an enterprise in connection with the borrowing of funds, and may include (IAS 23, par. 4):

1. Interest on bank overdrafts and short-term and long-term borrowings.

2. Amortization of discounts or premiums relating to borrowings.

3. Amortization of ancillary costs incurred in connection with the arrangement of borrowings.

4. Finance charges in respect of finance leases recognized in accordance with IAS 17, "Leases."

5. Exchange differences arising from foreign currency borrowings to the extent that they are regarded as an adjustment of interest costs.

6. Costs of preferred capital classified as a liability.

☞ **PRACTICE POINTER:** Item 5 above may cause difficulties, since the wording leaves it open to the enterprise to determine the extent to which the exchange differences are "regarded as an adjustment of interest costs," and opinions on this may differ.

In principle, any exchange loss or gain on foreign currency borrowings is a component (positive or negative) of the cost of those borrowings. The only issues here would appear to concern (a) the recognition of unrealized exchange gains or losses on borrowings; and (b) the treatment of unrealized but hedged exchange losses.

Regarding (a), paragraph 15 of IAS 21, "The Effects of Changes in Foreign Exchange Rates" (see Chapter 17), makes it clear that foreign exchange differences arising on reporting an enterprise's monetary items (excluding net investments in foreign entities) at rates different from those at which they were initially recorded or reported in previous financial statements, should be recognized as income or expense in the period in which they arise. Because they are to be recognized as income or expense, it would seem logical to recognize them as part of borrowing costs.

Regarding (b), IAS 21 is silent. However, according to IAS 39, "Financial Instruments: Recognition and Measurement," paragraphs 142 and 153 (see Chapter 16), it seems clear that exchange losses should be recognized in income (and hence treated as a component of borrowing costs) only to the extent that they are not hedged.

A *qualifying asset* (for the purposes of the "alternative" treatment) is an asset that *necessarily* takes a substantial period of time to get ready for its intended use or sale. Examples of qualifying assets given in the standard are inventories that require a substantial period of time to bring them to a saleable condition, manufacturing plants, power generation facilities, and investment properties (IAS 23, pars. 5–6). Examples of inventory items that would be qualifying assets include wine and spirits being aged, ships and aircraft being built, and long-term construction contracts in general. Intangibles such as capitalized development costs and other internally generated intangibles that meet the recognition criteria of IAS 38 (see Chapter 21) may also be qualifying assets.

Qualifying assets (and borrowing costs) include the investor's share of the qualifying assets (and borrowing costs) in a joint venture accounted for using proportionate consolidation. This does not apply if the equity method (the alternative treatment under IAS 31, "Financial Reporting of Interests in Joint Ventures") is used to account for the investment in the joint venture.

BORROWING COSTS: BENCHMARK TREATMENT

Borrowing costs should be recognized as an expense of the period in which they are incurred (IAS 23, par. 7).

BORROWING COSTS: ALLOWED ALTERNATIVE TREATMENT

Borrowing costs that are *directly attributable* to the acquisition, construction, or production of a *qualifying asset* should be capitalized as part of the cost of that asset when they can be measured reliably and when it is probable that they will result in future economic benefits to the enterprise. Borrowing costs that do not meet these conditions should be recognized as an expense of the period in which they are incurred (IAS 23, pars. 10–12). This alternative treatment may not be applied selectively; it must be applied to all qualifying assets or to none at all (SIC-2, "Consistency—Capitalization of Borrowing Costs").

BORROWING COSTS ELIGIBLE FOR CAPITALIZATION

Borrowing costs that are directly attributable to obtaining a qualifying asset are those borrowing costs that would have been avoided if the expenditure on the qualifying asset had not been made. This is straightforward when funds are borrowed specifically for the purpose of obtaining a particular qualifying asset. In that case, the amount of borrowing costs eligible for capitalization as part of the cost of that asset for the period are the actual costs of that borrowing during the period, less any investment income from temporary investment of the funds borrowed (IAS 23, pars. 13 and 15).

In other circumstances, the determination of the amount of borrowing costs that are directly attributable to obtaining a qualifying asset may be difficult, and judgment may need to be exercised. To the extent that funds that have been borrowed for general purposes are used for obtaining a qualifying asset, the amount of borrowing costs that are eligible for capitalization should be determined by applying a capitalization rate to the expenditures on that asset. This capitalization rate should be calculated as the weighted average of the borrowing costs applicable to the *general borrowings* of the enterprise during the period (any borrowings made specifically for the purpose of obtaining a qualifying asset are by definition not part of "general borrowings").

Thus, borrowing costs capitalizable in respect of a qualifying asset should be identified, first, as those of any borrowings made specifically for the purpose of obtaining the asset. If there were no specific borrowings, or these account for less than all of the expenditure on the asset, then "general borrowings" should be applied to the balance of the expenditure on the asset.

The amount of borrowing costs capitalized during a period should not exceed the total amount of borrowing costs incurred during that period.

It may be appropriate in some circumstances (such as when a group of companies manages borrowings centrally) to use an overall group capitalization rate. In other circumstances (such as when an entity in a group has substantial financial autonomy), an entity's capitalization rate should be based on its own borrowings (IAS 23, pars. 17–18).

COMMENCEMENT, SUSPENSION, AND CESSATION OF CAPITALIZATION

Capitalization should commence when:

1. Expenditures on the qualifying asset are being incurred.

2. Borrowing costs are being incurred.

3. Activities that are necessary to prepare the asset for its intended use or sale are in progress.

"Necessary activities" include technical, administrative, and legal work (as well as aging or maturing certain types of inventory); but simply holding an asset (such as development land or other property or finished items in inventory) does not allow attributable borrowing costs to be capitalized (IAS 23, pars. 20–22).

Moreover, during extended periods in which necessary activities are interrupted, *suspension* of capitalization is required. This does not apply, however, in the case of a temporary delay that is a necessary part of the process of getting the asset ready, such as an unavoidable delay in the construction of a bridge because of high water levels (IAS 23, pars. 23–24).

Capitalization of borrowing costs should *cease* when *substantially all* the activities necessary to prepare the qualifying asset for its intended sale or use are complete (IAS 23, par. 25).

> **OBSERVATION:** The term *substantially all* applies to assets that are complete apart from "minor modifications such as the decoration of a property to the purchaser's or user's specification," or which are "[physically] complete even though routine administration work might still continue" (IAS 23, par. 26). But it is also presumably meant to prevent an enterprise from intentionally keeping the work on an asset slightly incomplete in order to continue the capitalization of borrowing costs until the asset is sold, leased, or put to use.

When a qualifying asset is completed in parts or stages, and each part is capable of being sold or used while work continues on other parts, the capitalization of borrowing costs on a substantially completed part should cease. An example is a property development that is completed in stages, consisting of buildings capable of being used separately (IAS 23, pars. 27–28).

Capitalization should not cease on the grounds that further capitalization would lead to the carrying amount or expected ultimate cost of a qualifying asset exceeding its recoverable amount or net realizable value. Instead, the excess amount should be either written off in accordance with the impairment requirements applicable to the asset in question or written off as a loss in the case of a construction contract (IAS 23, par. 29).

DISCLOSURE

An enterprise should disclose in the notes to its financial statements:

1. The accounting policy adopted for borrowing costs.
2. In the case of the allowed alternative treatment:
   (a) the amount of borrowing costs capitalized during the period, and
   (b) the capitalization rate (or rates) used to determine the amount of borrowing (IAS 23, par. 29).

> **OBSERVATION:** Paragraph 29 refers to "rate" in the singular, but in practice more than one rate may be used, because different qualifying assets may be funded by different borrowings. This may occur because subsidiaries are treated as financially autonomous and have different capitalization rates or because one qualifying asset is funded by specific borrowings while another is funded out of general borrowings.

CHAPTER 6
BUSINESS COMBINATIONS

CONTENTS

OVERVIEW

A business combination is the bringing together of separate enterprises into one economic entity under unified control, as a result of either:

- An *acquisition,* that is, one enterprise obtaining control over the net assets and operations of another enterprise (in IAS GAAP, control means *de facto control,* see Chapter 9); or

- A *uniting of interests,* that is, one enterprise uniting with another in such a way that neither can be identified as the acquirer.

An acquisition may take place through one enterprise acquiring control over another by an acquisition of voting rights (and possibly other powers discussed further below), resulting in *de facto* control. The enterprise acquiring control may be one of the original enterprises or a new one established for the purpose of effecting the combination. In either case, a parent–subsidiary relationship will result, and consolidated financial statements (see Chapter 9) will normally be required. An acquisition may also take place through one enterprise simply acquiring the net assets of another enterprise or through a legal merger, neither of which will give rise to a need for consolidated financial statements. In a legal merger, one enterprise is used as the merger vehicle, and the other combinee is dissolved.

Acquisitions should be accounted for by using the purchase method, as follows:

- The acquirer's interest in the identifiable assets and liabilities of the acquiree is recorded at fair value.

- Goodwill (positive or negative) is recognized and treated as described below.

- A distinction is made between precombination and postcombination profits of the acquiree for the financial period in which the combination took place, only the latter being included as profits of the combined business (group).

Fair value is defined as "the amount for which an asset could be exchanged or a liability settled between knowledgeable, willing parties in an arm's-length transaction" (IAS 22, par. 9).

A uniting of interests takes place when it is not possible to identify an acquirer in a business combination. In IAS GAAP, by virtue of the concept of *de facto* control, it is assumed that in substance virtually all business combinations involve an acquirer, as the identification of a *de facto* acquirer is impossible only in exceptional circumstances, which are discussed further below. Subject to this, a uniting of interests may take place by means of a share exchange in which one combinee becomes a subsidiary of the other, by a legal merger whereby one combinee absorbs the other (which is dissolved), or through the formation of a new entity that either acquires the shares of the combinees or absorbs them in a legal merger.

A uniting of interests should be accounted for by using the pooling-of-interests method, the rationale of which is that no acquisition has occurred and the separate businesses are continuing, albeit now jointly owned and managed. Hence, there is no restatement of assets and liabilities at fair value, no recognition of goodwill (positive or negative), and no distinction between precombination and postcombination profits for the financial period in which the combination took place.

The relevant IAS GAAP have been promulgated in:

- IAS 22, "Business Combinations"

- IAS 27, "Consolidated Financial Statements and Accounting for Investments in Subsidiaries" (see Chapter 9)

- IAS 12, "Income Taxes"

- SIC-9, "Classification of Business Combinations as Either Acquisitions or Unitings of Interests"

- SIC-22, "Business Combinations—Subsequent Adjustment of Fair Values and Goodwill Initially Reported"

BACKGROUND

Originally issued in November 1983, IAS 22 was subsequently revised in 1993 (as part of the IASC's Comparability/Improvements project following E32) and in 1998. References to IAS 22 in this chapter are to the revised standard. Although there are conceptual differences, in practice the revised IAS GAAP differ significantly from U.S. GAAP in only a few respects. The greatest differences concern the use of the pooling-of-interests method and negative goodwill (items 2, 4, and 5 below). The main differences are as follows:

1. *The concept of control.* IAS GAAP are based on *de facto* control, while U.S. GAAP are based on *de jure* control; see Chapter 9.

2. *Use of the pooling-of-interests method.* The IAS criteria for a "uniting of interests" are harder to satisfy than the twelve criteria set out in APB 16 for a "pooling of interests" (see *Miller GAAP Guide*, Chapter 3) and, indeed, are described as "exceptional" in IAS 22 (revised). The use of the pooling method under IAS GAAP is expected to be rarer than under U.S. GAAP. However, the use of the pooling method under U.S. GAAP is currently

under review, and it is likely that this method will cease to be accepted under either U.S. GAAP or IAS GAAP.

3. *Date of acquisition.* In IAS GAAP, this is the date of the establishment of effective (*de facto*) control. In U.S. GAAP, it is the date on which *de jure* control is achieved by the transfer of the consideration for the acquisition to the selling party or parties. In practice, *de facto* control may be achieved before or after *de jure* control.

4. *Treatment of positive goodwill.* Under U.S. GAAP, positive goodwill may be amortized over not more than 40 years. Under IAS GAAP, there is a rebuttable presumption that the useful life of goodwill will not exceed twenty years; rebuttal is expected to be rare and entails the use of annual impairment tests in accordance with IAS 36 (see below).

5. *Treatment of negative goodwill.* Under U.S. GAAP, negative goodwill is not recorded unless the value of the acquiree's noncurrent assets (excluding long-term investments in marketable securities) has been written down to zero. Any negative goodwill so recorded is treated effectively as deferred income ("bargain purchase element"), amortized systematically back to income over a period not exceeding forty years, and appears in the balance sheet as a deferred credit. Under IAS 22, the acquiree's noncurrent assets are accounted for at fair values and are not written down. Negative goodwill is released back to income according to the criteria used in its recognition (discussed further below) and is shown in the balance sheet as a deduction in the same balance sheet classification as goodwill, and not as a deferred credit.

SCOPE

Acquisitions and the Purchase Method

In IAS GAAP, "virtually all" business combinations are considered to be acquisitions, in which one of the combining enterprises obtains control over the other (IAS 22, pars. 11–13), and are accounted for by using the purchase method (see Chapter 9). Control is presumed to be obtained when one of the combining enterprises acquires more than half the voting rights of the other, unless, in exceptional circumstances, it can be clearly demonstrated that such ownership does not constitute control. Even when one of the combining enterprises does not acquire more than one-half of the voting rights of the other combining enterprise, it may still be possible to identify an acquirer when one of the combining enterprises, as a result of the business combination, acquires:

1. Power over more than half the voting rights by virtue of an agreement with other investors.
2. Power to govern the other enterprise's financial and operating policies under a statute or an agreement.
3. Power to appoint or remove a majority of the members of the board of directors or equivalent governing body of the other enterprise.
4. Power to cast the majority of votes at meetings of the board or equivalent governing body of the other enterprise.

Moreover, the following will point to the existence of an acquirer:

1. The fair value of one enterprise is significantly greater than that of the other, in which case the former is the acquirer (but see the observation below).
2. The business combination is effected through an exchange of voting common shares for cash, in which case the enterprise giving up cash is the acquirer.
3. The business combination results in the management of one enterprise being able to dominate the selection of the management of the combined enterprise, in which case the enterprise with the dominant management is the acquirer. However, the criterion is who chooses the management of the combined enterprise, not from which of the combinees a majority of the management of the combined enterprise comes.

> **OBSERVATION:** In deciding which of two combining enterprises is the acquirer, if one of the enterprises is significantly larger in terms of fair value than the other, the former will usually be the acquirer if the only consideration exchanged consists of voting shares. In certain circumstances, however, the smaller combinee in terms of fair value may be the acquirer, because the terms of the combination may be such as to give the former shareholders of the smaller combinee the power to appoint or remove a majority of the members of the board of directors of the larger enterprise; what counts is the actual position regarding control. Examples of such circumstances are:
>
> - A substantial part of the consideration given to the former shareholders of the larger enterprise consists of cash, or
> - The former shareholders of the smaller enterprise receive shares carrying multiple voting rights.

ACCOUNTING PROCEDURES—PURCHASE METHOD

Date of Acquisition

The date of acquisition for accounting purposes is the date on which *de facto* control over the net assets and operations of the acquiree is effectively transferred to the acquirer. In substance, the date of acquisition is the date from which the acquirer has the power to govern the financial and operating policies of the acquiree in order to obtain benefits from its activities. In the absence of arrangements to the contrary regarding the transfer of *de facto* control, this will occur on completion of the transaction that confers legal *(de jure)* control. This is normally the date on which consideration (which may include an obligation to make a subsequent payment) passes to the former shareholders of the acquiree. However, *de facto* control is not deemed to have been transferred to the acquirer until all the conditions necessary to protect the interests of the parties involved have been satisfied. On the other hand, this does not require that a transaction be finalized in law before control effectively passes. Assessment of whether control has effectively been transferred must be made by consideration of the substance of the acquisition (IAS 22, par. 19).

Cost of Acquisition

Cost is the amount of cash or cash equivalents paid or the fair value, at the date of exchange, of other purchase consideration given by the acquirer in exchange for control over the net assets of the acquiree, plus any incremental costs directly attributable to the acquisition. When an acquisition involves more than one exchange transaction, the cost of the acquisition is the aggregate of the individual transactions. When an acquisition is achieved in stages, cost or fair value is determined as at the date of each exchange transaction, not at the date of the acquisition itself, which is determined as described above (IAS 22, pars. 21 and 22).

When settlement of purchase consideration is deferred, the fair value of that consideration is its present value, taking into account any premium or discount likely to be incurred in settlement, and not the nominal or face value (IAS 22, par. 23).

Marketable securities issued by the acquirer are measured at their fair value, which is normally their market price at the date of the exchange transaction. Undue fluctuations or the thinness of the market, however, may make the market price an unreliable indicator. This may also be the case for shares issued by the in-substance acquiree in reverse acquisitions (see below). When the market price on one particular date is not a reliable indicator, price movements for a reasonable period before and after the announcement of the terms of the acquisition should be considered. If the market is unreliable or no quotation exists, the fair value of the securities issued by the acquirer will need to be estimated. This may be done by reference to the relevant proportion of the fair value of the net assets, either of the issuing enterprise or of the acquired enterprise, whichever is more clearly evident. Purchase consideration paid in the form of cash to shareholders of the acquiree as an alternative to securities may also provide evidence of the fair value of the latter. Independent valuations may also be used. All aspects of the acquisition, including significant factors influencing the negotiations, need to be considered (IAS 22, par. 24).

Initial Recognition of Identifiable Assets and Liabilities

The identifiable assets and liabilities acquired that are recognized under paragraph 19 should be those of the acquiree that existed at the date of the acquisition, together with any liabilities recognized under IAS 22, paragraph 31 (which deals with the circumstances in which a provision may be recognized that was not a liability of the acquiree at that date; see below). They should be recognized separately as at the acquisition date, if and only if:

1. It is probable that any associated economic benefits will flow to, or resources embodying economic benefits will flow from, the acquirer; and

2. A reliable measure is available of their cost or fair value (IAS 22, par. 26).

Assets and liabilities that meet these two criteria are described in IAS 22 as "identifiable assets and liabilities." If there are items in an acquiree's balance sheet that do not meet these criteria, they will not be included in the allocation of the cost of the acquisition, and this will affect the amount of cost allocated to goodwill (positive or negative) in the consolidated balance sheet, as discussed below. An example would be goodwill in the acquiree's balance sheet, which would not be recognized as an identifiable asset. Instead, goodwill on acquisition would be calculated as a residual after allocating the cost of the acquisition to identifiable assets and liabilities. Other intangible assets should be recognized only if they meet the criteria laid down in IAS 38, "Intangible Assets" (see Chapter 21).

Moreover, an acquirer may obtain control over identifiable assets or liabilities that were not recognized in the financial statements of the acquiree, either because they did not qualify for recognition before the acquisition or because the events giving rise to them occurred as part of the acquisition transactions. Examples of the first are unrelieved tax losses of the acquiree that can be relieved against profits of the acquirer; and research and development costs that did not meet the IAS 38 criteria for the acquiree's financial statements before the acquisition, but did so for the consolidated financial statements at the acquisition date. An example of the second is an obligation undertaken by the acquirer to compensate employees of the acquirer for services performed before the acquisition.

The recognition of a provision that was not a liability of the acquiree to cover *postacquisition losses* of the acquiree is not permitted, however, as that would contravene IAS 37, "Provisions, Contingent Liabilities and Contingent Assets" (see Chapter 28). A provision for restructuring or similar expenses may be recognized only subject to stringent conditions set out in IAS 22, paragraph 31. These are the same as those set out in IAS 37, paragraphs 63–83 (see Chapter 28). Such provisions must reflect only plans for terminating or reducing activities of the *acquiree*, not those of the acquirer. The main features of such a plan must have been announced on or before the date of acquisition, by the directors or senior management of the acquirer, in such a way that there is a "valid expectation in those affected by the plan" that it will be implemented. Moreover, the plan must be formalized in detail within three months (or by the date the next annual consolidated financial statements are approved, if earlier), and if this deadline is not met, the provision must be reversed (IAS 22, par. 75). These restrictions are intended to limit the recognition of a provision on acquisition that was not a liability of the acquiree to the cases where a constructive obligation to restructure has arisen (IAS 37, par. 72).

The effect of these restrictions is to prevent estimated future restructuring expenses (except if the conditions are met) or estimated future losses of the acquiree being reflected in an increased amount of positive goodwill on acquisition, and thus being spread over the "useful life" of that goodwill in the form of amortization. In some cases, the result may be that negative goodwill is recognized. Under certain circumstances (see below), such negative goodwill is released to income in a way similar to the release of a provision.

Determining the Fair Values of Identifiable Assets and Liabilities Acquired

Under IAS 22 as revised in 1998, the fair value attributed to assets and liabilities is not affected by the acquirer's intentions. Thus, a fixed asset of the acquiree may not be written down from its fair value in its existing use to its fair value in its intended use or its net realizable value *as part of the accounting for the acquisition.* Any such write-downs must be reflected in the consolidated income statement after the acquisition.

The intent of this requirement, as with that for the treatment of restructuring expenses discussed above, is to prevent acquirers from boosting postacquisition consolidated income by applying overly "conservative" valuations in initially accounting for the assets and liabilities acquired.

IAS 22, paragraph 39, sets out a number of requirements for identifying fair values. In general, these are straightforward. It is worth noting that:

- Inventories should be valued at net realizable value after allowing for costs of completion and disposal and "a reasonable allowance for selling effort of the acquirer based on profit of selling similar items."

- Intangible assets should be treated as required by IAS 38, "Intangible Assets," and should exclude amounts representing items that do not meet the criteria in IAS 38, paragraphs 9–11, and are thus equivalent to goodwill (sometimes termed "quasi-goodwill"). These criteria are identifiability, control over a resource, and the existence of future economic benefits.

- Assets relating to surpluses on employee pension or similar benefit plans should be recognized only to the extent that future economic benefits (refunds from the plan or reductions in future contributions) are probable.

- Tax assets and liabilities should be considered from the point of view of the acquirer and the combined entity. Previously unrecognized deferred tax assets may qualify for recognition on acquisition, subject to IAS 12, "Income Taxes."

Allocating Acquisition Cost

The total cost of the acquisition is allocated to the individual assets and liabilities that are recognized as discussed above, and any balance is recognized as goodwill, positive or negative. The way in which this is done, however, is affected by the treatment in the consolidated financial statements of any *minority interests in the acquiree,* that is, any share in the net assets and net results of operations of the acquiree that is not owned, directly or indirectly through subsidiaries, by the parent.

IAS 22 allows two treatments: a benchmark treatment and an allowed alternative.

Benchmark Treatment

The assets and liabilities recognized on acquisition should be "measured" (i.e., valued) on a pro rata basis as follows:

1. The proportion of the assets and liabilities acquired in the acquisition that corresponds to the acquirer's proportionate interest obtained in the exchange transaction should be measured at the fair values as at the date of the acquisition transaction.

2. Any proportionate interest in such assets and liabilities attributable to minority interests in the acquiree should be measured at the preacquisition carrying values of the assets and liabilities in the acquiree's accounts.

3. If the aggregate amount of 1 and 2, above, differs from the amount of the cost of the acquisition, then the difference is treated as goodwill (positive or negative) and accounted for as described further below (IAS 22, par. 31).

Allowed Alternative Treatment

The assets and liabilities recognized on acquisition should be measured at their fair values as at the date of acquisition, fair value being applied to both the majority and minority interests' proportionate shares in them. If the net amount recognized above, after deduction of the minority interest's proportionate share, differs from the amount of the cost of the acquisition, then the difference is treated as goodwill (positive or negative) and accounted for as described further below. The minority interest's proportionate share is accounted for as a minority interest in the consolidated financial statements (IAS 22, par. 33).

> **OBSERVATION:** The rationale of the benchmark treatment is that the proportion of the assets and liabilities corresponding to the minority interest has not "changed hands" in the acquisition, and that restatement of this proportion to fair value is therefore not called for. However, the treatment of the assets and liabilities of which a proportion is attributable to the minority interests will have been subjected to the recognition criteria discussed above, which may well differ from those applied by the acquiree in its preacquisition financial statements. Hence, the logic of the rationale of applying a different valuation basis to this proportion may be questioned, and the allowed alternative treatment is an answer to this question.

The benchmark treatment reflects a proprietary view of accounting for business combinations, while the allowed alternative treatment reflects an entity view.

Note that the amount of goodwill is the same under either method. In neither case is any goodwill (positive or negative) attributed to the minority interest.

Step-by-Step Acquisition

An enterprise may acquire a target enterprise in more than one transaction involving share purchases over an extended period of time. This may occur when, for example, the first share purchase does not result in control or significant influence over the investee enterprise being obtained, the second results in control, and the third increases the proportion of the subsidiary's equity held by the parent. This type of situation is considered in IAS 22, paragraph 34.

After the first share purchase, the investment would be accounted for according to IAS 39, "Financial Instruments: Recognition and Measurement," at fair value subject to review for impairment (unless it were unquoted shares whose fair value could not be reliably measured). At the time of the second transaction, the acquirer needs to determine the appropriate value for consolidation purposes of what is now a controlling interest in the investee and the amount of any goodwill arising. This means that the fair value of the investment needs to be broken down into the investor's proportionate share of the fair values of the investee's (i.e., subsidiary's) recognized assets and liabilities, and any goodwill arising. This would also be necessary if the second share purchase had resulted in joint control (requiring proportionate consolidation or, alternatively, the equity method, see Chapter 9) or significant influence (requiring the equity method, see Chapter 14) being obtained, since both proportionate consolidation and the equity method require the separate identification of goodwill.

The issue here is: fair value at what date? IAS 22 requires that, for the purpose of determining goodwill on consolidation, fair value in relation to each one of a number of successive share purchases is the proportionate share of the fair value of the assets and liabilities acquired in that share purchase, as at the date of that share purchase. This may be called the "historical fair value."

The "historical fair value" approach would also be applied in the case of the third share purchase mentioned above. Goodwill is thus the aggregate of the amounts calculated using the historical fair value approach, less any amounts previously written off by way of amortization or recognition of impairment (see below).

Illustration

P Company acquired an interest in S Company in three steps: (1) acquiring 10% of the outstanding common shares for $100,000; (2) the following year, acquiring an additional 60% for $700,000; (3) after another year, acquiring the remaining 30% for $350,000.

At the respective dates of acquisition, the fair values of S Company's recognized assets and liabilities were the following net amounts: (1) $900,000; (2) $1,100,000; (3) $1,300,000. Goodwill recognized as at the date of the second share purchase will be amortized over 10 years. (The treatment of goodwill is discussed in detail later in this chapter.)

Computation of goodwill

First share purchase: Not applicable—no goodwill recognized

Second share purchase:

Fair value at first share purchase	$ 900,000
Proportion acquired 10%	$ 90,000
Cost	100,000
Goodwill = excess of cost over fair value	$ 10,000
Fair value at second share purchase	$1,100,000
Proportion acquired 60%	$ 660,000
Cost	700,000
Goodwill	$ 40,000
Total goodwill after second share purchase	$ 50,000

Third share purchase:

Fair value at third share purchase	$1,300,000
Proportion acquired 30%	$ 390,000
Cost	350,000
Goodwill (negative)	$ (40,000)
Total goodwill after third share purchase:	
Amount after second share purchase	$ 50,000
Less—amortization for 1 year (1/10)	(5,000)
Unamortized balance	$ 45,000
Less—negative goodwill from third share purchase	(40,000)
Total goodwill after third purchase	$ 5,000

Reverse Acquisitions

A *reverse acquisition* occurs when one enterprise obtains ownership of the shares of another enterprise but as part of the transaction issues enough voting shares to the owners of the acquired enterprise to make control of the combined enterprise pass to them. The treatment of reverse acquisitions in IAS GAAP follows the principle of *substance over form*. The enterprise whose shareholders now control the combined enterprise is, in substance, the acquirer, although legally it is the acquiree. IAS GAAP require that the enterprise whose shareholders (and management) control the combined enterprise be treated as the acquirer, and that the latter apply the purchase method to the assets and liabilities of the enterprise issuing the voting shares.

> ☛ **PRACTICE POINTER:** A reverse acquisition may be identified by the fact that an enterprise has issued a large multiple of its previously outstanding shares to acquire shares of another enterprise. Where the number of shares issued is greater than the number previously outstanding, but not significantly so, there may be other factors that point to a reverse acquisition. One may be the different sizes of the combining enterprises, with the legal "acquiree" being significantly larger. Often, the reason for the reverse acquisition is that the legal "acquirer" has a stock exchange listing or similar rights that the legal "acquiree" wishes to obtain by this indirect method, as this is cheaper or easier than doing so directly.
>
> IAS 27 makes no reference to accounting for reverse acquisitions. Following the requirements of IAS 22 in this regard is not entirely straightforward. The following guidelines may be noted:
>
> 1. The consolidated financial statements will be issued by the enterprise that, while in substance the acquirer, is legally the subsidiary. The asset and liability values appearing in the consolidated balance sheet at the acquisition date will be the previous carrying values of the assets and liabilities of the in-substance acquirer, plus the fair values of the assets and liabilities of the legal parent treated as the acquiree. The equity accounts in the consolidated balance sheet, apart from share capital (see point 2 below), will also be the same as those shown in the in-substance acquirer's balance sheet.
>
> 2. However, the numbers and types of shares appearing in the consolidated balance sheet will have to be those of the *legal parent*, including any shares issued by it as part of the combination. On the other hand, consistently with point 1 above, the monetary amount attributed to the issued capital in the consolidated balance sheet (as with the other equity accounts) should in principle be equal to the amount previously shown by the enterprise treated as the acquirer, plus any amount attributable to shares issued by the latter as part

of the combination. Otherwise, the consolidated balance sheet would not balance. The law, however, may lay down what amounts are to be shown for issued share capital. If these are different, a separate item will be needed in shareholders' equity to account for this difference.

3. Valuing the shares issued by the legal parent as consideration in the combination may present problems, as the shares of targets in reverse acquisitions tend to be thinly traded, and market value may not reflect their fair value. This may be better estimated on the basis of the fair values of the legal parent's net assets, including, where appropriate, its stock exchange listing or similar valuable rights. See also the discussion under "Cost of Acquisition," above.

4. The results of operations of the legal parent should be included in the consolidated financial statements only as from the acquisition date.

5. Prior period comparative figures should be based on the prior period financial statements of the enterprise treated as the acquirer.

6. If some of the shareholders of the enterprise treated as the acquirer (the legal subsidiary) did not exchange their shares for shares in the legal parent, they constitute a minority interest in the legal subsidiary and, presumably, should be accounted for as such, even though it may seem paradoxical to treat shareholders in the controlling entity in this way.

Goodwill Arising on Acquisition

Goodwill in IAS GAAP is the difference between the fair value of the purchase consideration given and the aggregate fair values of the identifiable assets and liabilities of the acquiree that are recognized on acquisition, as discussed above. What is recognized as goodwill on acquisition is therefore a function of the recognition criteria and valuation rules applied to the identifiable assets and liabilities (and notably those in IASs 36, 37, 38, and 39). As such, it is therefore not itself an identifiable asset or liability but a residual amount. Nevertheless, IAS GAAP require it to be shown as an asset (or, if negative, a contra-asset or deduction from assets).

The IASC explains this by stating that "goodwill arising on acquisition represents a payment made by the acquirer in anticipation of future economic benefits…[which] may result from synergy between the identifiable assets acquired or from assets which, individually, do not qualify for recognition in the financial statements but for which the acquirer is prepared to make a payment in the acquisition" (IAS 22, par. 42). The latter category of items that "individually do not qualify for recognition" are sometimes (but not in IAS GAAP) referred to as "quasi-goodwill."

Positive Goodwill: Recognition and Measurement

Positive goodwill should be recognized as an asset and be carried at cost, less any accumulated amortization and impairment losses. Goodwill should be amortized on a systematic basis over its useful life, which should reflect the best estimate of the period during which future economic benefits are expected to flow to the enterprise. There is a rebuttable presumption that this will not exceed twenty years from initial recognition.

The amortization method used should reflect the pattern in which the future economic benefits arising from goodwill are expected to flow (or be consumed). There is a strong presumption in favor of the straight-line method for this purpose, and while "persuasive evidence" is required for any departure from this, such evidence will rarely, if ever, be available (IAS 22, par. 52). The amortization for each period is to be recognized as an expense (IAS 22, pars. 41–46).

IAS 22, paragraph 49, acknowledges that it is difficult to estimate the useful life of goodwill. Estimates become less reliable as the length of the useful life increases. This is given as a reason for the rebuttable presumption that useful life will not exceed twenty years. The amortization period and method should be reviewed annually. This review can affect the accounting treatment in the current and future periods only, and not past periods, as would be the case with a change in accounting policy having retrospective effects.

IAS 22 states that in rare cases there may be persuasive evidence that the useful life will be a specified period longer than twenty years. In such cases, systematic amortization over the best estimate of the useful life must be supplemented by "estimates of the recoverable amount of the goodwill at least annually to identify any impairment losses" (impairment tests, as laid down in IAS 36, "Impairment of Assets"; see Chapter 19). There must also be disclosure of the reasons why the presumption is considered to be rebutted and the factors that were significant in determining the (longer) useful life (par. 50). As goodwill is carried on the basis of cost, any impairment loss should be recognized in the income statement (IAS 36, par. 4).

Goodwill may not, in the name of prudence, be written off over a period that is unrealistically short. Factors to be considered in estimating the useful life of goodwill are set out in IAS 22, paragraph 48. They imply that useful life of goodwill should be assessed separately for each acquisition.

Negative Goodwill: Recognition and Measurement

In IAS GAAP, negative goodwill is conceptualized as a discount on the net fair value of identifiable assets and liabilities acquired. Such a discount may be attributable to two kinds of factors:

- The acquisition consideration reflected expenses that the acquirer is expected to incur subsequently in respect of the acquiree (such as subsequent losses or restructuring expenses)
- A "bargain purchase" element

In either case, negative goodwill is recognized as a "contra-asset" and is shown as a deduction from the consolidated assets in the same balance sheet classification as goodwill.

IAS 22, paragraph 60, emphasizes the need to check that no negative goodwill is recognized because of an erroneous overstatement of the net fair value of identifiable assets and liabilities.

Insofar as negative goodwill relates to *expectations of future losses and expenses that are recognized in the acquirer's plan for the acquisition and can be measured reliably but do not represent identifiable liabilities at the acquisition date* (according to the IAS 37 criteria restated in IAS 22, pars. 29–31), it will be recognized as a contra-asset and released to the income statement as and when the future losses and expenses are recognized (IAS 22, par. 61). This treatment is somewhat analogous to a type of "provision," but one that does not meet the criteria for recognition as a liability.

Any amount of negative goodwill that does not qualify to be treated as above is accounted for as a "bargain purchase element" and is treated as follows (IAS 22, pars. 62–63):

- The amount of negative goodwill not exceeding the fair values of the acquired identifiable nonmonetary assets is released back to income on a systematic basis over the remaining weighted average useful life of the identified acquired depreciable/amortizable assets.
- Any amount of negative goodwill in excess of the fair values of the acquired identifiable nonmonetary assets (i.e., any amount that is effectively attributed to monetary assets) should be recognized as income immediately.

> **OBSERVATION:** One effect of the relatively stringent criteria in IAS 37 for recognizing provisions as liabilities (restated in IAS 22, pars. 29–31) is to make it substantially harder for acquirers to create large restructuring provisions on acquisition, which are reflected in increased positive goodwill and which are released to income in the years following the acquisition with a resulting boost to consolidated net income. Insofar as the expectation of restructuring and related expenses is reflected in the acquisition consideration but does not meet the IAS 37 criteria, any resultant negative goodwill that meets the alternative criteria in IAS 22, paragraph 61, is recognized as a contra-asset, which might be termed a "quasi-restructuring provision." (Alternatively, it is recognized as a "bargain purchase element" according to IAS 22, pars. 62–63.) This excludes the cases where the expected restructuring and related expenses neither meet the IAS 37 criteria nor

are reflected in a "discount" to the net fair value of the identifiable assets acquired.

Adjustments to Purchase Consideration Contingent upon Subsequent Events, and Subsequent Changes in the Cost of Acquisition

Adjustments to purchase consideration contingent upon subsequent events, and subsequent changes in the cost of acquisition are covered in IAS 22, paragraphs 65–70. The terms of an acquisition may provide for an adjustment of the purchase consideration contingent upon one or more subsequent events. Typically, these events relate to one or both of the following: the operating results of the acquiree reaching or being maintained at a pre-agreed level; or the market price of securities issued as part of the purchase consideration being maintained. Such adjustments should be made when the following conditions are met:

- The events that trigger them are probable, and
- The amount of the adjustment can be estimated reliably.

The thrust of IAS 22 is that any such adjustments to the purchase consideration should be made as soon as possible, even if subsequent corrections become necessary. Thus, according to IAS 22, paragraph 67, it is usually possible to estimate the amount of any such adjustment *when initially accounting for an acquisition,* that is to say, when the next annual financial statements after the acquisition are prepared, even though some uncertainty may exist. If an adjustment is made and the specified events do not occur or the estimate turns out to require revision, the cost of the acquisition is adjusted, with a consequential effect on goodwill (positive or negative), except in the following case.

When additional consideration has to be given to the seller to compensate for a fall in the market price of securities (shares or debt) given as consideration subject to a price guarantee from the acquirer, the additional consideration is not treated as an increase in the cost of acquisition and is not reflected in the amount of goodwill recognized. Instead, it is treated as a reduction in the premium or an increase in the discount at which the securities were originally issued (IAS 22, par. 70).

Subsequent Identification, or Changes in Value, of Identifiable Assets or Liabilities

Assets and liabilities of an acquiree may not have been recognized at the time of acquisition, either because they did not satisfy the recognition criteria or because the acquirer was unaware of their existence. Alternatively, the fair values of assets or liabilities that were recognized may require adjustment in the light of new information relevant to estimating their fair values as at the acquisition date. The treatment of these items depends on whether the adjustments are made before or after the end of the first complete annual accounting period subsequent to the acquisition.

When an adjustment is made for these reasons subsequent to acquisition but before the end of the first complete annual accounting period (i.e., excluding interim periods) commencing after the acquisition, the amount should be reflected in goodwill (where appropriate) subject to the following condition: it is probable that the amount will be recovered from expected future economic benefits. This condition applies particularly in the case of previously unrecognized liabilities or overvalued assets, the adjustment for which might have as a counterpart an increase in positive goodwill. When such an increase cannot be justified in terms of expected future economic benefits, the adjustment should be recognized as an expense.

When such adjustments are made after the end of the first complete annual accounting period commencing after the acquisition, they are reflected in income or expense and not as an adjustment to goodwill. The objective of applying this cutoff date is "to prevent goodwill being reassessed and adjusted indefinitely" (IAS 22, pars. 71–72).

It is important to note that such adjustments should be calculated *as though the adjusted fair values had been applied from the date of acquisition.* Thus, the adjustments should include: (a) the effect of the change in the fair values initially assigned; and (b) the effect of depreciation and other changes that would have resulted had the adjusted fair values been applied from the date of acquisition (SIC-22, par. 5).

UNITINGS OF INTERESTS

A uniting of interests should be accounted for by using the pooling-of-interests method, the rationale of which is that no acquisition has occurred and the separate businesses are continuing, albeit now jointly owned and managed.

Use of the pooling-of-interests method recognizes this by accounting for the combined enterprises as though the separate businesses were continuing as before, though now jointly owned and managed (IAS 22, par. 64).

The broader concept of control in IAS GAAP (see Chapter 9) implies that it is quite unusual not to be able to identify an acquirer in a business combination. Hence, unitings of interests as recognized under IAS GAAP are expected to be very rare.

☞ **PRACTICE POINTER:** The SEC has held that a business combination entered into by a would-be foreign registrant, after which the two combinees' former shareholders ended up with 55% and 45%, respectively, of the equity of the combined business, should be accounted for as a purchase under IAS 22. The would-be registrant, in applying IAS GAAP, had accounted for the combination as a uniting of interests. However, when it applied for registration with a view to a U.S. listing, the SEC held that the combinee whose shareholders had ended up with 55% of the equity of the combined business was, in fact, the acquirer, so that purchase accounting should be used. The SEC required this latter treatment to be used in the registration statement.

Subject to this, unitings of interests may take different legal forms:

- One combinee may legally become the subsidiary and the other, the parent.
- A new enterprise might be formed to act as the legal parent.
- A legal merger may take place, with one of the combinees being legally dissolved.

In general, the choice of legal form will not affect the presentation of the financial statements of the combined business. However, in the third case mentioned above (legal merger), there will be no need to use the pooling-of-interests method to prepare financial statements of the combined business since only one legal entity will remain.

Accounting for Unitings of Interests: The Pooling Method

The pooling method consists simply of combining the financial statements of the combinees on a line-by-line basis. There is no restatement of assets and liabilities at fair value, no recognition of goodwill (positive or negative), no recognition of any share premium on shares issued as part of the combination, and no distinction between precombination and postcombination profits for the financial period in which the combination took place (IAS 22, pars. 78–81).

This is, however, subject to the following:

- A single set of accounting policies should be used, and any adjustments necessary to conform with these policies must be made in arriving at the combined amounts.
- The amount to be shown for issued share capital of the combined business (at nominal value) should, in general, be equal to the sum of the precombination issued share capitals of the combinees. This is because shares exchanged as part of the

combination transactions are accounted for at nominal values. In jurisdictions where there is a legal requirement to show a different amount, the difference should be shown as a separate adjustment in the shareholders' interests.

- There may be a limited number of shareholders in one of the combinees who do not participate in the share exchange or other business combination transactions. If this combinee ends up as a legal subsidiary under the form chosen for the uniting of interests, this shareholding constitutes a minority interest and should be shown as such in the balance sheet of the combination.

- The effects of any "intragroup" transactions between the combinees should be eliminated, including those relating to transactions that occurred in the period in which the uniting of interests took place, but prior to its taking place.

In applying the pooling-of-interests method, the financial statement items of the combining enterprises for the period in which the combination occurs (and for any comparative periods disclosed) should be included in the financial statements of the combined entity as if they had been combined from the beginning of the earliest period presented. If the date of a uniting of interests to which an enterprise is a party is later than that of the most recent financial statements of that enterprise, the financial statements of that enterprise should not (prospectively) reflect the uniting of interests.

Any expenses incurred in relation to a uniting of interests should be recognized as expenses in the period in which they are incurred.

Illustration

C1 Company and C2 Company have the following balance sheets (summarized) as at June 30, 20XX:

	C1	C2
Net current assets	$ 5,000	$ 2,000
Property, plant, and equipment	6,000	7,000
	$11,000	$ 9,000
Common shares of $1	$ 9,000	$ 6,000
Earned surplus	2,000	3,000
	$11,000	$ 9,000

On June 30, 20XX, C1 and C2 combine by means of a transaction in which C1 issues a further 6,000 common shares in exchange for 100% of the issued share capital of C2. The market price of both companies' shares on that date is $4.

The fair values of C2's identifiable assets on June 30, 20XX are:

Net current assets	$ 2,500
Property, plant and equipment	$ 8,000
Total	$10,500

Balance sheets of the combined entity using the purchase and pooling methods:

	Purchase	Pooling
Net current assets	$ 7,500	$ 7,000
Property, plant, and equipment	14,000	13,000
Goodwill (6000 x $4 – 10,500)	13,500	nil
	$35,000	$20,000
Common shares	$15,000	$15,000
Paid-in surplus (6,000 x $3)	18,000	nil
Earned surplus	2,000	5,000
	$35,000	$20,000

Notes

Net current assets and property, plant, and equipment:

The difference between the two sets of figures reflects the adjustment of C2's net assets to fair values.

Goodwill: The acquisition cost is represented by 6,000 common shares of a nominal value of $1 with a market value of $4 each, total $24,000. From this is subtracted the fair values of the identifiable net assets of C2, total $10,500.

Common shares: Under either method, these represent the nominal value of the issued share capital of C1, namely, the initial $9,000 plus the $6,000 issued as part of the business combination. This is equal to the total of the precombination issued share capitals of C1 and C2, since the shares of C2 that were exchanged for those of C1 had the same nominal value as the latter.

Paid-in surplus: Under the purchase method, the difference between the nominal value of the 6,000 shares issued by C1 and their market value, namely, $3 per share, or $18,000 in total, is accounted for as paid-in surplus (share premium). No share premium is recognized under the pooling method.

Earned surplus: Under the purchase method, the "preacquisition" earned surplus of C2 is excluded from the combined "postacquisition" amount. The pooling method does not recognize the distinction between pre- and postacquisition amounts.

ALL BUSINESS COMBINATIONS

Taxes on Income

Paragraph 85 of IAS 22 is concerned with the effects of tax loss carryforwards that were not recognized as identifiable assets on acquisition. Had they been recognized, the amount of (positive) goodwill recognized would have been less. The concern is that enterprises may "cash in" the tax loss carryforwards in the years immediately following the acquisition, while spreading the amortization of the goodwill over a much longer period, thereby boosting after-tax income in the immediate postacquisition years.

Hence, paragraph 85 requires the values of any tax loss carryforwards that were not recognized as identifiable assets on acquisition but that are realized subsequently to be reflected in adjustments to the gross carrying value and the accumulated amortization of goodwill. The reduction of the carrying value of goodwill should also be recognized as an expense in the same period.

The effect of this is to approximate the situation that would have obtained in the current period, if the tax loss carryforward had been recognized as an identifiable asset at the acquisition date, and thereby to prevent the boosting of postacquisition consolidated net income.

DISCLOSURE

The disclosure requirements relating to business combinations are extensive, and those set out in paragraphs 86–98 of IAS 22 are additional to those in paragraphs 15–26 of IAS 27 (see Chapter 9). The requirements set out in IAS 22 are as follows:

For all business combinations, the following disclosures should be made in the financial statements for the period during which the combination has taken place:

1. The names and descriptions of the combining enterprises,
2. The method of accounting for the combination,
3. The effective date of the combination for accounting purposes, and
4. Any operations resulting from the business combination that the enterprise has decided to dispose of.

For a business combination that is an acquisition, the following additional disclosures should be made in the financial statements for the period during which the acquisition has taken place:

1. The percentage of voting shares acquired, and
2. The cost of acquisition and a description of the purchase consideration paid or contingently payable.

For goodwill, the financial statements should disclose

1. The amortization period(s) adopted.
2. If goodwill is amortized over more than twenty years, the reasons why the presumption that the useful life of goodwill will not exceed twenty years from initial recognition is rebutted. In giving these reasons, the enterprise should describe the factor(s) that played a significant role in determining the useful life of the goodwill.
3. If goodwill is not amortized on the straight-line basis, the basis used and reason why that basis is more appropriate than the straight-line basis.
4. The line item(s) of the income statement in which the amortization is of goodwill is included.
5. A reconciliation of the carrying amount of goodwill at the beginning and end of the period showing:
   (a) the gross amount and the accumulated amortization (aggregated with accumulated impairment losses) at the beginning of the period;
   (b) any additional goodwill recognized during the period;
   (c) any adjustments resulting from subsequent identification or changes in value of identifiable assets and liabilities;
   (d) any goodwill derecognized on the disposal of all or part of the business to which it relates during the period;
   (e) amortization recognized during the period;
   (f) impairment losses recognized during the period under IAS 36, "Impairment of Assets" (if any);
   (g) impairment losses reversed during the period under IAS 36 (if any);
   (h) other changes in the carrying amount during the period (if any);
   (i) the gross amount and the accumulated amortization (aggregated with accumulated impairment losses), at the end of the period.

Comparative information is not required.

When an enterprise describes the factor(s) that played a significant role in determining the useful life of goodwill that is amortized over more than twenty years, the enterprise considers the list of factors in IAS 22, paragraph 48 (see "Positive Goodwill: Recognition and Measurement," above).

An enterprise discloses information on impaired goodwill under IAS 36 in addition to the information required in 5(f) and (g) above.

For negative goodwill, the financial statements should disclose:

1. To the extent that negative goodwill is treated as relating to expectations of future losses and expenses under IAS 22, paragraph 61, a description, the amount, and the timing of the expected future losses and expenses (see "Negative Goodwill: Recognition and Measurement," above).

2. The period(s) over which negative goodwill is recognized as income.

3. The line item(s) of the income statement in which negative goodwill is recognized as income.

4. A reconciliation of the carrying amount of negative goodwill at the beginning and end of the period showing:

   (a) the gross amount of negative goodwill and the accumulated amount of negative goodwill already recognized as income, at the beginning of the period;

   (b) any additional negative goodwill recognized during the period;

   (c) any adjustments resulting from subsequent identification or changes in value of identifiable assets and liabilities;

   (d) any negative goodwill derecognized on the disposal of all or part of the business to which it relates during the period;

   (e) negative goodwill recognized as income during the period, showing separately the portion of negative goodwill recognized as income under paragraph 61 (if any);

   (f) other changes in the carrying amount during the period (if any);

   (g) the gross amount of negative goodwill and the accumulated amount of negative goodwill already recognized as income, at the end of the period (IAS 22, par. 91).

Comparative information is not required.

The disclosure requirements of IAS 37, "Provisions, Contingent Liabilities and Contingent Assets," apply to provisions recognized under IAS 22, paragraph 31, for terminating or reducing the activities of an acquiree. These provisions should be treated as a separate class of provisions for the purpose of disclosure under IAS 37. In addition, the aggregate carrying amount of these provisions should be disclosed for each individual business combination.

In an acquisition, if the fair values of the identifiable assets and liabilities or the purchase consideration can only be determined on a provisional basis at the end of the period in which the acquisition took place, this should be stated and the reasons should be given. When there are subsequent adjustments to such provisional fair values, those adjustments should be disclosed and explained in the financial statements of the period concerned.

For a business combination that is a uniting of interests, the following additional disclosures should be made in the financial statements for the period during which the uniting of interests has taken place:

1. Description and number of shares issued, together with the percentage of each enterprise's voting shares exchanged to effect the uniting of interests.

2. Amounts of assets and liabilities contributed by each enterprise.

3. Sales revenue, other operating revenues, extraordinary items, and the net profit or loss of each enterprise prior to the date of the combination that are included in the net profit or loss shown by the combined enterprise's financial statements.

General disclosures required to be made in consolidated financial statements are contained in IAS 27, "Consolidated Financial Statements and Accounting for Investments in Subsidiaries."

For business combinations effected after the balance sheet date, the information required by IAS 22, paragraphs 86–94 (as outlined above), should be disclosed. If it is impracticable to disclose any of this information, this fact should be disclosed.

Business combinations that have been effected after the balance sheet date and before the date on which the financial statements of one of the combining enterprises are authorized for issue are disclosed if they are of such importance that nondisclosure would affect the ability of the users of the financial statements to make proper evaluations and decisions (see IAS 10, "Contingencies and Events Occurring after the Balance Sheet Date").

In certain circumstances, the effect of the combination may be to allow the financial statements of the combined enterprise to be prepared in accordance with the going concern assumption. This might not have been possible for one or both of the combining enterprises. This may occur, for example, when an enterprise with cash flow difficulties combines with an enterprise having access to cash that can be used in the enterprise with a need for cash. If this is the case, disclosure of this information in the financial statements of the enterprise having the cash flow difficulties is relevant.

CHAPTER 7
CASH FLOW STATEMENTS

CONTENTS

OVERVIEW

IAS 7, "Cash Flow Statements," requires that all sets of "financial statements" should include such a statement. It is designed to focus attention on cash and liquidity movements, in contrast to the income statement, which focuses on revenues and expenses. Issued in 1992, IAS 7 replaced the previous, significantly different IAS 7, called "Statement of Changes in Financial Position." IAS 7, "Cash Flow Statements," specifies processes and formats for the preparation and presentation of cash flow statements, as discussed below.

BACKGROUND

The traditional accounting process is an uncertain and complex process. Not only is profit determination complex, it is potentially misleading. In any accounting year, there will be a mixture of complete and incomplete transactions. Transactions are complete when they have led to a final cash settlement and cause no profit-measurement difficulties.

Considerable problems arise, however, in dealing with incomplete transactions, where the profit or loss figure can be estimated only by means of the accruals concept, whereby revenue and costs are matched with one another as far as their relationship can be established or justifiably assumed and dealt with in the income statement of the period to which they relate.

A statement that focuses on changes in liquidity rather than on profits has two potential advantages. First, it provides different and additional information on movements and changes in net liquid assets, which assists appraisal of an enterprise's progress and prospects, and second, it provides information that is generally more objective (though not necessarily more *useful*) than that contained in the income statement.

Opinion has varied sharply in the past three decades on exactly what aspect of "liquidity" should best be focused on in published financial statements. Consider the following two balance sheet extracts from A Co.

	000s	*000s*
	12/31/X2	*12/31/X1*
Inventory	4300	4600
Accounts receivable	2600	1300
Cash and bank	1200	2500
	8100	8400
Accounts payable	6500	7900
Working capital	1600	500

Identify the change in position.

If we look solely at cash, we could state that A Co. had experienced a decrease in cash of 1,300,000 over the year. On the other hand, looking at working capital indicates a much better position, an increase of 1,100,000 over the year. Which figure should users of accounts regard when taking decisions?

Practice through the 1970s and beyond was generally focused on working capital, that is, on the current assets and current liabilities. The original IAS 7 reflected this preference. Now, however, the focus is much more closely on cash. More strictly, it is changes in cash plus cash equivalents, that is, those items that are so liquid as to be "nearly cash" that are analyzed. IAS 7 carefully and precisely defines what it means by "nearly," but different national systems still have different views on this element.

IAS 7 is uncompromising in that it applies to all enterprises. It requires that a cash flow statement be presented as an integral part of all sets of enterprise financial statements. Such cash flow statements classify and distinguish cash flows under three headings: operating activities, investing activities, and financing activities.

IAS and U.S. GAAP are broadly similar, although there are differences of detail in the required formats. The U.S. definition of cash equivalents is similar to that in IAS, but under U.S. GAAP changes in the balances of overdrafts are classified as financing cash flows, rather than being included within cash and cash equivalents.

TERMINOLOGY

The standard defines a number of terms, mostly in a straightforward way, all of them already mentioned above. These are as follows (par. 6):

- *Cash* comprises cash on hand and demand deposits.
- *Cash equivalents* are short-term, highly liquid investments that are readily convertible to known amounts of cash and that are subject to an insignificant risk of changes in value.
- *Cash flows* are inflows and outflows of cash and cash equivalents.
- *Operating activities* are the principal revenue-producing activities of the enterprise and other activities that are not investing or financing activities.
- *Investing activities* are the acquisition and disposal of long-term assets and other investments not included in cash equivalents.
- *Financing activities* are activities that result in changes in the size and composition of the equity capital and borrowings of the enterprise.

As indicated above, cash equivalents require further clarification. Cash equivalents are held for the purpose of meeting short-term cash commitments rather than for investment or other purposes. For an investment to qualify as a cash equivalent it must be readily convertible to a known amount of cash and be subject to an insignificant risk of changes in value. Therefore, an investment normally qualifies as a cash equivalent only when it has a short maturity of, say, three months or less from the date of acquisition. Equity investments are excluded from cash equivalents unless they are, in substance, cash equivalents, for example, in the case of preferred shares acquired within a short period of their maturity and with a specified redemption date.

This means that cash equivalents must meet both of two criteria (par. 7), that is:

(a) it has a short maturity "of, say, three months or less"; *and*

(b) it is held to meet short-term cash requirements, not for investment or other purposes.

Bank borrowings are generally considered to be financing activities. In some countries, however, bank overdrafts that are repayable on demand form an integral part of an enterprise's cash management. In these circumstances, bank overdrafts are included as a component of cash and cash equivalents.

> **OBSERVATION:** Analysts and readers of financial statements should not assume that "cash and cash equivalents" are interpreted identically in different countries. For example, in the United States the definition of cash equivalents is similar to that in IAS, but under U.S. GAAP changes in the balances of overdrafts are classified as financing cash flows, rather than being included within cash and cash equivalents. Under U.K. GAAP, cash is defined as cash in hand and deposits receivable on demand, less overdrafts repayable on demand. Cash equivalents are not included but are dealt with in liquid resources and financing.
>
> Enterprises from other countries that report under IAS may interpret the IAS definition, necessarily somewhat subjective as the concept of "cash equivalents" inevitably must be, in accordance with local cultures and characteristics.

PRESENTATION OF CASH FLOW STATEMENTS

The key requirement is that the cash flow statement reports cash flows during the period classified by operating, investing, and financing activities in a manner that is most appropriate to the business.

IAS 7 gives long lists of examples of each of operating, investing, and financing activities (pars. 13–17). Here we leave the provision of detailed examples to the illustrations that follow. We restrict our discussion to principles and to particular difficulties.

Cash flows from *operating activities* are primarily derived from the principal revenue-producing activities of the enterprise. Therefore, they generally result from the transactions and other events that enter into the determination of net profit or loss. All cash flows from the sale of productive non-current assets, such as plant, however, are cash flows from investing activities.

It follows from the above, of course, that the nature of the business, that is, of the "principal revenue-producing activities," may differ significantly from one business to another, in which case the implications of apparently similar transactions may also differ. For example, an enterprise may hold securities and loans for dealing or trading purposes, in which case they are similar to inventory acquired specifically for resale. Therefore, cash flows arising from the purchase and sale of dealing or trading securities are classified as operating activities. Similarly, cash advances and loans made by financial institutions such as banks are usually classified as operating activities since they relate to the main revenue-producing activity of that enterprise.

It is worth emphasizing that reference to the definitions of operating, investing, and financing activities given earlier makes it clear that any "principal revenue-producing activity" that is not a financing or investing activity as defined is automatically an operating activity.

The standard says very little about *investing activities* except to give a list of examples. They consist essentially of cash payments to acquire, and cash receipts from the eventual disposal of, property, plant, and equipment and other long-term productive assets. Cash payments and receipts relating to future, forward, option, and swap contracts are generally investing activities, unless undertaken by a dealer or trader in such contracts. When a contract is accounted for as a hedge of an identifiable position, however, the cash flows of the contract are classified in the same manner as the cash flows of the position being hedged.

☛ **PRACTICE POINTER:** It should be noted that if a relevant asset is acquired by incurring debt directly from the seller, then this represents, *pro tem*, a non-cash transaction that, as such, will not appear in a cash flow statement at all. Subsequent payments could be argued, and have been argued by some commentators, to be investing cash outflows. In our view, this is incorrect and would be inconsistent with the substance of the transaction, which is that of a purchase and a loan. It follows that the subsequent payments off the principal of the debt are financing outflows. IAS 7 gives an illustration (in its Appendix 1), which is consistent with our argument, and supports it explicitly in paragraph 17.

Financing activities, those relating to the size of the equity capital whether by capital inflow, capital repayment, or arguably dividend payment, or to borrowings (other than any short-term borrowings accepted as cash equivalents), are in essence a simple concept. Note that while interest paid (and also taxes paid) are definitely operating activity items, dividends paid could be interpreted as either operating or as financing activities. The standard says (par. 33) that dividends paid may be classified as a financing cash flow because they are a cost of obtaining financial resources. Alternatively, dividends paid may be classified as a component of cash flows from operating activities in order to assist users to demonstrate the ability of an enterprise to pay dividends out of operating cash flows.

IAS 7 implies, but does not explicitly state, a preference for treating dividends as a financing activity. We concur with this view, which is consistent with U.K. and U.S. practice.

Reporting Cash Flows from Operating Activities

Enterprises are allowed to use either of two methods to analyze and report cash flows from operating activities. These are (par. 18):

(a) The direct method, whereby major classes of gross cash receipts and gross cash payments are disclosed; and

(b) The indirect method, whereby net profit or loss is adjusted for the effects of transactions of a non-cash nature, any deferrals or accruals of past or future operating cash receipts or payments, and items of income or expense associated with investing or financing cash flows.

Enterprises are encouraged to report cash flows from operating activities using the direct method, but this is not a requirement. The indirect method takes reported net profit and adjusts for, in effect removes, non-cash flow items included in the calculation of that profit figure. The direct method, in contrast, is in effect a direct analyzed summary of the cash book. As such, the direct method provides information that may be useful in estimating future cash flows and that is not available under the indirect method.

The workings of, and differences between, the two methods are best shown by an example.

Illustration of Calculation of Cash Flow from Operating Activities by the Direct Method

Cash received from customers	$144,750
Cash paid to suppliers and employees	(137,600)
Cash dividend received from affiliate	900
Other operating cash receipts	10,000
Interest paid in cash (net of amounts capitalized)	(5,200)
Income taxes paid in cash	(4,500)
Net cash provided (used) by operating activities	$ 8,350

Illustration of Calculation of Cash Flow from Operating Activities by the Indirect Method

Net income	$8,000
Adjustments to reconcile net income to net cash provided by operating activities:	
Depreciation and amortization	$8,600
Provisions for doubtful accounts receivable	750
Provision for deferred income taxes	1,000
Undistributed earnings of affiliate	(2,100)
Gain on sale of equipment	(2,500)
Payment received on installment sale of product	2,500
Changes in operating assets and liabilities net of effects from purchase of XYZ Company:	
Increase in accounts receivable	(7,750)
Increase in inventory	(4,000)
Increase in accounts payable and accrued expenses	3,850
Total adjustments to net income	350
Net cash provided (used) by operating activities	$8,350

A comparison of the above two illustrations makes it clear, we suggest, that the indirect method is at the same time more complicated and less informative in terms of actual cash flows than the direct method. U.S. GAAP, like IAS GAAP, encourage but do not require the use of the direct method. U.K. GAAP now require the indirect method, on the grounds that the benefits to users of the direct method are outweighed by the costs of preparing it. If one takes a user rather than a preparer perspective, it is difficult to support the U.K. view on this point.

Reporting Cash Flows from Investing and Financing Activities

The essential requirement is very simple, namely, that an enterprise should report separately major classes of gross cash receipts and gross cash payments. Netting off of cash receipts and payments is allowed (for investing, financing, and operating activities) only in limited circumstances. These are (par. 22):

(a) When using the indirect method to report operating cash flows;

(b) Cash receipts and payments on behalf of customers when the cash flows reflect the activities of the customer rather than those of the enterprise; and

(c) Cash receipts and payments for items in which the turnover is quick, the amounts are large, and the maturities are short.

Items (b) and (c) above are likely to be restricted in practice to financial institutions such as banks. IAS 7 clarifies this as follows (par. 24).

> Cash flows arising from each of the following activities of a financial institution may be reported on a net basis:
>
> (a) cash receipts and payments for the acceptance and repayment of deposits with a fixed maturity date;
>
> (b) the placement of deposits with and withdrawal of deposits from other financial institutions; and
>
> (c) cash advances and loans made to customers and the repayment of those advances and loans.

Note that in every respect, reporting cash flows on a net basis is *allowed* in all the above situations. It is never *required*.

A complication arises with the treatment of foreign currency cash flows. This is because IAS 21, "The Effects of Changes in Foreign Exchange Rates" (see Chapter 17), permits the use of an exchange rate that approximates the actual rate. For example, a weighted average exchange rate for a period may be used for recording foreign currency transactions or the translation of the cash flows of a foreign subsidiary. However, IAS 21 does not permit use of this exchange rate at the balance sheet date when translating the cash flows of a foreign subsidiary (par. 27). Unrealized gains and losses arising from changes in foreign currency exchange rates are not cash flows. The effect of exchange rate changes on cash and cash equivalents held or due in a foreign currency, however, is reported in the cash flow statement in order to reconcile cash and cash equivalents at the beginning and the end of the period. This amount is presented separately from cash flows from operating, investing, and financing activities and includes the differences, if any, had those cash flows been reported at end of period exchange rates.

Cash flows from extraordinary items (see IAS 8, "Net Profit or Loss for the Period, Fundamental Errors, and Changes in Accounting Policies," Chapter 26) are separately disclosed, within the appropriate classification of operating, investing, or financing activities (par. 30). Cash flows from interest and dividends received and paid should each be shown separately, as already discussed. Cash flows arising from taxes on income should be separately disclosed and should be classified as cash flows from operating activities, unless they can be specifically identified with financing and investing activities.

IAS 7 restricts cash flow reporting related to investments in subsidiaries or associates accounted for by use of the equity or cost method to cash flows that have actually moved between the enterprise and the investee. This also applies to a joint venture consolidated by the equity method. However, an enterprise that reports its interest in a jointly controlled entity (see IAS 31, "Financial Reporting of Interests in Joint Ventures," Chapter 9) using proportionate consolidation, includes in its consolidated cash flow statement its proportionate share of the jointly controlled entity's cash flows.

Other Disclosures

IAS 7 requires that the aggregate cash outflows arising from acquisitions of subsidiaries or other business units and the aggregate cash inflows arising from such disposals should be reported separately, classified as investing activities (pars. 39–40). In addition, an enterprise should disclose in relation thereto the aggregate amounts during the period of each of the following:

(a) The total purchase or disposal consideration,
(b) The portion of the purchase or disposal consideration discharged by means of cash and cash equivalents,
(c) The amount of cash and cash equivalents in the subsidiary or business unit acquired or disposed of, and
(d) The amount of the assets and liabilities other than cash or cash equivalents in the subsidiary or business unit acquired or disposed of, summarized by each major category.

Paragraph 44 makes it clear that investing and financing transactions, such as the creation of a finance lease or the conversion of debt to equity, which do not result in movements in cash or cash equivalents, are not included in a cash flow statement. They must, however, be disclosed elsewhere "in a way that provides all the relevant information about these investing and financing activities"—by narrative, note, or separate schedule.

> **OBSERVATION:** As we pointed out earlier, the substance of a finance lease transaction is that of a purchase and a loan. A purchase implies a payment, financed from the receipt of the loan. Similarly, the conversion of debt to equity is arguably, in substance, the receipt of cash from equity holders and the payment of cash to previous creditors.
>
> Because IASC supports the principle of substance over form (Framework, par. 35; see Chapter 2), it could be argued that such situations should be reflected by equal and opposite in-substance "cash flows," on opposite sides of the cash flow statement. Paragraphs 43 and 44, without discussion, clearly reject this argument.

Enterprises are required to disclose the various components of the total cash and cash equivalents (par. 45) and, if necessary, a reconciliation of any differences between the amounts of cash and cash equivalents in the cash flow statement and the amounts in the balance sheet. The policy adopted in determining the figures for cash and cash equivalents must be clearly stated in the appropriate place. An enterprise should also disclose, together with appropriate explanations (par. 48), the amount of cash and cash equivalent balances, if material, that are not available for immediate use "by the group," for example because of exchange controls (why "by the group" rather than "by the enterprise" is not clear). The standard concludes by suggesting several nonmandatory disclosures.

Reference may need to be made to several other International Accounting Standards in relation to matters possibly relevant to cash flow statements. These include:

- IAS 14, "Segment Reporting" (Chapter 31)
- IAS 34, "Interim Financial Reporting" (Chapter 22)
- IAS 35, "Discontinuing Operations" (Chapter 11)

We present below the consolidated statement of cash flows, together with the accompanying notes, for Deutsche Telekom for the Financial Year ended December 31, 1998.

Consolidated Statement of Cash Flows
(comparative figures omitted)

	Note	1998 millions of DM
Net income		4,388
Income applicable to minority shareholders		397
Income after taxes		**4,785**
Depreciation and amortization		17,674
Income tax expense		4,844
Net interest expense		5,794
Net losses from the disposition of noncurrent assets		1,010
Personnel restructuring accruals		—
Increase/(decrease) in pension accruals		70
Results from associated companies		748
Other noncash income		(101)
(Increase)/decrease in trade accounts receivable		10
(Increase)/decrease in inventories		112

	Note	1998 millions of DM
Increase/(decrease) in trade accounts payable		482
Changes in other current assets and liabilities		412
Income taxes paid		(3,936)
Dividends received		216
Cash generated from operations		**32,120**
Interest paid		(6,656)
Interest received		923
Net cash provided by operating activities	(30)	**26,387**
Capital expenditures		(9,371)
Purchase of subsidiaries, associated and related companies, net of cash acquired		(5,345)
Proceeds from sale of noncurrent assets		1,399
Net change in short-term investments and marketable securities		(1,371)
Other		(1)
Net cash used for investing activities	(31)	**(14,689)**
Change in short-term borrowing		(9,349)
Issuance of medium and long-term debt		3,120
Repayments of medium and long-term debt		(3,580)
Dividends		(3,450)
Changes in minority interests		(36)
Proceeds from share offering		—
Net cash (used for) provided by financing activities	(32)	**(13,295)**
Effect of foreign exchange rate changes on cash and cash equivalents		11
Net increase (decrease) in cash and cash equivalents		**(1,586)**
Cash and cash equivalents, at beginning of year		**5,623**
Cash and cash equivalents, at end of year		**4,037**
Liquid assets as shown in the balance sheet		
Cash and cash equivalents, Dec. 31		4,037
Temporary cash investments, Dec. 31		5,911
Total		**9,948**

Notes to the consolidated statement of cash flows

The consolidated statement of cash flows has been prepared in conformity with International Accounting Standard No. 7, "Cash Flow Statements." Liquid assets and short-term investments with original maturities of less than 3 months at the date of purchase are considered cash equivalents for cash flow reporting purposes. These cash and cash equivalents decreased by DM 1,586 million in 1998 to DM 4,037 million at December 31, 1998.

This is a result of the following developments:

(30) Net cash provided by operating activities

Net cash provided by operating activities increased in 1998 to DM 26,387 million. The increase of approximately DM 3.7 billion is mainly attributable to an increase in net income, in the level of income taxes not affecting liquidity, and in trade accounts payable. This is offset in particular by a decrease in depreciation of property, plant, and equipment and a minor loss related to associated companies.

(31) Net cash used for investing activities

Net cash used for investing activities increased to DM 14,689 million in 1998. This is a result of the outflow of short-term investments and of the considerable increase in investments in financial assets (attributable, in particular, to the acquisition of shares in France Telecom). This is offset by a reduction, compared with the previous year, in investments in property, plant, and equipment to DM 9.4 billion. As in previous years, it was possible to finance such investments, totaling approximately DM 15 billion, from cash provided by operating activities.

(32) Net cash (used for) provided by financing activities

The decrease in cash (used for) provided by financing activities in 1998 to DM (13,295) million is attributable to an offsetting effect. Cash decreases due to higher dividend payments and the continued repayment of debts according to plan are offset by cash increases resulting from the issuance of new debts, in particular from the issue of a debut benchmark bond with a volume of DM 2 billion in May 1998.

CHAPTER 8
CHANGING PRICES AND
HYPERINFLATIONARY ECONOMIES

CONTENTS

OVERVIEW

In IAS GAAP, the use of adjustments or restatement to reflect the effects of changing prices on an enterprise's financial position and result is not a requirement unless the reporting currency is that of a country with a hyperinflationary economy. Hyperinflation is not defined in IAS GAAP, but a cumulative rate of inflation that approaches or exceeds 100% over three years is given as an important indicator. When the rate of inflation affecting the reporting currency is lower than this but significant, IAS GAAP encourage, but do not require, reporting enterprises to adopt a method of restatement based on either the general purchasing power approach or the current cost approach. In a hyperinflationary situation, IAS GAAP require the use of restatement in terms of general purchasing power, even in the case of financial statements prepared on the basis of current costs.

IAS GAAP on changing prices and hyperinflationary economies are set out in IAS 15, "Information Reflecting the Effects of Changing Prices," IAS 29, "Financial Reporting in Hyperinflationary Economies," and SIC-19, "Reporting Currency—Measurement and Presentation of Financial Statements under IAS 21 and IAS 29."

BACKGROUND

Like its counterpart in U.S. GAAP (FAS-89, "Financial Reporting and Changing Prices"), IAS 15 looks back to the period in the late 1970s and early 1980s when rates of inflation in the developed economies were high enough to engender a considerable degree of preoccupation with methods of restating financial statements for the effects of inflation. FAS-33 in the United States and Statement of Standard Accounting Practice (SSAP) No. 16 in the United Kingdom were characteristic of that period. As levels of inflation fell in the 1980s, the use of such methods became optional. FAS-33 was replaced by the voluntary FAS-89, while SSAP 16 was withdrawn.

In 1977, the IASC issued IAS 6, "Accounting Responses to Changing Prices," which required the disclosure of the effect of any procedures applied to reflect the impact of specific or general price changes. Subsequently, the IASC replaced IAS 6 with IAS 15, which required the use of restatement on the basis of either the general price level or current costs when the reporting currency was subject to a significant (but unspecified) degree of inflation. In 1989, the IASC followed an approach similar to that of the FASB, by making IAS 15 optional. In the same year, the IASC issued IAS 29, which requires general price level restatement when the reporting currency is subject to hyperinflation. It is worth noting, however, that IAS GAAP are applied in a number of countries with less developed economies, where significant inflation (but not necessarily hyperinflation) may be prevalent. Yet IAS 15 appears to be little used in practice, and some commentaries simply mention it without further elaboration.

The main differences between IAS GAAP and U.S. GAAP on accounting for the effects of changing prices and hyperinflation are:

1. IAS 15 permits the adjustments or restatement to be made to items in the enterprise's primary financial statements if they are "presented on a basis that reflects the effects of changing prices." FAS-89 does not permit such information to be included in the primary financial statements; it should be disclosed only as supplementary information.

2. IAS 15 and IAS 29 use the measuring unit current at the balance sheet date (end-of-year units of general purchasing power) to express financial statements that are the result of general price-level restatement. For comprehensive restatement, FAS-89 uses end-of-year units of general purchasing power; for partial restatement, either average-for-year units, or units of general purchasing power of the base period used to calculate the Consumer Price Index, may be used.

3. IAS 29 is applied not merely by enterprises whose reporting currency is subject to hyperinflation but also (in accordance with IAS 21) to the financial statements of foreign entities that report in such a currency, prior to their translation into the group reporting currency for the purpose of consolidation or equitization. FAS-52 does not permit this "re-state and translate" approach. Instead, the group reporting currency should be considered the "functional currency" of a foreign operation in a hyperinflationary economy, and the financial statement items should be remeasured in the functional currency.

SCOPE

IAS 15, "Information Reflecting the Effects of Changing Prices," is an optional standard for presenting "information…designed to make users of an enterprise's financial statements aware of the effects of…changes in the general level of prices or…in specific prices…on the results of its operations" (IAS 15, par. 7). No particular level of price change is specified. The optional standard "applies to enterprises whose levels of revenues, profit, assets or employment are significant in the economic environment in which they operate" (IAS 15, par. 3), which appears to mean that only larger enterprises are encouraged to apply it. IAS 15 permits the adjustments or restatement to be made to items in the enterprise's primary financial statements if they are "presented on a basis that reflects the effects of changing prices." It is expected, however, that the information will normally be given as supplementary to the primary financial statements (IAS 15, par. 25).

In contrast, IAS 29, "Financial Reporting in Hyperinflationary Economies," should be applied to the primary financial statements, including the consolidated financial statements, of any enterprise that reports in the currency of a hyperinflationary economy (IAS 29, par. 1). IAS 29, paragraph 3, sets out five characteristics of the economic environment as indicators of hyperinflation, of which the fifth is the most frequently cited:

1. The general population prefers to keep its wealth in nonmonetary assets or in a relatively stable foreign currency.

2. The general population regards monetary amounts not in terms of the local currency but in terms of a relatively stable foreign currency.

3. Sales and purchases on credit take place at prices that compensate for the expected loss of purchasing power during the credit period even when it is short.

4. Interest rates, wages, and prices are linked to a price index.

5. The cumulative inflation rate over three years is approaching or exceeds 100%.

METHODS OF ADJUSTMENT OR RESTATEMENT

The optional IAS 15 distinguishes between two approaches to providing financial information that reflects the effects of changing prices: the general purchasing power approach and the current cost approach. Either of these approaches may be used.

The general purchasing power approach is related to the concept of maintaining real financial capital (see Chapter 2, "Framework for the Preparation and Presentation of Financial Statements"), and reflects the effects of changes in the general purchasing power of the monetary unit, as measured by some general price index. The financial statements are restated in monetary units of the same general purchasing power, using the measuring unit current at the balance sheet date. This approach is described further below.

> **OBSERVATION:** The current cost approach is related to the concept of maintaining real physical capital or operating capability (see Chapter 2, "Framework for the Preparation and Presentation of Financial Statements"), and reflects specific price changes of assets, using either replacement costs or specific price indexes. This approach may also include methods for reflecting the effects of price changes on the enterprise's requirements for monetary working capital, and the effects of using borrowings to finance assets (IAS 15, pars. 8–18).
>
> IAS 29 requires the use of the general purchasing power restatement approach. As stated in IAS 29, paragraph 7: "In a hyperinflationary economy, financial statements, whether they

are based on a historical cost approach or a current cost approach, are useful only if they are expressed in terms of the measuring unit current at the balance sheet date." The concern here goes beyond capital maintenance to the use of a meaningful measuring unit. The measuring unit employed, the unit that is "current at the balance sheet date," is sometimes called a "unit of current purchasing power" or "current purchasing power unit." (This useful term is not used in IAS GAAP but will be employed in this chapter.)

Use of the approach required by IAS 29 is therefore one way of meeting the (optional) requirements of IAS 15. This approach is illustrated in the Appendix to this chapter.

The focus of the remainder of this chapter will be on the requirements of IAS 29.

THE REQUIREMENTS OF IAS 29, "FINANCIAL REPORTING IN HYPERINFLATIONARY ECONOMIES"

IAS 29, together with SIC-19, requires that if the measurement currency used by an enterprise is the currency of a hyperinflationary economy, then the enterprise's financial statements should be restated in units of the same purchasing power, using the measuring unit current at the balance sheet dates (units of current purchasing power). According to IAS 29, paragraph 37, this restatement should be made using "a general price index that reflects changes in general purchasing power," and it is preferable that the same index be used by all enterprises that report in the currency of the same economy.

☛ **PRACTICE POINTER:** It should be noted that official price indexes sometimes deliberately understate the erosion of the purchasing power of the monetary unit. We may also note that for foreign currency translation in the consolidation process, U.S. GAAP do not permit the "restate and translate" approach of IAS 29, which is vulnerable to this problem.

One method of verifying the accuracy of an official price index is to compare the percentage change in it with the percentage change in the exchange rates of the national currency into "hard" currencies. In the presence of exchange controls and "official" rates of exchange that do not give a fair reflection of the relative loss of purchasing power of the national currency, changes in the "unofficial" rates of exchange into hard currencies may be used for the purposes of verifying the official price indexes. While this may identify a problem, however, it does not provide a solution. The "functional currency" approach of U.S. GAAP, whereby in such a situation the enterprise would report in a "hard" functional currency other than the national currency, such as the group reporting currency, offers a better chance of finding a solution.

The restated financial statements should be presented as the primary financial statements, and separate presentation of the unrestated financial statements is discouraged. The corresponding figures for the previous period required by IAS 1, "Presentation of Financial Statements" (see Chapter 3) and any information in respect of earlier periods should also be restated in terms of units of current purchasing power at the balance sheet date (IAS 29, pars. 7–8).

The gain or loss on net monetary position (see below) should be separately disclosed as part of net income (IAS 29, par. 9).

If the enterprise is a foreign entity as defined in IAS 21 (see Chapter 17) and is included in the financial statements of another reporting enterprise, its financial statements should be restated under IAS 29 before being translated into the reporting currency of the other reporting enterprise. If the currency of a country that does not have a hyperinflationary economy is chosen as an appropriate measurement currency by an enterprise, the enterprise is not required to restate its financial statements under IAS 29. However, such a measurement currency should be such that it provides information about that enterprise that is useful and reflects the economic substance of the underlying events and circumstances relevant to that enterprise. A measurement currency different from the currency of the country in which the enterprise is domiciled should not be used as a means to avoid the requirement to restate under IAS 29 (SIC-19, pars. 5 and 7–8).

Historical Cost Financial Statements

End-of-Period Balance Sheet

Monetary items are not restated because they are already expressed in terms of the monetary unit current at the balance sheet date (current purchasing power unit). In the case of monetary items that are linked by agreement to changes in prices, such as index-linked bonds and loans, their carrying amounts adjusted in accordance with the agreement are used in the restated balance sheet. Other balance sheet amounts are restated to amounts in units of current purchasing power by applying a general price index, unless they are already carried at amounts in units of current purchasing power, such as current market value or net realizable value (IAS 29, pars. 11–14).

For items carried at cost or cost less depreciation, the restated cost or cost less depreciation is determined by applying to the historical cost and accumulated depreciation (if any) the change in a selected general price index from the date of acquisition to the balance sheet date. For items carried at revalued amounts, the revalued amount and accumulated depreciation (if any) are restated by applying the change in the price index from the date of the latest revaluation to the balance sheet date.

If records of the acquisition of property, plant, and equipment do not permit the ascertainment or estimation of the acquisition dates, it may be necessary, when the standard is first applied, to use an independent professional valuation of the items concerned as a basis for their restatement. If no general price index is available to cover the period between acquisition and the balance sheet date, an estimate of the changes in general purchasing power of the reporting currency over that period may be made by using the changes in the exchange rate between the reporting currency and a relatively stable foreign currency (IAS 29, pars. 11–18).

The restated amount of a nonmonetary item is reduced (in accordance with the appropriate IAS) when it exceeds the amount recoverable from the item's future use, sale or disposal (IAS 29, par. 19).

It is not appropriate both to restate capital expenditure (fixed assets) financed by borrowing and to capitalize that part of the borrowing costs that compensates for inflation.

> **OBSERVATION:** The part of borrowing costs that compensates for inflation is the difference between borrowing costs on a nominal or money basis and borrowing costs on a real (inflation-adjusted) basis. For example, if the nominal borrowing cost for a year is 45% and annual inflation is 35%, the real annual borrowing cost is:
>
> $$(1.45/1.35 - 1) \times 100 = 7.407\%$$
>
> While the income statement will show the nominal borrowing cost, it will also show the gain or loss on net monetary position, which includes the effect of inflation on borrowings (see below). Thus, in effect, it is borrowing costs on a real basis that impact net income.

IAS 21 permits an enterprise, in certain circumstances following a recent severe devaluation of the reporting currency, to capitalize as part of the cost of a fixed asset the resultant foreign exchange losses on borrowings used to purchase that asset (see Chapter 17). IAS 29 does not permit such capitalization in financial statements prepared in the currency of a hyperinflationary economy, the carrying amount of the asset being restated from the date of its acquisition (IAS 29, par. 23).

At the beginning of the first period of application of IAS 29, the components of owners' equity are restated by applying a general price index from the dates on which the components were contributed or otherwise arose, except for retained earnings and any revaluation surplus. Any revaluation surplus from prior periods is eliminated, and restated retained earnings is the residual amount (balancing figure) in the restated balance sheet. Subsequently, all components of owners' equity are restated by applying a general price index from the beginning of the period (or the date of contribution, if later). The movements for the period in owners' equity should be disclosed in accordance with IAS 1, "Presentation of Financial Statements" (see Chapter 3) (IAS 29, pars. 24–25).

Income Statement for the Period

All items in the income statement should be expressed in terms of end-of-year current purchasing power units. Hence, all income statement amounts need to be restated by applying the change in the general price index between the dates at which the amounts were recorded and the balance sheet date.

> ☛ **PRACTICE POINTER:** In practice, average index values for sub-periods, such as months, would normally be used, as in the case of average exchange rates used for the translation of foreign currency amounts under IAS 21 (see Chapter 17). General price-level restatement has been likened to currency translation.

Gain or Loss on Net Monetary Position

According to IAS 29, paragraph 27, the gain or loss on the enterprise's net monetary position may be estimated by applying the change in the general price index to the weighted average for the period of the difference between monetary assets and monetary liabilities.

> **OBSERVATION:** IAS 29 is not very explicit on this point. The method described in the *Miller GAAP Guide*, Chapter 6, is slightly different but quite explicit and is used in the Illustration in the Appendix to this chapter.
>   Alternatively, the gain or loss on net monetary position could be derived as the balancing figure in the restated balance sheet, after the inclusion of net income (less any dividend paid) in retained earnings but before the inclusion of the net gain or loss on net monetary position in net income.

The gain or loss on the net monetary position should be included in net income. Any adjustment to index-linked assets or liabilities (as mentioned above in the section on the balance sheet) is offset against the gain or loss on net monetary position. It is suggested that the gain or loss in net monetary position should be presented in the income statement together with interest income and expense (see the Observation above) and foreign exchange differences related to invested or borrowed funds (IAS 29, pars. 27–28).

Investees Accounted for under the Equity Method

If an investee accounted for under the equity method reports in the currency of a hyperinflationary country, the financial statements of the investee are restated in accordance with IAS 29 in order to calculate the investor's share of its net assets and results of operations (IAS 29, par. 20).

Current Cost Financial Statements

End-of Period Balance Sheet

Items stated at current cost are already expressed in units of current purchasing power and so are not restated. Other items are restated as described for historical cost balance sheets above (IAS 29, par. 29).

Income Statement for the Period

The current cost income statement reports items in terms of the purchasing power of the monetary unit at the times when the underlying transactions or events occurred. For example, cost of goods sold and depreciation are recorded at their current costs at the time of consumption. Therefore, all amounts need to be restated into current purchasing power units at the balance sheet date (IAS 29, par. 30).

Gain or Loss on Net Monetary Position

Gain or loss on net monetary position should be calculated and accounted for as already described above (IAS 29, par. 31).

Cash Flow Statement

All items in the cash flow statement should be restated in terms of current purchasing power units at the balance sheet date (IAS 29, par. 33).

Corresponding Figures

Comparative figures from the previous reporting period, and other comparative information that is disclosed in respect of prior periods, should be restated in terms of units of current purchasing power at the balance sheet date (IAS 29, par. 34).

Consolidated Financial Statements

A parent that reports in the currency of a hyperinflationary economy may have subsidiaries that also report in currencies of hyperinflationary economies. The financial statements of such subsidiaries should be restated in accordance with IAS 29 as described above, before being included in the process of consolidation. In the case of foreign subsidiaries, financial statements (restated as described above if they are in the currency of a hyperinflationary economy) should be translated into the reporting currency at closing rates as required by IAS 21.

If financial statements with different reporting dates are consolidated, all items, whether monetary or nonmonetary, should be restated into units of current purchasing power at the date of the consolidated financial statements (IAS 29, pars. 35–36).

ECONOMIES CEASING TO BE HYPERINFLATIONARY

When an enterprise discontinues the preparation and presentation of financial statements in accordance with IAS 29 because the economy of its reporting currency is no longer hyperinflationary, the amounts that are expressed in current purchasing power units as at the end of the previous reporting period should be treated as the basis for the carrying amounts in its subsequent financial statements (IAS 29, par. 38).

DISCLOSURES

The following disclosures should be made:

1. The fact that the financial statements and the comparative figures have been restated for changes in the general purchasing power of the reporting currency and are stated in terms of the unit of purchasing power current at the balance sheet date.
2. Whether the underlying financial statements are based on historical costs or current costs.
3. The identity and level of the general price index used at the balance sheet date and the movement in this index during the current and previous reporting periods (IAS 29, par. 39).

The following information should be disclosed about currencies used for measurement and presentation:

1. When the measurement currency is different from the currency of the country in which the enterprise is domiciled, the reason for using a different currency.

2. If the presentation currency is different from the enterprise's measurement currency, (a) the measurement currency, (b) the reason for using a different presentation currency, and (c) the method used in translation from the measurement currency into the presentation currency.

3. The reason for any change in the measurement currency or presentation currency (SIC-19, par. 10).

APPENDIX:
ILLUSTRATION OF GENERAL PRICE-LEVEL RESTATEMENT

XYZ Company was established on January 1, 2000. Its beginning balance sheet on that date was as follows:

Land	$6,000
Plant and equipment	4,000
Inventories	2,000
	12,000
Stockholders' equity	12,000

Gain or Loss on Net Monetary Items

The gain or loss on net monetary items may be calculated in five steps. Note that throughout, a positive figure denotes a net monetary asset position, a negative figure denotes a net monetary liability position, and that if a minus sign is applied to an amount that is already negative, the operation becomes an addition.

1. Calculate the net monetary position at the beginning of the year, and restate it to end-of-year current purchasing power units using the change in the general price-level index.

2. Assemble all increases and decreases in net monetary position during the year and restate them to end-of-year current purchasing power units (as indicated above for income statement items).

3. Calculate an estimated end-of-year net monetary position as the sum of the restated amounts in current purchasing power units obtained in steps 1 and 2.

4. Calculate the actual net monetary position at the balance sheet date.

5. The gain or loss on net monetary position is the amount calculated in step 4 minus the amount calculated in step 3.

Illustration of General Price-Level Restatement

During the year 2000, the company made the following transactions:

1. Purchased extra inventory for $10,000
2. Sold inventory for $11,000 cash, which had a historical cost of $9,000
3. Ending inventory on December 31, 2000 had a historical cost of $3,000 and was bought when the general price index was 115 (average)
4. The plant and equipment have an expected life of 4 years, and nil residual value. The straight-line method of depreciation is used
5. The general price index stood at:

   100 on January 1, 2000

   110 on June 30, 2000

   120 on December 31, 2000

Note: The symbol $ is used to indicate the measuring unit, namely dollars of current purchasing power as at December 31, 2000.

General Price-Level Restated Income Statement for the Year 2000

		$\$_{CPP}$	$\$_{CPP}$
Sales	11,000 x 120/110		12,000
Beginning inventory	2,000 x 120/100	2,400	
Add purchases	10,000 x 120/110	10,909	
		13,309	
(Less) ending inventory	3,000 x 120/115	(3,310)	
			10,179
			1,821
(Less) depreciation			(1,200)
			621
(Less) loss on net monetary assets items			(91)
Net income after general price-level restatement			530

Calculation of loss on net monetary items:

		$	$\$_{CPP}$
Beginning balance of net monetary items		Nil	Nil
Sales	11,000 x 120/110		12,000
Purchases	10,000 x 120/110		(10,909)
Estimated ending balance of monetary items			1,091
Actual ending balance of net monetary items			(1,000)
Difference = loss			91

The net income before price-level restatement ($11,000 – $9,000 – $1,000 for depreciation $1,000) and after price-level restatement can be reconciled as follows:

Historical cost net income	$1,000

Inventories

Additional charge based on restating the cost of inventories at the beginning and end of the year in dollars of current purchasing power, thus taking the inflationary element out of the profit on the sale of inventory Beginning inventory + 400 minus ending inventory – 130	(270)

Depreciation

Additional depreciation based on restated cost, measured in dollars of current purchasing power of plant and equipment $1,200 – $1,000	(200)

Monetary items

Net loss in purchasing power resulting from the effects of inflation on the company's net monetary assets	(91)

Effect of restatement of sales, purchases, and all other costs

These are increased by the change in the index between the average date at which they occurred and the end of the year. This restatement increases profit as sales exceed the costs included in this heading	91
Net income after general price-level restatement	530

Value of stockholders' equity, January 1, 2000		$ 12,000
Restated in terms of $$_{CPP}$ at December 31, 2000	(12,000 x 120/100)	$$_{CPP}$ 14,400

General Price-Level Restated Balance Sheet as at December 31, 2000

		$_{CPP}	$_{CPP}
Land	6,000 x 120/100		7,200
Plant and equipment	4,000 x 120/100	4,800	
(less) depreciation	1,000 x 120/100	(1,200)	
			3,600
			10,800
Inventories	3,000 x 120/100	3,130	
Cash	(11,000 – 10,000)	1,000	
			4,130
			14,930
Stockholders' equity	($_{CPP} 14,400 + 530)		14,930

CHAPTER 9
CONSOLIDATED
FINANCIAL STATEMENTS

CONTENTS

OVERVIEW

Consolidated financial statements represent the results of operations (income statement), cash flow statement, and financial position (balance sheet) of a single entity (the group) that comprises more than one separate legal entity. Because of the relationships between the entities making up the group, consolidated financial statements are considered to provide a more meaningful picture than the financial statements of the separate entities. The concept of a group in IAS GAAP is based on the concept of control, as exercised by a parent company over a subsidiary company. Control is defined in IAS GAAP as having two essential components:

1. The power to govern the financial and operating policies of an enterprise, and hence
2. The ability to obtain benefits from the enterprise's activities.

It is a rebuttable presumption that control over an enterprise exists when the group (i.e., the parent company and/or other subsidiary companies) holds more than half the voting power in that enterprise. Control may also exist when less than half the voting power is held, if certain other conditions (discussed below) are met.

A parent company should issue consolidated financial statements unless it is itself a wholly owned subsidiary (or is virtually wholly owned and the minority interest has given permission for the non-issuance of consolidated financial statements). The consolidated financial statements should include all subsidiaries, except those acquired and held exclusively for disposal in the near future and those for which the group's control over their assets and operations is impaired by severe long-term restrictions on the transfer of funds.

Consolidated financial statements should also include jointly controlled entities, by means of the proportionate consolidation method as explained below. IAS GAAP also permit the use of the equity method in such cases, but only as a less preferred alternative.

The relevant IAS GAAP have been promulgated in:

- IAS 27, "Consolidated Financial Statements and Accounting for Investments in Subsidiaries"
- IAS 31, "Financial Reporting of Interests in Joint Ventures"
- IAS 39, "Financial Instruments: Recognition and Measurement" (which amended parts of IAS 27 and IAS 31)
- SIC-12, "Consolidation—Special Purposes Entities"

BACKGROUND

The IASC has issued separate standards for consolidated financial statements (IAS 27), for the equity method (IAS 28), and for business combinations (IAS 22). Consolidated financial statements and the equity method were originally covered by IAS 3, which was then superseded when IAS 27 and IAS 28 were issued. Proportionate consolidation in the case of joint ventures is also dealt with separately in IAS 31. IAS 27 does not cover the pooling-of-interests method of accounting for the results of a business combination brought about through a uniting of interests. This is dealt with in IAS 22, "Business Combinations" (see Chapter 6).

The main differences between IAS GAAP and U.S. GAAP concern:

1. *The concept of control.* U.S. GAAP effectively consider control as a controlling financial interest represented by the direct or indirect ownership of a majority voting interest (*de jure* control). IAS GAAP take account of other means of exercising control (discussed below), that is, *de facto* control. There is, however, an FASB exposure draft that proposes to extend the concept of control in U.S. GAAP.

2. *The treatment of interests in jointly controlled operations.* U.S. GAAP do not permit the use of proportionate consolidation when the jointly controlled operation is a legal entity (corporate joint venture). In such a case, U.S. GAAP require the equity method to be used. IAS GAAP permit the equity method, but prefer proportionate consolidation.

3. *Conditions for exclusion from consolidation.* There are differences of emphasis, rather than of substance, which are discussed below.

SCOPE

Consolidated Financial Statements

According to IAS GAAP, any company having one or more subsidiaries that do not meet the criteria for exclusion from consolidation is required to issue consolidated financial statements (IAS 27). In addition, any company having an investment in a jointly controlled operation (joint venture) with jointly controlled assets or liabilities, or in a jointly controlled entity, should issue consolidated financial statements in which its share of the joint venture is included by means of proportionate consolidation (IAS 31). The conditions for excluding a subsidiary from consolidation also apply to the exclusion of a jointly controlled entity from proportionate consolidation.

However, a parent company that is itself a wholly owned subsidiary need not issue consolidated financial statements if its parent does not require it to do so. A parent company that is virtually wholly owned (often taken to mean that its parent owns 90% or more of the voting power) need not issue consolidated financial statements, provided its parent agrees and has obtained the approval of the owners of the minority interest. In such cases, the parent company that does not issue consolidated financial statements should disclose the reasons for this, together with the bases on which subsidiaries are accounted for in its separate financial statements and the name and registered office of its parent, which publishes consolidated financial statements (IAS 27, pars. 8–10).

Recognition in the Investor's Separate Financial Statements

As well as consolidated financial statements, IAS GAAP cover accounting for investments in subsidiaries and jointly controlled operations in the parent company's or joint venturer's separate financial statements. For a subsidiary that is consolidated, the parent company's financial statements may reflect the investment either (a) by carrying it at cost or (b) using the equity method (IAS 28) or (c) as "available-for-sale financial assets" as described in IAS 39, "Financial Instruments: Recognition and Measurement" (see Chapter 16). In the case of a subsidiary that has been excluded from consolidation, IAS 39 amended IAS 27 to allow in the parent company's financial statements the same treatments as for a consolidated subsidiary.

In the case of jointly controlled assets, a joint venturer should recognize its share of the venture's assets, liabilities, income, and expense in its separate financial statements.

> ☞ **PRACTICE POINTER:** Where the joint venture is an entity, it will issue its own financial statements, and IAS 31 does not lay down any particular requirements as to how the investment of the joint venturer should be recognized in the latter's separate financial statements. According to IAS 39, "Financial Instruments: Recognition and Measurement," it would be recognized there as an "available-for-sale investment" and measured at fair value if this can be reliably determined or, if not, at cost subject to impairment review. Recognition by means of the equity method (per IAS 28, see Chapter 14) is required in the case of the financial statements of an investor in a joint venture over which it does not have joint control but has significant influence. Logically, therefore, the equity method would also be permitted for recognizing an investment in a joint venture entity in the separate financial statements of an investor with joint control.

SCOPE OF CONSOLIDATED FINANCIAL STATEMENTS

Criteria for Inclusion: The Concept of Control

It should be noted that IAS GAAP are written in terms of "enterprises" rather than "companies" or "corporations." Hence, unincorporated entities that are controlled (such as partnerships, unincorporated associations, and trusts) fall within the scope of consolidation. Thus, terms such as *voting rights* and *board of directors* may need to be modified to be applicable to unincorporated entities, as with the term *equivalent governing body* used below.

The concept of control takes account of indirect as well as direct parent–subsidiary relationships. Thus, the term *subsidiary* includes:

- A subsidiary of a subsidiary, and
- An entity in which a majority of the voting rights is held in aggregate by two or more enterprises that are controlled by the same ultimate parent, which thereby also controls the entity in question.

IAS GAAP do not require "horizontal consolidations" of the financial statements of enterprises that are managed on a unified basis without the existence of a parent–subsidiary relationship.

The concept of control employed in IAS GAAP is *de facto* control. As well as resulting from ownership by the parent company and/or subsidiary companies of a majority of voting power in an entity (*de jure* control), control may be exercised in any of the following ways (IAS 27, par. 12):

1. By virtue of majority voting power obtained through an agreement with other investors,

2. Through a power to govern an enterprise's financial and operating policies under a statute or an agreement,

3. Through a power to appoint or remove a majority of the members of the board of directors or equivalent governing body, or

4. Through a power to cast the majority of votes at meetings of the board or equivalent governing body.

> ☛ **PRACTICE POINTER:** Although control by agreement (as in item 2 above) is not legal in some countries because it effectively disenfranchises shareholders holding voting shares, a

parent company domiciled in such a country (e.g., the United Kingdom) may have an enterprise as a subsidiary by virtue of the fact that the enterprise is controlled by another subsidiary in a country in which such an agreement is legal (e.g., Germany).

Power to appoint or remove a majority of the board or other governing body raises some problems of interpretation in countries where a two-tier board structure (supervisory board and management board) may be used for some companies. The interpretation generally given is that control exists where one party can appoint or dismiss the majority of either board.

The power to cast a majority of votes at board meetings also requires interpretation if some directors have the right to vote on some issues but not on others. Control would presumably depend on power over directors having the right to vote on substantially all significant matters.

In deciding whether the power to cast a majority of votes exists, any right held by a director to a casting vote must be taken into account. Where the chairman has this right, and two 50% owners each have the right to appoint the chairman in alternate years, then control may be considered to be exercised jointly.

An investor may exercise control by virtue of being the most powerful shareholder, but if there is another potentially dominant shareholder, then control is exercised only subject to the acquiescence of the latter. In that case, the enterprise may not be effectively controlled in such a way as to make it a subsidiary.

Exercise of control over an enterprise by virtue of points 1 to 4, above, will result in it being a subsidiary of the company exercising that control only if the latter has the ability to obtain benefits from the enterprise's activities. Benefits could have a wider interpretation than income in the narrow sense and include the reduction of competition, the avoidance of costs, and so on.

A Special Purpose Entity (SPE), in the form of a corporation, trust, partnership, or unincorporated entity, may be set up to accomplish a narrow and well-defined objective (e.g., to effect a lease, research and development activities, or a securitization of financial assets), such that in substance the enterprise has the right to obtain the majority of the benefits from the SPE or retains the majority of the residual risks related to the SPE or its assets in order to obtain benefits from its activities. In such circumstances, the enterprise should consolidate the SPE, even if it owns little or none of the SPE's equity and the SPE operates in a predetermined way so that no enterprise has explicit decision-making authority over it (i.e., it operates on "autopilot") (SIC-12).

Illustration

P has percentage holdings in S_1 and S_2, and S_1 S_2 have holdings in S_3, as shown below:

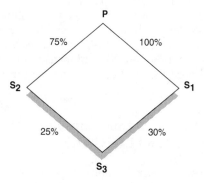

S_1 and S_2 are subsidiaries of P. P's percentage ownership of S_3 is 30% (via S_1) plus 18.75% (via S_2), totaling 48.75%. But P *controls* S_3 because it controls S_1 and S_2, which between them control 55% of the voting rights in S_3. Hence, S_3 is a subsidiary of P.

Conditions for Exclusion from Consolidation

A subsidiary should be excluded from consolidation when:

1. Control is intended to be temporary because the subsidiary is acquired and held exclusively with a view to its subsequent disposal in the near future, or
2. It operates under severe long-term restrictions that significantly impair its ability to transfer funds to the parent.

Such subsidiaries should be accounted for as if they were investments, in accordance with IAS 39 (IAS 27, par. 13, as amended by IAS 39). IAS 39 (par. 10) replaces the former distinction in IAS 25 between current and long-term investments, with a threefold distinction between: financial assets held for trading; held-to-maturity investments (with a fixed maturity); and available-for-sale financial assets. Subsidiaries excluded from consolidation for either of the reasons cited above would have to be accounted for in accordance with the rules for "available-for-sale financial assets," at fair value if this can be reliably measured and, if not, at cost subject to review for impairment (IAS 39, pars. 69–73).

A subsidiary should not be excluded from consolidation on the grounds that its business activities are dissimilar from those of the other enterprises within the group. Instead, additional information should be disclosed about the different business activities of subsidiaries, for example, in accordance with IAS 14, "Reporting Financial Information by Segment" (IAS 27, par. 14).

An investment in a jointly controlled entity should be excluded from proportionate consolidation if the joint venturer ceases to exercise joint control over the entity. This may happen when the venturer disposes of its interest or when external restrictions are placed on the jointly controlled entity such that it can no longer achieve its goals (IAS 31, pars. 30–31).

Conditions for Exclusion from Consolidation: Differences between U.S. GAAP and IAS GAAP

1. *Exclusion because control is only temporary.* U.S. GAAP do not state a requirement that, in order to be excluded, a subsidiary must have been acquired and held exclusively with a view to disposal in the near future. Such a requirement is stated in IAS GAAP (IAS 27, par. 13), which thus appear to be more restrictive on this point than U.S. GAAP.

2. *Exclusion because of impairment of control resulting from severe long-term restrictions on the transfer of funds.* In U.S. GAAP, such restrictions must be so severe that they "cast significant doubt on the parent's ability to control the subsidiary" (FAS 94). Logically, given the concept of *de facto* control employed in IAS GAAP, one might expect the latter to stipulate a similar requirement regarding the severity of the restrictions. However, this is not spelled out in IAS 27, which thus appears to be less restrictive on this point than U.S. GAAP.

3. *Exclusion because of the loss of control of a subsidiary in legal reorganization or bankruptcy, owing to control passing to a receiver or trustee.* This is specifically mentioned as a reason for exclusion in U.S. GAAP (FAS-94, par. 13) but not in IAS GAAP. However, such a situation could be considered as entailing a "severe long-term restriction which significantly impairs [the subsidiary's] ability to transfer funds to the parent" (IAS 27, par. 13(b)), and hence as a reason for exclusion.

CONSOLIDATION PROCEDURES AND ISSUES

Full versus Proportionate Consolidation

In preparing consolidated financial statements, the financial statements of the parent and its subsidiaries are combined on a line-by-line basis by adding together like items of assets, liabilities, equity, income, and expenses (IAS 27, par. 15). This is sometimes referred to as full consolidation. In proportionate consolidation, the venturer's shares of each of the assets, liabilities, income, and expenses of a jointly controlled entity are combined on a line-by-line basis with similar items in the venturer's financial statements. Or, they may be reported as separate line items in the venturer's financial statements (IAS 31, pars. 26–28). The Equity Method (see Chapter 14) is allowed as an alternative treatment to proportionate consolidation (IAS 31, pars. 32 –33).

The carrying amount of the parent's investment in each subsidiary and the parent's portion of the equity of each subsidiary are eliminated as set out in IAS 22, "Business Combinations," which also describes the treatment of any resultant goodwill (see Chapter 6).

Illustration

Company I holds 50% of the voting equity shares of company J jointly with another company, Q. Unless I controls J, for example by virtue of a contract with Q, I has joint control of J and the benchmark treatment is to use proportionate consolidation. If I has a contract with Q by virtue of which Q passes its control rights over to I, then J is a subsidiary of I and full consolidation will be used.

The balance sheets immediately following the acquisition of the 50% holding are as follows:

			Consolidated	
	I	J	Full	Proportionate
Sundry current assets	$28,600	$6,000	$34,600	$31,600
Investment in J:				
(4000 shares acquired at $1.50n per share)	6,000			
Property, plant, and equipment	50,000	4,000	54,000	52,000
Goodwill on consolidation ($6000 – 50% of $10,000)			1,000	1,000
	$84,600	$10,000	$89,600	$84,600
Shares of $1	$40,000	$ 8,000	$40,000	$40,000
Reserves	44,600	2,000	44,600	44,600
	$84,600	$10,000	$84,600	$84,600
Minority interest (50% of $10,000)			5,000	
	$84,600	$10,000	$89,600	$84,600

Note that the goodwill is the same under both full and proportionate consolidation, but that there is no minority interest in proportionate consolidation.

Calculation and Disclosure of Minority Interests in Full Consolidation

A minority interest is that part of the net results of operations and of the net assets of a subsidiary attributable to interests that are not owned, directly of indirectly, by the parent (IAS 27, par. 6).

Minority interests in the net income of consolidated subsidiaries are identified and adjusted against the income of the group in order to arrive at the net income attributable to the owners of the parent.

The calculation of minority interests in the net assets of consolidated subsidiaries at the date of the original combination follows IAS 22, "Business Combinations," paragraphs 31–34 (see Chapter 6). A benchmark treatment and an alternative treatment are described:

- Benchmark treatment (IAS 22, par. 32): When an acquirer purchases less than all the shares of the other enterprise, the resulting minority interest is stated at the minority's proportion of the preacquisition carrying amounts of the net assets of the subsidiary.

- Alternative treatment (IAS 22, par. 33): Any minority interest should be stated at the minority's proportion of the fair values of the assets and liabilities recognized as at the date of acquisition in accordance with IAS 22, par. 27. However, no share of any goodwill arising on the acquisition is attributed to the minority interest.

In addition to the amount calculated as described above, minority interests also include the minority's share of any movements in the subsidiary's equity since the date of the combination.

Minority interests should be presented in the consolidated balance sheet separately from liabilities and the parent company's equity. Minority interests in the income of the group should also be presented separately in the consolidated statement of income (IAS 27, par. 26).

> **OBSERVATION:** The wording of paragraph 26 regarding the presentation of minority interests is consistent with the treatment set out in IAS 1 (revised), which is illustrated in the Appendix to that standard (see Chapter 3). This implies that they are considered as an intermediate category between liabilities and equity.

If the losses applicable to the minority in a consolidated subsidiary exceed the minority interest in the subsidiary's equity, the excess and any further losses applicable to the minority must be charged against the majority interest (group net income), except insofar as the minority has both a binding obligation and the ability to make good the losses. If the subsidiary subsequently reports profits, the majority interest is allocated all such profits until the minority's share of losses previously charged against the majority has been recovered (IAS 27, par. 27).

Minority interests arise only through equity investments in subsidiaries (as defined in IAS 32, "Financial Instruments: Disclosures and Presentation," see Chapter 16) and not through investments in the form of debt.

If a subsidiary has cumulative preferred shares that are held outside the group, the subsidiary's preferred dividends (whether or not they have been declared) should be deducted in calculating the group's share of profits (IAS 27, par. 28).

Taxation

Taxes payable by either the parent or its subsidiaries on distribution to the parent out of their retained profits are accounted for in accordance with IAS 12 (revised), "Accounting for Taxes on Income" (IAS 27, par. 16). A current tax asset of one enterprise in a group may be offset against a current tax liability of another enterprise in the group only if the enterprises concerned have a legally enforceable right to make such an offset in settling their tax position and intend to do so (IAS 12, par. 73).

The treatment of deferred tax arising from a business combination is dealt with in IAS 12, paragraphs 66–68 (see Chapter 20).

Intragroup Balances

Intragroup balances and intragroup transactions and any resultant unrealized profits included in the carrying values of assets (e.g., inventory or fixed assets) should be eliminated in full. Unrealized losses reflected in carrying values should also be eliminated, except insofar as this would result in the carrying value of the asset exceeding the recoverable amount (IAS 27, par. 17). Timing differences resulting from such eliminations are to be dealt with in accordance with IAS 12 (see Chapter 20).

Unrealized profit on an "upstream" sale to the parent by a subsidiary with a minority interest, as well as on a "downstream" sale by the parent to a subsidiary with a minority interest, must therefore be fully eliminated. There is no requirement that the elimination of the profit on an "upstream" sale be allocated between the group and the minority interest.

The following illustration is adapted from the *Miller GAAP Guide*, Chapter 8.

Illustration of Profit in Inventory

P Company purchased $20,000 and $250,000 of merchandise in 20X1 and 20X2, respectively, from its 80% owned subsidiary S at 25% above cost. As of December 31, 20X1 and 20X2, P had on hand $25,000 and $30,000 of merchandise purchased from S. The following is the computation of intra-group profits:

In beginning inventory	25/125 of $25,000	=	$5,000
In ending inventory	25/125 of $30,000	=	$6,000

Consolidating adjustments at 12/31/X2:

1. Consolidated sales	$250,000	
Consolidated cost of sales		$250,000

To eliminate intragroup sales for the year 20X2.

2. Consolidated retained earnings	$5,000	
Consolidated cost of sales	$1,000	
Inventory		$6,000

To eliminate the intragroup profit in beginning and ending inventory.

Because consolidating adjustments are not booked, the intragroup profit in beginning inventory must again be eliminated in arriving at consolidated retained earnings. The additional unrealized intragroup profit arising in 20X2 is $1,000, and this is adjusted against consolidated cost of sales.

The two debit adjustments in 2 could be apportioned between the majority and minority interests in S in the proportions 80:20. In that case, the beginning balances of consolidated retained earnings and the minority interest would be adjusted downward by $4,000 and $1,000, respectively, and the parent company's and the minority interest's share of profit for 20X2 would be adjusted downward by $800 and $200, respectively. Since the whole $1,000 has been charged to consolidated cost of sales, the deduction of $200 from the minority interest's share of profit would reduce the amount borne by the majority interest (in arriving at the net income attributable to the parent company's shareholders) to $800.

These adjustments assume that the investment in the subsidiary has been accounted for in the parent company's financial statements on the basis of cost or revalued amounts. If the equity method had been used, the majority's 80% share of the intragroup profit would already have been eliminated (IAS 28, par. 16; SIC-3), and an adjustment different from 2, above, would be required.

Different Reporting Dates

When the financial statements of an enterprise included in a consolidation are drawn up at a date different from the group's financial reporting date, they may be used in the consolidation, provided that the difference does not exceed three months. In that case, adjustments should be made for any significant transactions or other events occurring between the two dates (IAS 27, pars. 19–20), for example, the accidental destruction of significant assets in a subsidiary after its balance sheet date but before that of the parent. If the difference between the dates exceeds three months, the requirements of the standard imply that the subsidiary should prepare interim financial statements for consolidation purposes.

Uniform Accounting Policies

Consolidated financial statements should be prepared by using uniform accounting policies for like transactions and other events in similar circumstances. In general, even if a consolidated enterprise employs accounting policies different from those of the group, appropriate adjustments can and should be made to its financial statements prior to consolidation. If this is not practicable, the fact must be disclosed together with the proportions of the items in the consolidated financial statements to which the different accounting policies have been applied (IAS 27, pars. 21–22).

> **OBSERVATION:** The exemption from the requirement for uniformity when it is "not practicable" introduces an element of arbitrariness into the procedure. For example, many U.K. companies state property assets at revalued amounts in both parent company and group financial statements, but if such a U.K. company has U.S. subsidiaries, the latters' property assets will be stated at historical cost. Should these be revalued before consolidation? The criterion of "practicability" is not defined.

The issue of comparability of financial statement information over time is dealt with in IAS 1 (revised), "Presentation of Financial Statements," paragraphs 27 and 40 (see Chapter 3).

Paragraphs 23–25 of IAS 27 address the issue of accounting for disposals of subsidiaries and related comparability issues. The results of operations of a subsidiary that is disposed of are included in the consolidated income statement until the date of disposal, which is the date on which the parent ceases to have control of the subsidiary. The difference between the proceeds from the disposal and the carrying amount of the subsidiary's assets less liabilities as of the date of the disposal is recognized in the consolidated income statement as the profit or loss on the disposal of the subsidiary.

> ☛ **PRACTICE POINTER:** IAS 27 gives no guidance on the treatment of goodwill related to subsidiaries in calculating the gain or loss on disposal. Failure to take account of such goodwill will result in gains being overstated and losses being understated. This also applies to goodwill written off directly against reserves, prior to this being barred by IAS 22 (revised) in 1995. Strictly speaking, any such goodwill should be disclosed and reintegrated in calculating the gain or loss on disposal.

IAS 27 states that, in order to ensure comparability from one financial reporting period to the next, supplementary information is often provided about the effect of the acquisition and disposal of subsidiaries on the financial position and results of the group for the reporting period and on the corresponding amounts for the preceding period. However, the standard does not lay down any requirements regarding such supplementary information. If a disposal meets the criteria for treatment as a discontinuing of operations, some disclosure requirements are laid down in IAS 35, "Discontinuing Operations" (see Chapter 11).

Partial Disposals

In the case of a partial disposal, the parent may:

1. Retain control or joint control of the subsidiary, or
2. Replace control by joint control, or
3. Retain an investment giving it a significant influence in the former subsidiary, or
4. Retain an investment not giving it a significant influence in the former subsidiary.

The standard (paragraph 24, as amended by IAS 39) makes it clear that in cases 3 and 4 above the equity method as set out in IAS 28 or the method of accounting for investments as set out in IAS 39 should be applied as from the date of disposal, as appropriate. Implicitly, in case 2, the provisions of IAS 31 should be applied.

> **OBSERVATION:** No reference is made to the calculation of the gain or loss on a partial disposal, or to such matters as the treatment of a dilution of the group's share of a subsidiary when the latter issues shares to a third party (equivalent to a partial disposal).

Shareholdings by a Subsidiary in Its Parent

IAS 27 does not deal with shareholdings by a subsidiary in its parent or with changes in these. IAS 1 (revised) paragraph 74 requires disclosure, in either the balance sheet or the notes, of shares in the enterprise held either by itself or by its subsidiaries or associates. SIC-D16, "Presentation of Treasury Shares," requires that when an enterprise acquires its own shares with a view to subsequent cancellation or resale, such shares should be presented in the consolidated balance sheet of the issuer as a deduction from equity; in the event of resale, any difference between the purchase cost and the resale price is treated as a change in equity, not as part of net income for the period. Shares held by a subsidiary in its parent may be considered from the perspective of the group as a form of treasury stock, and the appropriate presentation in the consolidated balance sheet would be as a deduction from equity.

This situation should be distinguished from that which occurs after a *reverse acquisition*, as discussed in Chapter 6.

In a situation in which a subsidiary owns shares in its parent, consolidated net income may be found algebraically. The following example is adapted from the *Miller GAAP Guide*, Chapter 8.

Company	Unconsolidated net income (excluding income from investees)	
A	$40,000	A (parent) owns 80% of B
B	20,000	B owns 70% of C
C	10,000	C owns 20% of A
	$70,000	

Let a, b, and c = the *consolidated basis* net income of A, B, and C, respectively.

We have: $a = 40{,}000 + 0.8b$

$b = 20{,}000 + 0.7c$

$c = 10{,}000 + 0.2a$

Solving for a:

$$a = 40{,}000 + 0.8(20{,}000 + 0.7c)$$
$$= 40{,}000 + 16{,}000 + 0.56(10{,}000 + 0.2a)$$
$$= 56{,}000 + 5{,}600 + 0.112a$$
$$(1 - 0.112)\ a = 61{,}600$$
$$a = 61{,}600/0.888 = 69{,}369.4$$

Consolidated (equity) net income of A = 0.8 × $69,369.4 = $55,496

The net income of C = $10,000 + 0.2 × 69,369 = $23,874, of which the 30% minority interest = $7,162

B's share of the net income of C = 0.7 × $23,847 = $16,712

B's net income = $20,000 + 16,712 = $36,712, of which the 20% minority interest = $7,342

Consolidated net income = $70,000 – (7,162 + 7,342) = $55,496

DISCLOSURE

In addition to those disclosures mentioned above, IAS 27 requires the following disclosures to be made:

1. In consolidated financial statements, a listing of significant subsidiaries, including the name, country of incorporation or residence, proportion of ownership interest, and, if different, proportion of voting power held.
2. In consolidated financial statements, where applicable:
   (a) the reasons for not consolidating a subsidiary;
   (b) the nature of the relationship between the parent and a subsidiary of which the parent does not own, directly or indirectly through subsidiaries, more than one half of the voting power;
   (c) the name of an enterprise in which more than one-half of the voting power is owned, directly or indirectly through subsidiaries, but which, because of the absence of control, is not a subsidiary; and
   (d) the effect of the acquisition and disposal of subsidiaries on the financial position at the reporting date, the results for the reporting period, and on the corresponding amounts for the preceding period.
3. In the parent's separate financial statements, a description of the method used to account for subsidiaries.

IAS 31 states the following disclosure requirements (pars. 45–49):

1. A venturer should disclose the aggregate amount of the following contingencies, unless the probability of loss is remote, separately from the amount of other contingencies:
   (a) any contingencies that the venturer has incurred in relation to its interests in joint ventures and its share in each of the

contingencies that have been incurred jointly with other venturers;

(b) its share of the contingencies of the joint ventures themselves for which it is contingently liable; and

(c) those contingencies that arise because the venturer is contingently liable for the liabilities of the other venturers of a joint venture.

2. The reference to IAS 10 in IAS 31, paragraph 45, should be replaced by a reference to IAS 37, "Provisions, Contingent Liabilities, and Contingent Assets," which superseded the relevant paragraphs of IAS 10. A venturer should disclose the aggregate amount of the following commitments in respect of its interests in joint ventures separately from other commitments:

(a) any capital commitments of the venturer in relation to its interests in joint ventures and its share in the capital commitments that have been incurred jointly with other venturers, and

(b) its share of the capital commitments of the joint ventures themselves.

3. A venturer should disclose a listing and description of interests in significant joint ventures and the proportion of ownership interest held in jointly controlled entities. A venturer that reports its interests in jointly controlled entities using the line-by-line reporting format for proportionate consolidation or the equity method should disclose the aggregate amounts of each of current assets, long-term assets, current liabilities, long-term liabilities, income and expenses related to its interests in joint ventures.

4. A venturer that does not issue consolidated financial statements, because it does not have subsidiaries, should disclose the information required in paragraphs 1, 2, and 3 above.

5. It is appropriate that a venturer that does not prepare consolidated financial statements because it does not have subsidiaries provide the same information about its interests in joint ventures as those venturers that issue consolidated financial statements.

CHAPTER 10
CONSTRUCTION CONTRACTS

CONTENTS

OVERVIEW

It is in the nature of construction contracts that they last over a long period of time, in general over more than one accounting period. The issue of determining the *total* profit on such a contract raises no new accounting problems over and above those of cost determination and allocation discussed in Chapter 23 in relation to inventory.

There is one important and difficult additional issue, however, which is the question of allocation of the total profit over the various accounting periods. If a contract extends over, say, three years, should the contribution to profits be 0%, 0%, and 100%, respectively, for the three years? Can we make profits on something before we have finished it? The realistic convention might seem to argue against doing so, and the prudent convention would certainly argue against it, too. But would this give a "fair presentation" of the results for each period? And would it be of any use? The various users want *regular* information on business progress. Can we not argue that we can be "reasonably certain," during the contract, of at least some profit—and if we can, then surely the matching principle is more important than an excessive slavishness to prudence?

Two alternative approaches have emerged over the years. These are the completed-contract method, which delays profit recognition until the end, and the percentage-of-completion method, which in defined conditions requires allocation over the accounting periods concerned. IAS GAAP are given in IAS 11, "Construction Contracts," as revised in 1993, and require the percentage-of-completion method.

BACKGROUND

The primary issue in accounting for construction contracts is the allocation of contract revenue, and of the contract costs to be matched against that revenue, between accounting periods. IAS 11 says that the problem is the allocation of these items to the "accounting periods in which construction work is performed," but this slightly begs the question. The key general accounting criteria such as relevance, reliability, matching, prudence, and usefulness, discussed in the IASC Framework (see Chapter 2), have to be applied, which of course means that the tensions and inconsistencies between them need to be resolved.

The effects of the two generally advanced methods of dealing with this problem, the completed-contract method and the percentage-of-completion method, are best shown by the comparative example below.

Illustration of Accounting for the Completed-Contract and Percentage-of-Completion Methods

The following data pertain to a $2,000,000 long-term construction contract:

	20X5	20X6	20X7
Costs incurred during the year	$500,000	$700,000	$300,000
Year-ended estimated costs to complete	1,000,000	300,000	—
Billing during the year	400,000	700,000	900,000
Collections during the year	200,000	500,000	1,200,000

The computation of realized gross profit under the percentage-of-completion method, assuming for simplicity that the degree of completion is determined on the basis of costs incurred, will be as follows.

The total expected profit is total revenue minus total expected costs at the end of year 1, that is, 2,000,000 − (500,000 + 1,000,000) = 500,000.

This is allocated over the 3 years as shown.

20X5

$$\frac{\$500,000}{\$1,500,000} \times \$500,000 - 0 = \qquad \$166,667$$

20X6

$$\frac{\$1,200,000}{\$1,500,000} \times \$500,000 - \$166,667 = \qquad \$233,333$$

20X7

$$\frac{\$1,500,000}{\$1,500,000} \times \$500,000 - (\$166,667 + \$233,333) = \$100,000$$

Total gross profit $\underline{\$500,000}$

The journal entries for both the completed-contract method and the percentage-of-completion method for the three years are as follows:

20X5	Completed Contract		% of Completion	
Construction in progress	$500,000		$500,000	
Cash or liability		$500,000		$500,000
Accounts receivable	400,000		400,000	
Advance billings		400,000		400,000
Cash	200,000		200,000	
Accounts receivable		200,000		200,000
Construction in progress	no entry		16,667	
Realized gross profit				
(P&L)				166,667

20X5	Completed Contract		% of Completion	
Construction in progress	$700,000		$700,000	
Cash or liability		$700,000		$700,000
Accounts receivable	700,000		700,000	
Advance billings		700,000		700,000
Cash	500,000		500,000	
Accounts receivable		500,000		500,000
Construction in progress	no entry		233,333	
Realized gross profit				
(P&L)				233,333

20X7	Completed Contract		% of Completion	
Construction in progress	$300,000		$300,000	
Cash or liability		$300,000		$300,000
Accounts receivable	900,000		900,000	
Advance billings		900,000		900,000
Cash	1,200,000		1,200,000	
Accounts receivable		1,200,000		1,200,000

20X7	Completed Contract	% of Completion
Construction in progress	no entry	100,000
Realized gross profit (P&L)		100,000
Advance billings	2,000,000	2,000,000
Construction in progress	1,500,000	2,000,000
Realized gross profit (P&L)	500,000	—

At the end of each year during which the contract is in progress, the excess of the construction-in-progress account over the advance billings account is presented as a current asset:

20X5: ($500,000 + $166,667) – $400,000 = $266,667

20X6: ($500,000 + $166,667 + $700,000 + $233,333)
       – ($400,000 + $700,000) = $500,000

In this illustration, the estimated gross profit of $500,000 was the actual gross profit on the contract. If changes in the estimated cost to complete the contract had been appropriate at the end of 20X5 and/or 20X6, or if the actual costs to complete had been determined to be different when the contract was completed in 20X7, those changes would have been incorporated into revised estimates during the contract period. For example, if at the end of 20X6 the costs to complete were estimated to be $400,000 instead of $300,000, the 20X6 gross profit would have been determined as follows:

$$\frac{\$1,200,000}{\$1,600,000} \times (2,000,000 - \$1,6000,000) = \$300,000$$

$$\$300,000 - \$166,667 = \$133,333$$

The 20X7 profit, assuming that the revised estimate of $400,000 for cost-of-completion turns out to be accurate, would be

$$\$400,000 - (\$166,667 + \$133,333) = \$100,000$$

The reason why, on these numbers, the 20X7 profit calculates to $100,000 in each circumstance is that (300/1,500) x 500 (circumstance 1)

$$= (400/1,600) \times 400 \text{ (circumstance 2)}$$

OBSERVATION: Looking at the above illustration, under the revised total contract cost figure of $1,600,000, it is clear that, with the advantage of hindsight, too high a proportion of the total profit (i.e., of $400,000) was allocated to 20X5, and too low a proportion to 20X6. Was this imprudent in 20X5? Was there a failure to fairly present in 20X5?

In one sense, yes it was imprudent. Clearly, the completed-contract method carries no such risks. But there was no failure of fair presentation in 20X5 under the percentage-of-completion method. The reality is that work had been done in 20X5 toward a profitable overall outcome. Estimates turned out to be imprecise. But to follow the completed-contract method and automatically report a profit of nil in 20X5 would arguably be the very negation of fair presentation. The amount $166,667 for 20X5 gross profit turned out to be subjectively inaccurate. A gross profit of $0 would be objective (reliable) but downright wrong! IAS 11, as we shall see below, attempts a reasonable path through the tensions inherent in the situation.

In practice, U.S. GAAP is usually similar to IAS GAAP. While under U.S. GAAP both the percentage-of-completion method and the completed-contract method are permitted (ARB 45), the percentage-of-completion method is generally used; the completed-contract method is used in circumstances when estimates of costs to completion and the extent of progress toward completion are not reasonably dependable.

SCOPE AND DEFINITIONS

IAS 11 is to be applied when accounting for construction contracts in the financial statements of contractors. We are given definitions of different types of contracts (par. 3).

- A *construction contract* is a contract specifically negotiated for the construction of an asset or a combination of assets that are closely interrelated or interdependent in terms of their design, technology, and function or their ultimate purpose or use.
- A *fixed price contract* is a construction contract in which the contractor agrees to a fixed contract price, or a fixed rate per unit of output, which in some cases is subject to cost escalation clauses.
- A *cost-plus contract* is a construction contract in which the contractor is reimbursed for allowable or otherwise defined costs, plus a percentage of these costs or a fixed fee.

Contractor is not defined. The word appears to be used in the general sense, that is, any enterprise that contracts. It is specifically stated (par. 5) that construction contracts are to include contracts for the rendering of services that are directly related to the construction of the asset, for example, those for the services of project managers and architects, and contracts for the destruction or restoration of assets, and the restoration of the environment after the demolition of assets.

It should be noted, however, that IAS 11 applies only to contracts "specifically negotiated." This seems to imply that only customized production is included. Also noteworthy is that the given definition implies no particular length of the construction period. We are talking about contracts, not long-term contracts. In practice, however, if no accounting period-ends are crossed, then no problems of revenue and expense recognition exist, so nothing remains to be resolved.

Sometimes one contract covers the construction of a number of assets. If three conditions are met, then each asset is required to be treated as a separate construction contract. These conditions are (par. 8):

1. Separate proposals have been submitted for each asset.
2. Each asset has been subject to separate negotiation, and the contractor and customer have been able to accept or reject that part of the contract relating to each asset.
3. The costs and revenues of each asset can be identified.

Conversely, a group of contracts, whether with one or with several different customers, may in substance be a single construction contract and is required to be treated as a single contract when, again, three conditions are met. These are (par. 9):

1. The group of contracts is negotiated as a single package.
2. The contracts are so closely interrelated that they are, in effect, part of a single project with an overall profit margin.
3. The contracts are performed concurrently or in a continuous sequence.

A typical example of this last case would be contracts for the design, and then building, of a particular project. Contracts may allow "add-in" options subject to further agreement. Such an add-on should be treated as part of the original contract unless either the asset differs significantly in design, technology, or function from the asset or assets covered by the original contract or the price of the asset is negotiated without regard to the original contract price.

CONTRACT REVENUE

The standard takes its time in arriving at the heart of the whole matter, which is, of course, the question of profit recognition. Consistent with the general logical progression of definition before measurement, we first need to define and consider contract revenues and contract costs. Naturally enough, the starting point for quantifying gross revenue is the "price" agreed in the contract. More fully, contract revenue should comprise (par. 11) the initial amount of revenue agreed in the contract and variations in contract work, claims, and incentive payments to the extent that it is probable that they will result in revenue and that they are capable of being reliably measured. Contract revenue is measured at the fair value of the consideration received or receivable.

It is the nature of long-term and unique customized projects that changes and unforeseen events are likely to occur. A variation is an instruction by the customer for a change in the work to be performed under the contract. The revenue from a variation is included in contract revenue when it is probable that the customer will approve the variation and the amount of revenue arising from the variation and the amount of revenue can be reliably measured.

A claim is an amount that the contractor seeks to collect from the customer or another party as reimbursement for costs not included in the contract price. A claim may arise from, for example, customer-caused delays, errors in specifications or design, and disputed variations in contract work. Claims are included in contract revenue only when negotiations have reached an advanced stage such that it is probable that the customer will accept the claim and the amount that the customer will probably accept can be measured reliably.

Incentive payments are additional amounts paid to the contractor if specified performance standards are met or exceeded, for example, for early completion of the contract. Incentive payments are included in contract revenue when the contract is sufficiently advanced and it is probable that the specified performance standards will be met or exceeded so that the amount of the incentive payment can be measured reliably.

It should be noted that there are, in theory, no options included in any of the above detail. Adjustments for variations, claims, and so on are required when the stated conditions are met and cannot be omitted on the grounds, for example, of conservatism. In practice, however, there are of course a large number of "probables" included in the specifications, so a degree of subjectivity and human or cultural bias is inevitably involved.

CONTRACT COSTS

The standard considers contract costs under three aspects. Contract costs should comprise (par. 16):

1. Costs that relate directly to the specific contract,
2. Costs that are attributable to contract activity in general and can be allocated to the contract, and
3. Such other costs as are specifically chargeable to the customer under the terms of the contract.

IAS 11 gives examples, and some sometimes pedantic detail, about each part in paragraphs 17–21. Allocatable costs, essentially design and construction overheads, are allocated using methods that are systematic and rational and are applied consistently to all costs having similar characteristics. The allocation is based on the normal level of construction activity. Construction overheads include such costs as the preparation and processing of construction personnel payroll. Costs that may be attributable to contract activity in general and can be allocated to specific contracts also include borrowing costs when the contractor adopts the allowed alternative treatment in IAS 23, "Capitalization of Borrowing Costs" (see Chapter 5).

Expenditures that one would not expect to be allowed to be charged to contract costs, such as general administration costs or research costs, "may" be included in contract costs when they are specifically chargeable to the customer under the terms of the contract. This is only sensible, as they will be included in revenues automatically. Costs incurred in securing a contract, that is, pre-contract costs, "are" included as part of the contract costs if they can be separately identified and measured reliably and it is probable that the contract will be obtained. When costs incurred in securing a contract are recognized as an expense in the period in which they are incurred, they are not included in contract costs when the contract is obtained in a subsequent period.

RECOGNITION OF CONTRACT REVENUE AND EXPENSES

Recognition of contract revenue and expenses, of course, is fundamentally what IAS 11 is all about. When profits are expected, the standard requires the percentage-of-completion method and does not allow the completed-contract method. This does not automatically mean, however, that profits are recognized in the early stages of a long-term construction contract.

The formal statement of the position is as follows (par. 22). When the outcome of a construction contract can be estimated reliably, contract revenue and contract costs associated with the construction contract should be recognized as revenue and expenses, respectively, by reference to the stage of completion of the contract activity at the balance sheet date. An expected loss on the construction contract should be recognized as an expense immediately when it becomes probable that total contract costs will exceed total contract revenue. Any such loss is determined and recognized irrespective of (par. 37):

1. Whether or not work has commenced on the contract,
2. The stage of completion of contract activity, or
3. The amount of profits expected to arise on other contracts that are not treated as a single construction contract.

The standard specifies, separately for fixed price and cost-plus contracts (as defined earlier in this chapter), when reliable estimation is possible. For a fixed price contract, it says that the outcome of a construction contract can be estimated reliably when all the following conditions are satisfied (par. 23):

1. Total contract revenue can be measured reliably.
2. It is probable that the economic benefits associated with the contract will flow to the enterprise.
3. Both the contract costs to complete the contract and the stage of contract completion at the balance sheet date can be measured reliably.
4. The contract costs attributable to the contract can be clearly identified and measured reliably so that actual contract costs incurred can be compared with prior estimates.

In the case of a cost-plus contract, the outcome of a construction contract can be estimated reliably when both the following conditions are satisfied (par. 24):

1. It is probable that the economic benefits associated with the contract will flow to the enterprise.
2. The contract costs attributable to the contract, whether or not specifically reimbursable, can be clearly identified and measured reliably.

It is important to understand and accept that "reliable estimation" is not the same as objective fact. As IAS 11 puts it (par. 29), an

> enterprise reviews and, when necessary, revises the estimates of contract revenue and contract costs as the contract progresses. The need for such revisions does not necessarily indicate that the outcome of the contract cannot be estimated reliably.

Clearly it is essential for the enterprise to have an efficient budgeting and costing system. The stage of completion is to be determined consistently in a manner appropriate to the contract, for example, proportion of cost basis, as used in our earlier illustration, by survey of work performed or by physical proportion. Proportion of cash received to a total contract price would not be appropriate, as it would not reflect the work performed.

It is, of course, highly likely that during the early stages of a long-term contract the outcome of the contract cannot be measured reliably under the required conditions stated above. When the outcome of a construction contract cannot be estimated reliably (par. 32):

1. Revenue should be recognized only to the extent of contract costs incurred that it is probable will be recoverable.

2. Contract costs should be recognized as an expense in the period in which they are incurred.

An expected loss on the construction contract should, of course, be recognized as an expense immediately.

The effect of this is that no profit is recognized when the outcome cannot be "estimated reliably," but also that a loss or net expense is recorded only if it is "expected." In other words, revenue equals expenses. Expenditures and costs are recorded, at cost, as assets until the later stages of the contract are reached.

> **OBSERVATION:** When the "early stage" treatment is being applied, the effect is identical to the effect of applying the completed-contract method, that is, no profits are recorded, but losses are recorded only if expected. Given also that the interpretation of words used in IAS 11 like "estimated reliably" and "probable" is inherently subjective and likely to be influenced by national norms and cultures, the way is open for national systems that would prefer, perhaps on the grounds of prudence, to use the completed-contract method, to interpret these subjective expressions in a way that would delay profit recognition, relative to other national norms. This is an inevitable part of international accounting. National cultural characteristics cannot be standardized by regulation.

The effect of a material change in estimates part way through the life of a construction contract is treated in accordance with IAS 8, "Net Profit or Loss for the Period, Fundamental Errors, and Changes in Accounting Policies" (see Chapter 26). The effects of the change in estimates are included in the net profit or loss for the period in which the change occurs, or if appropriate partly in that year and partly in future years.

DISCLOSURE

An enterprise should disclose (pars. 39–42):

1. The amount of contract revenue recognized as revenue in the period,

2. The methods used to determine the contract revenue recognized in the period, and

3. The methods used to determine the stage of completion of contracts in progress.

An enterprise should disclose each of the following for contracts in progress at the balance sheet date:

1. The aggregate amount of costs incurred and recognized profits (less recognized losses) to date,
2. The amount of advances received, and
3. The amount of retentions.

An enterprise should present:

1. The gross amount due from customers for contract work as an asset, and
2. The gross amount due to customers for contract work as a liability.

IAS 37, "Provisions, Contingent Liabilities, and Contingent Assets" (see Chapter 28), should also be applied if appropriate.

IAS 11 gives, as an appendix, a long example and illustration that is worthy of study.

CHAPTER 11
DISCONTINUING OPERATIONS

CONTENTS

OVERVIEW

A discontinuing operation is a relatively large component of an enterprise that is either being disposed of completely or substantially or is being terminated through abandonment or piecemeal sale. The effects of such discontinuation are likely to be significant both in their own right and in changing likely future results of the remaining components of the enterprise. The objective of IAS GAAP is to establish a basis for segregating information about a major operation that an enterprise is discontinuing from information about its continuing operations and to specify minimum disclosures about a discontinuing operation. Distinguishing discontinuing and continuing operations will improve the ability of investors, creditors, and other users of financial statements to make projections of the enterprise's cash flows, earnings generating capacity, and financial position.

IAS GAAP focus on how to present a discontinuing operation in an enterprise's financial statements and what information to disclose. It does not establish any new principles for deciding when and how to recognize and measure the income, expenses, cash flows, and changes in assets and liabilities relating to a discontinuing operation. Instead, it requires that enterprises follow the recognition and measurement principles in other relevant International Accounting Standards.

Originally, this area was dealt with briefly as part of IAS 8, "Net Profit or Loss for the Period, Fundamental Errors, and Changes in Accounting Policies." The relevant parts of IAS 8 have been withdrawn, and IAS GAAP is now contained in IAS 35, "Discontinuing

Operations," which is operative for financial statements covering periods beginning on or after January 1, 1999.

BACKGROUND

In essence, the results of enterprise operations need to be presented in a manner that will satisfy two objectives. First, the activities and results of the year under review must be reported fully and clearly. Second, readers should be able to glean, as effectively as possible, an impression of the implications of current period results for future periods. Much of IAS 8, mentioned above, is directed toward this latter objective, and IAS 35 is an extension and development of one aspect of this, requiring that the results of components of an enterprise that are not set to continue are distinguished from the results of those that are.

Philosophies, practices, and proposals in this whole area are under active discussion in a number of jurisdictions. As discussed in Chapter 3, IAS 1, "Presentation of Financial Statements," although recently extensively revised and effective from July 1, 1998, is likely to be further developed, as is the whole area of "reporting financial performance." This expectation of major changes applies to many jurisdictions, including U.K. and U.S. GAAP, as well as to IAS.

As far as the current position is concerned, an obvious difference relevant to this chapter is that IAS GAAP refer to discontinuing operations (present tense), whereas U.S. GAAP refer to discontinued operations (past tense). The definitions may be summarized as follows.

- IAS: A discontinuing operation is a separate major component (see below for detailed definition) of an enterprise that is being disposed of either substantially in its entirety or piecemeal or through abandonment. The disposal can take place over several months or longer but must be pursuant to a single plan.

- U.S. (APB 30, FAS-130): A discontinued operation is a segment of an enterprise that has been or will be sold, abandoned, or otherwise disposed of. It is normally envisaged that the disposal would be completed within a year of the "measurement" date (date of management commitment to a formal plan for discontinuance).

IAS 35 contains no specific measurement requirements, explicitly stating that the requirements of other IASC standards should be followed as relevant. U.S. GAAP (in APB 30) regarding measurement are to measure any gain or loss resulting from the discontinuance as at the measurement date and to provide at the measurement date for the estimated loss from operations during the wind-down period, together with the estimated loss on disposal. Gains are not recognized until realized.

SCOPE AND DEFINITIONS

The scope, subject as always to the materiality criterion, is universal. IAS 35 applies to all discontinuing operations of all enterprises. The key definitions (pars. 2 and 9) are as follows.

A *discontinuing operation* is a component of an enterprise:

1. That the enterprise, pursuant to a single plan, is:
   (a) disposing of substantially in its entirety, such as by selling the component in a single transaction, by demerger or spin-off of ownership of the component to the enterprise's shareholders;
   (b) disposing of piecemeal, such as by selling off the component's assets and settling its liabilities individually; or
   (c) terminating through abandonment;
2. That represents a separate major line of business or geographic area of operations; and
3. That can be distinguished operationally and for financial reporting purposes.

With respect to a discontinuing operation, the *initial disclosure event* is the occurrence of one of the following, whichever occurs earlier:

1. The enterprise has entered into a binding sale agreement for substantially all of the assets attributable to the discontinuing operation; or
2. The enterprise's board of directors or similar governing body has both (a) approved a detailed, formal plan for the discontinuance and (b) made an announcement of the plan.

The three elements of the definition of a discontinuing operation, all of which must be satisfied, need separate consideration. It must be emphasized that under element 1, there must be a single plan, although the discontinuance itself, that is, the disposal, may well be piecemeal or the abandonment gradual. Provided that there is such a plan and that there has been an "initial disclosure event," then the actual time for the "discontinuing" process can be quite long: "over a period of months or perhaps even longer" (par. 5). Straddling of a financial reporting year end may well occur. This is, of course, consistent with the usage of the present tense in the title of the standard.

The precise meaning of element 2 is inevitably somewhat subjective. It can normally be assumed that a reportable business segment or geographic segment as defined in IAS 14, "Reporting Financial Information by Segment," would normally satisfy criterion 2 of the definition of a discontinuing operation (par. 2(b)), that is, it would represent a separate major line of business or geographic area of operations. A part of a segment as defined in IAS 14 may also satisfy criterion 2 of the definition. However, for an enterprise that operates in a single business or geographic segment and therefore does not report segment information, a major product or service line may also satisfy the criteria of the definition.

Regarding element 3 of the definition, IAS 35 is more precise (par. 11). A component can be distinguished operationally and for financial reporting purposes if:

1. Its operating assets and liabilities can be directly attributed to it,

2. Its income (gross revenue) can be directly attributed to it, and

3. At least a majority of its operating expenses can be directly attributed to it.

Financial statement items, both assets/liabilities and income/expenses, are directly attributable if they would be eliminated as a result of the discontinuance. Only interest on "directly attributable" borrowing can be a directly attributable expense.

As a general point, it is important to distinguish a discontinuance of an operation, on the one hand, from the normal process of change and progression within a dynamic business operation. Business enterprises frequently close facilities, abandon products or even product lines, and change the size of their work force, in response to market forces. Whereas those kinds of terminations generally are not, in and of themselves, discontinuing operations as that term is used in IAS 35, they can occur in connection with a discontinuing operation.

Examples of activities that do not necessarily satisfy criterion (a) of paragraph 2, but that might do so in combination with other circumstances, include:

- Gradual or evolutionary phasing out of a product line or class of service,

- Discontinuing, even if relatively abruptly, several products within an ongoing line of business,

- Shifting of some production or marketing activities for a particular line of business from one location to another,

- Closing of a facility to achieve productivity improvements or other cost savings, or

- Selling a subsidiary whose activities are similar to those of the parent or other subsidiaries.

It is possible that a significant change, while not falling within the definition of a discontinuing operation within IAS 35, would be classified as a restructuring under IAS 37, "Provisions, Contingent Liabilities, and Contingent Assets." See the discussion in Chapter 28. Changes meeting neither of these definitions may still require disclosure under IAS 8 because their nature, size, or incidence makes disclosure necessary to explain the performance of the enterprise for the period.

RECOGNITION AND MEASUREMENT

As already indicated, IAS 35 introduces no new recognition and measurement criteria. The formal requirement is that (par. 17) an enterprise should apply the principles of recognition and measurement that are set out in other International Accounting Standards for the purpose of deciding when and how to recognize and measure the changes in assets and liabilities and the income, expenses, and cash flows relating to a discontinuing operation.

> **OBSERVATION:** It should not be assumed that this approach represents, in any sense, laziness or evasion on the part of IASC. Rather, it represents a deliberate view that the state of discontinuance does not lead to any measurement implications that are not fully and adequately dealt with within its comprehensive set of standards. IAS 35 itself gives four examples:
>
> - Employee termination benefits are dealt with as regards recognition in IAS 19, "Employee Benefits" (see Chapter 13).
> - Disposals of non-current assets are dealt with in IAS 16, "Property, Plant, and Equipment" (see Chapter 27).
> - Provisions are dealt with in IAS 37, "Provisions, Contingent Liabilities, and Contingent Assets" (see Chapter 28).
> - Impairment losses are dealt with in IAS 36, "Impairment of Assets" (see Chapter 19).

Two particular applications are worthy of comment. Although, as already discussed above, a restructuring as defined in IAS 37 may or may not fall within the definition of a discontinuing operation under IAS 35, it is explicitly stated in IAS 35 (par. 20) that a discontinuing operation *is* a restructuring as defined in IAS 37, paragraph 10. Paragraphs 70–83 of IAS 37 must therefore be followed, which define the measurement rules regarding provisions and also describe in some detail the requirements for the existence of a detailed formal plan (as required by both IAS 37, paragraph 72 and IAS 35, paragraph 2). Only expenditures directly arising from the restructuring, and not associated with the ongoing activities of the enterprise, may be included within the measurement of provisions. See the discussion in Chapter 28.

Although there is no requirement, nor indeed permission, to reduce relevant assets automatically to fair value or net realizable or break-up value, IAS 36, "Impairment of Assets," applies and is likely in many cases to need to be invoked. Where a discontinuing operation exists, an enterprise estimates the recoverable amount of each asset of the discontinuing operation (the higher of the asset's net selling price and its value in use) and recognizes an impairment loss or reversal of a prior impairment loss, if any.

In applying IAS 36 to a discontinuing operation, an enterprise determines whether the recoverable amount of an asset of a discontinuing operation is assessed for the individual asset or for the asset's cash-generating unit (defined in IAS 36 as the smallest identifiable group of assets that includes the asset under review and that generates cash inflows from continuing use that are largely independent of the cash inflows from other assets or groups of assets). This will be primarily determined by the nature of the process of discontinuance in the particular case under consideration. Impairment losses, or reversals of impairment losses, may, of course, become evident and necessary during the process of discontinuance, perhaps at several stages, not merely on the occurrence of the initial disclosure event.

PRESENTATION AND DISCLOSURE

The key activator regarding disclosures is the occurrence of the "initial disclosure event." In the financial statements for the year in which an initial disclosure event occurs, a series of disclosures is required. If an initial disclosure event occurs after the end of an enterprise's financial reporting period but before the financial statements for that period are approved by the board of directors or similar governing body, those financial statements should include the same disclosures for the period covered by those financial statements.

The disclosures required are defined by paragraph 27 as follows:

1. A description of the discontinuing operation;

2. The business or geographic segment(s) in which it is reported in accordance with IAS 14 (see Chapter 31);

3. The date and nature of the initial disclosure event;

4. The date or period in which the discontinuance is expected to be completed if known or determinable;

5. The carrying amounts, as of the balance sheet date, of the total assets and the total liabilities to be disposed of;

6. The amounts of revenue, expenses, and pre-tax profit or loss from ordinary activities attributable to the discontinuing operation during the current financial reporting period, and the income tax expenses relating thereto as required by paragraph 81(h) of IAS 12 (see Chapter 20); and

7. The amounts of net cash flows attributable to the operating, investing, and financing activities of the discontinuing operation during the current financial reporting period.

It should be remembered in the context of these disclosure requirements that any items expected to continue after completion of the discontinuance must not be allocated to the discontinuing operation. All the required information must be presented separately for each discontinuing operation if more than one discontinuance is happening in the same financial period.

When an enterprise actually disposes of assets or settles liabilities attributable to a discontinuing operation or enters into binding agreements for the sale of such assets or the settlement of such liabilities, it should include in its financial statements the following information when the events occur (par. 31):

1. For any gain or loss that is recognized on the disposal of assets or settlement of liabilities attributable to the discontinuing operation, (a) the amount of the pre-tax gain or loss and (b) income tax expense relating to the gain or loss, as required by paragraph 81(h) of IAS 12.

2. The net selling price or range of prices (which is after deducting the expected disposal costs) of those net assets for which the enterprise has entered into one or more binding sale agreements, the expected timing of receipt of those cash flows, and the carrying amount of those net assets.

It is, of course, inherent in the IASC approach to reporting discontinuing operations that the process may be spread over two or more periods. IAS 35, accordingly, requires all the disclosures described above to be continued in financial statements for periods up to and including the period in which the discontinuance is completed. A discontinuance is completed when the plan is substantially completed or abandoned, although payments from the buyer(s) to the seller may not yet be completed. If an enterprise abandons or withdraws from a plan that was previously reported as a discontinuing operation, that fact and its effect should be disclosed. An enterprise should also include in its financial statements for periods subsequent to the one in which the initial disclosure event occurs a description of any significant changes in the amount or timing of cash flows relating to the assets and liabilities to be disposed of or settled and the events causing those changes.

The disclosure of the amount of the pre-tax gain or loss recognized on the disposal of assets or settlement of liabilities attributable to the discontinuing operation (par. 31(a)) should be shown on the face of the income statement. All the other required disclosures may be shown either on the face of the financial statements or in the notes to the financial statements. However, IAS 35 "encourages" the information relating to income statement and cash flow items (par. 27(f) and (g)), to be presented on the face of the relevant statement.

IAS 35 notes explicitly that the event of having a discontinuing operation is not an extraordinary item. It also explicitly forbids any restructuring or other event that fails to meet its definition of a discontinuing operation from being called a discontinuing operation by enterprises following IAS GAAP.

IAS 35 also requires comparative information for prior periods that is presented in financial statements prepared after the initial disclosure event to be restated to segregate continuing and discontinuing assets, liabilities, income, expenses, and cash flows in a manner similar to that required for the current period. When interim financial reports are prepared, the notes to the interim financial report should describe any significant activities or events since the end of the most recent annual reporting report relating to a discontinuing operation and any significant changes in the amount or timing of cash flows relating to the assets and liabilities to be disposed of or settled.

CHAPTER 12
EARNINGS PER SHARE

CONTENTS

OVERVIEW

Earnings per share (EPS) is an important summary indicator of corporate performance for investors and other users of financial statements, relating the total earnings of the enterprise to the number of shares issued. It is an essential component in the Price/earnings (PE) ratio, which provides a basis of comparison between listed enterprises, and an indicator of market confidence, calculated as market price per share divided by EPS. High expectations of future performance lead to, and are indicated by, a higher share price and therefore a higher PE ratio.

Earnings per share figures are required by IAS GAAP to be presented in published financial statements in two forms. The basic EPS reports the EPS essentially as achieved in current circumstances. The diluted EPS calculates the EPS as if the dilutive effect of "potential" ordinary or common shares currently foreseeable had already taken place, that is, it assumes that a likely future increase in the number of shares has already happened. Intuitively, diluted EPS will be lower than basic EPS, but this need not be the case universally as the numerator may be increased as well as the denominator.

IAS 33, "Earnings per Share," became operative from January 1, 1998. There was considerable cooperation in this area between IASC, the U.S. FASB, and the U.K. ASB. IAS 33, FAS-128 in the United States, and FRS-14 in the United Kingdom were developed in cooperation and are consistent in all significant respects with each other. SIC-24 is now also relevant.

BACKGROUND

EPS is widely regarded as an important and convenient indicator of enterprise performance. In many ways, this is an unsatisfactory state of affairs. Accountants and regulators nationally and internationally have made enormous efforts to prescribe and increase transparency and clarity of reporting, but EPS goes out of its way to seek to reduce a voluminous and complex set of information to a single statistic. While in one sense wishing to downgrade the importance attached to EPS, regulators have inevitably found it necessary to make the EPS figure as reliable and consistent as possible. The earnings figure is relatively easy to regulate in terms of "which figure off the income statement to use," and impossible to regulate in terms of the inherent subjectivity involved in some aspects of revenue and expense calculation. Most of the detail of IAS 33, "Earnings per Share," is concerned with the calculation of the denominator in the EPS ratio, that is, with the actual or imputed number of shares.

SCOPE AND DEFINITIONS

IAS 33 must be applied by all enterprises whose ordinary shares or potential ordinary shares are publicly traded and by enterprises that are in the process of issuing ordinary shares or potential ordinary shares in public securities markets. When both parent and consolidated financial statements are presented, the information need be presented only on the basis of consolidated information.

An enterprise that has neither ordinary shares nor potential ordinary shares that are publicly traded but that voluntarily discloses earnings per share should calculate and disclose earnings per share in accordance with this standard. Thus, while only listed companies are required to follow IAS 33, any enterprise that does report EPS must do so in full accordance with the standard in order to comply with IAS GAAP.

The standard gives three definitions relating to shares, as follows (par. 6):

- An *ordinary share* is an equity instrument that is subordinate to all other classes of equity instruments.

- A *potential ordinary share* is a financial instrument or other contract that may entitle its holder to ordinary shares.

- *Warrants* or *options* are financial instruments that give the holder the right to purchase ordinary shares.

In addition, three definitions are imported from IAS 32, "Financial Instruments: Disclosure and Presentation" (par. 9).

- A *financial instrument* is any contract that gives rise to both a financial asset of one enterprise and a financial liability or equity instrument of another enterprise.
- An *equity instrument* is any contract that evidences a residual interest in the assets of an enterprise after deducting all of its liabilities.
- *Fair value* is the amount for which an asset could be exchanged, or a liability settled, between knowledgeable, willing parties in an arm's-length transaction.

The definition of an ordinary share as "subordinate to all other classes" implies that there is only one class of ordinary shares and, conversely, that all ordinary shares are of the same class. However, this is not in general the case. The standard states explicitly (par. 7) as follows.

> Ordinary shares participate in the net profit for the period only after other types of shares such as preference shares. An enterprise may have more than one class of ordinary shares. Ordinary shares of the same class will have the same rights to receive dividends.

Further ambiguity arises from a comparison of the above statement, which distinguishes ordinary shares in terms of their rights to participate in net profit, with the definition of an equity instrument, quoted above, which is couched purely in terms of rights to participate in a residual interest in net assets. The one need not automatically embrace the other.

It is possible to envisage complex equity structures creating apparently anomalous situations. For example, two types of shares could exist, A and B, both participating in residual net profits and having an interest in residual net assets, but with A also having an additional fixed preferential dividend entitlement. Clearly A, as a participating preference share, has some preference over B, so therefore B is subordinate to A. The definition of an ordinary share in IAS 33 would then clearly indicate that only B is an ordinary share, despite the fact that A also participates in residual net profit. On the other hand, two types of share could exist where the dividend entitlement of one, while neither fixed nor preferential, is stated as having a fixed proportional relationship to that of the other. Both types meet the definition (provided they also participate, whether equally or otherwise, in the residual net assets on dissolution also), so both are ordinary shares, but they are clearly distinguishable and would be expected to have different market values.

BASIC EARNINGS PER SHARE

Basic earnings per share should be calculated by dividing the net profit or loss for the period attributable to ordinary shareholders, the numerator, by the weighted average number of ordinary shares outstanding during the period, the denominator. Note that the numerator is the net result after deducting preference dividends (and in principle after deducting the returns to any other share class other than the ordinary shares).

The amount of preference dividends that is deducted from the net profit for the period is the amount of any preference dividends on noncumulative preference shares declared in respect of the period, and the full amount of the required preference dividends for cumulative preference shares for the period, whether or not the dividends have been declared. It follows that any dividends paid or declared during the current year in relation to cumulative preference shares in respect of previous period have been dealt with in earlier years, and should not be deducted in the current period EPS calculation.

> **OBSERVATION:** This simple definition of earnings for EPS purposes masks two issues that had caused some controversy in earlier years: tax considerations and unusual items. Under a number of jurisdictions the distribution policy affects the total taxation payable to a company on its income. Because "earnings" are supposed to be gross of dividends to ordinary shareholders and any effects thereof, it has been suggested that in such circumstances tax effects should be adjusted to give theoretical comparability between enterprises with different dividend policies. IAS 33 (like FAS-28 and FRS-14) ignores this issue, simply requiring earnings to be calculated after all tax effects of the actual activities have been taken into account.
>
> Unusual, and more specifically extraordinary, items are likewise not discussed in IAS 33. There had been much discussion in earlier years to the effect that EPS, as an indicator of likely repeatable performance, should exclude the effects of extraordinary items. However, the subjectivity of definition caused considerable difficulty and distortion (if not creativity) where this was tried. IAS 33 sweeps this issue, too, into oblivion by automatically requiring earnings to be calculated after the effects of all such items.

The denominator in the basic EPS calculation is potentially more difficult to calculate. It should be the weighted average number of ordinary shares outstanding during the period. This is the number of ordinary shares outstanding at the beginning of the period, adjusted by the number of ordinary shares bought back or issued during the period multiplied by a time-weighting factor. The time-weighting factor is the number of days that the specific shares are outstanding as a proportion of the total number of days in the period; a reasonable approximation of the weighted average is adequate in many circumstances. In most cases, shares are included in the weighted average number of shares from the date consideration is receivable (which is generally the date of their issue).

Some simple illustrations may be useful. Consider first the situation where an enterprise issues shares partway through the year at full market price.

I. Fullmar had total issued share capital on December 31, 20X1 as follows:

500,000 7% $1 preference shares

4,000,000 25¢ ordinary shares

Profit after tax for the year ended December 31, 20X1 was $435,000. On October 1, 20X1 Fullmar had issued 1 million 25¢ ordinary shares at full market price.

The EPS for the year ended December 31, 20X1 would be calculated as follows.

The number of ordinary shares in issue on January 1, 20X1 was 3 million, and 1 million were issued on October 1, 20X1. Thus, the time weighted average number of ordinary shares in issue for the year was

$$3,000,000 \times (9/12) + 4,000,000 \times (3/12) = 3,250,000$$

The earnings for the year attributable to the ordinary shareholders is $435,000 − 35,000 preference dividend = $400,000. Therefore,

$$\text{EPS} = (40,000,000/3,250,000)¢ \text{ per share} = 12.3¢ \text{ per share.}$$

A second situation is when the number of shares is increased by a capitalization or bonus issue, that is, the shares are issued for zero consideration, leading of course to no change in the resources available to the enterprise.

The standard (par. 20) logically requires that the weighted average number of ordinary shares outstanding during the period and for all periods presented should be adjusted for events, other than the conversion of potential ordinary shares, that have changed the number of ordinary shares outstanding, without a corresponding change in resources.

II. Using the same data as above, except that Fullmar issued the shares on October 1, 20X1 as bonus shares, EPS for 20X1 would be as follows.

We now have a capitalization issue, not a full market price issue, of shares and therefore we assume 4 million shares in issue for the whole of the year. (Note: This assumption would be the same no matter at what point during the year the capitalization was made.)

The number of shares in issue can also be calculated using the following:

$$3,000,000 \times (9/12) \times (4/3) + 4,000,000 \times (3/12)$$

(bonus factor)

$$= 3,000,000 + 1,000,000 = 4,000,000$$

$$\text{EPS} = (40,000,000/4,000,000) = 10\text{¢ per share}$$

The above calculation gives the EPS figure for the year 20X1. However, comparability (and paragraph 20 as quoted) requires the adjustment of all prior period EPS figures presented in the 20X1 financial statements.

If the EPS for the year ended December 31, 20X0 for Fullmar was 8¢, how would this figure have to be adjusted for the bonus issue for the 20XI financial statements?

The bonus issue represents a 1 for 3 share issue, that is, the number of shares has increased by one-third; therefore, we must have four-thirds times the original number of shares and the EPS will be multiplied by three-quarters, that is:

$$8\text{¢} \times (3/4) = 6\text{¢}$$

The third situation is where shares are issued partway through the year for consideration but at less than the full market price, as is likely to be the case with a "rights issue." In a rights issue, the exercise price is often less than the fair value of the shares. Therefore, such a rights issue includes a bonus element. The number of ordinary shares to be used in calculating basic earnings per share for all periods prior to the rights issue is the number of ordinary shares outstanding prior to the issue, multiplied by the following factor:

$$\frac{\text{Fair value per share immediately prior to the exercise of rights}}{\text{Theoretical ex-rights fair value per share}}$$

The theoretical ex-rights fair value per share is calculated by adding the aggregate fair value of the shares immediately prior to the exercise of the rights to the proceeds from the exercise of the rights and dividing by the number of shares outstanding after the exercise of the rights. Where the rights themselves are to be publicly traded separately from the shares prior to the exercise date, fair value for the purposes of this calculation is established at the close of the last day on which the shares are traded together with the rights.

Thus, a rights issue combines the characteristics of a capitalization issue and a full market price issue. New resources are passing into the business, so a higher earnings figure, related to these new resources, should be expected. At the same time, however, there is a bonus element in the new shares, which should be treated like a capitalization issue. To the extent that the rights issue provides new resources, that is, equates to an issue at full market price, we need to calculate the average number of shares weighted on a time basis. To the extent that the rights issue includes a discount or bonus element, we need to increase the number of shares deemed to have been in issue for the whole period.

III. Illustration of effect of a rights issue:

On June 30, 20X1, Trig has 6,000,000 $1 ordinary shares in issue with a current market value of $2 per share. On July 1, 20X1 Trig makes a four for six rights issue at $1.75, and all rights are taken up. Earnings for the year after tax and preference dividends are $81,579 and the previous year's EPS was declared as 9¢. Calculate the EPS figure that should be shown in the financial statements for the year ended December 31, 20X1.

We first need to calculate the theoretical ex-rights price of the shares:

Market value of
  equity before
  rights $=$ $600{,}000 \times \$2$ $= \$1{,}200{,}000$

Proceeds from
  rights issue $=$ $\underline{400{,}000 \times \$1.75} =$ $\underline{700{,}000}$
                        1,000,000 $\$1{,}900{,}000$

Theoretical ex-rights price = (1,900,000/1,000,000) = $1.90

Secondly, we calculate the weighted average number of shares:

$600{,}000 \times (1/2) \times (2/1.9) + 1{,}000{,}000 \times (1/2) = 815{,}789$
(time weighting)   (time weighting)

Therefore, EPS for year ending December 31, 20X1 = (8,157,900/ 815,789) = 10¢ per share

Third, we need to recalculate the previous year's EPS in order to make the comparative figure comparable with the current figure as reported.

$9 \times (1.9/2) = 8.55$¢ per share

A reduction has occurred in the previous year's EPS as we have retrospectively inserted the bonus element of the rights issue.

There are some exceptions to the general rule that shares are to be included in the weighted average number from the date consideration is receivable.

Ordinary shares issued as part of the purchase consideration of a business combination that is treated as an acquisition are included in the weighted average number of shares as of the date of the acquisition, because the acquirer incorporates the results of the operations of the acquiree into its income statement from the date of acquisition. Ordinary shares issued as part of a business combination that is treated as a uniting of interests are included in the calculation of the weighted average number of shares for all periods presented because the financial statements of the combined enterprise are prepared as if the combined entity had always existed. Therefore, the number of ordinary shares used for the calculation of basic earnings per share in a business combination that is a uniting of interests is the aggregate of the weighted average number of shares of the combined enterprises, adjusted to equivalent shares of the enterprise whose shares are outstanding after the combination.

Where ordinary shares are issued in partly paid form, these partly paid shares are treated as a fraction of an ordinary share (i.e., the proportion of payments received to date over the full subscription price) to the extent that they were entitled to participate in dividends relative to a fully paid ordinary share during the financial period.

Ordinary shares that are issuable upon the satisfaction of certain conditions (contingently issuable shares) are considered outstanding and included in the computation of basic earnings per share from the date when all necessary conditions have been satisfied. Outstanding ordinary shares that are contingently returnable (that is, subject to recall) are treated as contingently issuable shares.

Any different types of unusual share transaction should be treated in accordance with the substance of the situation and consistently with the principles outlined in the above text and illustrations. Further illustrations are given in IAS 33, paragraph 23.

DILUTED EARNINGS PER SHARE

Where there are securities existing at the year-end that will have a claim on equity earnings from some time in the future, then it is clear that at this future time the claim of each currently existing share will, other things equal, be reduced (or diluted). It is likely to be useful information to current shareholders and others to give them a picture of what the EPS would be if this dilution takes place. This is done by recalculating the current year's EPS as if the dilution had already occurred.

For the purpose of calculating diluted earnings per share, the net profit attributable to ordinary shareholders and the weighted average number of shares outstanding should be adjusted for the effects of all dilutive potential ordinary shares. This means that:

1. The net profit for the period attributable to ordinary shares is increased by the after-tax amount of dividends and interest recognized in the period in respect of the dilutive potential ordinary shares and adjusted for any other changes in income or expense that would result from the conversion of the dilutive potential ordinary shares, and

2. The weighted average number of ordinary shares outstanding is increased by the weighted average number of additional ordinary shares that would have been outstanding assuming the conversion of all dilutive potential ordinary shares.

Although this situation is by its nature more complicated than the calculation of basic earnings per share, the adjustments for the numerator, the earnings figure, are relatively straightforward, provided all aspects of the changes are considered. For example, if a convertible debenture exists, then the diluted EPS calculation requires the assumption that the conversion has already taken place. This assumption leads not only to an increase in the number of (assumed) shares, it also leads to the necessity to remove the interest charge on the debentures from the net profit calculation (after tax).

Formally, the net profit or loss attributable to ordinary shareholders is adjusted for the after-tax effect of the following (par. 26):

1. Any dividends on dilutive potential ordinary shares that have been deducted in arriving at the net profit attributable to ordinary shareholders as calculated for the basic EPS,

2. Interest recognized in the period for the dilutive potential ordinary shares, and

3. Any other changes in income or expense that would result from the conversion of the dilutive potential ordinary shares, such as bonus or profit-sharing schemes based on reported earnings.

Regarding the denominator in the diluted EPS calculation, that is, the number of shares, the number of ordinary shares should be the weighted average number of ordinary shares calculated as for the basic EPS, plus the weighted average number of ordinary shares that would be issued on the conversion of all the dilutive potential ordinary shares into ordinary shares. Dilutive potential ordinary shares should be deemed to have been converted into ordinary shares at the beginning of the period or, if later, the date of the issue of the potential ordinary shares. The calculation should be based on the terms of issue of the potential ordinary shares and should assume the most advantageous conversion rate or exercise price from the viewpoint of the holder.

Illustration of Calculation of Basic and Diluted EPS

The summarized income statement for the year ended 20X1 is as follows:

	$000	$000
Profit before taxation		1,000
Taxation		400
		600
Preference dividend	50	
Ordinary dividend	100	
		150
		450

The number of ordinary shares in issue is 2 million.

Calculate the basic EPS.

Basic EPS = (Profit after tax less preference dividend/Number of ordinary shares)

$$= (60{,}000{,}000 - 5{,}000{,}000)/2{,}000{,}000$$

$$= 27.5¢ \text{ per share}$$

Assume now that, in addition to the 2 million ordinary shares already in issue, however, there exists convertible loan stock of $500,000 bearing interest at 10%. This may be converted into ordinary shares between 20X3 and 20X6 at a rate of one ordinary share for every $2 of loan stock. Taxation is taken for convenience as 50%.

The fully diluted EPS is found as follows. If the conversion is fully completed, then there will be two effects:

1. The share capital will increase by 250,000 shares (1 share for every $2 of the $500,000 loans).
2. The profit after tax will increase by the interest on the loan no longer payable less the extra tax on this increase. The interest at 10% on $500,000 is $50,000, but the extra tax on this profit increase would be 50% of $50,000, that is, $25,000.

So profit after tax, and therefore "earnings," will increase by 50,000 – 25,000 = $25,000. Fully diluted EPS will therefore be:

$$(600{,}000 + 25{,}000 - 50{,}000)/(2{,}000{,}000 + 250{,}000)$$

$$= (57{,}500{,}000/2{,}250{,}000)¢$$

$$= 25.6¢ \text{ per share}$$

IAS 33 discusses a number of possible complications in some detail, in paragraphs 31–42.

As in the computation of basic earnings per share, ordinary shares whose issue is contingent upon the occurrence of certain events are considered outstanding and included in the computation of diluted earnings per share if the conditions have been met. Contingently issuable shares should be included as of the beginning of the period (or as of the date of the contingent share agreement, if later). If the conditions have not been met, the number of contingently issuable shares included in the diluted earnings per share computation is based on the number of shares that would be issuable if the end of the reporting period was the end of the contingency period (which, of course, could be zero).

If a group company other than the parent issues instruments that are potentially convertible into ordinary shares of the parent, then they should be included in the calculation of consolidated diluted EPS.

Options and other share purchase arrangements are dilutive when they would result in the issue of ordinary shares for less than fair value. The amount of the dilution is fair value less the issue price. Fair value for this purpose is calculated on the basis of the average price of the ordinary shares during the period. For the purpose of calculating diluted earnings per share, an enterprise should assume the exercise of dilutive options and other dilutive potential ordinary shares of the enterprise. The assumed proceeds from these issues should be considered to have been received from the issue of shares at fair value. The difference between the number of shares issued and the number of shares that would have been issued at fair value should be treated as an issue of ordinary shares for no consideration. Such ordinary shares generate no proceeds and have no effect on the net profit attributable to ordinary shares outstanding. Therefore, such shares are dilutive, and they are added to the number of ordinary shares outstanding in the computation of diluted earnings per share.

The illustration of the calculation of diluted EPS given above showed the common situation where, compared with the calculation of basic EPS, both the numerator and the denominator are increased. The effect in that case was a lower EPS figure, and indeed that is what the word *diluted* indicates. It is clearly possible, however, depending on the relative effect of the adjustments to numerator and denominator, for the effects to be antidilutive. Potential ordinary shares are antidilutive when their conversion to ordinary shares would increase earnings per share from continuing ordinary operations or decrease loss per share from continuing ordinary operations. The effects of antidilutive potential ordinary shares are ignored in calculating diluted earnings per share.

In considering whether potential ordinary shares are dilutive or antidilutive, each issue or series of potential ordinary shares is considered separately rather than in aggregate. The sequence in which potential ordinary shares is considered may affect whether or not they are dilutive. Therefore, in order to maximize the dilution of basic earnings per share, each issue or series of potential ordinary shares is considered in sequence from the most dilutive to the least dilutive.

It is important to note that, while EPS is based on net profit or loss, the determination of whether potential ordinary shares are dilutive or antidilutive is based on net profit from continuing operations. The net profit from continuing ordinary activities is the net profit from ordinary activities (as defined in IAS 8, "Net Profit or Loss for the Period, Fundamental Errors and Changes in Accounting Policies") after deducting preference dividends and after excluding items relating to discontinued operations; therefore, it excludes extraordinary items and the effects of changes in accounting policies and of corrections of fundamental errors.

The inclusion of potential ordinary shares in the denominator of a diluted EPS calculation when the enterprise has a loss from continuing ordinary activities as defined above would automatically have an antidilutive effect (as it would decrease loss per share). Such shares would therefore be ignored for calculating diluted EPS, even if the net profit (as opposed to net profit from continuing ordinary activities) is positive.

Potential ordinary shares are weighted for the period they were outstanding. Potential ordinary shares that were canceled or allowed to lapse during the reporting period are included in the computation of diluted earnings per share only for the portion of the period during which they were outstanding. Potential ordinary shares that have been converted into ordinary shares during the reporting period are included in the calculation of diluted earnings per share from the beginning of the period to the date of conversion; from the date of conversion, the resulting ordinary shares are included in both basic and diluted earnings per share.

SIC-24

SIC-24, "Earnings per Share—Financial Instruments and Other Contracts that May Be Settled in Shares," is effective from December 1, 2000. This SIC clarifies the application of the IAS 33 definition of potential ordinary shares, in the context of dilution, to the increasingly common situation of existing financial instruments or other contracts that may be settled by the reporting enterprise, either by payment in financial assets or by payment in the form of a transfer of ordinary shares in the reporting enterprise from that enterprise to the holder of the instrument. The SIC states that it makes no difference whether optionality is at the choice of the issuer or the holder.

Noting that a potential ordinary share is defined as a financial instrument or other contract that *may* entitle its holder to ordinary shares, SIC-24 confirms that all such financial instruments are potential ordinary shares. This means that if they are dilutive, they are to be included in the calculation of diluted EPS.

RESTATEMENT

As discussed above in relation to IAS 33 paragraph 20, and as shown in Illustration II above, if the number of ordinary or potential ordinary shares outstanding increases as a result of a capitalization or bonus issue or share split or decreases as a result of a reverse share split, the calculation of basic and diluted earnings per share for all periods presented should be adjusted retrospectively. If these changes occur after the balance sheet date but before issue of the financial statements, the per share calculations for those and any prior period financial statements presented should be based on the new number of shares. When per share calculations reflect such changes in the number of shares, that fact should be disclosed. In addition, basic and diluted earnings per share of all periods presented should be adjusted for (par. 43):

1. The effects of fundamental errors, and adjustments resulting from changes in accounting policies, dealt with in accordance with the benchmark treatment in IAS 8

2. The effects of a business combination that is a uniting of interests

Restatement of prior period diluted EPS to reflect a change in assumptions used is not allowed. Disclosure is "encouraged" of details of ordinary share transactions or potential ordinary share transactions that occur after the balance sheet date when nondisclosure "would" affect the ability of financial statement users to make "proper evaluations and decisions." Because the reported EPS (whether basic or diluted), relates to the reporting period, such events should not actually be incorporated in its calculation.

PRESENTATION AND DISCLOSURE

Separate EPS presentation is required, for each class of ordinary shares that has a different right to share in the net profit of the period, on the face of the income statement. Basic and diluted EPS should both be presented, with equal prominence, for all periods included, whether the EPS figures are positive or negative.

An enterprise may wish to disclose more information than IAS 33, "Earnings per Share," requires. Such information may help users to evaluate the performance of the enterprise and may take the form of per share amounts for various components of net profit. Such disclosures are encouraged. When such amounts are disclosed, however, the denominators are calculated in accordance with IAS 33 in order to ensure the comparability of the per share amounts disclosed.

Any such additional EPS calculations must not be presented with greater prominence than the basic and diluted EPS figures as calculated in accordance with IAS 33. If a component of net profit is used that is not reported as a line item in the income statement, a reconciliation should be provided between the component used and a line item that is reported in the income statement.

CHAPTER 13
EMPLOYEE BENEFITS

CONTENTS

OVERVIEW

Employee benefits take a variety of forms. Many of them are paid or provided concomitant with, or very shortly after, the provision of the service by the employee, and no particular accounting problems arise. However, important elements of the employee benefit package are likely to be significantly deferred—possibly by up to 50 years or more, and the treatment of pension rights is particularly problematic.

Many, though not all, pension plans are defined benefit plans, meaning that the amount the employee will be entitled to receive is predetermined (by formula, not usually by actual amount). This means that the employing enterprise is likely to be liable to make up any shortfall necessary to ensure that all relevant (ex-) employees can be fully provided for according to their rights. In other words, the risks, which are considerable given the inherent uncertainty of planning and investing decades in advance, fall on the employer. These risks must be estimated, and provided for, by the employer.

IAS GAAP in this area is provided in IAS 19, "Employee Benefits," issued in a revised—and significantly altered—form in 1998, effective from January 1, 1999, and revised again in 2000, effective from January 1, 2001. A separate standard, IAS 26, "Accounting and Reporting by Retirement Benefit Plans," deals with reporting by pension funds themselves.

BACKGROUND

Employment is based on an exchange agreement. The employee agrees to provide services for the employer; in exchange, the employer agrees to provide a current wage, a pension benefit, and possibly other benefits. Although pension benefits and some other benefits are not paid currently and may not be due for many years, they represent deferred compensation that must be accounted for as part of the employee's total compensation package. The deferred payments relate to current employment and must therefore be accounted for in the current period.

The major difficulties of accounting for employee benefits relate to the deferred elements. The IASC has had four relevant standards over the years (all numbered IAS 19). The first two, approved in 1983 and 1993, both had titles concerning "retirement benefit costs." The third, and also the current IAS 19 effective from January 1, 2001 have the broader title of this chapter. IAS 19 identifies five categories of employee benefits, as follows:

1. Short-term employee benefits, such as wages, salaries, and social security contributions, paid annual leave and paid sick leave, profit sharing and bonuses (if payable within 12 months of the end of the period), and nonmonetary benefits (such as medical care, housing, cars, and free or subsidized goods or services) for current employees;

2. Postemployment benefits such as pensions, other retirement benefits, postemployment life insurance, and postemployment medical care;

3. Other long-term employee benefits, including long-service leave or sabbatical leave, jubilee or other long-service benefits, long-term disability benefits, and, if they are payable 12 months or more after the end of the period, profit sharing, bonuses, and deferred compensation;

4. Termination benefits; and

5. Equity compensation benefits.

Item 2 takes up much of the length of the standard. Pension plans can take a variety of different forms; they can be either funded or unfunded, defined contribution or defined benefit.

An unfunded pension plan is one where the employer business itself undertakes to pay the pensions directly from its own resources as they fall due. With a funded plan, resources are accumulated in a separate legal entity (i.e., there is a separate fund). This separate fund may be a unique creation for the one employer or it may be operated by a specialist assurance company running many such plans. The two types of plan have obvious differences in terms of financial management and in terms of the bookkeeping entries. With a funded plan, money leaves the employer over the years of the employment and goes into the external fund. With an unfunded plan, no pension money leaves the employer at all until the employment has ceased and the actual pension begins to be paid.

Another distinction between different types of pension plans relates to the way in which the legal obligations under the plan are defined. In a defined contribution plan, the employer will normally discharge its obligation by making agreed contributions to a pension plan and the benefits paid will depend upon the funds available from these contributions and investment earnings thereon. The cost to the employer can, therefore, be measured with reasonable certainty.

In a defined benefit plan, however, the benefits to be paid will usually depend upon either the average pay of the employee during his or her career or, more typically, the final pay of the employee. In these circumstances, it is impossible to be certain in advance that the contributions to the pension plan, together with the investment return thereon, will equal the benefits to be paid. The employer may have a legal obligation to provide any unforeseen shortfalls in funds or, if not, may find it necessary to meet the shortfall in the interests of maintaining good employee relations. Conversely, if a surplus arises, the employer may be entitled to a refund of, or reduction in, contributions paid or payable into the pension plan. Thus, in this type of plan the employer's commitment is generally more open than with defined contribution plans, and the final cost is subject to considerable uncertainty.

There are no major differences of principle between IAS GAAP and U.S. GAAP. IAS GAAP, however, has no particular measurement requirement for equity (stock) compensation plans.

SCOPE AND DEFINITIONS

The scope of IAS 19 is wide. It should be applied by all employers in accounting for all employee benefits. It does not, however, deal with the preparation of financial reports by the actual employee benefit plans themselves. This highly specialized issue is covered by IAS 26, "Accounting and Reporting by Retirement Benefit Plans" (see the Appendix to this chapter).

The standard, as befits the complexity of the area and the variety of different types of employee benefit and pension plan likely to be found, finds it necessary to give a large number of definitions. Most are reasonably comprehensible, but all need to be clearly understood in order to apply the standard.

- *Employee benefits* are all forms of consideration given by an enterprise in exchange for service rendered by employees.
- *Short-term employee benefits* are employee benefits (other than termination benefits and equity compensation benefits) that fall due wholly within 12 months after the end of the period in which the employees render the related service.
- *Postemployment benefits* are employee benefits (other than termination benefits and equity compensation benefits) that are payable after the completion of employment.
- *Postemployment benefit plans* are formal or informal arrangements under which an enterprise provides postemployment benefits for one or more employees.
- *Defined contribution plans* are postemployment benefit plans under which an enterprise pays fixed contributions into a separate entity (a fund) and will have no legal or constructive obligation to pay further contributions if the fund does not hold sufficient assets to pay all employee benefits relating to employee service in the current and prior periods.
- *Defined benefit plans* are postemployment benefit plans other than defined contribution plans.
- *Multi-employer plans* are defined contribution plans (other than state plans) or defined benefit plans (other than state plans) that:
  (a) pool the assets contributed by various enterprises that are not under common control; and
  (b) use those assets to provide benefits to employees of more than one enterprise, on the basis that contribution and benefit levels are determined without regard to the identity of the enterprise that employs the employees concerned.
- *Other long-term employee benefits* are employee benefits (other than postemployment benefits, termination benefits, and equity compensation benefits) that do not fall due wholly within 12 months after the end of the period in which the employees render the related service.
- *Termination benefits* are employee benefits payable as a result of either:
  (a) an enterprise's decision to terminate an employee's employment before the normal retirement date, or
  (b) an employee's decision to accept voluntary redundancy in exchange for those benefits.

- *Equity compensation benefits* are employee benefits under which either:

  (a) employers are entitled to receive equity financial instruments issued by the enterprise (or its parent), or

  (b) the amount of the enterprise's obligation to employees depends on the future price of equity financial instruments issued by the enterprise.

- *Equity compensation plans* are formal or informal arrangements under which an enterprise provides equity compensation benefits for one or more employees.

- *Vested* employee benefits are employee benefits that are not conditional on future employment.

- The *present value of a defined benefit obligation* is the present value, without deducting any plan assets, of expected future payments required to settle the obligation resulting from employee service in the current and prior periods.

- *Current service cost* is the increase in the present value of the defined benefit obligation resulting from employee service in the current period.

- *Interest cost* is the increase during a period in the present value of a defined benefit obligation that arises because the benefits are one period closer to settlement.

- *Plan assets* comprise:

  (a) assets held by a long-term employee benefit fund; and

  (b) qualifying insurance policies.

- *Assets held by a long-term employee benefit fund* are assets (other than non-transferable financial instruments issued by the reporting enterprise) that:

  (a) are held by an entity (a fund) that is legally separate from the reporting enterprise and exists solely to pay or fund employee benefits; and

  (b) are available to be used only to pay or fund employee benefits, are not available to the reporting enterprise's own creditors (even in bankruptcy), and cannot be returned to the reporting enterprise, unless either:

    (i) the remaining assets of the fund are sufficient to meet all the related employee benefit obligations of the plan or the reporting enterprise, or

    (ii) the assets are returned to the reporting enterprise to reimburse it for the employee benefits already paid.

- *A qualifying insurance policy* is an insurance policy issued by an insurer that is not a related party (as defined in IAS 24, "Related

Party Disclosures") of the reporting enterprise, if the proceeds of the policy:

(a) can be used only to pay or fund employee benefits under a defined benefit plan;

(b) are not available to the reporting enterprise's own credits (even in bankruptcy) and cannot be paid to the reporting enterprise, unless either:

  (i) the proceeds represent surplus assets that are not needed for the policy to meet all the related employee benefit obligations, or

  (ii) the proceeds are returned to the reporting enterprise to reimburse it for employee benefits already paid.

- *Fair value* is the amount for which an asset could be exchanged or a liability settled between knowledgeable, willing parties in an arm's-length transaction.

- The *return on plan assets* is interest, dividends, and other revenue derived from the plan assets, together with realized and unrealized gains or losses on the plan assets, less any costs of administering the plan and less any tax payable by the plan itself.

- *Actuarial gains and losses* comprise:

  (a) experience adjustments (the effects of differences between the previous actuarial assumptions and what has actually occurred), and

  (b) the effects of changes in actuarial assumptions.

- *Past service cost* is the increase in the present value of the defined benefit obligation for employee service in prior periods, resulting in the current period from the introduction of, or changes to, postemployment benefits or other long-term employee benefits. Past service cost may be either positive (where benefits are introduced or improved) or negative (where existing benefits are reduced).

SHORT-TERM EMPLOYEE BENEFITS

The treatment of short-term employee benefits is straightforward. Paragraph 10 requires that where an employee has rendered service to an enterprise during an accounting period, the enterprise should recognize the undiscounted amount of short-term employee benefits expected to be paid in exchange for that service:

1. As a liability (accrued expense), after deducting any amount already paid, and

2. As an expense, unless another International Accounting Standard requires or permits the inclusion of the benefits in the cost of an asset (see, for example, IAS 2, "Inventories," Chapter 23, and IAS 16, "Property, Plant, and Equipment," Chapter 27).

There are no specific disclosure requirements in this respect in IAS 19. Other standards may be relevant, such as the requirement to show employee benefits for key management personnel under IAS 24, "Related Party Disclosures" (see Chapter 29) and the general requirement to disclose staff costs under IAS 1, "Presentation of Financial Statements" (see Chapter 3).

The standard addresses two particular applications, short-term compensated absences and profit sharing and bonus plans. In the former case, IAS 19 gives an illustration that is worthy of comment.

An enterprise has 100 employees, who are each entitled to 5 working days of paid sick leave for each year. Unused sick leave may be carried forward for one calendar year. Sick leave is taken first out of the current year's entitlement and then out of any balance brought forward from the previous year (a LIFO basis). At December 31, 20X1, the average unused entitlement is 2 days per employee. The enterprise expects, based on past experience, that 92 employees will take no more than 5 days of paid sick leave in 20X2 and that the remaining 8 employees will take an average of 6-1/2 days each.

The enterprise expects that it will pay an additional 12 days of sick pay as a result of the unused entitlement that has accumulated at December 31, 20X1 (1-1/2 days each, for 8 employees). Therefore, the enterprise recognizes a liability equal to 12 days of sick pay.

> **OBSERVATION:** The creation of this liability of 12 days of sick pay creates an expense, in the year to December 31, 20X1, additional to that already recorded. There is, of course, a much greater "entitlement," carried forward into 20X2, giving a total of 2 days of sick pay for each of the 100 employees. In effect, this additional entitlement is valued at nil because, on the basis of past experience, it is not expected to be taken up. If the liability, as calculated above, is obviously going to be immaterial, then IAS 19 notes (par. 15) that the calculations will not need to be made.

The second issue addressed specifically by IAS 19 is the treatment of profit sharing and bonus plans. An enterprise should recognize the expected cost of profit sharing and bonus payments as a short-term employee benefit when, and only when:

1. The enterprise has a present legal or constructive obligation to make such payments as a result of past events, and

2. A reliable estimate of the obligation can be made.

A present obligation exists when, and only when, the enterprise has no realistic alternative but to make the payments.

A problem arises if the employees are entitled to a payment in the future related to the current year's profits, but only if they remain with the enterprise for a specified period. Such plans create a constructive obligation as employees render service that increases the amount to be paid if they remain in service until the end of the specified period. The measurement of such constructive obligations reflects the possibility that some employees may leave without receiving profit sharing payments, that is, it is likely to be measured at less than the entire theoretical entitlement. Note that if a "reliable estimate" of the obligation cannot be made, then no provision can be recognized at all.

POSTEMPLOYMENT BENEFITS

We have already discussed the important distinction between defined contribution plans and defined benefit plans, and given the formal IAS 19 definitions. The major distinction, as the names accurately indicate, is that with a defined contribution plan the employer's obligations are fixed, and the employee takes the risk of the eventual pension being inadequate; with a defined benefit plan, the eventual pension payments are fixed (by formula, not necessarily by amount), and the employer takes the risk of the pension fund being inadequate and is responsible for making up any shortfall.

IAS 19 goes into some length (pars. 29–42) to "explain" the distinction between defined contribution plans and defined benefit plans in the context of multi-employer plans, state plans, and insured benefits.

With a multi-employer plan that is a defined benefit plan, the enterprise should account for its proportionate share of the defined benefit obligation, plan assets, and cost associated with the plan in the same way as for any other defined benefit plan. If sufficient information is not available to use defined benefit accounting for a multi-employer plan that is a defined benefit plan, an enterprise should account for the plan as if it were a defined contribution plan and disclose:

1. The fact that the plan is a defined benefit plan, and
2. The reason why sufficient information is not available to enable the enterprise to account for the plan as a defined benefit plan.

To the extent that a surplus or deficit in the plan may affect the amount of future contributions, additional disclosure is required of:

1. Any available information about that surplus or deficit,

2. The basis used to determine that surplus or deficit, and

3. The implications, if any, for the enterprise.

> ☛ **PRACTICE POINTER:** With a multi-employer defined benefit plan, an enterprise may in certain circumstances incur an obligation in respect of other employers involved within the plan. This could create a contingent liability (see IAS 37, "Provisions, Contingent Liabilities, and Contingent Assets," Chapter 28).

State plans are established by legislation to cover all enterprises (or all enterprises in a particular category, for example, a specific industry) and are operated by national or local government or by another body (for example, an autonomous agency created specifically for this purpose) that is not subject to control or influence by the reporting enterprise.

Despite the fact that the IASC definition of multi-employer plans (given above) explicitly excludes state plans, IAS 19 requires that an enterprise account for a state plan in the same way as for a multi-employer plan. The standard notes that state plans are usually defined contribution plans.

An enterprise may fund a postemployment benefit plan indirectly by means of the regular payment of insurance premiums. In such circumstances, the enterprise should treat such a plan as a defined contribution plan unless the enterprise will have (either directly or indirectly through the plan) a legal or constructive obligation to either:

1. Pay the employee benefits directly when they fall due, or

2. Pay further contributions if the insurer does not pay all future employee benefits relating to employee service in the current and prior periods.

If the enterprise retains such a legal or constructive obligation, the enterprise should treat the plan as a defined benefit plan. Whether or not there is a legal or constructive obligation is a question of fact.

DEFINED CONTRIBUTION PLANS

As we have implied above, there are no major difficulties involved in measuring the obligation or the expense as far as the reporting employer enterprise is concerned. The enterprise recognizes the contribution payable to the plan in relation to service rendered to the enterprise by an employee during the period as a liability, net of payments already made (which could lead to a net asset) and as an expense, unless another International Accounting Standard requires or permits the inclusion of the contribution in the cost of an asset (see, for example, IAS 2, "Inventories" (Chapter 23) and IAS 16, "Property, Plant, and Equipment" (Chapter 27). Where contributions to a defined contribution plan do not fall due wholly within 12 months after the end of the period in which the employees render the related service, they should be discounted as described below. The expense should be disclosed separately.

DEFINED BENEFIT PLANS

Accounting for defined benefit plans is much more complex because actuarial assumptions are required to measure the obligation and the expense, and there is a possibility of actuarial gains and losses. The obligations are measured on a discounted basis because they may be settled many years after the employees render the related service. IAS 19 takes no fewer than 78 paragraphs to cover this area. We attempt to provide a thorough coverage of the important aspects, without becoming too immersed in the detail.

In summary, the following steps are typically necessary in accounting by an enterprise for each defined benefit plan.

- Using actuarial techniques to make a reliable estimate of the amount of benefit that employees have earned in return for their service in the current and prior periods. This requires an enterprise to determine how much benefit is attributable to the current and prior periods and to make estimates (actuarial assumptions) about demographic variables (such as employee turnover and mortality) and financial variables (such as future increases in salaries and medical costs) that will influence the cost of the benefit.

- Discounting that benefit using the projected unit credit method (described below) in order to determine the present value of the defined benefit obligation and the current service cost.

- Determining the total amount of actuarial gains and losses and the amount of those actuarial gains and losses that should be recognized.

- Where a plan has been introduced or changed, determining the resulting past service cost.

- Determining the fair value of any plan assets.

- Where a plan has been curtailed or settled, determining the resulting gain or loss.

The amount recognized in the balance sheet as a defined benefit liability should be the net total of the following amounts (par. 54):

1. The present value of the defined benefit obligation (both legal and constructive) at the balance sheet date,

2. Plus any actuarial gains (less any actuarial losses) not recognized because of the "corridor" treatment set out below,

3. Minus any past service cost not yet recognized,

4. Minus the fair value at the balance sheet date of plan assets (if any) out of which the obligations are to be settled directly.

The present value of the defined benefit obligation is the present value of the total obligation less the fair value of plan assets (if any). Both these amounts should be determined regularly so that the proper estimates at balance sheet date are not materially departed from. The involvement of a qualified actuary is "encouraged."

One of the purposes of the 2000 revision of IAS 19 was to clarify the treatment of insurance policies. The definition of asset plans, given earlier in this chapter, has been revised to make it clear that qualifying insurance policies, as defined, *are* plan assets for all purposes, as under them the insurer will pay some or all of the defined benefit obligation.

When an insurance policy is not "qualifying," then it is not a plan asset. However, it is still an asset, and the enterprise recognizes its rights to reimbursement under the insurance policy as a separate asset, and not as a deduction in calculating the net defined benefit liability under paragraph 54. More formally, IAS 19 now states (par. 104A) that when, and only when, it is virtually certain that another party will reimburse some or all of the expenditure required to settle a defined benefit obligation, an enterprise should recognize its right to reimburse as a separate entity. The enterprise should measure the asset at fair value. In all other respects, an enterprise should treat that asset in the same way as plan assets. In the income statement, the expense relating to a defined benefit play may be presented net of the amount recognized for a reimbursement.

In essence, therefore, qualifying insurance policies are valued at fair value and treated as a deduction in calculating the net defined benefit liability under paragraph 54, through their inclusion in plan assets. Non-qualifying insurance policies are valued at fair value and treated separately as assets.

The amount determined under paragraph 54 may be negative. An enterprise should measure the resulting asset at the lower of:

1. The amount determined under paragraph 54.

2. The net total of

    (a) any unrecognized actuarial losses and past service cost, and

(b) the present value of any economic benefits available in the form of refunds from the plan or reductions in future contributions to the plan.

In the income statement, the enterprise should recognize the net total of the following amounts as expense (or income), except to the extent that another International Accounting Standard requires or permits their inclusion in the cost of an asset:

1. Current service cost,
2. Interest cost,
3. The expected return on any plan assets,
4. Actuarial gains and losses, to the extent that they are recognized,
5. Past service cost, to the extent required,
6. The effect of any curtailments or settlements.

The enterprise needs to calculate the present value of its defined benefit obligations. The increase in this figure over that of the previous year gives the current service cost to the extent that the increase results from employee service in the current period and gives the past service cost to the extent that it results from employee service in past periods (this increase—or decrease—being caused by changes in eventual benefit rights).

The method of calculation required by IAS 19 is the projected unit credit method. Each period of service increases the eventual benefit (by a "unit"), and the total obligation builds up period by period. The detailed procedure is much more effectively illustrated than described. The following example shows the general principles.

Illustration of Projected Unit Credit Method

A lump sum benefit is payable on termination of service and equal to 1% of final salary for each year of service. The salary in year 1 is 10,000 and is assumed to increase at 7% (compound) each year. The discount rate used is 10% per annum. The following table shows how the obligation builds up for an employee who is expected to leave at the end of year 5, assuming that there are no changes in actuarial assumptions.

Year	1	2	3	4	5
Benefit attributed to:					
Prior years	0	131	262	393	524
Current year (1% of final salary)	131	131	131	131	131
Current and prior years	131	262	393	524	655

Year	1	2	3	4	5
Opening obligation	—	89	196	324	476
Interest cost at 10%	—	9	20	33	48
Current service cost	89	98	108	119	131
Closing obligation	89	196	324	476	655

Note:

1. The opening obligation is the present value of benefit attributed to prior years.
2. The current service cost is the present value of benefit attributed to the current year (i.e., discounted at 10% per annum).
3. The closing obligation is the present value of benefit attributed to current and prior years.

The calculations are likely to be significantly affected by actuarial assumptions and by the discount rate used. The actuarial assumptions are largely outside the accounting domain. They must be unbiased and mutually compatible. Regarding the discount rate, however, IAS 19 is specific (par. 78). The rate used to discount postemployment benefit obligations (both funded and unfunded) should be determined by reference to market yields at the balance sheet date on high quality corporate bonds. In countries where there is no deep market in such bonds, the market yields (at the balance sheet date) on government bonds should be used. The currency and term of the corporate bonds or government bonds should be consistent with the currency and estimated term of the postemployment benefit obligations.

> **OBSERVATION:** There has been considerable debate and controversy over the appropriate discount rate to use. A number of commentators on the discussions and the exposure draft leading up to the standard argued that the discount rate used should reflect the expected long-term return on plan assets. The IASC has rejected this argument, essentially on the grounds that the measurement of an obligation should be independent of the measurement of the plan assets that happen to be held by a plan. The IASC position seems correct in principle.

The issue of whether, when, and how to recognize actuarial gains and losses is another aspect that has been extremely troublesome to the IASC (and to other regulatory authorities). The formal requirements (pars. 92 and 93) are convoluted and are quoted here verbatim.

> In measuring its defined benefit liability under paragraph 54, an enterprise should recognize a portion of its actuarial gains and losses as income or expense if the net cumulative unrecognized

actuarial gains and losses at the end of the previous reporting period exceeded the greater of:

1. 10% of the present value of the defined benefit obligation at that date (before deducting plan assets); and
2. 10% of the fair value of any plan assets at that date.

These limits should be calculated and applied separately for each defined benefit plan.

The portion of actuarial gains and losses to be recognized for each defined benefit plan is the excess determined as above, divided by the expected average remaining working lives of the employees participating in that plan. There is a 10% "corridor" inside which nothing need be recognized. However, an enterprise may adopt any systematic method that results in faster recognition of actuarial gains and losses, provided that the same basis is applied to both gains and losses and the basis is applied consistently from period to period. An enterprise may apply such systematic methods to actuarial gains and losses even if they fall within the limits specified above. Thus, if the net cumulative unrecognized actuarial gains at the end of the previous reporting period are 140, the present value of the defined benefit obligation is 1000, the fair value of plan assets is 900, and the expected average remaining working lives of the participating employees is 10 years, then the minimum actuarial gain to be recognized as income in the year is:

$$[140 - (10\% \times 1000)] \times 10\% = 4$$

The enterprise can choose any faster method of income (and expense) recognition up to, and including, immediate recognition of all actuarial gains and losses, provided of course that the chosen method is used consistently.

> **OBSERVATION:** This matter is discussed at some length in the standard and in an explanatory appendix issued with the standard. It is clear that a good deal of pragmatic compromise has taken place. The point of the 10% "corridor" seems to be to accept that the estimates of postemployment benefit obligations are at best approximate shots at an uncertain target, and that to alter reported earnings directly by the effects of these uncertainties might be misleading. If this is accepted (and the 10% figure is arbitrary, apparently selected for consistency with U.S. GAAP— itself equally arbitrary, of course), it seems less clear why *all* the gains or losses outside this "corridor" should not be recognized immediately. This does seem like income smoothing on a fairly heroic scale.
>
> A further problem is the treatment of the unrecognized actuarial gain or loss. This has to appear on the balance sheet. In the

case of the example given immediately above, the unrecognized gain of 140 – 4 = 136 (probably combined with further adjustments relating to the current reporting year) will appear on the balance sheet as a liability. But according to the IASC definition of a liability in the Framework (see Chapter 2), the 136 simply is not a liability, as the above-mentioned explanatory appendix explicitly confirms. Similarly, an unrecognized loss, recorded as an asset, fails to meet the Framework definition of asset.

It is made clear that the IASC Board prefers, in principle, a requirement to recognize the complete actuarial gains and losses immediately as income or expense in each and every annual financial statement but considered that some important issues remained to be resolved. An expectation of a decision to "revisit the treatment of actuarial gains and losses" is signaled (appendix, par. 41). As we write, there are signs of a change in U.S. thinking toward immediate recognition.

As already explained, past service cost arises when an enterprise introduces a defined benefit plan or changes the benefits payable under an existing defined benefit plan. Such changes are argued to be in return for employee service over the period until the benefits concerned are vested (i.e., are no longer conditional on future employment). Therefore, past service cost is recognized over that period, up to the vesting date, regardless of the fact that the cost refers to employee service in previous periods. Past service cost is measured as the change in the liability resulting from the amendment. To the extent that the benefits are already vested immediately following the introduction of, or changes to, a defined benefit plan, an enterprise should recognize past service cost immediately. Thus, if employees have unequivocal pension rights after 3 years of service, all past service costs arising in relation to employees who have served their 3-year period are an immediate expense. If the average period until vesting for certain employees is 2 years, then past service costs in relation to them are expensed on a straight-line basis over the following 2 years.

In principle, the fair value of plan assets is the market value. When no market price is available, the fair value of plan assets is estimated, for example, by discounting expected future cash flows by using a discount rate that reflects both the risk associated with the plan assets and the maturity or expected disposal date of those assets (or, if they have no maturity, the expected period until the settlement of the related obligation).

Plan assets exclude unpaid contributions due from the reporting enterprise to the fund, as well as any nontransferable financial instruments issued by the enterprise and held by the fund. Where plan assets include insurance policies that exactly match the amount and timing of some or all of the benefits payable under the plan, the plan's rights under those insurance policies are measured at the same amount as the related obligations.

The expected return on plan assets is based on market expectations, at the beginning of the period, for returns over the entire life of the related obligation. The expected return on plan assets reflects changes in the fair value of plan assets held during the period as a result of actual contributions paid into the fund and actual benefits paid out of the fund.

The difference between the expected return on plan assets and the actual return on plan assets is an actuarial gain or loss. It is included with the actuarial gains and losses on the defined benefit obligation in determining the net amount that is compared with the limits of the 10% "corridor" specified in paragraph 92.

In a business combination that is an acquisition, an enterprise recognizes assets and liabilities arising from postemployment benefits at the present value of the obligation less the fair value of any plan assets. The present value of the obligation includes all of the following, even if the acquiree had not yet recognized them at the date of the acquisition:

1. Actuarial gains and losses that arose before the date of the acquisition (whether or not they fell inside the 10% "corridor"),

2. Past service cost that arose from benefit changes, or the introduction of a plan, before the date of the acquisition, and

3. Amounts that, under the transitional provisions of IAS 19, the acquiree had not recognized.

An enterprise should recognize gains or losses on the curtailment or settlement of a defined benefit plan when the curtailment or settlement occurs. A curtailment occurs when the enterprise is committed to a material reduction in the scope of the plan, either by reducing the number of employees included, or by reducing the benefits per employee. A settlement occurs when an enterprise enters into a transaction that eliminates all further legal or constructive obligation for part or all of the benefits provided under a defined benefit plan, for example, when a lump-sum cash payment is made to, or on behalf of, plan participants in exchange for their rights to receive specified postemployment benefits.

Presentation and disclosure requirements regarding the treatment of defined benefit plans are extensive, and are as follows.

An enterprise should offset an asset relating to one plan against a liability relating to another plan when, and only when, the enterprise:

1. Has a legally enforceable right to use a surplus in one plan to settle obligations under the other plan; and

2. Intends either to settle the obligations on a net basis, or to realize the surplus in one plan and settle its obligation under the other plan simultaneously.

An enterprise should disclose the following information about defined benefit plans:

1. The enterprise's accounting policy for recognizing actuarial gains and losses.
2. A general description of the type of plan.
3. A reconciliation of the assets and liabilities recognized in the balance sheet, showing at least:
    (a) the present value at the balance sheet date of defined benefit obligations that are wholly unfunded;
    (b) the present value (before deducting the fair value of plan assets) at the balance sheet date of defined benefit obligations that are wholly or partly funded;
    (c) the fair value of any plan assets at the balance sheet date;
    (d) the net actuarial gains or losses not recognized in the balance sheet;
    (e) the past service cost not yet recognized in the balance sheet;
    (f) any amount not recognized as an asset;
    (g) the fair value at the balance sheet date of any reimbursement right recognized as an asset; and
    (h) the other amounts recognized in the balance sheet.
4. The amounts included in the fair value of plan assets for:
    (a) each category of the reporting enterprise's own financial instruments; and
    (b) any property occupied by, or other assets used by, the reporting enterprise.
5. A reconciliation showing the movements during the period in the net liability (or asset) recognized in the balance sheet.
6. The total expense recognized in the income statement for each of the following, and the line item(s) of the income statement in which they are included:
    (a) current service cost;
    (b) interest cost;
    (c) expected return on plan assets;
    (d) expected return on any reimbursements recognized as an asset;
    (e) actuarial gains and losses;
    (f) past service cost; and
    (g) the effect of any curtailment or settlement.

7. The actual return on plan assets as well as the actual return on any reimbursement right recognized as an asset.

8. The principal actuarial assumptions used as at the balance sheet date, including, where applicable:

   (a) the discount rates;

   (b) the expected rates of return on any plan assets for the periods presented in the financial statements;

   (c) the expected rates of return for the periods presented in the financial statements on any reimbursement right recognized as an asset;

   (d) the expected rates of salary increases (and of changes in an index or other variable specified in the formal or constructive terms of a plan as the basis for future benefit increases);

   (e) medical cost trend rates; and

   (f) any other material actuarial assumptions used.

An enterprise should disclose each actuarial assumption in absolute terms (for example as an absolute percentage) and not just as a margin between different percentages or other variables.

ACCOUNTING FOR OTHER LONG-TERM EMPLOYEE BENEFITS

A variety of items could be included under this heading, such as bonuses or profit-sharing payments payable 12 months or more after the period of the related service, or long-service or sabbatical leave. There is usually little uncertainty of calculation, and little or no past service cost. For these reasons, actuarial gains and losses are recognized immediately and no "corridor" is applied, and all past service cost is recognized immediately.

The amount recognized as a liability for other long-term employee benefits should be the net total of the present value of the defined benefit obligation at the balance sheet date minus the fair value at the balance sheet date of plan assets (if any) out of which the obligations are to be settled directly.

TERMINATION BENEFITS

The point about termination, as the definition given earlier in the chapter makes clear, is that it is not related to employee service. Indeed, it arises because of a cessation of employee service. It follows that termination benefits do not provide an enterprise with future economic benefits and they must therefore be recognized as an expense immediately.

The IASC, however, is obviously as concerned to prevent the creation of excessive provisions as to prevent the nonreporting of expenses. An enterprise should immediately recognize termination benefits as a liability and an expense when, and only when, the enterprise is demonstrably committed to either

1. Terminate the employment of an employee or group of employees before the normal retirement date, or
2. Provide termination benefits as a result of an offer made in order to encourage voluntary redundancy.

Demonstrable commitment requires a detailed formal plan and that the enterprise, either for legal or constructive reasons, is "without realistic possibility of withdrawal." Where termination benefits fall due more than 12 months after the balance sheet date, they should be discounted by using the discount rate specified in paragraph 78. In the case of an offer made to encourage voluntary redundancy, the measurement of termination benefits should be based on the number of employees expected to accept the offer.

> ☞ **PRACTICE POINTER:** Other International Accounting Standards may require disclosures relating to termination benefits, such as IAS 37, "Provisions, Contingent Liabilities, and Contingent Assets" (see Chapter 28) if a nonremote contingency arises, IAS 8, "Net Profit or Loss for the Period, Fundamental Errors, and Changes in Accounting Policies" (see Chapter 26) if the "size, nature or incidence" requires it, and IAS 24, "Related Party Disclosures" (see Chapter 29) in the case of key management personnel.

EQUITY COMPENSATION BENEFITS

Typically, equity compensation benefits will involve share or share options, or cash payments related to future share market prices, which are transferred to employees at less than the fair value at which they would be issued to an independent third party. IAS 19 does not specify any recognition and measurement requirements for equity compensation benefits, nor does it require disclosure of the fair value for employee share options. This is said to be "in view of the lack of international consensus."

> **OBSERVATION:** The above explanation is somewhat disingenuous. If equity compensation benefits are really benefits then they represent a transfer of resources (sooner or later) out of the

enterprise, that is, they are, conceptually, expenses. The attempt to produce a GAAP requirement consistent with this in the United States, in FAS-123, was met with a storm of political criticism, resulting in, in effect, an optional standard. The IASC silence may be sensible, but it is pragmatic rather than theoretically justified.

Perhaps in partial compensation for the lack of specification regarding principles, a whole series of disclosure requirements are specified. These are as follows (pars. 147–148).

- The nature and terms (including any vesting provisions) of equity compensation plans.
- The accounting policy for equity compensation plans.
- The amounts recognized in the financial statements for equity compensation plans.
- The number and terms (including, where applicable, dividend and voting rights, conversion rights, exercise dates, exercise prices, and expiration dates) of the enterprise's own equity financial instruments that are held by equity compensation plans (and, in the case of share options, by employees) at the beginning and end of the period. The extent to which employees' entitlements to those instruments are vested at the beginning and end of the period should be specified.
- The number and terms (including, where applicable, dividend and voting rights, conversion rights, exercise dates, exercise prices, and expiration dates) of equity financial instruments issued by the enterprise to equity compensation plans or to employees (or of the enterprise's own equity financial instruments distributed by equity compensation plans to employees) during the period and the fair value of any consideration received from the equity compensation plans or the employees.
- The number, exercise dates, and exercise prices of share options exercised under equity compensation plans during the period.
- The number of share options held by equity compensation plans, or held by employees under such plans, that lapsed during the period.
- The amount and principal terms of any loans or guarantees granted by the reporting enterprise to, or on behalf of, equity compensation plans.
- The fair value, at the beginning and end of the period, of the enterprise's own equity financial instruments (other than share options) held by equity compensation plans.

- The fair value, at the date of issue, of the enterprise's own equity financial instruments (other than share options) issued by the enterprise to equity compensation plans or to employees, or by equity compensation plans to employees, during the period.

If it is not practicable to determine the fair value of the equity financial instruments (other than share options), that fact should be disclosed.

TRANSITIONAL PROVISIONS

IAS 19 in its third version, valid from January 1, 1999, was significantly different from its predecessor and contained a number of transitional provisions (pars. 153–156). Retrospective calculation of the "corridor" is not required. The 2000 revisions are valid from January 1, 2001.

APPENDIX:
ACCOUNTING AND REPORTING BY
RETIREMENT BENEFIT PLANS

IASC has issued a separate standard, IAS 26, "Accounting and Reporting by Retirement Benefit Plans," dealing with this matter. It was effective on January 1, 1988, and thus predates IAS 19 in its current version, and indeed many of the standards in their current versions. Its subject matter is clearly highly specialized, applying to retirement plans, not to employers of potential retirees. Note, however, that IAS 26 applies to retirement plans even if they are not legally separate from the employer. IAS 26 does not require the preparation of reports by retirement benefit plans. Rather, it specifies how such reports should be prepared when they are prepared.

Readers involved in the preparation of such reports should read the whole standard. The major disclosure requirements are summarized below. A series of definitions are given in paragraph 8, generally consistent with, though different in detail from, those in IAS 19.

For defined contribution plans the report should contain a statement of the net assets available for the benefits and a description of the funding policy. The retirement benefit plan investments, for both defined contribution and defined benefit plans, should be carried at fair value. In the case of marketable securities, fair value is market value. Where plan investments are held for which an estimate of fair value is not possible, disclosure should be made of the reason why fair value is not used.

The report of a defined benefit plan should contain either:

1. A statement that shows:

    (a) the net assets available for benefits;

    (b) the actuarial present value of promised retirement benefits, distinguishing between vested benefits and nonvested benefits; and

    (c) the resulting excess or deficit; or

2. A statement of net assets available for benefits including either:

    (a) a note disclosing the actuarial present value of promised retirement benefits, distinguishing between vested benefits and nonvested benefits; or

(b) a reference to this information in an accompanying actuarial report.

If an actuarial valuation has not been prepared at the date of the report, the most recent valuation should be used as a base and the date of the valuation disclosed. The actuarial present value of promised retirement benefits should be based on the benefits promised under the terms of the plan on service rendered to date by using either current salary levels or projected salary levels with disclosure of the basis used. The effect of any changes in actuarial assumptions that have had a significant effect on the actuarial present value of promised retirement benefits should also be disclosed. The report should explain the relationship between the actuarial present value of promised retirement benefits and the net assets available for benefits, and the policy for the funding of promised benefits.

IAS 26 discusses advantages and disadvantages of the two alternative salary levels—current or projected, in paragraphs 24 and 25. The advantages of using projected salary levels appear greater, being more relevant to the likely outcome, but IAS 26 is careful not to state a clear preference (probably a function of the standard having had no update since 1988).

Three different "formats" for reports on defined benefit plans are given. Again, all are acceptable, but it should be noted that all three require information about the net assets available for benefits and a quantification of the actuarial present value of the promised retirement benefits.

The report of a retirement benefit plan, whether defined benefit or defined contribution, should also contain the following information:

1. A statement of changes in net assets available for benefits.
2. A summary of significant accounting policies.
3. A description of the plan and the effect of any changes in the plan during the period.

CHAPTER 14
THE EQUITY METHOD

CONTENTS

OVERVIEW

The equity method is a method of accounting by an enterprise for an investment in the equity capital (typically, voting shares) of another enterprise. The method is considered in IAS GAAP to be appropriate in cases where the investment enables the investor to exercise significant influence over the investee, with the power to participate in its financial and operating policy decisions but not to exercise control over it. In these circumstances, the investor has some responsibility for the return on its investment, and it is considered appropriate to include in the investor's results of operations its share of the profits or losses of the investee. In IAS GAAP, such an investee is referred to as an "associate." The equity method may be used in the separate financial statements of the investor and should be used in its consolidated financial statements.

The equity method is not a substitute for full consolidation when the criteria for the use of the latter method are met. It is allowed as an alternative treatment to proportionate consolidation in the case of joint control.

The relevant IAS GAAP have been promulgated in:

- IAS 28 , "Accounting for Investments in Associates"
- IAS 31, "Financial Reporting of Interests in Joint Ventures"
- IAS 27, "Consolidated Financial Statements and Accounting for Investments in Subsidiaries"
- IAS 22, "Business Combinations"
- IAS 36, "Impairment of Assets"
- IAS 39, "Financial Instruments: Recognition and Measurement"
- SIC-3, "Elimination of Unrealized Profits and Losses on Transactions with Associates"
- SIC-20, "Equity Accounting Method—Recognition of Losses"

BACKGROUND

IAS 28 was originally issued in 1988, following the issue of IAS 27. It was reformatted in 1994 without substantial changes to its contents. In 1998, it was amended twice, first to reflect the requirements of IAS 36 and again to reflect those of IAS 39. References in this chapter are to IAS 28 as amended in 1998.

Both as a technique and in terms of its scope of application (including the definition of "significant influence"), the use of the equity method in IAS GAAP is similar to that in U.S. GAAP. The main differences are as follows:

1. An investment consisting of between 20% and 50% of the voting equity capital of an investee, but over which the investor exercises de facto control, would under U.S. GAAP be accounted for by the equity method, but under IAS GAAP it would be consolidated. IAS GAAP refer to "voting power" in order to include investees that are not stock corporations, while U.S. GAAP refer to "voting stock."

2. In the case of corporate joint ventures (i.e., jointly controlled entities in IAS 31 terminology), IAS GAAP have proportionate consolidation as the benchmark method and the equity method as a less preferred alternative, while under U.S. GAAP only the equity method is permitted.

3. IAS 28 deals with the use of the equity method as an optional method in the separate financial statements of the investor, when the latter issues consolidated financial statements. In U.S. GAAP, it is the consolidated financial statements that are of interest in such a case; the parent enterprise's separate financial statements are not a matter for concern (and are not normally issued).

4. On some issues (such as the application of the equity method on a step-by-step basis) U.S. GAAP are more specific, while on other issues (such as applying uniform accounting policies and dealing with different reporting dates) IAS GAAP are more specific.

5. For investments accounted for by the equity method, U.S. GAAP (APB-18, par. 20) require more extensive disclosure than IAS GAAP (IAS 28, par. 27).

SCOPE

Significant Influence and the Definition of an *Associate*

The criterion for the application of the equity method is the exercise of significant influence by the investor over the investee, with the power to participate in its financial and operating policy decisions but not to exercise control over it (IAS 28, par. 3). In this case, the investee is classed as an associate.

If an investor holds, either directly or indirectly through subsidiaries, 20% or more of the voting power of the investee, there is a rebuttable presumption that the investor has significant influence. Conversely, if the investor holds, either directly or indirectly through subsidiaries, less than 20% of the voting power of the investee, there is a rebuttable presumption that the investor does not have significant influence. The existence of a substantial or majority ownership by another investor does not of itself serve to rebut the presumption of significant influence (IAS 28, par. 4).

Conditions that provide evidence of "significant influence" are set out in paragraph 5 of IAS 28, as follows:

1. Representation on the board of directors or other governing body of the investee,

2. Participation in policy making processes,

3. Material transactions between the investor and the investee,

4. Interchange of managerial personnel between the investor and the investee, and

5. Provision of essential technical information.

☛ **PRACTICE POINTER:** In the case where the investor holds 20% or more of the voting power of the investee, if neither of the conditions 1 and 2 above are met, this would be likely to constitute a rebuttal of the presumption of significant influence. In particular, this would be the case if the investee had successfully resisted the investor's attempts to gain board representation or its equivalent, or a "standstill agreement" had been signed between the investor and the investee that provided evidence of a lack of significant influence. If the investor could be shown to exercise significant influence because conditions 3 to 5 were met, however, the rebuttal could be rejected.

Conversely, in the case where the investor holds less than 20% of the voting power of the investee, if conditions 1 and 2 or most of the conditions 1 to 5 above were met, the presumption of no significant influence could be rebutted, especially if the investee publicly acknowledges the significant influence.

Treatment in Consolidated Financial Statements

An investment in an associate should be accounted for in consolidated financial statements under the equity method, unless one of the following conditions prevails:

1. The investment was acquired and is held exclusively with a view to its disposal in the near future.

2. The investee operates under severe long-term restrictions that significantly impair its ability to transfer funds to the investor.

In either of these cases, it should be accounted for under the cost method (IAS 28, pars. 8 and 10). If an investee ceases to meet the criteria for an associate, or starts to operate under the restrictions mentioned in condition 2 above, the equity method should be discontinued and the cost method adopted (with the carrying value at the relevant date being treated as cost for this purpose). The cost method is described in IAS 39, "Financial Instruments: Recognition and Measurement."

> **OBSERVATION:** Given the amendments to IAS 28 in the light of IAS 39, "Financial Instruments: Recognition and Measurement," and the remark in IAS 39, paragraph 69 that "[a]fter initial recognition, an enterprise should measure its financial assets...at their fair values," it may seem strange that in case of condition 1 above, IAS 28 requires the cost method rather than the method required for "available for sale financial assets," namely fair value. The initial recording of the investment at cost, however, involves the same recognition and measurement procedures as in the case of consolidation, with recognition of goodwill or negative goodwill as the difference between cost and the investor's share of the net fair value of

identifiable assets and liabilities acquired (see below and Chapter 6). If a requirement to use fair value rather than cost in condition 1 above were interpreted as entailing the nonrecognition of any goodwill on acquisition, this would thereby entail the recognition of an immediate loss (for positive goodwill) or gain (for negative goodwill). In addition, the assumption in condition 1 is that the investment will be held only for a relatively short period, during which cost and share of net fair value of identifiable assets and liabilities acquired would not be expected to differ materially except by the amount of goodwill.

EQUITY ACCOUNTING PROCEDURES

The accounting procedures for the equity method are largely similar to those required for consolidation (IAS 28, par. 16). In fact, the equity method is sometimes referred to as "one-line consolidation."

Under the equity method, the investment is initially recorded at cost, with a distinction being made between the investor's share of the net fair value of the identifiable assets and liabilities acquired and any goodwill (positive or negative). Subsequently, the carrying amount is increased or decreased to recognize the investor's share of changes in the investee's net assets. Such changes will result from profits retained or losses of the investee but may also be from other sources, as follows. Adjustments to the carrying amount may be needed to reflect changes in the investee's equity that have not been included in its income statement. These include revaluations of property, plant, and equipment and of investments; foreign exchange translation differences; and adjustments for the differences arising on business combinations, such as those for goodwill and its amortization and for depreciation based on fair values (IAS 28, pars. 6 and 17).

Illustration of the Equity Method

On December 31, 20X1, X Company acquired 600 common shares in Y Company (out of a total of 2,000 common shares outstanding) at a cost of $1.50 per share, that is, a 30% interest. At that date, Y's stockholders' equity was $2,800, comprising share capital of $2,000 and retained earnings of $800. Goodwill in Y is thus:

$900 − 30% of $2,800 = $840. This will be amortized over (say) 10 years, that is, $84 per year.

X Company is required to issue consolidated financial statements and decides to apply equity accounting for its investment in Y Company in its separate financial statements prior to consolidation. The balance sheets of X (before and after equity accounting for Y) and of Y at December 31, 20X2 are given below. The retained earnings of Y increased by $2,200 during the financial year.

	X Before Equity Accounting	Y	X After Equity Accounting
Net current assets	$ 1,000	$1,800	$ 1,000
Property, plant, and equipment	15,000	3,200	15,000
Investment in Y:			
At cost 600 x 1.50 = 900			
Investment in associate:			
Equity 900 + 30% of 2,200			
= 1,560, less goodwill			
amortization of 84 =			1,476
	$16,900	$5,000	$17,476
Share capital	$ 8,000	$2,000	$ 8,000
Reserves:	8,900	3,000	
8,900 + 30% of 2,200 – 84			9,476
	$16,900	$5,000	$17,476

X Company's income statement would include its share of Y's net income (after adjusting for goodwill amortization) under the caption "Income from associates" after "Profit from operations" and before "Income tax expense" (IAS 1, par. 75). Assuming that Y had paid no dividend, this share would be $1,476; X's share of any dividend would be added to this.

As "Income from associates" is reported before "Income tax expense," it would seem preferable to report it gross of income tax and to include the applicable income tax under the caption "Income tax expense" as is required in the United Kingdom under FAS-9. However, neither IAS 1 nor IAS 28 (nor APB 18) requires this.

If an associate has outstanding cumulative preferred shares held by outside interests, the investor's share of the associate's net income or loss should be calculated after adjusting for the preferred dividends, whether declared or not (IAS 28, par. 21). This is consistent with the treatment of a subsidiary's results in a similar situation (IAS 27, par. 28).

The Treatment of Loss-Making Associates and Impairment Losses

If an investor's share of an associate's losses is equal to or greater than the carrying amount of the investment prior to such losses being incurred, the carrying amount will be reduced to zero so that the investment is reported at a nil value. Additional losses need to be recognized only to the extent that the investor has made, or has incurred obligations to make, payments on behalf of the associate, for example, in accordance with a guarantee given by the investor. If the associate subsequently reports profits, the investor first applies its share of these against its share of the net losses that it has not recognized and should not resume including its share of the associate's profits in net income until the unrecognized share of losses has been covered by its share of subsequent profits (IAS 28, par. 22).

For the purpose of applying IAS 28, paragraph 22, the carrying amount of an investment should include only the carrying amount of instruments that provided unlimited rights of participation in earnings or losses and a residual interest in the investee. Continuing losses of an investee should be considered objective evidence that financial interests in that investee (both the financial instruments of the kinds mentioned above and other financial interests) may be impaired (SIC-20, pars. 5–8).

If there is an indication that the value of an investment in an associate may be impaired, the investor should apply IAS 36, "Impairment of Assets" (see Chapter 19). The recoverable amount of an investment in an associate is assessed for each individual associate, unless it does not generate cash flows that are largely independent of those from other assets of the investor. Cash flows that are not largely independent of those from other assets should be excluded to avoid double counting (IAS 36, par. 36).

If the investor has guaranteed or is otherwise committed to obligations of the investee or to satisfying such obligations, in addition to continuing to recognize its share of losses of the investee, the investor should determine whether a provision should be recognized in accordance with IAS 37 (SIC-20, par. 9).

In determining the value in use of the investment, the investor estimates one of the following:

1. Its share of the present value of the estimated future cash flows expected to be generated by the investee as a whole, including the cash flows from its operations and the proceeds of ultimate disposal, or

2. The present value of the estimated future cash flows expected to be received, in the form of dividends from the investee and from its ultimate disposal.

Under appropriate assumptions, 1 and 2 will produce similar estimates.

Any resultant impairment loss will be applied first against any positive goodwill (IAS 28, pars. 23–24).

Inter-enterprise Eliminations

IAS 28, "Accounting for Investments in Associates," does not specify how the results of transactions between an investor and investee should be accounted for under the equity method. This matter is dealt with in SIC-3, "Elimination of Unrealized Profits and Losses on Transactions with Associates." In the case of a "downstream" transaction in which the investor has sold an asset to the investee that the latter still holds, only the investor's proportionate share of the profit from the transaction should be treated as "unrealized." Thus, the carrying value of the asset and the net income or retained earnings in the investor's financial statements (consolidated and, where relevant, individual) should be adjusted by the amount of this proportionate share. This is sometimes referred to as "proportional elimination."

The same proportional method is logically applied in the case of an "upstream" transaction, after which the investor holds an asset purchased from the investee at a cost that includes a profit to the latter of which the investor's share is "unrealized."

An illustration of "downstream" and "upstream" transactions, adapted from the *Miller GAAP Guide*, is given below.

Illustration of "Downstream" and "Upstream" Transactions

An investor sells inventory "downstream" to an associate during a financial reporting period. At the end of the period, the associate's inventory includes an amount of $50,000, which is the investor's profit on the sales. The investor's share of the equity capital of the associate is 40%. The entries for the elimination of inter-enterprise profits are as follows:

Share of income of associate (40% of $50,000)	$20,000	
Investment in associate		$20,000

If the inter-enterprise sales were "upstream," the entries would be as follows:

Share of income from associate	$20,000	
Inventory		$20,000

Separate Financial Statements of the Investor

An enterprise with an investment in an associate may have one or more subsidiaries and be required to issue consolidated financial statements, or it may not be required to do so. An enterprise that issues consolidated financial statements may also issue its separate financial statements. In some countries this is a requirement, while in other countries it is neither required nor normally done. According to IAS 28 (pars. 12–15), the required treatment of an investment in an associate by an enterprise that issues its separate financial statements is much the same, whether or not that enterprise also issues consolidated financial statements.

If the investor issues both consolidated financial statements and separate financial statements, and the investment in the associate is not held exclusively with a view to its disposal in the near future (see the Practice Pointer below), then the investment should be treated in one of the following ways:

1. Carried at cost,

2. Accounted for using the equity method, or

3. Accounted for as an "available for sale financial asset" as described in IAS 39, paragraphs 68–73 (see Chapter 14), that is, at fair value unless this is unascertainable, in which case the cost method is used.

If the investor does not issue consolidated financial statements, the requirements are the same, except that:

1. The equity method should be used only if it would have been appropriate in consolidated financial statements had the investor issued them.

2. As an alternative to being accounted for as an "available for sale financial asset" according to IAS 39, an investment in an associate may be treated as a "financial asset held for trading." In either case, IAS 39 requires the use of fair value unless this is unascertainable, in which case the cost method is used.

☛ **PRACTICE POINTER:** If an investment in an associate is held exclusively with a view to its disposal in the near future, according to IAS 28, paragraph 10, it should be carried using the cost method in the consolidated financial statements.

In the case where the investor issues consolidated financial statements, IAS 28, paragraph 12 does not make it clear that this treatment is also required in the investor's separate financial statements, but it seems logical that it should be.

In the case where the investor does not issue separate financial statements, there is also some ambiguity. IAS 28, paragraph 14, does not make it clear what treatment is appropriate for the case where an investment in an associate is held exclusively with a view to its disposal in the near future. Use of the equity method would appear to be excluded, but paragraph 14 admits as alternatives both the cost method and treatment either as an "available for sale financial asset" or as a "financial asset held for trading" (both of the latter entailing the same treatment using fair value if ascertainable, according to IAS 39). As noted above, the required treatment in consolidated financial statements in such a case would be the use of the cost method. It is not clear why the rationale for using the cost method in consolidated financial statements would not apply in the case of the investor's separate financial statements, whether or not the investor issues consolidated financial statements.

> ☞ **PRACTICE POINTER:** Because IAS 28, paragraphs 12 and 14 both allow the use of the cost method in the investor's separate financial statements, we suggest that, for the sake of consistency, this be used in the case where the investment is held exclusively with a view to its disposal in the near future.

Finally, it should be noted that the use of fair value rather than cost in the investor's separate financial statements would have tax implications in a number of countries.

DISCLOSURE

According to IAS 28, paragraphs 26–28, the following disclosures are required:

1. An appropriate listing and description of significant associates, including the proportion of ownership interest and, if different, the proportion of voting power held.
2. The methods used to account for such investments.
3. The investor's share of any contingencies and capital commitments of an associate for which the investor is contingently liable, and any contingencies that arise because the investor is severably liable for all the associate's liabilities (as required by IAS 10, "Contingencies and Events Occurring after the Balance Sheet Date," see Chapter 15).

If an investor discontinues recognition of its share of losses of an investee, the investor should disclose the amount of its unrecognized share of the investee's losses, for the reporting period and cumulatively, in the notes to its financial statements (SIC-20, par. 10).

Investments in associates should be disclosed as a separate item in the balance sheet, following IAS 1, paragraphs 66–72. Those accounted for using the equity method should be classified as noncurrent assets. The investor's share of the profits or losses of such investments should be disclosed as a separate item in the income statement, following IAS 1, paragraphs 75–76 (but see the comments in the illustration above). The investor's share of any extraordinary items, or of the effects of any fundamental errors or changes in accounting policy, should be separately disclosed.

CHAPTER 15
EVENTS AFTER THE BALANCE SHEET DATE

CONTENTS

OVERVIEW

The purpose of the published financial statements of an enterprise is to give information about its results for the financial year under review and about its position at the balance sheet date. In principle, therefore, the financial statements should reflect those events that occurred during that year, and only those events. However, the financial statements are obviously not finalized until a considerable period after the actual balance sheet date, and events that occur between the balance sheet date and the date of the finalization of the financial statements may have implications for the information in those financial statements.

IAS 10, "Events after the Balance Sheet Date," deals with the appropriate treatment of these events. In broad terms, three situations can be distinguished, each with its own implications, as follows.

1. The event between balance sheet date and finalization date may provide new evidence or information about a situation that already existed on or before the balance sheet date, that is, the new event provides information concerning an earlier event. Because the effects of the earlier event are to be reported in the financial statements for the year under review, the accounts *should* be adjusted to take account of the new evidence or information.

2. The event between balance sheet date and finalization date may relate to a situation or condition that is new and that did not exist at the date of the balance sheet. This is a matter,

therefore, for the following year, and the financial statements currently under preparation should *not* be adjusted to reflect the new situation.

3. There is one exception to 2 above, in that if the new event seems likely to render the going concern assumption invalid (i.e., to suggest that the enterprise is shortly to be liquidated, see the discussion in Chapter 2), then this would be so fundamental that the basis of the preparation of the accounts *would* be changed, to reflect the likelihood of imminent liquidation.

IAS 10 was originally issued in 1978 under the title "Contingencies and Events Occurring after the Balance Sheet Date." Much of the content of this standard was replaced by IAS 37, "Provisions, Contingent Liabilities, and Contingent Assets," which is effective for accounting periods beginning on or after July 1, 1999 (fully discussed in Chapter 28). The remainder, very confusingly in terms of the numbering system, was replaced by a new IAS 10 (revised 1999), with the same title as this chapter, which is effective for accounting periods beginning on or after January 1, 2000. With one exception, the new IAS 10 does not involve major changes from the post-balance-sheet event parts of the old IAS 10. All references to IAS 10 in this chapter are to the new 1999 version.

BACKGROUND

As outlined above in the "Overview," IAS 10 seeks to ensure logical consistency in the extent to which events occurring in an enterprise between the date of the annual financial statements and the date of the finalization of those statements are, or are not, taken into account in the published annual financial statements. The standard should be applied in accounting for, and to the disclosure of, all events occurring after the reporting balance sheet date. IAS 10 is on the whole simple, clear, and succinct.

There are no differences of principle between IAS GAAP and U.S. GAAP. However, IAS 10 now requires that dividends proposed or declared after the balance sheet date are not adjusting events. Under U.S. GAAP the declaration of a cash dividend is nonadjusting, but the declaration of a stock dividend is adjusting.

DEFINITIONS

The definitions of the two types of post-balance sheet events can be simply stated (par. 2).

Events after the balance sheet date are those events, both favorable and unfavorable, that occur between the balance sheet date and the date when the financial statements are authorized for issue. Two types of events can be identified:

1. Those that provide evidence of conditions that existed at the balance sheet date (*adjusting events after the balance sheet date*); and

2. Those that are indicative of conditions that arose after the balance sheet date (*nonadjusting events after the balance sheet date*).

Events after the balance sheet date include all events up to the date when the financial statements are authorized for issue, even if those events occur after the publication of a profit announcement or of other selected financial information.

Care may need to be taken in determining the date of "authorization" for this purpose. Inevitably, the standard has to allow for a variety of different national systems of corporate governance and of management structure. As a general rule, the date of authorization is the date on which the executive directors approve the financial statements. If the financial statements are, for example, required to be submitted to the shareholders for approval after issue or required to be approved by a nonexecutive supervisory board after acceptance by the executive management of the enterprise, then these later dates are not relevant for IAS 10 purposes. IAS 10 gives two simple examples illustrating these points (pars. 4–5).

The standard gives some indicative illustrations of adjusting and nonadjusting events, which require logical application of the above definitions (pars. 8 and 10). For example, the resolution after the balance sheet date of a court case that, if it confirms that an enterprise already had a present obligation at the balance sheet date, may require the enterprise to adjust a provision already recognized or to recognize a provision instead of merely disclosing a contingent liability. This would, therefore, be an adjusting event. Similarly, information about the realizability of accounts receivable in existence at the balance sheet date, or about the net realizable value of items held in inventory at the balance sheet date, would be regarded as adjusting events. The discovery of errors, or the results of fraud, that show that the draft financial statements were incorrect is also specifically stated to be an adjusting event.

On the other hand, an example of a nonadjusting event after the balance sheet date is a decline in market value of investments between the balance sheet date and the date when the financial statements are authorized for issue. The fall in market value would not normally relate to the condition of the investments at the balance sheet date but would reflect circumstances that had arisen in the following period. Therefore, an enterprise would not adjust the amounts recognized in its financial statements for the investment, except in the rare situation of the going concern assumption being put at risk (see "Going Concern," below).

RECOGNITION AND MEASUREMENT

Now obvious, the formal requirements can be very briefly stated (pars. 7 and 9). An enterprise should adjust the amounts recognized in its financial statements to reflect adjusting events after the balance sheet date. It should not adjust the amounts recognized in its financial statements to reflect nonadjusting events after the balance sheet date.

The one major change introduced by the 1999 revision to IAS 10 concerns the treatment of dividends. IAS 10 now states that if dividends to holders of equity instruments (as defined in IAS 32, "Financial Instruments: Disclosure and Presentation," see Chapter 16) are proposed or declared after the balance sheet date, then an enterprise should not recognize those dividends at the balance sheet date (par. 11). This reflects the normal existing treatment in some countries, Germany for example, but will be a significant change from previous practice in other countries, for example, the United Kingdom.

The issue is as follows. It is common practice for an enterprise to announce dividends that are stated to be in respect of the period covered by the financial statements but that are proposed or declared after the balance sheet date and before the financial statements are authorized for issue. This leads to the question as to whether or not such announcements create a liability as of the balance sheet date. The definition of a liability given in IAS 1 (see Chapter 3) and in the IASC Framework (see Chapter 2) needs to be applied. Does an obligation exist as of the balance sheet date?

The logical answer to this question is no. At the balance sheet date the enterprise was under no contractual obligation, express or constructive, to declare any dividend at all. Even an announcement to seek formal approval for the payment of a certain dividend does not, of itself, create an obligation. It is only the formal declaration of the dividend itself that creates the obligation. It therefore follows that only a dividend already formally declared (and, of course, not paid) by the balance sheet date would create an obligation on that date.

> **OBSERVATION:** The above argument is entirely logical. The alternative, more pragmatic argument previously followed by many countries was that the dividend related to the reporting period and was an intended payment, thereby creating an in-substance liability. The choice between these two arguments, allowed by the previous International Standard, is now withdrawn, as indicated above. No liability should be recognized for dividends not formally declared by the balance sheet date.

It should be noted that IAS 1, "Presentation of Financial Statements," requires an enterprise to *disclose* the amount of dividends that were proposed after the balance sheet date but before the financial statements were authorized for issue. IAS 1 permits an enterprise to make this disclosure either on the face of the balance sheet *as a separate component of equity* (i.e., not amongst the liabilities) or in the notes to the financial statements.

GOING CONCERN

As already discussed in the "Overview" at the beginning of this chapter, if the going concern assumption is no longer appropriate, the effect is so pervasive that IAS 10 requires a fundamental change in the basis of accounting, rather than an adjustment to the amounts recognized within the original basis of accounting.

In effect, therefore, if management determines after the balance sheet date either that it intends to liquidate the enterprise or to cease trading, or that it has no realistic alternative but to do so, then the accounts are to be completely redrawn on a non-going-concern basis. As stated in Chapter 3, IAS 1, "Presentation of Financial Statements," requires specified disclosures in such circumstances.

DISCLOSURE

It is important for users to know when the financial statements were authorized for issue, as the financial statements do not reflect events after this date. An enterprise should, therefore, disclose the date when the financial statements were authorized for issue and who gave that authorization. If the enterprise's owners or others have the power to amend the financial statements after issuance, the enterprise should disclose that fact.

Disclosure requirements contained in other standards, concerning conditions that existed at the balance sheet date, may themselves need to be updated. One example is when evidence becomes available after the balance sheet date about a contingent liability that existed at the balance sheet date. In addition to considering whether it should now recognize a provision under IAS 37, "Provisions, Contingent Liabilities, and Contingent Assets," an enterprise should update its disclosures about the contingent liability in light of that evidence.

NONADJUSTING EVENTS AFTER THE BALANCE SHEET DATE

Although, by definition, nonadjusting events should not have any effect on the numbers included in the financial statements for the reporting year, some nonadjusting events after the balance sheet date may be of such importance that nondisclosure would affect the ability of users of the financial statements to make proper evaluations and decisions (par. 20). In such cases, the enterprise should disclose in the Notes the following information for each significant category of nonadjusting event after the balance sheet date:

1. The nature of the event, and
2. An estimate of its financial effect, or a statement that such an estimate cannot be made.

This is clearly likely in some cases to be a subjective matter. The standard gives a list of examples, reproduced below (par. 21):

1. A major business combination after the balance sheet date (IAS 22, "Business Combinations," requires specific disclosures in such cases, see Chapter 6) or disposing of a major subsidiary.
2. Announcing a plan to discontinue an operation, disposing of assets or settling liabilities attributable to a discontinuing operation or entering into binding agreements to sell such assets or settle such liabilities (see IAS 35, "Discontinuing Operations," discussed in Chapter 11).
3. Major purchases and disposals of assets or expropriation of major assets by government.
4. The destruction of a major production plant by a fire after the balance sheet date.
5. Announcing, or commencing the implementation of, a major restructuring (see IAS 37, "Provisions, Contingent Liabilities, and Contingent Assets," discussed in Chapter 28).
6. Major ordinary share transactions and potential ordinary share transactions after the balance sheet date (IAS 33, "Earnings per Share," encourages an enterprise to disclose a description of such transactions, other than capitalization issues and share splits, see Chapter 12).
7. Abnormally large changes after the balance sheet date in asset prices or foreign exchange rates.
8. Changes in tax rates or tax laws enacted or announced after the balance sheet date that have a significant effect on current and deferred tax assets and liabilities (see IAS 12, "Income Taxes," discussed in Chapter 20).
9. Entering into significant commitments or contingent liabilities, for example, by issuing significant guarantees.
10. Commencing major litigation arising solely out of events that occurred after the balance sheet date.

It should not be assumed that this list is in any way exhaustive.

☞ **PRACTICE POINTER:** The subjectivity inherent in this question of possible disclosure of nonadjusting events is not removed by the inclusion in IAS 10 of this list of examples. Words like "major" or "significant" appear in nearly all the examples given, so the expert subjective judgment of the accountants responsible for the preparation of the financial statement package remains crucial.

CHAPTER 16
FINANCIAL INSTRUMENTS

CONTENTS

OVERVIEW

IAS GAAP on financial instruments aim to deal comprehensively with issues both of presentation and disclosure and of recognition and measurement. Financial instruments are defined broadly: In IAS GAAP, a financial instrument is any contract (written or oral) which gives rise both to a financial asset of one enterprise and to a financial liability or an equity instrument of another enterprise. Financial instruments, thus, include all financial assets and financial liabilities, whether securitized or not, as well as derivatives.

In addition to their broad scope in terms of the recognition of financial instruments, IAS GAAP broke new ground in the application of fair value accounting to such instruments. Fair value is stated to be "a more appropriate measure for most financial assets than amortized cost," but, in fact, IAS GAAP require certain items to be accounted for at cost or amortized cost. Moreover, in the case of items that after initial recognition are remeasured at fair values, some assets may be classified so that gains and losses on their remeasurement are recognized in the statement of changes in equity, rather than in net income.

Historically, IAS GAAP on presentation and disclosure of financial instruments (IAS 32) were promulgated before those on recognition and measurement (IAS 39). This was because of the difficulty encountered in arriving at a consensus over the issues of measurement at fair value and the related issues of the recognition of the resultant remeasurement gains and losses (see "Background" below). However, this chapter maintains the order of presentation adopted in this Guide, that is, measurement requirements are dealt with below before disclosure requirements.

Considerable attention is given in IAS GAAP to issues of derecognition of financial assets and liabilities (and of gains or losses that may arise on derecognition), and to accounting for hedging relationships. These are dealt with fairly comprehensively, and IAS 39 is a standard of daunting length and complexity.

IAS GAAP on financial instruments are set out in:

- IAS 32, "Financial Instruments: Presentation and Disclosure" (effective date January 1, 1996)

- IAS 39, "Financial Instruments: Recognition and Measurement" (effective date January 1, 2001 or earlier application permitted for fiscal years ending after March 15, 1999 or later)

- SIC-5, "Classification of Financial Instruments—Contingent Settlement Provisions"

- SIC-16, "Share Capital—Reacquired Own Equity Instruments (Treasury Shares)"

- SIC-17, "Equity—Costs of an Equity Transaction"

In addition, in January 2001 IASC published IAS 39, "Implementation Guidance: Questions and Answers." According to IASC, the Questions and Answers in this document "do not have the status of…a Standard or Interpretation" (i.e., of IAS GAAP), but "enterprises should consider this guidance as they select and apply accounting policies in accordance with IAS 1 ("Presentation of Financial Statements"; see Chapter 3). Accordingly, we have included extracts from this guidance in the 2002 *Miller IAS Guide* (as additional "Practice Pointers," unless very short) where we consider that this would be helpful for the reader.

BACKGROUND

The last two decades have seen considerable innovation in the field of financial instruments, which now include interest rate swaps, caps and floors, forward contracts, repurchase agreements, and various forms of financial guarantees. These innovations have raised new accounting issues of disclosure, recognition, and measurement that have proven to be challenging to accounting standard-setters.

IAS GAAP on financial instruments have arisen out of the IASC's financial instruments project, which started in 1988 following an OECD symposium in which accounting for financial instruments had been discussed. There was an agreement between the IASC and the Canadian Institute of Chartered Accountants (CICA) to cooperate in the development of international and Canadian accounting standards on financial instruments. The CICA also provided support staff for the project. An eight-member project steering committee, consisting mainly of accountants from major firms, and a special consultation group with a wider membership were established. One important aim of the project was to produce a standard that would deal comprehensively with all types of financial instruments for all types of business, and would cover recognition and disclosure issues as well as those of presentation and disclosure.

The history of the financial instruments project was to be marked by difficulties concerning the extent to which fair values should be used as a basis for measurement.

The IASC produced a "Draft Statement of Principles" (DSOP), that is, a pre-exposure draft, which was approved by the steering committee in March 1990. The DSOP required that financial assets and financial liabilities held for trading should be measured on the basis of fair values, but this was not permitted for items held for investing and financing purposes. The IASC approved the DSOP in November 1990, but without resolving the issue of how investing and financing items should be measured. The IASC Board asked the steering committee to prepare exposure drafts on two alternative bases: one with a benchmark treatment consisting of fair value for trading items and cost for other items, with an allowed alternative treatment consisting of fair value for all items; and the other with a benchmark treatment of fair value for all items with an allowed alternative treatment consisting of fair value for trading items and cost for other items.

In June 1991, the IASC approved E40, which essentially followed the first of the two alternatives, but with the stipulation that hedging items should be measured on the same basis as the items they hedge. The CICA also produced an exposure draft, which differed from E40 by not allowing the alternative treatment whereby non-trading items could be measured at fair values. The two drafts also differed in their criteria for designating a hedge. The need to offer alternatives regarding the use of fair value, and the differences between the two exposure drafts on this point can, in retrospect, be seen as signs of serious difficulties to come.

There then ensued a period of two and a half years during which the IASC reviewed comments on E40 and the CICA exposure draft, invited comments on its tentative conclusions, and prepared a revised exposure draft, E48, which was published in January 1994. The corresponding CICA exposure draft was published in April 1994. In November 1994, following review of comments on these exposure drafts, and consideration of input from representatives of standard-setting bodies in twenty countries, the IASC decided to split its financial instruments project into two stages. The first stage would deal with presentation and disclosure and would aim to produce a standard by March 1995. The second stage would deal with the more controversial issues of recognition and measurement, with the hope of producing a standard by 1996 at the latest. The first of these target dates was met with the approval of IAS 32 in March 1995. However, the other target date was not to be achieved. (It may be noted that the FASB adopted a step-by-step approach from the outset in its financial instruments project.)

In 1995, a new project steering committee was set up with the objective of producing a progress report to the IASC Board in March 1996. A new advisory group was also formed which was to channel advice received from representatives of major national standard-setting bodies. It became apparent that the original target date for the second stage of the project was not going to be met. The extent of national differences and controversy over recognition and measurement issues and their interrelationships were felt to be such as to require a more comprehensive, long-term approach in order to produce a durable solution.

As a result, a discussion paper, "Accounting for Financial Assets and Financial Liabilities," was published jointly with the CICA in March 1997. In spite of its acknowledged intellectual quality, this discussion paper did not succeed in creating consensus, especially regarding the issue of how far a standard could practicably go in the direction of fair value accounting, and the related issue of the extent to which the resultant unrealized remeasurement gains and losses should be included in net income.

The longer-term, more comprehensive approach advocated by the new project steering committee was then overtaken by the need of the IASC to complete its program of "core standards," which included financial instruments, for approval by IOSCO by early 1999. In order to meet this deadline for the standard on recognition and measurement of financial instruments, a short-term approach was adopted, taking into account the work being done by the FASB on a major new standard, the future FAS-133, due to be issued in 1998. At the same time, the longer-term, more comprehensive approach was to be pursued with the aim of producing a harmonized international standard, in a joint project including the FASB and other national standard-setters. A Joint Working Group was set up with the aim of producing an exposure draft for issuance in 2000 and a proposed final standard in 2001.

E62, "Financial Instruments: Recognition and Measurement," was approved in April 1998 and IAS 39 was approved in December 1998 and published in March 1999. The speed with which the comments on E62 were considered and IAS 39 was approved was unusual, especially as IAS 39 departs from the proposals in E62 in a number of significant respects, which might have been considered to require re-exposure. On the other hand, the differences between IAS 39 and the earlier exposure drafts, E40 and E48, are matters of detail rather than substance, except that IAS 39 does not permit the full fair value approach and is thus more "cautious." The price to be paid for this "caution" is in the complexities of "hedge accounting," which would be avoided if both hedging items and hedged items were measured at fair value and the resultant remeasurement gains and losses were reflected in income.

In July 2000, IASC issued a 16-page exposure draft, E66, setting out a number of proposed "limited revisions" to IAS 39 and other related standards. A final set of limited revisions was issued in November 2000, "to improve specific paragraphs and help ensure that [IAS 32 and 39 and related Standards, IAS 27, IAS 28 and IAS 31] are applied consistently."

During 2000, IASC approved an approach to publish implementation guidance on IAS 39 in the form of Questions and Answers (Q&A) drafted by IASC staff and reviewed and approved by an IAS 39 Implementation Guidance Committee (IGC). The final Q&A document, issued on January 15, 2001, is 224 pages long, and is available on the IASC Web site. (As noted in the "Overview" above, extracts from the Q&A document have been included in this Guide.)

IAS 39 must be applied to accounting periods beginning on or after January 1, 2001, and may be applied voluntarily for accounting periods ending after March 15, 1999. Retrospective application is not permitted. The requirements of IAS 39 also entail revisions to several other IASs.

The aim of the project—to produce a standard that would deal comprehensively with all types of financial instruments for all types of business, and would cover recognition and measurement issues as well as those of presentation and disclosure—may be considered to have been largely met. However, IAS 39 is regarded as an interim measure, and it is still planned for the Joint Working Group to produce a new, internationally harmonized standard.

The main differences from U.S. GAAP are as follows:

1. With respect to recognition and measurement, the scope of IAS 39, which covers financial liabilities and unsecuritized debt, is wider than the combined scopes of FAS-133, "Accounting for Derivative Activities and Hedging Activities," and FAS-115, "Investments in Debt and Equity Securities," which do not cover these items.

2. IAS 39 requires financial liabilities that are neither held for trading nor derivatives to be measured at amortized cost. Liabilities that are held for trading or are derivatives are required to be measured at fair value, subject to the requirements of hedge accounting where applicable. Except for those that are derivatives, FAS-133 does not apply to financial liabilities.

3. IAS 39 lays down measurement rules for "loans and receivables originated by the enterprise and not held for trading."

These are to be measured at amortized cost (subject to impairment review), irrespectively of whether or not the enterprise intends to hold them to maturity. Because FAS-115 does not apply to unsecuritized debt, it lays down no measurement rules for such items. However, FAS-114 lays down rules for dealing with impairment of loans that are similar to those in IAS 39.

4. FAS-133 requires that, to be recognized as a derivative, a financial instrument must require or permit net settlement. IAS 39 makes no such requirement.

5. IAS 39 includes gains and losses on fair value hedges in net income (profit or loss), while FAS-133 includes them in comprehensive income but excludes them from net income.

6. IAS 39 treats foreign currency hedges as a type of cash flow hedge, while FAS-133 treats them as a separate category. Gains or losses on the ineffective portion of a cash flow hedge are included in net income under both standards, but under FAS-133 gains or losses on the ineffective portion of a foreign currency hedge are treated like those on a fair value hedge and excluded from net income.

7. IAS 39 treats hedges of a net investment in a foreign entity in the same way as it treats cash flow hedges. FAS-133 treats gains or losses on such hedges as part of the cumulative translation adjustment that is included in comprehensive income, but they are not separately disclosed.

8. Under IAS 39, a forecasted foreign currency transaction that is hedged need only be "highly probable" in order for any effectively hedged gain or loss not to be included in current net income but recognized directly in equity. U.S. GAAP (FAS-52) require a hedged foreign currency transaction to be "a firm commitment" in order for any effectively hedged gain or loss to be recognized directly in equity. In U.S. GAAP, being "highly probable" is acceptable for hedge accounting of forecasted transactions in the case of cash flow hedges, but not in the case of foreign currency hedges.

9. In the case of cash flow hedges, FAS-133 lays down more detailed and stringent criteria than IAS 39 for forecasted transactions to be recognized as hedged items.

10. FAS-133 effectively prohibits hedging on a portfolio basis (macro-hedging), which is allowed by IAS 39 in some cases.

SCOPE

Describing the scope of IAS GAAP on financial instruments is somewhat complex because, although some categories of items are excluded, there are exceptions to those exclusions. In addition, while IAS 32 and IAS 39 have almost the same scope, there are a few exceptions (see point 5 below). Most of the exclusions, however, result from categories of items being covered by other IASs (see points 1, 2, 3, 6, and 7 below).

The scope of IAS GAAP on financial instruments is set out in IAS 32, paragraphs 1–6 and IAS 39, paragraphs 1–7.

IAS GAAP on financial instruments apply to all enterprises, including banks and insurance companies, and to all financial instruments, *with the following exclusions*:

1. Interests in subsidiaries, associates, and joint ventures that are accounted for under IAS 27, "Consolidated Financial Statements and Accounting for Investments in Subsidiaries," IAS 28, "Accounting for Investments in Associates," and IAS 31, "Financial Reporting of Interests in Joint Ventures" (see Chapter 9). However, an enterprise should apply IAS 39 in its consolidated financial statements to account for an interest in a subsidiary, associate or joint venture that: (a) is acquired and held *exclusively* with a view to its subsequent disposal in the *near* future; or (b) operates under severe long-term restrictions that significantly impair its ability to transfer funds to the enterprise. In these cases, the disclosure requirements in IAS 27, IAS 28, and IAS 31 also apply.

2. Rights and obligations under leases, to which IAS 17, "Leases," applies. However, lease receivables recognized in a lessor's balance sheet are subject to the derecognition provisions of IAS 39, and IAS 39 also applies to derivatives that are embedded in leases (see Chapter 25).

3. Employers' assets and obligations under employee benefit plans, to which IAS 19, "Employee Benefits," and IAS 26, "Accounting and Reporting by Retirement Benefit Plans," apply (see Chapter 13).

4. Rights and obligations under insurance contracts, that is, contracts that expose the insurer to identified risks of loss from events or circumstances occurring or discovered within a specified period, *except for* financial instruments that take the form of an insurance contract but principally involve the transfer of financial risks, and derivatives that are embedded in insurance contracts. Thus, some types of financial reinsurance and guaranteed investment contracts issued by insurance companies and other enterprises are within the scope of IAS GAAP on financial instruments.

5. Equity instruments issued by the reporting enterprise, including options, warrants, and other financial instruments classified as shareholders' equity of the reporting enterprise, are not

subject to the recognition and measurement requirements of IAS 39 as applied by the issuing enterprise. However, they are subject (a) to the presentation and disclosure requirements of IAS 32 as applied by the issuing enterprise and (b) to the full requirements of IAS GAAP on financial instruments as applied by the holder of such instruments. (See also point 23 under "Definitions," below.)

6. The type of financial guarantee contracts, including letters of credit, that provide for payments to be made if the debtor *to the holder of the guarantee contract* fails to make payment when due, and to which IAS 37, "Provisions, Contingent Liabilities and Contingent Assets," is applicable (see Chapter 28). If the holder of the debt asset is a third party, the guarantee contract is not excluded from IAS GAAP on financial instruments. Also, the type of financial guarantee contract that provides for payments to be made in response to changes in a specified underlying variable (such as an interest rate, security price, commodity price, foreign exchange rate, price index, credit rating, etc.) is subject to IAS GAAP on financial instruments.

7. Contracts for contingent consideration in a business combination, to which IAS 22, "Business Combinations," applies (see Chapter 6).

8. Contracts that require a payment based on climatic, geological, or other physical variables. However, IAS GAAP on financial instruments apply to derivatives that are embedded in such contracts and are required by IAS GAAP to be separated from the host contract.

IAS GAAP on financial instruments apply to commodity-based contracts that give either party the right to settle in cash or some other financial instrument, but *not* to the type of commodity contracts (forward contracts) that: (a) were entered into, and continue, to meet the enterprise's expected requirements for purchase, sale, or usage; (b) were designated for that purpose at their inception; and (c) are expected to be settled by delivery. However, if an enterprise follows the practice of using offsetting contracts that effectively achieve settlement on a net basis, such contracts cannot be considered as having been "entered into in order to meet the enterprise's expected requirements for purchase, sale or usage" (IAS 39, pars. 6–7).

DEFINITIONS

The definitions given in IAS 32, paragraphs 5–17, are repeated in IAS 39, paragraphs 8–26, where a considerable number of additional definitions are also given. In view of the complexity of the subject matter, these definitions play an important role in contributing to the clarity of the standards. They are as follows (note that the term "enterprise" as used below may refer to individuals as well as to incorporated bodies, partnerships, and government agencies).

Definitions from IAS 32

1. A *financial instrument* is any contract that gives rise to a financial asset of one enterprise and a financial liability of another enterprise.

2. A *financial asset* is any asset that is any of the following:
   a. cash (but not gold bullion, which is a commodity);
   b. a contractual right to receive cash or another financial asset from another enterprise;
   c. a contractual right to exchange financial instruments with another enterprise under conditions that are potentially favorable;
   d. an equity instrument of another enterprise.

3. A *financial liability* is any liability that is a contractual obligation:
   a. to deliver cash or another financial asset to another enterprise; or
   b. to exchange financial instruments with another enterprise under conditions that are potentially unfavorable.

4. An *equity instrument* is any contract that is evidence of a residual interest in the assets of an enterprise after deducting all of its liabilities.

5. *Fair value* is the amount for which an asset could be exchanged, or a liability settled, between knowledgeable, willing parties in an arm's-length transaction. IAS 39, paragraph 10, provides the further definitions given below, and IAS 39, paragraph 11, provides extensive elaboration on a number of definitions.

Definition of a Derivative

6. A *derivative* is a financial instrument:
   a. the value of which changes in response to the change in a specified underlying variable, such as an interest rate, security price, commodity price, foreign exchange rate, index of prices or rates, credit rating or credit index, or any similar variable;
   b. which requires no, or little, initial net investment relative to other types of contracts that have a similar response to changes in market conditions; and
   c. which is settled at a future date.

☛ **PRACTICE POINTER:** The prepayment on a prepaid pay-fixed, receive-variable interest rate swap is not considered as an initial net investment for this purpose, so that the swap contract is a derivative. However, the prepayment on a prepaid pay-variable, receive-fixed interest rate swap *is* considered as an initial net investment, and the swap contract is not a derivative. Margin accounts do not constitute an initial net investment, as they are a form of collateral, not a prepayment.

Definitions of Four Categories of Financial Assets (and of Liabilities Held for Trading)

7. A *financial asset (or financial liability) held for trading* is one which was acquired (or incurred) principally for the purpose of generating a profit from short-term fluctuations in price or from a dealer's margin. A financial asset should also be classified as "held for trading" if, regardless of why it was acquired, it is part of a portfolio of assets in respect of which there is evidence of a recent actual pattern of short-term profit-taking from short-term fluctuations in price or a dealer's margin.

   Derivative financial assets and derivative financial liabilities are always deemed to be "held for trading" unless designated as effective hedging instruments (see under "Hedge Accounting" below). In addition to derivatives, liabilities held for trading include an obligation to deliver securities borrowed by a short seller (an enterprise which has sold securities that it does not own). Being used to fund trading activities does not mean that a liability is "held for trading."

8. *Held-to-maturity investments* are financial assets with fixed or determinable payments and fixed maturity that an enterprise has the positive intent and ability to hold to maturity, other than loans and receivables originated by the enterprise. (This definition receives further elaboration in the section on "Measurement," below.)

9. *Loans and receivables originated by the enterprise* are financial assets that are created by the enterprise by providing money, goods, or services directly to a debtor, except for those which are originated with the intent of their being sold immediately or in the short term for the purpose of generating a profit, which should be classified as "held for trading." Loans and receivables originated by the enterprise are distinguished from held-to-maturity investments in IAS GAAP by virtue of their being originated by the enterprise and not acquired from another lender, and include such items when acquired in a business combination provided they were similarly classified by the acquiree. (This definition receives further elaboration in point 25, below.)

10. *Available for sale financial assets* are those financial assets that are not included in any of the three categories described above, held for trading, held to maturity, or loans and receivables originated by the enterprise.

Definitions Relating to Recognition and Measurement

11. *Amortized cost of a financial asset or financial liability* is the amount at which the item was measured on its initial recognition, minus any repayments of principal, plus or minus the cumulative amortization of any difference between that amount and the amount due on maturity, and minus any write-down (directly or by using an allowance account) for impairment or uncollectability.

12. The *effective interest method* is a method of calculating amortization using the effective interest rate of a financial asset or liability. The *effective interest rate* of a financial instrument is that rate which, when used in a present value calculation, results in the carrying amount of the instrument. The present value calculation applies the interest rate to the expected stream of future cash receipts or payments for the period to maturity (or to the next market-based repricing date) and to the principal amount due (or expected carrying amount) at that date. The effective interest rate is thus the internal rate of return on the instrument for that period, sometimes known as the yield to maturity (or to the next repricing date). The computation should include all fees and points paid or received between the contracting parties. (The rate is a historical rate for a fixed rate instrument carried at amortized cost, and a current market rate for a floating rate instrument carried at fair value.) (IAS 32, par. 61; IAS 39, par. 10.)

13. *Transaction costs* are incremental costs that are directly attributable to the acquisition or disposal of a financial instrument. They include fees and commissions paid to agents, advisers, brokers, and dealers; levies by regulatory agencies and securities exchanges; and transfer taxes and duties. They do not include debt premium or discount, financing costs, or allocations of internal administrative or holding costs.

14. A *firm commitment* is a binding agreement for the exchange of a specified quantity of resources at a specified price on a specified date or dates.

15. *Control* of an asset is the power to obtain the future economic benefits that are expected to flow from the asset.

16. *Derecognition* is the removal of a financial asset or liability, or a portion thereof, from an enterprise's balance sheet.

Definitions Relating to Hedge Accounting

(These definitions are further elaborated in the section on "Hedging," below.)

17. *Hedging*, for accounting purposes, means designating one or more hedging instruments so that the change in their fair values is an offset, in whole or in part, to the change in the fair value of, or the cash flows from, a hedged item.

18. A *hedged item* is an asset, liability, firm commitment, or forecasted future transaction which (a) exposes the enterprise to risk of changes in fair value or in future cash flows and (b) for hedge accounting purposes is designated as being hedged.

19. A *hedging instrument*, for hedge accounting purposes, is a designated derivative or (in the limited circumstances indicated below) non-derivative financial asset or liability, for which changes in its fair value or cash flows are expected to offset changes in the fair value or cash flows of a designated hedged item. In IAS GAAP, a non-derivative financial instrument may be designated as a hedging instrument for hedge accounting purposes only if it hedges the risk of changes in foreign currency exchange rates.

20. *Hedge effectiveness* is the degree to which offsetting changes in fair value or cash flows attributable to a hedged risk are achieved by the hedging instrument.

Other Definitions

21. *Securitization* is the process whereby financial assets are transformed into securities.

22. A *repurchase agreement* is an agreement to transfer a financial asset to another party in exchange for cash or other consideration and a concurrent obligation to reacquire the financial asset at a future date for an amount equal to the cash or other consideration exchanged plus interest.

Elaboration on the Definitions

23. *Equity instruments.* An enterprise may have a contractual obligation that it can settle by payment in the form either of financial assets or of its own equity securities. In such a case, if the number of equity securities required to settle the obligation varies with changes in their fair value, so that the total fair

value of the equity securities used as payment always equals the amount of the contractual obligation, then the holder of the obligation is not exposed to gain or loss from fluctuations in the price of the equity securities. The obligation should therefore be accounted for as a financial liability of the enterprise, and it is not covered by the exclusion of equity instruments issued by the enterprise from the scope of IAS GAAP on financial instruments (see point 5 in the "Scope" section, above). Note that, for such an obligation (for example, a forward contract, option, or other derivative), its value is unrelated to changes in the value of the equity of the enterprise, and it is thus not itself an equity instrument.

24. *Derivatives.* Typical examples of derivatives are futures, forward, swap, and option contracts. A derivative usually has a notional amount, such as an amount of currency, a number of shares, a number of units of weight or volume, or of other units, specified in the contract; but the holder or writer of the derivative is not required to invest or receive this notional amount at the inception of the contract. A currency swap contract, in which the amount of currency to be swapped at a pre-determined exchange rate depends on sales made in that currency, is a derivative. A fixed payment may be required contingent upon some future event that is unrelated to the notional amount. The fixed price commitment between trade date and settlement date in a "regular way" contract for the purchase of a financial asset is a forward contract that meets the definition of a derivative. (This is further elaborated under "'Regular Way' Contracts" in the section on "Recognition," below.)

Commitments to buy or sell non-financial assets and liabilities that are intended to be settled by the reporting enterprise by making or taking delivery in the normal course of business, and for which there is no practice of settling net (either with the counterparty or by entering into offsetting contracts), are accounted for as executory contracts, not as derivatives. "Settling net" means making a cash payment based on the change in fair value.

25. *Loans and Receivables Originated by the Enterprise.* A loan acquired as a participation in a loan from another lender is considered to be originated by the enterprise, provided the enterprise funds its participation in the loan on the date on which the loan is originated by the other lender. Likewise, a loan acquired through syndication is an originated loan, as each lender shares in the origination. However, the acquisition of an interest in a pool of existing loans or receivables (for example, in a securitization) is a purchase, not an origination. Likewise, a transaction that is, in substance, a purchase of an existing loan or receivable (such as a loan to an unconsolidated special

purpose entity made to provide funding for its purchases of loans originated by others), is not a loan or receivable originated by the enterprise.

26. *Available-to-Sale Financial Assets.* A financial asset is classified as available for sale if it does not properly belong in one of the three other categories of financial assets. A financial asset is classified as held for trading, rather than available for sale, if it is part of a portfolio of similar assets for which there is a pattern of trading for the purpose of generating a profit from short-term price fluctuations or dealer's margin.

Embedded Derivatives

An "embedded derivative" is a component of a hybrid financial instrument that comprises both the derivative and a "host contract," with the effect that some of the cash flows of the combined instrument vary like those of a stand-alone derivative. It causes some or all of the cash flows that would otherwise be required by the host contract to be modified, based on the behavior of a specified variable such as an interest rate, security price, commodity price, foreign exchange rate, index of prices or rates, or other variable (IAS 39, par. 22).

☛ **PRACTICE POINTER:** A separately transferable derivative that is attached to a non-derivative financial instrument (such as a transferable call option) is not an embedded derivative.

An embedded derivative should be separated from the host contract and treated as a derivative in IAS GAAP if all of the following conditions are met (IAS 39, par. 23):

1. The economic characteristics and risks of the embedded derivative are not closely related to those of the host contract;

2. A separate instrument with the same terms as the embedded derivative would meet the definition of a derivative in IAS GAAP; and

3. The hybrid instrument is not itself measured at fair value with changes in fair value being included in net profit or loss.

In those circumstances, the host contract should be accounted for, either under IAS 39 if it is a financial instrument, or under the applicable IAS if it is not, unless the enterprise is unable to measure the embedded derivative separately either initially or at a subsequent reporting date. In case of such inability, the enterprise should treat the entire combined contract as a financial instrument held for trading.

☛ **PRACTICE POINTER:** The host contract and an embedded derivative that can be measured separately at fair value do not need to be separately disclosed, unless the former is measured at cost (IAS 32, pars. 46 and 77). If separation between a host contract and an embedded derivative is required, the initial carrying amount assigned to the host contract on separation is the difference between the cost of (i.e., the fair value of consideration given for) the hybrid instrument and the fair value of the embedded derivative.

Examples of embedded derivatives with economic characteristics and risks not closely related to the host contract are given in 1–7 below.

1. A put option on an equity instrument held by an enterprise is not closely related to the host equity instrument.

2. A call option embedded in an equity instrument held by an enterprise is not closely related to the host equity instrument from the holder's perspective. If the issuer is required or has the right to require settlement in its own shares, the call option is an equity instrument of the issuer, and therefore fails to meet the condition of not being closely related to the host instrument for the issuer's accounting purposes.

3. An option or automatic provision to extend the term of debt is not closely related to the host debt contract, unless there is a concurrent adjustment of the interest rate to the market rate at the time of the extension.

4. Contracts involving payments of interest or principal that are equity-indexed (that is, the amount payable is indexed to the value of equity shares), or commodity-indexed (that is, the amount payable is indexed to the price of a commodity), are not closely related to the host debt or insurance contract because the risks of the embedded derivative and the host contract are dissimilar.

5. An equity conversion feature embedded in a debt instrument is not closely related to the debt instrument.

6. A call or put option on debt that is issued at a significant discount or premium is not closely related to the debt, except for debt (such as a zero coupon bond) that is callable or puttable at its accreted amount.

7. Credit derivatives that are embedded in a host debt instrument, and allow one party (the beneficiary) to transfer the credit risk of an asset which the beneficiary may or may not actually own to another party (the guarantor), are not closely related to the debt instrument. Such derivatives allow the guarantor to assume the credit risk associated with an asset without purchasing it.

☞ **PRACTICE POINTER:** With reference to item 4 above, the same applies to purchases and sales denominated in a foreign currency that is neither the currency of the primary economic environment of either party nor the currency in which the product is routinely priced in international commerce. An example would be sales of oil (routinely priced in U.S.$) by a Norwegian supplier to a French customer priced in Swiss francs. Both companies have embedded forward contracts in Swiss francs: the Norwegian company to buy them and the French company to sell them. Moreover, these embedded forward currency contracts are not closely related in terms of economic characteristics and risks to the host supply contract.

Examples of embedded derivatives with economic characteristics and risks that are closely related to those of the host contract are given in items 1–8 below. Such derivatives are not accounted for separately from the host instrument under IAS GAAP (IAS 39, par. 25).

1. The embedded derivative that is linked to an interest rate or interest rate index that can change the amount of interest that would otherwise have been paid or received on the host debt contract is closely linked to the latter. Thus, floating rate debt cannot be split into fixed rate debt plus an embedded derivative.

2. An embedded floor or cap on interest rates is closely related to the interest rate on a debt instrument if the cap (floor) is at or above (below) the market rate of interest when the instrument is issued, and is not leveraged in relation to the host instrument.

3. An embedded derivative that is a stream of principal or interest payments denominated in a foreign currency is not separated from the host contract under IAS GAAP, because IAS 21, "The Effects of Changes in Foreign Exchange Rates," requires that foreign currency translation gains and losses on the entire host monetary item be recognized in net profit or loss.

4. A contract that is not a financial instrument, and that requires payments denominated in either (a) the currency of the primary economic environment in which any substantial party to the contract operates or (b) the currency routinely used in international commerce to denominate the price of the related good or service (such as the U.S.$ for crude oil), is not regarded as a host contract with an embedded foreign currency derivative.

5. The embedded derivative is a prepayment option with an exercise price that would not result in a significant gain or loss.

6. The embedded derivative is a prepayment option embedded in an interest-only or principal-only strip that (a) initially resulted from splitting the right to receive contractual cash flows of a financial instrument that did not, of itself, contain such an embedded derivative and (b) does not contain any terms not present in the original host debt contract.

7. The host contract is a lease, and the embedded derivative is either (a) the indexing of lease payments based on an inflation-related index such as a consumer price index (provided the index relates to inflation in the enterprise's own economic environment and the lease is not leveraged), (b) contingent rentals based on related sales, or (c) contingent rentals based on variable interest rates.

8. The embedded derivative links interest payments to an interest rate or interest rate index that does not alter the amount of the net interest payments that would otherwise be paid on the host contract in such a way as to disadvantage either the holder or the issuer as follows: the holder of the host asset would not recover substantially all of its recorded investment, or (in the case of a liability) the issuer would pay a rate more than twice the market rate at inception.

☛ **PRACTICE POINTER:** The equity conversion option of a convertible bond (a hybrid instrument) is an embedded derivative that should be separated from the host contract *only if* the latter is not accounted for at fair value with remeasurement gains or losses being reported in net profit or loss for the period.

RECOGNITION AND DERECOGNITION

Recognition of financial instruments is covered in IAS 39, paragraphs 27–34, and derecognition is covered in IAS 39, paragraphs 35–36.

Recognition

The basic rule for initial recognition is that an enterprise should recognize a financial asset or a financial liability on its balance sheet when, and only when, the enterprise becomes a party to the contractual provisions of the instrument (IAS 39, par. 27). Thus, planned future transactions of an enterprise, no matter how likely, are not assets or liabilities of that enterprise (IAS 39, par. 29).

Assets to be acquired and liabilities to be incurred as a result of a firm commitment to purchase or sell goods or services are not recognized as assets or liabilities until at least one of the parties has performed under the agreement so as to be either entitled to receive an asset or obligated to disburse an asset (such as when ordered goods are delivered) (IAS 39, par. 29).

However, a forward contract is recognized as an asset or liability on the commitment date, rather than on the closing date on which the exchange actually takes place. Although the fair values of the right and the obligation under the forward contract are generally equal on the commitment date (that is, the net fair value is zero), each party is exposed to the price risk inherent in the contract as from the commitment date, and the net fair value is unlikely to remain equal to zero. Hence, the recognition principle stated above is satisfied, from the perspectives of the buyer and the seller, at the time they become parties to the contract. Likewise, financial options are recognized as assets or liabilities when the holder or writer becomes a party to the contract (IAS 39, par. 29).

"Regular Way" Contracts: Trade Date versus Settlement Date

"Regular way" contracts are dealt with in IAS 39, paragraphs 30–34. A "regular way" contract is a contract for the purchase or sale of financial assets that requires delivery of the assets *within the time frame generally established* by regulation or convention in the market concerned. The fixed price commitment between the *trade date* (on which the contract is established) and the *settlement date* (on which the asset is delivered) is similar to that under a forward contract and meets the definition of a derivative. However, the duration of the commitment is short, and therefore such a contract is not recognized as a derivative in IAS GAAP.

> ☞ **PRACTICE POINTER:** A bank's commitment to make a loan at a specified rate of interest during a fixed period is a derivative (an option issued by the bank); but if the commitment allows drawdown of the loan within the time-frame generally established (the period expected to be needed for the bank to perform the underwriting, and for the transaction that is the subject of the loan to be scheduled and executed), then the "regular way" exemption applies.

For purchases or sales of financial assets under "regular way" contracts, IAS GAAP allow enterprises a choice between a policy of *trade date accounting* and a policy of *settlement date accounting*. The policy chosen should be applied consistently for all purchases and sales of financial assets that belong to the same category of financial assets defined in IAS 39, paragraph 10 (see points 7–10 in "Definitions," above).

Under trade date accounting, the asset to be received and the liability to pay for it are both recognized by the buyer, and the asset to be delivered is derecognized and the receivable from the buyer is recognized by the seller, on the trade date; however, interest generally does not start to accrue on either the asset or the liability until the settlement date.

Under settlement date accounting, the asset and the corresponding liability are not recognized by the buyer, and the asset is not derecognized and the receivable is not recognized by the seller, until the settlement date. When settlement date accounting is used for purchases under "regular way" contracts, the issue arises of how any change in the fair value of the purchased asset during the period between trade date and settlement date should be treated. In IAS GAAP, the treatment of value changes that occur during this period (the settlement period) depends on the classification of the related asset (see IAS 39, pars. 103–106). Thus, value changes that occur during the settlement period are not recognized for assets carried at cost or amortized cost. For assets classified as held for trading, value changes that occur during the settlement period are recognized in net profit or loss and, for assets classified as available-for-sale, value changes are recognized either in net profit or loss or directly in equity, according to the enterprise's chosen accounting policy.

In IAS GAAP, the treatment of a change in fair value during this period follows that of the asset itself, depending on its classification. That is, the value change is not recognized for assets carried at cost or amortized cost; it is recognized in net profit or loss for assets classified as trading; and it is recognized either in net profit or loss or directly in equity (in accordance with IAS 39, pars. 103–106) for assets classified as available for sale.

Illustration—Settlement Date or Trade Date Accounting

The following example, adapted from IAS 39, paragraph 34, illustrates the application of the above. On December 29, 2001, an enterprise commits to purchase a financial asset for $1,000 (including transaction costs), which is its fair value on the trade (commitment) date. On December 31, 2001 (fiscal year end) and on January 4, 2002 (settlement date) the fair value of the asset is $1,002 and $1,003, respectively. The amounts to be recorded in respect of the asset will depend on how it is classified and whether trade date accounting or settlement date accounting is used. This is illustrated in the two tables below. (Note: brackets denote credits.)

Settlement Date Accounting

Balances	Held-to-Maturity Investments— Carried at Amortized Cost	Available-for- Sale Assets— Remeasured to Fair Value with Changes in Equity	Assets Held for Trading and Available-for- Sale Assets— Remeasured to Fair Value with Changes in Profit or Loss
December 29, 20X1			
Financial asset	—	—	—
Liability	—	—	—
December 31, 20X1			
Receivable	—	$2	$2
Financial asset	—	—	—
Liability	—	—	—
Equity (fair value adjustment)	—	(2)	—
Retained earnings (through net profit or loss)	—	—	(2)
January 4, 20X2			
Receivable	$1,000	$1,003	$1,003
Financial asset	—	—	—
Liability	—	—	—
Equity (fair value adjustment)	—	(3)	—
Retained earnings (through net profit or loss)	—	—	(3)

Trade Date Accounting

Balances	Held-to-Maturity Investments— Carried at Amortized Cost	Available-for- Sale Assets— Remeasured to Fair Value with Changes in Equity	Assets Held for Trading and Available-for- Sale Assets— Remeasured to Fair Value with Changes in Profit or Loss
December 29, 20X1			
Financial asset	$1,000	$1,000	$1,000
Liability	(1,000)	(1,000)	(1,000)
December 31, 20X1			
Receivable	$1,000	$1,002	$1,002
Financial asset	(1,000)	(1,000)	(1,000)
Liability	—	—	—
Equity (fair value adjustment)	—	(2)	—
Retained earnings (through net profit or loss)	—	—	(2)
January 4, 20X2			
Receivable	$1,000	$1,003	$1,003
Financial asset	—	—	—
Liability	—	—	—
Equity (fair value adjustment)	—	(3)	—
Retained earnings (through net profit or loss)	—	—	(3)

Derecognition

The term *to derecognize* is used in IAS GAAP to mean "to cease to recognize," that is, to remove from the balance sheet. The issue of the derecognition of financial assets and financial liabilities, in whole or in part, is covered in IAS 39, paragraphs 35–65. The issue is complex because of the various ways in which such items may be transferred or discharged, wholly or partly, with the possibility of repurchase options or other derivatives being involved.

Derecognition of a Financial Asset

An enterprise should derecognize a financial asset or a portion of a financial asset when, and only when, the enterprise loses control of the contractual rights that comprise that asset or portion of an asset. Such loss of control occurs if one of the following three conditions is satisfied: (a) the enterprise realizes the rights to benefits specified in the contract; (b) the rights expire without being realized; or (c) the enterprise surrenders those rights. Determining whether an enterprise has lost control of a financial asset depends on the position of the transferee as well as that of the transferor.

A financial asset may be transferred to another enterprise without any of the three conditions (a)–(c) cited above being satisfied. In that case, the transfer is treated as part of a collateralized borrowing, and the transferor's right to reacquire the asset is not a derivative (IAS 39, pars. 35–37).

Examples of situations in which the transfer of a financial asset does not entail loss of control, and hence the asset should not be derecognized, are:

1. The transferor has the right to reacquire the transferred asset and neither of the following conditions (which would effectively nullify the value of that right) obtains: (a) the asset can be readily obtained in the market; or (b) the reacquisition price is fair value at the date of reacquisition.

2. The transferor is both entitled and obligated to repurchase the transferred asset on terms that effectively provide the transferee with a lender's return on the asset or asset exchanged for the transferred asset, that is, a return not materially different from that which could be obtained on a loan to the transferor fully secured on the transferred asset.

3. The asset transferred is not readily obtainable in the market and the transferor has retained substantially all of either: (a) the risks of, and returns from, ownership through a total return swap with the transferee (a total return swap provides the market returns and credit risks to one party in return for a payment based on an interest index such as LIBOR to the other party); or (b) the risks of ownership through an unconditional put option on the transferred asset issued by the transferor and held by the transferee (IAS 39, par. 38).

In general, control of a transferred asset is lost by the transferor only if the transferee has the ability to obtain the benefits of the asset. Evidence of this ability might be provided by the transferee being able to sell or pledge approximately the full fair value of the asset; however, this would not be conclusive evidence in all cases. For example, a bank might transfer a loan to another bank, but, in order to preserve its relationship with the customer to whom the loan was made, might stipulate that the transferee cannot sell or pledge the loan. In spite of this stipulation, provided the transferor has neither the right nor the ability to reacquire the transferred asset, the transfer is a sale and the transferor should derecognize the asset (IAS 39, pars. 41–42).

> ☛ **PRACTICE POINTER:** The same applies if the transferee has the ability to sell or pledge its *beneficial interest* in the transferred financial assets, even though it is unable to sell or pledge the *underlying* financial assets (as in the case of a sale through a special purpose entity).

Gains or Losses on Derecognition of an Asset

On derecognition, the difference between:

(1) the carrying amount of an asset (or portion of an asset) transferred to another party, and

(2) the sum of (i) the proceeds received or receivable and (ii) in the case of an asset classified as available for sale, the cumulative amount of any adjustments to reflect changes in the fair value of that asset which had been recognized directly in equity, should be included in net profit or loss for the period (IAS 39, par. 43).

Derecognition of Part of a Financial Asset

An enterprise may transfer part of a financial asset to one or more other parties, while retaining another part of that asset. Examples are:

1. Stripping the cash flows of the payment of interest on a bond from those of the repayment of principal, and selling one to another party while retaining the other; or

2. Selling a portfolio of receivables while retaining the right to service the receivables profitably for a fee, resulting in an asset for the servicing right.

If an enterprise transfers part of a financial asset to one or more other parties, while retaining another part, the carrying amount of the asset should be allocated between the part retained and the part sold on the basis of their relative fair values on the date of sale, and a gain or loss should be recognized on the proceeds of the part sold.

If the fair value of the part retained cannot be ascertained reliably, then it should be valued at zero and the entire carrying amount of the asset should be attributed to the part sold. In that case, a gain or loss should be recognized equal to the difference between: (a) the proceeds from the part sold; and (b) the entire carrying amount of the asset, adjusted in the case of an asset classified as available for sale by adding back or subtracting any prior losses or gains from changes in fair value which had been recognized directly in equity (IAS 39, pars. 47–48).

Illustration—Sale or Securitization in Which Servicing Is Maintained

This example illustrates how a transferor accounts for a sale or securitization in which servicing is retained. An enterprise originates $1,000 of loans that yield 10% interest for their estimated lives of 9 years. The enterprise sells the $1,000 principal plus the right to receive interest income of 8% of another enterprise for $1,000. The transferor will continue to service the loans, and the contract stipulates that its compensation for performing the servicing is the right to receive half of the interest income not sold (that is, 100 of the 200 basis points). The remaining half of the interest income not sold is considered an interest-only strip receivable. At the date of the transfer, the fair value of the loans, including servicing, is $1,100, of which the fair value of the servicing asset is $40 and the fair value of the interest-only strip receivable is $60. Allocation of the $1,000 carrying amount of the loan is computed as follows:

	Fair Value	Percentage of Total Fair Value	Allocated Carrying Amount
Loans sold	$1,000	91.0%	$ 910
Servicing asset	40	3.6	36
Interest-only strip receivable	60	5.4	54
Total	$1,100	100.0%	$1,000

The transferor will recognize a gain of $90 on the sale of the loan—the difference between the net proceeds of $1,000 and the allocated carrying amount of $910. Its balance sheet will also report a servicing asset of $36 and an interest-only strip receivable of $54. The servicing asset is an intangible asset subject to the provisions of IAS 38, "Intangible Assets."

Asset Derecognition Coupled with Recognition of a New Asset or Liability

An enterprise may transfer control of an entire financial asset but in the process create a new financial asset or assume a new financial liability (IAS 39, pars. 51–52). Examples are:

1. Selling a portfolio of receivables while assuming an obligation to compensate the purchaser if collections are below a certain level, thus assuming a guarantee liability; or

2. Selling a portfolio of receivables while retaining the right to service them for a fee which is greater than the cost of servicing, thus creating an asset representing the profit on servicing.

> **OBSERVATION:** The second example given in IAS 39, paragraph 52, is of the sale of a portfolio of receivables when retaining the right to service them for a fee which is less than the cost of doing so, thus creating a liability. As no further example is given of the creation of a new asset, we have modified the second example so as to do so.

Illustration—Asset Derecognition

To illustrate the first example given above, consider the following. Company A transfers certain receivables to Company B for a single, fixed cash payment. Company A is not obligated to make future payments of interest on the cash it has received from Company B. However, Company A guarantees Company B against default loss on the receivables up to a specified amount. Actual losses in excess of the amount guaranteed will be borne by Company B. As a result of the transaction, Company A has lost control over the receivables and Company B has obtained control. Company B now has the contractual right to receive cash inherent in the receivables, as well as a guarantee from Company A. Hence, under IAS GAAP:

1. The receivables are recognized by Company B on its balance sheet, and are derecognized (removed from its balance sheet) by Company A;

2. The guarantee is treated as a separate financial instrument, created as a result of the transfer. It is recognized as a financial liability by Company A, and as a financial asset by Company B (which, for practical purposes, might include the guarantee with the receivables). Note that this illustration assumes that the fair value of Company A's guarantee to Company B can be reliably estimated or measured (IAS 39, par. 53).

If the fair value of a new financial asset or financial liability created in a transfer transaction cannot be measured reliably, then (IAS 39, pars. 54–55):

1. In the case of a financial asset, its initial carrying amount is zero, and a gain or loss is recognized equal to the difference

between (i) the proceeds from the transaction and (ii) the previous carrying amount of the derecognized financial asset, plus or minus any prior losses or gains from changes in the fair value of the asset which had been recognized directly in equity;

2. In the case of a new financial liability that cannot be measured reliably, its initial carrying amount should be such that no gain is recognized on the transaction, any excess of the proceeds over the carrying amount being recognized as a liability; and if the circumstances are such that IAS 37, "Provisions, Contingent Liabilities and Contingent Assets" (see Chapter 28), requires the additional recognition of a provision, this will entail recognition of a loss.

> **OBSERVATION:** If no recognition of a provision and a concomitant loss is required, there may be a need under IAS 37 for disclosure of a contingent liability.

If a guarantee is recognized as a liability of the guarantor, it continues to be so recognized and is measured at fair value (or, if fair value cannot be reliably estimated, at the greater of its originally recorded amount and any provision required under IAS 37), until it expires. If the guarantee involves a large population of items, its fair value should be estimated by calculating a probability-weighted average of all possible outcomes (IAS 39, par. 56).

Derecognition of a Financial Liability

A financial liability (or part of a financial liability) should be derecognized when, and only when, it is extinguished by the obligation specified in the contract being discharged or canceled, or expiring. This condition is met when either:

1. The debtor discharges the liability (or part thereof) by paying the creditor, normally with cash, other financial assets, or services; or

2. The debtor is legally released from primary responsibility for the liability (or part thereof) either by process of law or by the creditor. If the debtor has given a guarantee, this does not necessarily prevent the condition from being met.

☛ **PRACTICE POINTER:** This includes the case in which an enterprise buys back one of its own bonds, even if it has the intention to re-sell it. The liability should be derecognized.

Payment to a third party, such as a trust (as in the case of "in-substance defeasance"), does not by itself relieve the debtor of its primary obligation to the creditor, in the absence of legal release (IAS 39, pars. 57–59).

Moreover, while legal release, either judicially or by the creditor, results in derecognition of a liability, recognition of a new liability may be required when non-cash financial assets are transferred to secure that release without the transfer meeting the derecognition criteria for such assets. In such a case, the transferred assets are not removed from the transferor's balance sheet, and the transferor recognizes a new liability related to the transferred assets which may be equal in amount to the liability that was derecognized (IAS 39, par. 60).

An exchange between an existing borrower and lender of debt instruments with substantially different terms is an extinguishment of the old debt that should result in its derecognition and the creation of a new debt instrument that should be recognized as such. The same treatment consisting of extinction and derecognition of an old debt instrument, and recognition of a new debt instrument, should be applied to a "substantial modification" of the terms of an existing debt instrument, whether or not this is due to financial difficulty on the part of the debtor. The criterion for deciding whether the terms are "substantially different" is that the discounted present value of the cash flows under the new terms, including any fees paid net of any fees received, differs by at least 10% from the discounted present value of the original debt instrument.

If an exchange of debt instruments or a modification of terms is accounted for as an extinguishment in accordance with the above, any costs or fees are recognized as part of the gain or loss on the extinguishment. However, if the transaction is not accounted for as an extinguishment, any costs or fees are treated as an adjustment to the carrying amount of the liability and are amortized over the remaining term of the modified loan (IAS 39, pars. 61–62).

The difference between (a) the carrying amount of a liability (or part of a liability) that is derecognized because it has been extinguished or transferred to another party, including any related unamortized costs, and (b) the amount paid in respect of its extinction or transfer, should be included in profit or loss for the period (IAS 39, par. 63).

If a creditor releases a debtor from its present obligation to make payments, but the debtor assumes an obligation (guarantee) to pay if the party assuming primary responsibility defaults, the debtor recognizes: (a) a new financial liability based on the fair value of the guarantee obligation; and (b) a gain or loss based on the difference between (i) any proceeds and (ii) the carrying amount of the original financial liability (including any related unamortized costs) minus the fair value of the new financial liability (IAS 39, par. 64).

Derecognition of Part of a Financial Liability, or of an Entire Financial Liability Coupled with Recognition of a New Financial Asset or Liability

The required accounting treatment for such transactions follows that for the corresponding transactions involving asset derecognition, that is, derecognition of part of a financial asset or derecognition of an entire financial asset coupled with recognition of a new financial asset or liability, as set out in IAS 39, paragraphs 47–56, and described above (IAS 39, par. 65).

MEASUREMENT

The section on measurement in IAS 39 extends to no less than one hundred paragraphs (pars. 66–165) and 30 pages, and deals with the issues that have caused the most controversy within the IASC's financial instruments project, that is, the use of fair value and the recognition of the resultant remeasurement gains and losses. In addition, the recognition of hedges and hedge accounting are covered.

Initial Measurement of Financial Assets and Financial Liabilities

Initial measurement is a relatively straightforward issue. When a financial asset or financial liability is initially recognized, an enterprise should measure it at its "cost," which is the fair value of the consideration given (for an asset) or received (for a liability) in exchange for it, including any transaction costs. Where the consideration is not cash, its fair value is normally determinable by reference to market prices. If no such market prices are reliably determinable, the fair value of the consideration is estimated as the sum of all future cash payments or receipts due in exchange for the asset or liability, discounted at the prevailing rate(s) of interest for a similar instrument (as to currency, term, type of interest rate, and other relevant factors) of an issuer with a similar credit rating (see IAS 18, par. 11, discussed in Chapter 30). Discounting may be omitted if its effect would be immaterial (IAS 39, pars. 66–67).

There is an exception to the above general rule in the case of hedged assets, for which IAS 39, paragraph 160, requires that certain hedging gains and losses be included in their initial measurement (see under "Cash Flow Hedges," below).

Subsequent Measurement of Financial Assets

For measurement subsequent to initial recognition, IAS 39, paragraph 68, classifies financial assets into four categories:

1. Loans and receivables originated by the enterprise and not held for trading;
2. Held-to-maturity investments;
3. Available-for-sale financial assets; and
4. Financial assets held for trading.

Assets in categories 1 and 2 above are exempt from the general requirement that, after initial recognition, an enterprise should measure financial assets, including derivatives, at their fair values. Instead, assets in these categories are required to be measured at cost or amortized cost, as indicated below. Financial assets that are designated as hedges are subject to measurement under the hedge accounting provisions described under "Hedge Accounting," below (IAS 39, pars. 68–69).

For assets in categories 3 and 4 above, there is a *presumption* that their fair values can be reliably determined, and they should be measured at their fair values, without any deduction for any transaction costs incurred on sale or disposal. (Measurement at fair values is discussed further under "Fair Value Measurement Considerations," below.)

However, this presumption may be rebutted for an asset which, although classified as available for sale or held for trading, does not have a quoted market price in an active market, and whose value cannot be reliably estimated. Examples are: (a) an equity instrument, or one which is, in substance, an equity instrument that is not quoted in an active market and for which other methods of reasonably estimating fair value are clearly inappropriate or unworkable; and (b) a derivative linked to, and requiring to be settled by delivery of, such an equity instrument. Such assets should be measured at cost or amortized cost, as described below (IAS 39, pars. 70–71).

If a financial asset is required to be measured at fair value and this is below zero, it is treated as a financial liability as set out under "Subsequent Measurement of Financial Liabilities," below (IAS 39, par. 72).

Financial Assets Excluded from Valuation at Fair Value

The valuation of such assets, subsequent to initial recognition, under IAS GAAP, depends on whether or not they have a fixed maturity.

Those which do should be measured at amortized cost using the effective interest rate method. Those with no fixed maturity should be measured at cost. In both cases, valuation is subject to review for impairment as set out under "Impairment and Uncollectability of Financial Assets," below (IAS 39, par. 73).

There are some exceptions to the above (IAS 39, pars. 74–75):

1. Loans and receivables originated by the enterprise and not held for trading are measured at amortized cost whether or not the enterprise intends to hold them to maturity.

2. Short duration receivables with no stated interest rate are normally measured at the invoice amount unless the effect of discounting would be material.

Illustration of Valuation at Amortized Cost

The following example is adapted from the *Miller GAAP Guide*, Chapter 17. On January 1, 2000, an enterprise acquires $100,000 par value 9% bonds of Paper Co., priced to yield 10%, with a maturity date of 12/31/2004. The value of the bonds on acquisition is:

Present value of interest payments 9% of $100,000 x annuity factor for $1 at 10% p.a. for 5 years (= 3.79079)	$ 34,117
Present value of maturity value $100,000 x present value factor for $1 in 5 years at 10% p.a. (= 0.62092)	62,092
Market value	$ 96,209
Discount from par value	3,791
Par value	$100,000

In the present example, the discount from par value reflects the fact that the coupon rate is 9% p.a., whereas the market interest rate on such an instrument on the acquisition date was 10% p.a. and the bond was priced accordingly.

Amortized cost using the effective interest method is as shown in column E below. The effect of this method is to amortize any discount from, or premium over, par value over the periods to maturity, and to recognize as periodic interest income (column A) the market rate (i.e., the periodic yield rate to maturity) at acquisition on the market value at acquisition. The periodic difference between the cash received, based on the coupon rate of 9%, and the interest income (effective yield) recognized, constitutes the periodic amortization of the discount.

Year	(A) Interest Income (E* x 10%)	(B) Cash Rec'd	(C) Discount Amortizn. (A – B)	(D) Remaining Discount (D* – C)	(E) Carrying Amount
1/1/00				$3,791	$96,209
12/31/00	$9,621	$9,000	$621	3,170	96,830
12/31/01	9,683	9,000	683	2,487	97,513
12/31/02	9,951	9,000	751	1,736	98,264
12/31/03	9,826	9,000	826	910	99,090
12/31/04	9,910	9,000	910	—	100,000

Note: D* and E* are the previous year's values in columns D and E, respectively.

Transaction Costs and Financial Assets Held for Trading

The following is an example of how transaction costs should be treated in relation to initial and subsequent measurement of a financial asset held for trading.

Example

An asset is acquired for $100 plus a purchase commission of $2. It is initially recorded at a cost of $102. At the next reporting date, the quoted market price of the asset is still $100. If the asset were sold, a commission of $3 would be payable. The commission payable on sale being disregarded, the asset should be measured at $100, which entails a remeasurement loss of $2 that will be included in net profit or loss for the period (IAS 39, par. 77).

> **OBSERVATION:** In the above example, the commission paid on purchase is initially recognized as part of the carrying amount of the asset (cost), but is subsequently written off as a remeasurement loss when the market price of the asset remains the same. This does not seem entirely logical, since the commission paid on purchase continues to be recognized as part of the carrying amount *only to the extent that the market price subsequently rises to a level at least equal to the market price on acquisition plus the amount of the commission paid.* It would seem more logical to recognize the purchase commission immediately as an expense of the period of purchase. However, that would conflict with the general principle in IAS GAAP that transaction costs incurred in the acquisition of an asset are recognized as part of the cost of that asset (see, for example IAS

16, par. 15, Chapter 27). In the above example of a financial asset held for trading, adherence to this general principle has the consequence of deferring recognition of an expense to the end of the period in a way that is somewhat illogical. The application of this general principle to financial assets held for trading (and to some that are held as available for sale) is a matter that may need to be reconsidered.

☞ **PRACTICE POINTER:** In the case of financial assets held as available for sale, the treatment of the transaction costs will depend on what policy the enterprise has adopted for recognizing remeasurement gains and losses. If the policy is to recognize these in net profit or loss for the period in which they arise, the treatment of transaction costs will be the same as in the case of financial assets held for trading (see above). If the policy is to recognize remeasurement gains and losses directly in equity: (a) if the asset has fixed or determinable payments and a fixed maturity, the transaction costs will be amortized periodically to net profit or loss using the effective interest rate method (see the Illustration above); (b) otherwise, the transaction costs will be recognized in net profit or loss at the time of sale.

Foreign Currency Financial Assets That Are Monetary Items under IAS 21

Under IAS 21, "The Effects of Changes in Foreign Exchange Rates" (see Chapter 17), any foreign exchange gains and losses on monetary assets are reported in net profit or loss, with the exception of a monetary item that is designated as a *cash flow hedge*. For a foreign currency monetary asset that is so designated, changes in its fair value in the reporting currency need to be treated differently depending on whether they are: (a) foreign exchange gains or losses; or (b) changes in its fair value in the foreign currency, for reasons such as interest rate movements and other market conditions. The former changes should be accounted for under the provisions of IAS 39, paragraphs 121–165, for "Hedge Accounting," while the latter changes should be accounted for under the provisions of IAS 39, paragraphs 103–107, for "Gains and Losses on Remeasurement to Fair Value," both of which are discussed below under those respective headings (IAS 39, par. 78).

Held-to-Maturity Investments

Held-to-maturity investments are an exception to the general requirement for subsequent measurement at fair value under IAS GAAP, but only if the holder has both the *positive intent* and the *ability* to hold the investment to maturity. IAS 39 envisages the problem that enterprises may seek to use the held-to-maturity category as widely as possible, in order to avoid the fair value requirement. In order to contain this problem, the criteria for a financial asset being classified as held-to-maturity are given extensive discussion in IAS 39, paragraphs 79–92.

These criteria are not met for a financial asset with a fixed maturity if:

1. The enterprise holding the asset intends to do so for only an undefined period;
2. The enterprise stands ready to sell the asset (except in a situation of a type that is non-recurring and could not have been reasonably anticipated by the enterprise) in response to changes in market interest rates or risks, liquidity needs, changes in the availability of and yield on alternative investments, changes in financing sources and terms, or changes in foreign currency risk;
3. The issuer has a right to settle the financial asset at an amount significantly below its amortized cost (IAS 39, par. 79).

With respect to held-to-maturity investments, fixed or determinable payments and fixed maturity mean a contractual arrangement that defines the amounts and dates of payments to the holder. A debt security with a variable interest rate can thus satisfy the criteria for a held-to-maturity investment, and re-estimating the future interest payments would normally have no significant effect on the carrying amount, as the effective market interest rate used to discount future cash flows would vary similarly (IAS 39, par. 80).

A financial asset that is callable by the issuer meets the criteria for a held-to-maturity investment provided:

1. The holder intends and is able to hold the asset until it matures or is called;
2. The holder would, on its being called, recover "substantially" all of its carrying amount.

If the second proviso is not satisfied, the asset should not be classified as held-to-maturity. The holder should consider any premium paid and capitalized transaction costs in determining whether the carrying amount would be "substantially" recovered.

A financial asset that is puttable is classified as held-to-maturity only if the holder has the positive intent and ability to hold it to maturity and not to exercise the put option (IAS 39, par. 82).

There are restrictions on an enterprise having the right to classify financial assets as held-to-maturity if, during the current or two preceding financial years, it has sold, transferred, or exercised a put option on more than an "insignificant" amount of held-to-maturity investments before maturity, other than by:

1. Sales close enough to maturity or exercised call date so that changes in the market rate of interest had no significant effect on the asset's fair value;
2. Sales after the holder had already collected "substantially" all of the asset's original principal through scheduled payments or prepayments; or
3. Sales due to an isolated event that is beyond the enterprise's control, is non-recurring, and could not have been reasonably anticipated by the enterprise.

> ☛ **PRACTICE POINTER:** IAS 39 offers no guidance on what is meant by "substantially" here. The meaning may perhaps be linked to that of "material," in the sense that the carrying amount would not be "substantially" recovered if a "material" amount of it were not recovered. The IAS Framework, paragraph 30 (see Chapter 2), considers materiality as an aspect of relevance, and states that "information is material if its omission or misstatement could influence the economic decisions of users taken on the basis of the financial statements...the size of the item or error [being] judged in the particular circumstances of its omission or misstatement." The materiality of the difference between the carrying amount and the amount that would be or has been recovered, and whether the latter is "substantially all" of the former, may perhaps be considered in that light. The Implementation Guideline mentions 90% of the asset's original principal as "generally qualifying" for exception from the restrictions on the right to classify an asset as held-to-maturity.

When the conditions that disposals must either have been "insignificant" in amount, or have met conditions 1–3 above, are not satisfied, the enterprise's actions in disposing of the investments cast doubt on its intent and ability to hold such investments to maturity, and hence its right to use the held-to-maturity classification is suspended. "Insignificant" is to be interpreted in relation to the total held-to-maturity portfolio (IAS 39, pars. 83–84).

> ☛ **PRACTICE POINTER:** If an enterprise sells a significant amount of financial assets classified as held-to-maturity, it loses the right to classify the remaining assets as held-to-maturity, and must reclassify them as either available for sale or held for trading. This is the so-called "tainting rule."

In IAS 39, paragraphs 85–86, a number of scenarios are set out in which sales before maturity could satisfy conditions 1–3 mentioned above. These range from: (a) "disaster scenarios," such as a run on a bank or a significant deterioration in the creditworthiness of the issuer, through (b) tax law changes that remove or significantly reduce the tax exempt status of interest on a held-to-maturity investment, or (c) changes in statutory or regulatory requirements regarding what constitutes a permissible investment or maximum level of certain kinds of investment, to (d) changes in the enterprise's investment portfolio in the context of a major business combination or restructuring that are necessary in order to maintain its interest rate risk or credit risk position, and (e) significant increases in regulatory capital requirements, or in the risk weights of assets, that cause an enterprise to sell held-to-maturity investments, in order either to "downsize" or to avoid a significant increase in capital required for "capital adequacy" purposes.

An enterprise fails to demonstrate the ability to hold an investment in a financial asset until maturity if:

1. It lacks the financial resources required to continue financing the investment until maturity; or

2. It is subject to an existing legal or other constraint that could frustrate its intention to hold the asset to maturity. As noted above, an issuer's call option constitutes such a constraint *only* if it can be used to settle the asset at an amount significantly below its amortized cost (IAS 39, par. 87).

There may be circumstances other than those mentioned above which indicate that an enterprise does not have the positive intent or ability to hold an investment to maturity (IAS 39, par. 88). No examples are given.

IAS 39, paragraph 80, stipulates that the positive intent and ability of an enterprise to hold its held-to-maturity investments to maturity should be reassessed at each balance sheet date. IAS 39, paragraphs 90–92, deal with circumstances in which the classification of an investment may be altered in such a way as to change its required accounting treatment as between fair value and amortized cost:

1. An enterprise may cease to demonstrate the positive intent or ability to hold to maturity an investment that has been classified as held-to-maturity. Alternatively, a reliable measure of fair value may become available for a financial asset for which such a measure was previously unavailable. In either of these cases, the investment should be remeasured at fair value, and any remeasurement gain or loss should be treated as described below under "Gains and Losses on Remeasurement to Fair Value."

2. Conversely, there may be circumstances in which it becomes appropriate to reclassify an asset measured at fair value so as to

remeasure it at amortized cost. Such circumstances are: (a) the enterprise has now become able to demonstrate the intent or ability to hold the asset to maturity; (b) a reliable measure of fair value for the asset has ceased to be available; or (c) the enterprise had its right to use the held-to-maturity category suspended for the reasons described above, but that period of suspension has now ended. In these circumstances, the carrying amount of the asset at fair value becomes its new amortized cost.

In the case of 2 above, if the asset has been classified as available-for-sale, and there have previously been gains or losses on remeasurement of the asset to fair value that have been recognized directly in equity in accordance with IAS 39, paragraph 103, such gains or losses should be treated as follows (see below, under "Gains and Losses on Remeasurement to Fair Value"):

1. In the case of an asset with a fixed maturity, such previously recognized gains or losses should be amortized over the remaining life of the asset until maturity. Any difference between the new amortized cost and the maturity amount should be amortized over the remaining life as an adjustment of yield, similar to amortization of premium or discount (see the "Illustration of Valuation at Amortized Cost," above).

2. In the case of a financial asset that does not have a fixed maturity, a previous gain or loss on that asset that has been recognized directly in equity should be left in equity until the asset has been disposed of, at which time it should be recognized in net profit or loss.

Subsequent Measurement of Financial Liabilities

After initial recognition, the required treatment of financial liabilities depends on whether or not they are held for trading or derivatives, and whether they are designated as hedged items (IAS 39, par. 93).

1. Those that are neither held for trading nor derivatives should be measured at amortized cost (using the effective interest method).

2. Those that are held for trading or are derivatives (and are not hedged items) should be measured at fair value, *except for*:

    (a) Derivatives that are linked to and must be settled by the delivery of an unquoted equity instrument whose fair value cannot be reliably measured, which should be measured at cost.

(b) Financial liabilities designated as hedged items should be accounted for under the provisions for Hedge Accounting described in the section on "Hedging," below.

For financial liabilities designated in a foreign currency that are not monetary items as defined in IAS 21, "The Effects of Changes in Foreign Exchange Rates" (see Chapter 17), any recognized change in fair value, including any component that may relate to changes in foreign exchange rates, is accounted for under IAS 39, paragraph 103. The example given of such a liability is mandatorily redeemable preferred stock, issued by the enterprise designated in a foreign currency (IAS 39, par. 94).

Foreign Currency Financial Liabilities That Are Monetary Items under IAS 21

Under IAS 21, any foreign exchange gains and losses on monetary liabilities are reported in net profit or loss, with the exception of a monetary item that is designated as a *cash flow hedge*. For a foreign currency monetary liability that is so designated, changes in its fair value in the reporting currency need to be treated differently depending on whether they are: (a) foreign exchange gains or losses; or (b) changes in its fair value in the foreign currency, for reasons such as interest rate movements and other market conditions. The former changes should be accounted for under the provisions of IAS 39, paragraphs 121–165, for "Hedge Accounting," while the latter changes should be accounted for under the provisions of IAS 39, paragraph 103, for "Gains and Losses on Remeasurement to Fair Value," which are discussed below under those respective headings (IAS 39, par. 94).

Fair Value Measurement Considerations

IAS 39, paragraphs 95–102, deal with the criteria for deciding whether the fair value of a financial instrument can be measured or estimated reliably. The fair value of a financial instrument can be estimated reliably if either (a) the variability in the range of reasonable fair value estimates is not significant or (b) the probabilities attaching to the various estimates in that range can be reasonably assessed and used to make an estimate of fair value (as a probability-weighted average of the various estimates). If the variability of the range of reasonable fair value estimates is so great, and the probabilities of the various possible outcomes are so difficult to assess that neither of the conditions (a) and (b) is met, then no reliable single estimate of fair value can be made. The assumption in IAS 39 seems to be that this will only be the case "occasionally" (IAS 39, par. 95).

IAS 39, paragraph 96, gives three examples of situations in which the fair value of a financial instrument can be reliably measured or estimated: (a) there is a published price quotation for it in an active public securities market; (b) it is a debt instrument rated by an independent rating agency, and its cash flows can be reasonably estimated; and (c) there exists an appropriate valuation model for it, and the data inputs required by that model can be measured reliably because they come from active markets.

Underlying the definition of *fair value* is a presumption that the enterprise is a going concern without any need to undertake a transaction on adverse terms. Subject to that, an enterprise takes its current circumstances into account in determining the fair values of its financial assets and financial liabilities. For example, the fair value of a financial asset that an enterprise has decided to sell for cash in the immediate future is determined by the amount that it may reasonably expect to receive from such a sale, and this will be affected by factors such as the current liquidity and depth of the market for the asset (IAS 39, par. 98).

There are several generally accepted methods for determining or estimating the fair value of a financial asset or financial liability (IAS 39, pars. 97–101). These include: (a) the use of published price quotations in an active market (which normally provide the best evidence of fair value); (b) where the market for the instrument is not active, (i) published price quotations that have been appropriately adjusted, (ii) price quotations from a market maker, or (iii) estimation techniques such as reference to the current market value of an instrument that is similar, discounted cash flow analysis and option pricing models; (c) if a market price does not exist for an instrument in its entirety, but markets exist for its component parts, construction of fair value on the basis of the relevant market prices for the component parts. It is important that valuation techniques incorporate the assumptions that market participants would use in their estimates of fair values, and IAS 39, paragraph 167(a), requires disclosure of the methods and significant assumptions applied in estimating fair values.

☛ **PRACTICE POINTER:** The appropriate quoted market price for an asset held or liability to be issued is normally the current bid price, and for an asset to be acquired or liability held, the current offer or asking price. When current bid and offer prices are unavailable, the price of the most recent transaction may be used to estimate fair value provided there has not been a significant change in market conditions since the date of that transaction. When asset and liability positions are matched, mid-market prices may be used.

If the market for a financial instrument is not active, and published price quotations are not available or cannot be used because they are not indicative of current fair value, estimation techniques may be used. Some of these techniques involve discounted cash flow analysis, and in such cases the discount rate to be used is a rate equal to the prevailing rate of return for financial instruments having substantially the same characteristics, including credit risk, the remaining term over which the interest rate is fixed, the remaining term to maturity, and the currency in which payments are to be made.

IAS 39, paragraph 102, states that there are many situations other than those enumerated above in which the variability in the range of reasonable fair value estimates is likely not to be significant. In the case of a financial instrument that has been acquired from another party, it is unlikely that an enterprise would purchase such an asset if it does not expect to be able subsequently to obtain a reliable measure of its fair value. The IASC Framework, paragraph 86, is quoted: "[T]he use of reasonable estimates is an essential part of the preparation of financial statements and does not undermine their reliability."

Gains and Losses on Remeasurement to Fair Value

The treatment of gains and losses on remeasurement to fair value was one of the most controversial issues in the development of IAS 39, particularly since it entailed the recognition in income of unrealized gains on remeasurement of items measured at fair values. The controversy led to a compromise (IAS 39, par. 103), whereby:

1. Unrealized remeasurement gains and losses are *required* to be recognized immediately in income (net profit or loss for the period) *only* in the case of financial assets and liabilities *held for trading*, including all derivatives except when designated as hedging instruments;

2. In the case of *available-for-sale financial assets*, the enterprise may choose its accounting policy from the two following alternatives: (a) immediate recognition in income, as for items held for trading; or (b) immediate recognition directly in equity, through the statement of changes in equity (IAS 1, pars. 86–88; see Chapter 3), until the asset is disposed of or determined to be impaired (see below), at which time the cumulative gain or loss previously recognized in equity should be included in net profit or loss for the period.

IAS 39, paragraph 104, requires the accounting policy choice between (a) and (b) above to be consistently applied to all such financial assets classified as available for sale. The IASC (IAS 39, par. 105) considers it highly unlikely that a voluntary change of accounting policy from (a) to (b) above could be justified on the grounds that it would result in a more appropriate presentation of events or transactions. Such a justification is necessary to meet the requirements of IAS 8, "Net Profit or Loss for the Period, Fundamental Errors and Changes in Accounting Policies" (see Chapter 26).

Moreover, a financial asset classified as held for trading should not be reclassified, since its classification is based on the objective for which it was initially acquired. A financial asset should be reclassified as held for trading only if there is evidence of an actual recent pattern of short-term trading for a profit in a portfolio of assets of which it is a part (IAS 39, par. 107).

In the case of financial assets purchases of which are recognized using settlement date accounting (see above under "'Regular Way' Contracts: Trade Date versus Settlement Date"), any change in the fair value of the asset to be received between the trade date and the settlement date (the settlement period), should be recognized as indicated in 1 or 2 above, unless the asset is being carried at cost or amortized cost. In the case of such assets, only impairment losses during the settlement period will be recognized, as discussed below (IAS 39, par. 106).

Gains and Losses on Financial Assets and Liabilities Not Remeasured to Fair Value

For financial assets and financial liabilities carried at cost or amortized cost, a gain or loss is recognized in net profit or loss when the item is derecognized or impaired (as well as a result of the amortization process for those carried at amortized cost). However, if there is a hedging relationship between such items and a hedging instrument, accounting for the gain or loss should follow the provisions for hedge accounting described in the section on "Hedging," below (IAS 39, par. 108).

Impairment and Uncollectability of Financial Assets

A financial asset is impaired if its carrying value is in excess of its estimated recoverable amount. At each balance sheet date, an enterprise should assess whether there is any objective evidence of the possible impairment of any of its financial assets or groups of such assets. If any such evidence exists, the relevant recoverable amount should be estimated, and any resultant impairment loss should be recognized in accordance with the relevant provisions, either for financial assets carried at amortized cost or for financial assets remeasured to fair value, as appropriate (see below) (IAS 39, par. 109).

IAS 39, paragraph 110, enumerates various types of objective evidence that may indicate the possible impairment of a financial asset or group of assets. These include: (a) significant financial difficulty, or a high probability of bankruptcy or other financial reorganization, of the issuer (but not, of itself, the downgrading of the issuer's credit rating); (b) default or delinquency in payments, or other breach of contract; (c) a concession granted by the lender to the borrower, which the lender would not otherwise consider, for reasons relating to the borrower's financial difficulties; (d) previous recognition of an impairment loss on the asset in a prior period; (e) disappearance of an active market for the asset owing to financial difficulties (but not just because the asset is a security that has ceased to be publicly traded); or (f) a historical pattern of collections of receivables that indicates that the entire face amount of a portfolio of receivables is very unlikely to be collected.

Financial Assets Carried at Amortized Cost

In the case of loans, receivables, or held-to-maturity investments carried at amortized cost, impairment (or a bad debt loss) has occurred if it becomes "probable" that not all amounts contractually due in respect of principal or interest will be collectable by the holder. The amount of the impairment loss is the difference between the asset's carrying amount and its estimated recoverable amount. The recoverable amount is equal to the present value of the expected future cash flows from the asset discounted at its original effective market interest rate. The current interest rate is not used, as this would equate to measurement at fair value of an asset carried at amortized cost. (Discounting of cash flows from short-term receivables is normally not practiced because of its immaterial effect.) The carrying amount of the asset should be reduced to its estimated recoverable amount either by direct deduction or through the use of an allowance (contra-asset) account. The amount of the loss should be included in net profit or loss for the period. Impairment and uncollectability are measured and recognized individually for financial assets that are individually significant, and may be measured and recognized on a portfolio basis for a group of similar financial assets *that are not individually identified as impaired* (IAS 39, pars. 111–112).

> ☞ **PRACTICE POINTER:** Note that the portfolio basis should be used *only if* the impairment cannot be identified with one or more individual assets in the group. In the case of debt restructuring, there is impairment if the present value of the future payments of principal and interest discounted at the loan's original effective interest rate (i.e., its recoverable amount) is lower than its carrying value.

For loans, receivables, or held-to-maturity investments with a variable or floating interest rate, the discount rate for estimating recoverable amount is the current effective interest rate or rates as determined under the contract. This will effectively result in an estimate of fair value, and the holder may use the observable market price of the instrument instead. If an asset is collateralized and foreclosure is probable, then the holder should measure impairment on the basis of the fair value of the collateral (IAS 39, par. 113).

An impairment or bad debt loss may be partly or entirely made good in a subsequent period. Provided the reversal can be objectively related to an event occurring after the write-down which provides evidence that the once probable loss will not occur or will be significantly smaller, the write-down of the financial asset should be reversed. This should be effected either by directly adjusting the carrying amount of the asset or by adjusting the allowance (contra-asset) account. The reversal should not result in a carrying amount in excess of what the amortized cost would have been at the date of the reversal, had the impairment not been recognized. The amount of the reversal should be included in net profit or loss for the period (IAS 39, par. 114).

In the case of a financial asset that is not carried at fair value because this cannot be reliably measured, its carrying amount should be reviewed for impairment at each balance sheet date on the basis of an analysis of expected net cash inflows. In such a case, the amount of any impairment loss is the difference between the carrying amount and the recoverable amount, which for such assets is equal to the present value of the expected future cash flows discounted at the current market rate of interest for a similar instrument (IAS 39, par. 115).

> **OBSERVATION:** The recoverable amount estimated as just described above is effectively an estimate of fair value. It is not clear how such an estimate could be feasible for an asset which "is not carried at fair value because [this] cannot be reliably measured."

Interest Income after Recognition of Impairment

Once a financial asset has been written down to its estimated recoverable amount, interest income from the asset is recognized on the basis of the interest rate used to discount the cash flows for the purpose of estimating the recoverable amount.

As noted above, once an impairment loss has been recognized on a financial asset, the holder should review the asset for any further impairment at each subsequent financial reporting date (IAS 39, par. 116).

Impairment Losses on Available-for-Sale Financial Assets

For assets classified as available for sale, losses on remeasurement to fair value may be recognized directly in equity. For such assets, IAS GAAP require that impairment losses be distinguished from normal remeasurement losses. An impairment loss is recognized when there is objective evidence that the asset's *recoverable amount* (for debt instruments) or current fair value (for equity instruments) *is less than its original acquisition cost* (net of any principal repayment or amortization).

In case of impairment loss, any cumulative net loss from remeasurement at fair value that has previously been recognized directly in equity should be removed from equity and recognized in net profit or loss for the period. The amount of the loss that should be treated as just described is the excess of the asset's original acquisition cost (net of any principal repayment or amortization) over the asset's recoverable amount (for debt instruments) or current fair value (for equity instruments), less any impairment loss on that asset already recognized in net profit or loss. The recoverable amount of a debt instrument remeasured to fair value is the present value of expected future cash flows from the asset discounted at the current market rate of interest for a similar asset (IAS 39, pars. 117–118).

> **OBSERVATION:** This treatment results in consistency of the treatment of impairment losses for all categories of financial assets, as it prevents part of the impairment loss from bypassing the income statement in the case of available-for-sale financial assets for which remeasurement losses have been recognized directly in equity.

Subsequently, there may be objective evidence, relating to an event occurring after the impairment loss was recognized in net profit or loss, that the fair value or recoverable amount has increased, making good the impairment loss entirely or in part. In such a case, the impairment write-down should be reversed (entirely or in part), and the amount of the reversal should be included in net profit or loss for the period (IAS 39, par. 119).

Fair Value Accounting in Certain Financial Services Industries

In some countries, enterprises in certain financial services industries, such as mutual funds or unit trusts, securities brokers and dealers, and insurance companies, measure substantially all of their financial assets at fair value (marking-to-market). Under IAS GAAP, such enterprises will be able to continue this practice by classifying the financial assets in question as either held for trading or available for sale (IAS 39, par. 120).

HEDGING

IAS 39 devotes paragraphs 121–165 to the implications of hedging in accounting for financial instruments. First, the criteria for identifying items as hedging instruments and hedged items within a hedging relationship are given; then the provisions for hedge accounting, to be applied to items so identified (IAS 39, par. 121), are set out. Hedging relationships are analyzed for accounting purposes into three categories: (a) fair value hedges, where the hedged exposure is to changes in fair value; (b) cash flow hedges, where the hedged exposure is to variability in cash flows; and (c) hedges of a net investment in a foreign entity (IAS 39, par. 137).

Hedging Instruments

Hedging involves a proportionate income offset between changes in the fair value of, or the cash flows attributable to, the hedging instrument and the hedged item. For hedge accounting purposes, this proportionate income offset constitutes the essence of the hedging relationship.

Under IAS GAAP, any derivative may be designated as a hedging instrument for hedge accounting purposes, with the following exception: a *written option* is a hedging instrument *only* when designated as an offset to a purchased option, including an embedded one (such as a written option used to hedge callable debt). The reason for the exception is that, otherwise, a written option may entail a loss to the writer significantly greater than the potential gain on the item that it is supposed to hedge.

A nonderivative financial asset or liability may be designated as a hedging instrument for hedge accounting purposes only when used to hedge foreign currency risk. This is because, unlike derivatives, under IAS GAAP nonderivatives are not systematically measured at fair value with resultant remeasurement gains and losses being systematically recognized in net profit or loss. Therefore, the designation of nonderivatives as hedging instruments, except in limited circumstances, would lead to inconsistencies in measurement. As an example of such limited circumstances, held-to-maturity investments carried at amortized cost may be effective hedging instruments against foreign currency exchange rate risk.

An enterprise's own equity securities are not financial assets or financial liabilities of the enterprise and are thus not hedging instruments.

A financial asset or financial liability whose fair value cannot be reliably measured or estimated cannot be a hedging instrument, unless it is a non-derivative instrument which is (a) denominated in a foreign currency and with a foreign currency component that is reliably measurable and (b) designated as a hedge of a foreign currency risk (IAS 39, pars. 122–126).

Hedged Items

A hedged item may be any of the following: a recognized asset or liability, a firm commitment not recognized in the balance sheet, or an uncommitted but highly probable future ("forecasted") transaction; and these may be considered as hedged either singly or as a group of like items with similar risk characteristics.

Unlike originated loans and receivables, held-to-maturity investments cannot be hedged with respect to interest rate risk, because their designation as held to maturity means that their carrying values are unaffected by changes in interest rates. However, held-to-maturity investments can be hedged items with respect to other risks, namely credit risk and foreign currency exchange rate risk (IAS 39, par. 127).

> ☛ **PRACTICE POINTER:** If an enterprise forecasts that it will purchase a financial asset that will be classified as held to maturity when it is acquired, enters into a derivative contract with the intent to lock in the current interest rate, and designates the derivative as a hedge of the forecasted purchase of the financial asset, then the hedging relationship can qualify for hedge accounting because although the financial asset *will* be classified as held-to-maturity, it is *not yet* so classified.

A hedged item that is a financial asset or financial liability may be a hedged item with respect to the risks associated with only a portion of its cash flows or fair value, provided the effectiveness of a partial hedge can be measured. In contrast, a hedged non-financial asset or non-financial liability should be designated as a hedged item either (a) for foreign currency risks or (b) in its entirety for all risks. This is because changes in the price of a component of a non-financial asset generally do not have a predictable and separately measurable effect on the price of the item itself, unlike (for example) the effect of a change in market interest rates on the price of a bond (IAS 39, pars. 128–130).

A single hedging instrument may be designated as a hedge of more than one type of risk provided that: (a) the risks hedged can be clearly identified; (b) the effectiveness of the hedge against each of these risks can be demonstrated; (c) the specific designation of the hedging instrument in respect of each of the risk positions can be ensured (IAS 39, par. 131).

If similar assets or liabilities are aggregated and hedged as a group, the individual assets or liabilities in the group will share in the designated risk exposure. Any change in fair value of an individual item in the group that is attributable to the hedged risk will be expected to be approximately proportional to the overall change in fair value of the group attributable to the hedged risk of the group (IAS 39, par. 132).

> ☛ **PRACTICE POINTER:** If an enterprise acquires a portfolio of shares to replicate a stock index and also a put option on the index to hedge against fair value losses on the portfolio, the put may not be designated as a hedging instrument in a hedge of the portfolio. This is because the changes in the individual fair values of the shares in the portfolio cannot be expected to be approximately proportional to the overall change in fair value of the portfolio.

Hedge effectiveness is a condition for the use of hedge accounting (see under "Assessing Hedge Effectiveness," below), and must be assessed by comparing the change in value or cash flow of a hedging instrument (or group of similar instruments) and a hedged item (or group of similar items). Hence, comparing a hedging instrument to an overall net position (such as the net of all fixed rate assets and fixed rate liabilities with similar maturity dates), rather than to a specific hedged item or group of items, does not qualify for hedge accounting. However, approximately the same effect on profit or loss in hedge accounting may be achieved by designating part of the underlying items as the hedged position, so as effectively to treat the net position as hedged (IAS 39, par. 133).

Illustration

An enterprise has $100 of assets and $90 of liabilities with risks and terms of a similar nature and wishes to hedge the net $10 asset exposure. In that case, it can designate $10 of assets as the hedged item. If both the assets and the liabilities are fixed rate instruments, such a designation may be used for a fair value hedge; if both are variable rate instruments, it may be used for a cash flow hedge.

Similarly, if the enterprise wishes to net the exposures of a firm commitment to make a purchase in a foreign currency of (say) 100 euros and a firm commitment to make a sale for 90 euros, it may hedge the net exposure of 10 euros by acquiring a derivative (such as a forward or option contract) for that amount and designating it as a hedging instrument for 10 euros out of the 100 euros of the firm purchase commitment.

Intra-group or intra-company hedging transactions do not qualify for hedge accounting treatment in the consolidated financial statements.

> ☛ **PRACTICE POINTER:** However, a parent company in country A (for example) can hedge a foreign currency exposure of a subsidiary in country B to a payable in the currency of a supplier in country C, and that hedge can qualify for hedge accounting in the consolidated financial statements. IAS 39 does not require that the operating unit that is exposed to the risk being hedged be a party to the hedging instrument. Also, an intra-group monetary item that is eliminated on consolidation can be designated as the hedged item in a foreign currency fair value hedge or cash flow hedge at the consolidated level, *but only if* the item results in an exposure to exchange differences that cannot be eliminated on consolidation. A forecasted intra-group transaction may also be designated as the hedged item in a foreign currency cash flow hedge if it relates to an intra-group monetary item that would qualify as a hedged item; it must be highly probable and result in the recognition of an intra-group monetary item for which exchange differences cannot be eliminated on consolidation.

A firm commitment to acquire a business in a business combination cannot be a hedged item (except with respect to exchange risk, if applicable), since no other risks can be specifically identified and measured (IAS 39, pars. 134–135).

Hedge Accounting

Hedge accounting is covered in IAS 39, paragraphs 136–145. By virtue of hedge accounting, there is symmetrical recognition of the offsetting effects on net profit or loss of changes in the fair values of the hedging instrument and the related hedged item within a hedging relationship.

> **OBSERVATION:** The need for hedge accounting in IAS 39 arises from the fact that fair value accounting is not comprehensively employed in accounting for financial instruments, so that a derivative used as a hedging instrument is accounted for at fair value but the hedged item may not be. Moreover, even when the hedged item is accounted for at fair value, there are different rules for reflecting remeasurement gains and losses on assets in different classifications (held for trading or available for sale). Consequently, special rules are needed to ensure that the gain or loss on the hedging instrument is correctly offset against the

loss or gain on the hedged item, and to specify the hedging relationships that qualify for such treatment.

Hedging relationships are of three types:

1. *Fair value hedge*—a hedge of the exposure to changes in the fair value of a recognized asset or liability, or of an identified portion of such an asset or liability, that is attributable to a particular risk and will affect reported net income.

   ☛ **PRACTICE POINTER:** In the case of originated loans, while these are carried at amortized cost and *unrealized* changes in their fair value from interest rate changes do not affect reported net income, they can be hedged items with respect to interest rate risk, because they are not designated as held to maturity and if they were sold the changes in fair value would be realized and would affect earnings.
   Inventories of a commodity may also be hedged for changes in fair value due to changes in the commodity price. Although the inventories are measured at the lower of cost and net realizable value, the change in their fair value affects profit and loss when they are sold or their carrying amount is written down. The hedging instrument could also be designated as a cash flow hedge (see below) of the future sale of the inventory.

2. *Cash flow hedge*—a hedge of the exposure to variability in cash flows that: (a) is attributable to a particular risk associated with (i) a recognized asset or liability, such as interest payments on variable rate debt, or (ii) a forecasted transaction, such as an anticipated purchase or sale; and (b) will affect reported net profit or loss. A hedge of a firm commitment (unrecognized in the balance sheet) to buy or sell an asset in the enterprise's reporting currency is accounted for as a cash flow hedge even though it is actually a fair value exposure, for reasons explained below.

   ☛ **PRACTICE POINTER:** The cash flow from a *forecasted* fixed rate debt issue can be hedged, because an increase in interest rates can lead to the debt being issued at a greater discount or lower premium than originally expected, and this would affect net profit or loss as the effective interest rate method is applied in calculating amortized cost.

3. *Hedge of a net investment in a foreign entity*—as defined in IAS 21, "The Effects of Changes in Foreign Exchange Rates" (see Chapter 17). Under IAS 21, all foreign exchange differences that result from translating the financial statements of a foreign entity are recognized directly in equity until disposal of the net investment.

An example of a fair value hedge is a hedge of exposure to changes in the fair value of fixed interest debt as a result of changes in interest rates; such a hedge could be entered into by either the issuer or the holder. Examples of cash flow hedges for the purposes of IAS GAAP are:

1. A hedge of a future currency risk arising from a contractual commitment by an airline (unrecognized in its balance sheet) to purchase an aircraft for a fixed amount of foreign currency;

2. Use of an interest rate swap to convert, effectively, floating rate debt to fixed rate debt, which is a hedge of the exposure to the variability of future interest cash flows; or

3. A hedge of the exposure of an electric utility to a change in the price of fuel which it has a contractual commitment (unrecognized in its balance sheet) to purchase at a fixed price with payment in its domestic currency.

Item 3 above is a hedge of the exposure to *changes in the fair value* of the fuel to be purchased at a fixed price in the enterprise's own currency. Strictly speaking, therefore, it is a type of fair value hedge, not a cash flow hedge. But such hedges are accounted for as cash flow hedges under IAS GAAP, since accounting for fair value hedges requires the hedged item to be a recognized asset or liability (or a portion of such an asset or liability), and the contractual commitment is not so recognized (IAS 39, pars. 136–141).

A hedging relationship qualifies for special hedge accounting as set out in IAS 39 if, and only if, all of the following conditions are met (IAS 39, par. 142):

1. The hedging relationship and the enterprise's risk management objective and strategy in undertaking the hedge should be formally documented from the inception of the hedge, providing identification of the hedging instrument and the related hedged item or transaction, the nature of the hedged risk, and the manner in which the effectiveness of the hedging instrument's effectiveness will be assessed.

2. The hedge is expected to be "highly effective" (see under "Assessing Hedge Effectiveness," below) in a manner consistent with the risk management strategy documented as required in 1 above.

3. For cash flow hedges, the forecasted transaction which is hedged must be *highly probable*, and must present exposure to variations in cash flows (or variations in the fair value of items that are the object of a contractual commitment to a future fixed price purchase or sale—see above) that could ultimately affect net reported profit or loss.

☛ **PRACTICE POINTER:** The term "highly probable" indicates a significantly greater likelihood of occurrence than the term "more likely than not" (i.e., the probability of occurrence should be significantly greater than 50%). A transaction's probability should be supported by observable facts and by the attendant circumstances. Other things being equal, the more distant in time a forecasted transaction is, the less likely that it would be considered highly probable and the stronger the evidence that would be needed to support an assertion that it is highly probable. If a forecasted transaction is no longer "highly probable" it may still be "expected to occur," but hedge accounting is discontinued.

4. The effectiveness of the hedge can be reliably measured (for fair value hedges, see "Fair Value Measurement Considerations," above).

5. The hedge is assessed on an ongoing basis and has been determined to have been highly effective throughout the relevant financial reporting period.

For a fair value hedge, a hedging relationship is normally designated by an enterprise for a hedging instrument in its entirety, except that: (a) the intrinsic value and the time value of an option may be split, and only the change in the intrinsic value may be designated as the hedging instrument; and (b) the interest element and the spot price element on a forward contract may be split, and only the price element may be designated as the hedging instrument.

A proportion of an entire hedging instrument, such as 50% of the notional amount, but not a proportion of the time period for which the instrument is outstanding, may be designated in a hedging relationship (IAS 39, pars. 142–145).

☛ **PRACTICE POINTER:** However, a derivative may be designated as hedging only a portion of the time period to maturity of a hedged item in the following circumstances, provided that effectiveness can be measured and the other hedge criteria are met. An enterprise acquires a 10% fixed interest government bond with a remaining term to maturity of 10 years, and classifies it as available for sale. To hedge against fair value exposure associated with the present value of the interest rate payments until year five, the enterprise enters into a 5-year pay-fixed receive-floating swap. The swap may be designated as hedging fair value exposure relating to (a) the fair value of the fixed interest rate payments on the bond until year 5, and (b) the change in fair value of the principal amount due on maturity, to the extent affected by changes in the yield curve for the 5 years of the swap.

Assessing Hedge Effectiveness

As noted above, a hedging relationship qualifies for hedge accounting in IAS GAAP only if it is expected to be "highly effective." IAS GAAP do not specify a single method for assessing hedge effectiveness; rather, an enterprise is required to make a documentation of its hedging strategy, including its procedures for assessing effectiveness. Effectiveness should be assessed, at a minimum, at each financial reporting date. The assessment should normally be made taking the time value of money into consideration (IAS 39, pars. 151–152).

The general criterion proposed for being "highly effective" is that, at the inception and throughout the life of the hedge, changes in the fair value or the cash flows of the hedged item (a) are expected to be "almost fully offset" by the changes in the fair value or the cash flows of the hedging instrument and (b) have been offset in practice within a range of 80% to 125%. For example, if a gain on a cash instrument of $100 is offset (in fact, rather more than fully offset) by a loss on the hedging instrument of $120, offset may be measured as 120/100, which is 120% and thus in the "highly effective" range (IAS 39, par. 146).

> ☞ **PRACTICE POINTER:** Some partial hedges may be "highly effective" as such and may qualify for hedge accounting by virtue of an appropriate portion if the hedged items are being designated as hedged. See the Illustration under "Hedged Items," above.

On the other hand, a hedge would not be "highly effective" if the hedging instrument and the hedged items were designated in different foreign currencies whose exchange rates do not move in tandem. Similarly, a hedge of interest rate risk would not be "highly effective" if the hedging instrument were a derivative whose fair value was exposed to a counterparty's credit risk (IAS 39, pars. 147–148).

To qualify for hedge accounting purposes, a hedge must relate to a specific, designated risk with a clear exposure in terms of the enterprise's net income. Hedges of more general economic, technological, or political exposure do not qualify, since such risks cannot be measured reliably and, therefore, hedge effectiveness cannot be adequately assessed (IAS 39, par. 149).

An investment accounted for under the equity method cannot be the hedged item in a fair value hedge, because the profit and loss exposure of the investor is not to changes in the fair value of the equity investment, but to the investor's share of the associate's profit or loss. Similar considerations apply to an investment in a consolidated subsidiary. In contrast, a net investment in a foreign subsidiary may be a hedged item in a foreign currency hedge under IAS 21, since this involves a hedge of a foreign currency exposure, not of a fair value exposure. (See below, under "Hedges of a Net Investment in, a Foreign Entity.") (IAS 39, par. 150.)

Fair Value Hedges

A fair value hedge that meets the criteria set out above should be accounted for as follows:

1. The gain or loss from remeasuring the hedging instrument at fair value should be recognized immediately in net profit or loss.

2. The loss or gain on the hedged item *attributable to the hedged risk* should be (a) applied as an adjustment to the carrying amount of the hedged item and (b) recognized immediately in net profit and loss. This applies to both hedged available-for-sale items for which the normal policy is to recognize gains and losses from remeasurements at fair value directly in equity, and to items which are otherwise measured at cost (IAS 39, par. 153). If, however, only certain risks attributable to a hedged item have been hedged, recognized changes in the fair value of the item *unrelated to the hedge* are accounted for in accordance with the enterprise's normal accounting policy for the item (following the requirements set out above, under "Gains and Losses on Remeasurement to Fair Value") (IAS 39, par. 155).

Illustration

The following example illustrates hedge accounting for a hedge of exposure to changes in the fair value of an investment in fixed rate debt from changes in market interest rates (market risk), by the holder of the investment. The investor classifies such investments as available for sale, and has the policy of recognizing gains or losses from remeasurement of available-for-sale items directly in equity.

On January 1, 2000, an investor purchases a fixed interest debt security for $100. At December 31, 2000 its current fair value is $110. The carrying amount in the balance sheet is increased to $110, and the remeasurement gain of $10 is recognized directly in equity.

To protect the value of $110, the holder enters into a hedge by acquiring a derivative. By December 31, 2001, the fair value of the derivative has increased by $5, while the fair value of the hedged debt security has declined by the same amount to $105. Note that the illustrative joined entries below do not include recording the acquisition of the derivative asset.

Investor's Journal Entries for the year 2000

1/1

Investment in debt security	$100	
Cash		$100

12/31

Investment in debt security	$ 10	
Equity (increase in fair value)		$ 10

Investor's Journal Entries for the year 2001

12/31

Derivative asset	$ 5	
Gain included in net profit/loss		$ 5
Loss included in net profit/loss	$ 5	
Investment in debt security		$ 5

The entries for the year 2001 illustrate the effect of hedge accounting: (a) the remeasurement gain and loss are included in net profit/loss (which was not the case for the unhedged remeasurement gain of $10 in 2000, which was recognized directly in equity); (b) both the fair value remeasurement gain on the hedging instrument and the fair value remeasurement loss on the hedged asset are included in net profit/loss. The fair value remeasurement loss is exactly offset by the fair value remeasurement gain.

At 12/31/2001, the carrying amount of the investment in the debt security is $105, and the carrying amount of the derivative is $5.

The gain of $10 recognized directly in equity at 12/31/2000 is reported as part of equity until the asset is disposed of, but is amortized to profit and loss over the remaining term to maturity of the asset, as from the date on which the asset ceases to be hedged, if not earlier (IAS 39, par. 157).

Cash Flow Hedges

If a cash flow hedge is, during a financial reporting period, a hedging relationship that meets the conditions for hedge accounting set out above, it should be accounted for as follows:

1. That portion of the gain or loss on the hedging instrument which is determined to be an "effective hedge" should be recognized directly in equity, as follows: the component of equity associated with the hedged item should be adjusted to the lower of (a) the fair value of the cumulative change in expected future cash flows of the hedged item from the inception of the hedge, and (b) the cumulative gain or loss on the hedging instrument needed to offset the cumulative change in expected cash flows of the hedged item from the inception of the hedge.

2. Any remaining gain or loss on the hedging instrument constitutes the ineffective portion, and should be reported (a) if the hedging instrument is a derivative, immediately in net profit or loss, and (b) if the hedging instrument is not a derivative, in accordance with the requirements for reporting fair value remeasurement gains and losses for the type of instrument involved (see above, under "Gains and Losses on Remeasurement to Fair Value").

If an enterprise's documented risk strategy for a particular hedging relationship excludes a specific component of the gain or loss on, or related cash flows on, the hedging instrument from the assessment of hedge effectiveness, that excluded component is recognized in accordance with the requirements for reporting fair value remeasurement gains and losses for the type of instrument involved (see above, under "Gains and Losses on Remeasurement to Fair Value") (IAS 39, pars. 158–159).

> ☛ **PRACTICE POINTER:** If an enterprise makes an export sale at a price denominated in a foreign currency, obtains an account receivable to be settled in 90 days, and takes out a 90-day foreign exchange contract to hedge the foreign currency exposure, it may designate the hedge as either a cash flow hedge or a fair value hedge.
>
> Under IAS 21, the sale is recorded at the spot rate at the date of sale, and the receivable is restated during the 90-day period to net profit or loss. If the foreign exchange contract is designated as a fair value hedge, the gain or loss from remeasuring the forward exchange contract at fair value is also recognized immediately in net profit or loss, and the effects of the hedge are thereby recognized. If the foreign exchange contract is designated as a cash flow hedge of the foreign currency risk on the receivable, the portion of the gain or loss that is determined to be an effective hedge is recognized directly in equity, and the ineffective portion in net profit or loss. The amount that has been recognized directly in equity (the effective portion) is transferred to net profit or loss in the same period or periods in which remeasurement gains or losses on the receivable are recognized in net profit or loss (IAS 39, pars. 158 and 162).

A hedged firm commitment or forecasted transaction may result in the recognition of an asset or liability. In that case, any related gains or losses on the hedging instrument that had been recognized directly in equity as indicated in 1 above should be removed from equity and be included in the initial measurement of the item being recognized. In all other cases, gains or losses on the hedging instrument that had been recognized directly in equity should be included in net profit or loss in the same period or periods during which the hedged item affects net profit or loss (IAS 39, pars. 160–162).

Hedge accounting as just specified should be discontinued if any of the following occurs (IAS 39, par. 163):

1. The hedging instrument expires or is sold, terminated or exercised, or the hedge no longer meets the criteria for hedge accounting. In these cases, the cumulative gain or loss on the hedging instrument that had been reported directly in equity when the hedge was effective (or met the criteria) should remain separately in equity until the forecasted transaction occurs, at which time it should be accounted for as described above. For this purpose, a replacement or rollover of a hedging instrument, provided it is part of the enterprise's documented hedging strategy, does not count as an expiry or termination.

2. The committed or forecasted transaction is no longer expected to occur, in which case any related net cumulative gain or loss that has been reported directly in equity should be reported in net profit or loss for the period.

Hedges of a Net Investment in a Foreign Entity

Hedges of a net investment in a foreign entity, in accordance with IAS 21, "Accounting for the Effects of Changes in Foreign Exchange Rates" (see Chapter 17), should be accounted for similarly to cash flow hedges, as follows (IAS 39, par. 164):

1. The portion of gain or loss on the hedging instrument that is determined to be an "effective hedge" should be recognized directly in equity.

2. Any gain or loss on the ineffective portion should be reported (a) if the hedging instrument is a derivative, immediately in net profit or loss, or (b) if it is not a derivative, in equity until the disposal of the net investment, when it should be recognized in net profit or loss accordance with IAS 21.

Hedges That Do Not Qualify for Special Hedge Accounting

A hedge will not qualify for the hedge accounting provisions just described if it fails to meet the criteria in IAS 39, paragraph 142, that were set out above. In that case, gains or losses arising from changes in the fair value of a hedged item which is remeasured at fair value should be reported according to the enterprise's normal accounting policy for items that are classified as held for trading or as available-for-sale, as appropriate. Fair value adjustments of a hedging instrument that is a derivative should be reported in net profit or loss.

PRESENTATION AND DISCLOSURE

Presentation

Liabilities and Equity

The issuer of a financial instrument should classify the instrument, or its component parts, as a liability or as equity in accordance with the substance of the contractual arrangement on initial recognition and the definitions of a financial liability and an equity instrument.

The substance of a financial instrument, rather than its legal form, governs its classification on the issuer's balance sheet. While substance and legal form are commonly consistent, this is not always the case. For example, some financial instruments take the legal form of equity but are liabilities in substance, and others may combine features associated with equity instruments and features associated with financial liabilities. The classification of an instrument is made on the basis of an assessment of its substance when it is first recognized. That classification continues at each subsequent reporting date until the financial instrument is removed from the enterprise's balance sheet.

The critical feature in differentiating a financial liability from an equity instrument is the existence of a contractual obligation on one party to the financial instrument (the issuer) either to deliver cash or another financial asset to the other party (the holder) or to exchange another financial instrument with the holder under conditions that are potentially unfavorable to the issuer. When such a contractual obligation exists, that instrument meets the definition of a financial liability regardless of the manner in which the contractual obligation will be settled. A restriction on the ability of the issuer to satisfy an obligation, such as lack of access to foreign currency or the need to obtain approval for payment from a regulatory authority, does not negate the issuer's obligation or the holder's right under the instrument.

When a financial instrument does not give rise to a contractual obligation on the part of the issuer to deliver cash or another financial asset or to exchange another financial instrument under conditions that are potentially unfavorable, it is an equity instrument. Although the holder of an equity instrument may be entitled to receive a pro rata share of any dividends or other distributions out of equity, the issuer does not have a contractual obligation to make such distributions.

When a preferred share provides for mandatory redemption by the issuer for a fixed or determinable amount at a fixed or determinable future date or gives the holder the "right to require the issuer to redeem the share at or after a particular date for a fixed or determin-

able amount, the instrument meets the definition of a financial liability
and is classified as such. A preferred share that does not establish
such a contractual obligation explicitly may establish it indirectly
through its terms and conditions. For example, a preferred share that
does not provide for mandatory redemption or redemption at the
option of the holder may have a contractually provided accelerating
dividend such that, within the foreseeable future, the dividend yield
is scheduled to be so high that the issuer will be economically com-
pelled to redeem the instrument. In these circumstances, classification as a financial liability is appropriate because the issuer has little,
if any, discretion to avoid redeeming the instrument. Similarly, if a
financial instrument labeled as a share gives the holder an option to
require redemption upon the occurrence of a future event that is
highly likely to occur, classification as a financial liability on initial
recognition reflects the substance of the instrument (IAS 32, pars. 18–
22).

Classification of Compound Instruments by the Issuer

The issuer of a financial instrument that contains both a liability and
an equity element should classify the instrument's component parts
separately.

IAS GAAP require the separate presentation on an issuer's balance sheet of liability and equity elements created by a single financial instrument. It is more a matter of form than substance that both
liabilities and equity interests are created by a single financial instrument rather than by two or more separate instruments. An issuer's
financial position is more faithfully represented by separate presentation of liability and equity components contained in a single instrument according to their nature.

For purposes of balance sheet presentation, an issuer recognizes
separately the component parts of a financial instrument that creates
a primary financial liability of the issuer and grants an option to the
holder of the instrument to convert it into an equity instrument of the
issuer. A bond or similar instrument convertible by the holder into
common shares of the issuer is an example of such an instrument.
From the perspective of the issuer, such an instrument comprises two
components: a financial liability (a contractual arrangement to deliver cash or other financial assets); and an equity instrument (a call
option granting the holder the right, for a specified period of time, to
convert into common shares of the issuer). The economic effect of
issuing such an instrument is substantially the same as issuing simultaneously a debt instrument with an early settlement provision and
warrants to purchase common shares, or issuing a debt instrument
with detachable share purchase warrants. Accordingly, in all such
cases, the issuer presents the liability and equity elements separately
on its balance sheet.

Classification of the liability and equity components of a convertible instrument is not revised as a result of a change in the likelihood that a conversion option will be exercised, even when exercise of the option may appear to have become economically advantageous to some holders. Holders may not always act in the manner that might be expected because, for example, the tax consequences resulting from conversion may differ among holders. Furthermore, the likelihood of conversion will change from time to time. The issuer's obligation to make future payments remains outstanding until it is extinguished through conversion, the maturity of the instrument or some other transaction.

A financial instrument may contain components that are neither financial liabilities nor equity instruments of the issuer. For example, an instrument may give the holder the right to receive a nonfinancial asset, such as a commodity in settlement and an option to exchange that right for shares of the issuer. The issuer recognizes and presents the equity instrument (the exchange option) separately from the liability components of the compound instrument, whether the liabilities are financial or non-financial (IAS 32, pars. 23–27).

Interest, Dividends, Losses, and Gains

Interest, dividends, losses, and gains relating to a financial instrument, or a component part, classified as a financial liability should be reported in the income statement as expense or income. Distributions to holders of a financial instrument classified as an equity instrument should be charged by the issuer directly to equity.

The classification of a financial instrument in the balance sheet determines whether interest, dividends, losses, and gains relating to that instrument are classified as expenses or income and reported in the income statement. Thus, dividend payments on shares classified as liabilities are classified as expenses in the same way as interest on a bond and reported in the income statement. Similarly, gains and losses associated with redemptions or refinancings of instruments classified as liabilities are reported in the income statement, while redemptions or refinancings of instruments classified as equity of the issuer are reported as movements in equity.

Dividends classified as an expense may be presented in the income statement either with interest on other liabilities or as a separate item. Disclosure of interest and dividends is subject to the requirements of IAS 1, "Presentation of Financial Statements"; IAS 30, "Disclosures in the Financial Statements of Banks and Similar Financial Institutions"; and IAS 39, "Financial Instruments: Recognition and Measurement." In some circumstances, because of significant differences between interest and dividends with respect to matters such as tax deductibility, it is desirable to disclose them separately within the income statement. Disclosures of the amounts of tax effects are made in accordance with IAS 12, "Income Taxes" (IAS 32, pars. 30–32).

Offsetting of a Financial Asset and a Financial Liability

A financial asset and a financial liability should be offset and the net amount reported in the balance sheet when an enterprise:

1. Has a legally enforceable right to set off the recognized amounts; and

2. Intends either to settle on a net basis, or to realize the asset and settle the liability simultaneously.

IAS GAAP require the presentation of financial assets and financial liabilities on a net basis when this reflects an enterprise's expected future cash flows from settling two or more separate financial instruments. When an enterprise has the right to receive or pay a single net amount and intends to do so, it has, in effect, only a single financial asset or financial liability. In other circumstances, financial assets and financial liabilities are presented separately from each other consistent with their characteristics as resources or obligations of the enterprise.

Offsetting a recognized financial asset and a recognized financial liability and presenting the net amount differs from ceasing to recognize a financial asset or a financial liability. While offsetting does not give rise to recognition of a gain or a loss, ceasing to recognize a financial instrument not only results in the removal of the previously recognized item from the balance sheet but may also result in recognition of a gain or a loss.

Simultaneous settlement of two financial instruments may occur through, for example, the operation of a clearinghouse in an organized financial market or a face-to-face exchange. In these circumstances the cash flows are, in effect, equivalent to a single net amount and there is no exposure to credit or liquidity risk. In other circumstances, an enterprise may settle two instruments by receiving and paying separate amounts, becoming exposed to credit risk for the full amount of the asset or liquidity risk for the full amount of the liability. Such risk exposures may be significant even though relatively brief. Accordingly, realization of a financial asset and settlement of a financial liability are considered simultaneous only when the transactions occur at the same moment.

Offsetting is usually inappropriate when:

1. Several different financial instruments are used to emulate the features of a single financial instrument (i.e., a "synthetic instrument");

2. Financial assets and financial liabilities arise from financial instruments having the same primary risk exposure (for example, assets and liabilities within a portfolio of forward contracts or other derivative instruments) but involve different counterparties;

3. Financial or other assets are pledged as collateral for non-recourse financial liabilities;

4. Financial assets are set aside in trust by a debtor for the purpose of discharging an obligation without those assets having been accepted by the creditor in settlement of the obligation (for example, a sinking fund arrangement); or

5. Obligations incurred as a result of events giving rise to losses are expected to be recovered from a third party by virtue of a claim made under an insurance policy.

An enterprise that undertakes a number of financial instrument transactions with a single counterparty may enter into a "master netting arrangement" with that counterparty. Such an agreement provides for a single net settlement of all financial instruments covered by the agreement in the event of default on, or termination of, any one contract. These arrangements are commonly used by financial institutions to provide protection against loss in the event of bankruptcy or other events that result in a counterparty being unable to meet its obligations. A master netting arrangement commonly creates a right of set-off that becomes enforceable and affects the realization or settlement of individual financial assets and financial liabilities only following a specified event of default or in other circumstances not expected to arise in the normal course of business. A master netting arrangement does not provide a basis for offsetting unless the enterprise has a legally enforceable right of set-off and intends to use it (IAS 32, pars. 33–41).

Disclosure

Transactions in financial instruments may result in an enterprise's assuming or transferring to another party one or more of the financial risks described below. The required disclosures provide information that assists users of financial statements in assessing the extent of risk related to both recognized and unrecognized financial instruments.

1. *Price risk*—There are three types of price risk: currency risk, interest rate risk, and market risk.

   (a) Currency risk is the risk that the value of a financial instrument will fluctuate due to changes in foreign exchange rates.

(b) Interest rate risk is the risk that the value of a financial instrument will fluctuate due to changes in market interest rates.

(c) Market risk is the risk that the value of a financial instrument will fluctuate as a result of changes in market prices whether those changes are caused by factors specific to the individual security or its issuer or factors affecting all securities traded in the market.

The term "price risk" embodies not only the potential for loss, but also the potential for gain.

2. *Credit risk*—Credit risk is the risk that one party to a financial instrument will fail to discharge an obligation and cause the other party to incur a financial loss.

3. *Liquidity risk*—Liquidity risk, also referred to as funding risk, is the risk that an enterprise will encounter difficulty in raising funds to meet commitments associated with financial instruments. Liquidity risk may result from an inability to sell a financial asset quickly at close to its fair value.

4. *Cash flow risk*—Cash flow risk is the risk that future cash flows associated with a monetary financial instrument will fluctuate in amount. In the case of a floating rate debt instrument, for example, such fluctuations result in a change in the effective interest rate of the financial instrument, usually without a corresponding change in its fair value (IAS 32, pars. 42–43).

Disclosure of Risk Management Policies

An enterprise should describe its financial risk management objectives and policies, including its policy for hedging each major type of forecasted transaction for which hedge accounting is used.

IAS GAAP do not prescribe either the format of the information required to be disclosed or its location within the financial statements. With regard to recognized financial instruments, to the extent that the required information is presented on the face of the balance sheet, it is not necessary for it to be repeated in the notes to the financial statements. With regard to unrecognized financial instruments, however, information in notes or supplementary schedules is the essential means of disclosure. Disclosures may include a combination of narrative descriptions and specific quantified data, as appropriate to the nature of the instruments and their relative significance to the enterprise.

Management of an enterprise group's financial instruments into classes that are appropriate to the nature of the information to be disclosed, taking into account matters such as the characteristics of the instruments, whether they are recognized or unrecognized and, if they are recognized, the measurement basis that has been applied. In general, classes are determined on a basis that distinguishes items carried on a cost basis from items carried at fair value. When amounts disclosed in notes or supplementary schedules relate to recognized assets and liabilities, sufficient information is provided to permit a reconciliation to relevant line items on the balance sheet. When an enterprise is a party to financial instruments not dealt with by IAS GAAP on financial instruments, such as obligations under retirement benefit plans or insurance contracts, these instruments constitute a class or classes of financial assets or financial liabilities disclosed separately from those dealt with by IAS GAAP on financial instruments (IAS 32, pars. 44–46).

Terms, Conditions, and Accounting Policies

For each class of financial asset, financial liability, and equity instrument, both recognized and unrecognized, an enterprise should disclose:

1. Information about the extent and nature of the financial instruments, including significant terms and conditions that may affect the amount, timing, and certainty of future cash flows.

2. The methods and significant assumptions applied in estimating fair values of financial assets and financial liabilities that are carried at fair value, separately for significant classes of financial assets, including prepayment rates, rates of estimated credit losses, and interest or discount rates.

3. Whether gains and losses arising from changes in the fair value of those available-for-sale financial assets that are measured at fair value subsequent to initial recognition are included in net profit or loss for the period or are recognized directly in equity until the financial asset is disposed of.

4. For each of the four categories of financial assets defined in IAS 39, paragraph 10 (see points 7–10 under "Definitions," above), whether "regular way" purchases of financial assets are accounted for at trade date or settlement date (IAS 39, par. 167).

The contractual terms and conditions of a financial instrument are an important factor affecting the amount, timing, and certainty of future cash receipts and payments by the parties to the instrument. When recognized and unrecognized instruments are important, either individually or as a class, in relation to the current financial position of an enterprise or its future operating results, their terms and conditions are disclosed. If no single instrument is individually significant to the future cash flows of a particular enterprise, the essential characteristics

of the instruments are described by reference to appropriate groupings of like instruments.

When financial instruments held or issued by an enterprise, either
individually or as a class, create a potentially significant exposure to
any of the four types of risks described above, terms and conditions
that may warrant disclosure include:

1. The principal, stated, face or other similar amount which, for
   some derivative instruments, such as interest rate swaps, may
   be the amount (referred to as the notional amount) on which
   future payments are based;

2. The date of maturity, expiry, or execution;

3. Early settlement options held by either party to the instrument,
   including the period in which, or date at which, the options
   may be exercised and the exercise price or range of prices;

4. Options held by either party to the instrument to convert the
   instrument into, or exchange it for, another financial instrument or some other asset or liability, including the period in
   which, or date at which, the options may be exercised and the
   conversion or exchange ratio(s);

5. The amount and timing of scheduled future cash receipts or
   payments of the principal amount of the instrument, including
   installment repayments and any sinking fund or similar requirements;

6. Stated rate or amount of interest, dividend or other periodic
   return on principal, and the timing of payments;

7. Collateral held, in the case of a financial asset, or pledged, in the
   case of a financial liability;

8. In the case of an instrument for which cash flows are denominated in a currency other than the enterprise's reporting currency, the currency in which receipts or payments are required;

9. In the case of an instrument that provides for an exchange,
   information described in items 1 to 8 for the instrument to be
   acquired in the exchange; and

10. Any condition of the instrument or an associated covenant that,
    if contravened, would significantly alter any of the other terms
    (for example, a maximum debt-to-equity ratio in a bond cov-
    enant that, if contravened, would make the full principal amount
    of the bond due and payable immediately).

When the balance sheet presentation of a financial instrument
differs from the instrument's legal form, it is desirable for an enterprise to explain in the notes to the financial statements the nature of
the instrument.

The usefulness of information about the extent and nature of financial instruments is enhanced when it highlights any relationships between individual instruments that may affect the amount, timing, or certainty of the future cash flows of an enterprise. For example, it is important to disclose hedging relationships such as might exist when an enterprise holds an investment in shares for which it has purchased a put option. Similarly, it is important to disclose relationships between the components of "synthetic instruments" such as fixed rate debt created by borrowing at a floating rate and entering into a floating to fixed interest rate swap. In each case, an enterprise presents the individual financial assets and financial liabilities in its balance sheet according to their nature, either separately or in the class of financial asset or financial liability to which they belong. The extent to which a risk exposure is altered by the relationships among the assets and liabilities may be apparent to financial statement users from information of the type described above but, in some circumstances, further disclosure is necessary.

In accordance with IAS 1, "Presentation of Financial Statements" (see Chapter 3), an enterprise provides clear and concise disclosure of all significant accounting policies, including both the general significant transactions and circumstances arising in the enterprise's business. In the case of financial instruments, such disclosure includes:

1. The criteria applied in determining when to recognize a financial asset or financial liability on the balance sheet and when to cease to recognize it;

2. The basis of measurement applied to financial assets and financial liabilities both on initial recognition and subsequently; and

3. The basis on which income and expense arising from financial assets and financial liabilities is recognized and measured.

Types of transactions for which it may be necessary to disclose the relevant accounting policies include:

1. Transfers of financial assets when there is a continuing interest in, or involvement with, the assets by the transferor, such as securitizations of financial assets, repurchase agreements, and reverse repurchase agreements;

2. Transfers of financial assets to a trust for the purpose of satisfying liabilities when they mature without the obligation of the transferor being discharged at the time of the transfer, such as in a substance defeasance trust;

3. Acquisition or issuance of separate financial instruments as part of a series of transactions designed to synthesize the effect of acquiring or issuing a single instrument;

4. Acquisition or issuance of financial instruments as hedges of risk exposures; and

5. Acquisition or issuance of monetary financial instruments bearing a stated interest rate that differs from the prevailing market rate at the date of issue.

To provide adequate information for users of financial statements to understand the basis on which financial assets and financial liabilities have been measured, disclosures of accounting policies indicate not only whether cost, fair value, or some other basis of measurement has been applied to a specific class of asset or liability but also the method of applying that basis. For example, for financial instruments carried on the cost basis, an enterprise may be required to disclose how it accounts for:

1. Costs of acquisition or issuance;

2. Premiums and discounts on monetary financial assets and financial liabilities;

3. Changes in the estimated amount of determinable future cash flows associated with a monetary financial instrument such as a bond indexed to a commodity price;

4. Changes in circumstances that result in significant uncertainty about the timely collection of all contractual amounts due from monetary financial assets;

5. Declines in the fair value of financial assets below their carrying amount; and

6. Restructured financial liabilities.

For financial assets and financial liabilities carried at fair value, an enterprise indicates whether carrying amounts are determined from quoted market prices, independent appraisals, discounted cash flow analysis, or another appropriate method, and discloses any significant assumptions made in applying those methods.

An enterprise discloses the basis for reporting in the income statement realized and unrealized gains and losses, interest, and other items of income and expense associated with financial assets and financial liabilities. This disclosure includes information about the basis on which income and expense arising from financial instruments held for hedging purposes are recognized. When an enterprise presents income and expense items on a net basis even though the corresponding financial assets and financial liabilities on the balance sheet have not been offset, the reason for that presentation is disclosed if the effect is significant (IAS 32, pars. 47–55; IAS 39, par. 167).

Interest Rate Risk

For each class of financial asset and financial liability, both recognized and unrecognized, an enterprise should disclose information about its exposure to interest rate risk, including:

1. Contractual repricing or maturity dates, whichever dates are earlier; and

2. Effective interest rates, when applicable.

An enterprise provides information concerning its exposure to the effects of future changes in the prevailing level of interest rates. Changes in market interest rates have a direct effect on the contractually determined cash flows associated with some financial assets and financial liabilities (cash flow risk) and on the fair value of others (price risk).

Information about maturity dates, or repricing dates when they are earlier, indicates the length of time for which interest rates are fixed and information about effective interest rates indicates the levels at which they are fixed. Disclosure of this information provides financial statement users with a basis for evaluating the interest rate price risk to which an enterprise is exposed and thus the potential for gain or loss. For instruments that reprice to a market rate of interest before maturity, disclosure of the period until the next repricing is more important than disclosure of the period to maturity.

To supplement the information about contractual repricing and maturity dates, an enterprise may elect to disclose information about expected repricing or maturity dates when those dates differ significantly from the contractual dates. Such information may be particularly relevant when, for example, an enterprise is able to predict, with reasonable reliability, the amount of fixed rate mortgage loans that will be repaid prior to maturity and it uses this data as the basis for managing its interest rate risk exposure. The additional information includes disclosure of the fact that it is based on management's expectations of future events and explains the assumptions made about repricing or maturity dates and how those assumptions differ from the contractual dates.

An enterprise indicates which of its financial assets and financial liabilities are:

1. Exposed to interest rate price risk, such as monetary financial assets and financial liabilities with a fixed interest rate;

2. Exposed to interest rate cash flow risk, such as monetary financial assets and financial liabilities with a floating interest rate that is reset as market rates change; and

3. Not exposed to interest rate risk, such as some investments in equity securities.

The effective interest rate (effective yield) of a monetary financial instrument is the rate that, when used in a present value calculation, results in the carrying amount of the instrument. The present value calculation applies the interest rate to the stream of future cash receipts or payments from the reporting date to the next repricing (maturity) date and to the expected carrying amount (principal amount) at that date. The rate is a historical rate for a fixed rate instrument carried at amortized cost and a current market rate for a floating rate instrument or an instrument carried at fair value. The effective interest rate is sometimes termed the level yield to maturity or to the next repricing date, and is the internal rate of return of the instrument for that period.

The requirement for disclosure of effective interest rates applies to bonds, notes, and similar monetary financial instruments involving future payments that create a return to the holder and a cost to the issuer reflecting the time value of money. The requirement does not apply to financial instruments such as nonmonetary and derivative instruments that do not bear a determinable effective interest rate. For example, while instruments such as interest rate derivatives, including swaps, forward rate agreements, and options, are exposed to price or cash flow risk from changes in market interest rates, disclosure of an effective interest rate is not relevant. However, when providing effective interest rate information, an enterprise discloses the effect on its interest rate risk exposure of hedging or "conversion" transactions such as interest rate swaps.

An enterprise may retain an exposure to the interest rate risks associated with financial assets removed from its balance sheet as a result of a transaction such as a securitization. Similarly, it may become exposed to interest rate risks as a result of a transaction in which no financial asset or financial liability is recognized on its balance sheet, such as a commitment to lend funds at a fixed interest rate. In such circumstances, the enterprise discloses information that will permit financial statement users to understand the nature and extent of its exposure. In the case of a securitization or similar transfer of financial assets, this information normally includes the nature of the assets transferred, their stated principal, interest rate and term to maturity, and the terms of the transaction giving rise to the retained exposure to interest rate risk. In the case of a commitment to lend funds, the disclosure normally includes the stated principal, interest rate and term to maturity of the amount to be lent and the significant terms of the transaction giving rise to the exposure to risk.

The nature of an enterprise's business and the extent of its activity in financial instruments will determine whether information about interest rate risk is presented in narrative form, in tables, or by using a combination of the two. When an enterprise has a significant number of financial instruments exposed to interest rate price or cash flow risks, it may adopt one or more of the following approaches to presenting information.

1. The carrying amounts of financial instruments exposed to interest rate price risk may be presented in tabular form, grouped by those that are contracted to mature or be repriced:

   (a) within one year of the balance sheet date;

   (b) more than one year and less than five years from the balance sheet date; and

   (c) five years or more from the balance sheet date.

2. When the performance of an enterprise is significantly affected by the level of its exposure to interest rate price risk or changes in that exposure, more detailed information is desirable. An enterprise such as a bank may disclose, for example, separate groupings of the carrying amounts of financial instruments contracted to mature or be repriced:

   (a) within one month of the balance sheet date;

   (b) more than one and less than three months from the balance sheet date; and

   (c) more than three and less than twelve months from the balance sheet date.

3. Similarly, an enterprise may indicate its exposure to interest rate cash flow risk through a table indicating the aggregate carrying amount of groups of floating rate financial assets and financial liabilities maturing within various future time periods.

4. Interest rate information may be disclosed for individual financial instruments or weighted average rates or a range of rates may be presented for each class of financial instrument. An enterprise group's instruments denominated in different currencies or having substantially different credit risks into separate classes when these factors result in instruments having substantially different effective interest rates.

In some circumstances, an enterprise may be able to provide useful information about its exposure to interest rate risks by indicating the effect of a hypothetical change in the prevailing level of market interest rates on the fair value of its financial instruments and future earnings and cash flows. Such interest rate sensitivity information may be based on an assumed 1% change in market interest rates occurring at the balance sheet date. The effects of a change in interest rates includes changes in interest income and expense relating to floating rate financial instruments and gains or losses resulting from changes in the fair value of fixed rate. The reported interest rate sensitivity may be restricted to the direct effects of an interest rate change on interest-bearing financial instruments on hand at the balance sheet date since the indirect effects of a rate change on financial markets and individual enterprises cannot normally be predicted reliably. When disclosing interest rate sensitivity information, an enterprise indicates the basis on which it has prepared the information, including any significant assumptions (IAS 32, pars. 56–65).

Credit Risk

For each class of financial asset, both recognized and unrecognized, an enterprise should disclose information about its exposure to credit risk, including:

1. The amount that best represents its maximum credit risk exposure at the balance sheet date, without taking account of the fair value of any collateral, in the event other parties fail to perform their obligations under financial instruments; and

2. Significant concentrations of credit risk.

An enterprise provides information relating to credit risk to permit users of its financial statements to assess the extent to which failures by counterparties to discharge their obligations could reduce the amount of future cash inflows from financial assets on hand at the balance sheet date. Such failures give rise to a financial loss recognized in an enterprise's income statement. An enterprise is not required to disclose an assessment of the probability of losses arising in the future.

The purposes of disclosing amounts exposed to credit risk without regard to potential recoveries from realization of collateral ("an enterprise's maximum credit risk exposure") are:

1. To provide users of financial statements with a consistent measure of the amount exposed to credit risk for both recognized and unrecognized financial assets; and

2. To take into account the possibility that the maximum exposure to loss may differ from the carrying amount of a recognized financial asset or the fair value of an unrecognized financial asset that is otherwise disclosed in the financial statements.

In the case of recognized financial assets exposed to credit risk, the carrying amount of the assets in the balance sheet, net of any applicable provisions for loss, usually represents the amount exposed to credit risk. For example, in the case of an interest rate swap carried at fair value, the maximum exposure to loss at the balance sheet date is normally the carrying amount since it represents the cost, at current market rates, of replacing the swap in the event of default. In these circumstances, no additional disclosure beyond that provided on the balance sheet is necessary. On the other hand, as illustrated by the examples described below, an enterprise's maximum potential loss from some recognized financial assets may differ significantly from their carrying amount and from other disclosed amounts such as their fair value or principal amount. In such circumstances, additional disclosure is necessary.

A financial asset subject to a legally enforceable right of set-off against a financial liability is not presented on the balance sheet net of the liability unless settlement is intended to take place on a net basis or simultaneously. Nevertheless, an enterprise should disclose the existence of the legal right of set-off when providing information. For example, when an enterprise is due to receive the proceeds from realization of a financial asset before settlement of a financial liability of equal or greater amount against which the enterprise has a legal right of set-off, the enterprise has the ability to exercise that right of set-off to avoid incurring a loss in the event of a default by the counterparty. However, if the enterprise responds, or is likely to respond, to the default by extending the term of the financial asset, an exposure to credit risk would exist if the revised terms are such that collection of the proceeds is expected to be deferred beyond the date on which the liability is required to be settled. To inform financial statement users of the extent to which exposure to credit risk at a particular point in time has been reduced, the enterprise discloses the existence and effect of the right of set-off when the financial asset is expected to be collected in accordance with its terms. When the financial liability against which a right of set-off exists is due to be settled before the financial asset, the enterprise is exposed to credit risk on the full carrying amount of the asset if the counterparty defaults after the liability has been settled.

An enterprise may have entered into one or more master netting arrangements that serve to mitigate its exposure to credit loss but do not meet the criteria for offsetting. When a master netting arrangement significantly reduces the credit risk associated with financial assets not offset against financial liabilities with the same counterparty, an enterprise provides additional information concerning the effect of the arrangement. Such disclosure indicates that:

1. The credit risk associated with financial assets subject to a master netting arrangement is eliminated only to the extent that financial liabilities due to the same counterparty will be settled after the assets are realized; and

2. The extent to which an enterprise's overall exposure to credit risk is reduced through a master netting arrangement may change substantially within a short period following the balance sheet date because the exposure is affected by each transaction subject to the arrangement.

It is also desirable for an enterprise to disclose the terms of its master netting arrangements that determine the extent of the reduction in its credit risk.

When there is no credit risk associated with an unrecognized financial asset or the maximum exposure is equal to the principal, stated, face, or other similar contractual amount of the instrument or the fair value, no additional disclosure is required. However, with some unrecognized financial assets, the maximum loss that would be recognized upon default by the other party to the underlying instrument may differ substantially from the amounts disclosed. For example, an enterprise may have a right to mitigate the loss it would otherwise bear by setting off an unrecognized financial asset against an unrecognized financial liability. In such circumstances, additional disclosure is required.

Guaranteeing an obligation of another party exposes the guarantor to credit risk that would be taken into account in making the disclosures required. This situation may arise as a result of, for example, a securitization transaction in which an enterprise remains exposed to credit risk associated with financial assets that have been removed from its balance sheet. If the enterprise is obligated under recourse provisions of the transaction to indemnify the purchaser of the assets for credit losses, it discloses the nature of the assets removed from its balance sheet, the amount, and timing of the future cash flows contractually due from the assets, the terms of the recourse obligation, and the maximum loss that could arise under that obligation. (See also IAS 37, "Provisions, Contingent Liabilities, and Contingent Assets," Chapter 28.)

Concentrations of credit risk are disclosed when they are not apparent from other disclosures about the nature and financial position of the business and they result in a significant exposure to loss in the event of default by other parties. Identification of significant concentrations is a matter for the exercise of judgment by management taking into account the circumstances of the enterprise and its debtors. IAS 14, "Reporting Financial Information by Segment" (see Chapter 31) provides useful guidance in identifying industry and geographic segments within which credit risk concentrations may arise.

Concentrations of credit risk may arise from exposures to a single debtor or to groups of debtors having a similar characteristic such that their ability to meet their obligations is expected to be affected similarly by changes in economic or other conditions. Characteristics that may give rise to a concentration of risk include the nature of the activities undertaken by debtors, such as the industry in which they operate, the geographic area in which activities are undertaken, and the level of creditworthiness of groups of borrowers. For example, a manufacturer of equipment for the oil and gas industry will normally have trade accounts receivable from sale of its products for which the risk of non-payment is affected by economic changes in the oil and gas industry. A bank that normally lends on an international scale may have a significant amount of loans outstanding to less developed nations and the bank's ability to recover those loans may be adversely affected by local economic conditions.

Disclosure of concentrations of credit risk includes a description of the shared characteristic that identifies each concentration and the amount of the maximum credit risk exposure associated with all recognized and unrecognized financial assets sharing that characteristic (IAS 32, pars. 66–76).

Fair Value

For each class of financial asset and financial liability, both recognized and unrecognized, *other than those carried at fair value,* an enterprise should disclose information about fair value. When it is not practicable within constraints of timeliness or cost to determine the fair value of a financial asset or financial liability with sufficient reliability, that fact should be disclosed together with information about the principal characteristics of the underlying financial instrument that are pertinent to its fair value.

The fair value of a financial asset or financial liability may be determined by one of several generally accepted methods. Disclosure of fair value information includes disclosure of the method adopted and any significant assumptions made in its application.

When an instrument is not traded in an organized financial market, it may not be appropriate for an enterprise to determine and disclose a single amount that represents an estimate of fair value. Instead, it may be more useful to disclose a range of amounts within which the fair value of a financial instrument is reasonably believed to lie.

When disclosure of fair value information is omitted because it is not practicable to determine fair value with sufficient reliability, information is provided to assist users of the financial statements in making their own judgments about the extent of possible differences between the carrying amount of financial assets and financial liabilities and their fair value. In addition to an explanation of the reason for the omission and the principal characteristics of the financial instruments that are pertinent to their value, information is provided about the market for the instruments.

The historical cost carrying amount of receivables and payables subject to normal trade credit terms usually approximates fair value. Similarly, the fair value of a deposit liability without a specified maturity is the amount payable on demand at the reporting date.

Fair value information relating to classes of financial assets or financial liabilities *that are carried on the balance sheet at other than fair value* is provided in a way that permits comparison between the carrying amount and the fair value. Accordingly, the fair values of recognized financial assets and financial liabilities are grouped into classes and offset only to the extent that their related carrying amounts are offset. Fair values of unrecognized financial assets and financial liabilities are presented in a class or classes separate from recognized items and are offset only to the extent that they meet the offsetting criteria for recognized financial assets and financial liabilities (IAS 32, pars. 77–87; IAS 39, par. 166).

Financial Assets Carried at an Amount in Excess of Fair Value

When an enterprise carries one or more financial assets at an amount in excess of their fair value, the enterprise should disclose:

1. The carrying amount and the fair value of either the individual assets or appropriate groupings of those individual assets; and

2. The reasons for not reducing the carrying amount, including the nature of the evidence that provides the basis for management's belief that the carrying amount will be recovered.

Management exercises judgment in determining the amount it expects to recover from a financial asset and whether to write down the carrying amount of the asset when it is in excess of fair value. The information just specified provides users of financial statements with a basis for understanding management's exercise of judgment and assessing the possibility that circumstances may change and lead to a reduction in the asset's carrying amount in the future. When appropriate, the information required is grouped in a manner that reflects management's reasons for not reducing the carrying amount.

An enterprise's accounting policies with respect to recognition of declines in value of financial assets assist in explaining why a particular financial asset is carried at an amount in excess of fair value. In addition, the enterprise provides the reasons and evidence specific to the asset that provide management with the basis for concluding that the asset's carrying amount will be recovered. For example, the fair value of a fixed rate loan intended to be held to maturity may have declined below its carrying amount as a result of an increase in interest rates. In such circumstances, the lender may not have reduced the carrying amount because there is no evidence to suggest that the borrower is likely to default (IAS 32, pars. 88–90).

Other Disclosures

Financial statements should include all of the following additional disclosures relating to hedging. The enterprise should:

1. Describe the enterprise's financial risk management objectives and policies, including its policy for hedging each major type of forecasted transaction.

   For example, in the case of hedges of risks relating to future sales, that description indicates the nature of the risks being hedged, approximately how many months or years of expected future sale have been hedged, and the approximate percentage of sales in those future months or years.

2. Disclose the following separately for designated fair value hedges, cash flow hedges, and hedges of a net investment in a foreign entity:

   (a) a description of the hedge;

   (b) a description of the financial instruments designated as hedging instruments for the hedge and their fair values at the balance sheet date;

   (c) the nature of the risks being hedged; and

   (d) for hedges of forecasted transactions, the periods in which the forecasted transactions are expected to occur, when they are expected to enter into the determination of net profit or loss, and a description of any forecasted transaction for which hedge accounting had previously been used but that is no longer expected to occur.

3. If a gain or loss on derivative and non-derivative financial assets and liabilities designated as hedging instruments in cash flow hedges has been recognized directly in equity, through the statement of changes in equity, disclose:

   (a) the amount that was so recognized in equity during the current period;

   (b) the amount that was removed from equity and reported in net profit or loss for the period; and

   (c) the amount that was removed from equity and added to the initial measurement of the acquisition cost or other carrying amount of the asset or liability in a hedged forecasted transaction during the current period.

Financial statements should include all of the following additional disclosures relating to financial instruments. The enterprise should:

1. If a gain or loss from remeasuring available-for-sale financial assets to fair value (other than assets relating to hedges) has been recognized directly in equity, through the statement of changes in equity, disclose:

(a) the amount that was so recognized in equity during the current period; and

(b) the amount that was removed from equity and reported in net profit or loss for the period.

2. If the presumption that fair value can be reliably measured for all financial assets that are available for sale or held for trading has been overcome and the enterprise is, therefore, measuring any such financial assets at amortized cost, disclose that fact together with a description of the financial assets, their carrying amount, an explanation of why fair value cannot be reliably measured, and, if possible, the range of estimates within which fair value is highly likely to lie. Further, if financial assets whose fair value previously could not be measured reliably are sold, that fact, the carrying amount of such financial assets at the time of sale, and the amount of gain or loss recognized should be disclosed.

3. Disclose significant items of income, expense, and gains and losses resulting from financial assets and financial liabilities, whether included in net profit or loss or as a separate component of equity. For this purpose:

   (a) total interest income and total interest expense (both on a historical cost basis) should be disclosed separately;

   (b) with respect to available-for-sale financial assets that are adjusted to fair value after initial acquisition, total gains and losses from derecognition of such financial assets included in net profit or loss for the period should be reported separately from total gains and losses from fair value adjustments of recognized assets and liabilities included in net profit or loss for the period (a similar split of "realized" versus "unrealized" gains and losses with respect to financial assets and liabilities held for trading is not required);

   (c) the enterprise should disclose the amount of interest income that has been accrued on impaired loans and that has not yet been received in cash.

4. If the enterprise has entered into a securitization or repurchase agreement, disclose, separately for such transactions occurring in the current financial reporting period and for remaining retained interests from transactions occurring in prior financial reporting periods:

   (a) the nature and extent of such transactions, including a description of any collateral and quantitative information about the key assumptions used in calculating the fair values of new and retained interests;

(b) whether the financial assets have been derecognized.

5. If the enterprise has reclassified a financial asset as one required to be reported at amortized cost rather than at fair value, disclose the reason for that reclassification.

6. Disclose the nature and amount of any impairment loss or reversal of an impairment loss recognized for a financial asset, separately for each significant class of financial asset (IAS 39, pars. 169–170).

IAS 32, paragraph 94, encourages additional disclosures when they are likely to enhance financial statement users' understanding of financial instruments. It may be desirable to disclose information such as:

1. The total amount of the change in the fair value of financial assets and liabilities that has been recognized as income or expense for the period;

2. The average carrying amount during the year of recognized financial assets and liabilities, the average aggregate principal, stated or nominal amount during the year of unrecognized financial assets and liabilities and the aggregate fair value during the year of all financial assets and liabilities, especially when the amounts at the balance sheet date are unrepresentative of amounts during the year.

EFFECTIVE DATE AND TRANSITION

IAS 39, "Financial Instruments: Recognition and Measurement," became operative for financial statements covering financial years beginning on or after January 1, 2001. Earlier application is permitted only as of the beginning of a financial year that ends after March 15, 1999 (the date of issuance of this Standard). Retrospective application is not permitted.

The transition to IAS 39 should be as follows:

1. Recognition, derecognition, measurement, and hedge accounting policies followed in financial statements for periods prior to the effective date of the Standard should not be reversed and, therefore, those financial statements should not be restated.

2. For those transactions entered into before the beginning of the financial year in which this Standard is initially applied that the enterprise did previously designate as hedges, the recognition, derecognition, and measurement provisions of this Standard

should be applied prospectively. Therefore, if the previously designated hedge does not meet the conditions for an effective hedge and the hedging instrument is still held, hedge accounting will no longer be appropriate starting with the beginning of the financial year in which this Standard is initially applied. Accounting in prior financial years should not be retrospectively changed to conform to the requirements of this Standard.

3. At the beginning of the financial year in which IAS 39 is initially applied, an enterprise should recognize all derivatives in its balance sheet as either assets or liabilities and should measure them at fair value (except for a derivative that is linked to and that must be settled by delivery of an unquoted equity instrument whose fair value cannot be measured reliably). Because all derivatives, other than those that are designated hedging instruments, are considered held for trading, the difference between previous carrying amount (which may have been zero) and fair value of derivatives should be recognized as an adjustment of the balance of retained earnings at the beginning of the financial year in which IAS 39 is initially applied (other than for a derivative that is a designated hedging instrument).

4. At the beginning of the financial year in which IAS 39 is initially applied, an enterprise should apply the criteria in the Standard to identify those financial assets and liabilities that should be measured at fair value and those that should be measured at amortized cost, and it should remeasure those assets as appropriate. Any adjustment of the previous carrying amount should be recognized as an adjustment of the balance of retained earnings at the beginning of the financial year in which IAS 39 is initially applied.

5. At the beginning of the financial year in which IAS 39 is initially applied, any balance sheet positions in fair value hedges of existing assets and liabilities should be accounted for by adjusting their carrying amounts to reflect the fair value of the hedging instrument.

6. If an enterprise's hedge accounting policies prior to initial application of IAS 39 had included deferral, as assets and liabilities, of gains or losses on cash flow hedges, at the beginning of the financial year in which this Standard is initially applied, those deferred gains and losses should be reclassified as a separate component of equity to the extent that the transactions meet the criteria in the Standard and, thereafter, should be accounted for as set out in the Standard.

7. Transactions entered into before the beginning of the financial year in which IAS 39 is initially applied should not be retrospectively designated as hedges.

8. If a securitization, transfer, or other derecognition transaction was entered into prior to the beginning of the financial year in which IAS 39 is initially applied, the accounting for that transaction should not be retrospectively changed to conform to the requirements of IAS 39.

9. At the beginning of the financial year in which IAS 39 is initially applied, an enterprise should classify a financial instrument as equity or as a liability in accordance with IAS GAAP (see point 23 in the section on "Definitions," above) (IAS 39, pars. 171–172).

CHAPTER 17
FOREIGN CURRENCY TRANSLATION

CONTENTS

OVERVIEW

Changes in foreign currency exchange rates affect financial reporting in two ways. There are effects on:

1. Accounting for transactions in foreign currencies and the carrying amounts in the reporting currency of financial assets and liabilities denominated in foreign currencies and of the net investment in a foreign entity; and

2. Translating the financial statements of foreign operations that are included in the financial statements of a reporting enterprise through full or proportionate consolidation or the equity method. A foreign operation may be a subsidiary, joint venture, or branch of the reporting enterprise.

IAS GAAP require foreign currency transactions to be accounted for by applying the spot exchange rate in effect at the transaction date. An average rate for the period (e.g., week or month) in which the transaction occurred may be used, in the absence of significant fluctuations in the spot rate. Foreign currency monetary items should be translated at the closing (spot) rate at the balance sheet date. Nonmonetary items carried at historical cost continue to be translated at the historical rate originally used, while those carried at fair value denominated in foreign currency are carried at the spot rate on the date on which the fair value was determined. For monetary items, exchange differences between the closing rate and the rate previously used should be recognized immediately in income, except in certain situations involving hedge accounting or in the case of unavoidable exchange losses on a liability incurred in the recent acquisition of an asset invoiced in foreign currency, where an allowed alternative treatment is permitted.

A net investment in a foreign entity should be translated at the closing rate, and exchange differences (gains or losses) arising on the translation should be recognized directly in equity, until the investment is disposed of and the gain or loss on disposal is recognized, at which time the exchange gains or losses should be included in the calculation of the gain or loss on disposal.

For foreign operations, a distinction is made between those that are an integral part of the parent's own operations and those that are separate and self-sustaining (foreign entities). The financial statements of foreign operations that are an integral part of the parent's operations should be translated as if their transactions had been those of the parent.

For foreign entities, IAS GAAP require assets and liabilities to be translated at closing rates and income statements to be translated at a reasonable approximation to actual rates (such as monthly average rates). However, goodwill and fair value adjustments to nonmonetary items arising on an acquisition may, alternatively, be translated at the historical rate at the acquisition date. Exchange differences should be recognized directly in equity. If the foreign entity's reporting currency is that of a hyperinflationary economy, its financial statements should be restated in accordance with IAS 29, "Financial Reporting in Hyperinflationary Economies" (see Chapter 8), before translation at the closing rate.

BACKGROUND

The main problem areas in accounting for the effects of changes in foreign exchange rates have been (a) the translation into the reporting currency of the financial statements of foreign entities in the consolidation process and (b) the particular problem when a foreign entity reports in the currency of a hyperinflationary economy (dealt with in IAS 29; see Chapter 8).

Historically, several methods have existed for translating the financial statements of a foreign entity into the reporting currency, with distinctions being made between those balance sheet items to be translated at closing rates and those to be translated at historic rates. Thus, there were distinctions between monetary and nonmonetary items, or between current and non-current items, or between items (including monetary items) carried at current fair values and those carried at historical costs; with the first-named of each pair being translated at closing rates and the second at historical rates. A major issue was the treatment of gains or losses arising on translation because of exchange rate changes: should these be included in income or not?

FAS-52 resolved most of these issues by requiring that all balance sheet items be translated at current (closing) rates and that the resultant translation gains and losses be recognized directly in equity, bypassing net income. Essentially, this represented a recognition that, in the consolidation or equitization of an independent foreign entity, such gains and losses are merely artifacts of the accounting process of translation and do not necessarily reflect any value changes that are relevant to the measurement of consolidated net income.

IAS GAAP have followed that lead. There are differences between IAS GAAP and U.S. GAAP, however, of which the most significant are set out below.

IAS GAAP on foreign currency translation are set out in:

- IAS 21, "Accounting for the Effects of Changes in Foreign Exchange Rates"
- SIC-7, "Introduction of the Euro"
- SIC-11, "Foreign Exchange—Capitalization of Losses Resulting from Severe Currency Devaluations"
- SIC-19, "Reporting Currency—Measurement and Presentation of Financial Statements under IAS 21 and IAS 29"

The main differences from U.S. GAAP (FAS-52 and FIN-37) are:

1. IAS 21 permits the translation of goodwill and fair value adjustments arising on acquisitions to be made at either current (closing) or historical exchange rates. FAS-52 requires the use of current (closing) rates.

2. IAS 21 permits (as an allowed alternative treatment) the capitalization as part of acquisition cost of unavoidable exchange losses on a foreign currency liability incurred in the recent acquisition of an asset invoiced in a foreign currency. This is not permitted by FAS-52.

3. IAS 21 requires the financial statements of a foreign entity that reports using the currency of a hyperinflationary country to be restated for general price-level changes prior to translation into the reporting entity's currency. FAS-52 requires remeasurement of the elements of the entity's financial statements into the reporting entity's currency, as though the latter were its functional currency. Whether the two methods produce similar results depends on how closely the change in the general price-level in the hyperinflationary economy is reflected in the change in the exchange rate between the two currencies. More generally, IAS 21 does not use the term or concept "functional currency."

4. IAS 21 does not deal with foreign currency hedges, which are dealt with in IAS 39. There are some differences between the treatment of foreign currency hedges in IAS 39 and in FAS-52 (see Chapter 16).

SCOPE

IAS 21 sets out the requirements for (a) accounting for transactions in foreign currencies and the carrying amounts in the reporting currency of financial assets and liabilities denominated in foreign currencies and of the net investment in a foreign entity; and (b) translating in the financial statements of foreign operations that are included the financial statements of a reporting enterprise through full or proportionate consolidation or the equity method.

A foreign operation may be a subsidiary, joint venture, or branch of the reporting enterprise.

IAS 21 does not deal with the following:

1. Hedge accounting for foreign currency items, dealt with in IAS 39 (see Chapter 16).

2. Specifying the currency in which financial statements are presented.

3. "Convenience translations" of financial statements from the reporting currency into another currency for the benefit of some users.

4. Presentation of foreign exchange difference in cash flow statements arising from transactions in a foreign currency, which are dealt with in IAS 7, "Cash Flow Statements" (see Chapter 7) (IAS 21, pars. 1–6).

DEFINITIONS

- The *reporting currency* is the currency that an enterprise uses to present its financial statements. Normally, this is the currency of the country in which the reporting entity is domiciled, but this is not required. If this is not the case, the standard requires disclosure of the reason. For example, an enterprise may be domiciled in the United Kingdom but have only very limited U.K. operations, while its non-U.K. operations are predominantly in U.S. dollars. In that case, the enterprise may choose the U.S. dollar as its reporting currency (or "functional currency" in the terminology of FAS-52). In such a case, IAS 1 requires the reporting currency to be prominently displayed in the financial statements to avoid any misunderstanding.

  For groups, the reporting currency is that used by the parent to present the consolidated financial statements.

- A *foreign currency* is a currency other than the enterprise's reporting currency.

- The *closing rate* is the spot exchange rate of the foreign currency and the reporting currency at the reporting (balance sheet) date.

- A *foreign operation* is a subsidiary, associate, joint venture, or branch of the reporting enterprise, the activities of which are based or conducted in a different country from that of the reporting enterprise.

- A *foreign entity* is a foreign operation, the activities of which are not an integral part of those of the reporting enterprise (IAS 21, par. 7).

MEASUREMENT CURRENCY AND PRESENTATION CURRENCY

The term "reporting currency" as used in IAS 21 does not distinguish between an enterprise's "measurement currency" and another currency that it might choose for the presentation of its financial statements ("presentation currency"). The "measurement currency" is the currency used by an enterprise for measuring items in its financial statements.

The measurement currency used by an enterprise should be such that it provides information about that enterprise that is useful and reflects the economic substance of the underlying events and circumstances relevant to that enterprise. Normally, this will be the currency of the country in which the enterprise is domiciled, but another currency may be used to a significant extent in, or have a significant impact on, the enterprise, and this currency may be an appropriate currency to be used as the measurement currency. All transactions in currencies other than the measurement currency should be treated as transactions in foreign currencies when applying IAS 21. Once the measurement currency has been chosen, it should not be changed unless there is a change in the underlying events and circumstances relevant to the enterprise (SIC-19, pars. 1–6).

Although the measurement currency is normally used as the presentation currency, an enterprise may (subject to legal requirements) choose to present its financial statements (or its consolidated financial statements) in a different currency. In order for the resultant financial statements to present fairly the financial position, performance, and cash flows, the method used to translate the financial statements from the measurement currency into the presentation currency should not lead to reporting in a manner that is inconsistent with the measurement of items in the measurement currency. IAS GAAP do not specify any particular method of translation (SIC-19, par. 9).

If the enterprise is a foreign entity as defined in IAS 21 and is included in the financial statements of another reporting enterprise, its financial statements should be restated under IAS 29 before being translated into the reporting currency of the other reporting enterprise. If the currency of a country that does not have a hyperinflationary economy is chosen as an appropriate measurement currency by an enterprise, the enterprise is not required to restate its financial statements under IAS 29 (SIC-19, pars. 7–8).

FOREIGN CURRENCY TRANSACTIONS

A foreign currency transaction is one that is denominated or requires settlement in a foreign currency, including:

1. Buying or selling goods or services at a price denominated in a foreign currency.

2. Borrowing or lending funds if the amounts payable or receivable are denominated in a foreign currency.

3. Becoming a party to an unperformed foreign exchange contract.

4. Otherwise acquiring or disposing of assets and incurring or settling of liabilities denominated in a foreign currency (IAS 21, par. 8).

Initial Recognition

A foreign currency transaction should be recorded, on initial recognition in the reporting currency, by applying to the foreign currency amount the exchange rate between the foreign currency and the reporting currency at the date of the transaction. This exchange rate should in principle be the spot rate. For practical reasons, however, where there is a large number of transactions during a relatively short period such as a week or a month, a reasonable approximation of it may be used, such as the average rate over the period, provided the fluctuations in the exchange rate are not such as to make such an approximation unreliable (IAS 21, pars. 9–10).

Reporting at Subsequent Balance Sheet Dates

Monetary items should be translated into the reporting currency at the closing rate. Nonmonetary items carried at fair value *in the foreign currency* should be translated at the rate prevailing on the date when the fair values were determined; there will be no subsequent retranslation unless a new fair value in the foreign currency is subsequently determined. Nonmonetary items carried at historical cost in the foreign currency should be translated at the rate prevailing at the date of the transaction; there is no subsequent retranslation (IAS 21, par. 11).

Recognition of Exchange Differences

IAS 21 does not deal with hedge accounting, except for the classification of exchange differences arising on a foreign currency liability accounted for as a hedge of a net investment in a foreign entity (see below). Hedge accounting is dealt with in IAS 39, "Financial Instruments: Recognition and Measurement" (see Chapter 16). The requirements set out below may be modified by IAS 39 when the requirements for hedge accounting are met.

Exchange differences arising on the settlement of monetary items, or on translating an enterprise's monetary items at rates different from those at which they were previously translated, should be recognized in net profit or loss in the period in which they arise, with the exception of the items described below under "Net Investment in a Foreign Entity." When a transaction is settled in a subsequent accounting period, an exchange difference will be recognized on translation or retranslation at each balance sheet date, and at settlement the difference to be recognized will be that between the rate on settlement and that at the previous balance sheet date (IAS 21, pars. 15–16).

The above is the benchmark treatment of exchange differences on liabilities arising on the acquisition of an asset invoiced in a foreign currency. There is an allowed alternative treatment in cases where the differences (that is, losses) result from a "severe devaluation or depreciation" of an enterprise's currency against which there is "no practical means of hedging" and that affects liabilities that "cannot be settled" and that "arise directly on the recent acquisition" of an asset invoiced in a foreign currency. The allowed alternative treatment is that the exchange losses may be capitalized as part of the acquisition cost of the related asset, provided that the resultant carrying amount does not exceed the replacement cost or the recoverable amount of the asset, whichever is lower (IAS 21, pars. 21–22).

The rationale behind this alternative treatment is that, in some countries, exchange controls impede both prompt settlement and hedging of foreign currency liabilities. In such circumstances, it may be impossible to take timely action to hedge or settle the liability prior to the "severe devaluation or depreciation," so that the exchange losses are "an unavoidable consequence of buying the asset and therefore...to be considered as part of its acquisition cost" (SIC-11, par. 7). If this condition is met, there is the further question of what is meant by "recent." SIC-11, paragraph 6, interprets "recent acquisition" as "acquisition within twelve months prior to the severe devaluation or depreciation."

Net Investment in a Foreign Entity

An enterprise may have a monetary item that is receivable from, or payable to, a foreign entity, settlement of which is neither planned nor likely to occur in the foreseeable future. Such an item is, in substance, an extension to or deduction from the enterprise's net investment in that foreign entity, and IAS GAAP require exchange differences arising on such items to be recognized directly in equity until the net investment in the foreign entity is disposed of, at which time they should be taken into account as part of the overall gain or loss on disposal (IAS 21, pars. 17–18).

When a foreign currency liability is accounted for as a hedge of an enterprise's net investment in a foreign entity, any exchange differences arising on that liability should be recognized directly in equity until the net investment in the foreign entity is disposed of, at which time they should be taken into account as part of the overall gain or loss on disposal (IAS 21, par. 19).

FINANCIAL STATEMENTS OF FOREIGN OPERATIONS

Classification of Foreign Operations

Foreign operations may be classified either as "integral to the operations of the reporting enterprise" or as "foreign entities." The classification affects the method required under IAS GAAP to be used in translating the financial statements of the foreign operations into the reporting currency.

Foreign Operations That Are Integral to Those of the Reporting Enterprise

A foreign operation is integral to the operations of the reporting enterprise if it effectively functions as an extension of the latter, so that *the cash flows of the reporting enterprise are directly affected by the activities of the foreign operation.* It may, for example, be a "captive" sales unit that sells only or mainly goods supplied by the reporting entity, or a "captive" production unit that supplies only or mainly the reporting entity (IAS 21, pars. 24–25).

Under IAS GAAP, the financial statements of a foreign operation that is integral to the operations of the reporting enterprise should be translated into the reporting currency by using the same rules and procedures for initial recognition, subsequent reporting, and treatment of exchange differences (described above under "Foreign Currency Transactions") that would be applied if the transactions of the foreign operation had been those of the reporting enterprise (IAS 21, pars. 27–28).

Foreign Entities

In contrast to a foreign operation that is not a foreign entity, a foreign entity exercises a significant degree of operational autonomy (that is, autonomy in carrying out its day-to-day activities), and its transactions with the reporting enterprise are not a predominant proportion of the foreign entity's activities. A significant proportion of its sales and purchases are likely to be in currencies other than the reporting currency. A foreign operation that is controlled in a *strategic* sense by the reporting enterprise may well exercise a significant degree of *operational* autonomy; most foreign subsidiaries fall into the category of foreign entities.

As noted above, a key criterion is whether the activities of the foreign operation directly affect the cash flows of the reporting enterprise. Related to this is the criterion of how much financial autonomy the foreign operation has: is it obliged to remit any surplus cash to, as well as being entirely dependent for funding on, the parent (reporting) enterprise? If the answers to these questions are negative, the foreign operation is properly classified as a foreign operation.

Under IAS GAAP, the following procedures should be used by the reporting enterprise to translate the financial statements of a foreign entity:

1. The assets and liabilities, both monetary and nonmonetary, of the foreign entity should be translated at the closing rate.
2. Income and expense items of the foreign entity should in principle be translated at exchange rates at the dates of the related

transactions (in practice, a reasonable approximation such as weekly or monthly average rate generally may be used), except when the foreign entity reports in the currency of a hyperinflationary economy. In the latter case, income and expense items should be translated at the closing rate.

3. All resulting exchange differences should be recognized directly in equity (and, when appropriate, in minority interests) until the disposal of the net investment in the foreign operation. Such exchange differences may result from (a) translating income and expense items at rates at transaction dates and assets and liabilities at closing rates; (b) retranslating the beginning-of-period net investment at the end-of-period closing rate; or (c) retranslating capital movements during the period at end-of-period closing rates.

4. Any goodwill, and any fair value adjustments to the carrying values of assets and liabilities, arising on the acquisition of a foreign entity may be either (a) treated as assets and liabilities of the foreign entity, translated and retranslated at closing rates; or (b) treated as assets and liabilities of the reporting entity or group, which are either (i) already expressed in the reporting currency and not requiring translation or (ii) nonmonetary items denominated in a foreign currency, translated at the exchange rate at the transaction date and not subsequently retranslated (IAS 21, pars. 30–33).

> **OBSERVATION:** The rationale of treatment (b) above is not clear in the case of fair value adjustments, since the underlying assets and liabilities in the foreign operation are translated at closing rates, and the treatment results in their being translated partly at closing rates and partly (to the extent of the fair value adjustments) at historical rates, which hardly seems logical. In the case of goodwill, the conceptual problem is not so obvious; but since goodwill is the residual between the fair values of the assets and liabilities acquired and the fair value of the acquisition consideration given, the same doubts about the rationale of treatment (b) must apply.

In the consolidation process, intragroup monetary balances are eliminated as laid down in IAS 27, "Consolidated Financial Statements and Accounting for Investments in Subsidiaries" (see Chapter 9). Where an intragroup monetary item is designated in a currency other than the reporting currency, however, an exchange difference is likely to arise when this item is eliminated against a counterpart item designated in the reporting currency or in a third currency. Such exchange differences are recognized in net profit or loss, unless they arise on an item that is either (a) a monetary item that, in substance, forms part of an enterprise's net investment in a foreign entity; or (b) a foreign currency liability accounted for as a hedge of an enterprise's net investment in a foreign entity. In the case of (a) or (b), the exchange gain or loss is recognized directly in equity until the disposal of the net investment, at which time it is accounted for as part of the profit or loss on disposal (IAS 21, par. 34).

The financial statements of a foreign entity may be drawn up at a different reporting date from that of the reporting enterprise. For consolidation purposes, another set of financial statements for the foreign entity will, if practicable, be prepared as of the reporting entity's reporting date. If, however, this is not practicable, and the difference between the two reporting dates does not exceed three months, IAS 27 permits the foreign entity's financial statements drawn up at a different date to be used for consolidation purposes. In this case, the assets and liabilities of the foreign entity are translated at the closing rate on the foreign entity's balance sheet date. Adjustments are made for significant movements in exchange rates between the two reporting dates, when appropriate, in accordance with IAS 27 or IAS 28, "Accounting for Investments in Associates" (see Chapters 9 and 14) (IAS 21, par. 36).

Disposal of a Foreign Entity

An enterprise may dispose of its interest in a foreign entity through sale, liquidation, repayment of share capital, or other means. On disposal, the cumulative amount of any exchange differences (gains or losses) that were recognized directly in equity should be brought into account as part of the gain or loss on disposal. In the case of a partial disposal, the relevant proportion of the cumulative amount of exchange differences should be included in the gain or loss on disposal.

Payment of a dividend out of the foreign entity is not considered to be a partial disposal unless it is a constructive return of the investment in share capital.

> ☛ **PRACTICE POINTER:** Normally, a dividend would not be considered to be a partial disposal unless the distribution reduced the distributable reserves of the foreign entity below their level at the acquisition date (that is, there was a distribution of preacquisition reserves).
>
> A write-down in the carrying amount of the net investment in a foreign entity is not a disposal and does not result in any cumulative exchange differences, previously recognized directly in equity, being recognized in profit or loss of the period (IAS 21, pars. 37–38).

Change in the Classification of a Foreign Operation

A change in the way in which a foreign operation is financed and operates in relation to the reporting enterprise may be such as to require a change in the classification of that foreign operation: it may either (a) become, or (b) cease to be, a foreign entity.

1. In case (a), exchange differences arising on the translation of nonmonetary assets at the date of the reclassification (as a foreign entity) should be recognized directly in equity.

2. In case (b), the translated amounts of the nonmonetary items at the date of the reclassification (as a foreign operation that is integral to those of the reporting entity) should be treated as their historical costs in the period of change and subsequently.

3. Monetary items will be translated at closing rates in either case and are not affected by the reclassification (IAS 21, par. 39–40).

Tax Effects of Exchange Differences

Gains and losses on foreign currency transactions, and exchange differences arising on the translation of financial statements of foreign operations, may have tax effects, which should be dealt with according to IAS 12, "Income Taxes" (see Chapter 20).

> **OBSERVATION:** In fact, IAS GAAP have little to say about this matter, which is addressed briefly in IAS 12, paragraphs 41 and 62–63. One problem for an international accounting standard on such a topic is the different tax treatment of such items in different jurisdictions.

DISCLOSURE

An enterprise should disclose:

1. The amount of exchange differences included in the net profit or loss for the period;

2. Net exchange differences classified as equity as a separate component of equity, and a reconciliation of the amount of such exchange differences at the beginning and end of the period; and

3. The amount of exchange differences arising during the period that is included in the carrying amount of an asset in accordance with the allowed alternative treatment in paragraph 21.

The following information should be disclosed about currencies used for measurement and presentation:

1. When the measurement currency is different from the currency of the country in which the enterprise is domiciled, the reason for using a different currency.

2. If the presentation currency is different from the enterprise's measurement currency, (a) the measurement currency, (b) the reason for using a different presentation currency, and (c) the method used in translation from the measurement currency into the presentation currency.

3. The reason for any change in the measurement currency or presentation currency.

When there is a change in the classification of a significant foreign operation, an enterprise should disclose:

1. The nature of the change in classification;

2. The reason for the change;

3. The impact of the change in classification on shareholders' equity; and

4. The impact of the net profit or loss for each prior period presented had the change in classification occurred at the beginning of the earliest period presented.

An enterprise should disclose the method selected in accordance with paragraph 33 (see above) to translate goodwill and fair value adjustments arising on the acquisition of a foreign entity.

An enterprise discloses the effect on foreign currency monetary items on the financial statements of a foreign operation of a change in exchange rates occurring after the balance sheet date if the change is of such importance that nondisclosure would affect the ability of users of the financial statements to make proper evaluations and decisions (see IAS 10, "Contingencies and Events Occurring after the Balance Sheet Date," discussed in Chapter 15).

Disclosure is also encouraged of an enterprise's foreign currency risk management policy (IAS 21, pars. 42–47; SIC-19, par. 10).

Transitional Provisions

On the first occasion that an enterprise applies this standard, the enterprise should, except when the amount is not reasonably determinable, classify separately and disclose the cumulative balance, at the beginning of the period, of exchange differences deferred and classified as equity in previous periods.

CHAPTER 18
GOVERNMENT GRANTS AND
GOVERNMENT ASSISTANCE

CONTENTS

OVERVIEW

Enterprises that receive a material amount of assistance from government or state sources are clearly in a different economic position from otherwise comparable enterprises that receive no such assistance. In order to allow proper appraisal of the results of the enterprise activities, and to facilitate comparisons, disclosure of this government assistance in as much detail as practicable is necessary.

More specifically, government *grants* are usually easily quantifiable, and the general principle of transparency requires that they be both properly accounted for and clearly disclosed. Government grants typically represent a reduction in net cash outflows, and therefore, at least ultimately, an increase in enterprise earnings. Some interesting issues of definition and alternative treatments arise, which need to be addressed and regulated. IAS GAAP are given in IAS 20, "Accounting for Government Grants and Disclosure of Government Assistance," effective from 1984. SIC-10, "Government Assistance—No Specific Relation to Operating Activities," is also relevant.

BACKGROUND

The issues of disclosure have already been summarized in the overview given above. The issues of measurement and definition are more complex, particularly in respect of grants related to the purchase of non-current assets. Under historical cost accounting, cost is obviously the basis of carrying value. IAS 16, "Property, Plant, and Equipment," for example, requires that an item of property, plant, and equipment that qualifies for recognition as an asset should initially be measured at its cost (see Chapter 27). The question is, what *is* its cost?

Suppose a government grant is paid to an enterprise because, and under the condition that, the enterprise purchases a depreciable non-current asset. The figures concerned are as follows:

Purchase price of asset	$12,000
Expected useful life	4 years
Expected residual value	Nil
Government grant	$2,000
Annual profits before depreciation, and grants relating to the asset	$20,000

It is possible to suggest at least four possible different ways of treating the grant.

1. To credit the total amount of the grant immediately to the income statement.
2. To credit the amount of the grant to a nondistributable reserve.
3. To credit the amount of the grant to revenue over the useful life of the asset by:
   (a) reducing the cost of the acquisition of the non-current asset by the amount of the grant, or
   (b) treating the amount of the grant as a deferred credit, a portion of which is transferred to revenue annually.

The first two methods may be rejected on the ground that they provide no correlation between the accounting treatment of the grant and the accounting treatment of the expenditure to which the grant relates. The first method would increase the profits in the first year by the entire amount of the grant, failing to associate the grant with the useful life of the asset. It thus ignores both the prudence convention and the matching convention. The second method means that the grant will *never* affect the profit figure. It also, therefore, ignores the matching convention and additionally leaves the "nondistributable reserve" in the balance sheet, presumably forever, that is, it is treated as paid-in surplus.

The third and fourth methods both follow and apply the matching convention. They both have exactly the same effect on reported annual profits, the differences being concerned only with balance sheet presentation.

Illustration of Different Accounting Treatments

Using the data given above, the two "acceptable" methods give the following results.

Method 3(a)

Profit before depreciation, etc.	$20,000	$20,000	$20,000	$20,000
Depreciation	(2,500)	(2,500)	(2,500)	(2,500)
Profit	$17,500	$17,500	$17,500	$17,500

Balance sheet extract at year-end

Non-current asset at (net)

cost	$10,000	$10,000	$10,000	$10,000
Depreciation	2,500	5,000	7,500	10,000
Carrying amount	$ 7,500	$ 5,000	$ 2,500	$ 0

Method 3(b)

Profit before depreciation, etc.	$20,000	$20,000	$20,000	$20,000
Depreciation	(3,000)	(3,000)	(3,000)	(3,000)
Grant released	500	500	500	500
Profit	$17,500	$17,500	$17,500	$17,500

Balance sheet extract at year-end

Non-current asset at cost	$12,000	$12,000	$12,000	$12,000
Depreciation	3,000	6,000	9,000	12,000
Carrying amount	$ 9,000	$ 6,000	$ 3,000	$ 0

Deferred credit

Government grant	$ 1,500	$ 1,000	$ 500	$ 0

Thus, method (a) shows assets of 7,500, 5,000, 2,500, and 0 over the four years, and method (b) shows assets of 9,000, 6,000, 3,000, and 0, together with "liabilities" of 1,500, 1,000, 500, and 0.

From a pragmatic point of view, method (a) has the obvious advantage of simplicity. No entries, and no thought, are required in the second and subsequent years. Method (b), however, has the advantage that assets acquired at different times and locations are recorded on a uniform basis, regardless of changes in governmental policy. But what *is* the cost of the asset? Is it 12,000 or is it 10,000? IAS 16, "Property, Plant, and Equipment" (see Chapter 27) states that cost is the amount of cash or cash equivalents paid, net of any trade discounts and rebates. This statement does not seem to categorically resolve the question. The government grant is not a trade discount. It is not a *trade* rebate, but it is a rebate. This would seem to imply that the cost in the sense of IAS 16 is 10,000. This is surely the net outflow arising because of the purchase. Yet IAS 20, as discussed in detail below, allows both methods.

> **OBSERVATION:** A difficult conceptual problem arises with the deferred credit under method (b), for example, the 1,500 at the end of year 1. We described it above as a "liability." As discussed in Chapter 2, IASC defines a liability as a present obligation of the enterprise arising from past events, the settlement of which is expected to result in an outflow of resources embodying economic benefits. On the assumption that the grant cannot be reclaimed by the governmental body concerned (the usual situation), the 1,500 is clearly *not* a liability, as no outflow of resources is foreseeable. It is more logically either a reserve (not yet realized), or a contra-asset. It could be suggested that this leads to a different possible treatment, that is, regular inclusion in the balance sheet as a visible contra-asset (i.e., included as a negative balance among the "assets" instead of as a positive balance amongst the liabilities). This would raise its own problems—not least the lack of user-friendliness involved in the concept of a negative asset. Such conceptual difficulties do not appear to worry either IASC or other national regulators.

U.S. GAAP, or at least promulgated U.S. GAAP, appear to be silent on this whole area. FAS-116, "Accounting for Contributions Received and Contributions Made," applies to not-for-profit organizations and explicitly excludes transfer of assets from governments to businesses. The U.S.-promulgated GAAP for the treatment of investment tax credits, perhaps analogous, permits either deferral and gradual release of the benefit to income, or instant release to income.

U.K. GAAP, in SSAP 4, does not permit the netting out of capital grants in the balance sheet and allows only the treatment retaining a separate deferred income balance. This is under the stated, but mistaken, belief that U.K. law, following European Directive wording, prohibits such setting off. U.K. (and European) legal requirements forbid the netting out of assets and liabilities, but of course deferred income is not a liability, as already discussed, so therefore netting would be perfectly legal!

SCOPE AND DEFINITIONS

IAS 20, "Accounting for Government Grants and Disclosure of Government Assistance," should be applied in accounting for, and in the disclosure of, government grants and in the disclosure of other forms of government assistance.
It does not deal with:

1. The special problems arising in accounting for government grants in financial statements reflecting the effects of changing prices or in supplementary information of a similar nature;
2. Government assistance that is provided for an enterprise in the form of benefits that are available in determining taxable income or are determined or limited on the basis of income tax liability (such as income tax holidays, investment tax credits, accelerated depreciation allowances, and reduced income tax rates);
3. Government participation in the ownership of the enterprise; and
4. Government grants covered by IAS 41, "Agriculture." (See Chapter 32. IAS 41, and therefore this exclusion from IAS 20, is effective for financial statements covering periods beginning on or after January 1, 2003.)

Government assistance is action by government designed to provide an economic benefit specific to an enterprise or range of enterprises qualifying under certain criteria. Government assistance for the purpose of this standard does not include benefits provided only indirectly through action affecting general trading conditions, such as the provision of infrastructure in development areas or the imposition of trading constraints on competitors.

A specific subset of government assistance is government grants. *Government grants* are assistance by government in the form of transfers of resources to an enterprise in return for past or future compliance with certain conditions relating to the operating activities of the enterprise. They exclude those forms of government assistance that cannot reasonably have a value placed upon them and transactions with government that cannot be distinguished from the normal trading transactions of the enterprise.

The notion of government is to be interpreted broadly. *Government* refers to government, government agencies, and similar bodies, whether local, national, or international.

Government grants may be related to revenue/expense items, such as repayment of 10% of the wages bill, or to capital/asset items, such as repayment of 10% of the cost of a machine. These two types are formally distinguished by IAS 20.

- *Grants related to assets* are government grants whose primary condition is that an enterprise qualifying for them should purchase, construct, or otherwise acquire long-term assets. Subsidiary conditions may also be attached restricting the type or location of the assets or the periods during which they are to be acquired or held.

- *Grants related to income* are government grants other than those related to assets.

The standard gives two other definitions, including the familiar fair value.

- *Forgivable loans* are loans of which the lender undertakes to waive repayment under certain prescribed conditions.

- *Fair value* is the amount for which an asset could be exchanged between a knowledgeable, willing buyer and a knowledgeable, willing seller in an arm's-length transaction.

GOVERNMENT ASSISTANCE

Despite the inclusion of government assistance in the title of IAS 20, the statements about it are brief and rather obscure. The definitions given above suggest, in effect, that government grants are government assistance that is distinguishable and quantifiable. Turning this around, references to government assistance in the standard are to government activities that cannot be quantified or clearly distinguished. It follows, of course, that government assistance in this sense cannot be included numerically in the financial statements.

Examples of assistance that cannot reasonably have a value placed upon it are free technical or marketing advice and the provision of guarantees. An example of assistance that cannot be distinguished from the normal trading transactions of the enterprise is a government procurement policy that is responsible for a portion of the enterprise's sales. The existence of the benefit might be unquestioned, but any attempt to segregate the trading activities from government assistance could well be arbitrary.

The significance of the benefit in the above examples may be such that disclosure of the nature, extent, and duration of the assistance is necessary in order that the financial statements may not be misleading (par. 36). The standard explicitly states (par. 37) that while loans at nil or low interest rates are a form of government assistance, the "benefit is not quantified by the imputation of interest."

The disclosure requirement implied in the above seems rather weakly stated. Nonquantified government support, which explicitly includes loans at low or zero interest, need not be disclosed at all unless its omission would be so serious as to be "misleading."

GOVERNMENT GRANTS

The major portion of IAS 20 is concerned with the treatment of government grants. The first issue to deal with is the timing of recognition. The IAS requirement (par. 7) is that government grants, including nonmonetary grants at fair value, should not be recognized until there is reasonable assurance that the enterprise will comply with the conditions attaching to them and that the grants will be received. Receipt of a grant does not of itself provide conclusive evidence that the conditions attaching to the grant have been or will be fulfilled.

"Reasonable assurance" is not, of course, definable or defined, but it is clearly less rigorous or demanding than, for example, "virtual certainty" or "beyond all reasonable doubt." The standard confirms (par. 10) that a forgivable loan (as defined earlier) is treated as a government grant when there is reasonable assurance that the enterprise will meet the terms for forgiveness of the loan. Once a government grant is recognized, any related contingency would be treated in accordance with IAS 37, "Provisions, Contingent Liabilities, and Contingent Assets" (see Chapter 28).

Perhaps rather surprisingly, IAS 20 discusses at some length (pars. 13–16) the ostensible advantages of two alternative approaches to the accounting treatment of government grants after recognition, namely the capital approach, under which a grant is credited directly to shareholders' interests, and the income approach, under which a grant is taken to income over one or more periods. Presumably there were members of the board at the time who felt some sympathy with the "capital approach," but by implication most board members must have tended toward the "net cost" argument of IAS 16, discussed above, as use of the capital approach is not permitted. The standard requires (par. 12) that government grants be recognized as income over the periods necessary to match them with the related costs that they are intended to compensate, on a systematic basis, that is, following method 3(a) or 3(b) as discussed at the beginning of this chapter. They should not be credited directly to shareholders' interests. SIC-10, "Government Assistance— No Specific Relation to Operating Activities," effective from August 1,

1998, has confirmed that government assistance to enterprises is a grant under IAS 20, even if granted generally to all enterprises within certain regions or industry sectors.

The matching principle will usually be simple to apply, as illustrated earlier in this chapter. Grants related to nondepreciable assets may also require the fulfillment of certain obligations and would then be recognized as income over the periods that bear the cost of meeting the obligations. As an example, a grant of land may be conditional upon the erection of a building on the site, and it may be appropriate to recognize it as income over the life of the building. A government grant that becomes receivable as compensation for expenses or losses already incurred or for the purpose of giving immediate financial support to the enterprise with no future related costs should be recognized as income of the period in which it becomes receivable. Separate disclosure and explanation may be required.

Usually, a careful reading of the contract with the governmental body will determine the appropriate accounting treatment, although an intelligent appraisal of the in-substance thrust of the contract may be required. For example a grant toward building a factory that stipulates that the factory must remain operating and employing at least 30 people for at least 3 years is clearly in essence a grant toward building a factory, not a revenue grant toward reducing net wage costs. However, where a grant clearly relates in material terms to both specific capital and specific revenue items, the standard is silent on appropriate treatment. Accounting common sense obviously requires an apportionment in such cases.

The standard is surprisingly vague about nonmonetary government grants, such as land donated by a government. IAS 20 merely notes (par. 23) that:

> it is usual to assess the fair value of the non-monetary asset and to account for both grant and asset at that fair value. An alternative course that is sometimes followed is to record both asset and grant at a nominal amount.

This is worded as a description, not as a requirement, although the preference is clear enough. Our view is that merely to record the event at nominal amount lacks transparency to an unacceptable degree. Also, it is not consistent with the substance over form principle and would lead to an inconsistent treatment of assets affecting both inter-enterprise and intra-enterprise comparisons.

PRESENTATION OF GOVERNMENT GRANTS

Regarding the presentation of grants related to assets, IAS 20 allows both methods (a) and (b) as discussed and illustrated earlier in this chapter. Thus, government grants related to assets, including non-monetary grants at fair value, should (pars. 24–28) be presented in the balance sheet either by setting up the grant as deferred income or by deducting the grant in arriving at the carrying amount of the asset. The standard spells out that separate disclosure of the gross cash flows in the cash flow statement is likely to be necessary, whatever treatment is followed in the balance sheet. IAS 7, "Cash Flow Statements" (see Chapter 7), is more explicit in making this grossing up of cash flows a requirement.

Regarding the presentation of grants related to income, the standard again accepts either of two alternatives (pars. 29–31). It states, with approval, that grants related to income are sometimes presented as a credit in the income statement, either separately or under a general heading such as "Other income"; alternatively, they are deducted in reporting the related expense.

A proper understanding of the financial statements may require separate disclosure of the grant and of its effects on particular items of income or expense.

REPAYMENT OF GOVERNMENT GRANTS

A grant to which conditions were attached may have been properly recognized under the "reasonable assurance" criterion discussed above. It may still become repayable in whole or in part, however, if, in fact, the conditions are not met. IAS 20 requires (par. 32) that such a grant, as soon as the repayment becomes foreseeable (which might be significantly earlier than when the repayment actually occurs), should be accounted for as a revision to an accounting estimate, under IAS 8, "Net Profit or Loss for the Period, Fundamental Errors and Changes in Accounting Policies," see Chapter 26. This essentially requires that the entries be made in the financial statements of the year concerned. Repayment of a grant related to income should be applied first against any unamortized deferred credit set up in respect of the grant. To the extent that the repayment exceeds any such deferred credit, or where no deferred credit exists, the repayment should be recognized immediately as an expense. Repayment of a grant related to an asset should be recorded by increasing the carrying amount of the asset or reducing the deferred balance by the amount repayable. The cumulative additional depreciation that would have been recognized to date as an expense in the absence of the grant should be recognized immediately as an expense. Circumstances giving rise to repayment of a grant related to an asset may require consideration to be given to the possible impairment of the new carrying amount of the asset (see IAS 36, "Impairment of Assets," discussed in Chapter 19).

DISCLOSURE

The following matters should be disclosed:

1. The accounting policy adopted for government grants, including the methods of presentation adopted in the financial statements,

2. The nature and extent of government grants recognized in the financial statements and an indication of other forms of government assistance from which the enterprise has directly benefited, and

3. Unfulfilled conditions and other contingencies attaching to government assistance that has been recognized.

CHAPTER 19
IMPAIRMENT OF ASSETS

CONTENTS

OVERVIEW

Very broadly speaking, purchase transactions are recorded in accounting terms first by including the purchased item as an asset at its cost price, then by expensing the item over one or a number of accounting periods according to its usage or consumption pattern. The going concern convention supports this treatment, as it explicitly assumes that there will be future operational accounting periods in which present assets can be transferred to expenses.

Strictly, this means that there is no need, at an intermediate stage in this process, to compare the temporary balance sheet number with any form of value—using the word *value* in its proper sense of monetary benefit to be derived. This would not be in accordance with the prudence convention, however, and would arguably be dangerously misleading to creditors and lenders. Over the years accounting has dealt with the inherent tension and conflict here in a variety of ways, all more or less *ad hoc,* depending on the accounting issue involved (and often depending also on the country involved).

The IASC has quite properly attempted to provide a general standard, IAS 36, "Impairment of Assets," to provide consistency and coherence to this whole matter. The principle of the standard is clear and simple. First, the carrying amount of an asset is determined in accordance with accounting principles and other relevant International Standards. Second, the "recoverable amount" of the asset is determined as of that date, being the *higher* of net selling price and the asset's value in use (to the existing enterprise). If the recoverable amount is lower than the carrying value as recorded, then an impairment loss must be recognized immediately, that is, the carrying value is lowered to the recoverable amount. Otherwise, no impairment loss is required. It is important to emphasize that recoverable amount is a very different concept from fair value and, for noncurrent assets, will often be significantly higher than fair value. IAS 36 does not require assets within its scope to be recorded at the lower of cost and market or fair value.

The question of which assets IAS 36 does apply to is rather complicated, and the "Scope" section below should be read carefully. Unfortunately, although the principle of IAS 36 is simply stated, the IASC, perhaps influenced by American tradition, found it necessary to specify considerable operational detail in relation to its application. We consider these details below.

BACKGROUND

The essential objective of IAS 36 is to ensure that assets are not carried at a figure greater than their recoverable amount. The standard itself says nothing about possible or normal methods of arriving at carrying value. The standard applies whatever the underlying basis of valuation of the asset is. It explicitly states (par. 4) that it applies to assets carried at revalued amount (e.g., under IAS 16, see Chapter 27), as well as to assets recorded on a cost basis. It will also apply to relevant assets where the carrying value is arrived at in accordance with IAS 15, "Information Reflecting the Effects of Changing Prices" (see Chapter 8) or with IAS 29, "Financial Reporting in Hyperinflationary Economics" (see Chapter 8).

The general principles of IAS 36, although the standard itself was only formally operative for accounting periods beginning on or after July 1, 1999, were already well established in IAS 16, "Property, Plant, and Equipment," in its 1993 version and can be traced back at least as far as IAS 15, issued in 1981. IAS 36 is essentially a set of "how-to" instructions.

IAS GAAP require first of all an investigation for indications of impairment. If such exist, then the assets should be tested for impairment and, if necessary, written down to their recoverable amount— the higher of net selling price or value in use, calculated on the basis of discounted future pretax cash flows related to the asset or the income-generating unit. Impairment losses are recognized in the income statement unless they relate to revalued assets. Under IAS such losses are accounted for in accordance with the standard relating to that asset.

U.S. GAAP requires a numerical calculation. An entity assesses whether impairment has occurred on the basis of the future cash flows (undiscounted and excluding interest) expected to result from use and eventual disposal of the asset. An impairment loss exists if the sum of these cash flows is less than the carrying amount of the asset.

The impairment loss recognized in the income statement is based on the asset's fair value, being either market value or the sum of discounted future cash flows. IAS GAAP requires the reversal of impairment losses when the change is due to changes in estimates of the asset's recoverable amount. U.S. GAAP does not allow reversals of impairment losses.

SCOPE

The standard begins by saying that it applied to all assets except…, and then gives a significant number of exceptions (par. 1). These are generally items that are covered in detail by other International Accounting Standards. Thus, IAS 36 does not apply to:

1. Inventories (see IAS 2, "Inventories," discussed in Chapter 23);
2. Assets arising from construction contracts (see IAS 11, "Construction Contracts," discussed in Chapter 10);
3. Deferred tax assets (see IAS 12, "Income Taxes," discussed in Chapter 20);
4. Assets arising from employee benefits (see IAS 19, "Employee Benefits," discussed in Chapter 13);
5. Financial assets that are included in the scope of IAS 32, "Financial Instruments: Disclosure and Presentation" (see Chapter 16).

In relation to the last point, it must be noted that financial assets excluded from IAS 32 are automatically excluded from the exclusion! Thus, investments in:

1. Subsidiaries, as defined in IAS 27, "Consolidated Financial Statements and Accounting for Investments in Subsidiaries,"
2. Associates, as defined in IAS 28, "Accounting for Investments in Associates," and
3. Joint ventures, as defined in IAS 31, "Financial Reporting of Interests in Joint Ventures"

are financial assets but are excluded from the scope of IAS 32. Therefore, IAS 36 applies to such investments.

> **OBSERVATION:** The standard very deliberately describes itself as dealing with impairment of assets, not with impairment of non-current assets. However, it then excludes inventories and construction contracts (IAS 2 and IAS 11) and accounts receivable and cash (both covered by IAS 32). In many if not most businesses, this will mean that all current assets are excluded from consideration under IAS 36. However, the IAS definition of current assets (discussed in Chapter 3) is more generally expressed, and IAS 36 could be applicable to certain current assets in special cases.

TERMINOLOGY

IAS 36 gives a number of definitions of key terms. Many of these definitions are interrelated, one term being used in the definition of another (par. 5). Most of the terms have been included also in other standards, with similar if not identical definitions.

- *Recoverable amount* is the higher of an asset's net selling price and its value in use.
- *Value in use* is the present value of estimated future cash flows expected to arise from the continuing use of an asset and from its disposal at the end of its useful life.
- *Net selling price* is the amount obtainable from the sale of an asset in an arm's-length transaction between knowledgeable, willing parties, less the costs of disposal.
- *Costs of disposal* are incremental costs directly attributable to the disposal of an asset, excluding finance costs and income tax expense.
- An *impairment loss* is the amount by which the carrying amount of an asset exceeds its recoverable amount.
- *Carrying amount* is the amount at which an asset is recognized in the balance sheet after deducting any accumulated depreciation (amortization) and accumulated impairment losses thereon.
- *Depreciation (amortization)* is the systematic allocation of the depreciable amount of an asset over its useful life.
- *Depreciable amount* is the cost of an asset, or other amount substituted for cost in the financial statements, less its residual value.

- *Useful life* is either:
  - (a) the period of time over which an asset is expected to be used by the enterprise, or
  - (b) the number of production or similar units expected to be obtained from the asset by the enterprise.

These terms should be easy to understand, but they can be difficult to calculate, and much of the standard is, almost, a manual of calculation instructions for the necessary figures. Two further definitions are given, as follows.

- A *cash-generating unit* is the smallest identifiable group of assets that generates cash inflows from continuing use that are largely independent of the cash inflows from other assets or groups of assets.
- *Corporate assets* are assets other than goodwill that contribute to the future cash flows of both the cash-generating unit under review and other cash-generating units.

When several assets are interrelated in their usage in a way that makes it impossible to meaningfully attribute cash inflows to each individual asset, they are to be considered together as a single cash-generating unit as defined above. In effect, therefore, a cash-generating unit is "an asset" for the purposes of IAS 36. Corporate assets do not generate their own cash flows, but, as described above, are necessary for the generation of cash flows by other units. Special considerations, discussed below, apply to such assets.

IDENTIFYING AN ASSET THAT MAY BE IMPAIRED

It is important to be clear that IAS 36 does not require that the recoverable amount of all assets must be determined annually in order to test for impairment. Rather, it postulates a two-stage process. The first stage is to assess, at each balance sheet date, whether there is any indication that an asset may be impaired. If any such indication exists, the enterprise should estimate the recoverable amount of the asset.

In assessing whether there is any indication that an asset may be impaired, an enterprise should consider, *as a minimum*, the following indications (par. 9):

External sources of information:

1. During the period, an asset's market value has declined significantly more than would be expected as a result of the passage of time or normal use.

2. Significant changes with an adverse effect on the enterprise have taken place during the period, or will take place in the near future, in the technological, market, economic, or legal environment in which the enterprise operates or in the market to which an asset is dedicated.

3. Market interest rates or other market rates of return on investments have increased during the period, and those increases are likely to affect the discount rate used in calculating an asset's value in use and decrease the asset's recoverable amount materially.

4. The carrying amount of the net assets of the reporting enterprise is more than its market capitalization.

Internal sources of information:

1. Evidence is available of obsolescence or physical damage of an asset.

2. Significant changes with an adverse effect on the enterprise have taken place during the period, or are expected to take place in the near future, in the extent to which, or manner in which, an asset is used or is expected to be used. These changes include plans to discontinue or restructure the operation to which an asset belongs or to dispose of an asset before the previously expected date.

3. Evidence is available from internal reporting that indicates that the economic performance of an asset is, or will be, worse than expected.

Only if such an indication of likely impairment exists do we need to move on to the second stage and actually measure the recoverable amount.

Several of the above considerations require some comment. Items 1 and 2 (under "External sources of information") are fairly obviously indicators of a possible fall in recoverable amount, relating directly to net selling price and value in use, respectively. In neither case, however, does a low or lower recoverable amount *necessarily* follow, as recoverable amount is the *higher* of net selling price and value in use. The relevance of item 3 is that value in use, as defined above, is the *present value* of future cash flows. Discounting is thus central to the calculation or recoverable amount, and an increase in discount rate may significantly reduce the value in use of an asset, as defined, if the new discount rate is regarded as relevant in the long term. Item 4, again, is a fairly obvious indicator that something is widely perceived as being wrong somewhere, though not, of course, that every, or any one particular, asset is impaired.

Note that other International Accounting Standards may require an impairment test to be carried out in other circumstances. For example, if goodwill or another intangible asset is to be amortized over a period greater than 20 years, then an *annual* impairment test is automatically required under IAS 38, "Intangible Assets" (see Chapter 21).

MEASUREMENT OF RECOVERABLE AMOUNT

IAS 36 devotes no less than 42 paragraphs to the measurement of recoverable amount, not including another 29 paragraphs on cash-generating units, and sets out what it described as "detailed computations." Nevertheless, a number of simplifications may be justified. If either net selling price or value in use exceeds the asset's carrying amount, then the other figure need not be determined at all. If net selling price is unobtainable even by reliable estimate, because of the absence of an active market, then the recoverable amount can be taken as equal to value in use. Conversely, the recoverable amount may be taken or given by the net selling price if the nature of the asset or the nature of its usage by the enterprise is such that value in use is unlikely to differ materially from net selling price, which will usually be the case with active and competitive factor markers (i.e., in developed economies).

Net Selling Price

Net selling price will often be straightforward to determine, being fair value less any incremental costs that would be directly attributable to the disposal of the asset. Fair value may need to be estimated by reference to comparable transactions. Costs of disposal, other than those that have already been recognized as liabilities, are deducted in determining net selling price. Examples of such costs are legal costs, stamp duty and similar transaction taxes, costs of removing the asset, and direct incremental costs to bring an asset into condition for its sale. However, termination benefits (as defined in IAS 19, "Employee Benefits," see Chapter 13) and costs associated with reducing or reorganizing a business after the disposal of an asset are not direct incremental costs to dispose of the asset (see IAS 37, "Provisions, Contingent Liabilities, and Contingent Assets," discussed in Chapter 28).

Value in Use

Estimating the value in use in a realistic way is often likely to be rather more difficult. It involves the following steps (par. 26):

1. Estimating the future cash inflows and outflows to be derived from continuing use of the asset and from its ultimate disposal; and

2. Applying the appropriate discount rate to these future cash flows.

In measuring value in use:

1. Cash flow projections should be based on reasonable and supportable assumptions that represent management's best estimate of the set of economic conditions that will exist over the remaining useful life of the asset. Greater weight should be given to external evidence.

2. Cash flow projections should be based on the most recent financial budgets/forecasts that have been approved by management. Projections based on these budgets/forecasts should cover a maximum period of five years, unless a longer period can be justified.

3. Cash flow projections beyond the period covered by the most recent budgets/forecasts should be estimated by extrapolating the projections on the basis of the budget/forecasts by using a steady or declining growth rate for subsequent years, unless an increasing rate can be justified.

This is all common sense stuff, although inevitably somewhat subjective.

Estimates of future cash flows should include:

1. Projections of cash inflows from the continuing use of the asset, net of projections of cash outflows that are necessarily incurred to generate the cash inflows (including cash outflows to prepare the asset for use) and that can be directly attributed, or allocated on a reasonable and consistent basis, to the asset; and

2. Net cash flows, if any, to be received (or paid) for the disposal of the asset at the end of its useful life.

☞ **PRACTICE POINTER:** Two practical points need to be observed in relation to the above. First, it is essential that estimates of future cash flows, and the discount rate used, be consistent regarding the treatment of inflation. It is consistent to estimate future cash flows in real terms (i.e., including specific price increases or decreases but excluding the effect of price increases due to general inflation) and to use a real discount rate (again, excluding the effects of general inflation). It is also consistent to estimate future cash flows in nominal terms (i.e., in number of inflated currency units) and then use a nominal discount rate, (i.e., a discount rate that includes inflation effects). No other pairing would be acceptable.

The second point is that double counting must be avoided. For example, if a physical asset creates cash inflows via receivables, we cannot count the cash inflow from the asset *and* the cash inflow from the receivable. Cash outflows via purchases and via payables would involve a similar double-counting.

Future cash flows should be estimated for the asset in its current condition. It follows that estimates of future cash flows should not include estimated future cash inflows or outflows that are expected to arise from:

1. A future restructuring to which an enterprise is not yet committed, or

2. Future (uncommitted) capital expenditure that will improve or enhance the asset in excess of its originally assessed standard of performance.

The issue of when an enterprise is "committed to a future restructuring" is discussed in IAS 37, "Provisions, Contingent Liabilities, and Contingent Assets" (see Chapter 28). If it is so committed, then obviously the related cash inflows and outflows *are* to be included.

The estimate of net cash flows to be received (or paid) for the disposal of an asset at the end of its useful life is determined in a similar way to an asset's net selling price, except that, in estimating those net cash flows:

1. An enterprise uses prices prevailing at the date of the estimate for similar assets that have reached the end of their useful life and that have operated under conditions similar to those in which the asset will be used.

2. Those prices are adjusted for the effect of both future price increases due to general inflation and specific future price increases (decreases). However, if estimates of future cash flows from the asset's continuing use and the discount rate exclude the effect of general inflation, this effect is also excluded from the estimate of net cash flows on disposal.

The standard briefly mentions the treatment of foreign currency cash flows (par. 47). This is that they are estimated in the foreign currency, discounted at a rate appropriate to that currency, and then the resulting figure is translated into the reporting currency at the spot rate ruling at the balance sheet date (i.e., the closing rate, see IAS 21, "The Effects of Changes in Foreign Exchange Rates," discussed in Chapter 17).

Discount Rate

The key points can be briefly stated. The discount rate (or rates) should be a pretax rate (or rates) that reflect(s) current market assessments of the time value of money and risks specific to the asset (par. 48). The discount rate(s) should not reflect risks for which future cash flow estimates have been adjusted, as this would involve double-counting. The standard rightly makes no attempt to argue that this process is other than subjective. It does try to suggest a suitable thought process (pars. 51–52).

As a starting point, the enterprise may take into account the following rates:

1. The enterprise's weighted average cost of capital determined using techniques such as the Capital Asset Pricing Model;
2. The enterprise's incremental borrowing rate;
3. Other market borrowing rates.

These rates are adjusted:

1. To reflect the way that the market would assess the specific risks associated with the projected cash flows, and
2. To exclude risks that are not relevant to the projected cash flows.

Consideration is given to such risks as country risk, currency risk, price risk, and cash flow risk.

This makes it clear, for example, that the appropriate discount may be different for different types of asset or different circumstances within the same enterprise. What is crucial, above all else except basic rationality and common sense, is that the method used should be applied consistently.

RECOGNITION AND MEASUREMENT OF IMPAIRMENT LOSSES

After all the subjectivity, complexity, and detail of earlier sections of IAS 36, it is easy to lose sight of the importance of those paragraphs dealing with recognition and measurement of impairment losses. This is the point and purpose of the entire standard. The standard requires that if, and only if, the recoverable amount of an asset is less than its carrying amount, the carrying amount of the asset should be reduced to its recoverable amount. That reduction is an impairment loss (par. 58).

An impairment loss should be recognized immediately as an expense in the income statement, unless the asset is carried at revalued amount under another International Accounting Standard (for example, under the allowed alternative treatment in IAS 16, "Property, Plant, and Equipment," see Chapter 27). Any impairment loss of a revalued asset should be treated as a revaluation decrease under the other International Accounting Standard.

In the general case, if the estimated impairment loss is greater than the carrying value of the relevant asset, the asset is simply reduced to nil, with a corresponding expense. Only if so required by another International Accounting Standard should a liability be recognized.

Common sense indicates, but the standard feels it necessary to state, that after the impairment loss has been recognized, the depreciation charge for the asset should be adjusted to allocate the revised carrying amount, net of any expected residual value, on a systematic basis over its remaining useful life.

This is all very well when "an asset" means "an asset." But when "an asset" means "a cash-generating unit," as discussed earlier, the treatment is not so easy in practice—as the standard's need for 29 paragraphs on the topic would suggest. If it is not possible to estimate the recoverable amount of an individual asset, an enterprise should determine the recoverable amount of the cash-generating unit to which the asset belongs (the asset's cash-generating unit) (par. 65). Identification of an asset's cash-generating unit involves judgment. If the recoverable amount cannot be determined for an individual asset, an enterprise identifies the lowest aggregation of assets that generate largely independent cash inflows from continuing use.

In other words, an asset's cash-generating unit is the smallest group of assets that includes the asset and that generates cash inflows from continuing use that are largely independent of the cash inflows from other assets or groups of assets.

Perhaps inevitably, the standard resorts to a series of examples in order to try and indicate more precisely how the analysis of any particular situation should proceed. Common sense and economic substance are perhaps the key watchwords. Thus, if an active market exists for the output produced by an asset or a group of assets, this asset or group of assets should be identified as a cash-generating unit, even if some or all of the output is used internally. If this is the case, management's best estimate of future market prices for the output should be used (par. 69):

1. In determining the value in use of this cash-generating unit, when estimating the future cash inflows that relate to the internal use of the output; and

2. In determining the value in use of other cash-generating units of the reporting enterprise, when estimating the future cash outflows that relate to the internal use of the output.

As an indicative illustration, we quote below the example given by IAS 36 in relation to this specification.

Illustration

A significant raw material used for plant Y's final production is an intermediate product bought from plant X of the same enterprise. X's products are sold to Y at a transfer price that passes all margins to X. Eighty percent of Y's final production is sold to customers outside of the reporting enterprise, 60% of X's final production is sold to Y, and the remaining 40% is sold to customers outside of the reporting enterprise.

For each of the following cases, what are the cash-generating units for X and Y?

Case 1: X could sell the products it sells to Y in an active market. Internal transfer prices are higher than market prices.

Case 2: There is no active market for the products X sells to Y.

Case 1

X could sell its products on an active market and, so, generate cash inflows from continuing use that would be largely independent of the cash inflows from Y. Therefore, it is likely that X is a separate cash-generating unit, although part of its production is used by Y.

It is likely that Y is also a separate cash-generating unit. Y sells 80% of its products to customers outside of the reporting enterprise. Therefore, its cash inflows from continuing use can be considered to be largely independent.

Internal transfer prices do not reflect market prices for X's output. Therefore, in determining value in use of both X and Y, the enterprise adjusts financial budgets/forecasts to reflect management's best estimate of future market prices for those of X's products that are used internally (see par. 69 of IAS 36).

Case 2

It is likely that the recoverable amount of each plant cannot be assessed independently from the recoverable amount of the other plant because:

1. The majority of X's production is used internally and could not be sold in an active market. So, cash inflows of X depend on demand for Y's products. Therefore, X cannot be considered to generate cash inflows that are largely independent from those of Y.
2. The two plants are managed together.

As a consequence, it is likely that X and Y together is the smallest group of assets that generates cash inflows from continuing use that are largely independent.

Readers who are actually engaged in the process of defining cash-generating units in real enterprises are advised to read all the illustrations given in IAS 36 carefully.

> **OBSERVATION:** In the context of Case 1 of this illustration, one might wonder why Y pays *more* than the market price. Economics might suggest that paying *less* than the market price is more likely, though other considerations such as multinational tax optimization could point either way. The issue is unimportant here as, either way, if internal transfer prices do not reflect market prices for X's output, then adjustment to estimated future *market* prices is required.

Once the cash-generating unit has been defined, the next step is to determine, and compare, the recoverable amount and carrying amount of that unit. It should go without saying, but the standard reminds us that the carrying amount of a cash-generating unit should be determined consistently with the way the recoverable amount of the cash-generating unit is determined.

This means, for example, that the carrying amount of a cash-generating unit includes the carrying amount of only those assets that can be attributed directly, or allocated on a reasonable and consistent basis, to the cash-generating unit and that will generate the future cash inflows estimated in determining the cash-generating unit's value in use and does not include the carrying amount of any recognized liability, unless the recoverable amount of the cash-generating unit cannot be determined without consideration of this liability. However, the standard notes that in practice the recoverable amount of a cash-generating unit may be considered either including or excluding assets or liabilities that are not part of the cash-generating unit—for example a net selling price of a business segment might be determined on the assumption that either the vendor or the purchaser accepts certain obligations. Consistency requires that if the obligation is included in the evaluation of the recoverable amount, it is the *net* carrying value with which this recoverable amount must be compared in determining whether an impairment loss exists.

There are two problems that need special consideration, namely goodwill and corporate assets (as already defined). In essence, these two problems are related. Goodwill, by definition, does not generate cash flows independently from other assets or groups of assets and, therefore, the recoverable amount of goodwill as an individual asset cannot be determined. As a consequence, if there is an indication that goodwill may be impaired, the recoverable amount is determined for the cash-generating unit to which the goodwill belongs. This amount is then compared to the carrying amount of this cash-generating unit, and any impairment loss is recognized, attributed first to the goodwill, as discussed below.

Similarly, corporate assets, also by definition, do not generate independent cash flows, and, again, the recoverable amount is determined by reference to the cash-generating unit to which the corporate asset belongs. In both cases, IAS 36 potentially requires a two-stage process. We give the wording of the requirement for goodwill, but that for corporate assets, although expressed separately and slightly differently in IAS 36, is in effect all the same. Notice that only goodwill recognized in the financial statements as an asset needs to be considered. We are not concerned with unrecorded assets (however significant they may actually be). If such goodwill relates to a cash-generating unit, an enterprise should (par. 80):

1. Perform a "bottom-up" test, that is, the enterprise should:

   (a) identify whether the carrying amount of goodwill can be allocated on a reasonable and consistent basis to the cash-generating unit under review; and

   (b) then, compare the recoverable amount of the cash-generating unit under review to its carrying amount (including the carrying amount of allocated goodwill, if any) and recognize any impairment loss.

   The enterprise should perform the second step of the "bottom-up" test even if none of the carrying amount of goodwill can be allocated on a reasonable and consistent basis to the cash-generating unit under review.

2. If, in performing the "bottom-up" test, the enterprise could not allocate the carrying amount of goodwill on a reasonable and consistent basis to the cash-generating unit under review, the enterprise should also perform a "top-down" test, that is, the enterprise should:

   (a) identify the smallest cash-generating unit that includes the cash-generating unit under review and to which the carrying amount of goodwill can be allocated on a reasonable and consistent basis (the "larger" cash-generating unit); and

   (b) then, compare the recoverable amount of the larger cash-generating unit to its carrying amount (including the carrying amount of allocated goodwill) and recognize any impairment loss.

This sounds complicated at first reading but is actually sensible enough. Appendix A of IAS 36, in examples 7 and 8, gives comprehensive illustration of the application of these requirements in practice for goodwill and corporate assets, respectively.

Once the impairment loss for a cash-generating unit has been determined, it has to be deducted from the carrying amounts of specific assets that are part of that unit, in some systematic manner. IAS 36 specifies its requirements with precision (pars. 88–89).

An impairment loss should be recognized for a cash-generating unit if, and only if, its recoverable amount is less that its carrying amount. The impairment loss should be allocated to reduce the carrying amount of the assets of the unit in the following order:

1. First, to goodwill allocated to the cash-generating unit (if any);

2. Then, to the other assets of the unit on a pro rata basis, based on the carrying amount of each asset in the unit.

In allocating an impairment loss, the carrying amount of an asset should not be reduced below the *highest* of:

1. Its net selling price (if determinable),

2. Its value in use (if determinable), or

3. Zero.

The amount of the impairment loss that would otherwise have been allocated to the asset should be allocated to the other assets of the unit on a pro rata basis. A liability should be recognized for any remaining amount of an impairment loss for a cash-generating unit, if, and only if, that is required by other International Accounting Standards.

The effect of this is, first, to eliminate goodwill, but then to ensure that the carrying amount of any individual asset is not reduced so far as to produce a figure not economically relevant to that asset.

REVERSAL OF AN IMPAIRMENT LOSS

The whole point, in a sense, of impairment losses is that they represent unusual or "extra" reductions in asset numbers (carrying values) as used in financial statements. If regular depreciation is a downward slope, then an impairment loss is a step downward. The basic cause of this downward step is something unusual and/or extraneous to the asset and its regular accounting treatment. It follows that this cause, this unusual or extraneous factor, may be removed over time. In such a situation, as explained and defined in IAS 36, the original impairment loss *must* be reversed.

We again, as with impairment losses, have a two-stage process. An enterprise first checks to see whether there is any *indication* that an impairment loss recognized in earlier years may have decreased significantly. IAS 36 spells out a series of likely indicators (par. 96) that mirror those discussed earlier under "Identifying an Asset That May Be Impaired."

The formal requirement for reversing impairment losses (par. 99) is that an impairment loss recognized for an asset in prior years should be reversed if, and only if, there has been a change in the estimates used to determine the asset's recoverable amount since the last impairment loss was recognized. If this is the case, the carrying amount of the asset should be increased to its recoverable amount. That increase is a reversal of an impairment loss. It is important to note that an asset's value in use may become greater than the asset's carrying amount simply because the present value of future cash inflows increases as they become closer. However, the service potential of the asset has not increased. Therefore, such an impairment loss is not reversed, even if the recoverable amount of the asset becomes higher than its carrying amount.

The reversal of an impairment loss should in no circumstances increase the carrying value of an asset above what it would have been at this balance sheet date if no impairment loss had been recognized in prior years. This means, in particular, that the carrying value of assets subject to depreciation cannot be increased above the figure that the pre-impairment depreciation policy applied to the pre-impairment recoverable amount would have given at this balance sheet date, that is, the amount of the reversal will be less than the amount of the original impairment. The new carrying value forms the basis for a systematic depreciation policy to allocate the carrying value, less estimated residual value if any, over the remaining useful life.

A reversal of an impairment loss for an asset should be recognized as income immediately in the income statement, unless the asset is carried at revalued amount under another International Accounting Standard (for example, under the allowed alternative treatment in IAS 16, "Property, Plant, and Equipment"; see Chapter 27). Any reversal of an impairment loss on a revalued asset should be treated as a revaluation increase under that other International Accounting Standard.

The required process for allocating the reversal of impairment losses by cash-generating units is the reverse of the sequence required for allocating the original impairment loss, as one might expect.

A reversal of an impairment loss for a cash-regenerating unit should be allocated to increase the carrying amount of the assets of the unit in the following order (pars. 107–108):

1. First, assets other than goodwill on a pro-rata basis based on the carrying amount of each asset in the unit;

2. Then, to goodwill allocated to the cash-generating unit (if any).

In allocating a reversal of an impairment loss for a cash-generating unit, the carrying amount of an asset should not be increased above the *lower* of:

1. Its recoverable amount (if determinable);

2. The carrying amount that would have been determined (net of amortization or depreciation) had no impairment loss been recognized for the asset in prior years.

The amount of the reversal of the impairment loss that would otherwise have been allocated to the asset should be allocated to the other assets of the unit on a pro rata basis.

IAS 36, however, is at pains to discourage the reversal of impairment losses with respect to goodwill. Such a reversal is not permitted unless (par. 109):

1. The impairment loss was caused by a specific external event of an exceptional nature that is not expected to recur, and

2. Subsequent external events have occurred that reverse the effect of that event.

It should be noted that the recognition of self-generated goodwill is not permitted under IAS 38, "Intangible Assets" (see Chapter 21), and the above restriction is presumably intended to ensure consistency with this.

DISCLOSURE

The disclosure requirements of IAS 36, like much else in the standard, are extensive. They are also quite straightforward, and we simply repeat them here.

For each class of assets, the financial statements should disclose:

1. The amount of impairment losses recognized in the income statement during the period and the line item(s) of the income statement in which those impairment losses are included;

2. The amount of reversals of impairment losses recognized in the income statement during the period and the line item(s) of the income statements in which those impairment losses are reversed;

3. The amount of impairment losses recognized directly in equity during the period; and

4. The amount of reversals of impairment losses recognized directly in equity during the period.

An enterprise that applies IAS 14, "Reporting Financial Information by Segment," should disclose the following for each reportable segment based on an enterprise's primary format (as defined in IAS 14; see Chapter 31):

1. The amount of impairment losses recognized in the income statement and directly in equity during the period, and

2. The amount of reversals of impairment losses recognized in the income statement and directly in equity during the period.

If an impairment loss for an individual asset or a cash-generating unit is recognized or reversed during the period and is material to the financial statements of the reporting enterprise as a whole, an enterprise should disclose:

1. The events and circumstances that led to the recognition or reversal of the impairment loss;

2. The amount of the impairment loss recognized or reversed;

3. For an individual asset:

   (a) the nature of the asset, and

   (b) the reportable segment to which the asset belongs, based on the enterprise's primary format (as defined in IAS 14, "Reporting Financial Information by Segment," if the enterprise applied IAS 14);

4. For a cash-generating unit:

   (a) a description of the cash-generating unit (such as whether it is a product line, a plant, a business operation, a geographic area, a reportable segment as defined in IAS 14, or other),

   (b) the amount of the impairment loss recognized or reversed by class of assets and by reportable segment based on the enterprise's primary format (as defined in IAS 14, if the enterprise applies IAS 14), and

   (c) if the aggregation of assets for identifying the cash-generating unit has changed since the previous estimate of the cash-generating unit's recoverable amount (if any), the enterprise should describe the current and former way of aggregating assets and the reasons for changing the way the cash-generating unit is identified;

5. Whether the recoverable amount of the asset (cash-generating unit) is its net selling price or its value in use;

6. If recoverable amount is net selling price, the basis used to determine net selling price (such as whether selling price was determined by reference to an active market or in some other way);

7. If recoverable amount is value in use, the discount rate(s) used in the current estimate and previous estimate (if any) of value in use.

If impairment losses recognized (reversed) during the period are material in aggregate to the financial statements of the reporting enterprise as a whole, an enterprise should disclose a brief description of the following:

1. The main classes of assets affected by impairment losses (reversals if impairment losses) for which no information is disclosed as above; and

2. The main events and circumstances that led to the recognition (reversal) of these impairment losses for which no information is disclosed as above.

CHAPTER 20
INCOME TAXES

CONTENTS

OVERVIEW

In the case of many transactions, the accounting treatment is likely to be the same as the tax treatment. This means that the effect on taxable net income is the same as the effect on reported accounting income in the particular period under consideration. The current year's current liability for taxes on income will, in such cases, be what one would expect from the reported accounting profit. Sometimes, however, the recognition and measurement requirements of tax laws differ from the recognition and measurement requirements of relevant accounting GAAP. Differences arise between the tax bases of assets and liabilities and their carrying amounts in the annual financial statements.

These differences are temporary, and they give rise to deferred tax assets and liabilities. Such temporary differences will generally reverse in later years when the related asset is used or the related liability is settled. A deferred tax liability or deferred tax asset represents the increase or decrease in taxes payable or refundable in future years as a result of temporary differences arising in, and carryforwards at the end of, the current year.

The principle applied is that full provision in the current financial statements should be made for the tax effects of the year's transactions and events, whether these effects are current or postponed (deferred) into the future.

IAS GAAP are contained in IAS 12, "Income Taxes." The original IAS 12 was replaced by a revised version, effective for accounting periods beginning on or after January 1, 1998. There were significant differences between the two versions. Although the basic issue is a simple one, the area has created a number of theoretical controversies over the years. Broadly speaking, IAS and U.S. GAAP are now reasonably consistent. The U.S. standard, FAS-109, is similar to IAS 12 in all essential details. For many years, U.K. GAAP have been significantly different as outlined below, but they are now moving back into line. SIC-21, "Income Taxes—Recovery of Reimbursed Non-Deductible Assets, and SIC-25, "Income Taxes—Changes in the Tax Status of an Enterprise or Its Shareholders," are also part of IAS GAAP.

It must be remembered that taxation is generally regarded as very much a national issue. Tax systems and tax rates differ significantly among different countries. It follows that if countries with different tax regimes all implement IAS GAAP, then the differences between tax and accounting effects are themselves likely to be different among the countries.

BACKGROUND

As outlined above, there is an accounting problem arising when, in any particular year, the tax effects of transactions differ from the accounting effects in a manner that is temporary, that is, expected to reverse in later years. There are many possible causes of this, as, depending on national tax regulations, there are many possible differences between tax and accounting effects. As an example of major significance in many countries, consider non-current assets.

It is common to apply the straight-line method of depreciation to non-current assets in financial statements. It is common in national tax systems to regulate the tax allowance for such non-current assets in a precise way, often based on the reducing balance basis, applying a given percentage to the net tax written down value brought forward.

Timing differences are differences between taxable profit and accounting profit that originate in one period and reverse in one or more subsequent periods. Temporary differences are differences between the tax base of an asset or liability and its carrying amount in the balance sheet. The tax base of an asset or liability is the amount attributed to that asset or liability for tax purposes.

All timing differences are temporary differences. Temporary differences also arise in the following circumstances, which do not give rise to timing differences, although the original IAS 12 treated them in the same way as transactions that do give rise to timing differences:

1. Subsidiaries, associates, or joint ventures have not distributed their entire profits to the parent or investor.

2. Assets are revalued, and no equivalent adjustment is made for tax purposes.

3. The cost of a business combination that is an acquisition is allocated to the identifiable assets and liabilities acquired, by reference to their fair values, but no equivalent adjustment is made for tax purposes.

The principle followed by the revised IAS 12 is that it requires an enterprise to account for the tax consequences of transactions and other events in the same way that it accounts for the transactions and other events themselves. Thus, for transactions and other events recognized in the income statement, any related tax effects are also recognized in the income statement. For transactions and other events recognized directly in equity, any related tax effects are also recognized directly in equity. Similarly, the recognition of deferred tax assets and liabilities in a business combination affects the amount of goodwill or negative goodwill arising in that business combination.

There are no major differences between IAS GAAP and U.S. GAAP regarding the treatment of deferred tax assets and liabilities.

Illustration of Fundamental Issues

Consider a non-current asset costing $100. It has an expected life of five years, at the end of which it is estimated it can be sold for $25. Straight-line depreciation is applied in the financial statements. For tax purposes the asset attracts an annual allowance of 25% on the reducing balance basis. Assume that the company concerned has a constant accounting profit (i.e., after charging the depreciation) of $100 per annum. For the calculation of taxable profit, the depreciation effect is removed and replaced by the tax allowances. Assume that taxation is payable at the rate of 33% of the taxable profit. In terms of the taxation payable as a current liability in respect of each of the five years, this would lead to the following results.

	Year				
	1	2	3	4	5
Accounting profit (after depreciation charge)	100	100	100	100	100
+ Depreciation	15	15	15	15	15
Taxation allowance	(25)	(18)	(14)	(11)	(8)
Taxable profit	90	97	101	104	107
Profit before tax	100	100	100	100	100
Taxation 33% of taxable profit	(30)	(32)	(33)	(34)	(36)
Profit after tax	70	68	67	66	64

The implication of a falling profit (i.e., earnings) figure is false, as the reality is that management has produced an identical profit each year using identical resources. Inspection indicates that the reality of the situation is that total tax payable over the five years is $165, and intuitively this should be spread equally each year, in proportion to the (equal) accounting results (i.e., $33 each year). The income effect of the taxation regulations should be equalized.

Consideration of balance sheet effects is also important. The illustration shows that in relation to the earnings of year 1, two tax effects follow, that is,

1. There is a current tax liability of $30.

2. There is an eventual further tax liability of $3 (33 − 30), which becomes current in years 4 or 5. Under the accruals principle (see Chapter 2), it is clear that this $3 arises as a result of the activities and earnings of year 1 and is therefore a liability at the end of year 1 (see the definition of liability in Chapter 2). Because it is not a current liability (the current taxation creditor being $30), it must be a deferred liability, which is settled by the end of year five. The amount to be transferred to the credit of the deferred tax account can be formally calculated as follows.

Amount equals:

Tax rate x (taxation allowances given − depreciation disallowed)

Thus for year 1:

33% x (25 − 15) = 3

and year 2:

33% x (18 − 15) = 1

	Year					
	1	*2*	*3*	*4*	*5*	*Total*
Profit before tax	$100	$100	$100	$100	$100	$500
Taxation: payable for year	30	32	33	34	36	165
Additional charge (credit) to deferred tax account	3	1	0	(1)	(3)	0
Total tax charge	33	33	33	33	33	165
Profit after tax	$ 67	$ 67	$ 67	$ 67	$ 67	$335

In this simple situation, it seems to make no difference whether we make the argument in terms of the income statement (equalizing the tax charge) or in terms of the balance sheet (recording all liabilities—or possibly assets) according to the general definitions of IAS GAAP. In the general case, as discussed later, it can make a difference. The original version of IAS 12 focused essentially on the income statement; the revised version now in force focuses on the balance sheet.

One practical consideration much argued by businesses in some jurisdictions is that, given (a) a stable tax regime, (b) a tendency for rising price levels, and (c) a tendency toward capital intensive expansion, it follows that the deferred tax account is likely to grow and grow, as the reversal of earlier temporary differences is more than counterbalanced by the originating temporary differences on new non-current assets. Formally, three approaches can be distinguished to this consideration:

1. *The flow-through approach,* which accounts only for that tax payable in respect of the period in question, that is, temporary differences are ignored.

2. *Full deferral,* which accounts for the full tax effects of differences, that is, tax is shown in the published accounts based on the full accounting profit, and the element not immediately payable is recorded as a liability until reversal.

3. *Partial deferral,* which accounts only for those differences where reversal is likely to occur in aggregate terms (because, for example, replacement of assets and expansion is expected to exceed depreciation).

Approach 1, which ignores deferred tax considerations altogether, is the old system before the 1970s. Approach 2 is that required by IAS 12 and in the United States. Approach 3, for many years, was required in the United Kingdom, but full deferral will be required there from 2002.

Another issue of principle arises because it is quite likely that, over the years during which a tax liability is deferred, tax rates are likely to change. Two approaches can be distinguished, known as the deferral method and the liability method. Under the *deferral method* of provision for deferred tax, the tax effects of temporary differences are calculated by using the tax rates current when the differences arise. No adjustments are made subsequently if tax rates change. Reversals are accounted for by using the tax rates in force when the temporary differences originated, although in practice the effects of reversal and new temporary differences are sometimes accounted for as one item.

Those who support this method recognize that, when tax rates change, this method will not give an indication of the amount of tax payable or recoverable. Any deferred tax balance will, therefore, be a deferred charge or credit rather than a liability or asset. When tax rates change, there is no need to revise the deferred tax already provided. Thus the tax charge or credit for the period relates solely to that period and is not distorted by any adjustments relating to prior periods.

Alternatively, it could be argued that the balances on the deferred tax account should be regarded as liabilities payable in the future or as assets receivable in the future. The best available estimate of the tax rate ruling in the future when the amount is to be paid or received will generally be the current tax rate. This means that the liability balance will need to be continually revised whenever the current tax rate changes. This is known as the *liability method*. Thus, the tax charge or credit for the period may include adjustments of accounting estimates relating to prior periods. The deferred tax provision represents the best estimate of the amount that would be payable or receivable if the relevant differences reversed.

The original IAS 12 had, in broad terms, an income statement focus, although with considerable optionality. It permitted either full or partial deferral using either the deferral method or a version of the liability method that focused on temporary differences between various income statement years. The revised IAS 12 requires full deferral, using a different variant of the liability method, which it terms the balance sheet liability method, described in detail below, which takes account of all temporary differences. The distinction is again one of income statement versus balance sheet.

SCOPE

IAS 12 applies to accounting for taxes on income, that is, taxes based on taxable profit. This includes all domestic and foreign income taxes, including taxes, such as withholding taxes, which are payable by a subsidiary, associate, or joint venture on distributions to the reporting enterprise. The 1998 version of IAS 12 did not, however, deal with the tax consequences of dividends and other distributions made by the reporting entity itself, which in some jurisdictions can have a significant effect on the amount of tax payable. Additional paragraphs dealing with this matter have been introduced, as discussed below, effective January 1, 2001.

DEFINITIONS

The definitions given in IAS 12 (par. 5) are reproduced below.

- *Accounting profit* is net profit or loss for a period before deducting tax expense.
- *Taxable profit* (*tax loss*) is the profit (loss) for a period, determined in accordance with the rules established by the taxation authorities, upon which income taxes are payable (recoverable).
- *Tax expense* (*tax income*) is the aggregate amount included in the determination of net profit or loss for the period in respect of current tax and deferred tax.
- *Current tax* is the amount of income taxes payable (recoverable) in respect of the taxable profit (tax loss) for a period.
- *Deferred tax liabilities* are the amounts of income taxes payable in future periods in respect of taxable temporary differences.

- *Deferred tax assets* are the amounts of income taxes recoverable in future periods in respect of:

  (a) deductible temporary differences,

  (b) the carryforward of unused tax losses, and

  (c) the carryforward of unused tax credits.

- *Temporary differences* are differences between the carrying amount of an asset or liability in the balance sheet and its tax base. Temporary differences may be either:

  (a) *taxable temporary differences,* which are temporary differences that will result in taxable amounts in determining taxable profit (tax loss) of future periods when the carrying amount of the asset or liability is recovered or settled; or

  (b) *deductible temporary differences,* which are temporary differences that will result in amounts that are deductible in determining taxable profit (tax loss) of future periods when the carrying amount of the asset or liability is recovered or settled.

- The *tax base* of an asset or liability is the amount attributed to that asset or liability for tax purposes.

Most of these definitions are straightforward. The distinction between taxable temporary differences and deductible temporary differences is made to sound complicated, but it is not. Taxable temporary differences lead in principle to a deferred tax liability, whereas deductible temporary differences lead to a deferred tax asset.

The standard discusses and illustrates the concept of the tax base at some length (pars. 7–11). The tax base of an asset is the amount that will be deductible for tax purposes against any taxable economic benefits (revenues or gains) that will flow to an enterprise when it recovers the carrying amount of the asset. If those economic benefits will not be taxable, the tax base of the asset is equal to its carrying amount.

Thus, for example, an enterprise shows interest receivable in its balance sheet with a carrying amount of 200 and dividends receivable with a carrying amount of 300. The revenue from the interest to be received will be taxed in full on a cash basis. The dividends receivable are from a subsidiary and are not taxable. The interest receivable has a tax base of nil, and the dividends receivable have a tax base of 300. The effect, as the above definitions make clear, is to create a taxable temporary difference of 200 in respect of the interest receivable and zero temporary difference (300 – 300) in respect of the dividends receivable.

The tax base of a liability is its carrying amount, less any amount that will be deductible for tax purposes in respect of that liability in future periods. In the case of revenue that is received in advance, the tax base of the resulting liability is its carrying amount, less any amount of the revenue that will not be taxable in future periods. Thus, if current liabilities include accrued expenses with a carrying amount of 1000, and if the related expenses are deductible for tax purposes on a cash basis (i.e., in future years), then the tax base of the accrued expenses is nil, but if the related expense has already been deducted for tax purposes, then the tax base of the accrued expenses is 1000. If current liabilities include interest revenue received in advance with a carrying amount of 400, and the related interest revenue has already been taxed on a cash basis, the tax base is the carrying amount of 400, reduced by the revenue not taxable in future periods, which is all of the 400. In this case the tax base of the current liability of interest received in advance is therefore nil.

Some items may have a tax base but will not be recognized as assets or liabilities in the balance sheet, that is, they have a carrying amount of nil. In such circumstances, a temporary difference will necessarily result. Business start-up costs and some types of research costs are examples that may occur in some jurisdictions of items that create tax assets but not accounting assets. A deductible temporary difference leading to a deferred tax asset would logically result.

☛ **PRACTICE POINTER:** In the case of consolidated financial statements, it is the consolidated carrying amount that needs to be compared with the corresponding tax base. The tax base is determined by reference to a consolidated tax return in those jurisdictions in which such a return is filed. In other jurisdictions, the tax base is determined by reference to the tax returns of each enterprise in the group.

RECOGNITION OF CURRENT TAX LIABILITIES AND ASSETS

Recognition of current tax liabilities and assets is perfectly straightforward. Unpaid current tax relating to current or earlier periods should be recognized as a liability. If the amount already paid in respect of current and prior periods exceeds the amount due for those periods, the excess should be recognized as an asset. The benefit relating to a tax loss that can be carried back to recover current tax of a previous period should be recognized as an asset.

RECOGNITION OF DEFERRED TAX LIABILITIES

The principle is again simple, in that a deferred tax liability should be recognized for all taxable temporary differences, as defined above. IAS 12 gives two exceptions, however, and then an exception to one of the exceptions. In summary, a deferred tax liability should not be recognized (i.e., there is no liability), if it arises from (par. 15):

1. Goodwill for which amortization is not deductible for tax purposes; or
2. The initial recognition of an asset or liability in a transaction that:
   (a) is not a business combination; and
   (b) at the time of the transaction, affects neither accounting profit nor taxable profit (tax loss).

However, for taxable temporary differences associated with investments in subsidiaries, branches, and associates, and interests in joint ventures, a deferred tax liability should be recognized in certain circumstances. All this is discussed in more detail below.

It is important not to lose sight of the general principle, which is if the carrying amount of an asset (in the financial statements) is greater than the tax base, then a taxable temporary difference arises and a deferred tax liability must be recognized. Thus, in the example given earlier (see "Illustration of Fundamental Issues"), the cost of the asset is $100, and at the end of year 1 the carrying amount is $85 (100 – 15) and the tax base is $75 (100 – 25). IAS 12 requires the recognition (and recording) of the resulting deferred tax liability of $10 multiplied by the tax rate (25% in the example).

The standard discusses a number of differently caused temporary differences at some length. The most common cause of temporary differences in most jurisdictions will be timing differences, that is, differences that arise when income or expense is included in accounting profit in one reporting period but is included in taxable profit in a different period. Common examples are depreciation, as already illustrated, interest revenues, which may be assessed on a cash basis for tax purposes but not for accounting purposes, and development costs, which may be capitalized for accounting purposes but not for tax purposes.

IAS 12 does not explicitly refer to timing differences as a subset of temporary differences. It discusses five circumstances, however, where temporary differences arise that are not timing differences, which we address below.

1. The cost of a business combination that is an acquisition is allocated to the identifiable assets and liabilities acquired by reference to their fair values, but no equivalent adjustment is made for tax purposes. For example, when the carrying amount of an asset is increased to fair value at the date of acquisition but the tax base of the asset remains at the original figure with the previous enterprise, then a taxable temporary difference

arises resulting in the recognition of a deferred tax liability. The amount of this recognized liability would affect the calculation of goodwill on acquisition on a dollar-for-dollar basis.

2. Assets are revalued and no equivalent adjustment is made for tax purposes. In some jurisdictions, when the carrying amount of an asset is changed to fair value or revalued amount, the difference is effective for tax purposes also, in which event the tax base of the asset will be altered correspondingly and no temporary difference will arise. In other jurisdictions, there would be no tax effects and the tax base for the asset is not adjusted. In the latter case, there is a temporary difference between the carrying value (which has altered) and the tax base (which has not), and so a deferred tax liability or asset appears to arise. The standard explicitly states that such a deferred tax effect should be recognized. This temporary difference exists even if (par. 20):

(a) the enterprise does not intend to dispose of the asset. In such cases, the revalued carrying amount of the asset will be recovered through use, and this will generate taxable income that exceeds the depreciation that will be allowable for tax purposes in future periods (i.e., the asset increase does logically create a corresponding deferred tax liability); or

(b) tax on capital gains is deferred if the proceeds of the disposal of the asset are invested in similar assets by virtue of "rollover" relief. In such cases, the tax will ultimately become payable on sale or use of the similar assets (i.e., when the "rolling-over" ceases).

OBSERVATION: The logic of the IAS 12 position on this revaluation issue can be criticized. Given the explicit claims by IASC that a balance sheet approach is being taken, the definition of a liability seems crucial. Since by definition in the relevant jurisdictions a revaluation has no tax effects, it seems extremely difficult to argue that a further tax obligation (or benefit) can arise. The statement by IAS 12 in (a) immediately above that usage "will generate" taxable income is correct, but it is also logically irrelevant, as the future taxable income cannot be the "past event" required by the definition of a liability accepted and used by IASC (see Chapter 2).

IASC has issued SIC-21, "Income Taxes—Recovery of Revalued Non-Depreciable Assets," effective from July 15, 2000, to clarify the implications of the term "recovery" as used in (a) above. The conclusion is that the deferred tax liability or asset that arises from the revaluation of a non-depreciable asset should be measured based on the tax consequences that would follow from recovery of the carrying amount of that asset through sale, regardless of the basis of measuring the carrying amount of that asset. Accordingly, if the tax law specifies a tax rate applicable to the taxable amount derived from the sale of an asset that differs from the tax rate applicable to the taxable amount derived from using an asset, the former rate is applied in measuring the deferred tax liability or asset related to a non-depreciable asset.

3. Goodwill or negative goodwill arises on consolidation. In many jurisdictions, the amortization of goodwill is not regarded as a deductible expense in calculating taxable profit, and the cost of goodwill is not deductible for taxation purposes when a subsidiary disposes of its underlying business. In such jurisdictions, goodwill has a tax base of nil, leading to a possibly large difference between carrying value and tax base, and therefore to a large taxable temporary difference. However, IAS 12 explicitly forbids the recognition of the deferred tax amount arising. The justification given is as follows (par. 21).

   However, this Standard does not permit the recognition of the resulting deferred tax liability because goodwill is a residual and the recognition of the deferred tax liability would increase the carrying amount of goodwill.

   > **OBSERVATION:** At first glance, this rationale again seems suspect. But it is correct to say that recognizing the calculated deferred tax liability would increase the carrying amount of the goodwill, calculated as a residual. This would then lead to an increase in the taxable temporary difference arising, leading to some extra deferred tax liability that, if recorded, would further increase the carrying amount of the goodwill. And so ad infinitum! Perhaps the fundamental point is that goodwill is seen as "a residual" rather than as an asset. Nevertheless, in an environment where fair value accounting is practiced, it is difficult to disagree with the suggestion that goodwill as calculated on acquisition is the fair value of the cost of acquisition, that is, something with economic meaning. The whole issue is more complicated than IAS 12 implies.

4. The tax base of an asset or liability on initial recognition differs from its initial carrying amount. In the case of a business combination, the resulting deferred tax number is recognized as discussed in point 1, above. If the transaction affects either accounting profit or taxable profit, an enterprise recognizes any deferred tax liability or asset and recognizes the resulting deferred tax expense or income in the income statement. If neither of these circumstances exists, that is, neither accounting profit nor tax profit are immediately affected, then the general rule would suggest the recognition of the resulting deferred tax liability or asset, and the adjustment of the carrying amount of

the asset or liability by the same amount. However, as already summarized above, this is neither required nor allowed. Paragraph 22(c) explains this as follows.

Such adjustments would make the financial statements less transparent. Therefore, this Standard does not permit an enterprise to recognize the resulting deferred tax liability or asset, either on initial recognition or subsequently. Furthermore, an enterprise does not recognize subsequent changes in the unrecognized deferred tax liability or asset as the asset is depreciated.

IAS 12 gives an example, with explanation, which we reproduce below.

Example Illustrating Paragraph 22(c)

An enterprise intends to use an asset which cost 1,000 throughout its useful life of five years and then dispose of it for a residual value of nil. The tax rate is 40%. Depreciation of the asset is not deductible for tax purposes. On disposal, any capital gain would not be taxable and any capital loss would not be deductible.

As it recovers the carrying amount of the asset, the enterprise will earn taxable income of 1,000 and pay tax of 400. The enterprise does not recognize the resulting deferred tax liability of 400 because it results from the initial recognition of the asset.

In the following year, the carrying amount of the asset is 800. In earning taxable income of 800, the enterprise will pay tax of 320. The enterprise does not recognize the deferred tax liability of 320 because it results from the initial recognition of the asset.

The tax base of the asset referred to, that is, the amount deductible for tax purposes against taxable economic benefits from the asset's use, is nil. It is the difference between carrying value and tax base, that is, $1,000 - nil = 1,000$, which would lead to the theoretical deferred tax liability of 400. However, this 400 is not recognized because it results "from the initial recognition of the asset," and this in turn arises because the (deferred tax) "adjustments would make the financial statements less transparent."

OBSERVATION: Taking the figures of the IASC example, there are two possible presentations on the initial recognition of the asset. The asset could be recorded at 1,000 and deferred tax not recorded. Second, the asset could be recorded at its "gross" cost of 1,400, together with a deferred tax liability of 400. This latter is the version stated to be "less transparent." Because it provides more information, this seems a peculiar comment. More fundamentally, *is* there a liability? A sum of $1,000 has been spent that has no tax effects. If it has no tax effects, how can it increase the liabilities for taxation? This, surely, is both a clearer and a simpler justification for not recognizing deferred taxation than the statements of IAS 12. More pragmatically, it seems unlikely that, apart from goodwill, expenditures will arise that create assets that are not recognized for tax purposes either as capital expenditure or as allowable expenses.

5. The carrying amount of investments in subsidiaries, branches, and associates or interests in joint ventures becomes different from the tax base of the investment or interest. In many cases the tax base will be cost, but the carrying amount may change, for example because of:

— the existence of undistributed profits of subsidiaries, branches, associates, and joint ventures;

— changes in foreign exchange rates when a parent and its subsidiary are based in different countries; and

— a reduction in the carrying amount of an investment in an associate to its recoverable amount.

The general rule is that deferred tax should be recognized as a liability for all such taxable temporary differences except (par. 39) to the extent that *both* of the following conditions are satisfied:

(a) the parent, investor, or venturer is able to control the timing of the reversal of the temporary difference; and

(b) it is probable that the temporary difference will not reverse in the foreseeable future.

Regarding subsidiaries (and also branches), the parent will, by definition, normally be able to control the dividend policy of the foreign enterprise and therefore to control the timing of the reversal of temporary differences relating to its investment. If the parent has determined that the profits will not be distributed in the foreseeable future, then no deferred tax liability is to be recognized. In the general case, an investor in a foreign associate (see Chapter 17) will not be in a posi-tion to control the dividend policy, so the above argument would not apply (although the issue of whether or not control exists is in the end a pragmatic matter). In the case of, for example, changes in foreign exchange rates, the timing of the reversal of temporary differences is obviously outside the control of the investor, and recognition of deferred tax is required.

RECOGNITION OF DEDUCTIBLE TEMPORARY DIFFERENCES

In principle, a deductible temporary difference, which gives rise to a deferred asset, is the exact mirror image of a taxable temporary difference, so it should arguably be treated as such. The difficulty, however, is that the "asset" is not in general repayable by the taxation authorities. Rather, it is deductible from the taxation charges relating to later years, if there are any. If future taxable profits do not in fact arise, then the "asset" will have no beneficial value, in which case of, course, it is not an asset at all and should not be recognized. Given the inherent uncertainty, at least in the case of unprofitable enterprises, of future taxable profits, a degree of caution and prudence is required.

The general requirement of IAS 12 (pars. 24 and 28) is that a deferred tax asset should be recognized for all deductible temporary differences to the extent that it is probable that taxable profit will be available against which the deductible temporary difference can be utilized. It is probable that taxable profit will be available against which a deductible temporary difference can be utilized when there are sufficient taxable temporary differences relating to the same taxation authority and the same taxable entity which are expected to reverse:

1. In the same period as the expected reversal of the deductible temporary difference, or

2. In periods into which a tax loss arising from the deferred tax asset can be carried back or forward.

The asset can (and should) be recognized on a partial basis if a positive but inadequate amount of future taxable profit is probable.

> ☞ **PRACTICE POINTER:** The meaning of "probable" is both important and uncertain. In IAS 37, "Provisions, Contingent Liabilities, and Contingent Assets" (see Chapter 28), it is stated (pars. 15 and 23) that an event is "probable" if the probability that the event will occur is greater than the probability that it will not. However, IAS 37 also explicitly states that this interpretation "does not necessarily apply in other International Accounting Standards." It should also be noted that the IAS 37 statement is presented in the context of liabilities, not of assets.
>
> It is in our view inevitable that "probable" in the IAS 12 context, and indeed in many contexts, is likely to be interpreted differently in different countries and cultures. For an "expectation" of reversal in the context of IAS 12, we suggest that significantly more than a 50–50 likelihood is required.

There are two circumstances in which, notwithstanding the above, a deferred tax asset should not be recognized (par. 24). These exactly mirror the exceptions to the recognition of deferred tax liabilities given in paragraph 15 and discussed above. A deferred tax asset should not be recognized if it arises from:

1. Negative goodwill that is treated as deferred income in accordance with IAS 22, "Business Combinations"; or

2. The initial recognition of an asset or liability in a transaction that:

   (a) is not a business combination; and

   (b) at the time of the transaction, affects neither accounting profit nor taxable profit (tax loss).

The reasons given for this, and the possible doubts about those reasons, are the same as those discussed above in relation to liabilities.

Further, again, consistently with the considerations in respect of deferred liabilities, an enterprise (par. 44) should recognize a deferred tax asset for all deductible temporary differences arising from investments in subsidiaries, branches, and associates and interests in joint ventures to the extent that, and only to the extent that, it is probable that:

1. The temporary difference will reverse in the foreseeable future, and

2. Taxable profit will be available against which the temporary difference can be utilized.

Deferred tax assets can arise not only through the existence of deductible temporary differences, as discussed at length above, but also through unused tax losses or unused tax credits that, in many jurisdictions, can be carried forward for a limited period or without limit. The criteria for recognizing deferred tax assets arising from the carryforward of unused tax losses and tax credits are the same as the criteria for recognizing deferred tax assets arising from deductible temporary differences, namely that a deferred tax asset should be recognized for the carryforward of unused tax losses and unused tax credits to the extent that it is probable that future taxable profit will be available against which the unused tax losses and unused tax credits can be utilized.

The implications are likely to be different, however, because the existence of unused tax losses suggests an unprofitable enterprise. The onus is therefore on the enterprise to verify and demonstrate that an expectation of future taxable profits is justifiable. When an enterprise has a history of recent losses, the enterprise recognizes a deferred tax asset arising from unused tax losses or tax credits only to the extent that the enterprise has sufficient taxable temporary differences or there is other convincing evidence that sufficient taxable profit will be available against which the unused tax losses or unused tax credits can be utilized by the enterprise. In such circumstances, disclosure of the amount of the deferred tax asset and the nature of the evidence supporting its recognition is required.

IAS 12 suggests "criteria" for assessing the probability of future taxable profits against which unused tax losses or credits can be utilized, though in truth these are little more than signposts. They are (par. 36):

1. Whether the enterprise has sufficient taxable temporary differences relating to the same taxation authority and the same taxable entity, which will result in taxable amounts against which the unused tax losses or unused tax credits can be utilized before they expire;

2. Whether it is probable that the enterprise will have taxable profits before the unused tax losses or unused tax credits expire;

3. Whether the unused tax losses result from identifiable causes that are likely to recur;

4. Whether tax planning opportunities are available to the enterprise that will create taxable profit in the period in which the unused tax losses or unused tax credits can be utilized.

Where unrecognized deferred tax assets exist, the situation should be reviewed at each successive balance sheet date. The enterprise recognizes a previously unrecognized deferred tax asset to the extent that it has now become probable that future taxable profit will allow the deferred tax asset to be recovered.

MEASUREMENT

As we discussed earlier in this chapter, the current version of IAS 12 requires, consistent with its focus on the balance sheet rather than on the income statement, the liability method of measurement to be used. This means that, at any particular balance sheet date, the deferred tax assets or liabilities should in principle represent the actual amounts recoverable or payable at the expected relevant date. Current (balance sheet date) tax rates will usually be used as proxies, though announced tax rates should be used in jurisdictions when they "have the substantive effect of actual enactment." The formal statement of the general principle (pars. 46, 47, and 51) is as follows:

> Current tax liabilities (assets) for the current and prior periods should be measured at the amount expected to be paid to (recovered from) the taxation authorities, using the tax rates (and tax laws) that have been enacted or substantively enacted by the balance sheet date.
>
> Deferred tax assets and liabilities should be measured at the tax rates that are expected to apply to the period when the asset is

realized or the liability is settled, based on tax rates (and tax laws) that have been enacted or substantively enacted by the balance sheet date.

The measurement of deferred tax liabilities and deferred tax assets should reflect the tax consequences that would follow from the manner in which the enterprise expects, at the balance sheet date, to recover or settle the carrying amount of its assets and liabilities.

This last point means, necessarily, that the reported figure will, in such circumstances, be dependent on management intentions or stated intentions. IAS 12 gives a series of examples that make this clear, and we produce the simplest one below:

An asset has a carrying amount of 100 and a tax base of 60. A tax rate of 20% would apply if the asset were sold and a tax rate of 30% would apply to other income.

The enterprise recognizes a deferred tax liability of 8 (40 at 20%) if it expects to sell the asset for its carrying amount without further use and a deferred tax liability of 12 (40 at 30%) if it expects to retain the asset and recover its carrying amount through use.

The question of whether or not long-term liabilities and long-term monetary assets should be discounted is a difficult and complex one, which is going to cause world standard-setters much angst over the next few years. It has implications for a number of IASC standards, and IASC has set up a project team to consider the whole matter. Early results should not be expected.

The major purpose of the latest revision to IAS 19, operative from January 1, 2001, is to deal with the taxation implications of dividend payments, which had been explicitly excluded from the scope of the previous version. In some jurisdictions, income taxes are payable at a higher or lower rate if part or all of the net profit or retained earnings is paid out as a dividend to shareholders of the enterprise. In these circumstances, current and deferred tax assets and liabilities are measured at the tax rate applicable to undistributed profits, and the income tax consequences of dividends are recognized when a liability to pay the dividend is recognized. The income tax consequences of dividends are more directly linked to past transactions or events than to distributions to owners. Therefore, the income tax consequences of dividends are recognized in net profit or loss for the same period as the dividend is recognized, as discussed in the next section.

IAS 12 does not allow discounting of deferred tax assets or liabilities. Its stated reasons are distinctly pragmatic (par. 54), namely, in effect,

1. Reliable calculation is impracticable or highly complex.

2. Therefore, discounting should not be *required*.

3. Comparability between enterprises is necessary.

4. Therefore, discounting should not be *permitted*.

After the deferred tax balances have been revised under the liability method as of the balance sheet date, the carrying amount of deferred tax assets must additionally be reviewed and reduced to the extent that it is no longer probable that sufficient taxable profit will be available to allow the benefit of part of all of that deferred tax asset to be utilized. Any such reduction should be reversed to the extent that it becomes probable that sufficient taxable profit will be available.

RECOGNITION OF CURRENT AND DEFERRED TAX

Although the whole focus of IAS 12 is on the balance sheet numbers, it is obviously necessary also to consider the implications of the "other entry." The principle is that current and deferred tax effects should be accounted for consistently with the underlying transactions or events. This means that the tax effect is included:

- In the income statement in most cases,
- In equity if the item is itself recognized directly in equity,
- In goodwill, for business combinations accounted for as acquisitions.

In the majority of cases, deferred tax will arise because of timing differences between years in relation to expense and revenue items. The tax effect of these occurrences will be a part of the current year tax charge in the income statement. We have already noticed that the carrying amount of deferred tax asset or liability balances may change even though there is no change in the amount of the related temporary differences, for example, from a change in tax rates or tax laws, a reassessment of the recoverability of deferred tax assets, or a change in the expected manner of recovery of an asset. The resulting deferred tax is likewise recognized in the income statement except to the extent that it relates to items previously charged or credited to equity.

Examples of items that IAS GAAP permit or require to be charged or credited directly to equity are as follows:

1. A change in carrying amount arising from the revaluation of property, plant, and equipment (see IAS 16, "Property, Plant, and Equipment," discussed in Chapter 27);

2. An adjustment to the opening balance of retained earnings resulting from either a change in accounting policy that is applied retrospectively or the correction of a fundamental error (see IAS 8, "Net Profit or Loss for the Period, Fundamental Errors, and Changes in Accounting Policies," discussed in Chapter 26);

3. Exchange differences arising on the translation of the financial statements of a foreign entity (see IAS 21, "The Effects of Changes in Foreign Exchange Rates," discussed in Chapter 17); and

4. Amounts arising on initial recognition of the equity component of a compound financial instrument (see IAS 32, "Financial Instruments: Disclosure and Presentation," discussed in Chapter 16).

Where items are charged or credited directly to equity, then current tax and deferred tax should also be so credited or charged, whether it arises in the same or a different accounting period. If it proves impossible to isolate the amount of tax that relates to items put directly to equity, then rational apportionment is permitted (par. 63). When an asset is revalued for tax purposes and that revaluation is related to an accounting revaluation of an earlier period or to one that is expected to be carried out in a future period, the tax effects of both the asset revaluation and the adjustment of the tax base are credited or charged to equity in the periods in which they occur. However, if the revaluation for tax purposes is not related to an accounting revaluation of an earlier period, or to one that is expected to be carried out in a future period, the tax effects of the adjustment of the tax base are recognized in the income statement.

IASC has noted, in SIC-25, "Changes in the Tax Status of an Enterprise or Its Shareholders," that a change in tax status, as for example, for a public listing, a restructuring, or a change in domicile of a controlling shareholder, may cause an immediate change in tax liabilities or assests. The SIC confirms that a change in the tax status of an enterprise or its shareholders does not give rise to increases or decreases in amounts recognized directly in equity. The current and deferred tax consequences of a change in tax status should be included in net profit or loss for the period, unless those consequences relate to transactions and events that result, in the same or different period, in a direct credit or charge to the recognized amount of equity. Those tax consequences that relate to changes in the recognized amount of equity, in the same or a different period (not included in net profit or loss), should be charged or credited directly to equity.

It is perhaps helpful to summarize the position related to deferred tax arising from a business combination, which requires considerable clarity of thought. A business combination that is an acquisition is likely to lead to temporary differences, leading in turn (subject to the recognition criteria discussed above) to identifiable deferred tax liabilities or assets that will affect the calculation of goodwill. As also indicated above, however, an enterprise does not recognize deferred tax liabilities arising from goodwill itself (if amortization of the goodwill is not deductible for tax purposes) or deferred tax assets arising from nontaxable negative goodwill that is treated as deferred income.

PRESENTATION

Tax assets and tax liabilities should be presented separately from other assets and liabilities in the balance sheet. Deferred tax assets and liabilities should be distinguished from current tax assets and liabilities. If the enterprise presents a classified balance sheet, all deferred tax assets and liabilities must be classified as non-current.

Current tax assets and current tax liabilities should be offset and shown as a net figure if, but only if, the enterprise (par. 71):

1. Has a legally enforceable right to set off the recognized amounts; and
2. Intends either to settle on a net basis, or to realize the asset and settle the liability simultaneously.

This requires in effect that offset items all relate to a single taxation authority, and that authority allows the enterprise to make or receive a single net payment. The word "enterprise" in the previous sentence includes a group in the case of consolidated financial statements.

The rules for offsetting deferred tax assets and deferred tax liabilities are broadly similar. An enterprise is required to offset deferred tax balance sheet items if, but only if (par. 74):

1. The enterprise has a legally enforceable right to set off current tax assets against current tax liabilities; and
2. The deferred tax assets and the deferred tax liabilities relate to income taxes levied by the same taxation authority on either:
   (a) the same taxable entity; or
   (b) different taxable entities that intend either to settle current tax liabilities and assets on a net basis or to realize the assets and settle the liabilities simultaneously, in each future period in which significant amounts of deferred tax liabilities or assets are expected to be settled or recovered.

In the income statement, the tax expense (or income) from ordinary activities—which includes the effect of both current and deferred items—must be shown on the face of the statement. Paragraph 78 notes that IAS 21, "Accounting for the Effects of Changes in Foreign Exchange Rates" (see Chapter 17), is silent as to where exchange differences should be presented in the income statement. IAS 12 states that exchange differences on deferred tax items that are recognized in the income statement may be included as part of the deferred tax expense or income or as part of foreign exchange losses or gains, whichever is "considered to be the most useful to financial statement users."

DISCLOSURE

The standard requires that the "major components" of tax expense or income should be disclosed separately (usually by way of note). Paragraph 80 gives a list of what such components "may include." Transparency should be the watchword, and we suggest all major elements should be separately disclosed. In addition, paragraph 81 gives a long and detailed list of additional disclosure requirements, which we reproduce. Disclosure is required of:

1. The aggregate current and deferred tax relating to items that are charged or credited to equity;

2. Tax expense (income) relating to extraordinary items recognized during the period;

3. An explanation of the relationship between tax expense (income) and accounting profit in either or both of the following forms:

   (a) a numerical reconciliation between tax expense (income) and the product of accounting profit multiplied by the applicable tax rate(s), disclosing also the basis on which the applicable tax rate(s) is (are) computed, or

   (b) a numerical reconciliation between the average effective tax rate and the applicable tax rate, disclosing also the basis on which the applicable tax rate is computed;

4. An explanation of changes in the applicable tax rate(s) compared to the previous accounting period;

5. The amount (and expiration date, if any) of deductible temporary differences, unused tax losses, and unused tax credits for which no deferred tax asset is recognized in the balance sheet;

6. The aggregate amount of temporary differences associated with investments in subsidiaries, branches, and associates and interests in joint ventures, for which deferred tax liabilities have not been recognized (see par. 39);

7. In respect of each type of temporary difference and in respect of each type of unused tax losses and unused tax credits:

    (a) the amount of the deferred tax assets and liabilities recognized in the balance sheet for each period presented,

    (b) the amount of the deferred tax income or expense recognized in the income statement, if this is not apparent from the changes in the amounts recognized in the balance sheet;

8. In respect of discontinued operations, the tax expense relating to:

    (a) the gain or loss on discontinuance, and

    (b) the profit or loss from the ordinary activities of the discontinued operation for the period, together with the corresponding amounts for each prior period presented;

9. The amount of income tax consequences of dividends to shareholders of the enterprise that were proposed or declared before the financial statements were authorized for issue, but are not recognized as a liability in the financial statements.

Further, as already indicated earlier, an enterprise should disclose the amount of a deferred tax asset and the nature of the evidence supporting its recognition, when:

1. The utilization of the deferred tax asset is dependent on future taxable profits in excess of the profits arising from the reversal of existing taxable temporary differences.

2. The enterprise has suffered a loss in either the current or preceding period in the tax jurisdiction to which the deferred tax asset relates.

An enterprise should disclose the nature of any potential income tax consequences that would result from the payment of dividends to its shareholders. In addition, the enterprise should disclose the amounts of the potential income tax consequences practicably determinable and whether there are any potential income tax consequences not practicably determinable.

> **OBSERVATION:** Deferred taxation is a complex area in principle, and IAS 12 is a complex standard. The emphasis on the balance sheet and the liability method (which is consistent with the Framework) seems to have forced some strained logic in places in order to produce the treatment that IASC first thought of. It is not obvious that the requirements of IAS 12 are always fully consistent with the Framework criteria for liabilities (see Chapter 2). The discounting ban may be reconsidered in principle. The U.K. ASB has produced a new U.K. standard, which broadly swings into line with IAS and U.S. thinking but explicitly permits discounting. Further discussion can be expected.

CHAPTER 21
INTANGIBLE ASSETS

CONTENTS

OVERVIEW

In IAS GAAP, an intangible asset is defined as "an *identifiable* non-monetary asset without physical substance held for use in the production or supply of goods or services, for rental to others or for administrative purposes." This excludes goodwill, which is by definition nonidentifiable, being the difference between the fair value of the purchase consideration given for, and the aggregate fair values of the *identifiable* assets and liabilities of, an acquired business that are recognized on acquisition.

Identifiability in IAS GAAP does not equal separability, since an asset of an enterprise is defined as "a *resource* [that is] (a) *controlled* by the enterprise as a result of past events; and (b) from which future economic benefits are expected to flow to the enterprise." For an intangible asset to be recognized, the future economic benefits must be "probable," and it must be possible to measure the cost of the asset reliably. "Control" encompasses both the right to obtain the benefits and the ability to restrict access to them by others. It is not considered to imply the ability to sell the item separately from other assets of the enterprise. These criteria thus permit the recognition as assets, in appropriate circumstances, of nonseparable items such as development costs that have not been converted into (separable) patents. As well as internally generated goodwill, expenditure on the following is not recognized as an intangible asset: brands, mastheads, publishing titles, customer lists and items similar in substance, start-ups, training, advertising and/or promotion, and relocation or reorganization. When such items are reflected in the cost of acquiring a business, they should be included in the amount of goodwill on acquisition. The position taken in IAS GAAP is that intangible items should be accounted for in the same manner whether they are acquired or internally generated.

IAS GAAP require intangible assets to be amortized on a systematic basis over their estimated useful life and to be subject to tests for impairment of value. The preferred (benchmark) basis for measurement is historical cost; restatement at fair value is permitted as a (less preferred) alternative treatment, provided (a) it can be determined by reference to an active market for the asset and (b) revaluation is carried out frequently enough to ensure that the carrying amount does not differ materially from fair value.

The relevant IAS GAAP have been promulgated in:

- IAS 38, "Intangible Assets" (July 1998), which superseded IAS 9, "Research and Development Costs," from July 1, 1999
- SIC-6, "Costs of Modifying Existing Software"
- IAS 36, "Impairment of Assets" (see Chapter 19)
- IAS 22, "Business Combinations" (recognition criteria for acquired intangibles, see Chapter 6)

This chapter is concerned with IAS 38 (as amplified by SIC-6), which restates the relevant provisions of IAS 22.

BACKGROUND

IAS 38 originated in the revision of the Exposure Draft E50 and its replacement by E60 in 1996. In this revision, the IASC decided to include the requirements on research and development (R&D) costs with those on other intangibles because R&D costs are intangible in nature, any value attributable to them being due to the know-how embodied in them rather than to physical items such as prototypes. The IASC was concerned to achieve, as far as possible, uniformity of treatment for all long-term nonfinancial assets, whether tangible or intangible, and for intangibles whether internally generated or acquired. This concern is manifested in IAS 38 in the following ways: (a) many of the paragraphs of IAS 38 are similar in wording, and in places virtually identical, to paragraphs of IAS 16, "Property, Plant, and Equipment"; (b) the recognition as assets of internally generated intangibles is allowed, subject to stringent and cumbersome criteria. Although the principle is that any intangibles that meet the asset recognition criteria should be recognized (except in the case of the "alternative treatment" discussed below), it remains to be seen whether the effect of these criteria acts as a deterrent to a reporting entity from so doing, in the absence of a powerful reason.

The treatment of R&D costs has been the subject of particular controversy internationally. While there is general agreement that research does not give rise to intangible values that can be recognized as assets, there is disagreement as to whether development may do so, subject to certain criteria. In its 1993 revision of IAS 9, "Research and Development Costs," the IASC changed its preferred (benchmark) treatment from that proposed in its Exposure Drafts E32 and E47, namely, the immediate expensing of all development costs, to capitalization (i.e., recognition as an asset), provided certain criteria were met. It was thought that this was more consistent with the concept of an asset as set out in the IASC's Framework. In IAS 38, capitalization is maintained, but the criteria for recognition have been tightened up; immediate expensing is not allowed as an alternative treatment if these criteria are met.

Another area of controversy has been the treatment of brands. Here, however, the IASC has felt able to take a firm line: internally generated brands are not to be recognized as assets, and brands acquired in a business combination are not considered to be separately identifiable assets and are thus assimilated to goodwill.

The main differences between IAS GAAP and U.S. GAAP regarding intangibles are the following:

1. With the exception of certain software development costs, which are required to be capitalized in accordance with FAS-86, "Accounting for the Costs of Computer Software to be Sold, Leased or Otherwise Marketed," U.S. GAAP (FAS-2) require all R&D costs to be immediately expensed. Under IAS GAAP, the required treatment of development costs is that they should be capitalized if certain recognition criteria are met.

2. IAS GAAP permit, as an alternative treatment, the restatement of intangible assets to their fair values, provided fair value can be determined by reference to an active market for that type of asset. This is not permitted by U.S. GAAP.

3. U.S. GAAP permit useful lives of identified intangibles to have a duration of up to 40 years, like goodwill acquired in a business combination. IAS GAAP incorporate a "rebuttable assumption" that useful lives of identified intangibles, as with goodwill acquired in a business combination, cannot exceed 20 years. If the assumption is rebutted, tests for impairment of value must be systematically applied.

SCOPE

The term *intangible assets* raises the major issue of which intangible items should be recognized as assets and which should not. Hence, IAS 38 mentions numerous items of expenditure on what may be termed *intangible resources*, many of which do not meet its asset recognition criteria. These items include expenditure on advertising, training, start-up, research and development activities (IAS 38, par. 4), and computer software, patents, copyrights, motion picture films, customer lists, mortgage servicing rights, fishing licenses, import quotas, franchises, customer or supplier relationships, customer loyalty, market share, and marketing rights (IAS 38, par. 8). A good number of these do not qualify for recognition as assets in terms of the criteria set out in the IASC's Framework, and one of the main purposes of IAS 38 is to distinguish between those that do and those that do not. The Introduction to IAS 38 cites several of the items mentioned above as examples of expenditure that does not meet these criteria, namely, start-ups, research, training, advertising and/or promotion, and relocation or reorganization. Paragraph 51 adds internally generated brands, mastheads, publishing titles, customer lists, and items similar in substance as items not qualifying for recognition as assets.

According to IAS 38, paragraph 5, an intangible asset held by a lessee under a finance lease is considered, after initial recognition, to be an asset falling within the scope of IAS 38.

> **OBSERVATION:** There is a rationale for this, in that the asset that is held by a lessee under a finance lease is an intangible property right or usufruct, rather than a physical asset. However, the statement is potentially confusing, since IAS 38 is also stated not to apply to items falling within the scope of IAS 17, "Leases" (IAS 38, par. 2; see below). The reference in IAS 38, paragraph 5, to assets held under a finance lease by a lessee is not to be interpreted as removing such items from the scope of

IAS 17. The latter specifically deals with a lessee's accounting for assets held under a finance lease (IAS 17, pars. 12–24; see Chapter 25) but contains no specific requirements for the depreciation of such items. Thus, the reference to assets held under a finance lease by a lessee in IAS 38, paragraph 5, is intended to indicate that, for these items, the requirements for depreciation set out in IAS 4, "Depreciation Accounting," are superseded by those in IAS 38 (as noted in IAS 4, footnote 1).

The scope of IAS 38 is clarified in paragraphs 1 and 2 by stating which categories of item are not included, namely:

1. Intangible assets covered by other accounting standards:
   (a) intangible assets held by an enterprise for sale in the ordinary course of business, covered by IAS 2, "Inventories," or IAS 11, "Construction Contracts,"
   (b) deferred tax assets (IAS 12, "Income Taxes"),
   (c) leases falling within the scope of IAS 17, "Leases,"
   (d) assets arising from employee benefits (IAS 19, "Employee Benefits"),
   (e) goodwill arising on a business combination (IAS 22),
   (f) financial assets as defined in IAS 32, "Financial Instruments: Disclosure and Presentation." The recognition of some financial assets is covered by IAS 27, "Consolidated Financial Statements and Accounting for Investments in Subsidiaries"; IAS 28, "Accounting for Investments in Associates"; IAS 31, "Financial Reporting of Interests in Joint Ventures"; and IAS 39, "Financial Instruments: Recognition and Measurement";
2. Mineral rights and expenditure on the exploration for, or development and extraction of, minerals, oil, natural gas, and similar nonregenerative resources;
3. Intangible assets arising in insurance enterprises from contracts with policyholders.

RECOGNITION

The key criteria for recognition of an intangible asset are *identifiability* and *control*, but *reliable measurability* is also a requirement.

Identifiability (IAS 38, pars. 10–12 and 17) is necessary in order to distinguish an intangible asset from goodwill. Separability is a sufficient condition for identifiability, but in IAS GAAP not a necessary one. An asset is separable if the enterprise could rent, sell, exchange, or distribute the specific future economic benefits attributable to the asset without also disposing of other assets or future economic benefits that flow from them. (Future economic benefits include both revenues and cost savings.)

An enterprise, however, may be able to identify an intangible asset in some other way. If an intangible asset is acquired together with a set of other assets, it may be separately identifiable by virtue of separate legal rights attaching to it. An internally generated intangible asset may also result from an internal project that gives rise to legal rights for the enterprise. Nevertheless, usually legal rights are transferable, so that such assets are separable (an exception is rights resulting from a legal duty on employees to maintain confidentiality). But identifiability in IAS GAAP can be achieved even if an asset generates future economic benefits only in combination with other assets, that is, it is not separable, provided the enterprise can identify the future economic benefits that will flow from the asset. In that case, however, the second criterion, control, is particularly crucial.

Control (IAS 38, pars. 13–16) is exercised by an enterprise over an asset if the enterprise (a) has the power to obtain the future economic benefits flowing from the underlying resource and (b) can also restrict the access of others to such benefits. The reference to the "underlying resource" should be interpreted as indicating that the resource itself is not recognizable as an asset unless the criterion of control (as well as that of identifiability) is met. Control will generally result from legal rights enforceable in law, and such rights provide a sufficient condition for control. But IAS GAAP do not exclude the possibility that control over the future economic benefits could be exercised in some other way.

> **OBSERVATION:** For example, development expenditure may give rise to an intangible asset if the criteria in IAS 38, paragraph 45, are met (see below), even though no legal rights to intellectual property such as a patent or a copyright have been created. However, in such a case another type of legal right, resulting from a legal duty on employees to maintain confidentiality, would presumably exist. It is hard to envisage control in the absence of some kind of related legal right, and IAS 38 provides no examples of this.

In the case of such intangible resources as benefits arising from a team of skilled staff and from training, even if the identifiability criterion can be satisfied, the criterion of controllability will most likely not be met in the absence of protection by legal rights. The same is true for customer lists or market shares. Such intangible resources therefore do not usually qualify for recognition as intangible assets.

IAS 38, paragraphs 19 and 22, state that an intangible asset (that has met the other recognition criteria) should be recognized only if its cost can be measure reliably, and that it should be measured initially at cost.

INITIAL MEASUREMENT OF ACQUIRED INTANGIBLE ASSETS

For the purpose of determining cost, four different modes of acquisition are considered (pars. 23–35): separate acquisition; acquisition as part of a business combination; acquisition by way of a government grant; and acquisition by exchange of assets.

In the case of separate acquisition, the rules for determining cost are the same as those for assets generally and do not call for comment here. The rules for determining cost in the case of acquisition as part of a business combination are given in IAS 22 (see Chapter 6). In the case of acquisition by way of a government grant, the rules in IAS 20 are applicable (see Chapter 18). These permit the following alternatives: (a) both the asset and the grant to be recognized at fair value, with amortization of the asset over its useful life unless it is nondepreciable (e.g., land), and the grant being recognized as income over the periods necessary to match them with related costs; (b) the asset to be recognized at a nominal value plus any expenditure that is directly attributable to preparing it for its intended use.

In general, exchanges of assets are accounted for at fair value, the fair value of the asset given being treated as the cost of the asset acquired, subject to any necessary adjustments for any other partial consideration such as cash. In the case of an intangible asset that is exchanged for an equity interest in a similar asset (such as a share in a research and development joint venture), the cost of the new asset is the carrying amount of the asset given up, with no gain or loss being recognized on the transaction, unless the fair value of the asset received is less than the carrying amount of the asset given up. In the latter case, this may provide evidence of an impairment loss relating to the latter. Any such impairment loss should be recognized, and the carrying amount after adjustment for impairment of the asset given up should be treated as the cost of the new asset (IAS 38, pars. 34–35).

INTERNALLY GENERATED INTANGIBLE ASSETS

Recognition

In order to assess whether an internally generated intangible resource meets the criteria for recognition as an asset, IAS 38 set out the following methodology (pars. 40–50):

1. The enterprise classifies the internal project resulting in the generation of the resource into two phases: a research phase and a development phase. If this distinction cannot be made for the internal project, then the entire project should be considered as a research phase.

2. Research is defined as original and planned investigation under-taken with the prospect of gaining new scientific or technical knowledge and understanding. Development is the application of research findings or other knowledge to a plan or design for the production of new or substantially improved materials, de-vices, products, processes, systems, or services prior to the com-mencement of commercial production or use (IAS 38, par. 7).

3. No intangible asset should be recognized as resulting from research or from the research phase of an internal project. Expenditure on research should be recognized as an expense when incurred.

4. An intangible resource arising from development (or from the development phase of an internal project) should be recog-nized as an intangible asset if, and only if, an enterprise can demonstrate all of the following:

   (a) the technical feasibility of completing the intangible asset so that it will be available for use or sale;

   (b) its intention to complete the intangible asset and use or sell it;

   (c) its ability to use or sell it;

   (d) how the intangible asset will generate probable future eco-nomic benefits. Among other things, the following should be demonstrated: the existence of a market for the intan-gible asset or its output or, if it is to be used internally, its usefulness to the enterprise;

   (e) the availability of adequate technical, financial, and other resources to complete the development and to use or sell the intangible asset, which may be demonstrated by an appropriate business plan; and

   (f) the enterprise's ability to measure reliably the expenditure attributable to the intangible asset during its development, for example, by means of the enterprise's costing system.

5. To demonstrate how an intangible asset will generate probable future economic benefits, the principles set out in IAS 36, "Im-pairment of Assets," especially paragraphs 26–56 on "Value in Use" (see Chapter 19) should be applied. If the asset will gener-ate economic benefits only in combination with other assets, the principles for "cash generating units" set out in IAS 36 should be followed.

Expenditure on internally generated resources that does not meet these asset recognition criteria includes the following: start-ups, re-search, training, advertising and/or promotion, relocation or reorga-nization, internally generated brands, mastheads, publishing titles, customer lists, and items similar in substance.

Cost of an Internally Generated Intangible Asset

The cost of an internally generated asset is the sum of the expenditure incurred from the date when the intangible asset first meets the recognition criteria set out above. Cost includes all expenditure that is either directly attributable to generating the asset or has been allocated on a reasonable and consistent basis to the activity of generating it. Allocations of overheads should follow the principles set out in IAS 2, "Inventories" (see Chapter 23). With regard to the recognition of interest as a cost, IAS 23, "Borrowing Costs" (see Chapter 5) sets out the applicable principles.

Expenditure that is not part of the cost of the intangible asset includes that on selling, administration, and training staff to operate the asset.

Expenditure on an intangible resource that was initially recognized as an expense in previous financial statements or reports (for example, expenditure during the "research phase" of an internal project) should not be recognized as part of the cost of an intangible asset at a later date (IAS 38, par. 59).

Illustration

An enterprise is developing a new production process. During 20X5, expenditure incurred was 1,000, of which 900 was incurred before December 1, 20X5 and 100 was incurred between December 1, 20X5 and December 31, 20X5. The enterprise is able to demonstrate that, at December 1, 20X5, the production process met the criteria for recognition as an intangible asset. The recoverable amount of the know-how embodied in the process (including future cash outflows to complete the process before it is available for use) is estimated to be 500.

At the end of 20X5, the production process is recognized as an intangible asset at a cost of 100 (expenditure incurred since the date when the recognition criteria were met, that is, December 1, 20X5). The 900 expenditure incurred before December 1, 20X5 is recognized as an expense because the recognition criteria were not met until December 1, 20X5. This expenditure will never form part of the cost of the production process recognized in the balance sheet.

During 20X6, expenditure incurred is 2,000. At the end of 20X6, the recoverable amount of the know-how embodied in the process (including future cash outflows to complete the process before it is available for use) is estimated to be 1,900.

At the end of 20X6, the cost of the production process is 2,100 (100 expenditure recognized at the end of 20X5 plus 2,000 expenditure recognized in 20X6). The enterprise recognizes an impairment loss of 200 to adjust the carrying amount of the process before impairment loss (2,100) to its recoverable amount (1,900). This impairment loss will be reversed in a subsequent period if the requirements for the reversal of an impairment loss in IAS 36, "Impairment of Assets," are met.

SUBSEQUENT EXPENDITURE

The view taken in IAS 38 is that only rarely will expenditure incurred after the initial recognition of a purchased intangible asset, or after the completion of an internally generated intangible asset, result in an addition to the amount of its capitalizable cost. This is because it is generally difficult (a) to attribute such expenditure to a particular intangible asset rather than to the business as a whole; and (b) even when that difficulty does not arise, to determine whether such expenditure will enhance, rather than merely maintain, the probable economic benefits that will flow from the asset.

Consequently, subsequent expenditure should be recognized as an expense, except in the rare cases where (a) probable enhancement of the economic benefits that will flow from the asset can be demonstrated and (b) the expenditure can be measured and attributed to the asset reliably (IAS 38, pars. 60–61).

SIC-6, "Costs of Modifying Existing Software," makes it clear that such costs, when incurred in relation to software that is not produced for sale, in order to restore or maintain the future economic benefits to be expected from its originally assessed standard of performance, should be recognized as expense.

MEASUREMENT SUBSEQUENT TO INITIAL RECOGNITION

The "benchmark" treatment is that an intangible asset should be carried at cost less any accumulated depreciation and (if any) accumulated impairment losses (IAS 38, par. 63).

The alternative treatment is to carry the intangible asset at a revalued amount. The revalued amount should be the fair value of the asset at the date of revaluation less any subsequent accumulated depreciation and (if any) subsequent accumulated impairment losses (IAS 38, par. 64).

If an intangible asset is revalued, this should also be done to all the other assets in its class (i.e., those of similar nature and use within the enterprise's operations), except those for which there is no active market, which should be carried at cost less accumulated amortization and impairment losses (IAS 38, pars. 70–72).

Fair value should be determined by reference to an active market, and revaluations should be made with sufficient regularity so that the carrying amount does not diverge materially from the fair value at the balance sheet date (IAS 38, par. 64). An active market is defined as one where all the following conditions exist: (a) the items traded within it are homogeneous, (b) willing buyers and sellers can normally be found at any time (within reason), and (c) prices are public information (IAS 38, par. 7). It is considered unlikely that such an active market would exist for an intangible asset (IAS 38, par. 67), although there may be exceptions to this generalization; for example, there may be active markets in freely transferable taxi licenses, fishing licenses, production quotas, or airport takeoff and landing "slots."

The alternative treatment does not apply to initial recognition, which should be at cost, or to intangible resources that were not previously recognized as assets. However, if only part of the cost of an intangible resource was recognized as an asset because it did not meet the criteria for recognition until part of the way through an internal project, the alternative treatment may be applied to the whole of the asset and not just to that proportion of it that would be represented by the amount recognized as its cost. The alternative treatment may also be applied to an intangible asset received by way of a government grant and initially recognized at a nominal amount (IAS 38, par. 66).

An active market that has existed for an intangible asset may cease to exist. In that case, if the asset has been accounted for by using the alternative treatment, then its carrying amount should be its revalued amount at the date of the last revaluation by reference to the formerly active market less any accumulated depreciation and impairment losses. The cessation of the active market may be an indication of possible impairment of the asset's value, and this should be tested in accordance with IAS 36, "Impairment of Assets" (see Chapter 19). If, at a subsequent measurement date, an active market is available again so that the fair value of the asset can be determined, the asset should be revalued at its fair value as of that date (IAS 38, pars. 73–75).

Recognition of Revaluation Gains and Losses

The usual prudence and realization conventions prevail. Increases in an intangible asset's carrying amount (gains) should be credited directly to owners' equity under the heading of revaluation surplus, except to the extent that the increase is a reversal of a previous revaluation decrease (loss) recognized as an expense in respect of the same asset, in which case the amount of the reversal is recognized as income.

Revaluation decreases (losses) are recognized as expenses except to the extent that the decrease is a reversal of a revaluation increase (gain) that was previously credited to revaluation surplus in respect of the same asset, in which case the amount of the reversal should be charged against the revaluation surplus (IAS 38, pars. 73–77).

According to IAS 38, paragraph 78, the cumulative revaluation surplus may be transferred directly to retained earnings when the surplus is realized. Realization of the surplus may occur (a) through retirement or disposal of the asset; or (b) through the process of using up the asset, insofar as the amortization based on the revalued carrying amount exceeds that which would have been calculated on the basis of the asset's historical cost. The transfer from revaluation surplus to retained earnings is not made through the income statement.

> ☞ **PRACTICE POINTER:** While it is clear that such transfers may not be made through the income statement, paragraph 78 does not make it entirely clear whether such transfers from revaluation surplus to retained earnings *should* be made in the appropriate conditions or whether they *may* be made. The corresponding paragraph of IAS 16, "Property Plant, and Equipment" (par. 39), has almost identical wording. The issue is potentially important, since revaluation reserves may not be legally distributable. Moreover, such transfers may have implications regarding accounting for income taxes, as indicated in IAS 12, "Income Taxes," paragraphs 62–65 (see Chapter 20). The wording of the relevant paragraphs of IAS 12 implies that such transfers from revaluation surplus to retained earnings *do not have to be made*. Presumably, the choice of accounting treatment for these items should be consistent.

AMORTIZATION AND DEPRECIATION

IAS 38 uses the terms *amortization* and *depreciation* interchangeably with reference to intangible assets to refer to the process of systematic allocation of an asset's cost or revalued amount, less any residual value, over its useful life. The residual value should be assumed to be zero, unless either (a) there is a commitment by a third party to purchase the asset at the end of its estimated useful life to the enterprise (i.e., the period of time over which it is being depreciated) or (b) there is an active market for the asset, such that the asset's residual value can be determined by reference to that market and it is probable that the market will exist at the end of asset's estimated useful life to the enterprise. The cost or revalued amount less any residual value of an asset is referred to as its "depreciable amount" (IAS 38, pars. 91–92).

Factors that need to be considered in estimating an intangible asset's useful life include the following (IAS 38, pars. 80 and 85):

1. The expected usage of the asset by the enterprise and whether the asset could be efficiently managed by another management team.

2. Typical product life cycles for the type of asset and public information on estimates of useful lives for similar types of assets that are used in a similar way.

3. Technical, technological, or other types of obsolescence.

4. The stability of the industry in which the asset operates and changes in the market demand for the outputs of the asset.

5. Expected actions by competitors or potential competitors.

6. The level of maintenance expenditure required to obtain the expected future economic benefits from the asset and the enterprise's intent and ability to spend such amounts.

7. The enterprise's period of control over the asset and legal and similar limits on control or use, such as the expiration dates of related patents, copyrights, or leases. If control over the future economic benefits from the asset is achieved though legal rights that have been granted for a finite period, the useful life of the asset should not exceed the duration of the legal rights unless they are renewable and renewal is virtually certain.

8. Whether the asset's useful life is dependent on that of other assets of the enterprise.

There is a rebuttable presumption that the useful life of an intangible asset will not exceed 20 years from the date at which the asset is available for use (IAS 38, par. 79). This presumption may be rebutted in rare cases, however, such as those in the following examples (IAS 38, par. 83).

Examples

A. An enterprise has purchased an exclusive right to generate hydroelectric power for sixty years. The costs of generating hydroelectric power are much lower than the costs of obtaining power from alternative sources. It is expected that the geographical area surrounding the power station will demand a significant amount of power from the power station for at least sixty years.

The enterprise amortises the right to generate power over sixty years, unless there is evidence that its useful life is shorter.

B. An enterprise has purchased an exclusive right to operate a toll motorway for thirty years. There is no plan to construct alternative routes in the area served by the motorway. It is expected that this motorway will be in use for at least thirty years.

The enterprise amortises the right to operate the motorway over thirty years, unless there is evidence that its useful life is shorter.

When the presumption is rebutted, the enterprise:

1. Amortizes the asset over the best estimate of its useful life;
2. Reviews the recoverable amount of the asset at least annually for impairment losses, even if there is no apparent indication of impairment; and
3. Discloses the reasons why the presumption is rebutted and the factors that were significant in determining the asset's useful life, with reference to the eight factors mentioned above.

IAS 38, paragraph 84, reminds the reader that the useful life of an intangible asset may be quite long, but it is always finite. Moreover, estimates of an intangible asset's useful life generally become less reliable as its length increases (par. 82). Estimates of useful life should therefore be prudent (especially where rapidly changing technology is involved), though not unrealistically short.

Amortization Method

IAS 38 envisages a variety of amortization methods that may be used to allocate systematically the depreciable amount of an intangible asset over the periods making up its useful life. The standard mentions the straight-line, diminishing balance, and units of production methods. The straight-line method should be used unless the time pattern of consumption of the asset's economic benefits can be determined reliably and clearly indicates that one of the other methods is more suitable. There will rarely, if ever, be persuasive evidence to support a method for intangible assets that is less conservative (that is, results in a lower amount of accumulated depreciation) than the straight-line method (IAS 38, pars. 88–90).

The amortization period and method should be reviewed at least at each financial year-end, and the amortization period should be changed if the expected useful life of the asset is significantly different from previous estimates (IAS 38, par. 94–96). If the expected time pattern of economic benefits has changed, the amortization method should be changed accordingly. Such changes should be accounted for as changes in accounting estimates under IAS 8, "Net Profit or Loss for the Period, Fundamental Errors, and Changes in Accounting Policies" (see Chapter 26).

Impairment Losses

The method to be used in making a review of an intangible asset's carrying amount for possible impairment (an impairment test) is set out in IAS 36, "Impairment of Assets" (see Chapter 19). There are also specific rules for the recognition of impairment losses in respect of intangible assets acquired in a business combination that are set out in IAS 22, "Business Combinations," paragraphs 58–60 (see Chapter 6).

In addition, IAS 38 requires impairment tests to be carried out at least at each financial year-end, even if there is no indication of impairment in value, in the following cases (IAS 38, pars. 99–102):

- The intangible asset is not yet ready for use (in which case its ability to generate sufficient future economic benefits to recover its cost is considered to be subject to much uncertainty).
- The intangible asset has an estimated useful life exceeding 20 years.

Retirements and Disposals

IAS 38, paragraph 104, states that gains or losses arising from the retirement or disposal of an intangible asset should (a) be determined as the difference between the disposal proceeds and the carrying amount of the asset; and (b) be recognized as income and expense in the income statement. The issue of the disposition of any revaluation surplus relating to the asset was addressed under "Recognition of Revaluation Gains and Losses," above.

DISCLOSURE

The financial statements should disclose the following for each class of intangible assets, distinguishing between internally generated intangible assets and other intangible assets (IAS 38, par. 107):

1. The useful lives or the amortization rates used;
2. The amortization methods used;
3. The gross carrying amount and the accumulated amortization (aggregated with accumulated impairment losses) at the beginning and end of the period;
4. The line item(s) of the income statement in which the amortization of intangible assets is included;
5. A reconciliation of the carrying amount at the beginning and end of the period, showing:
   (a) additions, indicating separately those from internal development and through business combinations,
   (b) retirements and disposals,
   (c) increases or decreases during the period resulting from revaluations under paragraphs 64, 76, and 77 and from

impairment losses recognized or reversed directly in equity under IAS 36, "Impairment of Assets" (if any),

(d) impairment losses recognized in the income statement during the period under IAS 36 (if any),

(e) impairment losses reversed in the income statement during the period under IAS 36 (if any),

(f) amortization recognized during the period,

(g) net exchange differences arising on the translation of the financial statements of a foreign entity,

(h) other changes in the carrying amount during the period.

Comparative information is not required.

A *class* of intangible assets is a grouping of assets of a similar nature and use in an enterprise's operations. Examples of separate classes may include:

1. Brand names,
2. Mastheads and publishing titles,
3. Computer software,
4. Licenses and franchises,
5. Copyrights, patents, and other industrial property rights, service and operating rights,
6. Recipes, formulas, models, designs, and prototypes,
7. Intangible assets under development.

The classes mentioned above are disaggregated (aggregated) into smaller (larger) classes if this results in more relevant information for the users of the financial statements.

An enterprise discloses information on impaired intangible assets under IAS 36 in addition to the information required as stated in IAS 38, paragraph 107(e)(iii)–(v); see 5(c)–(e) above.

An enterprise discloses the nature and effect of a change in an accounting estimate that has a material effect in the current period or that is expected to have a material effect in subsequent periods, under IAS 8, "Net Profit or Loss for the Period, Fundamental Errors, and Changes in Accounting Policy." Such disclosure may arise from changes in:

1. The amortization period,
2. The amortization method, or
3. Residual values.

The financial statements should also disclose:

1. If an intangible asset is amortized over more than 20 years, the reasons why the presumption that the useful life of an intangible asset will not exceed 20 years from the date when the asset is available for use is rebutted. In giving these reasons, the enterprise should describe the factor(s) that played a significant role in determining the useful life of the asset.

2. A description, the carrying amount, and remaining amortization period of any individual intangible asset that is material to the financial statements of the enterprise as a whole.

3. For intangible assets acquired by way of a government grant and initially recognized at fair value (see "Initial Measurement of Acquired Intangible Assets," above):

   (a) the fair value initially recognized for these assets,

   (b) their carrying amount, and

   (c) whether they are carried under the benchmark or the allowed alternative treatment for subsequent measurement.

4. The existence and carrying amounts of intangible assets whose title is restricted and the carrying amounts of intangible assets pledged as security for liabilities.

5. The amount of commitments for the acquisition of intangible assets.

When an enterprise describes the factor(s) that played a significant role in determining the useful life of an intangible asset that is amortized over more than 20 years, the enterprise considers the list of eight factors mentioned under "Amortization and Depreciation," above.

Intangible Assets Carried under the Allowed Alternative Treatment

If intangible assets are carried at revalued amounts, the following should be disclosed:

1. By class of intangible assets:

   (a) the effective date of the revaluation,

   (b) the carrying amount of revalued intangible assets,

   (c) the carrying amount that would have been included in the financial statements had the revalued intangible assets been carried under the benchmark treatment mentioned in "Measurement Subsequent to Initial Recognition," above.

2. The amount of the revaluation surplus that relates to intangible assets at the beginning and end of the period, indicating the changes during the period and any restrictions on the distribution of the balance to shareholders.

It may be necessary to aggregate the classes of revalued assets into larger classes for disclosure purposes. However, classes are not aggregated if this would result in the combination of a class of intangible assets that includes amounts measured under both benchmark and allowed alternative treatments for subsequent measurement.

Research and Development Expenditure

The financial statements should disclose the aggregate amount of research and development expenditure recognized as an expense during the period (IAS 38, par. 115).

Research and development expenditure comprises all expenditure that is directly attributable to research or development activities or that can be allocated on a reasonable and consistent basis to such activities (see "Cost of an Internally Generated Intangible Asset," above, for guidance on the type of expenditure to be included for the purpose of the disclosure requirement in par. 115).

Other Information

An enterprise is encouraged, but not required, to give the following information:

1. A description of any fully amortized intangible asset that is still in use;
2. A brief description of significant intangible assets controlled by the enterprise but not recognized as assets because they did not meet the recognition criteria in this standard or because they were acquired or generated before this standard was effective.

CHAPTER 22
INTERIM FINANCIAL REPORTING

CONTENTS

OVERVIEW

Annual financial statements are something of a blunt instrument. They cover a long period and do not appear until a considerable time after the end of that period. It is helpful to many users of financial statements to receive one or more progress reports at interim times and/or at shorter intervals. This is a requirement of most stock exchanges, which are likely to issue their own regulations on such statements for their own listed companies. It is also good public relations to appear to wish to keep an image of openness and transparency with one's investors, lenders, and customers.

The practice of issuing interim financial information has become more prevalent generally among listed enterprises in recent years. Clearly, as with the annual financial statements themselves, consistency, clarity of policy, and adherence to fair presentation are essential. IAS GAAP do not *require* the publication of interim financial reports. However, if an enterprise reporting under IAS GAAP does choose (or is required by other authorities) to issue such reports, then IAS prescribes the minimum content of an interim financial report, and the principles for recognition and measurement in complete or condensed financial statements for an interim period.

IASC GAAP are contained in IAS 34, "Interim Financial Reporting," effective for accounting periods beginning on or after January 1, 1999.

BACKGROUND

There are two possible ways of viewing the preparation of interim financial statements. The first, known as the discrete approach, views interim periods as just like any other accounting period, only shorter. The second, known as the integral approach, views an interim period as a component, or integral, part of the annual reporting period. Within this second approach, the purpose of interim financial reporting is to provide information over the course of the annual period that helps to anticipate annual results.

To some extent, IAS GAAP follow the second integral philosophy. They do not require that seasonal or cyclical revenues or expenses are smoothed out, as they can be properly interpreted as indicators of annual performance, given proper comparison figures plus further explanation if necessary. IAS 34 seeks to ensure that such meaningful comparison and necessary explanation are provided. There are no major differences between IAS and U.S. GAAP as promulgated in APB-28. It should be remembered as a general point, however, that many stock exchanges have their own rules in relation to enterprises quoted thereon.

SCOPE AND DEFINITIONS

As already indicated, IAS GAAP do not of themselves require the preparation and publication of interim financial reports by any enterprise, listed or otherwise. The fact that an enterprise may not have provided interim financial reports during a particular financial year or may have provided interim financial reports that do not comply with IAS 34 does not prevent the enterprise's annual financial statements from conforming to International Accounting Standards if they otherwise do so. If an enterprise's interim financial report is described as complying with International Accounting Standards, it must comply with all of the requirements of IAS 34. Thus, IAS 34 applies to all enterprises that are required, or elect, to publish an interim financial report in accordance with International Accounting Standards. IASC "encourages" publicly traded (listed) enterprises (par. 1) to provide interim financial reports at least as of the end of the first half of their financial year and to make their interim financial reports available not later than 60 days after the end of the interim period.

The standard gives two formal definitions, as follows (par. 4):

- *Interim period* is a financial reporting period shorter than a full financial year.

- *Interim financial report* means a financial report containing either a complete set of financial statements (as described in IAS

1, "Presentation of Financial Statements," see Chapter 3) or a set of condensed financial statements (as described in this standard) for an interim period.

IAS 34 makes it clear that it does not intend in any way to "discourage" the issue of an interim complete set of financial statements, that is, in full accord with IAS 1 (which requirement automatically embraces all other applicable IASs). The IAS itself, however, specifies the minimum components of an interim financial report as follows (par. 8):

1. Condensed balance sheet,
2. Condensed income statement,
3. Condensed statement showing either (a) all changes in equity or (b) changes in equity other than those arising from capital transactions with owners and distributions to owners,
4. Condensed cash flow statement,
5. Selected explanatory notes.

It is to be assumed that a reader of an interim financial report also has access to the previous full annual financial statements. The interim report, therefore, focuses on new circumstances and need not duplicate information previously reported.

FORM AND CONTENT OF INTERIM FINANCIAL STATEMENTS

As already discussed, an enterprise may, if it chooses, issue its interim financial statements in full accord with IAS 1. Otherwise, if an enterprise publishes a set of condensed financial statements in its interim financial report, those condensed statements should include, at a minimum, each of the headings and subtotals that were included in its most recent annual financial statements and the selected explanatory notes as required by IAS 34. Additional line items or notes should be included if their omission would make the condensed interim financial statements misleading. Basic and diluted earnings per share should be presented on the face of each income statement, complete or condensed, for each interim period.

The interim report should be as consistent as possible, for example, regarding consolidation, with the most recent annual financial statements. The condensed changes in equity statement (see component 3, above) should also be consistent with that of the annual statements.

This relatively brief comment deals with components 1–4 of the condensed interim report. The element of subjectivity involved in the question of "additional line items or notes" should be observed. However, IAS 34 deals with the content of required explanatory notes (note that component 5 does not include the word "condensed") in detail. Again, it is assumed that the previous full financial statements are available to the reader, so the notes in the interim reports should focus on an explanation of events and transactions that are significant to an understanding of the changes in financial position and performance of the enterprise since the last annual reporting date.

An enterprise should include the following information, as a minimum, in the notes to its interim financial statements, if material and if not disclosed elsewhere in the interim financial report (par. 16). The information should normally be reported on a financial year-to-date basis. However, the enterprise should also disclose any events or transactions that are material to an understanding of the current interim period:

1. A statement that the same accounting policies and methods of computation are followed in the interim financial statements as with the most recent annual financial statements or, if those policies or methods have been changed, a description of the nature and effect of the change;

2. Explanatory comments about the seasonality or cyclicality of interim operations;

3. The nature and amount of items affecting assets, liabilities, equity, net income, or cash flows that are unusual because of their nature, size, or incidence;

4. The nature and amount of changes in estimates of amounts reported in prior interim periods of the current financial year or changes in estimates of amounts reported in prior financial years, if those changes have a material effect in the current interim period;

5. Issuances, repurchases, and repayments of debt and equity securities;

6. Dividends paid (aggregate or per share) separately for ordinary shares and other shares;

7. Segment revenue and segment result for business segments or geographic segments, whichever is the enterprise's primary basis of segment reporting (disclosure of segment data is required in an enterprise's interim financial report only if IAS 14, "Reporting Financial Information by Segment," requires that enterprise to disclose segment data in its annual financial statements);

8. Material events subsequent to the end of the interim period that have not been reflected in the financial statements for the interim period;

9. The effect of changes in the composition of the enterprise during the interim period, including business combinations, acquisition or disposal of subsidiaries and long-term investments, restructurings, and discontinuing operations;

10. Changes in contingent liabilities or contingent assets since the last annual balance sheet date.

> ☞ **PRACTICE POINTER:** The requirement to present information on a financial year-to-date basis *and* to ensure an understanding of the current interim period should be noted carefully. It logically has no effect in the context of half-yearly interim statements, but if interim statements are issued quarterly, then its implications could be significant. The notes included must satisfy the requirements of providing an understanding of the latest quarter (and its comparatives) and also an understanding of the year-to-date (and its comparatives).

IAS 34 suggests (in par. 17) some brief examples of "the kinds of disclosure" required in the notes by the above. Disclosures should be consistent with the requirements of relevant individual International Accounting Standards. This is not to imply that all disclosure requirements of all standards are relevant. Items 1–10 above are an exhaustive list (of the required "minimum"), subject only to possible additions necessary to give "an understanding of the current interim period." A clear statement of disclosure of IAS compliance is required. This should specify either that the interim financial statements achieve *full* compliance with IAS 1, with all its implications, or specify that the interim financial statements achieve *full* compliance with IAS 34. No partial or "in all material respects" claims for compliance are permitted.

Interim reports are required to include interim financial statements as follows (par. 20):

1. Balance sheet as of the end of the current interim period and a comparative balance sheet as of the end of the immediately preceding financial year;

2. Income statements for the current interim period and cumulatively for the current financial year to date, with comparative income statements for the comparable interim periods (current and year-to-date) of the immediately preceding financial year;

3. Statement showing changes in equity cumulatively for the current financial year to date, with a comparative statement for the comparable year-to-date period of the immediately preceding financial year;

4. Cash flow statement cumulatively for the current financial year to date, with a comparative statement for the comparable year-to-date period of the immediately preceding financial year.

Illustration

To illustrate, suppose an enterprise's financial year ends December 31 (calendar year). The enterprise will present the following financial statements (condensed or complete) in its quarterly interim financial report as of June 30, 2001:

Balance Sheet:

At	June 30, 2001	December 31, 2000

Income Statement:

6 months ending	June 30, 2001	June 30, 2000
3 months ending	June 30, 2001	June 30, 2000

Cash Flow Statement:

6 months ending	June 30, 2001	June 30, 2000

Statement of Changes in Equity:

6 months ending	June 30, 2001	June 30, 2000

EPS figures would be required for each one of the four income statements presented. Enterprises whose business is highly seasonal are "encouraged to consider reporting," in addition to the above, financial information for the 12 months ending on the interim reporting date and comparative information for the prior twelve-month period. Presumably full compliance with IAS 34 does not strictly require this.

The question of materiality needs to be considered carefully. In deciding how to recognize, measure, classify, or disclose an item for interim financial reporting purposes, materiality should be assessed in relation to the interim period financial data. An event affecting an interim period may be material regarding that interim period but not material, or not expected to be material, in the context of a full financial year. Remember that "information is material if its omission or misstatement could influence the economic decisions of users" (Framework, par. 30). If it is material in the context of the interim period, then IAS 34 requires its disclosure.

☛ **PRACTICE POINTER:** Logically, if it is material for the interim period but possibly or probably not in the context of the whole year, the disclosure must be sufficiently detailed to make all the implications clear. Disclosure for the interim period, with no further comment, could be taken to imply a continuation of

the situation over the remainder of the year, and thus its
continuing materiality, which would be misleading. As IAS 34
puts it (par. 25), judgment must be exercised, remembering that
the overriding goal is to ensure that an interim financial report
includes all information that is relevant to understanding an
enterprise's financial position and performance during the
interim period.

Paragraph 16(d) (given as item 4 on page 22.04) requires, where
material, disclosure of changes in estimates used in previous interim
periods within the year, in the current interim period. However, IAS
34 does not require the preparation of separate interim reports for
the last interim period in the year (i.e., an enterprise reporting quarterly is required to present three quarterly reports and one annual
report, not four quarterly reports and one annual report). This creates a lacuna dealt with by paragraph 26, which requires that if an
estimate of an amount reported in an interim period is changed
significantly during the final interim period of the financial year but
a separate financial report is not published for that final interim
period, the nature and amount of that change in estimate should be
disclosed in a note to the annual financial statements for that financial year.

RECOGNITION AND MEASUREMENT

The key principle is that consistency of accounting policies is required between the annual statements and the interim statements.
However, change in accounting policy is allowed under IAS 8 (see
Chapter 26) and may be required by the issue of a new International
Accounting Standard or statement by the Standing Interpretations
Committee (SIC). The implications (par. 28) are that an enterprise
should apply the same accounting policies in its interim financial
statements as are applied in its annual financial statements, except
for accounting policy changes made after the date of the most recent
annual financial statements that are to be reflected in the next annual
financial statements. However, the frequency of an enterprise's reporting (annual, half-yearly, or quarterly) should not affect the measurement of its annual results. To achieve that objective, measurements for interim reporting purposes should be made on a year-to-date
basis.

The standard makes rather heavy weather of the implications of
this, but the principle is quite simple. This is that the definitions of
the elements, in particular, assets, liabilities, revenues, and expenses
given in the IASC Framework (see Chapter 2), must be applied
absolutely consistently between annual and interim statements. If an
expenditure does not create an asset capable of recognition under the

Framework as of the end of an interim period, then it must be treated as an expense in those interim results. Similarly, a liability can be recorded as such only if it represents an existing obligation as of the date of the interim period-end.

IAS 34 recognizes, as it must, that estimates and expectations, for example, concerning future benefits, will change as the full reporting year progresses, that is, they will change between interim reporting periods. An enterprise that reports more frequently than semiannually, measures income and expenses on a year-to-date basis for each interim period, using information available when each set of financial statements is being prepared. Amounts of income and expenses reported in the current interim period will reflect any changes in estimates of amounts reported in prior interim periods of the financial year. The amounts reported in prior interim periods are not retrospectively adjusted. Paragraphs 16(d) and 26 require, however, that the nature and amount of any significant changes in estimates be disclosed. These paragraphs also require, in the case of an enterprise that reports only semiannually, similar disclosure in the annual financial statements of significant changes in estimates used in the interim statements.

> **OBSERVATION:** Some uncertainties of detail arise. For example, suppose an enterprise has a policy of remeasuring certain assets to fair value on a frequent and regular basis. Such remeasurements will be reflected in interim reports. Is the base carrying amount, for the calculation of gain or loss on disposal, that of the latest interim report, or that of the last annual report? Logic would suggest the latter, at least as it will be shown in the next full annual report, as an optional interim report should not logically affect the position in and between compulsory annual reports. But the formal position is unclear. Additionally in this situation, and also with provisions, for example, for inventory write-down or doubtful debts, estimates may reverse between interim periods. Disclosure, if material, is of course required under paragraph 16(d)—presumably in the later interim period, but not, if the *net* movement is immaterial, in the eventual annual report. When these mobile interim figures become comparatives in the following year, the spirit of the standard will need to be followed, rather than the (absent) letter, in order to give adequate and nonmisleading disclosure.

IAS 34 explicitly confirms that revenues that are seasonal, cyclical, or occasional and costs that are incurred unevenly are (pars. 37 and 39) anticipated or deferred for interim reporting purposes if, and only if, it is also appropriate to anticipate or defer that type of item at the end of the financial year. In general, such items are recognized when they occur (with additional explanation under paragraph 16(b) as stated above or item 2 on page 22.04) if appropriate.

IAS 34 notes and effectively accepts that the use of estimation in interim reports is likely to be greater than might be acceptable in full annual financial statements. The trade-off between relevance and reliability, given that the whole point of interim reports is rapid and timely information, is likely to lead to a different balance. Appendix 3 to the standard gives a number of detailed suggestions ("illustrative and not part of the standard") as to what this might mean. For example, the existence of an annual stock-take does not imply the need for interim stock-takes.

RESTATEMENT OF PREVIOUSLY REPORTED INTERIM PERIODS

In general, IAS 8 will apply (see Chapter 26). IAS 34 states (par. 43) that a change in accounting policy, other than one for which the transition is specified by a new International Accounting Standard, should be reflected by:

1. Restating the financial statements of prior interim periods of the current financial year and the comparable interim periods of prior financial years (see par. 20), if the enterprise follows the benchmark treatment under IAS 8; or

2. Restating the financial statements of prior interim periods of the current financial year, if the enterprise follows the allowed alternative treatment under IAS 8. In this case, comparable interim periods of prior financial years are not restated.

The purpose and effect of paragraph 43 is to require that within the current financial year any change in accounting policy be applied retrospectively to the beginning of the financial year.

APPLYING THE RECOGNITION AND MEASUREMENT PRINCIPLES

IAS 34 contains an appendix, which gives a large number of examples of applying the principles of the standard. This appendix is only "illustrative" and not part of the standard. Many of the illustrations, paragraphs 12–22, relate to income taxes and discuss the application of the basic requirement to use the estimated weighted average annual effective tax rate expected for the full financial year. The examples are detailed and should be read in full by those seeking to apply IAS 34 in a complex scenario. Readers in jurisdictions with a prevalence of LIFO inventory valuations should note the lengthy argument in paragraph 27 of Appendix 2.

To reflect the nuances of difficulty at a more general level, we reproduce here just two of the examples given (IAS 34, Appendix 2, pars. 7–9):

- *Year-End Bonuses.* The nature of year-end bonuses varies widely. Some are earned simply by continued employment during a time period. Some bonuses are earned on the basis of a monthly, quarterly, or annual measure of operating result. They may be purely discretionary, contractual, or based on years of historical precedent. A bonus is anticipated for interim reporting purposes if, and only if, (a) the bonus is a legal obligation, or past practice would make the bonus a constructive obligation for which the enterprise has no realistic alternative but to make the payments, and (b) a reliable estimate of the obligation can be made. IAS 19, "Employee Benefits," provides guidance.

- *Contingent Lease Payments.* Contingent lease payments can be an example of a legal or constructive obligation that is recognized as a liability. If a lease provides for contingent payments based on the lessee achieving a certain level of annual sales, an obligation can arise in the interim periods of the financial year before the required annual level of sales has been achieved, if that required level of sales is expected to be achieved and the enterprise, therefore, has no realistic alternative but to make the future lease payment.

It is interesting to observe the strong emphasis on the balance sheet elements in the above arguments—the focus is on the existence and measurement of obligations (liabilities), not on the usage or consumption of resources (expenses). This is consistent with the general approach taken in the IASC Framework (see Chapter 2).

CHAPTER 23
INVENTORY PRICING AND METHODS

CONTENTS

OVERVIEW

The preparation of financial statements requires careful determination of an appropriate monetary amount of inventory. Usually, that amount is presented as a current asset in the balance sheet and is a direct determinant of cost of goods sold in the income statement; as such, it has a significant impact on the amount of net income. Because the matching convention is applied in determining net income, the measurement of inventories is of primary importance.

This measurement is also difficult, however. There is inevitable subjectivity involved in making assumptions about which costs "attach" to inventory items, and which "cost flows" are involved when they are used up or sold. The effect of this subjectivity is reduced, as far as possible, by requiring consistent application of the assumptions chosen.

IAS GAAP are given in IAS 2, "Inventories," and SIC-1, "Consistency—Different Cost Formulas for Inventories."

BACKGROUND

Inventory can include a number of different types or stages of item. These can be envisaged as:

- Goods or other assets purchased complete for resale;
- Consumable stores;
- Raw materials and components purchased for incorporation into products for sale;
- Products and services in intermediate stages of completion;
- Finished products for sale.

The key problem is how to evaluate the "cost" of an item at each and every stage in the production process, how to determine the cost of items sold, and, therefore, the cost of items not yet sold (i.e., still in inventory). The first major difficulty is the appropriate allocation of overhead costs (i.e., indirect costs) to particular items or products. The principle is that the cost of inventories should comprise all costs of purchase, costs of conversion, and other costs incurred in bringing the inventories to their present location and condition.

A moment's reflection will make it obvious that there are practical problems here. "Direct" items should present no difficulties, as figures can be related "directly" by definition. But overhead allocation necessarily introduces assumptions and approximations: What is the normal level of activity taking one year with another? Can overheads be clearly classified according to function? Which other (non-production) overheads are "attributable" to the present condition and location of an item of inventory? So, for any item of inventory that is not still in its original purchased state, it is a problem to determine the cost of a unit or even of a batch. Methods in common use include job, process, batch, and standard costing. All include, more or less, arbitrary overhead allocations.

Once we have found a figure for unit cost "in its present location and condition," the next difficulty will arise when we have to select an appropriate method for calculating the related cost where several identical items have been purchased or made at different times and therefore at different unit costs.

Consider the following transactions:

Purchases:	January	10 units at $25 each
	February	15 units at $30 each
	April	20 units at $35 each
Sales:	March	15 units at $50 each
	May	18 units at $60 each

How do we calculate inventory, cost of sales, and gross profit? There are several ways of doing this, based on different assumptions as to which unit has been sold, or which unit is deemed to have been sold. These are discussed in the next section.

INVENTORY COST ASSUMPTIONS

Five possible inventory cost assumptions are discussed below.

Unit Cost

Here we assume that we know the actual physical units that have moved in or out. Each unit must be individually distinguishable, for example, by serial numbers. In these circumstances, impractical in most cases, we simply add up the recorded costs of those units sold to give cost of sales and of those units left to give inventory. This needs no detailed illustration.

First-In, First-Out (FIFO)

With the FIFO method it is assumed that the units moving out are the ones that have been in the longest (i.e., came in first). The units remaining will therefore be regarded as representing the latest units purchased.

Illustration of FIFO Calculation

Calculate the cost of sales and gross profit based on FIFO inventory cost assumption from the data given above.

					Cost of Sales
January	10	at $25	=	$250	
February	15	at $30	=	450	
February total	25			700	
March	− 10	at $25 (Jan.)	=	250	
	− 5	at $30 (Feb.)	=	150	400

					Cost of Sales
March total		10 at $30	=	300	
April	+	20 at $35	=	700	
April total		30		1000	
May	−	10 at $30 (Feb.)	=	300	
	−	8 at $35 (Apr.)	=	280	580
May total		12 at $35		420	
					$980

Sales are 750 + 1080 = $1830
Purchases are 250 + 450 + 700 = $1400

This gives:	Sales		1830
	Purchases	1400	
	Closing inventory	420	
	Cost of sales		980
	Gross profit		$850

Last-In, First-Out (LIFO)

With the LIFO method, we reverse the assumption. We act as if the units moving out are the ones that came in most recently. The units remaining will therefore be regarded as representing the earliest units purchased.

Illustration of LIFO Calculation

Calculate the cost of sales and gross profit based on LIFO inventory cost assumption using the given data.

					Cost of Sales
January		10 at $25	=	$250	
February		15 at $30	=	450	
February total		25		700	
March	−	15 at $30 (Feb.)	=	450	450
March total		10	=	250	
April	+	20 at $35	=	700	
April total		30		950	
May	−	18 at $30 (Apr.)	=	630	630
		2 at $35 & 10 at $25		320	
					$1080

This gives:	Sales		1830
	Purchases	1400	
	Closing inventory	320	
	Cost of sales		1080
	Gross profit		$750

Weighted Average

With the weighted average method, we apply the average cost, weighted according to the different proportions at the different cost levels, to the items in inventory. The illustration below shows the fully worked out method, involving continuous calculations. In practice, an average cost of purchases figure is often used, particularly in manual systems, rather than an average cost of inventory figure. This approximation reduces the need for calculation to a periodic, maybe even annual, requirement.

Illustration of Weighted Average Calculation

Calculate the cost of sales and gross profit based on a weighted average inventory cost assumption.

					Cost of Sales
January		10 at $25	=	$250	
February		15 at $30	=	450	
February total		25 at $28*		700	
March	−	15 at $28	=	420	420
March total		10 at $28	=	280	
April	+	20 at $35	=	700	
April total		30 at $32*		980	
May	−	18 at $32	=	588	588
		12 at $32		392	
					$1008

*Working: $[(10 \times 25) + (15 \times 30)] / (10 + 15) = 28$

$[(10 \times 28) + (20 \times 35)] / (10 + 20) = 32$

This gives:	Sales		1830
	Purchases	1400	
	Closing inventory	392	
	Cost of sales		1008
	Gross profit		$822

Base Inventory

The base inventory approach is based on the argument that a certain minimum level of inventory is necessary in order to remain in business at all. Thus, it can be argued that some of the inventory, viewed in the aggregate, is not really available for sale and should therefore be regarded as a non-current asset. This minimum level, defined by management, remains at its original cost, and the remainder of the inventory above this level is treated, as inventory, by one of the other methods. In our example, the minimum level might be 10 units.

Illustration of Base Inventory Calculation

Calculate the cost of sales and gross profit based on a minimum inventory level of ten units and using FIFO.

January purchase of base inventory 10 at $25 = $250

					Cost of Sales
February		15 at $30	=	$450	
March	−	15 at $30	=	450	450
March total		0		0	
April	+	20 at $35	=	700	
April total		20	=	700	
May	−	18 at $35	=	630	630
May total		2 at $35	=	70	
					$1080
This gives:	Sales				1830
	Purchases			1150	
	Closing inventory			70	
	Cost of sales				1080
	Gross profit				$750

INVENTORY SYSTEMS

Periodic System

Inventory is determined by a physical count as of a specific date. As long as the count is made frequently enough for reporting purposes, it is not necessary to maintain extensive inventory records. The inventory shown in the balance sheet is determined by the physical count and is priced in accordance with the inventory method used. The net change between the beginning and ending inventories enters into the computation of the cost of goods sold.

Perpetual System

In a perpetual system, inventory records are maintained and updated continuously as items are purchased and sold. The system has the advantage of providing inventory information on a timely basis but requires the maintenance of a full set of inventory records. Theoretically, physical counts are not necessary, but they are normally taken to verify the inventory records. Audit practice will certainly require that a physical check of perpetual inventory records be made periodically.

There are no major differences of principle between IAS GAAP and U.S. GAAP. However, LIFO is significantly more widely used in the United States in practice than it is by enterprises following IAS GAAP.

IAS GAAP

IAS GAAP for this area are given in IAS 2, "Inventories." This standard was issued in 1993, effective January 1, 1995, and replaced the original standard issued in 1975. The scope of the standard is that it should be applied in financial statements prepared in the context of the historical cost system in accounting for inventories other than:

1. Work-in-progress arising under construction contracts, including directly related service contracts (see IAS 11, "Construction Contracts," discussed in Chapter 10);

2. Financial instruments (see Chapter 16);

3. Producers' inventories of agricultural and forest products, mineral ores, and agricultural produce to the extent that they are measured at net realizable value in accordance with well established practices in certain industries;

4. Biological assets related to agricultural activity (see IAS 41, "Agriculture," Chapter 32).

It is noteworthy that IAS 2 does not apply at all in the context of valuation bases other than historical cost.

In its "definitions" section, IAS 2 gives only two items, as follows (par. 4):

- *Inventories* are assets:
  (a) held for sale in the ordinary course of business,
  (b) in the process of production for such sale, or
  (c) in the form of materials or supplies to be consumed in the production process or in the rendering of services.

- *Net realizable value* is the estimated selling price in the ordinary course of business less the estimated costs of completion and the estimated costs necessary to make the sale.

In addition, costs of inventories, as already indicated, should comprise all costs of purchase, costs of conversion, and other costs incurred in bringing the inventories to their present location and condition.

The basic requirement of the entire standard is very simply stated (par. 6):

> Inventories should be measured at the lower of cost and net realizable value.

So, for each separate item, we need to determine both cost and net realizable value (NRV), as defined above.

The significance of the "separate items" point should be noted. Suppose there are three products, A, B, and C, with figures as shown in Table 23-1. The figure for inventory in the accounts is $30, not the lower of $33 and $36. This is, of course, a classic example of the prudence convention. It is also consistent with the requirements of IAS 18, "Revenue" (see Chapter 30).

Table 23-1: Lower Cost and NRV

Product	Cost	NRV	Lower
A	10	12	10
B	11	15	11
C	12	9	9
Total	33	36	30

COST OF INVENTORY

The costs of purchase of inventories comprise the purchase price, import duties and other taxes (if irrecoverable from the taxing authorities), and transport, handling, and other costs directly attributable to the acquisition of finished goods, materials, and services (par. 7). Trade discounts, rebates, and other similar items are deducted in determining the costs of purchase.

Although the matter is debatable from a theoretical perspective, a discount for prompt payment (which is not the same as a trade or volume discount) would probably be an "other similar item" in the context of the previous sentence.

IAS 2 permits foreign exchange differences to be included in the cost of inventory purchases in certain circumstances, as described as an allowed alternative treatment in IAS 21, "Accounting for the Effects of Changes in Foreign Exchange Rates" (see Chapter 17). Reference should also be made to SIC-11, "Foreign Exchange—Capitalization of Losses Resulting form Severe Currency Devaluations" (see Chapter 17). From a practical viewpoint, the required conditions would rarely be present.

The costs of conversion of inventory items are more problematic. They certainly include costs directly related to the units of production, such as direct labor. They also include a systematic allocation of fixed production overheads, such as depreciation, maintenance and administration of factory buildings and equipment, and of variable production overheads, that is, those indirect costs of production that vary directly, or nearly directly, with the volume of production, such as indirect materials and indirect labor.

> **OBSERVATION:** Although it does not say so in so many words, the standard makes it quite clear that direct or marginal costing methods, which treat overheads as a period cost related to time, rather than as a production cost related to units of product, are not permitted. The items stated above are *required* to be included, as "systematically allocated," in cost of conversion.

The allocation of variable production overheads is on the basis of the "actual use" of the production facilities, implying a machine-hour basis or some similar method. The allocation of fixed production overheads is explicitly required to be "based on the normal capacity of the production facilities." Normal capacity is the production expected to be achieved on average over a number of periods or seasons under normal circumstances, taking into account the loss of capacity resulting from planned maintenance. The actual level of production may be used if it approximates normal capacity. The standard thus makes it clear that normal capacity is to be a realistic expectation of practical outcomes, not an idealistic target or notional full capacity. Unallocated overheads arising as a result of production levels below normal capacity are treated as expenses of the period. In periods of abnormally high production, however, the amount of fixed overhead allocated to each unit of production is decreased so that inventories are not measured above cost.

An additional problem is the treatment of a production process that involves several products. Joint products occur when the production of one product necessarily results in the production of one or more other products. By-products are joint products of low or insignificant value. By-products are by definition immaterial. The standard suggests but does not seem to explicitly require (par. 12), that the net realizable value of by-products (which is obviously small) is deducted from the cost of the main product or products.

With other joint products, where both or all are significant, the costs of conversion of the production process as a whole need to be allocated between the products on a "rational and consistent" basis. The relative sales value of each product is suggested as an appropriate proportional allocation by the standard. Allocation according to gross contribution margin would be a sensible alternative. Once the products reach a stage in the production process where the conversion activities become separately identifiable, then individual allocation is required.

Any costs not covered by the above discussions are to be excluded from inventory costs, unless they are demonstrably incurred in bringing the inventories to their present location and condition. The distinction can sometimes be a fine one. For example, if wine is aged in the barrel prior to bottling, the cost of storing in the barrel is a cost of production. The later cost of storing the finished bottle is not. This still leaves open the issue of aging in the bottle, which in logic is a cost of production until the wine becomes finally "finished." It is explicitly stated that abnormal amounts of wasted materials, labor, or other production costs are to be treated as expenses, not as cost of inventory (thereby confirming that *normal* amounts of such wastages *are* cost of inventory and not expense). Borrowing costs may be included as cost of inventory in limited circumstances as defined in IAS 23, "Capitalization of Borrowing Costs" (see Chapter 5). Selling costs are never part of cost of inventory.

If the industry under consideration is a service provider rather than a product manufacturer, wholesaler, or retailer, then the same principles discussed above should be applied. In the case of a service provider, costs of inventories include the costs of the service (par. 16), that is, the labor and other costs of personnel directly engaged in providing the service, including supervisory personnel and attributable overheads for which the enterprise has not yet recognized the related revenue in accordance with IAS 18, "Revenue " (see Chapter 30). Broadly speaking, IAS 18 requires the recognition of revenue on a percentage-of-completion basis. Therefore the cost of services not yet recognized, that is, the "inventory" to be included in the closing balance sheet, is not likely to be large.

In the case of agricultural produce harvested from biological assets, the implications of IAS 41, "Agriculture" (see Chapter 32), must be considered. Under IAS 41, inventories comprising agricultural produce that an enterprise has harvested from its biological assets are measured on their initial recognition at their fair value less estimated point-of-sale costs at the point of harvest. It therefore follows that this "net fair value" figure is deemed "cost" of such agricultural produce inventories for the purposes of applying IAS 2.

IAS 2 recognizes that, in practice, cost may be measured by convenience methods such as standard costs, which take into account normal levels of activity and are reviewed regularly and kept up to date, or the retail method. This latter is often used in the retail industry for measuring inventories of large numbers of rapidly changing items that have similar margins and for which it is impracticable to use other costing methods. The cost of the inventory is determined by reducing the sales value of the inventory by the appropriate percentage gross margin. The percentage used takes into consideration inventory that has been marked down to below its original selling price. An average percentage for each retail department is often used.

> ☛ **PRACTICE POINTER:** Readers who work in commerce or industry will be well aware that the detailed discussion above about the calculation of cost of inventory masks some difficult, narrow, and often subjective decisions. The definition and calculation of normal capacity are crucial. What do we include in factory administration? There is no way in which such issues can be resolved in a uniform manner across industries or across national jurisdictions and differing local employment and production methods.
>
> What can be required, however, is consistency of policy and practice over time. It is necessary to be clear about the effect on reported annual earnings of changes in balance sheet inventory valuation. An "error" (i.e., a difference) of one dollar in closing inventory, everything else held constant, means a difference of one dollar in reported earnings. However, a difference of one dollar in opening inventory coupled with a difference of one dollar in the same direction in closing inventory means a difference of nil in reported earnings. For many practical purposes, consistency is quite enough.

FORMULAS FOR UNIT COST DETERMINATION

IAS 2 requires (not permits) the use of the unit cost method, as described earlier in this chapter, in certain circumstances. More formally, the inventory costs of items that are not ordinarily interchangeable and of goods or services produced and segregated for specific projects should be assigned by using specific identification of their individual costs (par. 19).

> ☛ **PRACTICE POINTER:** The above wording clearly indicates that a customized job lot, being by definition not interchangeable with other job lots, should be separately costed. However, it does not imply that identical items that are distinguishable, for example, by individual registration numbers, should be costed separately from each other. The criterion is interchangeability, not distinguishability.

In the majority of situations, individual noninterchangeability will not apply, so one of the more-or-less arbitrary cost formulas will need to be used. This is one of those situations where the IASC divides the allowed possibilities into two classes: the benchmark and the allowed alternative. The IASC explains the significance of the word *benchmark* as follows. The original proposal was to use the word *preferred*, but "the term 'benchmark' more closely reflects the Board's intention of identifying a point of reference when making its choice between alternatives." This sentence is remarkably opaque. We interpret it as suggesting that *benchmark* is not quite as strong as *preferred*. "Allowed alternatives" are fully acceptable under IAS GAAP, but it is likely that only a minority of the board wished to allow them.

The benchmark treatment for the cost of inventories where specific identification is not applicable is "by using the first-in, first-out (FIFO) or weighted average cost formulas." The allowed alternative treatment is "by using the last-in, first-out (LIFO) formula." No specific requirements are imposed on detailed calculations within the generalized formulas (pars. 21–24).

> **OBSERVATION:** No rationale is attempted as to the perceived pros and cons of these methods or of the two-level classification between benchmark and allowed alternative. If one takes the view that "old" historical costs are less relevant than "newer" historical costs, then it can be argued that LIFO is "better" for income calculation (as it tends to use "newer" cost figures as expenses) and FIFO is "better" for balance sheet purposes (as it tends to leave "newer" cost figures in closing inventory).
>
> None of this logical type argument appears to have influenced the final outcome of the board's debates as now enshrined in the standard. The majority of board members wished to delete LIFO, but several members wished to retain it and were able to block its deletion. LIFO is quite common in some countries, for example, Germany and the United States, though it is explicitly not normally acceptable under, for example, U.K. or French GAAP.

SIC-1, "Consistency—Different Cost Formulas for Inventories," states that a firm may use different cost formulas for different classes of inventory that have different characteristics regarding nature or use but must use the same formula within each "class." The method used for a class must be used throughout the worldwide operations of the enterprise and consistently over time.

NET REALIZABLE VALUE

Net realizable value is perhaps easier to define theoretically than cost but obviously contains elements of subjectivity in practice. As already illustrated, net realizable value must be calculated, and the "lower of cost and net realizable value" rule must be applied, on an item-by-item basis (pars. 25–30). Grouping of items is allowed only if they are "similar or related." This is interpreted restrictively to, for example, items from the same product line that have similar purposes or end uses, are produced and marketed in the same geographic area, and cannot be practicably evaluated separately from other items in that product line. It is not appropriate to write inventories down on the basis of a classification of inventory, for example, finished goods, or all the inventories in a particular industry or geographic segment. Service providers generally accumulate costs in respect of each service for which a separate selling price will be charged. Therefore, each such service is treated as a separate item.

Estimates of net realizable value should reflect the conditions existing at the balance sheet date. These estimates take into consideration fluctuations of price or cost directly relating to events occurring after the end of the period only to the extent that such events confirm conditions existing at the end of the period. Estimates of net realizable value also take into consideration the purpose for which the inventory is held. Raw materials are written down below cost only if it is expected that the resulting finished product itself will have a net realizable value less than its costs.

IAS 2 requires that when the circumstances that previously caused inventories to be written down below cost no longer exist, the amount of the write-down is reversed so that the new carrying amount is the lower of the cost and the revised net realizable value. In certain cases such as with commodities subject to significant market price changes, this requirement could, of course, lead to large swings in operating results due to unrealized gains and losses. However, this is arguably acceptable and even desirable if you take the view that management should be called to account for its success, or failure, in predicting price movements in those commodities in which it deals.

EXPENSE RECOGNITION

It is important, amidst all this welter of detail, not to lose sight of the simple central requirements of IAS 2, namely, that inventories should be measured at the lower of cost and net realizable value. When inventories are sold, the carrying amount of those inventories should be recognized as an expense in the period in which the related revenue is recognized (par. 31). The amount of any write-down of inventories to net realizable value, and of other losses of inventories, should be recognized as an expense in the period in which the write-down or loss occurs. The amount of any reversal of any write-down of inventories, arising from an increase in net realizable value, should be recognized as a reduction in the expense charge for inventories in the period in which the reversal occurs.

DISCLOSURE

The basic disclosure requirements are that the financial statements should disclose (pars. 34–36):

1. The accounting policies adopted in measuring inventories, including the cost formula used;
2. The total carrying amount of inventories and the carrying amount in classifications appropriate to the enterprise;
3. The carrying amount of inventories at net realizable value;
4. The amount of any reversal of any write-down that is recognized as income in the period;
5. The circumstances or events that led to the reversal of a write-down of inventories; and
6. The carrying amount of inventories pledged as security for liabilities.

The financial statements should disclose either:

1. The cost of inventories recognized as an expense during the period; or
2. The operating costs, applicable to revenues, recognized as an expense during the period, classified by their nature.

There is an additional requirement where the allowed alternative of LIFO is used. In this situation, the financial statements should disclose the difference between the amount of inventories as shown in the balance sheet and either:

1. The lower of the amount arrived at if FIFO or weighted average had been used and net realizable value, or
2. The lower of current cost at the balance sheet date and net realizable value.

This requirement seems to add weight to the suggestion that LIFO is accepted reluctantly within the standard.

CHAPTER 24
INVESTMENT PROPERTY

CONTENTS

OVERVIEW

Investment property is real estate (land or buildings) that is held to earn rentals, or for capital appreciation, i.e., it is held as an investment rather than for consumption or use. The treatment of investment properties in financial statements has been varied and controversial in recent years, and the debates are not yet over.

The IASC issued an exposure draft on investment properties, E64, in July 1999. This proposed a mandatory fair value model for investment properties. However, in the resulting debate, IAS was forced to backtrack, and the standard, IAS 40, gives a choice.

Investment property, as defined below, can be treated in either of two ways. The Board has agreed that the standard should permit enterprises to choose between a fair value model and a cost model. The fair value model is the model proposed in E64; investment property should be measured at fair value, and changes in fair value should be recognized in the income statement.

The cost model is the benchmark treatment in IAS 16, "Property, Plant, and Equipment"; investment property should be measured at depreciated cost (less any accumulated impairment losses). An enterprise that chooses the cost model should additionally disclose the fair value of its investment property in the notes to the financial statements.

IAS 40, "Investment Property," was issued in April 2000, effective for financial statements covering periods beginning on or after January 1, 2001. Before that date, IAS 25, "Accounting for Investments," applied (see Chapter 4). IAS 40 withdraws IAS 25.

BACKGROUND

The classic perception of a non-current asset is that of a long-term resource that is necessary to support the day-to-day operational activities of a business. It is used in production or administration, but is not itself sold. It gradually wears out, as its use-value, or service po-tential, is consumed, in recognition of which depreciation is charged in the annual profit calculation. The classic perception of an investment is that of an asset held so that the asset itself will earn positive returns, either through regular inflows such as interest, dividend, or rent or through capital appreciation. With an investment, the key issue is impairment, rather than consumption of use-value or service potential.

The specific problem with properties is that they can be held for either purpose or for both purposes at different times. Because of a general tendency, over the long term, for property prices to rise significantly in nominal terms, the distinction in practice is often particularly significant.

Until at least the 1970s, property held as an investment was generally treated for accounting purposes like any other property, with or without the possibility of revaluation and with or without the possibility of nondepreciation, depending on the jurisdiction. This approach began to be challenged, notably in the United Kingdom. It was argued that if a property is held as an investment, then:

1. The matching convention is arguably not relevant, as no service potential is being used up;
2. The current values of such investments, and any change therein, are of prime importance and relevance.

IAS 25, "Accounting for Investments," effective from January 1, 1987, was constructed to allow, but not to require, the treatment of an investment property as a long-term investment under IAS 25, rather than as property under IAS 16, "Property, Plant, and Equipment" (see Chapters 4 and 27, respectively). Even under IAS 25, such a property could be carried at either cost or revalued amount. Thus, there was a great deal of choice involved.

The proposals of E64 were designed to regularize this situation. E64 proposed a single required treatment for investment properties as defined, namely, measurement at fair value. As indicated in the overview to this chapter, the Board has been forced to backtrack from this position. Its long-term intentions were clear, as the Board's Introduction to IAS 40 indicates. We quote the relevant paragraphs in full so that readers can appreciate the nuances for themselves.

> This is the first time that the Board has introduced a fair value accounting model for non-financial assets. The comment letters on Exposure Draft E64 showed that although many support this step, many others still have significant conceptual and practical reservations about extending a fair value model to non-financial assets. Also, some believe that certain property markets are not yet sufficiently mature for a fair value model to work satisfactorily. Furthermore, some believe that it is impossible to create a rigorous definition of investment property and that this makes it impracticable to require a fair value model at present.

> For those reasons, the Board believes that it is impracticable, at this stage, to require a fair value model for investment property. At the same time, the Board believes that it is desirable to permit a fair value model. This evolutionary step forward will allow preparers and users to gain greater experience working with a fair value model and will allow time for certain property markets to achieve greater maturity.

> The Standard requires that an enterprise should apply the model chosen to all its investment property. A change from one model to the other model should be made only if the change will result in a more appropriate presentation. The Standard states that this is highly unlikely to be the case for a change from the fair value model to the cost model.

> In exceptional cases, there is clear evidence when an enterprise first acquires an investment property (or when an existing property first becomes investment property following the completion of construction or development, or after a change in use) that the enterprise will not be able to determine the fair value of the investment property reliably on a continuing basis. In such cases, the Standard requires an enterprise to measure that investment property using the benchmark treatment in IAS 16 until the disposal of the investment property. The residual value of the investment property should be assumed to be zero. An enterprise that has chosen the fair value model measures all its other investment property at fair value.

U.S. GAAP, as currently constituted (ARB-43, APB-6), require that investment properties be treated the same way as any other properties and are, therefore, squarely inconsistent with the original E64 proposals.

SCOPE

IAS 40 applies to all investment property. This includes investment properties held under a finance lease, in the books of the lessee, and those leased out under an operating lease, in the books of the lessor. IAS 40 does not apply to:

1. Forests and similar regenerative natural resources; or
2. Mineral rights, the exploration for and extraction of minerals, oil, natural gas, and similar non-regenerative resources.

DEFINITIONS

IAS 40 gives the following definitions, several of them familiar from other standards.

- *Investment property* is property (land or a building or part of a building—or both) held (by the owner or by the lessee under a finance lease) to earn rentals or for capital appreciation or both, rather than for:

  —use in the production or supply of goods or services or for administrative purposes, or

  —sale in the ordinary course of business.
- *Owner-occupied property* is property held (by the owner or by the lessee under a finance lease) for use in the production or supply of goods or services or for administrative purposes.
- *Fair value* is the amount for which an asset could be exchanged between knowledgeable, willing parties in an arm's-length transaction.
- *Cost* is the amount of cash or cash equivalents paid or the fair value of other consideration given to acquire an asset at the time of its acquisition or construction.
- *Carrying amount* is the amount at which an asset is recognized in the balance sheet.

It follows from the definition of investment property that an investment property will generate cash flows "largely independently" of other assets held by an enterprise. It is this which distinguishes investment property from owner-occupied property, as owner-occupied property only generates cash flows in conjunction with other operating assets necessary for the production or supply process. Examples of investment property include:

- Land held for long-term capital appreciation rather than for short-term sale in the ordinary course of business;
- Land held for a currently undetermined future use;
- A building owned by the reporting enterprise (or held by the reporting enterprise under a finance lease) and leased out under one or more operating leases; or
- A building that is vacant but is held to be leased out under one or more operating leases.

The following are examples of items that do not meet the IAS definition of investment property.

- Property held for sale in the ordinary course of business (see IAS 2, "Inventories," discussed in Chapter 23), for example, property held for trading by property traders or for development and resale by property developers;
- Property being constructed for third parties (see IAS 11, "Construction Contracts," discussed in Chapter 10);
- Owner-occupied property (see IAS 16, "Property, Plant, and Equipment," discussed in Chapter 27);
- Intangible assets associated with investment property, such as air rights and water rights (see IAS 38, "Intangible Assets," discussed in Chapter 21);
- Property that is being constructed or developed for future use as investment property.

> **OBSERVATION:** In marginal cases, judgment will be needed in distinguishing investment properties from owner-occupied properties. For example, an owner-managed hotel is essentially concerned with the provision of services to guests, so it is not an investment property. However, the owner of a building which is managed as a hotel by a third party, is in the position of holding an investment, with "largely independent" cash flows arising, hence creating an investment property. In complex intermediate situations, the substance of the situation, and the balance of emphasis, should be followed. Disclosure of the criteria used is required when classification is difficult.

An investment property within the definition should be recognized as an asset when, and only when:

1. It is probable that the future economic benefits that are attributable to the investment property will flow to the enterprise, and
2. The cost or fair value of the investment property can be measured reliably.

It seems difficult to envisage circumstances in which requirement 2 above would not be met. A government grant in kind, of an asset that has no active market, would be one such circumstance.

MEASUREMENT

The initial measurement is fairly straightforward. Under IAS 40, an investment property should be measured initially at its cost, which is the fair value of the consideration given for it. Transaction costs are included in the initial measurement. The cost of a purchased investment property comprises its purchase price and any directly attributable expenditure. Directly attributable expenditure includes, for example, professional fees for legal services and property transfer taxes.

When an investment property has already been recognized, subsequent expenditure on that investment property should be recognized as an expense when it is incurred unless:

1. It is probable that this expenditure will enable the asset to generate future economic benefits in excess of its originally assessed standard of performance, and

2. This expenditure can be measured and attributed to the asset reliably.

If these conditions are met, the subsequent expenditure should be added to the carrying amount of the investment property.

The question of measurement subsequent to the initial measurement is more complicated. As already outlined, two models are available: the fair value model and the cost model. An enterprise has a choice between these two models under IAS, and should apply the chosen model to all of its investment property.

> **OBSERVATION:** Although the choice given in IAS 40 between these two models is a free one, and there is no stated "benchmark" treatment, it is very clear that the preference indicated in E64 for a fair value model remains. Fair value has to be determined in *all* cases—for measurement in the financial statements if the fair value model is used, and for disclosure in the notes if the cost model is used. The standard notes that IAS 8, "Net Profit or Loss for the Period, Fundamental Errors and Changes in Accounting Policies," states that a voluntary change in accounting policy should be made only if the change will result in a more appropriate presentation of events or transactions in the financial statements of the enterprise. The standard explicitly states that it is highly unlikely that a change from the fair value model to the cost model will result in a more appropriate presentation.

Measurement Under the Fair Value Model

There is a rebuttable presumption that an enterprise will be able to determine the fair value of an investment property reliably on a continuing basis. After initial recognition, an enterprise that chooses the fair value model should measure all of its investment property at its fair value, unless this presumption is not valid.

A gain or loss arising from a change in the fair value of investment property should be included in net profit or loss for the period in which it arises. The standard makes it absolutely explicit that changes in fair value are to be taken directly to earnings, and not taken to or from reserves.

IAS 40 discusses the practicalities of measuring fair value at some length, dissecting the implications of "knowledgeable, willing parties," and "arm's length" in its definition. Much of this discussion is common sense. Note that the fair value figure used in a balance sheet should reflect the actual market state and circumstances as of the balance sheet date, not as of either a past or a future date. It follows, for example, that the cost of any anticipated future capital expenditure that will enhance the property, and any related expected increase in benefits, are both omitted from the estimation of fair value at the current date.

The best evidence of fair value is normally given by current prices on an active market for similar property in the same location and condition and subject to similar lease and other contracts. In the absence of current prices on an active market, an enterprise considers information from a variety of sources, including:

- Current prices on an active market for properties of different nature, condition or location (or subject to different lease or other contracts), adjusted to reflect those differences;

- Recent prices on less active markets, with adjustments to reflect any changes in economic conditions since the date of the transactions that occurred at those prices; and

- Discounted cash flow projections based on reliable estimates of future cash flows, supported by the terms of any existing lease and other contracts and by any external evidence such as current market rents for similar properties in the same location and condition, and using discount rates that reflect current market assessments of the uncertainty in the amount and timing of the cash flows.

IAS 40 recognizes that, in exceptional cases, an enterprise may not be able to determine the fair value of an investment property reliably on a continuing basis. This arises when, and only when, comparable market transactions are infrequent and alternative estimates of fair value (for example, based on discounted cash flow projections) are not available. In such cases, an enterprise should measure that investment property using the benchmark treatment in IAS 16, "Property, Plant, and Equipment" (see Chapter 27). The residual value of the investment property should be assumed to be zero. The enterprise should continue to apply IAS 16 until the disposal of the investment property. In such circumstances, the enterprise measures all its other investment properties at fair value. Once an enterprise has begun measuring an investment property at fair value, it should continue to do so, even if the measurements subsequently become less reliable.

> **OBSERVATION:** IASC, and indeed world accounting thought generally, is moving toward a greater support for the fair value concept, but not yet on a systematic basis. As the most recent IASC Standard, IAS 40 took the thinking a little further by discussing the concept, and we can usefully do the same. Fair value is an actual market price, theoretically identical for buyer and seller. It therefore differs from, and will in practice be greater than, net realizable value, which is net of realization expenses. It also differs from value in use, as defined in IAS 36, "Impairment of Assets" (see Chapter 19). Fair value reflects knowledge and estimates of participants in the market, as well as factors that are relevant to market participants in general. In contrast, value in use reflects the enterprise's knowledge and estimates, as well as entity-specific factors that may be specific to the enterprise and that are not applicable to enterprises in general. For example, fair value does not reflect any:
>
> * additional value derived from the creation of a portfolio of properties in different locations,
> * synergies between investment property and other assets,
> * legal rights or legal restrictions that are specific only to the current owner, or
> * tax benefits or tax burdens that are specific to the current owner.
>
> It follows from the above that fair value is also not the same as recoverable amount, which is the higher of net realizable value and value in use (see Chapter 27).

Measurement Using the Cost Model

After initial recognition, an enterprise that chooses the cost model should measure all of its investment property using the benchmark treatment in IAS 16, "Property, Plant, and Equipment," that is, at cost less any accumulated depreciation and any accumulated impairment losses. In other words, if choosing the cost model, an enterprise proceeds, in measurement (but not disclosure) terms to follow IAS 16 (see Chapter 27), as if IAS 40 did not exist.

TRANSFERS

According to IAS 40, transfers to or from investment property should be made when, and only when, there is a change in use, evidenced by:

- Commencement of owner-occupation, for a transfer from investment property to owner-occupied property,
- Commencement of development with a view to sale, for a transfer from investment property to inventories,
- End of owner-occupation, for a transfer from owner-occupied property to investment property,
- Commencement of an operating lease to another party, for a transfer from inventories to investment property,
- End of construction or development, for a transfer from property in the course of construction or development (covered by IAS 16, "Property, Plant, and Equipment," see Chapter 27) to investment property.

The wording indicates that this list is intended to be exhaustive.

☛ **PRACTICE POINTER:** When the cost model is being used for investment properties, transfers between investment property, owner-occupied property and inventories do not change the carrying amount of the property transferred and they do not change the cost of that property for measurement or disclosure purposes. The standard does not remind us, but we should note, that the fair value of investment properties measured under the cost model has to be disclosed in the notes, a requirement that does not extend to owner-occupied property or to inventory.

A transfer to or from investment properties which are being carried at fair value obviously has potentially very significant effects on the measurement process and the carrying amount of an asset.

If an investment property carried at fair value becomes an owner-occupied property, or is transferred to inventory, then the property's cost for subsequent accounting purposes is its fair value as at the date of the change in use. It will subsequently be dealt with under IAS 16, "Property, Plant, and Equipment" (see Chapter 27), or IAS 2, "Inventories" (see Chapter 23), as appropriate.

If an owner-occupied property becomes an investment property carried at fair value, then IAS 16 should be applied up to the date of the change of use, i.e., the enterprise continues to depreciate the property and to recognize any impairment losses. A difference between the carrying amount of the asset under IAS 16 at the date of the change of use, and the fair value at that date, is dealt with in the same way as a revaluation under IAS 16. This means that:

1. Any resulting decrease in the carrying amount of the property is recognized in net profit or loss for the period. However, to the extent that an amount is included in revaluation surplus in respect of that property, the decrease is charged against that amount of revaluation surplus; and

2. Any resulting increase in the carrying amount is treated as follows:

   (a) To the extent that the increase reverses a previous impairment loss for that property, the increase is recognized in net profit or loss for the period. The amount recognized in net profit or loss for the period does not exceed the amount needed to restore the carrying amount to the carrying amount that would have been determined (net of depreciation) had no impairment loss been recognized; and

   (b) Any remaining part of the increase is credited directly to equity under the heading of revaluation surplus. On subsequent disposal of the investment property, the revaluation surplus included in equity may be transferred to retained earnings. The transfer from revaluation surplus to retained earnings is not made through the income statement.

If a property classed as inventory is transferred to become an investment property carried at fair value, then the treatment is consistent with that of a sale of inventory under IAS 2. A difference between the fair value of the property at that date and its previous carrying amount is therefore part of net profit or loss for the period. Similarly, a self-constructed investment property that will be carried at fair value will give rise, on completion, to an effect on reported net profit or loss for the period equal to the difference between the fair value on the completion date and its previous (cost-based) carrying amount.

> **OBSERVATION:** Many readers may be struck by the apparent lack of prudence, and of strict adherence to the realization principle, inherent in the previous paragraph. However, this is the whole point of the fair value concept. There is, by definition,

reliable evidence to determine fair value, which is a market-based concept, and therefore it follows logically, and consistently with a true sale, that a gain relating to operating processes has been "made." Anybody who regards only a completed transaction as providing adequate evidence for fair value, should reject the whole notion of fair value accounting, not just a small aspect of the standard.

DISPOSALS

An investment property should be eliminated from the balance sheet (derecognized) on disposal. The disposal of an investment property may occur by sale or by entering into a finance lease. In determining the date of disposal for investment property, an enterprise applies the criteria in IAS 18, "Revenue" (see Chapter 30), for recognizing revenue from the sale of goods. IAS 17, "Leases" (see Chapter 25), applies on a disposal by entering into a finance lease or by a sale and lease-back. An investment property must also be derecognized when it is permanently withdrawn from use and no further economic benefits are expected from its disposal. Gains or losses arising on derecognition, i.e., the difference between the net disposal proceeds and the carrying amount, are recognized as income or expense in the income statement, unless IAS 17, "Leases," requires otherwise in the case of a sale and leaseback. This is, of course, consistent with the treatment of annual changes in fair value of a retained investment property.

If payment for an investment property is deferred, the consideration received is recognized initially at the cash price equivalent. The difference between the nominal amount of the consideration and the cash price equivalent is recognized as interest revenue on a time proportion basis under IAS 18, "Revenues" (see Chapter 30).

> **OBSERVATION:** If an investment property is disposed of by means of a finance lease, then there is likely to be a freehold reversion at the end of the lease period. In other words, the property is disposed of now, but may return to the possession and ownership of the disposing party at a known date in the future. This logically means that:
>
> (a) A tangible asset will (re)-appear eventually;
>
> (b) The right to receive (or re-receive) that tangible asset in the future represents an identifiable intangible asset now.
>
> It would seem that the intangible asset referred to in item b above would fall within the scope of IAS 38 (see Chapter 21). This would eventually be replaced by the tangible asset (as in item a above) to which IAS 40 or IAS 16 would apply, as

appropriate to its usage at that time. Under IAS 17, "Leases" (see Chapter 25), the lessor enterprise is supposed to include "any unguaranted residual value" in its receivable.

DISCLOSURE

The IAS 40 disclosure requirements are extensive and, as usual, incapable of effective summary. The requirements can usefully be considered under three headings, beginning with those requirements which apply in all cases, i.e., for both the fair value and the cost value models.

Certain requirements of IAS 17, "Leases" (see Chapter 25), may be relevant. Under IAS 17, the owner of an investment property gives a lessor's disclosures about operating leases. An enterprise that holds an investment property under a finance lease gives a lessee's disclosure about that finance lease and a lessor's disclosure about any operating leases that the enterprise has granted.

Disclosure requirements specified in all cases under IAS 40 are as follows:

- When classification is difficult, the criteria developed by the enterprise to distinguish investment property from owner-occupied property and from property held for sale in the ordinary course of business.

- The methods and significant assumptions applied in determining the fair value of investment property, including a statement whether the determination of fair value was supported by market evidence or was more heavily based on other factors (which the enterprise should disclose) because of the nature of the property and lack of comparable market data.

- The extent to which the fair value of investment property (as measured or disclosed in the financial statements) is based on a valuation by an independent valuer who holds a recognized and relevant professional qualification and who has recent experience in the location and category of the investment property being valued. If there has been no such valuation, that fact should be disclosed.

- The amounts included in the income statement for:

  —Rental income from investment property;

  —Direct operating expenses (including repairs and maintenance) arising from investment property that generated rental income during the period; and

—Direct operating expenses (including repairs and maintenance) arising from investment property that did not generate rental income during the period.

• The existence and amounts of restrictions on the realizability of investment property or the remittance of income and proceeds of disposal.

• Material contractual obligations to purchase, construct or develop investment property or for repairs, maintenance, or enhancements.

Additional disclosures required when the fair value model is used are that an enterprise should disclose a reconciliation of the carrying amount of investment property at the beginning and end of the period showing the following (comparative information is not required):

• Additions, disclosing separately those additions resulting from acquisitions and those resulting from capitalized subsequent expenditure;

• Additions resulting from acquisitions through business combinations;

• Disposal;

• Net gains or losses from fair value adjustments;

• The net exchange differences arising on the translation of the financial statements of a foreign entity;

• Transfers to and from inventories and owner-occupied property; and

• Other movements.

In the exceptional cases when an enterprise measures investment property using the benchmark treatment in IAS 16, "Property, Plant, and Equipment" (because of the lack of a reliable fair value), the reconciliation required by the previous paragraph should disclose amounts relating to that investment property separately from amounts relating to other investment property. In addition, an enterprise should disclose:

• A description of the investment property;

• An explanation of why fair value cannot be reliably measured;

• If possible, the range of estimates within which fair value is highly likely to lie;

- On disposal of investment property not carried at fair value:

  —The fact that the enterprise has disposed of investment property not carried at fair value,

  —The carrying amount of that investment property at the time of sale,

  —The amount of gain or loss recognized.

Additional disclosures are also required when the cost model is used. In this situation, an enterprise should also disclose:

- The depreciation methods used;

- The useful lives or the depreciation rates used;

- The gross carrying amount and the accumulated depreciation (aggregated with accumulated impairment losses) at the beginning and end of the period;

- A reconciliation of the carrying amount of investment property at the beginning and end of the period showing the following (comparative information is not required):

  —Additions, disclosing separately those additions resulting from acquisitions and those resulting from capitalized subsequent expenditure,

  —Additions resulting from acquisitions through business combinations,

  —Disposals,

  —Depreciation,

  —The amount of impairment losses recognized, and the amount of impairment losses reversed, during the period under IAS 36, "Impairment of Assets,"

  —The net exchange differences arising on the translation of the financial statements of a foreign entity,

  —Transfers to and from inventories and owner-occupied property,

  —Other movements.

- The fair value of investment property. In the exceptional cases when an enterprise cannot determine the fair value of the investment property reliably, the enterprise should disclose:

—A description of the investment property,

—An explanation of why fair value cannot be determined reliably,

—If possible, the range of estimates within which fair value is highly likely to lie.

TRANSITIONAL PROVISIONS

An enterprise adopting IAS 40 for the first time is changing an accounting policy. Normally when a change in accounting policy occurs, IAS 8, "Net Profit or Loss for the Period, Fundamental Errors, and Changes in Accounting Policies," applies (see Chapter 26). IAS 8 requires comparative information to be restated (benchmark treatment) or additional pro forma comparative information on a restated basis to be disclosed (allowed alternative treatment) unless it is impracticable to do so. IAS 40 confirms that if the reporting enterprise has chosen the cost model for investment properties, then IAS 8 should be applied.

However, if the fair value model is being used, then IAS 40 requires a different treatment, which does not require restatement of comparative information. In full, the details are specified as follows.

Under the fair value model, an enterprise should report the effect of adopting the standard on its effective date (or earlier) as an adjustment to the opening balance of retained earnings for the period in which the standard is first adopted. In addition:

- If the enterprise has previously disclosed publicly (in financial statements or otherwise) the fair value of its investment property in earlier periods (determined on a basis that satisfies the definition of fair value and the guidance in the standard), the enterprise is encouraged, but not required, to

  —Adjust the opening balance of retained earnings for the earliest period presented for which such fair value was disclosed publicly, and

  —Restate comparative information for those periods.

- If the enterprise has not previously disclosed publicly the information described above, the enterprise should not restate comparative information and should disclose that fact.

DECISION TREE

The following decision tree, reproduced from the appendix to IAS 40, provides a useful summary of the process of deciding on the appropriate IAS treatment of a property.

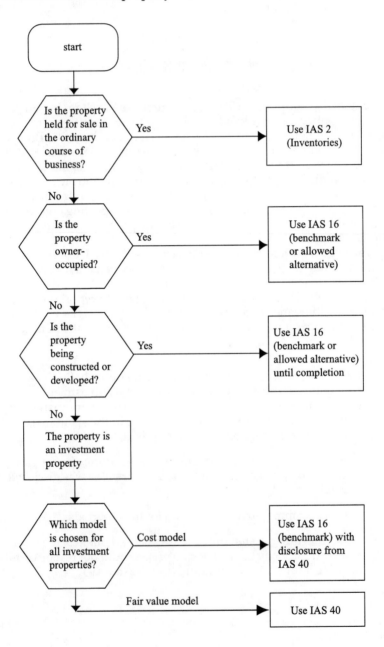

Note: In exceptional cases under the fair value model, evidence may indicate clearly that the enterprise will not be able to determine the fair value of the property reliably on a continuing basis. An enterprise measures the property using the benchmark treatment in IAS 16, and measures all its other investment properties at fair value.

> **OBSERVATION:** It seems clear to us that the failure by the IASC board to agree to the single fair value method proposed in E64 represents something of a setback to IASC, at least in the short term. The final outcome, allowing choice, is hardly consistent with the desire for harmonization, and perhaps uniformity, discussed in our introductory chapter. It may not be a coincidence that this outcome allows the United Kingdom, which requires fair value with no choice, and the United States, which requires cost with no choice, to carry on broadly as they had been before.
>
> However, there are wider issues involved. This situation could be regarded as a microcosm of the broader debate about the desirability of cost versus fair value as the basis for measuring assets and liabilities. This broader debate is, in turn, only an adjunct of the even more fundamental issues of for what and for whom financial reporting is actually intended. The debates will continue.

CHAPTER 25
LEASES

CONTENTS

OVERVIEW

A lease is an agreement that conveys to one party (the lessee) the right to use property but does not convey legal ownership of that property. It follows that if an asset is defined as something that is legally owned (i.e., that has been acquired in an exchange transaction), then leases will not give rise to an asset in the financial statements of the lessee. It also follows that if nothing has been "acquired," then nothing is unpaid for, that is, the lease agreement will also not give rise to a liability in the financial statements of the lessee.

If, however, the lease agreement allows the lessee to use the property for all or most of its useful life, requires the lessee to pay total amounts close to and possibly greater than the normal buying price of the item, and requires or assumes that the lessee will look after the item as if the item belonged to it (e.g., insurance, repairs, and maintenance), then it is clear that in substance the lessee would be in the same position, both economically and in terms of production and operating capacity, *as if* the lessee actually owned the asset. Furthermore, a contractual requirement to make future payments greater than the net cost of a straightforward purchase of the item means that the lessee is in the same position *as if* it had taken out a loan under agreed regular repayment terms and at an agreed rate of interest. Thus, in such circumstances, the economic substance of the situation is that the lessee has an asset and a liability, although the legal form of the agreement makes it quite clear that the legal ownership of the item remains with the other party (the lessor).

The general principle of substance over form discussed in Chapter 2 requires that, in such circumstances, the lessee *does* record an asset and a liability in its balance sheet, and the lessor also records a sale and an account receivable in its financial statements.

In broad terms, the whole issue of accounting for leases can be summarized quite simply. If a lease agreement essentially gives the parties rights and obligations similar to those arising from a legal purchase, then the accounting proceeds as if it *were* a legal purchase. This gives rise to a fixed asset and an obligation. If, on the other hand, a lease agreement is, in the context of the particular characteristics of the object in question, essentially a short-term rental, then the accounting treats it as such, giving rise in the books of the lessee to a simple expense, normally allocated on a time basis.

Unfortunately, this simple division masks a considerable amount of practical difficulty. There are problems involved in creating a clear demarcation line between the two situations, and a number of particular issues and problems have arisen over the years that IASC and various national standards have tried to tackle.

The main GAAP for accounting for leases is in IAS 17. This was originally issued in 1982, as "Accounting for Leases," but was replaced by a new standard, "Leases," agreed to in 1997 and standard from January 1, 1999, but still referred to as IAS 17. A more fundamental reconsideration of the standard is ongoing, but no time schedule has emerged.

SIC 15, "Incentives in an Operating Lease," is also relevant.

BACKGROUND

A lease agreement that puts the parties to the lease (the lessee and the lessor) into a relationship that is, in substance, that of buyer and borrower (the lessee) and of seller and lender (the lessor) is known as a finance lease. The accounting treatment of finance leases required by IAS GAAP follows the substance of the situation. All other leases are operating leases. Operating leases are treated as hire or rental contracts on a time basis.

There are no major differences of principle between IAS GAAP and U.S. GAAP regarding leases. There are some detailed differences, however, and U.S. GAAP are distinctly more prescriptive in some respects. IAS GAAP define a finance lease as a lease where the present value of the minimum lease payments is equal to "substantially all" of the fair value of the asset at the date of the lease. U.S. GAAP require a precise 90% threshold. Alternatively, IAS GAAP specify that a lease is a finance lease if it is for "a major part" of the economic life, whereas U.S. GAAP specify a precise 75%.

Both jurisdictions require the net investment method to allocate gross earnings over time by the lessor of a finance lease, which excludes the effect of cash flows arising from taxes and financing relating to a lease transaction. An exception to this is for leveraged leases under U.S. GAAP where such cash flows are included.

SCOPE AND TERMINOLOGY

The scope of IAS 17 is that it applies to all leases except as stated below. IAS 17 does not apply to:

- Lease agreements to explore for or use minerals, oils, natural gas, and similar non-regenerative resources, or
- Licensing agreements for items such as motion pictures, video recordings, plays, manuscripts, patents, and copyrights.

Additionally, IAS 17 should not be applied to the measurement by:

- Lessees of investment property held under finance leases (see IAS 40, "Investment Property," Chapter 24),
- Lessors of investment property leased out under operating leases (see IAS 40),
- Lessees of biological assets held under finance leases (see IAS 41, "Agriculture," Chapter 32), or
- Lessors of biological assets leased out under operating leases (see IAS 41).

In an attempt to impose a reasonable degree of logic, clarity, and precision on what are inevitably subjective (or arbitrary) distinctions, IAS GAAP, like major national GAAPs, have indulged in a certain amount of complication and complexity. A number of terms are defined in paragraph 3 of IAS 17, and an understanding of these definitions and terms is essential in order to appreciate the meaning and significance of the GAAP requirements. Explanations of these terms are now given.

- A *lease* is an agreement whereby the lessor conveys to the lessee in return for a payment or series of payments the right to use an asset for an agreed period of time.
- A *finance lease* is a lease that transfers to the lessee substantially all the risks and rewards incident to ownership of an asset. Title may or may not eventually be transferred at the end of the lease.
- An *operating lease* is a lease other than a finance lease.

The risks of ownership relating to a finance lease are those of breakdown, damage, wear and tear, theft, obsolescence, and so on. The rewards of ownership are extracted by using the asset for substantially all its productive usefulness, that is, its economic life, and by receiving its residual value at the time of its disposal.

- *Economic life* is either:
  (a) the period over which an asset is expected to be economically usable by one or more users, or
  (b) the number of production or similar units expected to be obtained from the asset by one or more users.
- *Useful life* is the estimated remaining period, from the beginning of the lease term, without limitation by the lease term, over which the economic benefits embodied in the asset are expected to be consumed by the enterprise currently using it.

Note that the useful life relates to the expected situation *for the lessee*. The economic life relates to the asset, whether or not the current lessee is the only presumed user. Thus, although the useful life can exceed the lease term, the useful life cannot exceed the economic life.

- The *lease term* is the noncancelable period for which the lessee has contracted to lease the asset, together with any further terms for which the lessee has the option to continue to lease the asset, with or without further payment, which option at the inception of the lease it is reasonably certain that the lessee will exercise.
- A *noncancelable lease* is a lease that is cancelable only in one of the following circumstances:
  (a) upon the occurrence of some remote contingency;
  (b) with the permission of the lessor;
  (c) if the lessee enters into a new lease for the same or an equivalent asset with the same lessor; or
  (d) upon payment by the lessee of an additional amount such that, at inception, continuation of the lease is reasonably certain.

- The *inception of the lease* is the earlier of the date of the lease agreement or of a commitment by the parties to the principal provisions of the lease.

One of the major criteria for deciding whether or not a finance lease exists is the total amount, or more accurately the total minimum amount, payable under the lease contract. This leads to a set of related terms, as follows:

- *Minimum lease payments* are the payments over the lease term that the lessee is, or can be, required to make, excluding contingent rent, costs for services, and taxes to be paid by and reimbursed to the lessor, together with:

  (a) in the case of the lessee, any amounts guaranteed by the lessee or by a party related to the lessee; or

  (b) in the case of the lessor, any residual value guaranteed to the lessor by either:

     (i) the lessee,

     (ii) a party related to the lessee, or

     (iii) an independent third party financially capable of meeting this guarantee.

However, if the lessee has an option to purchase the asset at a price that is expected to be sufficiently lower than the fair value at the date when the option becomes exercisable so that, at the inception of the lease, it is reasonably certain to be exercised, that is, a "bargain purchase option" exists, then the minimum lease payments comprise the minimum payments payable over the lease term and the payment required to exercise this purchase option.

- *Fair value* is the amount for which an asset could be exchanged or a liability settled, between knowledgeable, willing parties in an arm's-length transaction.

- From the viewpoint of the lessee, the *guaranteed residual value* is that part of the residual value that is guaranteed by the lessee or by a party related to the lessee (the amount of the guarantee being the maximum amount that could, in any event, become payable).

- From the viewpoint of the lessor, the *guaranteed residual value* is that part of the residual value that is guaranteed by the lessee or by a third party unrelated to the lessor who is financially capable of discharging the obligations under the guarantee.

- *Unguaranteed residual value* is that portion of the residual value of the leased asset, the realization of which by the lessor is not assured or is guaranteed solely by a party related to the lessor.

- The lessor's *gross investment in the lease* is the aggregate of the minimum lease payments under a finance lease from the standpoint of the lessor and any unguaranteed residual value accruing to the lessor.

- *Net investment in the lease* is the gross investment in the lease less unearned finance income.

- *Unearned finance income* is the difference between

   (a) the aggregate of the minimum lease payments under a finance lease from the standpoint of the lessor and any unguaranteed residual value accruing to the lessor; and

   (b) the present value of (a) above, at the interest rate implicit in the lease.

Some of the greatest technical difficulties are caused by the need, at least theoretically, to calculate backward the interest rates implicitly included in arriving at the total payments under the lease.

- The *interest rate implicit in the lease* is the discount rate that, at the inception of the lease, causes the aggregate present value of (a) the minimum lease payments; and (b) the unguaranteed residual value, to be equal to the fair value of the leased asset.

- The *lessee's incremental borrowing rate of interest* is the rate of interest the lessee would have to pay on a similar lease or, if that is not determinable, the rate that, at the inception of the lease, the lessee would incur to borrow over a similar term, and with a similar security, the funds necessary to purchase the asset.

- *Contingent rent* is that portion of the lease payments that is not fixed in amount but is based on a factor other than just the passage of time (e.g., percentage of sales, amount of usage, price indices, market rates of interest).

LEASE CLASSIFICATION

As already indicated, the form of words that determines the classification of a lease as either a finance lease or an operating lease is quite simple.

A lease is classified as a finance lease if it transfers substantially all the risks and rewards incident to ownership. A lease is classified as an operating lease if it does not transfer substantially all the risks and rewards incident to ownership. Because the transaction between a lessor and a lessee is based on a lease agreement common to both parties, it is appropriate to use consistent definitions. The application of these definitions to the differing circumstances of the two parties, however, may sometimes result in the same lease being classified differently by lessor and lessee.

The standard makes no attempt to define "substantially all." Some national GAAPs take a much more numerical approach to this question, for example, requiring the present value of the minimum lease payments to be 90% or more of the fair value of the asset at the inception of the lease (e.g., the United States, Germany). Others, such as the United Kingdom, suggest that 90% gives a "presumption" of a finance lease but make it clear that the determining factor is "substantially all," not 90%.

> **OBSERVATION:** The desirability of creating a precise numerical distinction is very much open to question. It has the obvious surface advantage of apparent objectivity and precision. However, the chosen figure is purely arbitrary. More importantly, the creation of a definitive numerical distinction allows, and arguably encourages, business enterprises to structure lease contracts so that they fall just marginally below the chosen criterion, even though the whole purpose may, quite visibly, be, in substance, to finance the "purchase" of major resources by borrowing. The use of a fixed numerical boundary may substantially reduce subjectivity for the accountant and the auditor, but it may at the same time substantially increase creative accounting and the likelihood of misleading or unfair financial statements.

What IAS 17 does do is to give a number of examples of situations that would normally (1–5) or that could (6–8) point to a lease being properly classified as a finance lease. These are as follows (pars. 8 and 9):

1. The lease transfers ownership of the asset to the lessee by the end of the lease term.

2. The lessee has the option to purchase the asset at a price that is expected to be sufficiently lower than the fair value at the date the option becomes exercisable such that, at the inception of the lease, it is reasonably certain that the option will be exercised (i.e., a bargain purchase option exists).

3. The lease term is for the major part of the economic life of the asset even if title is not transferred.

4. At the inception of the lease the present value of the minimum lease payments amounts to at least substantially all of the fair value of the leased asset.

5. The leased assets are of a specialized nature such that only the lessee can use them without major modifications being made.

6. If the lessee cancels the lease, the lessor's losses associated with the cancellation are borne by the lessee.

7. Gains or losses from the fluctuation in the fair value of the residual fall to the lessee (for example, in the form of a rent rebate equaling most of the residual sales proceeds at the end of the lease).

8. The lessee has the ability to continue the lease for a secondary period at a rent that is substantially lower than market rent (i.e., a bargain rental option).

Because, under situations 1 and 2, the lessee ends up with legal ownership, the validity of a finance lease classification is obvious. Situation 3 assumes, reasonably enough, that a major part of the economic life (measured in years) must imply transfer of substantially all the risks and rewards of ownership (measured in money). Situation 4 argues that payment of substantially all of the purchase price, after discounting to present value, must again imply that the substance of the transaction is a purchase on credit terms, and situation 5 indicates by definition that only the lessee can derive "rewards" from possession of the particular items. The remaining three situations, 6, 7, and 8, while perhaps less definitive, all clearly point to the likelihood of the lessee being in the in-substance ownership position of deriving the benefits and "paying the price."

Illustration of Lease Classification

Costa PLC uses three identical pieces of machinery in its factory. These were all acquired for use on the same date by the following means:

1. Machine 1 rented from Brava Corporation at a cost of $250 per month payable in advance and terminable at any time by either party

2. Machine 2 rented from Blanca Corporation at a cost of eight half-yearly payments in advance of $1500

3. Machine 3 rented from Sol Corporation at a cost of six half-yearly payment in advance of $1200

The cash price of this type of machine is $8000, and its estimated life is 4 years. Are the above machines rented by operating or finance leases?

Machine 1 is held on an operating lease, as there is no transfer of the risks or rewards of ownership. Machine 2 involves a total payment of $12,000. In present value terms this will almost certainly be more than the $8000 fair value of the asset, and therefore clearly more than "substantially all of the fair value of the leased asset" (see situation 4 above). Machine 2 is therefore held on a finance lease. Machine 3 involves a total payment of $7200, the present value of which will be significantly less than $8000, so situation 4 above will not apply. The question is whether or not situation 3 applies, that is, whether or not 3 years is a "major part of the economic life" of the machine (which is 4 years). Under U.S. GAAP, which specifies an arbitrary 75% ratio here, this would be a finance lease under situation 3 (in which circumstance the lease agreement would probably have been changed before signing in order to be a week or two shorter). Under U.K. GAAP, which focuses more exclusively on situation 4, machine 3 would, on the available information, be an operating lease. This example well illustrates the practical difficulties that may arise in lease classification.

☞ **PRACTICE POINTER:** Leases of land and buildings are classified in exactly the same way as leases of any other type of asset. The nature of land, however, with its unlimited life, is that only situations 1 and 2 above could logically be expected to give the possibility of a finance lease classification. The IAS implies, but does not explicitly state, that a single lease of "land and buildings" should be split into two for classification purposes if the effect of separating out the land would be significant. This is most rationally done by allocating the present value of the minimum lease payments between the two elements in the ratio of their fair values at the inception of the lease.

ACCOUNTING AND REPORTING BY
LESSEES—FINANCE LEASES

In the case of finance leases, the substance and financial reality are that the lessee acquires the economic benefits of the use of the leased asset for the major part of its economic life in return for entering into an obligation to pay for that right an amount approximating to the fair value of the asset and the related finance charge.

Lessees should recognize finance leases as assets and liabilities in their balance sheets at amounts equal at the inception of the lease to the fair value of the leased property or, if lower, at the present value of the minimum lease payments (par. 12). In calculating the present value of the minimum lease payments, the discount factor is the interest rate implicit in the lease, if this is practicable to determine; if not, the lessee's incremental borrowing rate should be used. At the inception of the lease, the asset and the liability for the future lease payments are recognized in the balance sheet at the same amounts.

During the lease term, each lease payment should be allocated between a reduction of the obligation and the finance charge to produce a constant periodic rate of interest on the remaining balance of the obligation over the amortization period. The asset initially recorded is depreciated in a manner consistent with that used by the lessee for owned assets.

If the circumstances described in situations 1 or 2 above are present, that is, a transfer of ownership is clearly foreseeable, then depreciation is usually based on the economic life of the leased asset; otherwise, it is based on the shorter of economic life and lease term. Contingent rentals are generally not included in the minimum lease payments and are not accounted for as part of the capitalized lease. They should be charged to expense in the period to which they relate.

Illustration of Finance Lease Accounting by the Lessee

A lessee leases an asset on a noncancelable lease contract with a primary term of 5 years from January 1, 20X1. The rental is $650 per quarter payable in advance. The lessee has the right to continue to lease the asset after the end of the primary term for as long as it wishes at a nominal rent. In addition, the lessee is required to pay all maintenance and insurance costs as they arise. The leased asset could have been purchased for cash at the start of the lease for $10,000 and has a useful life of 8 years.

The interest rate implicit in the lease can be found as follows:

From the definition of "interest rate implicit in the lease," we can state that:

1. $10,000 (fair value) = the present value at implicit interest rate of 20 quarterly rentals payable in advance of $650.
2. The present value of the first rental payable is $650 as it is paid now.
3. Thus, $9350 = the present value at implicit interest rate of 19 rentals of $650.
4. Therefore, 9350/650 = 14.385 = annuity present value factor at implicit interest rate of 19 rentals of $1.
5. Using discount tables and interpolating, we can determine the quarterly interest rate to be 2.95%.

Assuming the asset has a nil residual value and that the asset is to be leased for a further 2 years after the primary period, we can show the accounting entries over the life of the lease required in the lessee's books.

The lease falls within the definition of a finance lease; therefore, the "rights in the lease" will be capitalized at fair value of $10,000 and the obligation under the lease of $10,000 will be shown as a liability, as shown by the following journal.

1/1/X1	Fixed asset	10,000	
	Creditors (lessor)		10,000

The minimum lease payments amount to 20 x $650 = $13,000; the cash price was $10,000; hence, the total finance charge will be $3000.

Remembering that this total finance charge should be allocated to accounting periods during the lease to produce a constant periodic rate of charge on the remaining balance of the obligation for each accounting period, then an appropriate method of allocation would be the actuarial method as follows:

Period	Capital Sum at Start of Period	Rental Paid	Capital Sum during Period	Finance Charge (2.95% per Quarter)*	Capital Sum at End of Period
	$	$	$	$	$
1/X1	10,000	650	9,350	276	9,626
2/X1	9,626	650	8,976	265	9,241
3/X1	9,241	650	8,591	254	8,845
4/X1	8,845	650	8,195	242	8,437
				1,037	
1/X2	8,437	650	7,787	230	8,017
2/X2	8,017	650	7,367	217	7,584
3/X2	7,584	650	6,934	205	7,139
4/X2	7,139	650	6,489	191	6,680
				843	
1/X3	6,680	650	6,030	178	6,208
2/X3	6,208	650	5,558	164	5,722
3/X3	5,722	650	5,072	150	5,222
4/X3	5,222	650	4,572	135	4,707
				627	
1/X4	4,707	650	4,057	120	4,177
2/X4	4,177	650	3,527	104	3,631
3/X4	3,631	650	2,981	88	3,069
4/X4	3,069	650	2,419	71	2,490
				383	
1/X5	2,490	650	1,840	54	1,894
2/X5	1,894	650	1,244	37	1,281
3/X5	1,281	650	631	19	650
4/X5	650	650	—	—	—
				110	
		13,000		3,000	

We can now apportion the annual rental of $2600 (i.e., 4 x $650) between a finance charge and a capital repayment as follows:

	Total Rental	Finance Charge	Capital Repayments
	$	$	$
X1	2,600	1,037*	1,563
X2	2,600	843	1,757
X3	2,600	627	1,973
X4	2,600	383	2,217
X5	2,600	110	2,490
	13,000	3,000	10,000
	(a)	(b)	(a) – (b)

*As calculated using actuarial method.

We also need to calculate a depreciation charge. The period for depreciation will be 7 years as this is the lesser of economic life (8 years) and lease period (7 years). The annual depreciation charge on a straight-line basis is, therefore:

$$\$10,000 \div 7 = \$1429$$

The accounting entries in the lessee's books will be as follows, assuming year-end as December 31.

Profit and loss account charges

	Depreciation	Finance Charge	Total
X1	1,429	1,037	2,466
X2	1,429	843	2,272
X3	1,429	627	2,056
X4	1,429	383	1,812
X5	1,428	110	1,538
X6	1,428	—	1,428
X7	1,428	—	1,428
	10,000	3,000	13,000

Balance sheet entries:

Assets held under finance leases

	Cost $		Accumulated Depreciation $		Net Book Value of Assets Held under Finance Leases $
12/31/X1	10,000	−	1,429	=	8,571
12/31/X2	10,000	−	2,858	=	7,142
12/31/X3	10,000	−	4,287	=	5,713
12/31/X4	10,000	−	5,716	=	4,284
12/31/X5	10,000	−	7,145	=	2,855
12/31/X6	10,000	−	8,574	=	1,426
12/31/X7	10,000	−	10,000	=	—

Obligations under finance leases (i.e., the capital element of future rentals payable)

	Obligations under Finance Leases Outstanding at Start of Year $		Capital Repayment $		Obligations under Finance Leases Outstanding at Year-End $
12/31/X1	10,000	–	1,563	=	8,437
12/31/X2	8,437	–	1,757	=	6,680
12/31/X3	6,680	–	1,973	=	4,707
12/31/X4	4,707	–	2,217	=	2,490
12/31/X5	2,490	–	2,490	=	—
12/31/X6					—
12/31/X7					—

Note in the above illustration that, after inception, the net asset and net liability figures are different. This will be the usual situation. They are reduced on different bases for different reasons and related to different assumptions.

☛ **PRACTICE POINTER:** IAS 36, "Impairment of Assets," applies to finance lease assets. It may be necessary under IAS 36 to recognize, or to reverse, an impairment loss (see Chapter 19).

ACCOUNTING AND REPORTING BY LESSEES—OPERATING LEASES

Lease payments under an operating lease should be recognized as an expense in the income statement on a straight-line basis over the lease term unless another systematic basis is representative of the time pattern of the user's benefit (par. 25). Note that the pattern of payment is not relevant. Remember that contingent rent, as discussed above, is not included in the original calculations. It therefore follows that the rental expense for any year will consist of:

1. The minimum rent under the lease divided equally over the number of years, plus
2. Any contingent rent relating to that year.

Illustration of Operating Lease Accounting by the Lessee

If the lease given in the earlier illustration were to be treated as an operating lease, then the only entries in the financial statements would be the following annual journal entry:

Rental expense (4 x 650)	2,600	
Creditors (4 x 650)		2,600

> **OBSERVATION:** Consideration of the two illustrations, for finance lease and operating lease, respectively, will quickly suggest the potentially great differences in terms of the shape of the reported performance, and the reported balance sheet structure, that the two methods can give. Note again that these differences, especially in marginal cases, may not be indicative of fundamental realities that are anywhere near as different and distinctive as the accounting numbers might imply.

Lease Incentives in Operating Leases

During the negotiation of a new operating lease or the renewal of an existing one, the lessee may receive incentives to sign the agreement from the lessor. Incentives take many forms, including rent-free periods, reduced rents for a period of time, leasehold improvements on the lessor's account, or a cash signing fee. IAS 17 is silent on this matter, but the Standing Interpretations Committee has clarified the position in SIC-15, "Incentives in an Operating Lease." This requires that the benefit of such incentives be recognized at the inception of the lease and treated as a reduction of rental expense over the term of the lease. The benefit is recognized on a straight-line basis, unless another systematic basis is representative of the time pattern in which benefit is derived from the leased asset.

FINANCIAL STATEMENT DISCLOSURE—LESSEES

It must be remembered that leases are a specific type of financial instrument and, therefore, that the requirements of IAS 32, "Financial Instruments: Disclosure and Presentation," apply to leases (see Chapter 16). IAS 39, "Financial Instruments: Recognition and Measurement," does not apply to "rights and obligations under leases, to which IAS 17, Leases, applies."

In addition, the requirements on disclosure under IAS 16, "Property, Plant, and Equipment" (see Chapter 27), IAS 36, "Impairment of Assets" (see Chapter 19), IAS 38, "Intangible Assets" (see Chapter 21), IAS 40, "Investment Property" (see Chapter 24), and IAS 41, "Agriculture" (see Chapter 32) apply to the amounts of leased assets under finance leases that are accounted for by the lessee as acquisitions of assets.

Disclosure requirements specific to IAS 17 for finance leases are as follows (par. 23):

1. For each class of asset, the net carrying amount at the balance sheet date;

2. A reconciliation between the total of minimum lease payments at the balance sheet date and their present value. In addition, an enterprise should disclose the total of minimum lease payments at the balance sheet date, and their present value, for each of the following periods:

    (a) not later than one year,

    (b) later than one year and not later than five years,

    (c) later than five years.

3. Contingent rents recognized in income for the period;

4. The total of future minimum sublease payments expected to be received under noncancelable subleases at the balance sheet date;

5. A general description of the lessee's significant leasing arrangements including, but not limited to, the following:

    (a) the basis on which contingent rent payments are determined,

    (b) the existence and terms of renewal or purchase options and escalation clauses,

    (c) restrictions imposed by lease arrangements, such as those concerning dividends, additional debt, and further leasing.

For operating leases, in addition to the general requirements of IAS 32, IAS 17 requires disclosure of the following (par. 27):

1. The total of future minimum lease payments under noncancelable operating leases for each of the following periods:

    (a) not later than one year,

    (b) later than one year and not later than five years,

    (c) later than five years;

2. The total of future minimum sublease payments expected to be received under noncancelable subleases at the balance sheet date;

3. Lease and sublease payments recognized in income for the period, with separate amounts for minimum lease payments, contingent rents, and sublease payments;

4. A general description of the lessee's significant leasing arrangements including, but not limited to, the following:

   (a) the basis on which contingent rent payments are determined,

   (b) the existence and terms of renewal or purchase options and escalation clauses,

   (c) restrictions imposed by lease arrangements, such as those concerning dividends, additional debt, and further leasing.

ACCOUNTING AND REPORTING BY LESSORS—FINANCE LEASES

As is the case with the financial statements of lessees, the approach is to follow and record the substance of the situation. From the viewpoint of the lessor, the substance is that the lessor has an amount receivable, much of it usually non-current, due from the lessee. In direct relation to the lease contract, the lessor has no other assets or liabilities. The amounts received from the lessee will embrace two elements, that is, a repayment of "loan" and an interest revenue.

Lessors should recognize assets held under a finance lease in their balance sheets and present them as a receivable at an amount equal to the net investment in the lease (pars. 28–33). A lessor aims to allocate finance income over the lease term on a systematic and rational basis. This income allocation is based on a pattern reflecting a constant periodic return on the lessor's net investment outstanding in respect of the finance lease. Lease payments relating to the accounting period, excluding costs for services, are applied against the gross investment in the lease to reduce both the principal and the unearned finance income.

Estimated unguaranteed residual values used in computing the lessor's gross investment in a lease are reviewed regularly. If there has been a reduction in the estimated unguaranteed residual value, the income allocation over the lease term is reviewed and any reduction in respect of amounts already accrued is recognized immediately.

Initial direct costs, such as commissions and legal fees, are often incurred by lessors in negotiating and arranging a lease. For finance leases, these initial direct costs are incurred to produce finance income and are either recognized immediately in income or allocated against this income over the lease term. The latter may be achieved by recognizing as an expense the cost as incurred and recognizing as income in the same period a portion of the unearned finance income equal to the initial direct costs.

Finance Leasing by Manufacturers or Dealers

The manufacturer or dealer may be the person who actually provides the asset, as well as the finance. A finance lease of an asset by a manufacturer or dealer lessor gives rise to two types of income:

1. The profit or loss equivalent to the profit or loss resulting from an outright sale of the asset being leased, at normal selling prices, reflecting any applicable volume or trade discounts; and

2. The finance income over the lease term.

The sales revenue recorded at the commencement of a finance lease term by a manufacturer or dealer lessor is the fair value of the asset, or, if lower, the present value of the minimum lease payments accruing to the lessor, computed at a commercial rate of interest (par. 36). The cost of sale recognized at the commencement of the lease term is the cost, or carrying amount if different, or the leased property less the present value of the unguaranteed residual value. The difference between the sales revenue and the cost of sale is the selling profit, which is recognized in accordance with the policy followed by the enterprise for sales that will be consistent with IAS 18, "Revenue," see Chapter 30.

Manufacturer or dealer lessors sometimes quote artificially low rates of interest in order to attract customers. The use of such a rate would result in an excessive portion of the total income from the transaction being recognized at the time of sale. If artificially low rates of interest are quoted, selling profit must be restricted to that which would apply if a commercial rate of interest were charged. Initial direct costs should be charged as expenses at the inception of the lease.

Illustration of Finance Lease Accounting by the Lessor

A lessor leases out an asset on terms that constitute a finance lease. The primary period is 5 years commencing July 1, 20X0, and the rental payable is $3000 per annum (in arrears). The lessee has the right to continue the lease after the 5-year period referred to above for an indefinite period at a nominal rent. The cash price of the asset in question at July 1, 20X0 was $11,372, and one can calculate the rate of interest implicit in the lease to be 10%.

Show the entries in the lessor books.

The finance charge is simply the difference between the fair value of the asset (in this case being the cash price of the new asset) and the rental payments over the lease period, that is, of $15,000 less $11,372, or $3,628.

Using the actuarial method with an interest rate of 10%, the allocation of the finance charge will be as follows:

Year-ended June 30	Balance b/f $	Finance Charge (10%) $	Rental $	Balance c/f (in Year-end Balance Sheet) $
20X1	11,372	+ 1,137	(3,000) =	9,509
20X2	9,509	+ 951	(3,000) =	7,460
20X3	7,460	+ 746	(3,000) =	5,206
20X4	5,206	+ 521	(3,000) =	2,727
20X5	2,727	+ 273	(3,000) =	Nil
		$3,628	$15,000	

The relevant extracts from the income statements of the years in question will thus appear as follows:

	20X1	20X2	20X3	20X4	20X5	Total
Rentals	3,000	3,000	3,000	3,000	3,000	15,000
Less capital						
Repayments	1,863	2,049	2,254	2,479	2,727	11,372
Finance charges	1,137	951	746	521	273	3,628
Interest payable	(x)	(x)	(x)	(x)	(x)	
Overheads	(x)	(x)	(x)	(x)	(x)	

The relevant balance sheets will appear as follows:

	Year-ended June 30			
	20X1	20X2	20X3	20X4
Net investment in finance lease				
Current	2,049	2,254	2,479	2,727
Non-current	7,460	5,206	2,727	—
	9,509	7,460	5,296	2,727

ACCOUNTING AND REPORTING BY LESSORS—OPERATING LEASES

As IAS 17 (par. 41) unsurprisingly says, lessors should present assets subject to operating leases according to the nature of the asset. The asset subject to the operating lease is, in substance as well as in form, a non-current asset of the lessor. Such an asset should be depreciated on a basis consistent with the lessor's policy for similar assets. IAS 16, "Property, Plant, and Equipment," or IAS 38, "Intangible Assets," will apply (see Chapters 27 and 21). In addition IAS 36, "Impairment of Assets," will need to be considered (see Chapter 19).

Costs, including depreciation, incurred in earning the lease income are recognized as an expense. Lease income (excluding receipts for services provided such as insurance and maintenance) is recognized in income on a straight-line basis over the lease term even if the receipts are not on such a basis, unless another systematic basis is more representative of the time pattern in which use benefit derived from the leased asset is diminished. By definition, no element of selling profit can arise.

Initial direct costs incurred specifically to earn revenues from an operating lease are either deferred and allocated to income over the lease term in proportion to the recognition of rent income or are recognized as an expense in the income statement in the period in which they are incurred.

FINANCIAL STATEMENT DISCLOSURE—LESSORS

As with lessees, IAS 32, "Financial Instruments: Disclosure and Presentation," applies to both finance leases and operating leases in the financial statements of the lessor. Additional requirements are given below.

For finance leases (par. 39):

1. A reconciliation between the total gross investment in the lease at the balance sheet date and the present value of minimum lease payments receivable at the balance sheet date. In addition, an enterprise should disclose the total gross investment in the lease and the present value of minimum lease payments receivable at the balance sheet date, for each of the following periods:

   (a) not later than one year,

   (b) later than one year and not later than five years,

   (c) later than five years;

2. Unearned finance income;

3. The unguaranteed residual values accruing to the benefit of the lessor;

4. The accumulated allowance for uncollectible minimum lease payments receivable;

5. Contingent rents recognized in income;

6. A general description of the lessor's significant leasing arrangements.

For operating leases (par. 48):

1. The future minimum lease payments under noncancelable operating leases in the aggregate and for each of the following periods:

   (a) not later than one year,

   (b) later than one year and not later than five years,

   (c) later than five years;

2. Total contingent rents recognized in income;

3. A general description of the lessor's significant leasing arrangements.

In addition, the requirements on disclosure under IAS 16, "Property, Plant, and Equipment" (see Chapter 27), IAS 36, "Impairment of Assets" (see Chapter 19), IAS 38, "Intangible Assets" (see Chapter 21), IAS 40, "Investment Property" (see Chapter 24), and IAS 41, "Agriculture" (see Chapter 32) apply to operating leases in the lessor's financial statements.

SALE AND LEASEBACK TRANSACTIONS

A sale and leaseback transaction involves the sale of an asset by the vendor and the leasing of the same asset back to the vendor. The lease payment and the sale price are usually interdependent as they are negotiated as a package. The accounting treatment of a sale and leaseback transaction depends upon the type of lease involved.

If the leaseback is an operating lease and the lease payments and the sale price are established at fair value, there has, in effect, been a normal sale transaction and any profit or loss is recognized immediately. If the sale price is below fair value, any profit or loss should be recognized immediately except that, if the loss is compensated by future lease payments at below market price, it should be deferred and amortized in proportion to the lease payments over the period for which the asset is expected to be used. If the sale price is above fair value, the excess over fair value should be deferred and amortized over the period for which the asset is expected to be used. Also, for operating leases, if the fair value at the time of a sale and leaseback transaction is less than the carrying amount of the asset, a loss equal to the amount of the difference between the carrying amount and fair value should be recognized immediately.

If the leaseback is a finance lease, the transaction is a means whereby the lessor provides finance to the lessee, with the asset as security. For this reason it is not appropriate to regard an excess of sales proceeds over the carrying amount as income because there has, in substance, been no sale. Such excess is deferred and amortized over the lease term. For finance leases, if the fair value at the time of the sale and leaseback transaction is less than the carrying amount of the asset, then no recognition of the difference between the two is necessary (again, because there has in substance not been a sale). However, such a difference might indicate an impairment in accordance with IAS 36, "Impairment of Assets," which standard would then be applied (see Chapter 19).

IASC has issued a draft interpretation, not confirmed at the time of writing, SIC-D27, "Transactions in the Legal Form of a Lease and Leaseback." This appears to be a response to a complicated piece of attempted creative accounting involving a long-term lease from A to B and then a short-term lease of the same asset from B to A. The draft is structured around a long and detailed "example" instead of being structured around basic principles, which does not seem a very good way of doing things. In brief, the draft conclusion is that, in substance, the overall effect is that there is no lease and IAS 17 does not apply.

CHAPTER 26
NET PROFIT OR LOSS FOR THE PERIOD, FUNDAMENTAL ERRORS, AND CHANGES IN ACCOUNTING POLICIES

CONTENTS

OVERVIEW

The objective in this chapter is to prescribe the classification, disclosure, and accounting treatment of certain items in the income statement so that all enterprises prepare and present an income statement on a consistent basis. This enhances comparability both with the enterprise's financial statements of previous periods and with the financial statements of other enterprises. Accordingly, IAS GAAP require the classification and disclosure of extraordinary items and the disclosure of certain items within profit or loss from ordinary activities. They also specify the accounting treatment for changes in accounting estimates, changes in accounting policies, and the correction of fundamental errors.

IAS GAAP for this area are contained in IAS 8, "Net Profit or Loss for the Period, Fundamental Errors and Changes in Accounting Policies." The original IAS 8 was approved in 1977 but was replaced by a revised IAS 8 effective from January 1, 1995. IAS 8 as revised dealt, among other things, with discontinued operations, but the relevant sections have now been deleted (i.e., pars. 4, 19–22 and the definition in par. 6), and replaced by IAS 35, "Discontinuing Operations," effective for financial statements covering periods beginning on or after January 1, 1999 (see Chapter 11).

SIC-8, "First Time Application of IASs as the Primary Basis of Accounting," also relates to IAS 8.

BACKGROUND

As stated in the overview, the overall purpose of IAS 8 is to increase consistency and, therefore, comparability in the preparation and presentation of published financial statements. A number of different issues are involved, and IAS 8 is largely an omnibus collection of requirements relating to a series of only semi-related issues. It is perhaps symptomatic that the removal of the sections on discontinued operations (discussed above) has no implications for the remainder of the standard. The key issues remaining are given by the distinctly ungainly title of IAS 8.

Under IAS GAAP, comparatives and prior year opening retained earnings are restated (if practicable) for the effects of changes in accounting policies; alternatively, the cumulative amount of the change is accounted for and separately disclosed in income for the period of the change and the entity discloses pro forma comparatives as if the change had been applied retrospectively to those periods. The first approach is that adopted under U.K. GAAP, whereas the second is that used in most cases under U.S. GAAP (APB-20 and 30, FAS-16). U.K. GAAP also require the effect of the change on the current year to be given.

International Accounting Standards allow the same choice for the correction of fundamental errors—either restatement of comparatives or correction in income of the period in which the errors are identified. Restatement of comparatives for fundamental errors is mandatory under both U.S. and U.K. GAAP and may be required for nonfundamental but material errors under U.S. GAAP.

Under IAS GAAP, disclosure of individual extraordinary items can be made either on the face of the income statement or in the notes, provided the total of all such items is shown on the face of the income statement. Exceptional items are usually disclosed in the notes, although it is acceptable to present them on the face of the income statement.

Under U.S. GAAP, extraordinary items are presented separately on the face of the income statement net of taxes. Disclosure of the tax impact is either on the face of the income statement or in the notes to the financial statements. Items of an exceptional nature are treated separately in arriving at income from operations. Subtotals of income from operations before such items are prohibited.

SCOPE AND DEFINITIONS

IAS 8 specifies the appropriate definition and disclosure of five major topics. These are:

- Extraordinary items,
- Profit or loss from ordinary activities,
- Changes in accounting estimates,
- Fundamental errors,
- Changes in accounting policy.

Tax effects of these items are dealt with in accordance with IAS 12, "Income Taxes" (see Chapter 20).

The standard gives a series of key definitions. For convenience and completeness, these are given together here. Because of the episodic nature of IAS 8, however, they are discussed later in the appropriate section of this chapter. The definitions given are (par. 6):

- *Extraordinary items* are income or expenses that arise from events or transactions that are clearly distinct from the ordinary activities of the enterprise and therefore are not expected to recur frequently or regularly.

- *Ordinary activities* are any activities that are undertaken by an enterprise as part of its business and such related activities in which the enterprise engages in furtherance of, incidental to, or arising from these activities.

- *Fundamental errors* are errors discovered in the current period that are of such significance that the financial statements of one or more prior periods can no longer be considered to have been reliable at the date of their issue.

- *Accounting policies* are the specific principles, bases, conventions, rules, and practices adopted by an enterprise in preparing and presenting financial statements.

NET PROFIT OR LOSS FOR THE PERIOD

The essential requirement is that all items of income and expense recognized in a period should be included in the determination of the net profit or loss for the period unless an International Accounting Standard requires or permits otherwise.

This is actually a convoluted way of defining what is required. "Income" is not defined in IAS 8, but it is defined in the Framework, paragraph 70 (see Chapter 2) as increases in economic benefits during the accounting period in the form of inflows or enhancements of assets or decreases in liabilities that result in increases in equity, other than those relating to contributions from equity participants.

This definition includes gains, both realized and unrealized, as well as revenue. IAS 8 notes two other International Accounting Standards that require exclusions. These are revaluation surpluses (see IAS 16, "Property, Plant, and Equipment," Chapter 27) and gains and losses arising on the translation of the financial statements of a foreign entity (see IAS 21, "Accounting for the Effects of Changes in Foreign Exchange Rates," Chapter 17).

These examples should not necessarily be assumed to be exhaustive.

In principle, unusual, exceptional, and extraordinary items are all to be included in net profit or loss for the period, as are the effects of changes in accounting estimates. Circumstances may exist, however, when certain items may be excluded from net profit or loss for the current period. IAS 8 deals with two such circumstances: the correction of fundamental errors and the effect of changes in accounting policies, both discussed below.

Separate disclosure on the face of the income statement (i.e., not in the notes) is required of total figures for profit or loss from ordinary activities and for extraordinary items.

EXTRAORDINARY ITEMS

Extraordinary items have been defined above. IAS 8 says that their occurrence is "rare." In general terms, extraordinary items or, more accurately, items treated as extraordinary in financial statements were much more common ten or twenty years ago than is the case today. The standard suggests two examples that "generally" give rise to extraordinary items for "most" enterprises, that is, the expropriation of assets and an earthquake or other natural disaster. However, an event or transaction may be extraordinary for one enterprise but not extraordinary for another enterprise because of the differences in their respective ordinary activities. Claims from policyholders arising from an earthquake, for example, do not qualify as an extraordinary item for an insurance enterprise that insures against such risks.

IAS 8 requires that the nature and amount of each distinct extraordinary item must be disclosed separately. This is usually done in the notes (with only the total appearing on the face of the income statement) but can be done directly in the income statement.

PROFIT OR LOSS FROM ORDINARY ACTIVITIES

IAS 8 has already established that profit or loss from ordinary activities must be shown as a separate total on the face of the income statement and that the nature and amount of each extraordinary item must be disclosed separately within the financial statements as a whole. The standard continues to require that (par. 16):

> When items of income and expense within profit or loss from ordinary activities are of such size, nature or incidence that their disclosure is relevant to explain the performance of the enterprise for the period, the nature and amount of such items should be disclosed separately.

It goes without saying that this is necessarily a highly subjective requirement. In broad terms, anything unusual enough to disturb the trend of regular results from regular operations should be disclosed. What is relevant is clearly dependent on specific circumstances, as well as on the concept of materiality. Inventory write-downs may be rare or may be a regular annual event. Consistency and equitable treatment of losses and gains are required. IAS 8 gives a number of examples of circumstances that "may" give rise to the separate disclosure of items of income and expense in accordance with paragraph 16, as follows:

1. The write-down of inventories to net realizable value or property, plant, and equipment to recoverable amount, as well as the reversal of such write-downs;
2. A restructuring of the activities of an enterprise and the reversal of any provisions for the costs of restructuring;
3. Disposals of items of property, plant, and equipment;
4. Disposals of long-term investments;
5. Discontinued operations;
6. Litigation settlements;
7. Other reversals of provisions.

Note that there is no suggestion that any of the above give rise to extraordinary items. If reported separately, it must be absolutely clear that they are still part of the results of "ordinary activities."

CHANGES IN ACCOUNTING ESTIMATES

There are very few figures in a set of published financial statements that do not involve accounting estimates. IAS 8 states that the use of reasonable estimates is an essential part of the preparation of financial statements and does not undermine their reliability. This last phrase presumably expresses a claim or hope (or matter of convenient definition), rather than fact, but the earlier part of the statement is certainly correct.

By definition, estimates may need to be revised over the years in light of new or changing information. The revision of an estimate does not affect the original classification of the transaction, and the effect of a change in an accounting estimate should be included in the same income statement classification as was used previously for the estimate, that is, as ordinary or extraordinary item.

Revision of estimates should not be given retroactive effect. The effect of a change in an accounting estimate should be included in the determination of net profit or loss in (par. 26):

1. The period of the change, if the change affects the period only; or
2. The period of the change and future periods, if the change affects both.

For example, a change in the estimate of the amount of bad debts affects only the current period and therefore is recognized immediately. However, a change in the estimated useful life or the expected pattern of consumption of economic benefits of a depreciable asset affects the depreciation expense in the current period and in each period during the remaining useful life of the asset. In both cases, the effect of the change relating to the current period is recognized as income or expense in the current period. The effect, if any, on income of future periods is recognized in future periods.

If it is excessively difficult to distinguish between a change in estimate and a change in accounting policy, the change should be treated as a change in accounting estimate. For example, a change from capitalization to write-off of an item could be viewed as a change in policy or as a change in estimation of future outcomes, but if there is doubt it should be treated as the latter. The nature and amount of a change in an accounting estimate that has a material effect in the current period or that is expected to have a material effect in subsequent periods should be disclosed. If it is impracticable to quantify the amount, this fact should be disclosed.

FUNDAMENTAL ERRORS

The formal IASC definition was given earlier in the chapter. Notice that a change in estimate as discussed above is not an error. Errors may occur as a result of mathematical mistakes, mistakes in applying accounting policies, misinterpretation of facts, fraud, or oversights. The correction of these errors is normally included in the determination of net profit or loss for the period in which the error is discovered. Such errors are not usually "fundamental." An error becomes a fundamental error only when its significance is such that the financial statements of an earlier year can no longer be considered to have been reliable at the date of their original issue. The standard gives as an example the inclusion in the financial statements of a previous period of material amounts of work-in-progress and receivables in respect of fraudulent contracts, which cannot be enforced.

Two alternative courses of action are allowed when dealing with the existence of a fundamental error: a benchmark treatment and an allowed alternative. The benchmark treatment (par. 34) is that the amount of the correction of a fundamental error should be reported by adjusting the opening balance of retained earnings. Comparative information should be restated, unless it is impracticable to do so.

The following disclosures are required under the benchmark treatment (par. 37):

1. The nature of the fundamental error;
2. The amount of the correction for the current period and for each prior period presented;
3. The amount of the correction relating to periods prior to those included in the comparative information; and
4. The fact that comparative information has been restated or that it is impracticable to do so.

This all means, in effect, that the current financial statements, including the comparative information, are presented as if the fundamental error had in fact been corrected in the period in which it was made. As far as IASC is concerned, the actual reissue of a corrected version of the original (wrong) financial statements is not required, but the standard notes that national laws may require this to be done.

The allowed alternative treatment (par. 38) is that the amount of the correction of a fundamental error should be included in the determination of net profit or loss for the current period. Comparative information should be presented as reported in the financial statements of the prior period. Additional pro forma information, prepared in accordance with paragraph 34, should be presented unless it is impracticable to do so.

This is not very clear! No indication is given as to how the correction should be included in net profit or loss, and paragraph 34 makes no mention of pro forma information. The additional information, which is presented "often as separate columns," should show the net profit or loss of the current period and any prior periods presented as if the fundamental error had been corrected in the period when it was made. It may be necessary to apply this accounting treatment in countries where the financial statements are required to include comparative information that agrees with the financial statements presented in prior periods. This is probably the reason for allowing this alternative treatment in the standard.

Under this alternative treatment the enterprise is required to disclose the following (par. 40):

1. The nature of the fundamental error;
2. The amount of the correction recognized in net profit or loss for the current period; and
3. The amount of the correction included in each period for which pro forma information is presented and the amount of the correction relating to periods prior to those included in the pro forma information. If it is impracticable to present pro forma information, this fact should be disclosed.

Real-life applications of these principles are, by definition, likely to be rare. IAS 8 does give a (nonmandatory) illustration in an appendix, which adds significantly to the clarity of what IASC has in mind, so we reproduce that illustration here.

Illustration of Fundamental Errors

During 20X2, Beta Co. discovered that certain products that had been sold during 20X1 were incorrectly included in inventory at December 31, 20X1 at 6,500.

Beta's accounting records for 20X2 show sales of 104,000, cost of goods sold of 86,500 (including 6,500 for error in opening inventory), and income taxes of 5,250.

In 20X1, Beta reported:

Sales	73,500
Cost of goods sold	(53,500)
Profit from ordinary activities before income taxes	20,000
Income taxes	(6,000)
Net profit	14,000

20X1 opening retained earnings were 20,000, and closing retained earnings were 34,000.

Beta's income tax rate was 30% for 20X2 and 20X1.

Beta Co.
Extract from the Income Statement under the Benchmark Treatment

	20X2	20X1 (restated)
Sales	104,000	73,500
Cost of goods sold	(80,000)	(60,000)
Profit from ordinary activities before income taxes	24,000	13,500
Income taxes	(7,200)	(4,050)
Net profit	16,800	9,450

Beta Co.

Statement of Retained Earnings under the Benchmark Treatment

	20X2	20X1 (restated)
Opening retained earnings as previously reported	34,000	20,000
Correction of fundamental error (Net of income taxes of 1,950) (Note 1)	(4,550)	—
Opening retained earnings as restated	29,450	20,000
Net profit	16,800	9,450
Closing retained earnings	46,250	29,450

Extracts from Notes to the Financial Statements

1. Certain products that had been sold in 20X1 were incorrectly included in inventory at December 31, 20X1 at 6,500. The financial statements of 20X1 have been restated to correct this error.

Beta Co.

Extract from the Income Statement under the Allowed Alternative Treatment

			Pro forma	
	20X2	20X1	20X2 (restated)	20X1 (restated)
Sales	104,000	73,500	104,000	73,500
Cost of goods sold (Note 1)	(86,500)	(53,500)	(80,000)	(60,000)
Profit from ordinary activities before income taxes	17,500	20,000	24,000	13,500
Income taxes (including the effects of the correction of a fundamental error)	(5,250)	(6,000)	(7,200)	(4,050)
Net profit	12,250	14,000	16,800	9,450

Beta Co.

Statement of Retained Earnings under the Allowed Alternative Treatment

			Pro forma	
	20X2	20X1	20X2 (restated)	20X1 (restated)
Opening retained earnings as previously reported	34,000	20,000	34,000	20,000
Correction of fundamental error (Net of income taxes of 1,950)	—	—	(4,550)	—

	20X2	20X1	Pro forma 20X2 (restated)	Pro forma 20X1 (restated)
Opening retained earnings as restated	34,000	20,000	29,450	20,000
Net profit	12,250	14,000	16,800	9,450
Closing retained earnings	46,250	34,000	46,250	29,450

Extracts from Notes to the Financial Statements

1. Cost of goods sold for 20X2 includes 6,500 for certain products that had been sold in 20X1 but were incorrectly included in inventory at December 31, 20X1. Restated pro forma information for 20X2 and 20X1 is presented as if the error had been corrected in 20X1.

CHANGES IN ACCOUNTING POLICIES

Accounting policies were defined earlier in this chapter. They are discussed more fully in IAS 1, "Presentation of Financial Statements" (see Chapter 3). In simple terms, they indicate the ways in which an enterprise calculates the figures in its financial statements and the assumptions made.

The strong desire for consistency in financial statements over time, and preferably among enterprises too, means that changes in accounting policies should be minimized. IAS 8 allows only three reasons for a change in accounting policies, as follows (par. 42):

> A change in accounting policy should be made only if required by statute, or by an accounting standard setting body, or if the change will result in a more appropriate presentation of events or transactions in the financial statements of the enterprise. A more appropriate presentation of events or transactions in the financial statements occurs when the new accounting policy results in more relevant or reliable information about the financial position, performance or cash flows of the enterprise.

This last is likely, of course, to involve a considerable element of subjectivity. Note that a change from one already existing policy acceptable under IAS GAAP to another already existing acceptable policy is only permitted if a "more appropriate presentation" will result. A benchmark treatment is not, in this sense, preferable to an allowed alternative treatment. Neither the adoption of an accounting policy for events or transactions that differ in substance from previously occurring events or transactions, nor the adoption of a new accounting policy for events or transactions that did not occur previously or that were immaterial, are changes in accounting policies (as there were no corresponding previous accounting policies to "change"). The adoption of a policy of carrying assets at revalued amounts is a change in accounting policy but is dealt with in IAS 16, "Property, Plant, and Equipment" (see Chapter 27), or IAS 38, "Intangible Assets" (see Chapter 21), as appropriate, and IAS 8 does not apply.

IAS 8 manages to make the required treatment and presentation for dealing with the disclosure of changes in accounting policies extremely complicated. First of all, changes can be applied "retrospectively" or, if necessary, "prospectively." Retrospective application results in the new accounting policy being applied to events and transactions as if the new accounting policy had always been in use. Therefore, the accounting policy is applied to events and transactions from the date of origin of such items. Prospective application means that the new accounting policy is applied to the events and transactions occurring after the date of the change. No adjustments relating to prior periods are made either to the opening balance of retained earnings or in reporting the net profit or loss for the current period because existing balances are not recalculated. However, the new accounting policy is applied to existing balances as of the date of the change. For example, an enterprise may decide to change its accounting policy for borrowing costs and capitalize those costs in conformity with the allowed alternative treatment in IAS 23, "Capitalization of Borrowing Costs." Under prospective application, the new policy applies only to borrowing costs that are incurred after the date of the change in accounting policy. Strictly speaking, *prospective* is the wrong word; *nonretrospective* would be more accurate.

This is not quite as clear as it may sound. If there is a semi-depreciated balance brought forward, should it be continually depreciated under the old policy because "existing balances are not recalculated," or should it now be treated under the new policy because "the new policy is applied to existing balances as from the date of the change" (which might imply immediate write-off)? The logic of the principle of "prospective" application would suggest that new transactions or events, and existing balances, are to be treated in the future under the new policy, which implies that the old balance should be gradually eliminated under the new policy.

IAS 8 allows a benchmark treatment, preferably applied retrospectively, but "prospectively" if necessary, and an allowed alternative treatment, again preferably applied retrospectively, but "prospectively" if necessary. This gives four possible treatments, which we attempt to distinguish as clearly as possible.

The benchmark treatment is that (par. 49) a change in accounting policy should be applied retrospectively unless the amount of any resulting adjustment that relates to prior periods is not reasonably determinable. Any resulting adjustment should be reported as an adjustment to the opening balance of retained earnings. Comparative information should be restated unless it is impracticable to do so.

However, the change in accounting policy should be applied prospectively when the amount of the adjustment to the opening balance of retained earnings cannot be reasonably determined.

When a change in accounting policy has a material effect on the current period or any prior period presented, or may have a material effect in subsequent periods, an enterprise should disclose the following under the benchmark method:

1. The reasons for the change;

2. The amount of the adjustment for the current period and for each period presented;

3. The amount of the adjustment relating to periods prior to those included in the comparative information; and

4. The fact that comparative information has been restated or that it is impracticable to do so.

The allowed alternative treatment is that a change in accounting policy should be applied retrospectively unless the amount of any resulting adjustment that relates to prior periods is not reasonably determinable. Any resulting adjustment should be included in the determination of the net profit or loss for the current period. Comparative information should be presented as reported in the financial statements of the prior period. Additional pro forma comparative information, prepared in accordance with paragraph 49, should be presented unless it is impracticable to do so. Once again, the change in accounting policy should be applied prospectively when the amount to be included in net profit or loss for the current period cannot be reasonably determined.

When a change in accounting policy has a material effect on the current period or any prior period presented, or may have a material effect in subsequent periods, an enterprise should disclose the following under this allowed alternative method:

1. The reasons for the change;

2. The amount of the adjustment recognized in net profit or loss in the current period; and

3. The amount of the adjustment included in each period for which pro forma information is presented and the amount of the adjustment relating to periods prior to those included in the financial statements. If it is impracticable to present pro forma information, this fact should be disclosed.

The difference between the two treatments, assuming that retrospective application is considered in both cases, is that under the benchmark method a resulting adjustment is taken to the opening balance of retained earnings, thus having no effect on reported annual earnings in any year. Under the allowed alternative method, which is consistent with U.S. GAAP, a resulting adjustment is taken to, and obviously affects, reported annual earnings of the current year. Additional pro forma information is also required. This is illustrated in an appendix to IAS 8, not reproduced here, and is similar to the pro forma columnar statements shown earlier in the illustration of the two treatments of fundamental errors. IAS 8 notes again that the allowed alternative treatment may need to be applied in countries where the financial statements are required to include comparative information that agrees with the financial statements presented in prior periods. This is again, presumably, the reason for the existence of the alternative in the standard.

ADOPTION OF INTERNATIONAL ACCOUNTING STANDARDS

When a change in accounting policy arises because of the adoption by an enterprise of an International Accounting Standard, IAS 8 really states the obvious when it says that the change should be accounted for in accordance with the specific transitional provisions, if any, in that International Accounting Standard. In the absence of any transitional provisions, the change in accounting policy should be applied in accordance with the benchmark treatment or the allowed alternative treatment in IAS 8.

IAS 8 is silent, however, about how to record changes arising from a wholesale switch to IAS GAAP. This has been addressed in SIC-8, "First-time Application if IASs as the Primary Basis of Accounting," effective from August 1, 1998. The key points are that the relevant standards and interpretations should be applied retrospectively except when either:

1. Individual standards and interpretations say otherwise, or

2. The amount of the adjustment relating to prior periods cannot be reasonably determined.

Full comparative information is required. Only the benchmark treatment from IAS 8 is permitted in this situation; the allowed alternative treatment is specifically excluded by SIC-8. This means that an adjustment arising because of the transition to IASs must be treated as an adjustment to the opening balance of retained earnings in the year of the transition. It cannot be taken to reported current earnings, as it is likely to be significant and distorting.

In the period of transition to full IAS GAAP, the following disclosures are required:

1. The fact, if it is so, that the adjustment to the opening balance of retained earnings cannot be reasonably determined;
2. The fact, if relevant, that it is impracticable to provide comparative information; and
3. For each IAS that permits a choice of transitional accounting policies, the policy selected.

CHAPTER 27
PROPERTY, PLANT, AND EQUIPMENT

CONTENTS

OVERVIEW

The accruals (matching) convention requires that fixed assets with a finite useful life should be gradually expensed over that life, in a manner such that annual expenses are pro rata with annual benefits. This process is known as *depreciation*.

IAS GAAP come from a variety of sources. The key relevant standards are:

- IAS 16, "Property, Plant, and Equipment"
- IAS 22, "Business Combinations" (re goodwill)
- IAS 36, "Impairment of Assets"
- IAS 38, "Intangible Assets"

This chapter deals fully with IAS 16, and also with SIC-14 and SIC-23.

BACKGROUND

Assets have already been defined, as discussed in Chapter 2, as follows (Framework, par. 49a).

> An asset is a resource controlled by the enterprise as a result of past events and from which future economic benefits are expected to flow.

Assets are divided into fixed assets and current assets. The IAS terms are *non-current assets* and *current assets*, respectively. The distinction is formally defined in IAS 1 (par. 57).

An asset should be classified as a current asset when it:

1. Is expected to be realized in, or is held for sale or consumption in, the normal course of the enterprise's operating cycle; or
2. Is held primarily for trading purposes or for the short-term and is expected to be realized within 12 months of the balance sheet date; or
3. Is cash or a cash equivalent asset that is not restricted in its use.

All other assets should be classified as non-current assets.

The definition of non-current assets is often misunderstood. A non-current asset is not an asset with a long life. The essential criterion is the *intention* of the owner, the intended *use* of the asset. A non-current asset is an asset that the firm intends to use within the business, over an extended period, in order to assist its daily operating activities. A current asset, on the other hand, is usually defined in terms of time. A current asset is an asset likely to change its form, that is, likely to undergo some transaction, within 12 months.

☞ **PRACTICE POINTER:** Consider two firms, A and B. Firm A is a motor trader. It possesses some motor vehicles that it is attempting to sell, and it also possesses some desks used by the sales staff, management, and so on. Firm B is a furniture dealer. It possesses some desks that it is attempting to sell, and it also possesses some motor vehicles used by the sales staff and for delivery purposes. In the accounts of A, the motor vehicles are current assets and the desks are non-current assets. In the accounts of B, the motor vehicles are non-current assets and the desks are current assets. Note incidentally that a fixed asset that, after several years' use, is about to be sold for scrap, remains in the fixed asset part of the accounts even though it is about to change its form.

The crucial difference between IAS GAAP and U.S. GAAP is that IAS GAAP permit the upward revaluation of depreciable and non-depreciable non-current assets, whereas U.S. GAAP do not. U.S. GAAP also allow no distinction between investment properties and other properties.

PRINCIPLES OF ACCOUNTING FOR DEPRECIATION

The first major problem with depreciation, perhaps surprisingly, is to agree on what it is, and what it is for. The generally agreed view nowadays is that it is in essence a straightforward application of the matching, or accruals, convention. With a non-current asset, the benefit from the asset is spread over several years. The matching convention requires that the corresponding expense be matched with the benefit in each accounting period. This does not simply mean that the total expense for the asset's life is spread over the total beneficial life. It means, more specifically, that the total expense for the asset's life is spread over the total beneficial life *in proportion to the pattern of benefit*. Thus, to take a simple example, if a non-current asset gives half of its benefit, or usefulness, in year 1, one-third in year 2, and one-sixth in year 3, and the total expenses arising are $1200, then the matching convention requires the charging of $600 in year 1, $400 in year 2, and $200 in year 3, in the annual profit calculation. This charge is known as the *depreciation charge*.

In order to calculate a figure for this charge it is necessary to answer four basic questions:

1. What is the cost of the asset?

2. What is the estimated useful life of the asset to the business? (This may be equal to, or may be considerably less than, its technical or physical useful life.)

3. What is the estimated residual selling value ("scrap value") of the asset at the end of the useful life as estimated?

4. What is the pattern of benefit or usefulness derived from the asset likely to be (not the *amount* of the benefit)?

It is perfectly obvious that the second, third, and fourth of these involve a good deal of uncertainty and subjectivity. The "appropriate" figures are all dependent on future plans and future actions. It is important to realize that even if the first figure, the cost of the fixed asset, is known precisely and objectively, the basis of the depreciation calculation as a whole is always uncertain, estimated, and subjective. The estimates should, as usual, be reasonable, fair, and prudent (whatever precisely this implies).

But the first figure is often not at all precise and objective, for several reasons.

> ☛ **PRACTICE POINTER:** Problems in establishing a "cost" figure for a non-current asset include the following:
>
> 1. Incidental expenses associated with making the asset workable should be included, for example, installation costs carried out by the business's own staff, probably including some overhead costs.
>
> 2. The non-current asset may be constructed within the business by its own workforce, giving rise to all the usual costing problems of overhead definition and overhead allocation.
>
> 3. Depending on the accounting policies used by the firm generally, the "basic" figure for the fixed asset may be revalued periodically. Additionally, if land is not depreciated but the building on the land is, then this requires a split of the total cost (or value) figure for the land and buildings together into two possibly somewhat arbitrary parts.
>
> 4. Major alterations/improvements may be made to the asset part way through its life. If these appear to increase the benefit from the asset over the remaining useful life, and perhaps also to increase the number of years of the remaining useful life, and are material, then the costs of these improvements should also be capitalized (i.e., treated as part of the non-current asset from then on). Maintenance costs, however, including a major overhaul that does not occur frequently, are "running" expenses and should be charged to the income statement as incurred. In practice, this distinction can be difficult to make.

The total figure to be depreciated, known as the *depreciable amount*, will consist of the cost of the asset less the scrap value. This depreciable amount needs to be spread over the useful life in proportion to the pattern of benefit. Once the depreciable amount has been found, with revision if necessary to take account of material improvements, several recognized methods exist for spreading, or allocating, this amount to the various years concerned. The more important possibilities are outlined below. It is essential to understand the implicit assumption that each method makes about the pattern of benefit arising and therefore about the appropriate pattern of expense allocation.

Methods of Calculating Depreciation

Straight-Line Method

The depreciable amount is allocated on a straight-line basis, that is, an equal amount is allocated to each year of the useful life. If an asset is revalued or materially improved, then the new depreciable amount will be allocated equally over the remaining, possibly extended, useful life.

Illustration of Straight-Line Method

Using the straight-line method, calculate the annual depreciation charge from the following data.

Cost ("basic" value figure)	$12,000
Useful life	4 years
Scrap value	$2,000

Annual charge = ($12,000 – $2,000)/4
= $2,500

This is by far the most common method. It is the easiest to apply, and also the preparation of periodic (e.g., monthly) accounts for internal purposes is facilitated. This method assumes, within the limits of materiality, that the asset is equally useful, or beneficial, each year. Whether this assumption is as frequently justified as the common usage of the method suggests is an open question.

Reducing-Balance Method

Under this method, depreciation each year is calculated by applying a constant percentage to the NBV (net book value) brought forward from the previous year. (Note that this percentage is based on the cost less depreciation to date.) Given the cost (or valuation) starting figure, and the useful life and "scrap" value figures, the appropriate percentage needed to make the net book value at the end of the useful life exactly equal to the scrap value can be found from a formula:

$$d = \sqrt[n]{S/C}$$

where d is the depreciation percentage, n is the life in years, S is the scrap value, and C is the cost (or basic value).

This formula is rarely used. In practice, when this method is used a standard "round" figure is usually taken, shown by experience to be vaguely satisfactory for the particular type of asset under consideration. Notice, incidentally, that the formula fails to work when the scrap value is zero, and produces an extreme and possibly distorted allocation of expense when the scrap value is very small.

Illustration of Reducing-Balance Method

Using the data of the previous illustration and assuming a depreciation percentage of 40%, calculate the depreciation charge for each of the 4 years using the reducing balance method.

Year 1	Cost	$12,000
	Depreciation 40%	4,800
Year 2	NBV	7,200
	Depreciation 40%	2,880
Year 3	NBV	4,320
	Depreciation 40%	1,728
Year 4	NBV	2,592
	Depreciation 40%	1,037
	NBV	$1,555

If the estimated scrap value turns out to be correct, then a "profit" on disposal of $445 would be recorded also in year 4. This is an example of a reducing-charge method, or of an accelerated depreciation method. The charge is highest in the first year and gradually reduces over the asset's life.

Several arguments can be advanced for preferring this approach to the straight-line method, at least in theory, as follows:

1. It better reflects the typical benefit pattern, at least of some assets.

2. It could be argued that, where the pattern of benefit is assumed to be effectively constant, the appropriate "expense," which needs to be correspondingly evenly matched, is not the pure depreciation element, but the sum of:

   (a) the pure depreciation element, and

   (b) the maintenance and repair costs.

   Because (b) will tend to increase as the asset gets older, it is necessary for (a) to be reduced as the asset gets older, in the hope that the total of the two will remain more or less constant. This may be a valid argument in the most general of terms, but of course there is no reason why an arbitrary percentage applied in one direction should even approximately compensate for flexible and "chancy" repair costs in the other.

3. It better reflects the probable fact that the value (i.e., the market or resale value) of the asset falls more sharply in the earlier years. This argument, often advanced, is questionable in principle. Depreciation is concerned with appropriate allocation of expense, applying the matching convention. It is not concerned with an annual revaluation of the fixed assets, so whether or not a particular method is good or bad from this viewpoint is, or should be, irrelevant. As long as the original estimate of future benefit is still valid, the fact that current market value is small, at an intermediate time, is not of concern.

A particular variant found in practice in some countries is known as the double-declining balance method. This involves calculating the appropriate "straight line" depreciation percentage, then doubling it and applying the resulting percentage on the reducing balance basis.

Sum-of-the-Digits Method

The sum-of-the-digits method is another example of a reducing-charge method. It is based on a convenient "rule of thumb" and produces a pattern of depreciation charge somewhat similar to the reducing-balance method.

Using the same figures as before, we give the 4 years weights of 4, 3, 2, and 1, respectively, and sum the total weights. In general terms we give the n years weights of $n, n-1, \ldots, 1$, respectively, and sum the total weights, the sum being $n(n+1)/2$. The depreciable amount is then allocated over the years in the proportion that each year's weighting bears to the total.

Illustration of Sum-of-the-Digits Method

Using the data in the previous illustrations gives the following figures.

4 + 3 + 2 + 1 = 10 (the "sum" of the "digits")

Depreciable amount = $12,000 − $2,000 = $10,000

Depreciation charges are:

Year	1	4/10 x 10,000 = $4,000
	2	3/10 x 10,000 = $3,000
	3	2/10 x 10,000 = $2,000
	4	1/10 x 10,000 = $1,000

This gives NBV figures in the balance sheet of $8,000, $5,000, $3,000, and $2,000 for year ends 1–4, respectively.

Output or Usage Method

The output or usage method is particularly suitable for assets where the rate of usage or rate of output can be easily measured. For example, a motor vehicle might be regarded as having a life of 100,000 miles, rather than a life of 4 years. The depreciable amount can then be allocated to each year in proportion to the recorded mileage, for example, if 30,000 miles are covered in year 1, then 3/10 of the depreciable amount will be charged in year 1. The life of a machine could be defined in terms of machine hours. The annual charge would then be

$$\text{Depreciable amount} \times \frac{\text{Machine hours used in the year}}{\text{Total estimated life in machine hours}}$$

Revaluation or Arbitrary Valuation

The revaluation or arbitrary valuation approach is occasionally used with minor items such as loose tools. An estimated or perhaps purely arbitrary figure for the value of the items (in total) is chosen at the end of each year. Depreciation is then the difference between this figure and the figure from the previous year. Strictly, of course, this is not a method of depreciation at all, but a lazy alternative to it.

All of the above methods can be criticized on the grounds that they ignore the fact that the resources "tied up" in the fixed asset concerned have an actual cost to the business in terms of interest paid, or an implied (opportunity) cost in terms of interest foregone. This could well be regarded as an essential expense that should be matched appropriately against the benefit from the asset. The "actuarial" methods that attempt to take account of interest expense are complicated to apply and in financial accounting are hardly ever used.

> **OBSERVATION:** The process of depreciation calculation is not designed to produce balance sheet numbers that are either particularly meaningful or particularly useful as measurements of value; in fact, they are measurements of unexpired costs.
>
> It must be remembered that depreciation is a process of matching expenses in proportion to benefits. Given that the depreciable amount has been agreed, the annual charge is based on actual or implied assumptions as to the pattern of benefit being derived, and nothing else. In simple bookkeeping terms, all that is happening is that a transfer is being made from the non-current assets section in the balance sheet to the expenses section in the income statement. It is the expense that is being positively calculated, not the reduction in the asset figure. It follows from this that:
>
> 1. The asset figure for an intermediate year has no very obvious or useful meaning. It can only be defined in a roundabout way. For example, under historical cost (HC) accounting, it is the amount of the original cost not yet deemed to have been used or not yet allocated. This intermediate figure is often called "net book value," but it is *not* a value at all within the proper meaning of the word.
> 2. Depreciation has nothing to do with ensuring that the business can "afford" to buy another asset when the first one becomes useless. This is true even if we ignore the likelihood of rising price levels. Depreciation does not increase the amount of any particular asset, cash or otherwise.
> 3. However, depreciation, like any other expense figure, does have the effect of retaining *resources* (or total assets) in the business. By reducing profit, we reduce the maximum dividend payable (which would reduce resources) and, therefore, increase the "minimum resources remaining" figure. This is, in fact, a particular illustration of the idea of capital maintenance discussed in Chapter 8.

IAS GAAP

When it was originally issued in 1974, IAS 4 was *the* International Standard on depreciation. Later and more specific standards have removed much of its cover. In November 1999, IASC announced that it had decided to withdraw IAS 4, "Depreciation Accounting," as this subject is now addressed in IAS 16, "Property, Plant, and Equipment," IAS 22, "Business Combinations," and IAS 38, "Intangible Assets."

PROPERTY, PLANT, AND EQUIPMENT

IAS GAAP for the accounting treatment of property, plant, and equipment is provided by IAS 16. Originally issued in 1981, IAS 16 was revised in 1993, effective January 1, 1995, and revised again in 1998, effective accounting periods beginning on or after July 1, 1999. Here we consider only the latest version. The 1998 changes were essentially concerned with consequential amendments arising from the issue of IAS 36, "Impairment of Assets" (see Chapter 19) and IAS 37, "Provisions, Contingent Liabilities, and Contingent Assets" (see Chapter 28). Further minor amendments have since been made to allow for the issue of IAS 40 and IAS 41.

The standard notes that the general definition and recognition criteria for an asset given in the "Framework for the Preparation and Presentation of Financial Statements" (discussed in Chapter 2) must be satisfied before IAS 16 applies. Subject to that, IAS 16 applies to accounting for all property, plant, and equipment except when another IAS requires or permits a different accounting treatment (par. 1).

There are, in fact, a number of exclusions. It is explicitly stated (par. 2) that IAS 16 does not apply to biological assets related to agricultural activity (to which IAS 41 applies; see Chapter 32), nor to mineral rights, the exploration for and extraction of minerals, oil, natural gas, and similar nonregenerative resources. However, it does apply to property, plant, and equipment used to develop or maintain these activities or assets but separable from those activities or assets.

An enterprise applies IAS 40, "Investment Property," rather than IAS 16, to its investment property (see Chapter 24). IAS 16 applies to property being constructed or developed for future use as an investment property, but on its completion IAS 40 would apply. IAS 40 also applies to existing investment property being redeveloped for future continued use as investment property.

If any other IAS permits a particular approach to the initial recognition of the carrying amount of property, plant, and equipment, then that standard will prevail regarding this initial carrying value, but IAS 16 would then apply to all other aspects, including depreciation. An example of this would be IAS 22, "Business Combinations," which requires property, plant, and equipment acquired in a business combination to be measured initially at fair value (see Chapter 6).

IAS 16 also does not deal with certain aspects of the application of a comprehensive system reflecting the effects of changing prices (see IAS 15, "Information Reflecting the Effects of Changing Prices" (Chapter 8) and IAS 29, "Financial Reporting in Hyperinflationary Economies" (Chapter 8). However, enterprises applying such a system are required to comply with all aspects of IAS 16, except those that deal with the measurement of property, plant, and equipment subsequent to its initial recognition.

The standard gives a number of key definitions as follows:

- *Property, plant, and equipment* are tangible assets that:
  - (a) are held by an enterprise for use in the production or supply of goods or services, for rental to others, or for administrative purposes; and
  - (b) are expected to be used during more than one period.
- *Depreciation* is the systematic allocation of the depreciable amount of an asset over its useful life.
- *Depreciable amount* is the cost of an asset, or other amount substituted for cost in the financial statements, less its residual value.
- *Useful life* is either:
  - (a) the period of time over which an asset is expected to be used by the enterprise; or
  - (b) the number of production or similar units expected to be obtained from the asset by the enterprise.
- *Cost* is the amount of cash or cash equivalents paid or the fair value of the other consideration given to acquire an asset at the time of its acquisition or construction.
- *Residual value* is the net amount that the enterprise expects to obtain for an asset at the end of its useful life after deducting the expected costs of disposal.
- *Fair value* is the amount for which an asset could be exchanged between knowledgeable, willing parties in an arm's-length transaction.
- An *impairment loss* is the amount by which the carrying amount of an asset exceeds its recoverable amount.
- *Carrying amount* is the amount at which an asset is recognized in the balance sheet after deducting any accumulated depreciation and accumulated impairment losses thereon.

> **OBSERVATION:** Comparing the 1993 and 1998 versions of IAS 16, the 1998 version
>
> 1. inserts a definition of impairment loss that includes the term "recoverable amount," and
> 2. deletes a definition of "recoverable amount" and does not replace it.
>
> We assume that the definition in IAS 36 should now be applied (see Chapter 19), that is, that "recoverable amount" is the higher of an asset's net selling price and its value in use. This should be compared with the definition of "fair value" given above, which is, in effect, gross market price.

Recognition of Property, Plant, and Equipment

An item of property, plant, and equipment should be recognized (par. 7) as an asset when:

1. It is probable that future economic benefits associated with the asset will flow to the enterprise;
2. The cost of the asset to the enterprise can be measured reliably.

In determining whether an item satisfies the first criterion for recognition, an enterprise needs to assess the degree of certainty attaching to the flow of future economic benefits on the basis of the available evidence at the time of initial recognition. Existence of sufficient certainty that the future economic benefits will flow to the enterprise necessitates an assurance that the enterprise will receive the rewards attaching to the asset and will undertake the associated risks. The second criterion for recognition is usually readily satisfied because the exchange transaction evidencing the purchase of the asset identifies its cost. In the case of a self-constructed asset, a reliable measurement of the cost can be made from the transactions with parties external to the enterprise for the acquisition of the materials, labor, and other inputs used during the construction process.

IAS 16 allows for the aggregation of items that may individually be insignificant (par. 11), giving "moulds, tools and dies" as an example. The aggregation is then treated as *"an* asset" if the above recognition criteria are met. When it is clear that, although an asset may initially be acquired as a whole, significant components of it will have significantly different useful lines, then the expenditure on the asset should be allocated to the component parts, and each part should be accounted for as a separate item. An aircraft and its engines are given as a likely example. This separate treatment allows depreciation figures to properly reflect the different consumption patterns of the various components.

> ☛ **PRACTICE POINTER:** The standard goes out of its way to clarify that the criterion of probable future economic benefits from "the item" should be interpreted broadly. For example, resources acquired for safety or environmental reasons, whether legally required or only through custom or good public relations, will assist the enterprise to obtain future economic benefits from its other assets. Provided that the resultant carrying amount of the total assets does not exceed the recoverable amount from the total assets, the safety or environmental expenditures should be recognized as assets under IAS 16.

Recognition of Major Inspection or Overhaul Costs

The IASC has issued SIC-23, "Property, Plant, and Equipment—Major Inspection or Overhaul Costs," effective from July 15, 2000. This clarifies the situation whereby a major overhaul or service is needed to allow continued use of an asset, but only once every several years. In effect, SIC-23 allows and requires that the overhaul or service is treated as a separate component of the whole asset in certain circumstances. It follows from the discussion of significant components in the section above, that the overhaul is itself treated as a separate asset, to be depreciated over the period between each overhaul.

The SIC notes that the original purchase of the new total asset will, in effect, involve the purchase of the initial overhaul component; the cost of this can be estimated by reference to the expected cost of the first overhaul and adjusted to bring it to present day prices, thus establishing an opening carrying value for the separate "overhaul" component.

The SIC words its requirement the other way around, requiring that all major inspection or overhaul costs are recognized as an expense in the period in which they are actually incurred, unless all of three conditions are met. The formal wording is as follows.

> The cost of a major inspection or overhaul of an item of property, plant and equipment occurring at regular intervals over the useful life of an asset and made to allow the continued use of the asset should be recognised as an expense in the period in which it is incurred except when:
>
> (a) consistent with IAS 16.12, the enterprise has identified as a separate component of the asset an amount representing major inspection or overhaul and has already depreciated that component to reflect the consumption of benefits which are replaced or restored by the subsequent major inspection or overhaul (whether the asset is carried at historical cost or revalued);
>
> (b) it is probable that future economic benefits associated with the asset will flow to the enterprise; and
>
> (c) the cost of the major inspection or overhaul to the enterprise can be measured reliably.

If these criteria are met, the cost should be capitalized and accounted for as a component of the asset.

Measurement of Property, Plant, and Equipment

IAS 16 divides its consideration of measurement issues into several different stages, that is, initial measurement, subsequent expenditure, and measurement subsequent to the initial recognition.

Initial Measurement

The essential requirement is straightforward and can be simply stated (par. 14). An item of property, plant, and equipment that qualifies for recognition as an asset should initially be measured at its cost. The cost of an item of property, plant, and equipment comprises its purchase price, including import duties and nonrefundable purchase taxes, and any directly attributable costs of bringing the asset to working condition for its intended use. Any trade discounts and rebates are deducted in arriving at the purchase price. Examples of directly attributable costs are

1. The cost of site preparation
2. Initial delivery and handling costs
3. Installation costs
4. Professional fees such as for architects and engineers
5. The estimated cost of dismantling and removing the asset and restoring the site, to the extent that it is recognized as a provision under IAS 37, "Provisions, Contingent Liabilities, and Contingent Assets" (see Chapter 28)

In practice, however, a number of complications are likely to arise. The standard goes into some detail about several aspects (pars. 16–22). It notes that in cases where payment is deferred beyond normal credit terms, defined or imputed interest must be removed from the total of the payments, thus reducing the cost to the cash purchase price equivalent. It notes that general and administration overheads are not likely to be "directly attributable costs" as the term is used above.

The question of what is an essential cost of "bringing the asset to working condition" is likely to be difficult and subjective. Operating losses incurred "prior to an asset achieving planned performance" are to be treated as an expense. This implies that losses on such items as a shakedown cruise on a new liner are an expense, not a necessary cost of reaching the "working condition." But the cost of testing the engines to ensure that they have no leaks or faults is surely such a necessary cost, and the distinction is a narrow one. The standard also feels the need to discuss the calculation of cost of self-constructed assets—to exclude any internal profits or abnormal wastage, for example—though all this is only normal practice. Assets held under finance leases are costed in accordance with IAS 17, "Leases" (see Chapter 25) and government grants are to be dealt with in accordance with IAS 20, "Accounting for Government Grants and Disclosure of Government Assistance" (see Chapter 18).

If items of property, plant, and equipment are exchanged or partly exchanged for *dissimilar* items, then the cost of the acquired asset is its fair value, which will be "equivalent to the fair value of the asset given up adjusted by the amount of any cash or cash equivalents transferred" (or so the standard says!). However, if items are exchanged for a *similar* asset "that has a similar use in the same line of business and which has a similar fair value," or for an "equity interest in a similar asset," then the "earnings process is incomplete" (i.e., in substance, there is no sale) and the cost of the new asset is the carrying amount of the asset parted with.

> **OBSERVATION:** The above two paragraphs of text provide a good example of the perceived need by IASC in recent years to spell out details of the implications of its general requirements for particular situations in greater detail than used to be the case. The contrast with the approach in the old IAS 4, issued in 1974, makes the point clearly.

The question has recently arisen as to the appropriate treatment of revenues and expenses relating to operations incidental to the construction or development of property, plant, and equipment. Consider, for example, a building site which is used as a parking lot until construction commences. Is the operating profit (or loss) an adjustment to the cost of the eventual building?

IASC has issued a draft SIC-D26, "Property, Plant, and Equipment—Results of Incidental Operations," not confirmed at the time of writing. This proposes that results of such incidental operations should be recognized in net profit or loss for the period, with the various income and cost items included in their respective classifications on the face of the income statement. There should be no adjustment to the cost of the eventual property, plant, or equipment.

Subsequent Expenditure

Once again, the principle is straightforward but the detail can become complex. Subsequent expenditure relating to an item of property, plant, and equipment that has already been recognized should (par. 23) be added to the carrying amount of the asset when it is probable that future economic benefits, in excess of the originally assessed standard of performance of the existing asset, will flow to the enterprise. All other subsequent expenditure should be recognized as an expense in the period in which it is incurred. Examples of improvements that result in increased future economic benefits include:

1. Modification of an item of plant to extend its useful life, including an increase in its capacity;

2. Upgrading machine parts to achieve a substantial improvement in the quality of output; or

3. Adoption of new production processes enabling a substantial reduction in previously assessed operating costs.

In essence, therefore, anything that restores or maintains the originally expected level of future economic benefits must be treated as an expense. If, however, the cost (or carrying amount) of an asset has taken a loss of economic benefits into account, subsequent expenditure to reverse this loss could logically be capitalized. For example, suppose a house is purchased without a kitchen. The installation of a fitted kitchen should be added to the carrying value of the house. The later replacement of the fitted kitchen with a newly fitted kitchen would be an expense.

Unless, of course, the kitchen had originally been regarded as a separate asset to the house! To continue the earlier example of an aircraft and its engines, which had been treated as separate assets with different depreciation policies, a replacement engine is a new asset and would be recorded as such.

Measurement Subsequent to Initial Recognition

The IASC has always operated on the basis that a strict adherence to historical cost is not required and, indeed, has recognized the possibility of rejecting historical cost accounting as the normal basis (see Chapter 8). Consistent with this approach, two alternative approaches to subsequent measurement are allowed under IAS 16 (pars. 28 and 29). The first is described as the benchmark treatment and is simply stated.

> Subsequent to initial recognition as an asset, an item of property, plant, and equipment should be carried at its cost less any accumulated depreciation and any accumulated impairment losses.

Depreciation is discussed below, and impairment issues are addressed by IAS 36, "Impairment of Assets" (see Chapter 19).

The second, "alternative" treatment adds regular "fair value" revaluation to the system. Formally this is stated as follows:

> Subsequent to initial recognition as an asset, an item of property, plant and equipment should be carried at a revalued amount, being its fair value at the date of the revaluation less any subsequent accumulated depreciation and subsequent accumulated impairment losses. Revaluations should be made with sufficient regularity such that the carrying amount does not differ materially from that which would be determined using fair value at the balance sheet date.

The fair value of land and buildings will usually be their market value as determined by professional qualified appraisers. It is interesting to note that the explicit statement in the 1993 version of IAS 16 that such valuation should presume continued "use of the asset in the same or a similar business" has been dropped from the current version. Now it is the fair value on the open market that should be used. When there is no evidence of market value because of the specialized nature of the plant and equipment and because these items are rarely sold, except as part of a continuing business, they are valued at their depreciated replacement cost. Appropriate specific price indexes may, if necessary, be used to determine replacement cost.

The frequency of revaluation required is not precisely defined. It is suggested in the standard (par. 32) that items that "may experience significant and volatile movements in fair value" will require annual revaluation. For other items "every three or five years may be sufficient." All items within a class of property, plant, and equipment, however, are revalued simultaneously in order to avoid selective revaluation of assets and the reporting of amounts in the financial statements that are a mixture of costs and values at different dates. A class of assets may be revalued on a rolling basis, provided revaluation of the class of assets is completed within a short period of time and provided the revaluations are kept up to date. A class of property, plant, and equipment is a grouping of assets of a similar nature and use in an enterprise's operations.

IAS 16, paragraph 33, discusses the treatment of accumulated depreciation. The wording is obscure, and we quote the paragraph in full.

> When an item of property, plant and equipment is revalued, any accumulated depreciation at the date of the revaluation is either:
>
> (a) restated proportionately with the change in the gross carrying amount of the asset so that the carrying amount of the asset after revaluation equals its revalued amount. This method is often used when an asset is revalued by means of an index to its depreciated replacement cost; or
>
> (b) eliminated against the gross carrying amount of the asset and the net amount restated to the revalued amount of the asset. For example, this method is used for buildings that are revalued to their market value.
>
> The amount of the adjustment arising on the restatement or elimination of accumulated depreciation forms part of the increase or decrease in carrying amount which is dealt with in accordance with paragraphs 37 and 38.

Item (a) appears to suggest the following. Suppose we have an asset to which IAS 16 applies, cost 10,000, useful life 5 years, estimated residual value nil, now 3 years old. This will be recorded as:

Cost	Depreciation	Carrying Amount
10,000	6,000	4,000

The asset is now revalued, by index or otherwise, to a new gross figure of 15,000, that is, the new "cost" is 15,000. The depreciation is now "restated proportionately," that is, it is also increased by 50%. We thus end up with:

Gross Revaluation	Depreciation	Carrying Amount
15,000	9,000	6,000

This increase in carrying amount of 2,000 is then dealt with as discussed below.

Item (b) above suggests a different sequence. Suppose the asset is again recorded before revaluation:

Cost	Depreciation	Carrying Amount
10,000	6,000	4,000

It is now revalued to a current fair value *in its existing state* of 6,000. This means that the new carrying value is to be 6,000. Other balances will need to be altered or eliminated as shown.

Asset Revaluation Account		
Transfer of cost	10,000 | 6,000	Transfer of depreciation
Surplus (calculated)	2,000 | 6,000	New carrying value (given)
	12,000 | 12,000	

As indicated above, the treatment of increases and decreases arising on revaluation is dealt with in IAS 16, paragraphs 37 and 38. On the first revaluation after initial recognition:

- Decreases are charged to the income statement as an expense; and

- Surpluses are credited directly to equity, under the heading of revaluation surplus.

At subsequent revaluations (to the extent that there is a previous revaluation surplus in respect of the same asset held in equity), a decrease should be charged against it, but any excess of deficit over that previous surplus should be expensed to the income statement. Where a previous revaluation gave a deficit in respect of the same asset that was charged to expense, a subsequent revaluation surplus should be recognized as income to the extent of the previous deficit; any excess should be credited to equity.

Such a revaluation surplus reserve is not "realized," and is therefore not "earned," and not available for dividend. However, it is likely to become realized over time. Such revaluation surplus included in equity may be transferred directly to retained earnings when the surplus is realized. The whole surplus may be realized on the retirement or disposal of the asset. Some of the surplus, however, may be realized as the asset is used by the enterprise; in such a case, the amount of the surplus realized is the difference between depreciation based on the revalued carrying amount of the asset and depreciation based on the asset's original cost.

It is noteworthy that the word "may" is used three times in the last three sentences. The increase in carrying amount may be transferred to retained earnings eventually when the asset is disposed of, or gradually over the remaining useful life—thus in effect offsetting in the retained earnings balance the effect of "extra" depreciation. Note that in neither case is there any effect on the income statement for any year; this will be charged in full with the new depreciation expense. Alternatively, it appears that the increase could be left in revaluation surplus forever. Under a historical cost accounting philosophy, this last possibility seems illogical, although under a current cost philosophy it would be logically correct (see Chapter 8).

Depreciation

The formal requirement of IAS 16 for the calculation of depreciation should by now have a familiar ring (par. 41).

The depreciable amount of an item of property, plant, and equipment should be allocated on a systematic basis over its useful life. The depreciation method used should reflect the pattern in which the asset's economic benefits are consumed by the enterprise. The depreciation charge for each period should be recognized as an expense, unless it is included in the carrying amount of another asset (e.g., as part of the manufacturing cost of inventories).

The standard goes into detail about a number of aspects. Value of the asset above carrying amount does not obviate the requirement for annual depreciation. Useful life may be influenced by a number of factors (par. 43) including:

1. The expected usage of the asset by the enterprise;

2. The expected physical wear and tear, which depends on operational factors, such as the number of shifts for which the asset is to be used and the repair and maintenance program of the enterprise, and the care and maintenance of the asset while idle;

3. Technical obsolescence arising from changes or improvements in production, or from a change in the market demand for the product or service output of the asset;

4. Legal or similar limits on the use of the asset, such as the expiration dates of related leases; or

5. Management disposal policies.

Land and buildings are separable assets with different accounting characteristics and should be considered separately, even if acquired as a single purchase. When the "benchmark" measurement approach is used (i.e., when the asset continues to be recorded on the basis of its historical cost), the original estimated residual value (whether nil or otherwise) is not subsequently altered for changes in prices. When the allowed alternative treatment is adopted, however, a new estimate is made at the date of any subsequent revaluation of the asset. The estimate is based on the residual value prevailing at the date of the estimate for similar assets that have reached the end of their useful lives and that have operated under conditions similar to those in which the asset will be used.

> ☞ **PRACTICE POINTER:**   The residual value figure can be ignored (i.e., treated as zero) if "insignificant." It should be estimated (net of expected disposal costs) as at the date of acquisition (or the date of any subsequent revaluation) on the basis of realizable values prevailing at *that* date for similar worn out assets. Thus, no account should be taken of expected future inflation or changes in price levels. This is perhaps prudent but does not seem consistent. With so much estimation and subjectivity involved, would a little bit more do any harm?

The standard mentions three depreciation methods by name: straight-line, reducing (or diminishing) balance, and the sum-of-the-digits (par. 47). This list is neither exhaustive nor in order of preference. The method used for an asset is selected on the basis of the expected pattern of economic benefits and is consistently applied from period to period unless there is a change in the expected pattern of economic benefits from that asset. This implies that for any particular asset, with its own particular expected pattern of economic benefits, there is one particular appropriate method. Once the method has been chosen, consistency is required.

> **OBSERVATION:**   It is sometimes argued, for example in the case of hotels, that depreciation of the building is not necessary on the grounds that its fair value is being maintained by the incurrence of expensive maintenance costs that are being charged as expenses. To charge depreciation as well could appear to be "double-counting."

Standard-setters generally are at pains to counter this argument. It is not valid to argue that maintenance increases residual value at the end of economic life, so in principle the proposition is invalid, although maintenance is certainly a factor in determining the *length* of the economic life. It must be remembered, however, that the useful life could be significantly shorter than the economic life. It certainly seems theoretically valid for a hotel owner to argue that expected residual value at the end of the expected useful life (to him) is equal to or greater than the initial carrying value. This would suggest that, while depreciation needs to be provided, the "correct" figure will be nil! Auditors may be suspicious of this argument.

Both the estimate of useful life and the choice of depreciation method should be reviewed "periodically." Significant changes in estimated useful life, or in the expected pattern of economic benefits, will lead to adjustments of the depreciation charge, by longer life or by change in method, respectively, in respect of current and future periods. It may be necessary, in certain cases, to include an element of decommissioning costs, which will take place at the *end* of the useful life, in the original "cost" figure. This is dealt with in IAS 37, "Provisions, Contingent Liabilities, and Contingent Assets" (see Chapter 28).

It is necessary to determine whether or not an item of property, plant, and equipment has become impaired. This area is covered by IAS 36, "Impairment of Assets" (see Chapter 19). SIC-14, "Property, Plant, and Equipment—Compensation for the Impairment or Loss of Items," makes it clear that monetary or nonmonetary compensation from third parties for items of property, plant, and equipment impaired, lost, or given up should be included in the income statement when recognized, with separate disclosure. There is no question of a reversal of the impairment.

Retirements and Disposals

An item of property, plant, and equipment should be eliminated from the balance sheet on disposal or when the asset is permanently withdrawn from use and no future economic benefits are expected from its disposal (par. 55). Gains or losses arising from the retirement or disposal of an item of property, plant, and equipment should be determined as the difference between the estimated net disposal proceeds and the carrying amount of the asset and should be recognized as income or expense in the income statement. It thus follows that any element of revaluation reserve, whether or not transferred to earnings reserve from revaluation reserve, will not pass through the income statement, as discussed earlier. Property, plant, and equipment that is retired from active use and held for disposal is carried at its carrying amount at the date when the asset is retired from active use. At least at each financial year-end, an enterprise tests the asset for impairment under IAS 36, "Impairment of Assets" (see Chapter 19), and recognizes any impairment loss accordingly.

DISCLOSURE

The disclosure requirements are lengthy, and are as follows.

The financial statements should disclosure, for each class of property, plant, and equipment:

1. The measurement bases used for determining the gross carrying amount. When more than one basis has been used, the gross carrying amount for that basis in each category should be disclosed.
2. The depreciation methods used.
3. The useful lives or the depreciation rates used.
4. The gross carrying amount and the accumulated depreciation (aggregated with accumulated impairment losses) at the beginning and end of the period.
5. A reconciliation of the carrying amount at the beginning and end of the period showing:

   (a) additions;

   (b) disposals;

   (c) acquisitions through business combinations;

   (d) increases or decreases during the period resulting from revaluations and from impairment losses recognized or reversed directly in equity under IAS 36, "Impairment of Assets" (if any);

   (e) impairment losses recognized in the income statement during the period under IAS 36 (if any);

   (f) impairment losses reversed in the income statement during the period under IAS 36 (if any);

   (g) depreciation;

   (h) the net exchange differences arising on the translation of the financial statements of a foreign entity;

   (i) other movements.

Comparative information is not required for the reconciliation in 5 above.

The financial statements should also disclose:

1. The existence and amounts of restrictions on title, and property, plant, and equipment pledged as security for liabilities;
2. The accounting policy for the estimated costs of restoring the site of items of property, plant, or equipment;
3. The amount of expenditures on account of property, plant, and equipment in the course of construction;
4. The amount of commitments for the acquisition of property, plant, and equipment.

When items of property, plant, and equipment are stated at revalued amounts, the following should be disclosed:

1. The basis used to revalue the assets;
2. The effective date of the revaluation;
3. Whether an independent appraiser was involved;
4. The nature of any indexes used to determine replacement cost;
5. The carrying amount of each class of property, plant, and equipment that would have been included in the financial statements had the assets been carried under the benchmark treatment in paragraph 28;
6. The revaluation surplus, indicating the movement for the period and any restrictions on the distribution of the balance to shareholders.

CHAPTER 28
PROVISIONS, CONTINGENT
LIABILITIES, AND CONTINGENT ASSETS

CONTENTS

OVERVIEW

The major purpose of IAS 37, "Provisions, Contingent Liabilities, and Contingent Assets," is to deal with two of the more difficult aspects of liabilities. In principle, one can envisage three types of obligation situation. The first is where the existence of the obligation and the amount of the obligation are definite. This gives rise to a liability proper. The second is where the existence of the obligation is definite but the amount of the obligation is uncertain. This gives rise to a provision, which must be recorded as an estimated liability in the balance sheet. The final situation is when the existence of the obligation is uncertain (the amount probably, but not necessarily, being uncertain, too), and some future event, not wholly within the control of the enterprise, will determine whether an obligation does or does not eventually arise.

This last situation gives rise to a contingent liability. A contingent liability is not recorded in the balance sheet, but it is disclosed in the notes to the accounts unless the possibility of an outflow of resources is "remote." The distinction between a provision and a contingent liability may in practice be a difficult and subjective one, although the definitions discussed below are clear enough.

The standard also deals with contingent assets, which are possible assets that arise from past events but whose existence will be confirmed or denied only by the occurrence or nonoccurrence of one or more uncertain future events not wholly within the control of the enterprise. An example is a claim that an enterprise is pursuing through legal processes, where the outcome is uncertain. An enterprise should not recognize a contingent asset. A contingent asset should be disclosed where an inflow of economic benefits is "probable." When the realization of income is virtually certain, then the related asset is not a contingent asset and its recognition is appropriate.

By way of appendix, IAS 37 gives examples of the application of its principles.

Tables 28-1 and 28-2 give a summary and overview of the major requirements of the standard (with paragraph references to the standard itself).

BACKGROUND

As part of its original series of International Accounting Standards, IASC issued IAS 10, "Contingencies and Events Occurring after the Balance Sheet Date," in 1974. Most of the original IAS 10, that is, all those parts dealing with contingencies, was replaced by IAS 37, "Provisions, Contingent Liabilities, and Contingent Assets," which is operative for annual financial statements beginning on or after July 1, 1999. The remaining parts of the old IAS 10 have since also been superseded as discussed in Chapter 15.

IAS 37 deals with issues that must inevitably involve some difficult and subjective distinctions related to future expectations. It seeks to reduce the subjectivity by clear definitions and clearly stated requirements and by the inclusion of examples to illustrate the application of its principles. Nothing, however, can remove the need for intelligent and professional judgment on the part of accountants involved in the preparation and the auditing of the financial statements. The motto of the standard, though unstated, is perhaps that full necessary disclosure should always take place, whether or not the actual balance sheet itself is to be adjusted.

U.S. GAAP for provisions are broadly similar to IAS GAAP, though contained within several standards rather than one general one. U.S. GAAP for contingencies do not explicitly specify that a contingency should result from past events.

Table 28-1: Provisions and Contingent Liabilities

Where, as a result of past events, there may be an outflow of resources embodying future economic benefits in settlement of (a) a present obligation or (b) a possible obligation whose existence will be confirmed only by the occurrence or nonoccurrence of one or more uncertain future events not wholly within the control of the enterprise.

If:	If:	If:
There is a present obligation that probably requires an outflow of resources.	There is a possible obligation or a present obligation that may, but probably will not, require an outflow of resources.	There is a possible obligation or a present obligation where the likelihood of an outflow of resources is remote.
Then: A provision is recognized (par. 14).	**Then:** No provision is recognized (par. 27).	**Then:** No provision is recognized (par. 27).
Disclosures are required for the provision (pars. 84 and 85).	Disclosures are required for the contingent liability (par. 86).	No disclosure is required (par. 86).

A contingent liability also arises in the extremely rare case where there is a liability that cannot be recognized because it cannot be measured reliably. Disclosures are required for the contingent liability.

Table 28-2: Contingent Assets

Where, as a result of past events, there is a possible asset whose existence will be confirmed only by the occurrence or nonoccurrence of one or more uncertain future events not wholly within the control of the enterprise.

If:	If:	If:
The inflow of economic benefits is virtually certain.	The inflow of economic benefits is probable, but not virtually certain.	The inflow is not probable.
Then: The asset is not contingent (par. 33).	**Then:** No asset is recognized (par. 31).	**Then:** No asset is recognized (par. 31).
	Disclosures are required (par. 89).	No disclosure is required (par. 89).

SCOPE OF APPLICATION

In general, IAS 37 applies to all enterprises. However, there are a number of rather complicated exceptions to this, which need to be considered. These are as follows:

1. IAS 37 does not apply to provisions, contingent liabilities, or contingent assets that result from financial instruments that are carried at fair value. It does, however, apply to financial instruments, that are not carried at fair value. See the discussion on financial instruments in Chapter 16.

2. IAS 37 does not apply to provisions, contingent liabilities, or contingent assets that result from executory contracts, unless the contract is onerous. Executory contracts are contracts under which neither party has performed any of its obligations or both parties have partially performed their obligations to an equal extent. An onerous contract is a contract in which the unavoidable costs of meeting the obligations under the contract exceed the economic benefits expected to be received under it.

3. The standard does not apply to items arising in insurance enterprises from contracts with their policyholders, but it does apply to provisions, contingent liabilities, and contingent assets of insurance enterprises, other than those arising from contracts with policyholders.

4. Where another International Accounting Standard deals with a specific type of provision, contingent liability, or contingent asset, an enterprise applies that standard instead of IAS 37. For example, certain types of provisions are also addressed in standards on:

   (a) construction contracts (see IAS 11, "Construction Contracts," discussed in Chapter 10);

   (b) income taxes (see IAS 12, "Income Taxes," discussed in Chapter 20);

   (c) leases (see IAS 17, "Leases," discussed in Chapter 25). However, as IAS 17 contains no specific requirements to deal with operating leases that have become onerous, IAS 37 applies to such cases; and

   (d) employee benefits (see IAS 19, "Employee Benefits," discussed in Chapter 13).

With the above exceptions, IAS 37 applies to all provisions, contingent liabilities, and contingent assets as defined in the standard.

> ☛ **PRACTICE POINTER:** These terms, especially the word *provision*, may be used loosely in some jurisdictions with other

meanings. For example, the terms *provision for depreciation* and *provision for doubtful debts*, are in common use. Such items are not provisions in the sense used by this standard, and the standard does not deal with them.

DEFINITIONS AND MEANINGS

Liabilities are defined as in IAS 1. A *liability* is a present obligation of the enterprise arising from past events, the settlement of which is expected to result in an outflow from the enterprise of resources embodying economic benefits. A *provision* is a liability of uncertain timing or amount (but not of uncertain existence).

Two types of obligation can be distinguished.

- A *legal obligation* is an obligation that derives from:

    (a) a contract (through its explicit or implicit terms), or

    (b) legislation, or

    (c) other operation of law.

- A *constructive obligation* is an obligation that derives from an enterprise's actions where:

    (a) by an established pattern of past practice, published policies, or a sufficiently specific current statement, the enterprise has indicated to other parties that it will accept certain responsibilities; and

    (b) as a result, the enterprise has created a valid expectation on the part of those other parties that it will discharge those responsibilities.

A constructive obligation creates a liability just as much as a legal obligation does.

Again, contingent liabilities, as the term is used in the standard, can arise in two different ways.

- A *contingent liability* is:

    (a) a possible obligation that arises from past events and whose existence will be confirmed only by the occurrence or nonoccurrence of one or more uncertain future events not wholly within the control of the enterprise, or

    (b) a present obligation that arises from past events but is not recognized because:

        (i) it is not probable that an outflow of resources embodying economic benefits will be required to settle the obligation, or

(ii) the amount of the obligation cannot be measured with sufficient reliability.

The meaning of the word *probable* in this definition is of some significance. This is discussed further below.

- A *contingent asset* is a possible asset that arises from past events and whose existence will be confirmed only by the occurrence or nonoccurrence of one or more uncertain future events not wholly within the control of the enterprise.

The distinction between accruals and provisions is that accruals are liabilities to pay for goods or services that have been received or supplied but have not been paid, invoiced, or formally agreed with the supplier, including amounts due to employees (for example, amounts relating to accrued vacation pay). Although it is sometimes necessary to estimate the amount or timing of accruals, the uncertainty is generally much less than for provisions. Accruals are often reported as part of trade and other payables, whereas provisions are reported separately.

In a theoretical sense, the distinction between provisions and contingent liabilities is perhaps less clear, as uncertainty exists in both cases. It may be suggested that:

1. Provisions are *present* obligations (of uncertain amount).

2. Contingent liabilities are either:

    (a) *possible* obligations, because it has yet to be confirmed whether the enterprise has a present obligation that could lead to an outflow of resources embodying economic benefits; or

    (b) *present* obligations that do not meet the recognition criteria in the standard (because either it is not probable that an outflow of resources embodying economic benefits will be required to settle the obligation or a sufficiently reliable estimate of the amount of the obligation cannot be made).

In practice they can be quite easily distinguished by the reader of financial statements, in that provisions *are* included in the balance sheet and contingent liabilities are *not* included in the balance sheet.

RECOGNITION OF PROVISIONS

The standard states (par. 14) that a provision should be recognized when:

1. An enterprise has a present obligation (legal or constructive) as a result of a past event,

2. It is probable that an outflow of resources embodying economic benefits will be required to settle the obligation, and

3. A reliable estimate can be made of the amount of the obligation.

If these conditions are not met, no provision should be recognized.
Comparison of this statement with the definition of a liability given above shows that, in effect, all that paragraph 14 says is that a provision should be recognized when a liability exists and can be reliably estimated.

> **OBSERVATION:** The terminology used by the standard is rather confusing. It states, for example, in paragraph 14 that if certain conditions are not met, then "no provision should be recognized." However, it has already been stated that provisions are recognized as liabilities and that "contingent liabilities" are not recognized as liabilities. It follows that an "unrecognized provision" is not an unrecognized provision. Rather, it is a contingent liability (which is not recognized, by definition). There is some circularity going on here!

Several of the terms used in paragraph 14 warrant some consideration. First of all, there may in certain circumstances (in "rare cases" according to the standard) be real uncertainty as to whether or not a present obligation exists. A lawsuit that is being disputed is a likely example. The standard says that after obtaining and assessing all possible evidence, where it is more likely than not that a present obligation exists at the balance sheet date, the enterprise recognizes a provision (if the recognition criteria are met). Where it is more likely that no present obligation exists at the balance sheet date, the enterprise discloses a contingent liability, unless the possibility of an outflow of resources embodying economic benefits is remote (as discussed below).

"More likely than not" clearly suggests that a 51% probability of the existence, arising from the past event, of a present obligation creates a provision. Equally clearly, 49% probability in such circumstances creates a contingent liability, which will not be recorded in the balance sheet itself.

> **OBSERVATION:** It seems to us quite defensible in logic to argue that when something may or may not happen and there is no means of objective predetermination, the treatment should follow the simple balance of probabilities. It must be said, however, that this attitude is putting the demands of rationality and neutrality above the demands of prudence. On the other hand, since in either event full disclosure is ensured in one way or another, the reader of the financial statements should not be misled, which is arguably the crucial issue. The standard goes out of its way to state that the interpretation of "probable" as "more likely than

not" in IAS 37 is unique to that standard, and it should not necessarily be assumed that the word "probable" as used in any other IASC standard or publication has the same meaning as in IAS 37.

The standard discusses past events at considerable length, although some of its points seem to be statements of the obvious and not all are worthy of comment here. An obligation will arise from a past event only where the settlement of the obligation can be enforced by law or, in the case of a constructive obligation, where the event (which may be an action of the enterprise) creates a valid expectation in other parties that the enterprise will discharge the obligation. The only liabilities recognized in an enterprise's balance sheet are those that exist at the balance sheet date. It is only those obligations arising from past events existing independently of an enterprise's future actions (i.e., the future conduct of its business) that are recognized as provisions.

It follows from the above that, for example, unavoidable decommissioning costs at the end of a plant's useful life do give rise to a provision during the life of the plant. However, if an enterprise intends to spend money on amending its factory processes but could avoid spending by changing its mode of operation, then it has no present obligation for that future expenditure, and no provision is required—indeed under the theoretical logic of the standard, no provision is permitted.

The standard points out that a "reliable estimate" is, of course, still an estimate. Estimates based on knowledge and experience, and statistical probability in the case of large numbers of possible obligations within the same class (as with product warranties for example), do provide adequate reliability. Except in extremely rare cases, an enterprise will be able to determine a range of possible outcomes and can therefore make an estimate of the obligation that is sufficiently reliable to use in recognizing a provision.

In the extremely rare case where no reliable estimate can be made, a liability exists that cannot be recognized. That liability is disclosed as a contingent liability.

CONTINGENT LIABILITIES, CONTINGENT ASSETS, AND RECOGNITION

As already indicated, the rule is quite simple. No contingent liability or contingent asset should be recognized; no contingent liability or contingent asset should be recorded in the balance sheet. The requirements for disclosure in the notes to the financial statements are discussed below.

In respect of contingent items, it is necessary to reassess the situation regularly (the standard says "continually") to see whether the likelihood of inflows or outflows of resources has increased. If it becomes probable that an outflow of future economic benefits will be required for an item previously dealt with as a contingent liability, a provision is recognized in the financial statements of the period in which the change in probability occurs (except in the extremely rare circumstances where no reliable estimate can be made), that is, the item ceases to be a contingent liability. If it has become virtually certain that an inflow of economic benefits will arise, the asset and the related income are recognized in the financial statements of the period in which the change occurs, that is, the item ceases to be a contingent asset. If an inflow of economic benefits has become probable, an enterprise discloses the contingent asset (see the discussion on disclosure, below).

MEASUREMENT OF PROVISIONS

In essence, the amount recognized as a provision should be the best estimate of the expenditure required to settle the present obligation at the balance sheet date. It should be noted that, in principle, this is not necessarily the same as the best estimate of the expenditure likely to be required to settle the obligation at its likely date of settlement. Where the effect of the time value of money is material, however, the amount of a provision should be the present value of the expenditures expected to be required to settle the obligation. The discount rate should be a pretax rate that reflects current market assessments of the time value of money and the risks specific to the liability. The discount rate should not reflect risks for which future cash flow estimates have been adjusted. Note that where the effect of discounting would be material, discounting is a requirement, not an option.

Where the provision concerns a large population of items, then a statistical calculation of expected values is appropriate, with warranties on large volume sales, for example. If, say, experience suggests that 5% of sales will have minor faults at an average cost of $100 and 2% of sales will have major faults at an average cost of $1,000, and sales have been 20,000 units, then the provision would be calculated as follows:

$$(5\% \times 20,000 \times \$100) + (2\% \times 20,000 \times \$1,000)$$

$$= \$100,000 + \$400,000 = \$500,000$$

Where a single obligation is under consideration, the situation is more complicated. It is worth quoting the comment of the standard, paragraph 40, in full.

Where a single obligation is being measured, the individual most likely outcome may be the best estimate of the liability. However, even in such a case, the enterprise considers other possible outcomes. Where other possible outcomes are either mostly higher or mostly lower than the most likely outcome, the best estimate will be a higher or lower amount. For example, if an enterprise has to rectify a serious fault in a major plant that it has constructed for a customer, the individual most likely outcome may be for the repair to succeed at the first attempt at a cost of 1,000, but a provision for a larger amount is made if there is a significant chance that further attempts will be necessary.

> **OBSERVATION:** At first sight there seems a danger of some confusion and inconsistency here. It will be recalled that in the context of the *recognition* of a provision, that is, the issue of whether or not a provision exists to be recorded, the "more likely than not" criterion is to be used. In paragraph 40 as quoted, the phrase used is "if there is a significant chance." This is not strictly an inconsistency, as paragraph 40 refers only to *measurement*, not to recognition. The meaning of "significance chance" is not discussed, but intuitively a chance could be regarded as significant with a probability considerably (significantly!) less than 50%.
>
> The logical sequence must be carefully followed. First, is there a provision (more likely than not). If not, then measurement is not required. If yes, then measurement of a single obligation should follow paragraph 40, including the significant chance consideration.

The measurement of provisions needs to take full account of risk and uncertainty. Caution is needed in making judgments under conditions of uncertainty, so that income or assets are not overstated and expenses or liabilities are not understated. However, uncertainty does not justify the creation of excessive provisions or a deliberate overstatement of liabilities. Future events that may affect the amount required to settle an obligation should be reflected in the amount of a provision where there is sufficient objective evidence that they will occur.

The phrase "sufficient objective evidence" is an interesting one. IAS 37 gives the example of an expectation of future changes in technology reducing site clean-up costs on the future decommissioning of a plant. There would need to be independent (equals objective?) evidence of the expected existence and effectiveness of the technology involved.

Gains on the expected disposal of assets are not taken into account in measuring a provision, even if the expected disposal is closely linked to the event giving rise to the provision. Instead, an enterprise recognizes gains on expected disposals of assets at the time specified by the International Accounting Standard dealing with the assets concerned.

In some situations significant or even total reimbursement of the cash outflow necessary to settle a provision may be expected, for example, because of insurance contracts or supplier warranties. In most cases, however, the enterprise will remain liable for the whole of the amount in question so that the enterprise would have to settle the full amount if the third party failed to pay for any reason. In this situation, a provision is recognized for the full amount of the liability, and a separate asset for the expected reimbursement is recognized only when it is virtually certain that reimbursement will be received if the enterprise settles the liability.

Whatever the original procedure for the measurement of a provision, provisions should be reviewed at each balance sheet date and adjusted to reflect the current best estimate. If it is no longer probable that an outflow of resources embodying economic benefits will be required to settle the obligation, the provision should be reversed. Note that such reversal is a requirement, not an option. Where discounting is used, the carrying amount of a provision increases in each period to reflect the passage of time. This increase is recognized as an interest expense.

APPLICATION OF RECOGNITION AND MEASUREMENT RULES

IAS 37 gives, in the body of the standard itself, not as appendices, discussions of the application of its principles to three particular areas. The standard is obviously concerned that adequate provisions should be made as soon as they are necessary. But it is at least equally concerned to prevent the creation of unnecessary or unnecessarily high provisions. This is to prevent creative accounting techniques such as income smoothing by the creation of extra provisions in profitable years, or "big bath" techniques, where management artificially accentuates a bad year by creating excessive provisions, thereby earning a steadily improving profit in upcoming years.

Future operating losses are simply dealt with. They do not meet the definition of a liability (being *future* events) and a provision cannot be provided for them. Relevant assets should, however, be tested for impairment under IAS 36, "Impairment of Assets" (see Chapter 19).

As discussed and defined in the "Scope of Application" section of this chapter, IAS 37 does not apply to executory contracts unless they are onerous. If an enterprise has a contract that is onerous, the present obligation under the contract should be recognized and measured as a provision. Before a separate provision for an onerous contract is established, an enterprise recognizes any impairment loss that has occurred on assets dedicated to that contract (see IAS 36, "Impairment of Assets," discussed in Chapter 19).

The third area of application discussed in IAS 37 is that of restructuring. The standard goes into considerable detail, to try to specify the circumstances in which provisions are or are not required as tightly as possible. In this case in particular, IASC is concerned to minimize the possibility of excessive or unjustified provisions. The definition of a restructuring given by IAS 37 is that it is a program that is planned and controlled by management, and materially changes *either:*

1. The scope of a business undertaken by an enterprise, *or*
2. The manner in which that business is conducted.

Examples of events that "may" fall within this definition are given as follows:

1. Sale or termination of a line of business;
2. The closure of business locations in a country or region or the relocation of business activities from one country or region to another;
3. Changes in management structure, for example, eliminating a layer of management; or
4. Fundamental reorganizations that have a material effect on the nature and focus of the enterprise's operations.

A provision for restructuring costs is recognized only when the general recognition criteria for provisions set out in paragraph 14 are met. IAS 37 spends no less than 12 paragraphs discussing the application of paragraph 14 to restructurings. IAS 37 states that a constructive obligation to restructure arises *only* when an enterprise:

1. Has a detailed formal plan for the restructuring, identifying at least:
   (a) the business or part of a business concerned;
   (b) the principal locations affected;
   (c) the location, function, and approximate number of employees who will be compensated for terminating their services;
   (d) the expenditures that will be undertaken;
   (e) when the plan will be implemented; *and*
2. Has raised a valid expectation in those affected that it will carry out the restructuring by starting to implement that plan or announcing its main features to those affected by it.

Whether or not these criteria are met is a question of fact to be determined in each case. The mere announcement, however formal, of a management intention is certainly not by itself sufficient. No obligation can arise related to the sale of an operation until the enterprise is committed to the sale by means of a binding sale agreement. Any restructuring provision should include only the direct expenditure arising from the restructuring, which are those that are both:

1. Necessarily entailed by the restructuring, and
2. Not associated with the ongoing activities of the enterprise.

Any expenditures relating to the *future* activities of the business, such as relocating or retraining staff, marketing, or investment in new processes, cannot be included as part of a restructuring provision. Identifiable future operating losses up to the date of a restructuring are not included in a provision, unless they relate to an onerous contract as defined in the standard.

DISCLOSURE

The disclosure requirements of IAS 37 are extensive and incapable of effective summarization. They are as follows.

For each class of *provision*, an enterprise should disclose:

1. The carrying amount at the beginning and end of the period;
2. Additional provisions made in the period, including increases to existing provisions;
3. Amounts used (i.e., incurred and charged against the provision) during the period;
4. Unused amounts reversed during the period; and
5. The increase during the period in the discounted amount arising from the passage of time and the effect of any change in the discount rate.

Comparative information is not required.

An enterprise should disclose the following for each class of provision:

1. A brief description of the nature of the obligation and the expected timing of any resulting outflows of economic benefits;
2. An indication of the uncertainties about the amount or timing of those outflows. Where necessary to provide adequate information, an enterprise should disclose the major assumptions made concerning future events; and

3. The amount of any expected reimbursement, stating the amount of any asset that has been recognized for that expected reimbursement.

Unless the possibility of any outflow in settlement is "remote," an enterprise should disclose for each class of *contingent liability* at the balance sheet date a brief description of the nature of the contingent liability and, where practicable:

1. An estimate of its financial effect;
2. An indication of the uncertainties relating to the amount or timing of any outflow; and
3. The possibility of any reimbursement.

Where an inflow of economic benefits is probable, an enterprise should disclose a brief description of the nature of the *contingent assets* at the balance sheet date and, where practicable, an estimate of their financial effect.

The use of the phrase "where practicable" in relation to the disclosure of contingent liabilities and continent assets should be noted. What is "impracticable" is not discussed. If any of the required information is omitted on the grounds of impracticability, then that fact must be stated. In "extremely rare" cases, disclosure of some or all of the information required can be expected to prejudice seriously the position of the enterprise in a dispute with other parties on the subject matter of the provision, contingent liability, or contingent asset. In such cases, an enterprise need not disclose the information but should disclose the general nature of the dispute, together with the fact that, and reason why, the information has not been disclosed.

TRANSITIONAL PROVISIONS

The effect of adopting the standard should be reported as an adjustment to the opening balance of retained earnings for the period in which the standard is first adopted. Enterprises are encouraged, but not required, to adjust the opening balance of retained earnings for the earliest period presented and to restate comparative information. If comparative information is not restated, this fact should be disclosed.

APPENDICES TO THE STANDARD

As already indicated, IAS 37 gives a considerable number of examples of the application of the standard by way of appendix. These relate to the question of when a provision is to be *recognized*, and are not extended to the problems of the measurement of a recognized provision. Readers involved with difficult recognition decisions should read the appendix to IAS 37 carefully, and apply the examples directly or by analogy.

Also see the decision tree in Figure 28-1.

Figure 28-1: Decision Tree for Provisions and Contingent Liabilities

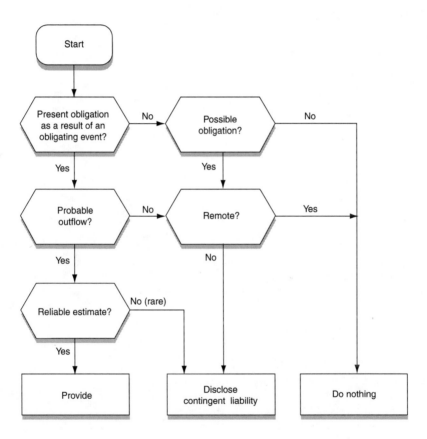

CHAPTER 29
RELATED PARTY DISCLOSURES

CONTENTS

OVERVIEW

The existence of related party relationships, that is, relationships where the independence necessary for "arm's-length" transactions does not exist, carries at least the possibility that transactions will take place that would not otherwise have done so or that the value of transactions may be different from what it would otherwise have been. The principle followed by IAS GAAP is that disclosure of the relationships and of the transactions is necessary, so that the reader of the financial statements is made aware of the lack of independence and its implications. There is no suggestion, however, that quantification of the monetary effect of the relationship is required. Disclosure is addressed, not measurement. The matter is dealt with by IAS 24, "Related Party Disclosures." Effective from January 1, 1986, IAS 24 is now one of the older standards.

BACKGROUND

As indicated above, the principle of IAS 24 is that disclosure of related party implications is necessary (subject always to the fact that International Accounting Standards are not intended to apply to immaterial items) to ensure an overall fair presentation in financial statements. U.S. GAAP (in FAS-57) are consistent in principle with IAS GAAP, but more detailed. Under U.S. GAAP the nature and extent of any transactions with all related parties should be disclosed, together with the amounts involved. All material related party transactions (other than compensation arrangements, expense allowances, and similar items) must be disclosed in the separate financial statements of wholly owned subsidiaries, unless these are presented in the same financial report that includes the parent's consolidated financial statements (including those subsidiaries).

DEFINITIONS

Two key definitions are as follows:

- *Related party*—parties are considered to be related if one party has the ability to control the other party or exercise significant influence over the other party in making financial and operating decisions.

- *Related party transaction*—a transfer of resources or obligations between related parties, regardless of whether a price is charged.

It should be noted that a transaction is here defined as a transfer of resources or obligations, even if no payment, in cash or otherwise, for the transfer is involved.

It is important to consider the difficult concepts of control and significant influence. IAS 24 defines control as follows:

> *Control*—ownership, directly, or indirectly through subsidiaries, of more than one half of the voting power of an enterprise, or a substantial interest in voting power and the power to direct, by statute or agreement, the financial and operating policies of the management of the enterprise.

> **OBSERVATION:** The IAS 24 definition of control (operative from January 1, 1986) should be contrasted with the definition given in IAS 27, "Consolidated Financial Statements and Accounting for Investments in Subsidiaries," operative from January 1, 1990 (par. 6). This states that control, "for the purpose of this standard," is the power to govern the financial and operating policies of an enterprise in order to obtain benefits from its activities. This IAS 27 definition is repeated *verbatim*, even down to the parenthesis, in IAS 28, "Accounting for Investments in Associates," operative also from January 1, 1990 but revised with effect from July 1, 1999 (par. 3).
>
> The IAS 24 definition is noticeably more restrictive than that used in IAS 27 and 28, the former requiring at least a "substantial interest" in voting power and the latter not necessarily requiring any voting power at all. The letter of the regulations explicitly states, of course, that the IAS 27 and 28 definitions apply only to those standards. But IAS GAAP are arguably more concerned

with the spirit of the regulations (compare the philosophy of substance over form, see Chapter 2), and as already pointed out, IAS 24, effective from 1986, comes from an earlier period and ethos in IASC history.

The whole spirit of IAS GAAP is to avoid financial statements being, considered as a totality, misleading. We suggest that the IAS 24 definition needs to be interpreted flexibly in that light.

IAS 24 also gives a definition of significant influence "for the purpose of this standard." This defines significant influence as participation in the financial and operating policy decisions of an enterprise but not control of those policies. Note that "participation" is not defined, but it would need to be "material participation" in order to give significant influence. IAS 24 notes that if the route to significant influence is via share ownership, then the definitions in IAS 28, "Accounting for Investments in Associates," apply (see Chapter 14). Other routes to significant influence are possible, however, statute and agreement being suggested by the standard.

SCOPE

Although the disclosure requirements described below are simply stated and the objective and definitions of the standard are clear in principle, IAS 24 goes to considerable length and complexity to prescribe and delineate when disclosure is or is not required.

The standard begins by saying that it should be applied in dealing with related parties and transactions between a reporting enterprise and its related parties. The requirements of the standard apply to the financial statements of each reporting enterprise. However, it then continues to give a list of related party relationships, notwithstanding the definitions discussed above, which are the "only" relationships with which the standard deals. These are as follows:

1. Enterprises that directly, or indirectly through one or more intermediaries, control, or are controlled by, or are under common control with, the reporting enterprise (this includes holding companies, subsidiaries, and fellow subsidiaries);

2. Associates (see IAS 28, "Accounting for Investments in Associates," see Chapter 14);

3. Individuals owning, directly or indirectly, an interest in the voting power of the reporting enterprise that gives them significant influence over the enterprise, and close members of the family of any such individual (close members of the family of an individual are those that may be expected to influence, or be influenced by, that person in their dealings with the enterprise);

4. Key management personnel, that is, those persons having authority and responsibility for planning, directing, and controlling the activities of the reporting enterprise, including directors and officers of companies and close members of the families of such individuals; and

5. Enterprises in which a substantial interest in the voting power is owned, directly or indirectly, by any person described in 3 or 4 or over which such a person is able to exercise significant influence. This includes enterprises owned by directors or major shareholders of the reporting enterprise and enterprises that have a member of key management in common with the reporting enterprise.

The standard explicitly emphasizes that it is the substance of the relationship that matters, not "merely" the legal form. Although this list is explicitly exhaustive rather than illustrative, it needs to be interpreted broadly. It certainly includes transactions that arise normally in the ordinary course of business, such as directors' remuneration and other emoluments, as well as any other transactions between such parties. The effect of 5 above should be noted. Thus if, for example, a member of the key management personnel is able to exercise significant influence over the holder of a substantial interest in another otherwise completely unconnected enterprise, then a related party situation exists.

The scope and application of IAS 24 is further complicated by a list of specific exclusions. Some of these relate to group financial statements. No disclosure of transactions is required in consolidated financial statements in respect of intragroup transactions in parent financial statements when they are made available or published with the consolidated financial statements and in financial statements of a wholly-owned subsidiary if its parent is incorporated in the same country and provides consolidated financial statements in that country. In addition, no disclosure is required in financial statements of state-controlled enterprises of transactions with other state-controlled enterprises.

Further, in the context of IAS 24, a number of enterprises are "deemed" not to be related parties as follows:

1. Two companies simply because they have a director in common, notwithstanding paragraphs 4 and 5 above (but it is necessary to consider the possibility, and to assess the likelihood, that the director would be able to affect the policies of both companies in their mutual dealings);

2. Providers of finance, trade unions, public utilities, government departments and agencies in the course of their normal dealings with an enterprise by virtue only of those dealings (al-

though they may circumscribe the freedom of action of an enterprise or participate in its decision-making process); and

3. A single customer, supplier, franchiser, distributor, or general agent with whom an enterprise transacts a significant volume of business merely by virtue of the resulting economic dependence.

IAS 24 spends six paragraphs (pars. 12–17) in discussing, but not appraising, methods that may be used in practice in determining the price to be used in related party transactions. Because it expresses no preferences, and its requirements do not require quantification of the effects of the "relatedness" of the relationship, the value added by these paragraphs seems arguable.

DISCLOSURE

Essentially there are two separate disclosure requirements to consider. The first exists when there is a related party relationship that involves control (the meaning of control having been discussed at length above). Where control exists, related party relationships should be disclosed (par. 20), whether or not any transactions have taken place between the parties. This is considered necessary so that readers of the financial statements can form a view about the actual or potential effects of the related party relationships.

The second disclosure requirement applies to any related party relationship. In other words, it applies to related party relationships with control, as does the first disclosure requirement, but in addition applies to related party relationships with significant influence. This second requirement (par. 22) is that if there have been transactions between related parties, the reporting enterprise should disclose the nature of the related party relationships as well as the types of transactions and the elements of the transactions necessary for an understanding of the financial statements.

The elements of transactions necessary for an understanding of the financial statements would normally include an indication of the volume of the transactions, either as an amount or as an appropriate proportion, amounts or appropriate proportions of outstanding items and pricing policies. Items of a similar nature may be disclosed in aggregate except when separate disclosure is necessary for an understanding of the effects of related party transactions on the financial statements of the reporting enterprise.

The above wording is, necessarily, somewhat imprecise. It clearly does not require monetary quantification of the effects of the "relatedness" of the parties to the transaction, although some indication is required in respect of "outstanding items." The substance and spirit of the requirements, we suggest, is that readers of the financial statements should not be misled as to the actual or potential significance and effect of the related party relationships.

National law may require disclosure in relation to some categories of related parties, transactions with directors being a common example. Other International Accounting Standards also contain specific requirements that are relevant to certain related party situations. IAS 27, "Consolidated Financial Statements and Accounting for Investments in Subsidiaries," and IAS 28, "Accounting for Investments in Associates," require various disclosures in relation to consolidated subsidiaries and associates, respectively (see Chapters 9 and 14). IAS 8, "Net Profit or Loss for the Period, Fundamental Errors, and Changes in Accounting Policies," requires disclosure of extraordinary items and items of income and expense within profit or loss from ordinary activities that are of such size, nature, or incidence that their disclosure is relevant to explain the performance of the enterprise for the period (see Chapter 26).

IAS 1, "Presentation of Financial Statements," requires disclosure concerning payables to and receivables from related enterprises (see Chapter 3). IAS 14, "Segment Reporting," where applicable, requires the disclosure of intersegment pricing (see Chapter 31), and IAS 31, "Financial Reporting of Interests in Joint Ventures," requires various disclosures in relation to joint ventures (see Chapter 14).

It should be noted, however, that IAS 24 specifically observes (par. 25) that consolidated financial statements treat the group, that is, the parent and subsidiaries, as a single reporting enterprise. It follows that details of transactions between members of the group need not be disclosed in such consolidated accounts. It also follows logically, of course, that this exemption does not apply to the individual accounts, where published, of either parent or subsidiary enterprises. Likewise, transactions with associated enterprises accounted for under the equity method (see Chapter 14) are not eliminated in consolidated accounts, and therefore such transactions do require disclosure as related party transactions as part of the consolidated financial statements.

An example of disclosure is given on the following page.

Illustration of Disclosure

Information Relating to the Board of Management and Supervisory Board of Hoechst AG

	1997 *DM*	*1996* *DM*
Supervisory Board emoluments	2,365,000	2,214,500
Board of Management emoluments	14,967,758	13,760,208
Pensions for former members of the Board of Management or their surviving dependents	12,757,904	12,459,677
Pension provisions for former members of the Board of Management or their surviving dependents	130,557,286	111,038,029
Loans to members of the Board of Management		44,740

Interest is charged on loans to Board of Management members at an annual rate of 4% or 6.5%. DM 14,160 was repaid in 1996. The loan balance was sold on November 1, 1997.

CHAPTER 30
REVENUE

CONTENTS

OVERVIEW

The primary issue in accounting for revenue is determining when to recognize revenue. Revenue is recognized when it is "probable" that future economic benefits will flow to the enterprise and these benefits can be measured reliably. IAS GAAP for this area are contained in IAS 18, "Revenue." This standard identifies the circumstances in which the criteria will be met and, therefore, revenue will be recognized. It also provides practical guidance on the application of these criteria.

BACKGROUND

The profit or earnings figure reported by an enterprise for an accounting period is in essence the result of a two-stage process. Stage 1 is to define and delineate the revenues to be recognized in the period. Stage 2 is to define and delineate the corresponding expenses, the net of the two figures being the profit. Many International Accounting Standards are directly or indirectly about aspects of expense determination. But revenue is logically the first issue to consider, as the timing of revenue recognition significantly affects the timing of expense recognition—sales and cost of sales being an obvious and significant example.

The general principles outlined above are included in the IASC Framework (see Chapter 2). Key distinctions are discussed in detail below. IAS GAAP regarding revenues are contained in IAS 18, "Revenues," effective from January 1, 1995. This standard replaced an earlier standard called "Revenue Recognition," also numbered 18, which had been effective since 1982.

Perhaps rather surprisingly, neither U.S. nor U.K. GAAP contain a standard dealing with general principles, as opposed to specific applications, of revenue and its recognition. There are no significant differences of principle between these jurisdictions. It should not necessarily be assumed, however, that the typical interpretation of "probable" is the same across the various jurisdictions.

SCOPE AND DEFINITIONS

IAS 18 should be applied in accounting for revenue arising from the following transactions and events:

1. The sale of goods,
2. The rendering of services, or
3. The use by others of enterprise assets yielding interest, royalties, and dividends.

Revenue is formally defined in paragraph 7 as follows:

> *Revenue* is the gross inflow of economic benefits during the period arising in the course of the ordinary activities of an enterprise when those inflows result in increases in equity, other than increases relating to contributions from equity participants.

There are some subtleties in this definition, which require careful consideration. Under IAS definitions, revenue is a subset of income. Income is defined in the "Framework for the Preparation and Presentation of Financial Statements" (see Chapter 2) as increases in economic benefits during the accounting period in the form of inflows or enhancements of assets or decreases of liabilities that result in increases in equity, other than those relating to contributions from equity participants. Income encompasses both revenue and gains. Revenue has been defined above. Gains (Framework, par. 75) represent "other items that meet the definition of income and may, or may not, arise in the course of the ordinary activities of an enterprise."

This is not entirely clear either. The Framework says that revenue is "referred to by a variety of different names including sales, fees, interest, dividends, royalties and rent." Gains "include, for example, those arising on the disposal of non-current assets." Unrealized gains that are recognized in the income statement are part of income but are not revenue.

> ☞ **PRACTICE POINTER:** The notion of "ordinary activities" is the central determinant of the distinction between revenue and gains. For example, sales of real estate would lead to revenue for a property development company, but to gains for an industrial or commercial enterprise.
>
> The position of a disposal of a depreciating non-current asset leading to a surplus on disposal over the depreciated carrying value, is not theoretically so clear. In our view this is logically seen as a correction to earlier depreciation estimates. Because these earlier depreciation charges are certainly operating expenses, then the surplus on disposal is logically an operating item too and therefore within the ordinary activities (but perhaps as negative expense not as revenue).

Revenue includes only the gross inflows of economic benefits received and receivable by the enterprise on its own account. Amounts collected on behalf of third parties such as sales taxes, goods and services taxes, and value-added taxes are not economic benefits that flow to the enterprise and do not result in increases in equity. Therefore, they are excluded from revenue. Under the same argument, the revenue of an agent is the commission earned, not the gross amount collected on behalf of the principal.

The standard comments on each of the three types of "transactions and events" included within its scope. The sale of goods embraces goods produced by the enterprise for the purpose of sale and goods purchased for resale, such as merchandise purchased by a retailer or land and other property held for resale. The rendering of services typically involves the performance by the enterprise of a contractually agreed task over an agreed period of time. The services may be rendered within a single period or over more than one period. Some contracts for the rendering of services are directly related to construction contracts, for example, those for the services of project managers and architects. Revenue arising from these contracts is dealt with under IAS 11, "Construction Contracts" (see Chapter 10), not under IAS 18.

The use by others of enterprise assets gives rise to revenue in the form of (par. 5):

1. Interest—charges for the use of cash or cash equivalents or amounts due to the enterprise;
2. Royalties—charges for the use of long-term assets of the enterprise, for example, patents, trademarks, copyrights, and computer software; and
3. Dividends—distributions of profits to holders of equity investments in proportion to their holdings of a particular class of capital.

It should be noted that this set of three "forms" of revenue is exhaustive as far as the application of IAS 18 to the use by others of enterprises' assets is concerned.

Apart from the implications for the scope and coverage of IAS 18 arising form the above discussion, IAS 18 gives a number of explicit exclusions in paragraph 6. IAS 18 does not deal with revenue arising from:

1. Lease agreements (see IAS 17, "Leases," Chapter 25);
2. Dividends arising from investments that are accounted for under the equity method (see IAS 28, "Accounting for Investments in Associates," discussed in Chapter 14);
3. Insurance contracts of insurance enterprises;
4. Changes in the fair value of financial assets and financial liabilities or their disposal (see IAS 39, "Financial Instruments: Recognition and Measurement," Chapter 16);
5. Changes in the value of other current assets;
6. Initial recognition of, or from fair value of, changes in the biological assets related to agricultural activity (see IAS 41, "Agriculture," Chapter 32);
7. Initial recognition of agricultural produce (see IAS 41, "Agriculture," Chapter 32); and
8. The extraction of mineral ores.

The only other definition given by IAS 18 is the familiar concept of fair value. It is repeated here for completeness.

> *Fair value* is the amount for which an asset could be exchanged, or a liability settled, between knowledgeable, willing parties in an arm's-length transaction.

MEASUREMENT OF REVENUE

The above definition of fair value leads to what is ostensibly a simple rule, namely, that revenue should be measured at the fair value of the consideration received or receivable, taking into account the amount of any trade discounts and volume rebates allowed by the enterprise. When the inflow of cash or cash equivalents is deferred, the fair value of the consideration may be significantly less than the nominal amount of cash received or receivable. When the arrangement effectively constitutes a financing transaction, the fair value of the consideration is determined by discounting all future receipts using an imputed rate of interest. The imputed rate of interest is the more clearly determinable of either:

1. The prevailing rate for a similar instrument of an issuer with a similar credit rating, or
2. A rate of interest that discounts the nominal amount of the instrument to the current cash sales price of the goods or services.

Remember that, as always, the concept of materiality applies when considering whether discounting is necessary.

Sometimes goods or services are exchanged, or swapped, without a cash movement. Two possible situations can arise. If the exchange or swap is for goods or services that are "of a similar nature and value," then the exchange is not regarded as a transaction that generates revenue. This is often the case with commodities like oil or milk where suppliers exchange or swap inventories in various locations to fulfil demand on a timely basis in a particular location. However, when goods are sold or services are rendered in exchange for dissimilar goods or services, the exchange is regarded as a transaction that generates revenue. The revenue is measured at the fair value of the goods or services received, adjusted by the amount of any cash or cash equivalents transferred. Note carefully that it is the fair value of what is received that has to be considered, not the fair value of what was rendered. Note also that although fair value is by definition the result that would arise in an arm's-length transaction, the requirement to measure revenue at fair value applies to both arm's-length and non-arm's-length transactions. Again, it is the fair value of goods or services received that must be used.

Care must be used in defining "a transaction" for the purpose of revenue measurement. The principle of substance over form is paramount. For example, when the selling price of a product includes an identifiable amount for subsequent servicing, that amount is deferred and recognized as revenue over the period during which the service is performed. Conversely, the recognition criteria are applied to two or more transactions together when they are linked in such a way that the commercial effect cannot be understood without reference to the series of transactions as a whole. For example, an enterprise may sell goods and, at the same time, enter into a separate binding agreement to repurchase the goods at a later date. In this latter situation the substance of the two transactions is that there is, in effect, no sale at all and, therefore, no revenue.

SALE OF GOODS

IAS 18 requires that five conditions be satisfied before revenue from the sale of goods is recognized. These are (par. 14):

1. The enterprise has transferred to the buyer the significant risks and rewards of ownership of the goods.

2. The enterprise retains neither continuing managerial involvement to the degree usually associated with ownership, nor effective control over the goods sold.

3. The amount of revenue can be measured reliably.

4. It is probable that the economic benefits associated with the transaction will flow to the enterprise.

5. The costs incurred or to be incurred in respect of the transaction can be measured reliably.

Several of these criteria require further comment. For typical retail sales, the transfer of the significant risks and rewards occurs on the transfer of possession or of legal title to the buyer. However, an enterprise may retain a significant risk of ownership in a number of ways. Examples of situations in which the enterprise may retain the significant risks and rewards of ownership are:

- When the enterprise retains an obligation for unsatisfactory performance not covered by normal warranty provisions;

- When the receipt of the revenue from a particular sale is contingent on the derivation of revenue by the buyer from its sale of the goods;

- When the goods are shipped subject to installation and the installation is a significant part of the contract, which has not yet been completed by the enterprise; or

- When the buyer has the right to rescind the purchase for a reason specified in the sales contract and the enterprise is uncertain about the probability of return.

Again, the risks retained must be significant, that is, material, for the above to apply.

Requirement 2 deals with what is theoretically a question of fact in each particular situation. For example, if the seller transfers title to a buyer but retains control over that buyer's own marketing and pricing policies, then the reality of the transaction might be that the buyer is in substance acting as agent for the seller.

Requirements 3 and 5 are straightforward in principle, as profit cannot be adequately quantified without reliable measurement of revenue and expense. Reliable is, of course, a relative term, not an absolute. Requirement 4 may give problems in the case, for example, of exchange control restrictions. It may be uncertain that a foreign governmental authority will grant permission to remit the consideration from a sale in a foreign country. When the permission is granted, the uncertainty is removed and revenue is recognized. However, when an uncertainty arises about the collectability of an amount already included in revenue, the uncollectable amount or the amount in respect of which recovery has ceased to be probable is recognized as an expense rather than as a reduction of the amount of revenue originally recognized.

RENDERING OF SERVICES

There are two situations to be considered under rendering of services, when the outcome of the service transaction can be measured "reliably" and when it cannot. During the early stages of a transaction, it is often the case that the outcome of the transaction cannot be estimated reliably. Nevertheless, it may be probable that the enterprise will recover the transaction costs incurred. Therefore, revenue is recognized only to the extent of costs incurred that are expected to be recoverable. As the outcome of the transaction cannot be estimated reliably, no profit is recognized. This is a long-winded way of saying that the costs incurred to date are carried forward as assets. Naturally, if recovery of the transaction costs is not reasonably foreseeable, then the costs to date must be written off as expenses.

The second situation to be considered is where the outcome of the transaction can be measured "reliably." In such cases, the revenue associated with the transaction should be recognized by reference to the stage of completion of the transaction at the balance sheet date. The outcome of a transaction can be estimated reliably when all the following conditions are satisfied:

1. The amount of revenue can be measured reliably.
2. It is probable that the economic benefits associated with the transaction will flow to the enterprise.
3. The stage of completion of the transaction at the balance sheet date can be measured reliably.
4. The costs incurred for the transaction and the costs to complete the transaction can be measured reliably.

This is the percentage-of-completion method, which is required and discussed in detail in relation to construction contracts (see Chapter 10). IAS 18 explicitly states that the requirements of IAS 11, "Construction Contracts," are generally applicable to the recognition of revenue and the associated expenses for a transaction involving the rendering of services.

The above criteria are likely to be met provided that the enterprise has an effective internal budgeting and reporting system and that a clear agreement on terms has been reached with the customer. In practice, where a large number of regular acts of service are to be performed, revenue can be recognized on a simple time basis.

INTEREST, ROYALTIES, AND DIVIDENDS

Two conditions are necessary for revenue arising from the use by others of enterprise assets leading to interest, royalties, or dividends. These are that (par. 29):

1. It is probable that the economic benefits associated with the transaction will flow to the enterprise, and

2. The amount of the revenue can be measured reliably.

Revenue should then be recognized on the following bases:

- Interest should be recognized on a time proportion basis that takes into account the effective yield on the asset.

- Royalties should be recognized on an accrual basis in accordance with the substance of the relevant agreement.

- Dividends should be recognized when the shareholder's right to receive payment is established.

The effective yield on an asset is the rate of interest required to discount the stream of future cash receipts expected over the life of the asset to equate to the initial carrying amount of the asset. Interest revenue includes the amount of amortization of any discount, premium, or other difference between the initial carrying amount of a debt security and its amount at maturity.

It is important to distinguish, in all cases of revenue recognition, between uncertainty of recognition and uncertainty of collection of receivables after recognition. Revenue is recognized only when it is probable that the economic benefits associated with the transaction will flow to the enterprise. However, when an uncertainty arises about the collectability of an amount already included in revenue, the uncollectable amount, or the amount in respect of which recovery has ceased to be probable, is recognized as an expense, rather than as a reduction of the amount of revenue originally recognized.

DISCLOSURE

The disclosure requirements are straightforward and are given below (par. 35). An enterprise should disclose:

1. The accounting policies adopted for the recognition of revenue, including the methods adopted to determine the stage of completion of transactions involving the rendering of services;
2. The amount of each significant category of revenue recognized during the period including revenue arising from:
   (a) the sale of goods,
   (b) the rendering of services,
   (c) interest,
   (d) royalties,
   (e) dividends; and
3. The amount of revenue arising from exchanges of goods or services included in each significant category of revenue.

ILLUSTRATIONS

IAS 18 contains an Appendix, which gives no less than twenty illustrations of the application of the standard to particular types of situation. The appendix is illustrative only, and the examples do not modify or override the principles in the standard itself. Many of the illustrations are simple and/or repetitive of statements within the standard. Readers who study all these examples in the standard should note that the examples generally assume that the amount of revenue can be measured reliably, it is probable that the economic benefits will flow to the enterprise, and the costs incurred or to be incurred can be measured reliably.

We reproduce below two of the more interesting applications given.

Layaway Sales under Which the Goods Are Delivered Only When the Buyer Makes the Final Payment in a Series of Installments

Revenue from layaway sales is recognized when the goods are delivered. However, when experience indicates that most such sales are consummated, revenue "may" be recognized when a significant deposit is received, provided the goods are on hand, identified, and ready for delivery to the buyer.

Initiation, Entrance, and Membership Fees

In the case of initiation, entrance, and membership fees, revenue recognition depends on the nature of the services provided. If the fee permits only membership and all other services or products are paid for separately, or if there is a separate annual subscription, the fee is recognized as revenue when no significant uncertainty as to its collectability exists. If the fee entitles the member to services or publications to be provided during the membership period or to purchase goods or services at prices lower than those charged to nonmembers, it is recognized on a basis that reflects the timing, nature, and value of the benefits provided.

CHAPTER 31
SEGMENT REPORTING

CONTENTS

OVERVIEW

The key objective of segment reporting is to assist the user of financial statements in making judgments about the opportunities and risks facing an enterprise by the disclosure of finer information than that provided in the primary financial statements. The information is finer in that it provides an analysis of the enterprise's financial performance in the various market areas in which it operates. Market areas may be understood in the sense of product markets (business segments) and geographic markets (geographic segments), and one of the issues in segment reporting is whether these two types of segment should be given equal weight in the analysis. Disclosure of appropriate segment information enables the user of financial statements to observe the enterprise's performance by market area, for example, in terms of returns on assets employed and on sales and of cash flows. In addition, the enterprise's performance in the various segments can be examined in light of changes in sales and in assets employed in each segment.

For segment reporting to be truly useful, however, it must be comparable both over time for the same enterprise and cross-sectionally between enterprises. The latter is hard to achieve, especially regarding business segments, as this requires the segments themselves to be comparable, that is, similar in composition. Other potential pitfalls in achieving cross-sectional comparability in segment reporting are those relating to accounting methods and particularly the treatments of: (a) costs and assets common to more than one reportable segment; and (b) intersegment sales, with the attendant issue of transfer prices.

IAS 14, "Reporting Financial Information by Segment," as revised in 1997, addresses the issue of cross-sectional comparability by providing sets of criteria to be used in arriving at the composition of a segment for financial reporting purposes. In addition, the basis of intersegment transfer pricing must be disclosed. The sets of criteria to be used in arriving at the composition of a segment differ depending on whether the segment is business or geographic. They may be expected to result in a reasonable degree of cross-sectional comparability.

IAS 14 emphasizes "similarity of risks and returns" as the overarching criterion in identifying the segments of an enterprise for financial reporting purposes. However, the structure of the enterprise's organization and internal financial reporting system are accepted as normally providing an acceptable basis for segment identification, including the choice of which type of segment, business or geographic, is treated as "primary" rather than "secondary." The latter choice is crucial, since the level of disclosure required for primary segments is much greater than that required for secondary segments, which latter does not permit comparisons of profitability or cash-generating performance.

BACKGROUND

FAS-14, "Financial Reporting for Segments of a Business Enterprise," was issued in 1976 and was the first financial reporting standard (national or international) on this subject. Five years later, IAS 14, "Reporting Financial Information by Segment," was issued. During the 1990s, there was increasing recognition of the importance of segment information in analyzing enterprise performance. In 1997, the Financial Accounting Standards Board (FASB) responded to the criticism that FAS-14 did not require sufficient disclosure by replacing it with FAS-131. In 1996, the IASC made a major revision to IAS 14 (and shortened its name to "Segment Reporting"). The revised

IAS 14 was finally approved in July 1997. There was substantial cooperation between the IASC, the FASB, and the Canadian Institute of Chartered Accountants (CICA) in deciding the content of the new standards. Consequently, there is much similarity between FAS-131 and the revised IAS 14, and both standards follow a "management approach" to identifying segments based on the structure of the internal financial reporting system. This approach is applied somewhat differently in the two standards, however, which may lead to differences in practice. Also, FAS-131 requires the disclosure of certain items not required by IAS 14.

The main differences are as follows:

1. Unlike IAS 14, FAS-131 does not have a category of "secondary" segments for which a lower level of disclosure is required. However, FAS-131 has a category of "enterprise-wide" information about products and services, geographic areas, and major customers, which must be disclosed separately if this has not been done as part of the segment reporting.

2. Operating segments that are reportable segments according to FAS-131 may be a mixture of business and geographic segments, if that is how the enterprise's management and internal financial reporting system is organized. In the case of "matrix" organizational structures, however, with overlapping geographic and business operating segments, the business segments are the reportable segments. IAS 14 does not permit a mixture of business and geographic segments in primary reportable segments, except in the case of "matrix" organizational structures (see below), but either category may be chosen as the primary segments, depending on the management structure of the enterprise and the dominant source and nature of its risks and returns. The category not chosen as the primary segments will be the secondary segments. In the case of "matrix" structures, both business and geographic segments may be treated as primary.

3. FAS-131 states that a component of an enterprise need not have any earned revenues to be a reportable segment, provided it is engaged in business activities from which revenues *may* be earned. FAS-133 also counts intersegment sales together with external sales in applying the size criteria for reportable segments. IAS 14 requires a reportable segment to have a majority of its revenues earned from sales to external customers, a condition that could not be met in the absence of earned revenues. IAS 14 also excludes intersegment sales in applying the size criteria.

4. FAS-131 states that the accounting methods and performance measures used internally (in the management accounting system) should be used for reporting segment performance but

requires reconciliations of segment information to consolidated information. IAS 14 specifies which performance measures are to be used in segment reporting and requires the accounting methods to be the same as those used in the enterprise's consolidated or own financial statements.

5. In addition to the information required by IAS 14 for primary segments, FAS-131 requires disclosure of interest income and expense, unusual items, and extraordinary items.

6. FAS-131 requires abbreviated segment information in interim financial statements, including segment revenues, profit or loss, and total assets. IAS GAAP (IAS 34, "Interim Financial Reporting") do not require interim disclosure of segment total assets, and disclosure of segment revenues and results is required for primary segments only. This means that when business segments are the primary segments, less information relevant to assessing geographic exposure is required than that required by FAS-131.

SCOPE

IAS 14 is applicable to the financial statements of all enterprises that have issued, or are in the process of issuing, publicly traded securities (equity or debt). Any other enterprises that choose to disclose segment information in financial statements prepared under IAS GAAP must also follow IAS 14.

Segment information is not required for parent financial statements when consolidated financial statements are published. However, subsidiaries with publicly traded securities should disclose their own segment information. If a single financial report contains both the financial statements or consolidated financial statements of an enterprise reporting under IAS GAAP and also the financial statements of another enterprise in which the reporting enterprise has an equity investment accounted for as an associate or joint venture, the segment information to be disclosed in that financial report is that based on the reporting enterprise's own or consolidated financial statements (IAS 14, pars. 1–7).

SEGMENTS

IAS 14 does not define "segment" or "operating segment" as such. Instead, it defines *business* segments, *geographic* segments, and *reportable* segments as follows (par. 9):

- A *business segment* is a distinguishable component of an enterprise that (a) is engaged in providing an individual product or service or a group of *related* products or services, and (b) is subject to risks and returns that are different from those of other business segments.

- A *geographic segment* is a distinguishable component of an enterprise that (a) is engaged in providing products or services within a particular economic environment, and (b) is subject to risks and returns that are different from those of components operating in other economic environments.

- A *reportable segment* is a business segment or a geographic segment as defined above for which IAS 14 requires segment information to be disclosed. The criteria for identifying reportable segments are discussed below.

Business Segments

Factors that should be considered in determining whether products and services are *related* include:

1. The nature of the products or services;
2. The nature of the production processes;
3. The type or class of customer for the products or services;
4. The methods used to distribute the products or provide the services; and
5. If applicable, the nature of the regulatory environment, for example, banking, insurance, or public utilities.

There is a presumption in IAS 14 that segments correspond to those organizational units for which information is reported to the board of directors and to the chief executive officer for the purpose of evaluating the unit's past performance and making decisions about future allocations of resources (IAS 14, par. 31). However, one or more internally reported business segments may be combined into a single segment when they are essentially similar in terms of long-term financial performance and the five factors listed above. In rare cases, the internally reported segments may not satisfy the criteria set out in IAS 14, in which case further subdivision is necessary, looking at the next lower level used for internal reporting purposes.

Geographic Segments

Factors that should be considered in identifying geographic segments include:

1. Similarity of economic and political conditions;
2. Relationships between operations in different geographic areas;

3. Proximity of operations;

4. Special risks associated with operations in a particular area;

5. Exchange control regulations; and

6. The underlying currency risks.

A geographic segment may be a country, a group of several countries, or a region within a country, provided that it does not include operations in economic environments with significantly differing risks and returns (IAS 14, par. 12). The standard allows geographic segments to be based on either: (a) the *source* of a segment's goods and services, that is, the location of its production or service facilities and other assets; or (b) the *destination* of a segment's goods and services, that is, the location of its markets and customers. The geographic segments should normally be those organizational units for which information is reported to the board of directors and the chief executive officer for performance appraisal and resource allocation decisions; this will determine the choice of source or destination as the basis of geographic segmentation.

As with business segments, IAS 14 envisages the possibilities that: (a) two organizational units may be combined into one geographic segment if they are "substantially similar" in terms of the six criteria given above; (b) an organizational unit may need to be subdivided in order to arrive at segments that meet those criteria, with reference to the next lower level of units used for internal reporting purposes.

Reportable Segments

The identification of reportable segments under IAS GAAP is a two-stage affair. One stage is concerned with identifying the primary and secondary categories of segment; that is, in the wording of IAS 14, with deciding to which category of segment (business or geographic) the primary, and to which the secondary, reporting format will be applied, if it is reportable (IAS 14, pars. 26–33). The other is concerned with the application of size criteria in order to identify those segments for which disclosure of segment information (whether primary or secondary) is required, that is, those that are reportable (IAS 14, pars. 34–43).

IDENTIFYING THE PRIMARY AND SECONDARY CATEGORIES OF SEGMENT

Normally, the basis for determining the primary and secondary reporting segments is the enterprise's internal organization and management structure and its system of internal financial reporting.

These will usually incorporate either a product–service market (business) or a geographic market orientation, which in turn will reflect management's identification of the predominant sources and nature of the enterprise's risks and returns. If the internal organization structure and reporting systems follow a "matrix approach," in which both a product–service market (business) focus and a geographic market focus are reflected on the enterprise's organization and systems, then IAS 14 prioritizes business segments over geographic segments as the choice for application of the primary reporting format. The standard permits an enterprise with a "matrix" organization structure and reporting system to apply the primary reporting format to both business and geographic segments but not to the latter only.

IAS 14 envisages a situation in which the enterprise's internal organization structure and reporting systems have neither a product–service nor a geographic market focus (for example, the focus might be on legal entities within a group). In such a case, the directors and management of the enterprise are required to make a choice between business and geographic segments for the application of the primary reporting format on the basis of their identification of the predominant sources and nature of the enterprise's risks and returns (IAS 14, pars. 26–30).

The internal reporting system may have segments, some of which satisfy the requirements of IAS 14 for identification as either business or geographic segments (see above) and some of which do not. In this case, the latter (unsuitable) segments should be analyzed into their next lower level of subsegment along either business or geographic lines, and the subsegments will then be identified as potentially reportable segments. This should be done "rather than construct[ing] segments solely for external reporting purposes" (IAS 14, par. 33). However, the resultant potentially reportable segments may be combined with other "substantially similar" ones in light of the size criteria discussed below.

MEETING THE SIZE CRITERIA FOR REPORTABLE SEGMENTS

Two or more internally reported segments of the same category (business or geographic) may be combined, provided they are "substantially similar." For this, they must (a) exhibit similar long-term financial performance; and (b) be similar in terms of the characteristics of the category of segment to which they belong, as set out above (IAS 14, par. 34).

Subject to this, a segment should be identified as a *reportable* segment if the conditions 1(a)–(c) below are satisfied or, if necessary in order to meet the "75% rule," condition 2 below (IAS 14, pars. 35–37):

1. A majority of its revenue is earned from sales to external customers, and at least one of the three conditions (a)–(c) below is satisfied:

   (a) its revenue from sales to external customers and from transactions with other segments is 10% or more of the total revenue, external and internal, of all segments; or

   (b) its segment result, whether profit or loss, is 10% or more of the combined result of all segments in profit, or 10% or more of the combined result of all segments in loss, whichever is the greater in absolute terms; or

   (c) its assets are 10% or more of the total assets of all segments (IAS 14, par. 35).

2. If the reportable segments that have been identified do not have attributable external revenue totaling at least 75% of the enterprise's consolidated revenue (or enterprise revenue if the enterprise does not issue consolidated financial statements), then additional reportable segments *must* be identified until at least 75% of the consolidated (or enterprise) revenue is included in reportable segments.

Condition 1(b) is somewhat complex. The segments must be partitioned into profit makers and loss makers, and their respective profits and losses combined and totaled. Whichever total is larger in absolute amount is then the number to be used as the denominator in calculating the 10% hurdle. The numerator is the segment's result, whether profit or loss. Thus, if the combined total loss of all the loss-making segments is larger than the combined total profit of all the profit-making segments, the combined total loss is used in calculating the 10% hurdle for profit-making, as well as loss-making, segments. Likewise, if the larger combined total is that of profits, this number is used in calculating the 10% hurdle for loss-making, as well as profit-making, segments.

If a segment meets none of the conditions 1(a)–(c) above, it *may* still be designated as a reportable segment or combined with other substantially similar segments to form a reportable segment. If a segment is neither separately reported nor combined, it is included as an unallocated item reconciling the grand totals of the reportable segments to the corresponding consolidated (or enterprise) totals (IAS 14, par. 36).

The 75% minimum threshold means that up to 25% of the operations of an enterprise may be unallocated to reportable segments. However, if a segment for which information is reported to the board of directors and the chief executive officer is not classed as a reportable segment because it earns a majority of its revenue from intersegment sales, even though its revenue from sales to external customers is 10% or more of total enterprise revenue from external customers, this fact should be disclosed, as should the amounts of revenue from the segment's sales to external customers and from its intersegment sales (IAS 14, par. 75).

If the reportable status of a segment changes, in terms of meeting the size criteria, the following rules should be observed for comparative purposes (IAS 14, pars. 42–43):

1. A segment identified as reportable in the immediately preceding reporting period because it satisfied the size criteria should continue to be treated as reportable in the current period, even if it no longer meets the size criteria, if management judges that it is of continuing significance.

2. A segment that meets the size criteria in the current period but that did not do so in the immediately preceding period should have the prior period segment data restated to reflect it as a separate reportable segment in the prior period, unless this is impracticable. This may involve splitting what was a single reportable segment in the prior period disclosures.

VERTICALLY INTEGRATED OPERATIONS

Because IAS 14 limits reportable segments to those that earn a majority of their revenues from sales to external customers, it does not require the "upstream" stages of vertically integrated operations to be identified as separate business segments. However, it does encourage the voluntary reporting of "upstream" and "downstream" stages of vertically integrated operations as separate segments, with appropriate description including the basis for intersegment transfer pricing. If the enterprise does not make this voluntary disclosure, in identifying reportable business segments it should combine the "upstream" (selling) segment with the "downstream" (buying) segment, unless there is no reasonable basis for doing so, in which case the upstream segment should be treated as unallocated (IAS 14, pars. 39–41).

ACCOUNTING POLICIES IN SEGMENT REPORTING

Segment information should be prepared in conformity with the accounting policies adopted for preparing the main financial statements of the group (consolidated) or of the enterprise if no consolidated financial statements are issued. This does not mean that these accounting policies should be applied to the reportable segments as if the latter were separate reporting entities. The results of a detailed calculation made in applying a particular accounting policy at the enterprise-wide level may be reflected at reportable segment level by means of allocations on some reasonable basis, provided such a basis exists. An example is pension calculations, the results of which may be allocated to segments on the basis of demographic data, rather than being recalculated for each segment (IAS 14, pars. 44–45).

Additional segment information, prepared on the basis of accounting policies other than those used in the main financial statements, may be disclosed provided: (a) it is used in internal financial reporting for performance assessment and resource allocation by the board of directors and the chief executive officer; and (b) the basis of accounting measurement used in this additional information is clearly described (IAS 14, par. 46).

Some asset, liability, revenue, or expense items may be shared between two or more reportable segments. IAS 14 does not require such items to be allocated between the segments concerned if the only basis for such allocation is arbitrary or difficult to understand. Allocations should reflect such factors as the nature of the items to be allocated, the activities conducted by the segment, and the relative autonomy of that segment. Related items should also be treated consistently; for example, assets that are used jointly by two or more segments should be allocated to those segments if, and only if, the related revenues and expenses are likewise allocated to those segments (IAS 14, pars. 47–48.)

Revenue from intersegment transactions should be measured and reported on the basis of the actual transfer prices used. This basis and any changes to it should be disclosed, as should any changes in accounting policies used in segment reporting that have a material effect on such information. Prior period information presented for comparative purposes should be restated to reflect such changes unless this is impracticable. Such disclosure should include a description of the nature of the change, the reasons for it, the fact that comparative information has been restated or that it is impracticable to do so, and the financial effect of the change if this is reasonably determinable (IAS 14, par. 74). Changes in the enterprise's accounting policies, including those at the enterprise level that affect segment information, fall within the scope of IAS 8, "Net Profit or Loss for the Period, Fundamental Errors, and Changes in Accounting Policies" (see Chapter 26). If the benchmark treatment set out in IAS 8 is followed, prior period segment information will be restated. If the alternative treatment is followed, the cumulative adjustment that is included in determining the enterprise's net profit or loss is also included in segment result if it is an operating item that can be attributed or reasonably allocated to segments. In the latter case, IAS 8 may require separate disclosure if its magnitude, nature, or incidence is relevant to the explanation of the enterprise's performance for the period.

Some changes in accounting policies relate specifically to segment reporting and do not affect the aggregate information in the main financial statements. Examples are changes in (a) identification of segments, and (b) the basis for allocating revenues and expenses to segments. For comparative purposes, prior period segment information should be restated to reflect any such changes unless this is impracticable. The same does not apply to the effects of changes in the method used to price intersegment transfers, as this does not count as a change in accounting policy; however, the change must be disclosed (IAS 14, pars. 77–79.)

An enterprise may change the identification of its segments and not restate prior period segment information on the new basis because it is impracticable to do so. In such a case, for comparative purposes the enterprise should, for the year in which the change in the identification of segments is made, report segment data using both the old and the new bases of segmentation (IAS 14, par. 76).

DISCLOSURE

An enterprise should indicate the types of products and services included in each reported business segment and indicate the composition of each reported geographic segment, both primary and secondary (IAS 14, par. 80).

The disclosures required under the primary and secondary reporting formats are as given below (IAS 14, pars. 50–72).

PRIMARY REPORTING FORMAT

The disclosure requirements in paragraphs 51–67 should be applied to each reportable segment on the basis of an enterprise's primary reporting format.

An enterprise should disclose segment revenue for each reportable segment. Segment revenue from sales to external customers and segment revenue from transactions with other segments should be separately reported.

An enterprise should disclose segment result for each reportable segment. Segment result is defined as segment revenue minus segment expenses, excluding: (a) extraordinary items; (b) interest and gains or losses on sales of investments and extinguishment of debt, unless the segment's operations are primarily of a financial nature; (c) shares of profits or losses of associates or joint ventures accounted for under the equity method; (d) income tax; (e) general administration expenses, head office expenses, and other enterprise-level expenses, unless they can be related to the segment's operating activities and directly attributed to it or allocated to it on some reasonable basis; (f) any adjustment for minority interests (IAS 14, par. 16).

If an enterprise can compute segment net profit or loss or some other measure of segment profitability other than segment result without arbitrary allocations, reporting of such amount(s) is "encouraged" in addition to segment result, appropriately described. If that measure is prepared on a basis other than the accounting policies adopted for the consolidated or enterprise financial statements, the enterprise must include in its financial statements a clear description of the basis of measurement.

An example of a measure of segment performance above segment result on the income statement is gross margin on sales. Examples of measures of segment performance below segment result on the income statement are profit or loss from ordinary activities (either before or after income taxes) and net profit or loss.

An enterprise should disclose the total carrying amount of segment assets for each reportable segment and should disclose segment liabilities for each reportable segment.

An enterprise should disclose the total cost incurred during the period to acquire segment assets that are expected to be used during more than one period (property, plant, equipment, and intangible assets) for each reportable segment. While this sometimes is referred to as capital additions or capital expenditure, the measurement required by this principle should be on an accrual basis, not a cash basis.

An enterprise should disclose the total amount of expense included in segment result for depreciation and amortization of segment assets for the period for each reportable segment (IAS 14, par. 58).

An enterprise is encouraged, but not required, to disclose the nature and amount of any items of segment revenue and segment expense that are of such size, nature, or incidence that their disclosure is relevant to explain the performance of each reportable segment for the period.

An enterprise should disclose, for each reportable segment, the total amount of significant noncash expenses, other than depreciation and amortization for which separate disclosure is required by paragraph 58, that were included in segment expense and, therefore, deducted in measuring segment result (IAS 14, par. 61).

An enterprise that provides the segment cash flow disclosures that are encouraged by IAS 7 need not also disclose depreciation and amortization expense pursuant to paragraph 58 or noncash expenses pursuant to paragraph 61.

An enterprise should disclose, for each reportable segment, the aggregate of the enterprise's share of the net profit or loss of associates, joint ventures, or other investments accounted for under the equity method if substantially all of those associates' operations are within that single segment.

While a single aggregate amount is disclosed pursuant to the preceding paragraph, each associate, joint venture, or other equity method investment is assessed individually to determine whether its operations are substantially all within a segment.

If an enterprise's aggregate share of the net profit or loss of associates, joint ventures, or other investments accounted for under the equity method is disclosed by reportable segment, the aggregate investments in those associates and joint ventures should also be disclosed by reportable segment.

An enterprise should present a reconciliation between the information disclosed for reportable segments and the aggregated information in the consolidated or enterprise financial statements. In presenting the reconciliation, segment revenue should be reconciled to enterprise revenue from external customers (including disclosure of the amount of enterprise revenue from external customers not included in any segment's revenue); segment result should be reconciled to a comparable measure of enterprise operating profit or loss as well as to enterprise net profit or loss; segment assets should be reconciled to enterprise assets; and segment liabilities should be reconciled to enterprise liabilities.

Paragraphs 69–72 identify the disclosure requirements to be applied to each reportable segment on the basis of an enterprise's secondary reporting format, as follows.

If an enterprise's primary format is geographic segments (whether based on the location of assets or that of customers), it should also report the following segment information for each business segment whose revenue from sales to external customers is 10% or more of total enterprise revenue from sales to external customers or whose segment assets are 10% or more of the total assets of all business segments:

1. Segment revenue from external customers;

2. The total carrying amount of segment assets; and

3. The total cost incurred during the period to acquire segment assets that are expected to be used during more than one period (property, plant, equipment, and intangible assets).

If an enterprise's primary format for reporting segment information is business segments, it should also report the following information:

1. Segment revenue from external customers by geographic area based on the geographic location of its customers, for each geographic segment whose revenue from sales to external customers is 10% or more of total enterprise revenue from sales to all external customers;

2. The total carrying amount of segment assets by geographic location of assets, for each geographic segment whose segment assets are 10% or more of the total assets of all geographic segments; and

3. The total cost incurred during the period to acquire segment assets that are expected to be used during more than one period (property, plant, equipment, and intangible assets) by geographic location of assets, for each geographic segment whose segment assets are 10% or more of the total assets of all geographic segments.

If an enterprise's primary format for reporting segment information is geographic segments that are based on location of assets, and if the location of its customers is different from the location of its assets, then the enterprise should also report revenue from sales to external customers for each customer-based geographic segment whose revenue from sales to external customers is 10% or more of total enterprise revenue from sales to all external customers.

If an enterprise's primary format for reporting segment information is geographic segments that are based on the location of customers, and if the enterprise's assets are located in different geographic areas from its customers, then the enterprise should also report the following segment information for each asset-based geographic segment whose revenues from sales to external customers or segment assets are 10% or more of related consolidated or total enterprise amounts:

1. The total carrying amount of segment assets by geographic location of the assets; and

2. The total cost incurred during the period to acquire segment assets that are expected to be used during more than one period (property, plant, equipment, and intangible assets) by location of the assets.

APPENDIX:
SEGMENT REPORTING

The following pages contain an example of segment reporting. In this example, the primary reporting format is applied to the business segments and the secondary reporting format to the geographic segments. Although compliance with the revised IAS 14 was not required for the 1997 annual report, the group in question (Hoechst) chose to do so.

5 Segment reporting

The realignment of the Group in 1997 has resulted in independent operating entities, whose managements are responsible for determining the operating strategies. The function of Hoechst AG is that of a holding company. The management of the Group and internal reporting were adjusted accordingly.

The segment information prepared in accordance with IAS 14 reflects this new approach.

Segment data

Segment	Life sciences Hoechst Marion Roussel		Behring Diagnostics[2]		Hoechst Schering AgrEvo		Hoechst Roussel Vet		Industry Celanese		Specialty Chemicals[3]	
	1997	1996[1]	1997	1996[1]	1997	1996[1]	1997	1996[1]	1997	1996[1]	1997	1996[1]
External sales	13 296	12 555	727	930	4 056	3 627	869	785	7 809	6 467	4 053	6 782
Intragroup sales	676	550		58	13	12	32		776	735	222	370
Total sales	13 972	13 105	727	988	4 069	3 639	901	785	8 585	7 202	4 275	7 152
Operating profit	1 652	2 038	19	88	314	194	124	73	816	728	283	685
Operating profit, comparable	1 881	1 742	19	57	408	265	129	73	936	786	348	212
Cash flow from operations	2 510	2 640	107	228	627	463	148	76	912	912	399	873
Cash flow from operating acitivities[5]	1 765				507	434	73		642			
Assets	22 944	17 746		1 010	4 428	3 832	531	398	4 916	4 168		5 341
Liabilities	5 334	5 650		232	1 116	963	271	140	1 588	1 496		1 382
Net assets	17 610	12 096		778	3 312	2 869	260	258	3 328	2 672		3 959
Capital expenditures	830	647	94	139	267	162	81	20	498	560	241	612
Research and development costs	2 377	2 155	85	129	511	434	72	52	68	50	91	168
Employees as of December 31,	40 670	39 595		3 234	8 550	7 427	2 090	1 759	12 214	13 820		24 563
Key figures (in %)												
Return on sales	11.8	15.6	2.6	8.9	7.7	5.3	13.8	9.3	9.5	10.1	6.6	9.6
Return on net assets	9.4	16.8		11.3	9.5	6.8	47.7	28.3	24.5	27.2		17.3

[1] Adjusted to comply with management approach
[2] Consolidated until September 30, 1997, see Note 6
[3] Consolidated until June 30, 1997, see Note 6
[4] Polypropylene businesses consolidated until June 30, 1997, see Note 6
[5] Reported for segments that prepare own financial statements at the respective balance sheet date(s)

Comments on the segments

The activities of the Group as at the end of 1997 are comprised of the following classes of activity:
- Life sciences, including Hoechst Marion Roussel (Pharmaceuticals), Hoechst Roussel Vet (Animal health) and Hoechst Schering AgrEvo (Crop protection, crop production, environmental health)
- Industry, including Celanese (Organic basic chemicals), Trevira (Polyester products), Plastics (Polyethylene), Ticona (Technical polymers), Messer (Industrial gases) and Herberts (Paints and coatings).

In 1997, the following segments were transferred to or combined with third parties: Behring Diagnostics (diagnostics) with Dade to form Dade Behring on October 1, and Specialty Chemicals with Clariant on July 1. In addition, the plastics segment was reorganized with the polypropylene businesses being combined with those of BASF to form Targor effective July 1. As the major part of the remaining plastics segment, the polyethylene business was established as a separate legal entity named Hostalen Polyethylen on July 1.

	Trevira 1997	Trevira 1996[1]	Plastics[4] 1997	Plastics[4] 1996[1]	Ticona 1997	Ticona 1996[1]	Messer 1997	Messer 1996[1]	Herberts 1997	Herberts 1996[1]	Other businesses 1997	Other businesses 1996[1]	Segment total 1997	Segment total 1996[1]
	6070	5599	2142	2454	1413	1322	2712	2354	2718	2342	6235	5710	52100	50927
	57	102		12	39		94	116			3564	155	5473	2110
	6127	5701	2142	2466	1452	1322	2806	2470	2718	2342	9799	5865	57573	53037
	282	84	123	203	160	195	370	330	173	120	-29	-120	4287	4618
	344	158	184	172	163	177	357	357	152	132	-53	-180	4868	3951
	505	395	212	321	144	-37	526	577	325	228	120	414	6535	7090
	711				178		473	521	246	188				
	4377	3936	788	1491	1394	1225	3503	2589	1764	1642	4724	4244	49369	47622
	1646	1273	370	529	897	823	886	703	563	456	3912	3083	16583	16730
	2731	2663	418	962	497	402	2617	1886	1201	1186	812	1161	32786	30892
	438	548	138	152	110	82	490	377	146	129	351	582	3684	4010
	106	129	30	33	54	54	53	43	66	64	477	569	3990	3880
	14771	15334	2930	5867	2356	2513	8282	7235	7538	7289	18458	18843	117859	147479
	4.6	1.5	5.7	8.2	11.0	14.8	13.2	13.4	6.4	5.1			7.4	8.7
	10.3	3.2	29.4	21.1	32.2	48.5	14.1	17.5	14.4	10.1			13.1	14.9

Comments on the segment data

Inter-segment sales represent sales to Group companies not belonging to the same segment. Transfer prices for inter-segment sales are set on an arm's length basis.

In calculating operating profit, comparable, certain components of income and expenses are eliminated (see Note 9).

Cash flow from operations is calculated by adjusting operating profit for non-cash operating revenues and expenses, as per the statements of cash flows.

Cash flow from operating activities is calculated by adjusting profit before taxes for non-cash revenues and expenses.

Assets, liabilities, net assets represent assets employed in operations and liabilities owed to third parties excluding corporate debt and taxes, and assets net of liabilities, respectively. Net assets represent the balance after deducting liabilities from assets.

Capital expenditures includes expenditure on property, plant and equipment and investments in intangible assets.

Other businesses includes those product areas and service operations that are not shown separately due to their insignificance (individually less than 10 % of total segment figures). The sales and operating profit of these businesses are explained further below.

31.18 Segment Reporting

Sales by region are segmented by customer domicile.
Operating margin is the operating profit divided by sales.
Return on net assets is the operating profit divided by net assets.

In 1997, operating profit of the plastics segment was lowered by DM 42 million due to the loss on the sale of the Australian plastics business to Kemcor. In 1996, operating profit of Hoechst Marion Roussel includes gains on the sale of Lutsia and of product rights totaling DM 275 million. The gain on the sale of the printing plates business of DM 250 million is included in the operating profit of Specialty Chemicals for 1996.

Other businesses

	Sales 1997	Sales 1996	Operating profit 1997	Operating profit 1996
Hoechst South Africa Group	709	559	31	16
Hoechst Research & Technology[1]	208		- 355	
Hoechst AG restructuring			- 160	
InfraServ companies/HiServ[1]	4936		79	
Generic Pharmaceuticals	740	737	1	- 116
SGL Carbon		411		85
Vaccines/Plasma	617	421	116	27
Vianova Resins	892	853	53	33
Kalle Nalo	170	225	113	20
Gain on sale of buildings in Tokyo			132	
Gain on sale of a 49 % interest in the vaccines business				142
Others	1527	2659	- 39	- 327[2]
Total	9799	5865	- 29	- 120

[1]Certain Group functions became separate legal entities in 1997. The services provided by these entities to other Group companies are reported as sales in 1997
[2]Includes DM -319 million operating loss of the research functions of Hoechst AG, Hoechst Celanese and Hoechst Japan, which became a separate legal entity in 1997

Hoechst South Africa, a publicly traded company in which the Group has a 73.7 % interest, operates in a variety of businesses, independent of the other segments. Its primary contributor to sales is plastics, accounting for 56 % of the total business.

During 1997, the InfraServ companies, providing infrastructure and other services to the operating companies, HiServ and Hoechst Research & Technology were established as separate legal entities.

In the course of setting up independent Group companies in 1997, some restructuring charges related to operating activities but not allocable to individual Group companies remained with Hoechst AG.

The generic pharmaceutical businesses Rugby, Copley, Cox and Biochimica Opos as well as Chiron Behring and the plasma business in Japan that was not contributed to Centeon are independently operated. Kalle Nalo was sold effective October 1, 1997. The operating profit includes the pretax profit from operating activities as well as the gain on the sale of shareholdings totaling DM 111 million. Separation Products and Food Ingredients were included in "Other Businesses" for the second half-year 1997 and 1996. For all other periods these businesses were included in "Specialty Chemicals".

In 1996, the sale of a 49 % interest in the vaccines business resulted in a gain of DM 142 million. The Group continues to own 51% of Chiron Behring.

In the following table, the segment totals are reconciled to the Group figures.

Reconciliation of segment to Group figures	Segment total		Reconciliation		Group	
	1997	1996	**1997**	1996	**1997**	1996
External sales	52 100	50 927			52 100	50 927
Intragroup sales	5 473	2 110	- 5 473	- 2 110	0	0
Total sales	57 573	53 037	- 5 473	- 2 110	52 100	50 927
Operating profit	4 287	4 618	- 634	- 605	3 653	4 013
Operating profit, comparable	4 868	3 951	- 634	- 491	4 234	3 460
Assets	49 369	47 622	11 536	7 503	60 905	55 125
Liabilities	16 583	16 730	25 213	20 313	41 796	37 043
Net assets	32 786	30 892	- 13 677	- 12 810	19 109	18 082
Capital expenditures	3 684	4 010	2	11	3 686	4 021
Research and development costs	3 990	3 880			3 990	3 880
Employees as of December 31,	117 859	147 479	353	383	118 212	147 862
Key figures (in %)						
Return on sales	7.4	8.7			7.0	7.9
Return on net assets	13.1	14.9			19.1	22.2

The reconciliation shows a) the elimination of intragroup sales, profits, receivables and payables as well as income and expenses, b) assets and liabilities not allocable to the individual segments, c) corporate items, e.g. Corporate Center costs, annual interest expense on pension liabilities for retirees of Hoechst AG and the goodwill resulting from the acquisition of the outstanding minority interest in Roussel Uclaf which is related to but not allocated to HR Vet and AgrEvo in accordance with the management approach.

The figures for 1996 included expenses of DM 173 million relating to the full recognition of previously deferred actuarial losses due to early-retirement programs for retirees from 1994 to 1996.

In addition to the information on business segments based on the structure of the Group, figures are presented for geographical segments in accordance with IAS 14.

Segment data Regions	Europe[2]		thereof Germany		Americas		thereof USA		Asia, Africa, Australasia		Segment total	
	1997	1996	**1997**	1996	**1997**	1996	**1997**	1996	**1997**	1996	**1997**	1996
External sales	25 451	25 415	10 019	9 169	18 933	17 335	11 502	11 231	7 716	8 177	52 100	50 927
Assets	23 067	21 122[1]	8 874	11 409[1]	22 506	22 124	18 001	18 766	3 796	4 376	49 369	47 622
Capital expenditures	2 112	2 388[1]	1 385	1 740[1]	1 377	1 202	961	817	195	420	3 684	4 010

[1] Adjusted to improve comparability, see Note 4
[2] Europe includes the countries of Eastern Europe as well as the Commonwealth of Independent States (CIS)

Part III

Industry-Specific Standards

CHAPTER 32
AGRICULTURE

CONTENTS

OVERVIEW

IAS 41, "Agriculture," is effective for annual financial statements beginning on or after January 1, 2003. It is a completely new standard dealing with the accounting treatment of agricultural activity. Agricultural activity is the management by an enterprise of the biological transformation of living animals or plants (biological assets) for sale, into agricultural produce or into additional biological assets. IAS 41 does not deal with the processing of agricultural produce after harvest.

IAS 41 requires that biological assets should be measured at their fair value less estimated point-of-sale costs, unless such market-based values are neither available nor capable of reliable estimation, when cost less depreciation and any impairment losses should be used. The standard requires that a change in fair value less estimated point-of-sale costs of a biological asset be included in the net profit or loss for the period in which it arises. This means, of course, that gains that are unrealized in transaction terms are to be included in operating profits.

IAS 41 was the last standard approved by the "old" IASC Board, at the end of 2000.

BACKGROUND

For a considerable time, IASC has been issuing standards that explicitly excluded agricultural activity from their scope. For example:

- IAS 2, "Inventories," excluded "producers' inventories of livestock, agricultural and forest products...to the extent that they are measured at net realizable value in certain industries."
- IAS 16, "Property, Plant, and Equipment," did not apply to "forests and similar regenerative natural resources."
- IAS 18, "Revenue," did not deal with revenue arising from "natural increases in herds, and agricultural and forest products."
- IAS 40, "Investment Property," did not apply to "forests and similar regenerative natural resources."

Thus, there was no harmonizing force at work regarding financial reporting for agricultural activities. Taking a global view, agriculture is generally a small business activity, but this is tending to change. Thirdly, agriculture is a very significant industry in many countries, particularly in developing economies, where the resources available to develop local techniques and regulation are likely to be lacking. For all of these reasons, a standard on agriculture was felt to be desirable.

Much agricultural activity involves either the gradual physical expansion, and therefore increase in value, of a specific item, such as a tree or a cow, or the creation, without any market transaction, of a new item, such as a sapling grown from seed or the birth of a calf. In both these situations, the traditional accounting process based on recording the historical cost-of-purchase transactions, and then waiting until revenue is "earned" by means of a sale transaction, fails to fairly present the economic reality of the accumulation of agricultural resources. For this reason, IAS 41 focuses on the use of fair values in both the balance sheet and the calculation of revenues.

SCOPE

IAS 41 becomes formally operative for annual financial statements covering periods beginning on or after January 1, 2003. Earlier application is "encouraged" by the IASC. The standard should be used to account for the following when they relate to agricultural activity:

- Biological assets,
- Agricultural produce at the point of harvest, or

- Government grants related to biological assets measured on the fair value basis, and to government grants that require enterprises not to engage in specified agricultural activity.

IAS 41 does not apply to:

- Land related to agricultural activity (see IAS 16, "Property, Plant, and Equipment," see Chapter 27, and IAS 40, "Investment Property," see Chapter 24);
- Intangible assets related to agricultural activity (see IAS 38, "Intangible Assets," see Chapter 21); and
- Government grants related to biological assets measured on the cost basis, to which IAS 20, "Accounting for Government Grants and Disclosure of Government Assistance" (see Chapter 18) is applied.

IAS 41 only applies to agricultural produce at the point of harvest. After that point, IAS 2, "Inventories" (see Chapter 23), or some other applicable IAS, is applied. It follows that IAS 41 does not apply to products associated with the processing of agricultural produce after the point of harvest. Consider, for example, a vintner who owns land on which vines are planted. These produce grapes, which he uses to produce wine. The land is not covered by IAS 41; the vines are, as biological assets; the grapes, as agricultural produce, are covered by IAS 41 at the point of harvest, but not thereafter; the wine, whether in process or completed, is not covered by IAS 41.

TERMINOLOGY AND DEFINITIONS

The standard gives a series of definitions of specifically agriculture-related terms, as follows.

- *Agricultural activity* is the management by an enterprise of the biological transformation of biological assets for sale, into agricultural produce, or into additional biological assets.
- *Agricultural produce* is the harvested product of the enterprise's biological assets.
- A *biological asset* is a living animal or plant.
- *Biological transformation* comprises the processes of growth, degeneration, production, and procreation that cause qualitative or quantitative changes in a biological asset.
- A *group of biological assets* is an aggregation of similar living animals or plants.
- *Harvest* is the detachment of produce from a biological asset or the cessation of a biological asset's life processes.

Agricultural activity can cover a wide range of diverse operations. Three factors are said to be common to all agricultural activity.

1. Biological assets are capable of biological transformation.
2. Agricultural activity, to fall within IAS 41, must be managed. Thus, fish farming is an agricultural activity, whereas ocean fishing is not.
3. Changes in quantity or quality brought about by biological transformation are monitored and measured routinely as part of the management process.

In addition to these agriculture-related definitions, a number of general terms are defined for completeness, as follows.

- An *active market* is a market where all the following conditions exist:

  —The items traded within the market are homogeneous;

  —Willing buyers and sellers can normally be found at any time; and

  —Prices are available to the public.

- *Carrying amount* is the amount at which an asset is recognized in the balance sheet.

- *Fair value* is the amount for which an asset could be exchanged or a liability settled between knowledgeable, willing parties in an arm's-length transaction.

- *Government grants* are as defined in IAS 20, "Accounting for Government Grants and Disclosure of Government Assistance" (see Chapter 18).

The fair value concept is developed in the standard (in par. 9), which states that the fair value of an asset is based on its present location and condition. As a result, for example, the fair value of cattle at a farm is the price for the cattle in the relevant market less the transport and other costs of getting the cattle to that market. The implications of this are discussed below.

RECOGNITION AND MEASUREMENT

The recognition criteria are straightforward, and logically follow from the definition of an asset given in the IASC Framework (see Chapter 2). An enterprise should recognize a biological asset or agricultural produce when, and only when, all three of the following are satisfied.

1. The enterprise controls the asset as a result of past events.

2. It is probable that future economic benefits associated with the asset will flow to the enterprise.

3. The fair value or cost of the asset can be measured reliably.

Control, in this context, implies demonstrating ownership or responsibility, not necessarily inculcating obedience(!).

The essential measurement requirement of IAS 41, which is the core of the whole standard, can be simply stated. A biological asset should be measured on initial recognition and at each balance sheet date at its fair value less estimated point-of-sale costs, except where the fair value cannot be measured reliably. Agricultural produce harvested from an enterprise's biological assets should be measured at its fair value less estimated point-of-sale costs at the point of harvest. This amount is used as a substitute for "cost" at that date when applying IAS 2, "Inventories," or another applicable International Accounting Standard. Point-of-sale costs include commissions to brokers and dealers, levies by regulatory agencies and commodity exchanges, and transfer taxes and duties. Point-of-sale costs exclude transport and other costs necessary to get assets to a market.

> **OBSERVATION:** The precise implications of this measurement requirement are not so straightforward as the succinct statement given above might suggest. The definition of fair value has been quoted above. As regards assets, this is identical to the definition given in IAS 40, "Investment Properties" (see Chapter 24). IAS 40 explicitly states (in par. 29) that the fair value of investment property is "usually its market value....It is the best price reasonably obtainable by the seller and the most advantageous price reasonably obtainable by the buyer."
>
> This statement from IAS 40 should be contrasted with the statement from IAS 41, already quoted, that the fair value of cattle at a farm is the price for the cattle in the relevant market less the transport and other costs of getting the cattle to that market. Since the fair value under IAS 40 is explicitly identical for both buyer and seller, and the fair value "of cattle at a farm" under IAS 41 is explicitly *not* identical for both buyer and seller (being different by the transport, etc. costs), it would seem that these two statements are inconsistent. The only way they can be made consistent is to impute into the IAS 40 statement the two additional points that:
>
> 1. Costs of "getting" the property to the market must be deducted from fair value in the seller's books, and
>
> 2. It is in the nature of the property market that such costs are always zero.
>
> It has to be said that IAS 40 gives no hint of this, and such an imputation seems somewhat far-fetched. Transport costs will indeed be zero, but "other" costs may not be.

The second point to underline is that, ignoring the above question of definition of fair value, IAS 40 requires the relevant properties to be measured at fair value, period. IAS 41, in contrast, requires the relevant agricultural or biological assets to be measured at fair value less point-of-sale costs as defined. This is not so much an inconsistency as an overt difference. It appears that fair value less point-of-sale costs is effectively identical to the more traditional concept of net realizable value, which is defined in IAS 2, "Inventories" (see Chapter 23) (par. 4), as the estimated selling price in the ordinary course of business less the estimated costs of completion and the estimated costs necessary to make the sale, and in IAS 15 (see Chapter 8) (par. 13), as the net current selling price of an asset. Net realizable value, and/or fair value less point-of-sale costs, are more prudent concepts than fair value, period. It might be that this more prudent approach was necessary to get adequate support from the (pre-2001) IASC Board for the issue of the standard. This comment is speculation, but seems to be supported by a statement in an Appendix to IAS 41 (at par. B26) that "failure to deduct estimated point-of-sale costs could result in a loss being deferred."

☛ **PRACTICE POINTER:** The required measurement basis is fair value less point-of-sale costs. It is important not to be confused by the statement that point-of-sale costs exclude transport and other costs necessary to get biological assets to market. The reason for this exclusion is that these costs have *already* been deducted in arriving at fair value for the purposes of IAS 41.

The practical effect of all this is that biological assets under IAS 41 should be measured at the arm's-length exchange price, less transport, etc. costs to market, and less point-of-sale costs such as commissions, levies, and taxes.

IAS 41 makes a number of detailed comments about the determination of fair value. Biological assets or agricultural produce may conveniently be grouped according to key attributes. Contracts specifying prices at a future date are not necessarily relevant to the determination of fair values related to current market conditions. If several active markets are available with different prices, the market expected to be eventually used will give the relevant price to act as the basis of fair value estimation.

If an active market does not exist, an enterprise uses one or more of the following, when available, in determining fair value:

- The most recent market transaction price, provided that there has not been a significant change in economic circumstances between the date of that transaction and the balance sheet date;

- Market prices for similar assets with adjustment to reflect differences; and

- Sector benchmarks such as the value of an orchard expressed per export tray, bushel, or hectare, and the value of cattle expressed per kilogram of meat.

If no market-determined prices or values are available in relation to a biological asset in its present condition, then the discounted present value of expected net cash receipts may be used. In certain circumstances, essentially for biological transformation since initial cost incurrence is small, cost may be a reasonable approximation to fair value.

There is a presumption that fair value can be measured reliably for a biological asset. That presumption can be rebutted, but only on initial recognition for a biological asset for which market-determined prices or values are not available and for which alternative estimates of fair value are determined to be clearly unreliable. In such a case, the biological asset should be measured at its cost less any accumulated depreciation and any accumulated impairment losses. Once the fair value of such a biological asset becomes reliably measurable, an enterprise should measure it at its fair value less estimated point-of-sale costs.

In all cases, agricultural produce at the point of harvest must be measured at its fair value less the estimated point-of-sale costs.

So far, measurement has been discussed in the context of the balance sheet. It follows, both from the logic of the notion of economic gain and from the accounting relationship between the income statement and the balance sheet that, in essence, gain is represented by the increase in the recorded value of net assets. The required treatment of gains arising from the application of IAS 41 is that such gains are income; that is, they are part of the operating results for the period. More formally, a gain or loss arising on initial recognition of a biological asset at fair value less estimated point-of-sale costs and from a change in fair value less estimated point-of-sale costs of a biological asset should be included in net profit or loss for the period in which it arises. A gain or loss arising on initial recognition of agricultural produce at fair value less estimated point-of-sale costs should be included in net profit or loss for the period in which it arises.

> **OBSERVATION:** There are several arguments in favor of this approach. It follows logically from the decision to base measurement on fair value in the first place. More pragmatically, but just as importantly, it reports on progress regarding the very purpose of carrying out agricultural activity, namely the growth, in quality and quantity, of biological assets. Nevertheless, there are also arguments against this approach. Such gains are not realized within the traditional accounting meaning of the term and, although a high degree of reliability of fair value figures is often obtainable, it is still true to say that value figures *after* sale will generally be more reliable still.

In our view, if the fair value is accepted at all as the foundation for the valuation of biological assets and the initial valuation of agricultural produce, then taking the gains to income, as required by IAS 41, is the only logical and useful conclusion.

The alternative would presumably have been the taking of these gains directly to equity. There are ideas emerging that consider reducing the distinction between these two alternatives through the creation of a single performance statement to replace both the income statement and the separate primary statement reflecting changes in equity as currently required by IAS 1 (see Chapter 3). These ideas are a long way from fruition at this time.

GOVERNMENT GRANTS

The fair-value-based valuation approach of IAS 41 gave the IASC a problem regarding the treatment of government grants. IAS 20, "Accounting for Government Grants and Disclosure of Government Assistance" (see Chapter 18), requires that government grants should not be recognized until there is reasonable assurance that:

- The enterprise will comply with the conditions attaching to them; and
- The grants will be received.

IAS 20 also requires that government grants should be recognized as income over the periods necessary to match them with the related costs that they are intended to compensate, on a systematic basis. As regards the presentation of government grants related to assets, IAS 20 permits two methods—setting up a government grant as deferred income or deducting the government grant from the carrying amount of the asset.

If the latter method is used in the context of a biological asset under IAS 41, then this will reduce the cost of the asset, and therefore increase the excess of a fair value over that "cost" on a dollar-for-dollar basis. Since this excess, under IAS 41, is taken directly to income, the effect is that the government grant itself is taken immediately to income, in direct conflict with the IAS 20 requirement to match the grant over the relevant periods.

IAS 41 resolves the conflict by requiring a delay in the recognition of such grants when the fair value basis is used. An unconditional government grant related to a biological asset measured at its fair value less estimated point-of-sale costs should be recognized as income when, and only when, the government grant becomes a receivable. If a government grant related to a biological asset measured at its fair value less estimated point-of-sale costs is conditional, including where a government grant requires an enterprise not to engage in specified agricultural activity, an enterprise should recognize the government grant as income when, and only when, the conditions attaching to the government grant are met.

To illustrate, if a government grant is received in relation to a herd of cattle, which is repayable if the herd is not kept for three years, then none of the grant can be recognized as income until the three years have expired. However, if the amount repayable is reduced to 40% of the grant after the end of year two, then 60% of the grant could and should be taken to income at that point.

☛ **PRACTICE POINTER:** The treatment of government grants denoted above applies under IAS 41 when the fair value less point-of-sale costs measurement basis applies (which will be the usual situation). However, if a government grant relates to a biological asset measured at its cost less any accumulated depreciation and any accumulated impairment losses, IAS 20, "Accounting for Government Grants and Disclosure of Government Assistance," is applied.

PRESENTATION AND DISCLOSURE

An enterprise should present the carrying amount of its biological assets separately on the face of its balance sheet. It should disclose the aggregate gain or loss arising during the current period on initial recognition of biological assets and agricultural produce and from the change in fair value less estimated point-of-sale costs of biological assets. The enterprise should also provide a description of each group of biological assets.

The standard discusses how this last, vaguely worded requirement is to be interpreted. The objective that should underlie the interpretation of the word "group" in this context is to provide information which may be helpful in assessing the timing of future cash flows. The "description" may be narrative or quantified, but quantified descriptions of each group of biological assets, distinguishing between consumable and bearer biological assets or between mature and immature biological assets, are "encouraged." Consumer biological assets are those that are intended to be harvested as agricultural produce or sold as biological assets. Bearer biological assets are all others, i.e., those likely to be self-regenerating. Thus, livestock intended for the production of meat are consumable biological assets. Livestock from which milk is produced are bearer biological assets. For example, an enterprise may disclose the carrying amounts of consumable biological assets and bearer biological assets by group. An enterprise may further divide those carrying amounts between mature and immature assets.

Further detailed disclosure requirements are given, as follows.

If not disclosed elsewhere in information published with the financial statements, an enterprise should describe:

- The nature of its activities involving each group of biological assets; and
- Non-financial measures or estimates of the physical quantities of:
  - —Each group of the enterprise's biological assets at the end of the period, and
  - —Output of agriculture produce during the period.

An enterprise should disclose the methods and significant assumptions applied in determining the fair value of each group of agricultural produce at the point of harvest and each group of biological assets.

An enterprise should disclose the fair value less estimated point-of-sale costs of agricultural produce harvested during the period, determined at the point of harvest.

An enterprise should disclose:

- The existence and carrying amounts of biological assets whose title is restricted, and the carrying amounts of biological assets pledged as security for liabilities;
- The amount of commitments for the development or acquisition of biological assets; and
- Financial risk management strategies related to agricultural activity.

An enterprise should present a reconciliation of changes in the carrying amount of biological assets between the beginning and the end of the current period. Comparative information is not required. The reconciliation should include:

- The gain or loss arising from changes in fair value less estimated point-of-sale costs;
- Increases due to purchases;
- Decreases due to sales;
- Decreases due to harvest;
- Increases resulting from business combinations;
- Net exchange differences arising on the translation of financial statements of a foreign entity; and
- Other changes.

An enterprise should disclose the following related to agricultural activity covered by IAS 41:

- The nature and extent of government grants recognized in the financial statements;
- Unfulfilled conditions and other contingencies attached to government grants; and
- Significant decreases expected in the level of government grants.

When an enterprise has biological assets whose fair value cannot be measured reliably, i.e., the use of a cost-based measurement is necessary, then a number of additional disclosures are required, as follows.

If an enterprise measures biological assets at their cost less any accumulated depreciation and any accumulated impairment losses at the end of the period, the enterprise should disclose for such biological assets:

- A description of the biological assets;
- An explanation of why fair value cannot be measured reliably;
- If possible, the range of estimates within which fair value is highly likely to lie;
- The depreciation method used;
- The useful lives or the depreciation rates used; and
- The gross carrying amount and the accumulated depreciation (aggregated with accumulated impairment losses) at the beginning and end of the period.

If, during the current period, an enterprise measures biological assets at their cost less any accumulated depreciation and any accumulated impairment losses, the enterprise should disclose any gain or loss recognized on disposal of such biological assets, and the reconciliation of changes in the carrying amount of biological assets should disclose amounts related to such biological assets separately. In addition, the reconciliation should include the following amounts included in net profit or loss related to those biological assets:

- Impairment losses;
- Reversals of impairment losses; and
- Depreciation.

If the fair value of biological assets previously measured at their cost less any accumulated depreciation and any accumulated impairment losses becomes reliably measurable during the current period, an enterprise should disclose for those biological assets:

1. A description of the biological assets;
2. An explanation of why fair value has become reliably measurable; and
3. The effect of the change.

TRANSITIONAL ARRANGEMENTS

IAS 41 contains no specific transitional requirements. It merely notes that, on first adoption of the Standard, IAS 8, "Net Profit or Loss for the Period, Fundamental Errors, and Changes in Accounting Policies," will apply (see Chapter 26).

CHAPTER 33
DISCLOSURES IN THE FINANCIAL STATEMENTS OF BANKS AND SIMILAR FINANCIAL INSTITUTIONS

CONTENTS

OVERVIEW

IAS GAAP do not, in general, include industry-specific financial reporting standards. IAS GAAP on financial reporting by banks and similar financial institutions are one exception (another being Agriculture; see Chapter 32). As one may note from the title of this chapter, however, they address only issues of disclosure. IAS GAAP on financial instruments (see Chapter 17) deal with a number of recognition and measurement issues (as well as further disclosure issues) that are of particular relevance to banks.

The disclosure requirements of IAS GAAP for banks and similar financial institutions include: (a) specific disclosures of accounting policies; (b) the contents of the income statement or of accompanying notes to it; (c) the contents of the balance sheet or of accompanying notes to it; and (d) off balance sheet items, including contingencies and commitments.

A significant feature of IAS GAAP is the tightly defined concept of a liability and its application to provisions as a type of liability, set out in the Framework (see Chapter 2) and further elaborated in standards such as IAS 37, "Provisions, Contingent Liabilities, and Contingent Assets," and IAS 22, "Business Combinations" (see Chapters 28 and 6). The issue of provisions is central in financial reporting for banks. In some jurisdictions, banks are permitted or even required to set aside amounts for losses on loans and advances, or for "general banking risks," in addition to those losses that have been specifically identified and those potential losses that, on the basis of past experience, may be reasonably anticipated on the portfolio of loans and advances. These amounts are sometimes known as "hidden reserves." IAS GAAP require such amounts to be disclosed as appropriations of retained earnings, and increases and decreases in the balances of such items are to be excluded from the determination of net profit or loss for the period. In other words, IAS GAAP do not permit "hidden reserves."

BACKGROUND

Since 1977, the IASC has collaborated with the Basle Committee of Banking Supervisors on the matter of the international harmonization of the financial reporting of banks. At the European level, other harmonization work took place during the 1980s in order to produce the EEC Bank Accounts Directive, which was approved in December 1986. The IASC issued IAS 30, "Disclosures in the Financial Statements of Banks and Similar Financial Institutions," in June 1990. The standard was reformatted in 1994, and a few amendments were made in 1998 to reflect implications of IAS 39, "Financial Instruments: Recognition and Measurement."

The IASC explained the attention it was paying to the banking industry by reference to the following: (a) banks represent a significant and influential sector of business worldwide; (b) they play a major role in maintaining confidence in the monetary system; (c) there is thus considerable and widespread interest in the well-being of banks and in particular their solvency and liquidity and the relative degree of risk that attaches to the different types of banking business; and (d) the operations of banks and, thus, their accounting and reporting requirements are different from those of other commercial enterprises.

IAS GAAP specifically directed toward the financial reporting of banks are set out in IAS 30, "Disclosures in the Financial Statements of Banks and Similar Financial Institutions." IAS 30 supplements other IASs, the requirements of which also apply to banks unless they are specifically exempted from them. In this context, particular mention may be made of IAS 1, "Presentation of Financial Statements," IAS 32 and IAS 39 on financial instruments, IAS 10, "Contingencies and Events Occurring after the Balance Sheet Date," IAS 14, "Segment Reporting," IAS 24, "Related Party Transactions," and IAS 37, "Provisions, Contingent Liabilities, and Contingent Assets" (the last named is not actually mentioned in IAS 30, whereas all the others are).

In the United States, as in other countries with developed economies, the standards for the financial reporting of banks are laid down by the national banking regulator. U.S. GAAP do include specialized industry GAAP for banking and thrift institutions, focussing on accounting for business combinations with particular reference to the determination of goodwill and other assets acquired: FAS-72 and FIN-9 (see *Miller GAAP Guide,* Chapter 48). The thrust of these standards is quite different from that of IAS 30, the purpose of which is to set an *international* standard of *disclosure.*

SCOPE

IAS 30 should be applied in the financial statements of "banks and similar financial institutions (subsequently referred to as banks)." As such, banks include all financial institutions meeting two criteria: (a) having among their principal activities the taking of deposits and borrowing with the objective of lending and investing; and (b) being within the scope of banking or similar legislation. IAS 30 applies to both the separate financial statements and the consolidated financial statements of a bank, and where a group undertakes banking operations, the standard is applicable in respect of those operations (but not necessarily other operations) in its consolidated financial statements. IAS 30 supplements other IASs, the requirements of which also apply to banks unless they are specifically exempted from them (IAS 30, pars. 1–5).

> **OBSERVATION:** An issue arises regarding the applicability of IAS 30 and certain other IASs to institutions referred to as Islamic banks, also sometimes called "interest free banks" since their statutes (based on Islamic Shari'a jurisprudence) forbid them to charge or receive interest. The financial instruments employed by Islamic banks differ from those used by conventional banks in ways other than the avoidance of interest, and the items in Islamic banks' financial statements do not correspond in a number of cases to the items specified in IAS 30.

Islamic banks do not fully meet criterion (a) above for inclusion within the scope of IAS 30, since they do not borrow or lend in a conventional sense, and the funds that they take on behalf of customers are not interest-bearing deposits but are either non-interest-bearing current accounts or a type of profit-and-loss-sharing managed fund.

International accounting standards for Islamic banks are issued by the Accounting and Auditing Organization for Islamic Financial Institutions (AAOIFI), whose activities are regarded by itself and IASC as being complementary to those of the latter.

ACCOUNTING POLICIES

Banks use differing methods for the recognition and measurement of items in their financial statements. While harmonization of these methods is desirable, it is beyond the scope of this standard. In order to comply with IAS 1, "Presentation of Financial Statements," accounting policies dealing with the following items may need to be disclosed:

1. The recognition of the principal types of income;

2. The valuation of investment and dealing securities;

3. The distinction between those transactions and other events that result in the recognition of assets and liabilities on the balance sheet and those transactions and other events that only give rise to contingencies;

4. The basis for the determination of losses on loans and advances and for writing off uncollectable loans and advances; and

5. The basis for the determination of charges for general banking risks and the accounting treatment of such charges.

These items are discussed further below. Some of these topics are the subject of existing International Accounting Standards, while others may be dealt with at a later date (IAS 30, par. 8).

Income Statement

A bank should present an income statement that groups income and expenses by nature and discloses the amounts of the principal types of income and expenses.

In addition to the requirements of other International Accounting Standards, the disclosures in the income statement or the notes to the financial statements should include, but are not limited to, the following items of income and expenses:

- Interest and similar income;
- Interest expense and similar charges;
- Dividend income;
- Fee and commission income;
- Fee and commission expense;
- Gains less losses arising from dealing securities;
- Gains less losses arising from investment securities;
- Gains less losses arising from dealing in foreign currencies;
- Other operating income;
- Losses on loans and advances;
- General administrative expenses; and
- Other operating expenses.

Such disclosures are in addition to those of the source of income required by IAS 14, "Reporting Financial Information by Segment."

Income and expense items should not be offset except for those relating to hedges and to assets and liabilities that have been offset in accordance with paragraph 23 (see below).

Gains and losses arising from each of the following are normally reported on a net basis:

1. Disposals and changes in the carrying amount of dealing securities;
2. Disposals of investment securities; and
3. Dealings in foreign currencies.

Net interest is a product of both interest rates and the amounts of borrowing and lending. It is desirable for management to provide a commentary about average interest rates, average interest earning assets, and average interest-bearing liabilities for the period. In some countries, governments provide assistance to banks by making deposits and other credit facilities available at interest rates that are substantially below market rates. In these cases, management's commentary often discloses the extent of these deposits and facilities and their effect on net income, and the standard encourages this (IAS 30, pars. 9–17).

Balance Sheet

A bank should present a balance sheet that groups assets and liabilities by nature and lists them in an order that reflects their relative liquidity. This may equate broadly to their maturities. Current and non-current items are not presented separately because most assets and liabilities of a bank can be realized or settled in the near future.

In addition to the requirements of other International Accounting Standards, the disclosures in the balance sheet or the notes to the financial statements should include, but are not limited to, the following assets and liabilities:

Assets

- Cash and balances with the central bank;
- Treasury bills and other bills eligible for rediscounting with the central bank;
- Government and other securities held for dealing purposes;
- Placements with, and loans and advances to, other banks;
- Other money market placements;
- Loans and advances to customers; and
- Investment securities.

Liabilities

- Deposits from other banks;
- Other money market deposits;
- Amounts owed to other depositors;
- Certificates of deposits;
- Promissory notes and other liabilities evidenced by paper; and
- Other borrowed funds.

The distinction between balances with other banks and those with other parts of the money market and from other depositors is relevant information because it gives an understanding of a bank's relations with, and dependence on, other banks and the money market. Hence, a bank discloses separately:

1. Balances with the central bank;
2. Placements with other banks;
3. Other money market placements;
4. Deposits from other banks;
5. Other money market deposits; and
6. Other deposits.

(IAS 30, pars. 18–21)

The amount at which any asset or liability is stated in the balance sheet should not be offset by the deduction of another liability or asset unless a legal right of set-off exists and the offsetting represents the expectation as to the realization or settlement of the asset or liability (IAS 30, par. 23).

A bank should disclose the fair values of each class of its financial assets and liabilities as required by IAS 32, "Financial Instruments: Disclosure and Presentation," and IAS 39, "Financial Instruments: Recognition and Measurement" (see Chapter 16). IAS 39 provides for four classifications of financial assets: loans and receivables originated by the enterprise, held-to-maturity investments, financial assets held for trading, and available-for-sale financial assets. A bank should disclose the fair values of its financial assets for these four classifications, as a minimum (IAS 30, pars. 24–25).

Contingencies and Commitments Including Off Balance Sheet Items

A bank should disclose the following contingencies and commitments required by IAS 10, "Contingencies and Events Occurring after the Balance Sheet Date" (see Chapter 15):

1. The nature and amount of commitments to extend credit that are irrevocable because they cannot be withdrawn at the discretion of the bank without the risk of incurring significant penalty or expense;

2. The nature and amount of contingencies and commitments arising from off balance sheet items, including those relating to:

   (a) direct credit substitutes, including general guarantees of indebtedness, bank acceptance guarantees, and standby letters of credit serving as financial guarantees for loans and securities,

   (b) certain transaction-related contingencies, including performance bonds, bid bonds, warranties, and standby letters of credit related to particular transactions,

   (c) short-term self-liquidating trade-related contingencies arising from the movement of goods, such as documentary credits where the underlying shipment is used as security,

   (d) those sale and repurchase agreements not recognized in the balance sheet,

   (e) interest and foreign exchange rate related items, including swaps, options, and futures, and

   (f) other commitments, note issuance facilities, and revolving underwriting facilities.

IAS 10, "Contingencies and Events Occurring after the Balance Sheet Date," is of particular relevance to banks because banks often become engaged in many types of contingencies and commitments, some revocable and others irrevocable, which are frequently significant in amount and substantially larger than those of other commercial enterprises. Many banks also enter into transactions that are currently not recognized as assets or liabilities in the balance sheet but that give rise to contingencies and commitments. Such off-balance-sheet items often represent an important part of the business of a bank and may have a significant bearing on the level of risk to which the bank is exposed.

Maturities of Assets and Liabilities

The maturities of assets and liabilities and the ability to replace, at an acceptable cost, interest-bearing liabilities as they mature, are important factors in assessing the liquidity of a bank and its exposure to changes in interest rates and exchange rates. In order to provide information that is relevant for the assessment of its liquidity, a bank should disclose, as a minimum, an analysis of assets and liabilities into relevant maturity groupings, based on the remaining period at the balance sheet date to the contractual maturity date.

The maturity groupings applied to individual assets and liabilities differ between banks and in their appropriateness to particular assets and liabilities. Examples of periods used include the following:

1. Up to 1 month;
2. From 1 month to 3 months;
3. From 3 months to 1 year;
4. From 1 year to 5 years; and
5. 5 years and over.

When repayment is spread over a period of time, each installment is allocated to the period in which contractually agreed or expected to be paid or received.

It is essential that the maturity periods adopted by a bank be the same for assets and liabilities. This makes clear the extent to which the maturities are matched and the consequent dependence of the bank on other sources of liquidity. Maturities could be expressed in terms of:

1. The remaining period to the repayment date,
2. The original period to the repayment date, or
3. The remaining period to the next date at which interest rates may be changed.

Management may also provide, in its commentary on the financial statements, information about interest rate exposure and about the way it manages and controls such exposures.

A bank should disclose an analysis expressed in terms of contractual maturities, even though the contractual repayment period is often not the effective period, because contractual dates reflect the liquidity risks attaching to the bank's assets and liabilities.

Some assets of a bank do not have a contractual maturity date. The period in which these assets are assumed to mature is usually taken as the expected date on which the assets will be realized.

In order to provide users with a full understanding of the maturity groupings, the disclosures in the financial statements may need to be supplemented by information as to the likelihood of repayment within the remaining period. Hence, management may provide, in its commentary on the financial statements, information about the effective periods and about the way it manages and controls the risks and exposures associated with different maturity and interest rate profiles (IAS 30, pars. 30–39).

CONCENTRATIONS OF ASSETS, LIABILITIES, AND OFF BALANCE SHEET ITEMS

A bank should disclose any significant concentrations of its assets, liabilities, and off balance sheet items. Such disclosures should be made in terms of geographic areas, customer or industry groups, or other concentrations of risk: A bank should also disclose the amount of significant net foreign currency exposures.

Geographic areas may comprise individual countries, groups of countries, or regions within a country; customer disclosures may deal with such sectors as governments, public authorities, and commercial and business enterprises. Such disclosures are made in addition to any segment information required by IAS 14, "Reporting Financial Information by Segment" (see Chapter 31).

The disclosure of significant net foreign currency exposures is also a useful indication of the risk of losses arising from changes in exchange rates (IAS 30, pars. 40–42).

Losses on Loans and Advances

A bank should disclose the following:

1. The accounting policy that describes the basis on which uncollectable loans and advances are recognized as an expense and written off.

2. Details of the movements in the provision for losses on loans and advances during the period. It should disclose separately the amount recognized as an expense in the period for losses on uncollectable loans and advances, the amount charged in the period for loans and advances written off, and the amount credited in the period for loans and advances previously written off that have been recovered.

3. The aggregate amount of the provision for losses on loans and advances at the balance sheet date.

4. The aggregate amount included in the balance sheet for loans and advances on which interest is not being accrued and the basis used to determine the carrying amount of such loans and advances.

Local circumstances or legislation may require or allow a bank to set aside amounts for losses on loans and advances in addition to those losses that have been specifically identified and those potential losses that experience indicates are present in the portfolio of loans and advances. *Any such amounts set aside represent appropriations of retained earnings and not expenses determining net profit or loss for the period. Similarly, any credits resulting from the reduction of such amounts result in an increase in retained earnings and are not included in the determination of net profit or loss for the period* (IAS 30, pars. 43–46).

As the time at which uncollectable loans and advances are written off differs, the gross amount of loans and advances and of the provisions for losses may vary considerably in similar circumstances. Hence, a bank should disclose its policy for writing off uncollectable loans and advances (IAS 30, pars. 47–49).

General Banking Risks

Local circumstances or legislation may require or allow a bank to set aside amounts for general banking risks, including future losses or other unforeseeable risks, in addition to the charges for losses on loans and advances. A bank may also be required or allowed to set aside amounts for contingencies in addition to those for which accrual is required by IAS 10, "Contingencies and Events Occurring after the Balance Sheet Date" (see Chapter 15). These charges may result in the overstatement of liabilities, understatement of assets, or undisclosed accruals and provisions. They present the opportunity to distort net income and equity.

Any amounts set aside in respect of general banking risks, including future losses and other unforeseeable risks or contingencies (in addition to those for which accrual must be made in accordance with IAS 10, "Contingencies and Events Occurring after the Balance Sheet Date") *should be separately disclosed as appropriations of retained earnings and not as charges to profit and loss. Any credits resulting from the reduction of such amounts result in an increase in retained earnings and are not included in the determination of net profit or loss for the period* (IAS 30, pars. 50–52).

Assets Pledged as Security

In some countries, banks are required, either by law or by national custom, to pledge assets as security to support certain deposits and other liabilities. The amounts involved are often substantial and so may have a significant impact on the assessment of the financial position of a bank.

A bank should disclose the aggregate amount of secured liabilities and the nature and carrying amount of the assets pledged as security (IAS 30, pars. 53–54).

Trust Activities

Banks commonly act as trustees and in other fiduciary capacities that result in the holding or placing of assets on behalf of individuals, trusts, retirement benefit plans, and other institutions. Provided the trustee or similar relationship is legally supported, these assets are not assets of the bank and, therefore, are not included in its balance sheet. If the bank is engaged in significant trust activities, disclosure of that fact and an indication of the extent of those activities are made in its financial statements because of the potential liability if it fails in its fiduciary duties. For this purpose, trust activities do not encompass safe custody functions.

Related Party Transactions

IAS 24, "Related Party Disclosures" (see Chapter 29), deals generally with the disclosures of related party relationships and transactions between a reporting enterprise and its related parties. In some countries, the law or regulatory authorities prevent or restrict banks entering into transactions with related parties, whereas in others such transactions are permitted. IAS 24 is of particular relevance in the presentation of the financial statements of a bank in a country that permits such transactions.

Certain transactions between related parties may be effected on different terms from those with unrelated parties. For example, a bank may advance a larger sum or charge lower interest rates to a related party than it would in otherwise identical circumstances to an unrelated party; advances or deposits may be moved between related parties more quickly and with less formality than is possible when unrelated parties are involved. Even when related party transactions arise in the ordinary course of a bank's business, information about such transactions is relevant to the needs of users and its disclosure is required by IAS 24.

When a bank has entered into transactions with related parties, it is appropriate to disclose the nature of the related party relationship, the types of transactions, and the elements of transactions necessary for an understanding of the financial statements of the bank. The elements that would normally be disclosed to conform with IAS 24 include a bank's lending policy to related parties and, in respect of related party transactions, the amount included in or the proportion of the following:

1. Each of loans and advances, deposits, and acceptances and promissory notes; disclosures may include the aggregate amounts outstanding at the beginning and end of the period, as well as advances, deposits, repayments, and other changes during the period;

2. Each of the principal types of income, interest expense, and commissions paid;

3. The amount of the expense recognized in the period for losses on loans and advances and the amount of the provision at the balance sheet date; and

4. Irrevocable commitments and contingencies and commitments arising from off balance sheet items (IAS 30, pars. 56–58).

APPENDIX:
USE OF IAS IN COUNTRIES
AROUND THE WORLD*

This information is reproduced from the IASB Web site as of April 12, 2001. Updated information can be found on their Web site: http://www.iasb.org.uk.

ALBANIA

IFAC Member: No

Stock Exchange:

Accounting Principles: We need information. <u>Can you help?</u>

ARGENTINA

IFAC Member: Yes

Stock Exchange: The **Buenos Aires Stock Exchange** requires domestic companies to follow Argentine GAAP. Foreign companies may follow Argentine GAAP. Alternatively, they may follow IAS or their national GAAP, in which case they must include a reconciliation to Argentine GAAP.

Accounting Principles: Two levels of accounting standards exist in Argentina: those adopted by the (local) Consejos Profesionales de Ciencias Economicas on the basis of the 'technical resolutions' of the Federacion de Consejos and those adopted under legal authority, primarily developed by the Comision Nacional de Valores (for listed companies) and specialised industry standards developed by regulatory agencies such as the Central Bank of the Argentine Republic. Both the Federacion and the Comision are planning to base most (but not all) of their accounting standards on IAS.

ARMENIA

IFAC Member: No

Stock Exchange:

Accounting Principles: The Government of Armenia decided in Decree 740 (26 November 1998) to adopt IAS. Most of the Standards are expected to be adopted by the Ministry of Finance by the end of 1999, with the remaining Standards adopted by 30 June 2000. A new Association of Accountants and auditors of the Republic of Armenia is also being organised.

AUSTRALIA

IFAC Member: Yes

Stock Exchange: The **Australian Stock Exchange** allows foreign issuers to use Australian GAAP (that is, standards adopted by the Australian Accounting Standards Board) or another set of accounting standards acceptable to ASX. A note to the relevant listing rule cites International Accounting Standards as the only example of "acceptable" non-Australian GAAP. ASX policy is to accept national standards that are based on IAS (such as those of Hong Kong, Singapore, and Malaysia) or that are largely compatible with IAS (such as those of the U.K.) The Australian Stock Exchange has allowed debt issuers to use U.S. GAAP without reconciliation to Australian GAAP, although the Australian Securities and Investments Commission has lately requested U.S. issuers to follow Australian GAAP. Domestic issuers must follow Australian GAAP.

Accounting Principles: New arrangements for setting Australian accounting standards came into effect on 1 January 2000, with the enactment of part of the legislative reform package contained in the Corporate Law Economic Reform Program Act 1999.

Under the new arrangements, a new body, the Financial Reporting Council (FRC) is established with the responsibility for the broad oversight of the accounting standard setting process for the private, public and not-for-profit sectors. It will set the broad strategic direction for the Australian Accounting Standards Board (AASB), approve and monitor its priorities and business plan, and oversee its operations. The FRC also has a statutory obligation to monitor the development of international accounting standards and accounting standards that apply in major international financial centers, to further the development of a single set of accounting standards for world-wide use with appropriate regard to international developments, and to promote the adoption of international best practice accounting standards in the Australian accounting standard setting process if doing so would be in the best interests of both the private and public sectors in the Australian economy. The FRC is monitoring and assessing the work of the IASB, national accounting standard setting bodies in Canada, France, Germany, Japan, New Zealand, the United Kingdom and the United States of America. It is also monitoring the work of the European Commission.

The AASB is a body corporate with power to formulate accounting standards for the purposes of the Corporations Law and for the public and not-for-profit sectors, and to participate in and contribute to the development of a single set of accounting standards for world-wide use. The legislation provides that the AASB may distribute the text of a draft international accounting standard (whether or not modified to take account of the Australian legal or institutional environment) for the purposes of consultation. Under the revised standard setting arrangements, the AASB is responsible for employing its own technical and administrative support staff. In addition to the FRC statutory obligation to monitor the development of international accounting standards and accounting standards that apply in major international financial centres, the AASB has stated in Policy Statement 6 "International Harmonisation Policy" which was issued in 1996 that to achieve the AASB's objective of pursuing the development of an internationally accepted set of accounting standards, the AASB will, in the interim, work towards ensuring that compliance with Australian accounting standards will result in compliance with IASs.

AUSTRIA

IFAC Member: Yes

Stock Exchange: Wiener Bourse (the Vienna Stock Exchange) requires all domestic and foreign companies listed on the A-Market and the Austrian Growth Market to submit consolidated financial statements that follow either IAS or US GAAP starting April 2001. Other listed companies (domestic and foreign) not on the A-Market or AGM may use IAS or US GAAP consolidated financial statements.

Accounting Principles: The Austrian commercial code prescribes accounting practices for Austrian companies and requires compliance with the EC Directives. In January 1999, the Parliament of Austria enacted a law that allows all Austrian companies to follow IAS or another internationally recognised body of accounting standards, rather than the Austrian commercial code accounting, in preparing their consolidated financial statements for domestic reporting purposes, provided that:

- the statements also comply with the EC Directives;

- the statements disclose the basis of accounting used and any significant differences from Austrian law; and

- the information value is deemed at least equivalent to that that would result from complying with Austrian law, and the auditor's report so states.

The law is effective for financial years beginning 1 January 1998 or later.

BAHAMAS

IFAC Member: Yes

Stock Exchange:

Accounting Principles: We need information. <u>Can you help?</u>

BAHRAIN

IFAC Member: Yes

Stock Exchange:

Accounting Principles: By law, banks in Bahrain are required to conform to IAS.

BANGLADESH

IFAC Member: Yes

Stock Exchange: All companies listed on the **Chittagong Stock Exchange** must follow International Accounting Standards.

Accounting Principles: We need information. <u>Can you help?</u>

BARBADOS

IFAC Member: Yes

Stock Exchange:

Accounting Principles: Effective January 1, 1996, The Institute of Chartered Accountants of Barbados (ICAB) fully adopted all International Accounting Standards as issued by IASC as the "benchmark" for generally accepted accounting principles in Barbados. Previously, many of those standards had been adopted on a selective basis as approved by the Council of the Institute.

BELGIUM

IFAC Member: Yes

Stock Exchange: Brussels Stock Exchange allows IAS financial statements. Domestic companies with significant foreign operations or foreign capital sources may follow IAS as well for consolidated financial statements.

EASDAQ (European Association of Securities Dealers Automated Quotation) **Exchange** allows IAS for all listed companies. EASDAQ's rulebook published in October, 1996 states that annual and quarterly financials of listed companies should be in accordance with one of the following standards:

- International Accounting Standards;

- the accepted standards of the issuer's home state (if the issuer is incorporated in, or has registered offices, in the European Union) with a reconciliation to International Accounting Standards; or

- US GAAP (issuers whose financial instruments were first, and continue to be, traded on NASDAQ, and issuers intending to seek admission of their financial instruments to trading on a US Stock Exchange or securities market, or to offer them in the USA).

Accounting Principles: Under Belgian Law, the King has authority to prescribe the form and content of financial statements. To implement that authority, the King has created a Commission for Accounting Principles.

BENIN

IFAC Member: No

Stock Exchange:

Accounting Principles: One of seven French-speaking West African countries (including Benin, Burkina Faso, Ivory Coast, Mali, Niger, Senegal, and Togo) that in 1998 signed a business harmonisation treaty that includes creation of a new accounting plan—Systeme Comptable Ouest-Africain (Plan SYSCOA). SYSCOA is not based on IAS.

BOLIVIA

IFAC Member: Yes

Stock Exchange:

Accounting Principles: In Bolivia, the National Technical Accounting and Auditing Committee (Consejo Tecnico Nacional de Auditoria y Contabilidad) within the Society of Auditors of Bolivia (Colegio de Auditores de Bolivia) is responsible for setting accounting and auditing standards for the profession.

BOTSWANA

IFAC Member: Yes

Stock Exchange:

Accounting Principles: IAS are recommended, although there is no legal requirement to apply them.

BRAZIL

IFAC Member: Yes

Stock Exchange: All companies listed on the **Rio de Janeiro Stock Exchange** and **Sao Paulo Stock Exchange** must submit financial statements that follow Brazilian GAAP.

Accounting Principles: The Brazilian Institute of Accountants [IBRACON] issues accountants standards influenced by IAS. The introduction to the standards handbook states:

"IBRACON is a member of the IFAC and IASC and has taken an active part in the projects undertaken by the two entities. However, IBRACON itself has issued a series of pronouncements concerning accounting and audit that are in resonance with Brazil's own reality. . . .[the IAS pronouncements] do not take precedence of those of IBRACON because, among other reasons, there is a similarity between them. The publication of the IAS's furnishes a wider source of consultation and study, and should contribute to the improvement and perfecting of our own standards of accounting and auditing."

The Securities Commission Law of 1976 established a Brazilian Securities Commission which has the power to issue regulations regarding financial accounting standards.

BRUNEI

IFAC Member: No

Stock Exchange:

Accounting Principles: The Brunei Darussalam Institute of Certified Public Accountants has begun to develop accounting standards.

BULGARIA

IFAC Member: Yes

Stock Exchange: National accounting standards are obligatory for all companies listed on the **Bulgarian Stock Exchange.**

Accounting Principles: According to the Accounting Law (enacted in 1991), the Council of Ministers approves National Accounting Standards (NAS) and a National Chart of Accounts in compliance with IAS, which are obligatory for all accounting entities. The Chart of Accounts has been in effect since April 1, 1991 and NAS have been in effect since January 1, 1993. NAS provide for conformity with National Accounting Legislation, uniform application of international accounting terminology, and application of IAS in accordance with specific accounting problems in Bulgaria. For issues that are not treated in NAS, the principles of IAS should be applied. As of January 1, 2000 the Institute of Certified Public Accountants in Bulgaria, upon request of the Ministry of Finance, shall develop and update the NAS, the corresponding methodology and guidelines. Up to 1 February 2000, 35 NAS have been approved (including those without analogue in IAS). The Institute of Certified Public Accountants in Bulgaria has also approved 20 National Audit Standards in compliance with International Audit Standards.

BURKINA FASO

IFAC Member: No

Stock Exchange:

Accounting Principles: One of seven French-speaking West African countries (including Benin, Burkina Faso, Ivory Coast, Mali, Niger, Senegal, and Togo) that in 1998 signed a business harmonisation treaty that includes creation of a new accounting plan—Systeme Comptable Ouest-Africain (Plan SYSCOA). SYSCOA is not based on IAS.

CAMBODIA

IFAC Member: No

Stock Exchange:

Accounting Principles: In 1998 Cambodia established a new accounting standards committee that intends to issue standards based on IAS.

CANADA

IFAC Member: Yes

Stock Exchange: For the **Toronto Stock Exchange** and **Alberta Stock Exchange**, all registrants must submit financial statements that follow Canadian GAAP. Pursuant to British Columbia law, the **Vancouver Stock Exchange** allows foreign companies to follow their national GAAP with a reconciliation to Canadian GAAP in the notes. Pursuant to Quebec law, the **Montreal Stock Exchange** allows foreign companies to use IAS or US, UK, or Australian GAAP, with advance permission and with a reconciliation to Canadian GAAP in the notes, because those GAAPs are generally comparable to Canadian GAAP. National GAAP from other countries may not be used.

The President and Chief Executive Officer of the Toronto Stock Exchange issued a statement that said: "It is therefore desirable, not only that Canadian companies disclose the fact that they have followed accounting principles generally accepted in Canada in preparing their financial statements, but also that they disclose conformity with, or identify deviations from, International Accounting Standards." Many public Canadian companies do so.

Accounting Principles: The Canada Business Corporations Act and various provincial corporation acts require financial statements to be prepared in conformity with generally accepted accounting principles. By regulation, GAAP is defined as the principles set out in the Handbook of the Canadian Institute of Chartered Accountants. For public companies, several of the provincial securities commissions have supplemented the CICA Handbook with additional disclosure provisions. Accounting Standards in the CICA Handbook are set by the Accounting Standards Board (AcSB) of the CICA. AcSB's policy is to conform Canadian GAAP to IAS unless there is a fundamental disagreement or particular circumstance that warrants a different approach. CICA has an Emerging Issues Committee that provides consensus interpretations of CICA standards.

CAYMAN ISLANDS

IFAC Member: No

Stock Exchange: All companies listed on the **Cayman Islands Stock Exchange**, including domestic, may follow IAS or US, Canadian, or UK GAAP, or other equivalent standards acceptable to the Exchange. The CSX specializes in mutual fund and debt security listings.

Accounting Principles: We need information. Can you help?

CHILE

IFAC Member: Yes

Stock Exchange: The **Santiago Stock Exchange** requires domestic listed companies to submit financial statements that follow Chilean accounting principles. Foreign listed companies must follow their own national principles and include a reconciliation to Chilean GAAP.

Accounting Principles: Accounting standards are set by the Chilean College of Accountants ("CCC"). Their pronouncements are known as Technical Bulletins. If no Chilean standard exists, Technical Bulletin No. 56, approved on September 23, 1997, calls for the use of International Accounting Standards, effective January 1, 1998.

CHINA, PEOPLE'S REPUBLIC

IFAC Member: Yes

Stock Exchange: Shanghai or Shenzen Stock Exchanges

Companies that have issued B-Shares [these trade in China and overseas] must follow IAS.

Companies that have issued H-Shares [these trade in Hong Kong only] may follow either IAS or Hong Kong accounting standards.

Companies that have issued A-Shares [these trade in China only] must follow accounting standards promulgated by the PRC Ministry of Finance.

Accounting Principles: Under the Accounting Law enacted in 1985 and revised in 1993, the Division of Administration of Accounting Affairs (DAAA) of the Ministry of Finance is responsible for setting accounting standards that all companies must follow. In 1993, the DAAA published "Accounting Standards for Business Enterprises" (ASBE), which sets out the general framework of accounting in China. Subsequently, DAAA has been developing specific accounting standards and regulations under the ASBE. Members of the Chinese Institute of CPAs must state in their audit reports whether or not the reporting enterprise has complied with ASBE. In 1998 an Accounting Standards Committee was created within the DAAA. That committee has primary responsibility for developing the standards, subject to MOF approval.

Listed companies must also comply with disclosure regulations issued by the China Securities and Regulatory Commission.

China has set a target for all enterprises to be subject to an independent CICPA audit by the year 2000. China has announced a policy of developing new Accounting Standards for Business Enterprises in harmony with IAS.

COLOMBIA

IFAC Member: Yes

Stock Exchange:

Accounting Principles: Colombian General Accepted Accounting Principles (Colombian GAAP) are currently included in Decree 2649 of 1993. This decree was issued by the Executive.

In addition, Law 43 of 1990 (Article 29) created the Consejo Técnico de la Contaduría Pública. The Consejo has several functions, including researching new accounting and auditing principles. However, its pronouncements are not mandatory for accountants. Nor are they binding on the government or the Congress in their function to establish general standards.

IAS are not formally adopted as Colombian standards or used as the basis for Colombian standards. Colombia generally tends to take into account US GAAP and FASB Rules when new regulations are issued.

As a general principle, all commercial companies in Colombia must adapt their financial statements to Decree 2649. However, article 136 allows a company to use a different but "comprehensive set of standards," if that company follows certain rules of disclosure in cases of incompatibility with Colombian GAAP.

The Securities Superintendency (the Colombian securities regulatory authority) has the authority (according to Decree 2739 of 1991, Article 3; Decree 2115 of 1992, Article 4; Decree 2649 of 1993, Article 137; and Decree 2337 of 1995, Article 5) to set special accounting rules that must be applied by issuers that have made a public offering in Colombia. The Superintendency has issued External Circular 2 of 1998 setting those special rules. The Securities Superintendency did not establish any different rules for foreign companies listing their securities on a Colombian exchange. Consequently, foreign companies must follow the same standards as Colombian companies to sell their securities in Colombia. However, because IAS Standards are generally regarded are "stronger" than the Superintendency's rules, there would not likely be a practical problem for a foreign company to use IAS in financial statements published in Colombia.

COSTA RICA

IFAC Member: Yes

Stock Exchange:

Accounting Principles: Accounting standards are established by the Institute of Public Accountants of Costa Rica. The Board of Management of the Institute has adopted a policy to implement IAS as Costa Rican accounting standards "with the purpose of bringing about transparency and clearness in the way companies present their financial statements." Consistent with that policy, the Board of Management in Ordinary Session 01-99 (05.01.99, Agreement 6.2) adopted a programme to implement IAS as the accounting standards of Costa Rica not later than 1 October 1999. Until the programme is implemented, Mexican GAAP is to be used. For financial years ending October 1999 or later, Costarican companies are encouraged to use IAS. For years ending October 2000 or later, it is mandatory.

CROATIA

IFAC Member: Yes

Stock Exchange: Zagreb Stock Exchange requires IAS financial statements for both domestic and foreign enterprises.

Accounting Principles: The Croatian Accounting Act fully recognises IAS for both domestic and foreign companies. To be used in Croatia, IAS have to be first printed in the National Gazette of the Republic of Croatia.

CYPRUS

IFAC Member: Yes

Stock Exchange: Regulation 78 of the **Cyprus Stock Exchange** requires that IAS be followed by all listed companies, both foreign and domestic.

Accounting Principles: The Institute of Certified Public Accountants of Cyprus adopts all IAS, and has done so since 1981. UK accounting standards are looked to if IAS do not address a particular issue.

CZECH REPUBLIC

IFAC Member: Yes

Stock Exchange: The **Prague Stock Exchange** requires audited financial statements compiled in accordance with IAS, including annexes to the financial statements, for the year preceding the filing of a listing application. The Exchange also requires three years of audited financial statements prepared in accordance with Czech accounting standards. A prospectus requires audited financial statements prepared in accordance with IAS. In addition, an Issuer is required to file quarterly financial information (although not necessarily in accordance with IAS) and audited annual financial statements prepared in accordance with IAS.

Accounting Principles: Czech accounting standards (CAS). Financial statements prepared using IAS are required for publicly listed enterprises.

DENMARK

IFAC Member: Yes

Stock Exchange: Copenhagen Stock Exchange allows Danish companies to use IAS or US or UK GAAP with a reconciliation to Danish GAAP. Foreign companies may follow their national GAAP with a reconciliation to Danish GAAP or, if their own national law allows the use of IAS, US, or UK GAAP, the foreign company may use that GAAP without reconciliation to Danish GAAP.

Accounting Principles: Danish accounting principles are contained in the Annual Accounts Act. The Law implements the EU Fourth and Seventh Directives. Banks, insurance companies, and certain mortgage and loan institutions follow in principle the Annual Accounts Act by separate industry laws specific for these types of institutions.

As no explicit Danish accounting framework exists, guidance is sought in International Accounting Standards (IASs). Since 1976 when the Danish Institute of State-Authorized Public Accountants (FSR) became member of IASC, FSR has supported the IASs.

A translation into Danish of the IASC Framework has been supported, indicating an implicit recognition of the IASC Framework. FSR has issued all IASC Standards with a preface prepared by the accounting committee of the FSR. This preface includes comparison of all significant differences from the Accounting Law and accounting practices generally accepted in Denmark.

As a supplement to the Accounting Law, accounting standards are issued by FSR. The development of accounting standards actually sets the details of the present Danish accounting disclosure. Generally, Danish accounting standards do not deviate significantly from IASC standards and are considered to be a supplement to the Accounting Law.

DOMINICAN REPUBLIC

IFAC Member: Yes

Stock Exchange:

Accounting Principles: In September 1999, the Board of Directors of the Dominican Republic Institute of Certified Public Accountants (Instituto de Contadores Publicos Autorizados de la Republica Dominicana) adopted International Accounting Standards as the accounting standards of the Dominican Republic effective 1 January 2000. The Board acted pursuant to its authority under Law 633 of 16 June 1944, which created the Institute and gave it power to establish accounting standards.

ECUADOR

IFAC Member: Yes

Stock Exchange:

Accounting Principles: In 1996 the National Federation of Accountants of Ecuador ("FNCE") passed resolution 09-01-96, which states that effective January 1, 1996, the application of IAS is mandatory in Ecuador. The FNCE has assumed the responsibility for regulating and clarifying the application of IAS in Ecuador.

EGYPT

IFAC Member: Yes

Stock Exchange: All companies listed on the **Cairo Stock Exchange** must follow IAS.

Accounting Principles: Applying IAS is mandatory for all companies reporting to the Capital Market Authority under the provisions of Law 95 (Capital Markets Law) in Egypt. This includes all companies listed on the Cairo Stock Exchange as well as all specialised investment companies. Commencing 1998, most other companies in Egypt are required to comply with Egyptian Accounting Standards, which are, in all material respects, the same as IAS. Egyptian Accounting Standards are issued by the Egyptian Society of Accountants and Auditors (ESAA) and are, essentially, Arabic versions of IAS. The preface to Egyptian Accounting Standards states: "The Egyptian Accounting Standards (EAS) have been prepared to comply with the International Accounting Standards (IAS) issued by the International Accounting Standards Committee (IASC) except for certain minor differences to adapt the Standards to the Egyptian economic environment." EAS have also been adopted as part of the Uniform Accounting System that forms the basis of financial reports prepared by government-owned enterprises.

EL SALVADOR

IFAC Member: Yes

Stock Exchange:

Accounting Principles: We need information. <u>Can you help?</u>

ESTONIA

IFAC Member: No

Stock Exchange: Tallinn Stock Exchange regulations, section 4.4.4., require that an issuer's financial statements comply with International Accounting Standards. In some cases the Accounting Standards Board of Estonia will limit the choices under IAS.

Accounting Principles: The Estonian Accounting Law (effective date 01.01.95) requires that the financial statements of all companies be prepared in accordance with Estonian GAAP. By law, the Estonian Accounting Standards Board, an autonomous government unit, is responsible for standard-setting in Estonia. The guidelines issued by the Board are generally in conformity with IASC and must be applied when drawing up the separate and consolidated accounts. In cases where IASC allows for alternative treatments, a single treatment is prescribed by Estonian GAAP. To date, the Board has approved 20 guidelines. A bound volume, including English translations, is published yearly.

A conceptual framework is set out in the Estonian Accounting Law. This generally results in automatic convergence with new IASC's standards or interpretations. The Estonian Accounting Standards Board is committed to harmonising its standards with international standards. The Board closely monitors developments in the IASC process and the work of other standard-setters such as FASB, ASB, AASB, CICA, and FRSB, that is, standard-setters concerned with developing standards under a cohesive and consistent conceptual framework.

FIJI

IFAC Member: Yes

Stock Exchange: Listed Companies are required to comply with disclosure requirements of the 1983 Companies Act, and all accounting standards approved by the Fiji Institute of Accountants (FIA). Interim statements are required, and annual financial reports must be published within four months of balance sheet date. Additional disclosure requirements relating to directors' interests also apply.

Accounting Principles: The Accounting Standards Committee of the FIA adopts Fiji accounting standards. The Committee has decided to adopt most International Accounting Standards as Fiji standards with effect for reporting periods beginning on or after 1st January 2000. Adoption of IAS 12, 35, 36, and 37 will be postponed for a year or so. Certain other IAS not deemed to have applicability in Fiji will not be adopted. Small reporting entities are exempted from complying with certain standards, but are encouraged to do so. Where International Accounting Standards permit alternative treatments, all alternatives are not necessarily allowed by the FIA.

National government has agreed through the Public Sector Finance Act that all public sector enterprises must conform to generally accepted accounting practices.

FINLAND

IFAC Member: Yes

Stock Exchange: Foreign companies listed on the **Helsinki Exchanges** may follow IAS or US or UK GAAP or their national GAAP, with advance permission of the regulatory authority and with reconciliation to Finnish GAAP. Also, domestic listed companies may follow IAS if more than 50% of the shares are owned by foreigners or if the company is listed in an OECD country outside the European Economic Area, again with reconciliation to Finnish GAAP.

Accounting Principles: The Finnish Accounting Board, an agency of the government Ministry of Trade and Industry, develops accounting principles under the Accounting Act of 1992. Also, the Association of Authorised Public Accountants has an accounting committee that advises the Board. Finnish accounting standards generally are based on IAS.

FRANCE

IFAC Member: Yes

Stock Exchange: Paris Stock Exchange allows IAS financial statements for foreign listed companies. Companies based in the EU are also allowed to follow their national accounting standards. Domestic companies may follow IAS for consolidated financial statements.

Accounting Principles: Under a law enacted 6 April 1998, listed French companies are allowed to elect to follow IASC Standards in their consolidated financial statements for domestic reporting purposes. That law permits companies to elect US GAAP until 2002, provided that an official translation into French is published and approved. However, before French companies can elect either IASC Standards or US GAAP, the Comité de la Réglementation Comptable (CRC) must vote to adopt IAS. This is not yet in process of being done and is not likely to happen before the end of 1999.

Publicly traded companies are subject to the requirements of the Commission des Opérations de Bourse (COB), the French securities regulatory agency. The COB's regulatory position, published in COB's January 1999 monthly Bulletin, is that listed companies still have to use French GAAP as their primary accounting framework, but they can publish supplemental financial statements in accordance with IAS if they wish to do so.

GEORGIA

IFAC Member: No

Stock Exchange:

Accounting Principles: On 5 February 1999, the Parliament of Georgia enacted a law (signed by the President 23 February) adopting

International Accounting Standards as the accounting standards of Georgia. IAS must be followed by all private entities, except small enterprises and non-commercial entities. Joint stock companies (public companies) must follow IAS starting 1 January 2000. Other limited liability companies must start 1 January 2001. The law also created a new Georgian Accounting Standards Commission to translate IAS and SIC Interpretations, to approve temporary standards in the absence of IAS, and to approve the structure of a chart of accounts based on IAS. The law also requires that educational institutions in Georgia reflect IAS in their accounting curricula.

The National Bank of Georgia, in cooperation with the Association of Banks of Georgia (which represents 35 banks), has begun a programme to "assist Georgian banks in strategic transition towards the western banking standards." That programme includes assisting local banks in transition to International Accounting Standards.

GERMANY

IFAC Member: Yes

Stock Exchange: Deutsche Börse, Frankfurt Stock Exchange, Bavarian Stock Exchange, and **Stuttgart Stock Exchange** all allow IAS financial statements. Domestic companies may follow IAS as well for consolidated financial statements.

Accounting Principles: A 1998 law, aimed at making the capital markets in Germany more competitive, allows companies whose securities are publicly traded to prepare their consolidated financial statements, for domestic reporting purposes, using International Accounting Standards or US GAAP rather than German GAAP.

In 1998, Germany also created a new, independent German Accounting Standards Committee (Deutsches Rechnungslegungsstan-dards Committee or DRSC), based in Berlin.

GHANA

IFAC Member: Yes

Stock Exchange:

Accounting Principles: Accounting standards are established by the Institute of Chartered Accountants (Ghana). Those standards are based on IAS with minor modifications.

GREECE

IFAC Member: Yes

Stock Exchange:

Accounting Principles: Accounting principles are set out in Company Law 2190/1920, as amended, which generally follows the guidelines of IASC. The government-sponsored Institute of Sworn-in Accountants (Syndesmos Orkoton Logiston, or SOL) has a committee, the National Accounting Standards Board (Ethniko Symboulio Loeistikis, or ESYL), that publishes non-binding guideliness on accounting issues.

GUATEMALA

IFAC Member: Yes

Stock Exchange:

Accounting Principles: The Guatemalan Institute of Public Accountants and Auditors ("IGCPA") issues accounting standards based in large part on both Mexican GAAP and IAS. Guatemala does not default to IAS in the absence of a domestic standard.

GUYANA

IFAC Member: Yes

Stock Exchange:

Accounting Principles: No information. Can you help?

HAITI

IFAC Member: Yes

Stock Exchange:

Accounting Principles: In September 1997, the Order of Professional Accountants of Haiti (OCPAH) passed a resolution adopting for Haiti the International Accounting Standards, subject to Haitian laws.

HONDURAS

IFAC Member: Yes

Stock Exchange:

Accounting Principles: The Honduran College of University Professionals in Public Accounting ("COHPUCP") fully adopted IAS in its meeting on May 26, 1996. Both IAS and International Standards of Auditing were mandatorily applicable in Honduras effective January 1, 1997.

HONG KONG, CHINA

IFAC Member: Yes

Stock Exchange: Stock Exchange of Hong Kong allows foreign listed companies to follow either Hong Kong GAAP or IAS with a reconciliation to Hong Kong GAAP. The Exchange allows some foreign companies to use UK GAAP, on a case by case basis. If the Stock Exchange of Hong Kong is the company's secondary listing, rather than primary listing, the company may follow the accounting principles of the market of primary listing. Domestic companies must follow Hong Kong GAAP.

Accounting Principles: The Companies Ordinance contains detailed provisions governing the form and content of financial statements, and supporting records.

The Hong Kong Society of Accountants (HKSA) has a Financial Accounting Standards Committee, which issues Statements of Standard Accounting Practice (SSAP). SSAP do not have any statutory backing, but the HKSA requires compliance by members. Before they are mandatory, SSAPs must be approved by the Council of the HKSA. HKSA also recommends, but does not require, the use of IAS in the absence of local standards. As a result of a major policy change by the HKSA in 1993, it became the policy of HKSA to harmonise its standards with IAS, rather than with the UK, and a programme to do so is under way.

An Urgent Issues and Interpretations Subcommittee of the Financial Accounting Standards Committee develops guidance on applying SSAPs. The listing rules of the Hong Kong Stock Exchange impose additional financial disclosure requirements on listed companies.

HUNGARY

IFAC Member: Yes

Stock Exchange: The **Budapest Stock Exchange** Regulations for Listing, Continued Trading and Disclosure require large multinational firms and Hungarian firms with cross-border activities to follow IASC Standards. Other listed companies are allowed to follow IAS.

Accounting Principles:

ICELAND

IFAC Member: Yes

Stock Exchange:

Accounting Principles: The Icelandic parliament (Althingi) enacted a new law on financial reporting (no. 144/1994) based on the 4th and 7th Directives from the European Union. Iceland was not a member of the European Union but was required to adopt the substance of the directives into law based on provisions in the European Economic Area agreeement. The 1994 law also established an Accounting Standards Board which is charged with the responsibility of supplementing the law with accounting standards. The board has issued several standards that are in an abbreviated form in conformity with standards issued by IASC.

Due to high inflation during the 1970s Iceland adopted the general price level model of accounting for financial reporting as well as for taxation purposes. The model was adopted in 1979 and is still being used despite low single digit rates of inflation in the 1990s. Currently, a separate committee appointed by the Ministry for Finance is studying whether the inflation accounting system should be abandoned.

INDIA

IFAC Member: Yes

Stock Exchange:

Accounting Principles: Financial reporting requirements for companies incorporated in India are set out in the Companies Act. An amendment to that Act that took effect 31 October 1998 requires compliance with accounting standards established by a new National Advisory Committee on Accounting Standards (NAC). Members of NAC are nominated by the Institute of Chartered Accountants of India (ICAI), the Institute of Cost and Works Accountants of India, the Institute of Company Secretaries of India, the central Government, the Reserve Bank of India, the Comptroller and Auditor-General of India, the SEBI, and others. Accounting standards specified by ICAI shall take precedence until NAC is established. Thereafter, accounting standards in India will be prescribed by the central government in consultation with the NAC.

In 1977, the ICAI created an Accounting Standards Board which publishes accounting standards. The ASB's policy is to take IAS into consideration in developing its standards. Most of those standards conform in all material respects to IAS; those on R&D, foreign exchange, borrowing costs, banks, and business combinations do not.

INDONESIA

IFAC Member: Yes

Stock Exchange: Jakarta Stock Exchange and Capital Market Supervisory Agency (BAPEPAM) requires public companies to [comply] with Statements and Interpretations of the Committee on Financial Accounting Standards.

Accounting Principles: The standard-setting body in Indonesia is Komite Standar Akuntaksi Keuangan (Committee on Financial Accounting Standards). After they issue a Statement of Financial Accounting Standards, it must be endorsed by the Indonesian Institute of Accountants, though their Interpretations need not be endorsed by IIA. Under Indonesian law, both public and private companies must comply with those accounting standards. Since 1994, it has been the policy of the Committee to use International Accounting Standards as the basis for developing Indonesian standards.

IRAN

IFAC Member: Yes

Stock Exchange: All companies must follow Iranian accounting principles.

Accounting Principles: We need information. <u>Can you help?</u>

IRAQ

IFAC Member: Yes

Stock Exchange:

Accounting Principles: We need information. <u>Can you help?</u>

IRELAND

IFAC Member: Yes

Stock Exchange: The **Dublin Stock Exchange** requires that listed companies prepare their financial statements using UK GAAP as promulgated in Ireland (see below). However, foreign issuers based in the EU may use their national GAAP.

Accounting Principles: Accounting standards issued by the Accounting Standards Board (ASB) of the United Kingdom are promulgated in the Republic of Ireland by the Institute of Chartered Accountants in Ireland, where appropriate modified to take account of the different legislative background in the Republic.

ISRAEL

IFAC Member: Yes

Stock Exchange: The **Tel Aviv Stock Exchange** requires listed companies to follow Israeli Accounting Standards, which are in line with U.S. GAAP.

Accounting Principles: The Israel Accounting Standards Board (IASB) was formed in April 1997 on joint agreement among the institute of Certified Public accountants in Israel, the Israel Securities Authority, and the Tel Aviv Stock Exchange. The IASB is independent and operates under a Public Council. The IASB has stated that its long-term objective is to harmonise Israeli GAAP with International Accounting Standards. IASB's current work programme includes projects to adopt a number of IAS. The Chairman of IASB has said that the board has recently started to evaluate each IAS with the intention of adopting the majority either verbatim or with slight modifications. The project is likely to take two years (through the end of 2000).

While, by law, all limited liability companies in Israel are required to publish financial statements, only those regulated by the Securities Authority or the Stock Exchange must follow IASB Standards. Legislation is being considered that would require all companies to follow IASB Standards.

ITALY

IFAC Member: Yes

Stock Exchange: The **Italian Exchange (Milan)** allows IAS financial statements by foreign listed companies. Domestic companies may follow IAS as well for consolidated financial statements.

Accounting Principles: Italian accounting standards are established, in part, by Italian Law and, in part, by principles issued by the Consiglio Nazionale dei Dottori Commercialisti e dei Ragionieri. If neither of those two sources has addressed an issue, companies generally follow IAS. In February 1998, Italy passed a law allowing companies whose securities are publicly traded in the EU and also in a non-EU country to prepare their consolidated financial statements, for domestic reporting purposes, using International Accounting Standards if IAS are not in conflict with the EU directives and are accepted by the non-EU country. (A recent EU study showed that by appropriate choice where IAS allow alternative practices, an enterprise can comply with EU directives and, at the same time, with IAS.)

IVORY COAST

IFAC Member: No

Stock Exchange:

Accounting Principles: One of seven French-speaking West African countries (including Benin, Burkina Faso, Ivory Coast, Mali, Niger, Senegal, and Togo) that in 1998 signed a business harmonisation treaty that includes creation of a new accounting plan—Systeme Comptable Ouest-Africain (Plan SYSCOA). SYSCOA is not based on IAS.

JAMAICA

IFAC Member: Yes

Stock Exchange: Jamaica Stock Exchange requires all registrants to submit financial statements that follow Statements and recommendations of the Institute of Chartered Accountants of Jamaica.

Accounting Principles: We need information. <u>Can you help?</u>

JAPAN

IFAC Member: Yes

Stock Exchange: By regulation of the Ministry of Finance, the financial statements submitted by a foreign company listed on the **Tokyo Stock Exchange** must be based on the accounting standards as follows:

(1) If the financial statements are the same as those used in its home country, a foreign issuer is allowed to submit these financial statements (known as "home country basis").

(2) If the financial statements used in its home country are not sufficient in disclosure quality and the issuer uses a different set of financial statements based on the different accounting standards for foreign listing purposes, the foreign issuer is allowed to submit these financial statements (known as "third country basis"). To illustrate, some Swiss companies that submit IAS financial statements for listing on the London Stock Exchange also submit financial statements based on IAS to the Tokyo Stock Exchange.

(3) If it is impossible to meet the above two criteria, the Minister of the Finance can specify the accounting standards on which the financial statements have to be based (known as "Minister of the Finance directed basis").

If financial statements based on IAS satisfy one of the above three, a foreign issuer can submit financial statements based on IAS.

Accounting Principles: Three laws affect financial reporting in Japan. The main law is the Commercial Code, which applies to all corporations and defines how assets, liabilities, revenue, expenses, and net income are calculated. The Securities and Exchange Law governs financial reporting by public companies. Measurements of assets, liabilities, revenue, expenses, and net income are the same as under the Commercial Code. The Corporate Income Tax Law also addresses some accounting measurement issues not covered in the Commercial Code or securities law. Taxable income is net income measured under the Commercial Code, with some adjustments.

The three laws are administered by the Ministry of Finance. Accounting standards are set by the Business Accounting Deliberation Council (BADC), an advisory committee to the Ministry of Finance. The Japanese Institute of Certified Public Accountants issues implementation guidance. In setting new standards or revising existing rules, BADC takes into consideration IASC standards and those issued by leading national standard-setters.

In March 2000, the Japanese Institute of CPAs and the Japan Federation of Economic Organizations (Keidanren, which is an organization of large Japanese companies) jointly announced that a new private sector accounting standard-setting body will be established in Japan, possibly before March 2001. Click here for the press release from JICPA describing the proposal for Restructuring Accounting Standard-Setting in Japan.

JORDAN

IFAC Member: Yes

Stock Exchange: The **Amman Stock Exchange** (formerly Amman Financial Market) requires both domestic and foreign listed companies to comply with IASC Standards.

Accounting Principles: We need information. Can you help?

KAZAKHSTAN

IFAC Member: No

Stock Exchange: Kazakhstan Stock Exchange requires that all companies must submit financial statements that comply with "A-listed" IASC Standards. Other listed companies follow Kazakhstan accounting principles.

Accounting Principles: Accounting principles are prescribed by the Ministry of Finance under the Accounting Statute of 1995.

KENYA

IFAC Member: Yes

Stock Exchange:

Accounting Principles: In 1998, the Institute of Certified Public Accountants of Kenya has resolved to adopt International Accounting Standards and phase out Kenyan Accounting Standards for financial years commencing on or after 1 January 2000, although earlier application of IAS is encouraged.

KOREA

IFAC Member: Yes

Stock Exchange: For the **Korean Stock Exchange,** under the requirements of the Korean Securities and Futures Commission (KSFC), foreign companies may submit financial statements in their own national GAAP with a note reconciling to Korean GAAP, or they may submit Korean GAAP financial statements. They may not submit IAS statements. Korean companies must follow Korean GAAP.

Accounting Principles: As a result of a 1998 agreement between the Korean Government and the World Bank, a new independent private-sector Korea Accounting Standards Board was created as of 1 July 1999 (to begin operations 1 September). The Board operates under a new Korea Accounting Institute, also created as of 1 July 1999. The Board's goal is to improve Korean accounting standards to a level consistent with international best practices.

KUWAIT

IFAC Member: Yes

Stock Exchange:

Accounting Principles: By a Ministerial Order of 1990, IAS are adopted as national standards, with explanatory material added.

KYRGYZ REPUBLIC

IFAC Member: Yes

Stock Exchange: Kyrgyz Stock Exchange requires that all listed companies must submit financial statements that follow Kyrgyz accounting principles.

Accounting Principles:

LATVIA

IFAC Member: No

Stock Exchange: Riga Stock Exchange listing rules require that all 'Official List' companies must follow IAS.

Accounting Principles: IAS are recommended, although there is no legal requirement to apply them.

LAOS

IFAC Member: No

Stock Exchange:

Accounting Principles: Laos accounting laws require that all business enterprises, whether domestic or foreign owned, must prepare financial statements. The Accounting Department of the Ministry of Finance is responsible for setting accounting standards. The use of International Accounting Standards is permitted.

LEBANON

IFAC Member: Yes

Stock Exchange:

Accounting Principles: We need information. Can you help?

LESOTHO

IFAC Member: Yes

Stock Exchange:

Accounting Principles: The Legal and Technical Committee and the Council of the Lesotho Institute of Accountants have considered IASC standards and recommended their adoption (with the exception of IAS 32). There is no legal requirement for companies to apply them.

LIBERIA

IFAC Member: Yes

Stock Exchange:

Accounting Principles: We need information. <u>Can you help?</u>

LIBYA

IFAC Member: Yes

Stock Exchange:

Accounting Principles: We need information. <u>Can you help?</u>

LITHUANIA

IFAC Member: No

Stock Exchange: National Stock Exchange of Lithuania requires that all companies on the 'Official Trading List' must follow IAS.

Accounting Principles: The Lithuanian Accounting Institute develops national accounting standards. The Law on Accounting Principles, which sets legal requirements for financial reporting practices, stipulates that companies must either (a) follow national accounting standards or (b) follow International Accounting Standards and EU accounting directives.

LUXEMBOURG

IFAC Member: Yes

Stock Exchange: Luxembourg Stock Exchange allows IAS financial statements for foreign companies, provided the EU directives are also complied with. Foreign listed companies may also follow US or UK GAAP. Foreign listed companies may also follow their national GAAP if they include a reconciliation of significant differences with IAS.

Accounting Principles: Companies follow the EC 4th and 7th Directives. National accounting standards are not established.

MACEDONIA

IFAC Member: No

Stock Exchange: The **Macedonia Stock Exchange** requires that all companies, foreign and domestic, follow IASC Standards.

Accounting Principles: Decree No. 08-6423/1, approved by the Minister of Finance of Macedonia on 7 July 1997, requires that "accounting standards implemented in the Republic of Macedonia are the International Accounting Standards promulgated by the International Accounting Standards Committee." Pursuant to that decree, the Ministry of Finance has adopted a number of specific IAS but some of the more recent IAS (issued in 1997 and 1998) have not yet been adopted.

MALAWI

IFAC Member: Yes

Stock Exchange:

Accounting Principles: We need information. Can you help?

MALAYSIA

IFAC Member: Yes

Stock Exchange: Kuala Lumpur Stock Exchange allows IAS financial statements pursuant to "Guidelines for the Public Offering of Securities of Foreign-Based Companies With Listing and Quotation on the Kuala Lumpur Stock Exchange" adopted by the Malaysian Securities Commission 1 April 1997. Those guidelines allow foreign issuers to follow IAS or Malaysian GAAP. "Under certain strict conditions," on special application to the Securities Commission, a foreign registrant's own national GAAP may be acceptable if a reconciliation of net profit or loss and shareholders' equity to Malaysian GAAP is provided.

Accounting Principles: The Malaysian Accounting Standards Board (MASB) is a statutory body established by the Financial Reporting Act (1997) with sole authority to set legally binding financial reporting standards in Malaysia. The following is from the MASB:

The MASB pursues a policy of internationalisation/ harmonisation of Malaysian concepts statements and accounting standards which will lead to those statements and standards being made compatible, in all material respects, with the standards of other national and international standard-setters, primarily the IASC.

The MASB will, where possible, use the work of the IASC but will review the IASC standards to assess their suitability in the context of structural exceptions in the economy, legislative or otherwise, peculiar to Malaysia. The MASB will modify those standards, as necessary, or develop new standards where the IASC has not addressed a matter or where standards are required to suit the Malaysian environment. The MASB's current work programme involves the review of all accounting standards issued in Malaysia.

MALI

IFAC Member: No

Stock Exchange:

Accounting Principles: One of seven French-speaking West African countries (including Benin, Burkina Faso, Ivory Coast, Mali, Niger, Senegal, and Togo) that in 1998 signed a business harmonisation treaty that includes creation of a new accounting plan—Systeme Comptable Ouest-Africain (Plan SYSCOA). SYSCOA is not based on IAS.

MALTA

IFAC Member: Yes

Stock Exchange: The by-laws of the **Malta Stock Exchange** Act of 1990 require all listed companies to publish interim (half-yearly) and yearly financial statements prepared in conformity with IAS.

Accounting Principles: Compliance with IAS is mandatory under the 1995 Companies Act for accounting periods beginning after 30 June 1996. An International Accounting Standards Advisory Board has been established by the Malta Institute of Accountants to assist members in applying IAS.

MAURITIUS

IFAC Member: No

Stock Exchange:

Accounting Principles: Accounting Standards and Guidelines are developed locally by the Mauritian Accounting and Auditing Standards Committee. IAS are used as a guide, with the goal that compliance with the requirements of Mauritius Accounting Standards will ensure compliance with the requirements of International Accounting Standards.

MEXICO

IFAC Member: Yes

Stock Exchange: The Comision Nacional de Valores (Mexican National Securities Commission) requires that listed companies comply with standards set by the Mexican Institute of Certified Public Accountants (see below).

Accounting Principles: Accounting standards are set by the Accounting Principles Commission (CPC) of the Mexican Institute of Certified Public Accountants. Their pronouncements are known as Bulletins. If no Mexican standard exists, Bulletin A-8 calls for the use of International Accounting Standards or the standards in the company's home country, effective 1 January 1995. CPC also issues Circulars that contain official interpretations and recommendations, but Circulars are not mandatory. The Mexican National Securities Commission also issues rules that must be followed by public companies. On 29 December 1995, the Mexican bank regulatory agency (CNBV) issued new Mexican bank accounting principles that are consistent with IAS.

MOLDOVA

IFAC Member: Yes

Stock Exchange:

Accounting Principles: Accounting is regulated by the Ministry of Finance and the National Accounting Standards Working Group. The first group of twelve IAS-conformed National Accounting Standards and a National Chart of Accounts became effective January 1, 1998.

MYANMAR

IFAC Member: No

Stock Exchange:

Accounting Principles: Accounting is regulated by the Myanmar Accountancy Council, part of the Auditor-General's office. The Council does not promulgate accounting standards but, rather, accepts financial statements prepared using either International Accounting Standards or UK GAAP.

NAMIBIA

IFAC Member: Yes

Stock Exchange:

Accounting Principles: Standards are developed locally. IAS used as a guide.

NEPAL

IFAC Member: No

Stock Exchange:

Accounting Principles: The Institute of Chartered Accountants of Nepal Act, 1996, makes the use of International Accounting Standards mandatory in Nepal.

NETHERLANDS

IFAC Member: Yes

Stock Exchange: Amsterdam Stock Exchange allows foreign companies to follow either IAS or US GAAP without reconciliation to Netherlands GAAP. Domestic companies may follow Netherlands GAAP or IAS, US GAAP, or UK GAAP with a reconciliation to Netherlands GAAP.

Accounting Principles: Accounting requirements are established by law. Additional accounting guidelines (not mandatory but strongly recommended and looked to under the law) are set by the Council for Annual Reporting (Raad voor de Jaarverslaggeving). Those guidelines are based increasingly on IAS. IAS are incorporated into the guidelines "to the extent considered acceptable and relevant."

Under the Netherlands Civil Code, a company that has multinational operations may prepare its financial statements in accordance with the GAAP of one of the member states of the European Community, as long as the financial statements still enable a sound judgement to be formed of the assets and liabilities and the results of the company.

NEW ZEALAND

IFAC Member: Yes

Stock Exchange: For the **New Zealand Stock Exchange**, domestic listed companies must follow NZ GAAP. Foreign listed companies may follow NZ GAAP, IAS, US GAAP, UK GAAP, or their national GAAP without reconciliation to NZ GAAP.

Accounting Principles: Accounting standards are set by the Financial Reporting Standards Board (FRSB), a committee of the Institute of Chartered Accountants of New Zealand. The Companies Act of 1993 created an Acounting Standards Review Board, which is responsible for reviewing and approving standards developed by FRSB. Once approved, standards of FRSB become mandatory for all companies. ASRB can approve standards developed and submitted by other than FRSB. ASRB has statutory obligation to liaise with the Australian Accounting Standards Board, with a view to harmonising New Zealand and Australian accounting standards. FSRB also has a policy of trying to develop standards that are consistent with IAS. All new standards must include a comparison with both Australian and IASC standards.

The foreword to the New Zealand Statements of Accounting Standards says: "The [Institute of Chartered Accountants of New Zealand] will incorporate International Accounting Standards within the body of financial reporting standards, wherever possible."

NICARAGUA

IFAC Member: Yes

Stock Exchange:

Accounting Principles: We need information. Can you help?

NIGER

IFAC Member: No

Stock Exchange:

Accounting Principles: One of seven French-speaking West African countries (including Benin, Burkina Faso, Ivory Coast, Mali, Niger, Senegal, and Togo) that in 1998 signed a business harmonisation treaty that includes creation of a new accounting plan—Systeme Comptable Ouest-Africain (Plan SYSCOA). SYSCOA is not based on IAS.

NIGERIA

IFAC Member: Yes

Stock Exchange:

Accounting Principles: We need information. <u>Can you help?</u>

NORWAY

IFAC Member: Yes

Stock Exchange: Oslo Stock Exchange allows foreign listed companies to follow IAS, US, or UK GAAP without reconciliation to Norwegian GAAP. With permission, they may also follow other national GAAP. Domestic listed companies must follow Norwegian GAAP.

Accounting Principles: The New Norwegian Accounting Act (July 1998) is generally consistent with IAS. The law includes basic accounting principles (revenue recognition, matching, etc.) and general measurement rules for assets (for example, lower of cost or market). Furthermore, the law includes reference to good accounting practice, and background papers to the law make reference to the Norwegian Accounting Standards Board and the Oslo Stock Exchange as the main sources to determine what is good accounting practice. With respect to listed companies, accounting standards and pronouncements from the Oslo Stock Exchange are, for all practical purposes, requirements and not just recommendations.

When the Parliament approved the New Norwegian Accounting Act, it made reference to IAS as part of the legal background material (Innst. O, number 61-1997-98, page 24): " ...the development of 'true and fair view' must be based on a harmonization to the IAS rules as a basis for Norwegian standard setting." Accordingly, a Norwegian company generally would be allowed to follow IAS, with certain allowed alternatives in cases where such alternative is considered to provide better information than IAS.

OMAN

IFAC Member: No

Stock Exchange:

Accounting Principles: IAS are mandatory in Oman. Sultani Decree 77 of 1986 requires all companies in the Sultanate of Oman to prepare financial statements in accordance with IASs.

PAKISTAN

IFAC Member: Yes

Stock Exchange: Karachi Stock Exchange requires that all companies must follow IASC Standards as well as comply with reporting requirements of the Companies Ordinance of 1984, the Banking Ordinance of 1964, and the Insurance Act of 1935.
Lahore Stock Exchange allows both domestic and foreign companies to file financial statements using IASC Standards or U.K. GAAP.

Accounting Principles: The Companies Ordinance of 1984 specifies detailed financial reporting rules. In the absence of a specific rule under the Ordinance, listed companies must follow International Accounting Standards. Special accounting rules have been established for banks and insurance companies. Non-listed companies must follow standards developed by the Institute of Chartered Accountants of Pakistan, which for the most part are based on IAS.

PANAMA

IFAC Member: Yes

Stock Exchange: Panama's Stock Exchange, the **Bolsa de Valores de Panamá**, requires that listed companies follow IAS starting in 2000.

Accounting Principles: By law, the Accounting Technical Board ("Junta Técnica de Contabilidad," JTC, a government agency) has responsibility to approve accounting standards in Panama. JTC has created a Financial Accounting Standards Commission—Comision de Normas de Contabilidad Financiera de Panama (NOCOFIN)—to develop the standards and to provide guidance for implementing them.

JTC officially adopted the International Accounting Standards, and ordered them to be applied for accounting activities in the Republic of Panama. The decision was made via Resolution No. 4 of 10 February 1998, officially approved on 27 March 1998, and published in issue No. 23,533 of the "Gaceta Oficial," the government's official journal, dated 30 April 1998. The Resolution also orders the adoption of the "International Standards and Guides of Auditing" in the Republic of Panama.

Here is a summary of the main provisions of Resolution No. 4, regarding the adoption of IAS:

1. The international accounting standards issued by the International Accounting Standards Committee, are adopted as "own and applicable" in the Republic of Panama.

2. The Financial Accounting Standards Commission of Panama (NOCOFIN) is authorised to issue regulations for the application of IAS in Panama.

3. JTC resolves to coordinate with the universities, professional associations and other national and international organisations, regarding the promulgation of IAS.

4. JTC resolves to promulgate (publish, maybe) all IAS adopted by this Resolution.

5. IAS go into effect "for those fiscal periods that begin in 1999" and thereafter.

6. JTC resolves that the national accounting standards previously approved by Panama are to be "eliminated from the registry," except for those that are considered applicable only in Panama.

When IAS are published in the Gaceta Oficial, they have the force of law. However, see below for recent court decision in Panama.

Under Accord 4-99 adopted by the Superintendent of Banks on 11 May 1999, banks in Panama are permitted to choose to follow either (a) IAS or (b) US GAAP starting with the year ended 31 December 1999. Banks must notify the Superintendent of Banks about which set of standards they have chosen. Also, Panamanian banks must be independently audited, and auditors of banks are permitted to follow either (a) International Standards of Auditing (ISAs) or (b) Statements of Auditing Standards (SAS) issued by the American Institute of Certified Public Accountants (AICPA).

Of 69 banks that published their financial statements for periods ended 31 December 1999, 61 presented them in accordance with IAS, 6 chose US GAAP, and 2 presented under "generally accepted accounting principles" without further description. Among the IAS banks is the Banco Nacional de Panamá, the government bank, which performs roles of central bank in Panama.

In August 1999, The Supreme Court of Justice in Panama ordered the "temporary suspension" of JTC Resolution No. 4, discussed above, that adopted IAS as the official accounting standards for businesses in Panama. The Court said that only the Ministry of Commerce and Industry, not the accounting board, has authority to adopt IAS. The ruling does not affect the similar requirement (Accord 4-99) adopted by the Superintendent of Banks that all Panamanian banks follow IAS starting next year.

Further, Panama's Stock Exchange (Bolsa de Valores de Panamá, or BVP) has sent a letter to its listed companies stating that its requirement for companies trading in the Exchange to present their financial statements in accordance with IAS will still be in place. Their letter states: "The Bolsa de Valores de Panamá, S. A., as the private entity that it is, decided to adopt IAS with the clearly defined objective of increasing transparency and equal the preparation, presentation and auditing of the financial statements of the companies whose instruments are registered and traded at this Exchange. This objective has not changed, so the Bolsa de Valores de Panamá, S. A. will keep on working in benefit of the national and international investing public, which forces us to continue with the process of adoption of International Accounting Standards as it has been programmed and widely divulged."

PAPUA NEW GUINEA

IFAC Member: No

Stock Exchange: A stock exchange is being organised.

Accounting Principles: The Papua New Guinea Institute of Accountants is in process of creating an accounting standards board.

PARAGUAY

IFAC Member: Yes

Stock Exchange:

Accounting Principles: We need information. <u>Can you help?</u>

PERU

IFAC Member: Yes

Stock Exchange: Domestic listed companies must follow IAS (or US GAAP in the absence of an IAS on the subject). Foreign listed companies must follow their own national GAAP with an explanation of differences with IAS.

Accounting Principles: Article 223 of the General Corporate Law of Peru requires that all Peruvian companies follow generally accepted accounting principles (GAAP) in preparing their financial statements. Resolution No. 013-98-EF/93.01 under that law, approved 17 July 1998, establishes International Accounting Standards as GAAP in Peru or, in the absence of an International Accounting Standard, U.S. GAAP.

PHILIPPINES

IFAC Member: Yes

Stock Exchange:

Accounting Principles: All public companies and all companies with more than 20 shareholders must follow rules of the Philippine Securities and Exchange Commission (SEC). The Accounting Standards Council (ASC) of the Philippines Institute of Certified Public Accountants (PICPA) issues accounting standards. The ASC has eight members: four from PICPA, one from the SEC, one from the Central Bank, one from the Professional Regulation Commission, and one from the Financial Executives Institute of the Philippines.

ASC standards are recognised by the SEC and Central Bank of Philippines. After approval by the Board of Accountancy and the Professional Regulation Commission (government bodies), ASC standards become mandatory. The ASC's policy is to review and adopt both existing and new IASC Standards as Philippine standards such that "compliance with Philippine GAAP would mean automatic compliance with IASC standards."

POLAND

IFAC Member: Yes

Stock Exchange: Warsaw Stock Exchange requires 3-years audited financial statements prepared in accordance with Polish 1994 Accountancy Act. Domestic companies must follow Polish GAAP but if their shares also trade in a foreign market they must include a reconciliation to either IAS or US GAAP. Foreign listed companies may follow IAS or US GAAP with a reconciliation to Polish GAAP.

Accounting Principles: Principles are set out in the 1994 Polish Accountancy Act, which also requires conformity with EU Directives. A Committee on Accounting Standards was established in 1997 by the President of the Polish Securities Commission under the Foundation for the Development of Capital Market Standards. The Committee consists of 9 members: representatives of academics, international and local auditing firms, Ministry of Finance, Polish Securities and Exchange Commission and Polish Chamber of Auditors. That committee sets standards that must be followed in accordance with the Accountancy Act of 1994. The committee has adopted the IASC conceptual framework as the basis for formulating Polish accounting standards. The committee has concluded that in the absence of a specific Polish accounting standard, compliance with IAS is appropriate under the Accountancy Act.

In addition to standards issued by the Committee, the Chairman of Polish Securities and Exchange Commission (KPWiG) issues regulations regarding specific disclosure requirements for publicly traded companies.

As of 1 January 1999, the Polish securities regulations and disclosure requirements were changed to require foreign issuers to present their financial statements in accordance with (1) the Polish Accountancy Act, (2) IAS or (3) US GAAP. Polish issuers whose shares or depositary receipts are also listed on a foreign stock exchange are required to present financial statements in accordance with Polish GAAP together with a reconciliation to either IAS or US GAAP.

Further, the Polish Accountancy Act is now under revision. Under the first draft of revised Act, for a Polish company or a foreign issuer following Polish GAAP, if an accounting matter is not covered by the Act or by Polish GAAP, IAS should be applied.

PORTUGAL

IFAC Member: Yes

Stock Exchange: Lisbon Stock Exchange (BVL - Bolsa de Valores de Lisboa) requires that financial statements follow Portuguese accounting standards.

Accounting Principles: Accounting standards are developed by the Ministry of Finance and the Commission for Accounting Normalisation (an independent agency of government). These standards conform to the directives of the EC and are not significantly different from IAS.

ROMANIA

IFAC Member: Yes

Stock Exchange: Bucharest Stock Exchange requires that listed companies prepare their financial statements using Romanian accounting standards. The BSE is testing the use of IAS for five companies for a trial period, after which they will consider expanding IAS to all companies—but in parallel with Romanian accounting standards.

Accounting Principles: Accounting standards are issued by the Ministry of Finance after consulting the CECCAR (National Commission of Accounting Experts). CECCAR is an independent association, not an agency of the government.

In June 1999, Romania adopted regulations under its Accountancy Law to (a) require companies to follow IAS and the IASC Framework in the absence of a national accounting standard and (b) begin a programme to develop national standards based on IAS. The regulations will be phased in starting with a few large companies in 1999, public companies and some others of national interest in 2000, large nonpublic companies in 2001, and by 2006 for smaller companies.

RUSSIA

IFAC Member: No

Stock Exchange:

Accounting Principles: A "Programme for the Reform of Russian Accounting" based on International Accounting Standards was approved by the government in March 1998, along the lines of a proclamation by the President of the Russian Federation in February 1997. There will be a national system of accounting standards rather than automatic adoption of IAS. The programme to develop a set of Russian accounting standards is expected to take at least three years.

The reform programme is a project of the American Chamber of Commerce in Russia. The U.S. Agency for International Development is providing over $1 million in funding for the creation of an International Center for Accounting Reform (ICAR) in Moscow. ICAR will work closely with the Russian Government's Interdepartmental Commission for Reform of Accounting and Auditing to bring Russian accounting and auditing rules into conformance with international standards. ICAR will perform the following three functions:

- Rework the normative base for the reform of the accounting and auditing systems;

- Prepare practical instructions for the application of the reform; and

- Develop training materials and re-training courses for practicing accountants.

ICAR plans to publish a newsletter in Russian and English, hold seminars and workshops which will present the work of the Center and establish a working group. ICAR is located in Moscow at Ul. Pokrovka 42/5, Moscow 103062, Tel: 937-7046, Fax: 937-7040.

The Ministry of Finance of Russia has issued Order No. 36n dated 12 July 1999, *Changes and Amendments to the Guidance on Preparing and Presenting Consolidated Financial Statements approved by Ministry of Finance Order No. 112 dated 30 December 1996.* Under Order No. 36n, a group is given a dispensation from its obligation to file Russian-based consolidated accounts if it produces consolidated accounts in compliance with International Accounting Standards that are true and fair including disclosures.

See also Russia: Use of IAS

SAUDI ARABIA

IFAC Member: Yes

Stock Exchange:

Accounting Principles: Accounting standards are established by the Ministry of Commerce.

SIERRA LEONE

IFAC Member: Yes

Stock Exchange:

Accounting Principles: We need information. <u>Can you help?</u>

SINGAPORE

IFAC Member: Yes

Stock Exchange: Stock Exchange of Singapore requires domestic companies to follow Singaporean GAAP. Foreign listed companies may follow IAS (no reconciliation to Singaporean GAAP is required) or US GAAP (reconciliation to Singaporean GAAP is required).

Accounting Principles: Statements of Accounting Standards (SAS) are issued by the Institute of Certified Public Accountants of Singapore (ICPAS). They are developed by the ICPAS's Accounting Standards Committee.

ICPAS stated policy, March 2000: "ICPAS considers the accounting standards of other major jurisdictions as part of the due process for setting accounting standards in Singapore. Where an accounting treatment prescribed by an IAS is consistent with that of major jurisdictions like the United States and the United Kingdom, the Institute would not generally adopt a treatment which is different from IAS. But where major jurisdictions require or allow differing accounting treatment, then it would be justifiable for the Institute to consider allowing a treatment which departs from the IAS and which is applicable in the Singapore context. Neverthelsss, such departures would be kept to a minimum. The Institute has also taken the position to accelerate the process of standard-setting and to harmonise with IASs. Our approach will be very much in line with the recommendations on 'Coordination with National Due Process' as contained in the Novembver 1999 IASC Report, *Recommendations on Shaping IASC for the Future.*"

SLOVAK REPUBLIC

IFAC Member: No

Stock Exchange: Bratislava Stock Exchange requires IAS for foreign listed companies and Slovak Accounting Standards for domestic listed companies.

Accounting Principles: The Act on Accounting (No. 563/1991) places responsibility for Slovak accounting standards with the Ministry of Finance. The accounting regime is similar to the European Accounting Directives.

SLOVENIA

IFAC Member: Yes

Stock Exchange: Ljubljana Stock Exchange allows domestic and foreign listed companies to follow IAS or US or UK GAAP or their national GAAP without reconciliation to Slovenian GAAP.

Accounting Principles: The Slovene Accounting Standards Committee of the Slovenian Institute of Auditors establishes Slovene Accounting Standards. Those standards are recognised under the 1993 Company Act. Slovene Accounting Standards "encompass a much wider scope than that currently covered by the IAS," including matters of financial records, bookkeeping, charts of accounts, and financial controls.

SOUTH AFRICA

IFAC Member: Yes

Stock Exchange: Paragraph 8.51(a) of the **Johannesburg Stock Exchange's** listing requirements requires compliance with GAAP, but GAAP is not defined. Under Exchange policy, a listed company may follow South African GAAP or IAS (without reconciliation to South African GAAP). As noted below, compliance with South African GAAP results also in compliance with IAS, though not vice versa.

Accounting Principles: In 1993, the Council of The South African Institute of Chartered Accountants and the Accounting Practices Board, which is the body that approves South African accounting standards, decided that Statements of Generally Accepted Accounting Practice should be based on IASs. To implement that decision, South Africa commeced a harmonisation and improvements project to revise its existing GAAP in line with IAS and to issue a new standard in all areas where an IAS exists but no equivalent South African standard exists. While the South African policy does not permit differences with IAS on fundamental issues, it does allow for elimination of alternative treatments, additional disclosures, guidance, and differences from IAS if IAS is in conflict with law or regulation. As a result of the harmonisation programme, compliance with South African GAAP results also in compliance with IAS, but not vice versa.

SPAIN

IFAC Member: Yes

Stock Exchange: Spanish companies listed on any of the four public securities exchanges in Spain **(Madrid, Barcelona, Bilbao, and Valencia)** must prepare their financial statements according to Spanish accounting principles. Listed companies that are domiciled in another European Union country may submit financial statements using their own national GAAP without reconciliation to Spanish GAAP. Listed companies from other countries may submit financial statements using IAS, US GAAP, or their own national GAAP but with an audited reconciliation to Spanish GAAP.

Accounting Principles: Accounting standards are established under law, particularly the Code of Commerce. Royal Decree 302, 17 March 1989, recognises the Instituto de Contabilidad y Auditoria de Cuentas (ICAC) as the national accounting standard setter. ICAC is a government agency that develops accounting standards within the Ministry of Finance. There is a national general accounting plan. Since 1998 it has been ICAC's stated policy to work to minimise differences between IAS and Spanish GAAP.

Guidance is also provided by the professional organisation, Asociacion Española de Contabilidad y Administracion de Empresas (AECA).

SRI LANKA

IFAC Member: Yes

Stock Exchange: Companies listed on the **Columbo Stock Exchange** must submit financial statements under Sri Lanka GAAP.

Accounting Principles: The Sri Lanka Accounting and Auditing Standards Act No. 15 of 1995, requires all specified business enterprises—including listed companies—to prepare and present financial statements in accordance with Sri Lanka Accounting Standards.

The Act empowers the Institute of Chartered Accountants of Sri Lanka to adopt suitable accounting standards from time to time and to publish them in the Gazette to have legal effect. The standards are developed by the Accounting Standards Committee of the Institute and are largely derived from IASs. However, the Institute has framed two national standards to deal with issues not covered under IASs, namely finance companies and plantation accounting. Accounting standards relating to banks must have the concurrence of the Banking Supervision Department of the Central Bank.

All IASC exposure drafts are examined by the Accounting Standards Committee, and comments are forwarded to IASC. IASs undergo due review process by the Committee before they are formally adopted by the Council of the Institute.

The Accounting Standards Committee consists of 12 members, including representatives of accountancy bodies, regulatory bodies, and user groups.

Under the Act, an independent body called the Sri Lanka Accounting and Auditing Standards Monitoring Board has been set up to monitor compliance with the accounting standards by all specified business enterprises. The Board has 13 members, including representatives of accountancy bodies, academics, capital market regulators, and industry and commerce.

SUDAN

IFAC Member: Yes

Stock Exchange:

Accounting Principles: We need information. Can you help?

SWAZILAND

IFAC Member: Yes

Stock Exchange:

Accounting Principles: The Swaziland Institute of Accountants issues Swaziland Accounting Standards that are identical to or conform with International Accounting Standards. There is no legislation that forces companies to use any particular accounting standards.

SWEDEN

IFAC Member: Yes

Stock Exchange: Stockholm Exchange requires domestic companies to follow Swedish GAAP. Foreign listed companies may follow Swedish GAAP; alternatively they may follow IAS, UK, or US GAAP with a reconciliation to Swedish GAAP.

Accounting Principles: Companies must follow the Annual Accounts Act of 1995 in preparing their financial statements. Accounting standards, which mirror IAS unless IAS is in conflict with the Act, are established primarily for public limited companies by the Financial Accounting Standards Council (Redovisiningsrådet, or RR). RR includes representatives of the accounting profession and industry.

SWITZERLAND

IFAC Member: Yes

Stock Exchange: Swiss Stock Exchange permits all listed companies, domestic and foreign, to follow Swiss GAAP (see below) or either IAS or their national GAAP with no reconciliation to Swiss GAAP required. Companies using IAS or national GAAP must also meet the disclosure requirements of Swiss GAAP.

Accounting Principles: The Swiss Foundation for Accounting and Reporting publishes accounting standards (ARR/FER) that are generally consistent with, but not as detailed as, IAS. Compliance with ARR/FER is required for listed companies. However, compliance with IAS ensures compliance with ARR/FER, and many large Swiss companies follow IAS. A foreign listed company using its own national GAAP may have to add supplemental disclosures to comply with Swiss GAAP.

SYRIA

IFAC Member: Yes

Stock Exchange: Damascus Stock Exchange currently closed. May reopen shortly.

Accounting Principles: Accounting principles and standards in Syria are established by the Association of Syrian Certified Accountants. They are based on IAS. Accounting laws and regulations are established by the Ministry of Internal Trade.

TAIWAN

IFAC Member: Yes

Stock Exchange: Domestic listed companies must submit financial statements that follow Taiwanese accounting principles. Foreign listed companies must follow their own national principles and include a reconciliation to Taiwanese GAAP.

Accounting Principles: The Securities and Exchange Commission of the Ministry of Finance sets the financial reporting requirements for public companies. The Ministry of Economic Affairs issues accounting regulations for both public and nonpublic companies. An independent accounting standards board (Accounting Research and Development Foundation, or ARDF), established in 1984, publishes Statements of Financial Accounting Stanards (SFAS) that are recognised by the Ministry of Finance. ARDF also publishes interpretive guidance in the form of Supplementary Explanation Statements.

TANZANIA

IFAC Member: Yes

Stock Exchange: Dar-es-Salaam Stock Exchange allows companies to submit IAS financial statements.

Accounting Principles: Accounting standards in Tanzania are set by the National Board of Accountants and Auditors (NBAA), a government agency. The standards are set out in Tanzanian Statements of Accounting Guidelines (TSAG). While the TSAGs are not the same as IAS, the introduction to the TSAGs states: "In the preparation of these Guidelines, account has been taken of the development of accounting standards on the international scene (i.e. the work of the International Accounting Standards Committee) as well as specific developments in various countries of accounting repute. Thus these Guidelines embrace the best international accounting practice adapted where necessary to cater for Tanzanian needs."

THAILAND

IFAC Member: Yes

Stock Exchange: The **Stock Exchange of Thailand** allows foreign listed companies to follow Thai GAAP, IAS, or US GAAP. Domestic companies must follow Thai GAAP or IAS if there is no Thai standard on the subject.

Accounting Principles: Currently, accounting standards are set by the Institute of Certified Accountants and Auditors of Thailand

(ICAAT). ICAAT has adopted several IAS as Thai standards. Their goal is to adopt most if not all IAS as Thai standards by 1999. The Thai government is expected to require companies to prepare financial statements using IAS starting 1999. The Finance Ministry will create a new independent self-regulatory board with responsibility both to set standards and to oversee compliance.

TOGO

IFAC Member: No

Stock Exchange:

Accounting Principles: One of seven French-speaking West African countries (including Benin, Burkina Faso, Ivory Coast, Mali, Niger, Senegal, and Togo) that in 1998 signed a business harmonisation treaty that includes creation of a new accounting plan—Systeme Comptable Ouest-Africain (Plan SYSCOA). SYSCOA is not based on IAS.

TRINIDAD & TOBAGO

IFAC Member: Yes

Stock Exchange:

Accounting Principles: IAS are adopted as national standards.

TUNISIA

IFAC Member: Yes

Stock Exchange:

Accounting Principles: Law No. 96-112 (30 Dec. 1996) adopted a new accounting system for Tunisian private enterprises, including a conceptual framework, intended to be broadly in harmony with IAS. The Ministry of Finance has authority to adopt individual accounting standards by decree. Most of the standards that have been adopted are similar to IAS, though not the standard on translating foreign currencies. Smaller companies are allowed to use simplified standards. Some foreign enterprises are allowed to use their national GAAP or IAS.

TURKEY

IFAC Member: Yes

Stock Exchange: For the **Istanbul Stock Exchange**, foreign companies may follow IAS Standards or US GAAP or UK GAAP (and also must comply with the 4th and 7th EC Directives). A foreign company may also follow its national GAAP, in which case the ISE may require a reconciliation to IAS. Domestic companies must follow Turkish national GAAP.

Accounting Principles: Public companies, banks, and companies with more than 100 shareholders must follow accounting standards issued by the Capital Market Board (CMB), a government agency within the Ministry of Finance. Accounting standards are set by an Accounting and Auditing Committee. The committee includes representatives of the government and the private sector. The accounting standards issued by CMB are generally similar to IAS. In the absence of a specific CMB standard, CMB recommends use of either the industry practice or International Accounting Standards. Some companies prepare two sets of financial statements, one following CMB standards and the other following IASB standards.

TURKMENISTAN

IFAC Member: No

Stock Exchange:

Accounting Principles: We need information. <u>Can you help?</u>

UGANDA

IFAC Member: Yes

Stock Exchange:

Accounting Principles: The Accounting Standards Committee of the Institute of Certified Public Accountants of Uganda encourages the use of International Accounting Standards.

UKRAINE

IFAC Member: No

Stock Exchange: For the **Ukraine Stock Exchange,** domestic listed companies must follow Ukrainian GAAP. Foreign listed companies may use either IAS or Ukrainian accounting standards.

Accounting Principles: Ukrainian GAAP is established by the Ministry of Finance. As part of an August 1998 agreement with the IMF, the Ukrainian Government adopted certain economic policies including a requirement that all commercial banks convert to IAS by end of 1998.

UNITED ARAB EMIRATES

IFAC Member: No

Stock Exchange:

Accounting Principles: A federal law passed in the United Arab Emirates in February 1999 requires that all banks and financial institutions prepare their financial statements using International Accounting Standards for periods beginning 1 January 1999.

UNITED KINGDOM

IFAC Member: Yes

Stock Exchange: London Stock Exchange allows IAS financial statements.

Accounting Principles: Financial Reporting Standards (FRS) are established by the Accounting Standards Board (ASB), a wholly-owned subsidiary of FRC Ltd., an independent not-for-profit corporation that promotes the best practice in financial reporting. ASB has been prescribed by the Secretary of State for Trade and Industry for the puporses of section 256(1) of the Companies Act of 1985 with the effect that accounting standards isued by the ASB are recognised as such for the purposes of the accounting requirements of the Acts in Great Britain.

The foreword to ASB standards states: "FRSs are formulated with due regard to international developments. The Board supports the

International Accounting Standards Committee in its aim to harmonise international financial reporting. As part of this support, an FRS contains a section explaining how it relates to the International Accounting Standard (IAS) dealing with the same topic. In most cases, compliance with an FRS automatically achieves compliance with the relevant IAS. Where the requirements of an accounting standard and an IAS differ, the accounting standard should be followed by entities reporting within the area of application of the Board's accounting standards."

ASB has established an Urgent Issues Task Force (UITF) to provide interpretive guidance. A related organisation, the Financial Reporting Review Panel, examines departures from accountancy requirements under the Companies Act.

The UK Department of Trade and Industry is currently studying the implications of allowing UK companies to follow IAS.

UNITED STATES

IFAC Member: Yes

Stock Exchange: New York Stock Exchange, NASDAQ, American Stock Exchange, Arizona Stock Exchange, Boston Stock Exchange, Chicago Stock Exchange, Chicago Board Options Exchange, Pacific Stock Exchange, Philadelphia Stock Exchange: Foreign listed companies may use US GAAP or IAS or their national GAAP. If not US GAAP, a note reconciling income statement and balance sheet items to US GAAP is required by regulation of the U.S. Securities and Exchange Commission. Domestic companies must follow US GAAP.

Accounting Principles: Since 1973, the Financial Accounting Standards Board has been the designated organization in the private sector for establishing standards of financial accounting and reporting. Those standards govern the preparation of financial reports. They are officially recognized as authoritative by the Securities and Exchange Commission (SEC) (Financial Reporting Release No. 1, Section 101) and the American Institute of Certified Public Accountants (Rule 203, Rules of Conduct, as amended May 1973 and May 1979).

The SEC has statutory authority to establish financial accounting and reporting standards for publicly held companies under the Securities Exchange Act of 1934. Throughout its history, however, the Commission's policy has been to rely on the private sector for this function to the extent that the private sector demonstrates ability to fulfill the responsibility in the public interest.

Excerpt from FASB Plan for International Activities

Over the coming years the FASB intends to engage in the following activities involving direct cooperation with other standard-setting bodies to resolve specific issues and to reduce differences in accounting standards between nations:

a. Pursue opportunities to engage in joint multinational standard-setting projects on mutually selected topics to arrive at separate national standards that are in substantial agreement with one another. The FASB has already begun a number of projects in this area, including the joint project on disaggregated disclosures with Canada and the parallel project with the IASC on earnings per share. In addition, while not formal FASB agenda projects, it is believed that the joint research study with Canada and Mexico on the North American accounting environment and the accounting concepts working group with Australia, Canada, the IASC, and the United Kingdom will lead to the identification of common problem areas that could benefit from joint consideration. Future activities will include:

—Adopting a common or substantially similar standard with Canada on disaggregated disclosures;

—Adopting a standard on earnings per share the same as or substantially similar to that of the IASC;

—Following up on the joint research study with Canada and Mexico to identify areas where differences can be reduced either by conforming existing standards or by creating common standards;

—Identifying projects that have promise for reaching broad international agreement.

b. Consider adopting foreign national or IASC standards that are judged through due process to be superior to their U.S. counterparts. The FASB will evaluate standards of other countries and of the IASC in areas where current U.S. GAAP is limited, problematic, or nonexistent. In the case of IASC standards, the focus will be on the IASC benchmark standard if a pronouncement permits alternative methods. Where it is believed that the adoption of another standard-setting body's high-quality standard would be more efficient and effective than developing a new FASB standard, formal consideration will be given to proposing its adoption. Earnings per share is an example of a proposed IASC standard that was tentatively judged to be superior to the existing U.S. standard.

FASB has established an Emerging Issues Task Force (EITF) to provide interpretive guidance.

URUGUAY

IFAC Member: Yes

Stock Exchange:

Accounting Principles: Law No. 16.060 requires that the financial statements of all companies must follow generally accepted accounting principles. By decree, most International Accounting Standards have been declared obligatory. In a few cases certain principles in an IAS have not been adopted, and Uruguayan regulations take precedence over IAS. Even if an IAS has not been adopted, if there is no national regulation companies generally look to IAS for guidance.

UZBEKISTAN

IFAC Member: Yes

Stock Exchange: Tashkent Republican Stock Exchange requires that foreign companies must submit financial statements that comply with U.S. GAAP. Domestic companies must follow Uzbek accounting standards.

Accounting Principles: Accounting standards are developed by the Ministry of Finance and issued jointly by the Ministry of Finance and the Ministry of Justice. Once issued, they have the force of law for all companies. Different standards apply to banks than to other enterprises. Uzbekistan accounting standards are closely based on IAS—compliance with UZ GAAP will usually result in compliance with IAS.

VENEZUELA

IFAC Member: Yes

Stock Exchange:

Accounting Principles: GAAP in Venezuela is determined by the Venezualan Federation of Colleges of Public Accountants and, in the case of companies traded on either of Venezuela's stock exchanges, by the National Securities Commission (CNV). If neither of those organisations has issued a pronuncement on a subject, International Accounting Standards are the first alternative for all accounting and disclosure matters. If there is no Venezuelan GAAP or an IASC Standard, then companies look to Mexican GAAP and then to U.S. GAAP.

VIETNAM

IFAC Member: Yes

Stock Exchange:

Accounting Principles: Decrees issued by the Ministry of Finance (MOF) provide some guidance on accounting standards that companies doing business in Vietnam must follow. Domestic companies must follow the Vietnamese Accounting System. Foreign companies generally are allowed to use their national GAAP, with approval by MOF.

YUGOSLAVIA

IFAC Member: Yes

Stock Exchange:

Accounting Principles: At a meeting of its Assembly in Belgrade on 24 December 1998, the Association of Accountants and Auditors of Yugoslavia (which has authority to set accounting standards in Yugoslavia pursuant to the Law on Accounting) voted for the direct implementation of International Accounting Standards in the Federal Republic of Yugoslavia. Moreover, the Association has agreed to develop and publish a translation of IAS.

ZAMBIA

IFAC Member: Yes

Stock Exchange:

Accounting Principles: The Zambia Institute of Certified Accountants has implemented a formal policy for the adoption of International

Accounting Standards, although there is no legal requirement for companies to apply them.

ZIMBABWE

IFAC Member: Yes

Stock Exchange: The **Zimbabwe Stock Exchange** requires both Zimbabwe and foreign listed companies to comply with both IAS and Zimbabwe accounting standards. Compliance with Zimbabwe standards means compliance with IAS since Zimbabwe Accounting Practices Board has adopted all International Accounting Standards (with guidance added for mining companies and related party transactions).

Section 8.51 (a) of the ZSE listing requirements states "the annual financial statements must have been prepared in accordance with the issuers national law and, in all significant respects with GAAP or IAS." For Zimbabwe companies whose principal listing is in Zimbabwe (64 out of 67 listed companies) they must use IAS standards and the local GAAP requirements. This is in terms of our requirements and the local professional accounting standards. I am not aware of any difference where applicable between our Companies Act as amended and IAS requirements. The local GAAP would cover the agricultural and mining listed companies in areas not covered by IAS.

Accounting Principles: The Zimbabwe Accounting Practices Board has stated the following: "All discussion papers and exposure drafts issued by the International Accounting Standards Committee are examined by the Institute and the Zimbabwe Accounting Practices Board and comments arising from such examination are communicated to the IASC by the Institute.

International accounting standards published by the IASC are re-examined by the Institute and the Board. Standards ratified by the Board bear the stamp of general acceptance by the organisations represented on the Board and assume the identity of 'Zimbabwe Accounting Standards.' The disclosure requirements of such standards are incorporated into a subsequent amendment to the Companies (Financial Statements) Regulations."

This effectively means that Zimbabwe standards are the International standards. The ZAPB has issued guidance in only two areas so far: IAS 12 for mining companies and IAS 24 as related parties can be complex in African society. Our standard audit opinion includes the wording: "In our opinion the financial statements are properly drawn up in compliance with the Companies Act (Chapter 24:03) and in conformity with International Standards as adopted for use in Zimbabwe. . . ."

USAGE OF IASC STANDARDS

Companies and Other Organizations Using IAS

The IASC Web site provides a continuously updated list of such organizations. This list is compiled based on information identified by the IASC Secretariat in published annual reports. To be included, the auditor's report, summary of accounting policies, or notes must state that the financial statements conform to IAS without qualification. That is, an enterprise is not included if it complies with IAS "except for" one or more Standards. The list excludes enterprises that simply present a reconciliation from another GAAP to IAS and that use a mixture of national and international standards.

As of April 2001 this list contained 143 enterprises. They can be analyzed by country as follows:

Austria	9	Hungary	3
Bahrain	6	International	2
Belgium	2	Kuwait	1
Botswana	3	Latvia	1
Bulgaria	1	Malta	2
China	2	Netherlands	3
Croatia	4	New Zealand	1
Cyprus	2	Norway	2
Czech Republic	2	Peru	1
Denmark	11	Slovenia	4
Estonia	1	South Africa	3
Europe (Pan-European)	2	Spain	1
Finland	3	Switzerland	50
France	1	Turkey	2
Germany	61	United Arab Emirates	4
Hong Kong	5	Zimbabwe	1

CROSS-REFERENCE

ORIGINAL PRONOUNCEMENTS TO
2002 *MILLER IAS GUIDE* CHAPTERS

This locator provides instant cross-reference between an original pronouncement and the chapter(s) in this publication in which a pronouncement is covered. Original pronouncements are listed on the left and the chapter(s) in which they appear in the 2002 *Miller IAS Guide* on the right.

INTERNATIONAL ACCOUNTING STANDARDS

ORIGINAL PRONOUNCEMENT	2002 *MILLER IAS GUIDE* REFERENCE
Framework for the Preparation and Presentation of Financial Statements	Issued 1989. See also SIC-6. Framework for the Preparation and Presentation of Financial Statements, ch. **2**
IAS 1 Presentation of Financial Statements	Revised 1997. Supersedes IAS 1 (1975), IAS 5 (1976), IAS 13 (1979). See also SIC-8. Presentation of Financial Statements, ch. **3**
IAS 2 Inventories	Revised 1993. Supersedes IAS 2 (1977). See also SIC-1. Inventory Pricing and Methods, ch. **23**
IAS 3 Consolidated Financial Statements	Superseded and withdrawn.
IAS 4 Depreciation Accounting	Issued 1976. Portions superseded by IAS 16 (revised 1993) and IAS 38 (1998). Property, Plant, and Equipment, ch. **27**
IAS 5 Information to Be Disclosed in Financial Statements	Superseded and withdrawn.
IAS 6 Accounting Responses to Changing Prices	Superseded and withdrawn.
IAS 7 Cash Flow Statements	Revised 1992. Supersedes IAS 7 (1977). Cash Flow Statements, ch. **7**

IAS 8

Net Profit or Loss for the Period, Fundamental
Errors and Changes in Accounting Policies

Revised 1993. Supersedes IAS 8 (1978). Part
superseded by IAS 35 (1998).

Net Profit or Loss for the Period, Fundamental
Errors, and Changes in Accounting Policies,
ch. **26**

IAS 9

Research and Development Costs

Superseded and withdrawn.

IAS 10

Events after the Balance Sheet Date

Revised 1999. Supersedes IAS 10 (1978) with
respect to events occurring after the balance
sheet date.

Events after the Balance Sheet Date, ch. **15**

IAS 11

Construction Contracts

Revised 1993. Supersedes IAS 11 (1979).

Construction Contracts, ch. **10**

IAS 12

Income Taxes

Revised 1996. Supersedes IAS 12 (1979).

Income Taxes, ch. **20**

IAS 13

Presentation of Current Assets and Current
Liabilities

Superseded and withdrawn.

IAS 14

Segment Reporting

Revised 1997. Supersedes IAS 14 (1981).

Segment Reporting, ch. **31**

IAS 15

Information Reflecting the Effects of
Changing Prices

Issued 1981. Made non-mandatory in 1989.

Changing Prices and Hyperinflationary
Economies, ch. **8**

IAS 16

Property, Plant, and Equipment

Revised 1993. Supersedes IAS 16 (1982).
Further amended in 1998. See also SIC-14.

Property, Plant, and Equipment, ch. **27**

IAS 17

Leases

Revised 1997. Supersedes IAS 17 (1982). See
also SIC-15.

Leases, ch. **25**

IAS 18

Revenue

Revised 1998. Supersedes IAS 18 (1982).

Revenue, ch. **30**

IAS 19

Employee Benefits

Revised 1998. Supersedes IAS 19 (1993).

Employee Benefits, ch. **13**

IAS 20

Accounting for Government Grants and
Disclosure of Government Assistance

Issued 1983. See also SIC-10.

Government Grants and Government
Assistance, ch. **18**

IAS 21

The Effects of Changes in Foreign Exchange
Rates

Revised 1993. Supersedes IAS 21 (1983). See
also SIC-7 and SIC-11.

Foreign Currency Translation, ch. **17**

IAS 22

Business Combinations

Revised 1998. Supersedes IAS 22 (1993). See
also SIC-9.

Business Combinations, ch. **6**

IAS 23

Borrowing Costs

Revised 1993. Supersedes IAS 23 (1984). See
also SIC-2.

Borrowing Costs, ch. **5**

IAS 24

Related Party Disclosures

Issued 1984.

Related Party Disclosures, ch. **29**

IAS 25

Accounting for Investments

Issued 1986. Replaced by IAS 39 and IAS 40
effective January 1, 2001.

Accounting for Investments, ch. **4**

IAS 26

Accounting and Reporting by Retirement
Benefit Plans

Issued 1987.

Employee Benefits, ch. **13**

IAS 27

Consolidated Financial Statements and
Accounting for Investments in Subsidiaries

Issued 1989. Amended by IAS 39 (1999). See
also SIC-12.

Consolidated Financial Statements, ch. **9**

IAS 28

Accounting for Investments in Associates

Revised 1998. Amended by IAS 39 (1999). See
also SIC-3.

The Equity Method, ch. **14**

IAS 29

Financial Reporting in Hyperinflationary
Economies

Issued 1989.

Changing Prices and Hyperinflationary
Economies, ch. **8**

IAS 30

Disclosures in the Financial Statements of
Banks and Similar Financial Institutions

Issued 1990. Amended by IAS 39 (1999).

Disclosures in the Financial Statements of
Banks and Similar Financial Institutions, ch. **33**

IAS 31
Financial Reporting of Interests in Joint
Ventures

Issued 1990. Amended by IAS 36 (1998) and
IAS 39 (1999). See also SIC-13.

Consolidated Financial Statements, ch. **9**

IAS 32
Financial Instruments: Disclosure and
Presentation

Revised 1999. Supersedes IAS 32 (1995).
Amended by IAS 39 (1999). See also SIC-5 and
SIC-16.

Financial Instruments, ch. **16**

IAS 33
Earnings per Share

Issued 1997.

Earnings per Share, ch. **12**

IAS 34
Interim Financial Reporting

Issued 1998.

Interim Financial Reporting, ch. **22**

IAS 35
Discontinuing Operations

Issued 1998. Supersedes part of IAS 8 (1993).

Discontinuing Operations, ch. **11**

IAS 36
Impairment of Assets

Issued 1998. Supersedes part of IAS 9 (1993),
IAS 16 (1993), and IAS 22 (1993).

Impairment of Assets, ch. **19**

IAS 37
Provisions, Contingent Liabilities and
Contingent Assets

Issued 1998. Supersedes part of IAS 10 (1978).

Provisions, Contingent Liabilities, and
Contingent Assets, ch. **28**

IAS 38
Intangible Assets

Issued 1998. Supersedes IAS 9 (1993).

Intangible Assets, ch. **21**

IAS 39
Financial Instruments: Recognition and
Measurement

Issued 1999. Supersedes part of IAS 25 (1986).

Financial Instruments, ch. **16**

IAS 40
Investment Property

Issued 2000. Supersedes part of IAS 25 (1986).

Investment Property, ch. **24**

IAS 41
Agriculture

Issued 2001.
Agriculture, ch. **32**

INDEX